Not For Tourists™ Guide to CHICAGO

2004

Not For Tourists Inc New York

published and designed by
Not For Tourists Inc
NFT$_{TM}$- Not For Tourists$_{TM}$- Guide to CHICAGO 2004
www.notfortourists.com

Concept by
Jane Pirone

Information Design
Jane Pirone
Rob Tallia
Scot Covey
Diana Pizzari

Editor
Jane Pirone

Managing Editors
Rob Tallia
Diana Pizzari

City Editor
Kathie Bergquist

Writing and Editing
Jane Pirone
Diana Pizzari
Rob Tallia
Kathie Bergquist

Database Design
Scot Covey

Graphic Design / Production
Scot Covey
James Martinez
Alex Still
Yun Zan
Ana Albu

Research/Data Entry
Diana Pizzari
Annie Holt
Shannon Browne
Aniela Srocynski
Sherry Wasserman
Anne-Cecile Bourget
Sharyn Jackson

Contributors
Richard Archambault
David Daruszka
Krista Ely
Harvey Henao
Stefanie Langer
Eric Mathiasen
Ricardo Nabholz
Jim Sprowl
Alice Tegtmeier
Emily Ziring

Printed in China
ISBN# 0-9740131-2-9 $16.95

Dear **NFT** User:

The more things stay the same in Chicago, the more things change. While Richard the Younger continues his father's legacy of a city run "of the Daleys, by the Daleys, and for the Daleys," he proves himself equally adept as Daley senior at getting his political points made (such as the late-night coup that put Meigs Field out of commission). Meanwhile, his Bridgeport homies and the rest of the south side say goodbye to a good guy from the 'hood, name of Comiskey, and dubiously greet his replacement, the suspiciously Northside-sounding US Cellular Field.

Nonetheless, the 'Sox still hold their own, the Bulls still are, um, "recovering" and the Cubs—well, maybe next year. In the meantime, 2004 should see the long-awaited and now nearly-forgotten completion of Frank Gehry's notorious Millenium Park bandshell and, hopefully, improved transportation connections to McCormick Place—we, Chicago's 2,900,000 citizens, will keep our collective fingers crossed.

As goes Chicago, so goes **NFT**. On the one hand, we've kept all the useful information from the 2003 edition. On the other hand, some things have changed—improved, expanded listings of nightlife, dining, shopping, and practical information, as well as new pages such as a guide to local media and a calendar of events. We hope you will find these improvements useful—but please bear in mind that while we try to be up-to-date, the rapidity with which things change make it impossible to be 100% accurate; in short: phone first.

Thanks for purchasing **NFT-Chicago**. We envision this as a practical, essential guide to Chicago urban existence and in the spirit of this truly Democratic city, we encourage your participation in the project as well. Please log on to our website at www.notfortourists.com, and give us a shout-out. Let us know what you like, and even more important, what you'd like to see changed and improved. And if there's something you feel is missing that would really make this *the* essential guide for Chicagoans, let us know that, too. I assure you that all suggestions are considered in the revision process. Furthermore, I have to give props to Kit Bernardi, the 2003 City Editor, without whose diligent hard work this edition would not be possible, and to the entire **NFT** staff who put up with me for some reason or another.

Yours in Civic Pride,
Kathie Bergquist
NFT-Chicago, City Editor, 2004

Neighborhoods

The North Side

Parks & Places

Colleges & Universities

Transit

Sports

General Information

Arts & Entertainment

Essential Phone Numbers 302

Map 1 • River North / Fulton Market District

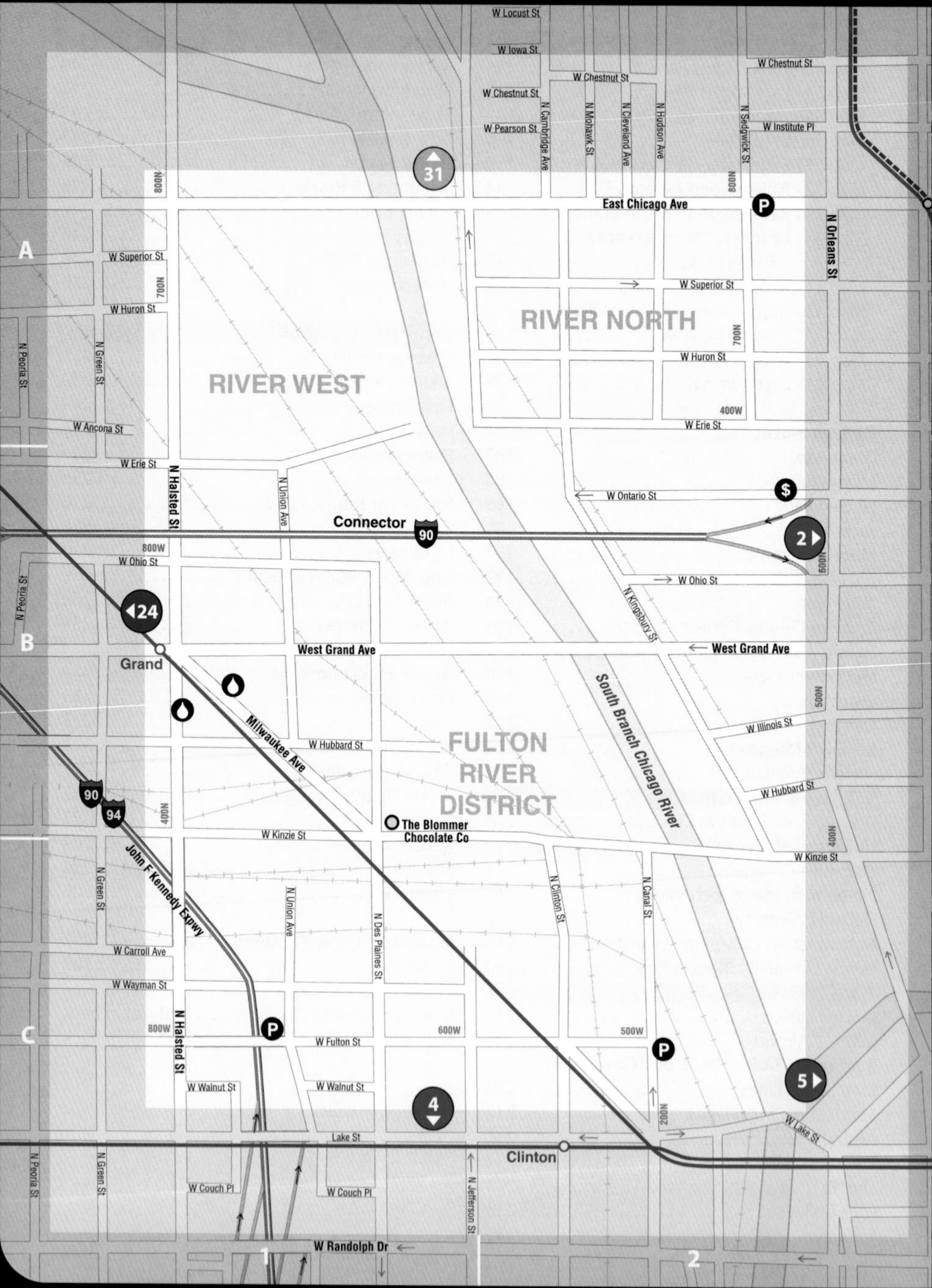

N

W Locust St
W Iowa St
W Chestnut St
W Chestnut St
W Chestnut St
W Pearson St
N Cambridge Ave
N Mohawk St
N Cleveland Ave
N Hudson Ave
N Sedgwick St
W Institute Pl
31
800N
800N
East Chicago Ave
N Orleans St
A
W Superior St
700N
W Superior St
W Huron St
RIVER NORTH
700N
W Huron St
N Peoria St
N Green St
RIVER WEST
400W
W Ancona St
W Erie St
W Erie St
N Halsted St
N Union Ave
W Ontario St
Connector
90
2
800W
W Ohio St
600N
W Ohio St
N Peoria St
24
N Kingsbury St
B
West Grand Ave
West Grand Ave
Grand
South Branch Chicago River
500N
W Illinois St
Milwaukee Ave
W Hubbard St
FULTON RIVER DISTRICT
W Hubbard St
90
94
400N
The Blommer Chocolate Co
400N
W Kinzie St
W Kinzie St
John F Kennedy Expwy
N Green St
N Union Ave
N Des Plaines St
N Clinton St
N Canal St
W Carroll Ave
W Wayman St
N Halsted St
800W
W Fulton St
600W
500W
C
W Walnut St
W Walnut St
5
4
200N
W Lake St
Lake St
Clinton
N Peoria St
N Green St
W Couch Pl
W Couch Pl
N Jefferson St
W Randolph Dr
1
2

Essentials

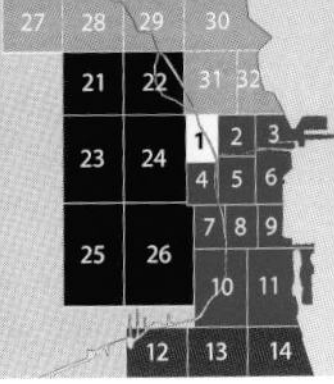

Crisscrossed by rail tracks, I-90/94, and the Chicago River, this area is transitioning from industrial to residential as the loft conversion craze in River North, Greek Town, and West Loop Gate expands. The Bloomer Chocolate Company pumps sweet, chocolate-coated air into the streets all day. If you're watching your weight, breathing it in is the next best thing.

Banks

- **New Century Bank** • 363 W Ontario St

Car Washes

- **River West Hand Car Wash** • 478 N Milwaukee Ave
- **We Wash III** • 453 N Halsted

Landmarks

- **The Blommer Chocolate Co** • 600 W Kinzie St

Parking

Map 1 • River North / Fulton Market District

Sundries / Entertainment

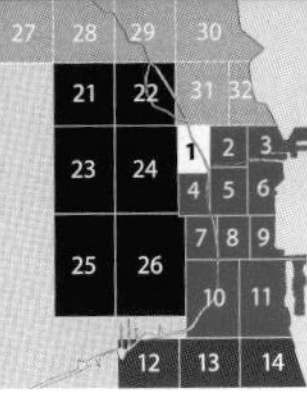

Map 1

Too bad, but the word has spread to the 'burbs about La Scarola serving whopping big bowls of homemade pasta for smallish prices. Go during the week to avoid the double dates. Reza's kebabs are killer. At Funky Buddha Lounge and Scoozi!, look for the buffed and beautiful from East Bank Club. Real people drink at Emmit's Pub.

Bars

- **Emmit's Irish Pub & Eatery** • 495 N Milwaukee Ave
- **Funky Buddha Lounge** • 728 W Grand Ave
- **Rednofive** • 440 N Halsted

Gyms

- **East Bank Club** • 500 N Kingsbury St

Restaurants

- **Chilpancingo** • 358 W Ontario St
- **Iguana Cafe** • 517 N Halsted St
- **La Scarola** • 721 W Grand Ave
- **Reza's** • 432 W Ontario St
- **Scoozi!** • 410 W Huron St
- **Thyme** • 464 N Halsted
- **Zealous** • 419 W Superior St

Map 2 • Near North / River North

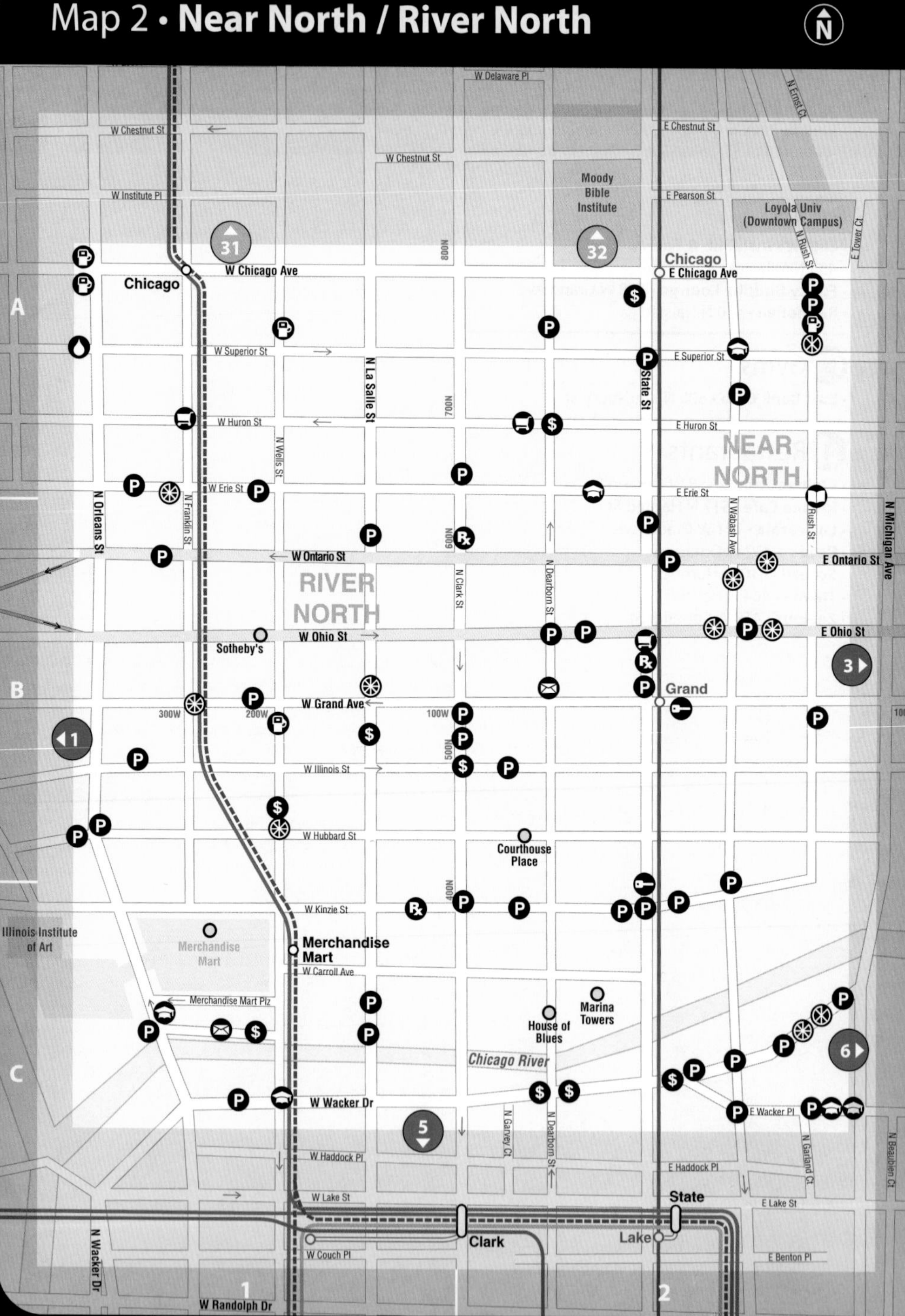

Essentials

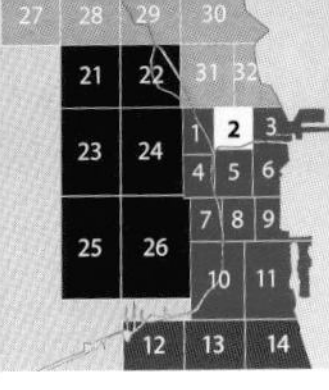

This trendy neighborhood has gone from abandoned warehouse district to artists' haven to tourist mecca. But thankfully, established eateries, comfy bars, independent shopkeepers, and historic architecture hold their ground in making this neighborhood a pulsating place to live. The graceful, old Courthouse Building is where some of Chicago's infamous criminals were tried. Service at the post office on Dearborn St stinks. Go to the Mail Boxes, Etc. on Wells St to get stamped.

Banks

- **Bank One** • 35 W Wacker Dr
- **Fifth Third Bank** • 222 Merchandise Mart Plz
- **Lakeside Bank** • 55 W Wacker Dr
- **LaSalle Bank** • 515 N La Salle St
- **MB Financial Bank** • 1 E Wacker Dr
- **North Community Bank** • 448 N Wells St
- **North Community Bank** • 800 N State St
- **North Bank** • 501 N Clark St
- **Oak Brook Bank** • 33 W Huron St

Car Rental

- **Enterprise** • 10 E Grand Ave • 312-670-7270
- **Hertz** • 401 N State St • 312-372-7600

Car Washes

- **River North Hand Car Wash** • 356 W Superior St

Gas Stations

- **Citgo** • 750 N Wells St
- **Shell** • 350 W Chicago Ave

Landmarks

- **Courthouse Place** • 54 W Hubbard St
- **Marina Towers** • 300 N State St
- **Merchandise Mart** • 222 Merchandise Mart Plz
- **Sotheby's** • 215 W Ohio St

Pharmacies

- **CVS Pharmacy** • 121 W Kinzie St
- **Osco Drug** • 550 N State St
- **Walgreens** • 641 N Clark St

Pizza

- **Bacino's** • 75 E Wacker Dr
- **California Pizza Kitchen** • 52 E Ohio St
- **Gino's East of Chicago** • 62 E Ontario St
- **Giordano's** • 730 N Rush St
- **Lou Malnati's Pizzeria** • 439 N Wells St
- **Pizzeria Due** • 619 N Wabash Ave
- **Pizzeria Ora** • 545 N La Salle St
- **Pizzeria Uno** • 29 E Ohio St
- **Rizzata's Pizzeria** • 300 W Grand Ave

Post Offices

- 222 Merchandise Mart Plz
- 540 N Dearborn St

Schools

- **Associated Colleges-Midwest** • 205 W Wacker Dr
- **Feltre School** • 22 W Erie St
- **Frances Xavier Ward School** • 730 N Wabash Ave
- **Illinois Institute of Art** • 350 N Orleans St
- **Insti-Clinical Social Work** • 68 E Wacker Pl
- **Loyola University** • 820 N Michigan Ave
- **Moody Bible Institute** • 820 N La Salle St
- **Urban Youth Prgrm Alternative** • 65 E Wacker Pl

Supermarkets

- **Jewel-Osco** • 550 N State St
- **Whole Foods Market** • 50 W Huron St

Parking

Map 2 • Near North / River North

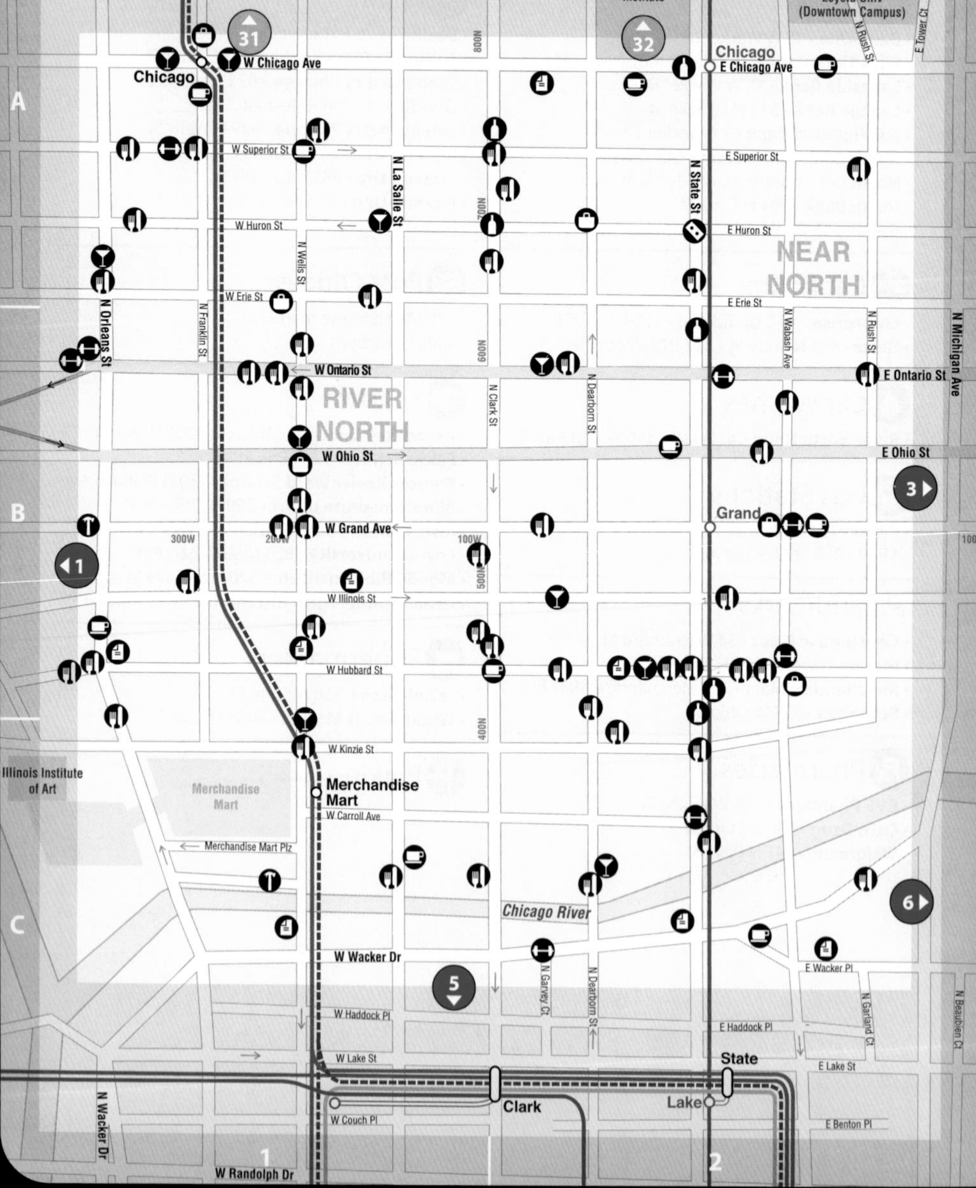

Make a cheap date of a Friday night by hitting the free booze at the many River North gallery openings. Red Head Piano Bar offers retro swigs to young swingers; Cyrano's serves up a steak frites par excellence.

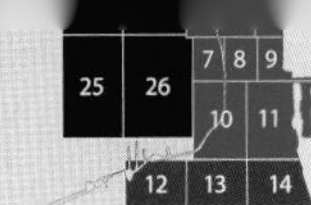

Bars

- **Bar Louie** • 226 W Chicago Ave
- **Bin 36** • 339 N Dearborn St
- **Blue Frog Bar & Grill** • 676 N La Salle Dr
- **Cyrano's Bistrot & Wine Bar** • 546 N Wells St
- **Green Door Tavern** • 678 N Orleans St
- **Harry's Velvet Room** • 56 W Illinois St
- **Martini Ranch** • 311 W Chicago Ave
- **Mother Hubbard's** • 5 W Hubbard St
- **Red Head Piano Bar** • 16 W Ontario St

Copy Shops

- **A Cut Rate Printers** • 1 E Wacker Dr
- **AlphaGraphics** • 154 W Hubbard St
- **Chicago Print** • 71 W Chicago Ave
- **Cushing & Co** • 325 W Huron St
- **Franklin's Printing** • 65 E Wacker Pl
- **Kinko's** • 444 N Wells St
- **Mail Boxes Etc** • 446 N Wells St
- **Sir Speedy** • 18 W Hubbard St

Coffee

- **Cosi** • 55 E Grand Ave
- **Dunkin' Donuts** • 20 E Chicago Ave
- **Seattle's Best** • 42 E Chicago Ave
- **Seattle's Best** • 701 N Wells St
- **Starbucks** • 345 N La Salle St
- **Starbucks** • 35 E Wacker Dr
- **Starbucks** • 414 N Orleans St
- **Starbucks** • 430 N Clark St
- **Starbucks** • 600 N State St
- **Starbucks** • 750 N Franklin St

Gyms

- **Crunch Fitness** • 350 N State St
- **Crunch Fitness** • 38 E Grand Ave
- **Executive Sports & Fitness Ctr** • 77 W Wacker Dr
- **Lakeshore Athletic Club** • 441 N Wabash Ave
- **Ontario Place Fitness Club** • 10 E Ontario St
- **Sharper Fitness** • 401 N Ontario St

Hardware Stores

- **Clark & Barlow Hardware** • 353 W Grand Ave
- **Hinges & Handles** • 222 Merchandise Mart Plz

Liquor Stores

- **Binny's Beverage Depot** • 213 W Grand Ave
- **Copperfield's** • 70 W Huron St
- **Dalal Food & Liquor** • 414 N State St
- **Holiday Wines & Spirits** • 6 W Chicago Ave
- **Rossi's Liquors** • 412 N State St
- **Superior Liquor** • 750 N Clark St
- **White Hen Pantry** • 645 N State St

Restaurants

- **Ace Grill** • 71 E Wacker
- **Bob Chinn's Crab House** • 321 N La Salle St
- **Brasserie Jo** • 59 W Hubbard St
- **Cafe Iberico** • 739 N La Salle St
- **Chicago Chop House** • 60 W Ontario St
- **Club Lago** • 331 W Superior St
- **Crofton on Wells** • 535 Wells St
- **Cyrano's Bistrot & Wine Bar** • 546 N Wells St
- **Erawan Royal Thai Cuisine** • 729 N Clark St
- **Frontera Grill** • 445 N Clark St
- **Gaylord India** • 678 N Clark St
- **Gene & Georgetti** • 500 N Franklin St
- **Harray Caray's** • 33 W Kinzie St
- **House of Blues** • 329 N Dearborn St
- **Jaipur Palace** • 22 E Hubbard St
- **Kevin** • 9 W Hubbard St
- **Kinzie Chophouse** • 400 N Wells St
- **Klay Oven** • 414 N Orleans St
- **Lawry's The Prime Rib** • 100 E Ontario St
- **Linos** • 222 W Ontario St
- **Lou Malnati's Pizzeria** • 439 N Wells St
- **Maggiano's Little Italy** • 516 N Clark St
- **Magnum's Prime Steakhouse** • 225 W Ontario St
- **Mr Beef** • 666 N Orleans St
- **Nacional 27** • 325 W Huron St
- **Narcisse** • 710 N Clark St
- **Original Gino's East** • 633 N Wells St
- **Pizzeria Due** • 619 N Wabash Ave
- **Pizzeria Uno** • 29 E Ohio St
- **Redfish** • 400 N State St
- **Rosebud on Rush** • 720 N Rush St
- **Rumba** • 351 W Hubbard St
- **Shaw's Crab House & Blue Crab Lounge** • 21 E Hubbard St
- **Smith & Wollensky** • 318 N State St
- **Sorriso** • 321 N Clark St
- **Star of Siam** • 11 E Illinois St
- **Sullivan's Steakhouse** • 415 N Dearborn St
- **Sushi Naniwa** • 607 N Wells St
- **Thai Star Cafe** • 660 N State St
- **Tizi Melloul** • 531 N Wells St
- **Topolobampo** • 445 N Clark St
- **Vong's Thai Kitchen** • 6 W Hubbard St
- **Wildfire** • 159 W Erie St
- **Zinfandel** • 59 W Grand Ave

Shopping

- **Jazz Record Mart** • 444 N Wabash Ave
- **Mary Wolf Gallery** • 705 Dearborn St
- **Mig and Tig Furniture** • 549 N Wells St
- **Montauk** • 223 W Erie St
- **Nordstrom** • 55 E Grand Ave
- **Paper Source** • 232 W Chicago Ave
- **Sportmart** • 620 N La Salle St

Video Rental

- **Blockbuster Video** • 700 N State St

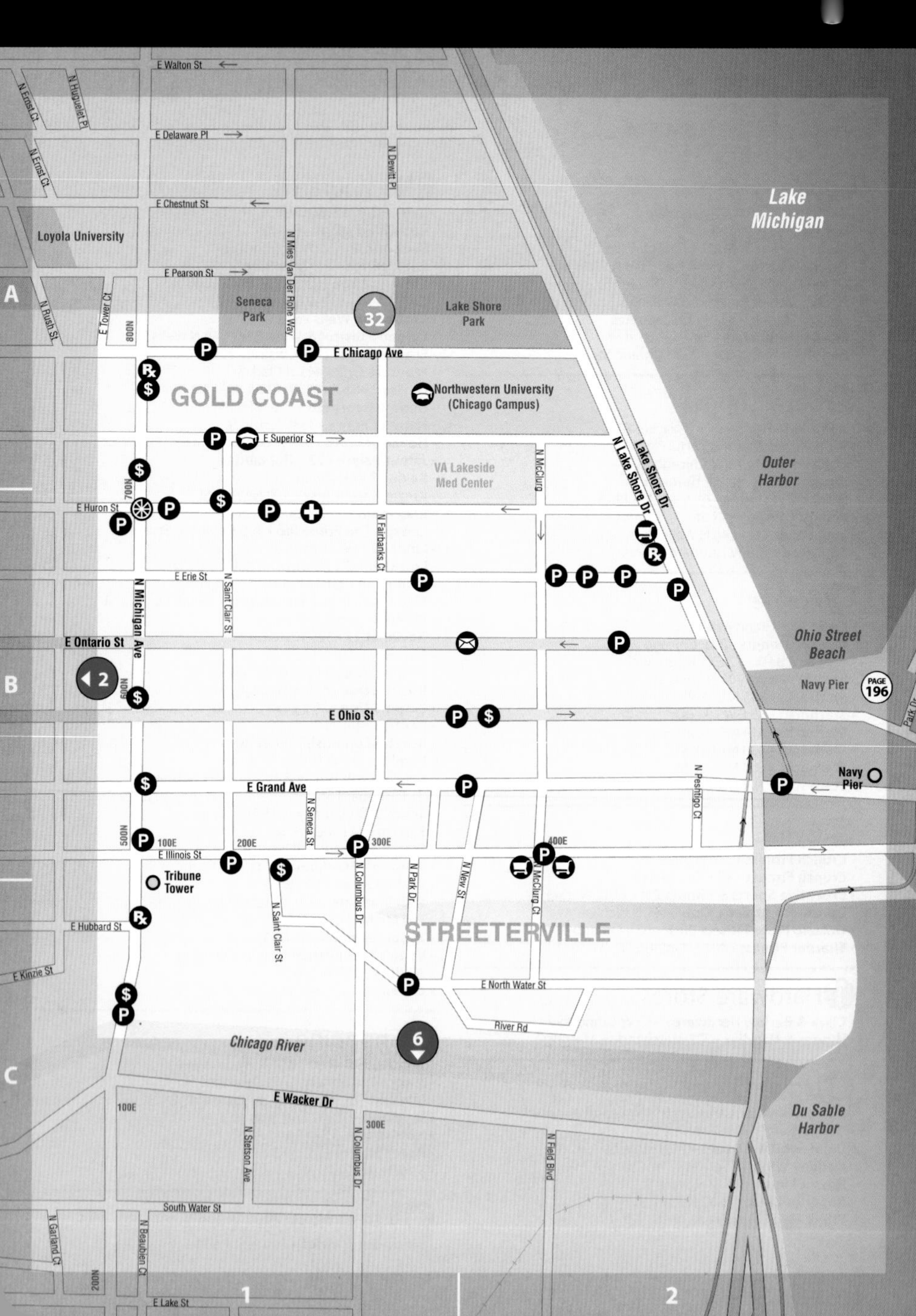

E Walton St
N Ernst Ct
N Huguelet Pl
E Delaware Pl
N Dewitt Pl
E Chestnut St
Lake Michigan
Loyola University
N Mies Van Der Rohe Way
E Pearson St
A
N Rush St
E Tower Ct
Seneca Park
32
Lake Shore Park
800N
E Chicago Ave
GOLD COAST
Northwestern University (Chicago Campus)
E Superior St
VA Lakeside Med Center
N McClurg
N Lake Shore Dr
Lake Shore Dr
Outer Harbor
700N
E Huron St
N Fairbanks Ct
E Erie St
N Saint Clair St
N Michigan Ave
E Ontario St
Ohio Street Beach
B
2
600N
Navy Pier
PAGE 196
E Ohio St
Park Dr
E Grand Ave
N Peshtigo Ct
Navy Pier
N Seneca St
500N
100E
200E
300E
400E
E Illinois St
Tribune Tower
N Columbus Dr
N Park Dr
N New St
N McClurg Ct
E Hubbard St
N Saint Clair St
STREETERVILLE
E Kinzie St
E North Water St
River Rd
Chicago River
6
C
E Wacker Dr
100E
300E
N Stetson Ave
N Columbus Dr
N Field Blvd
Du Sable Harbor
South Water St
N Garland Ct
N Beaubien Ct
200N
E Lake St
1
2

The tiny, densely populated blocks of Streeterville are home to lots of big stores, lots of big restaurants, and lots of big hotels, as well as the maze that is the Northwestern University Medical campus. Hoity-toity residents of the premier highrises sip their champagne and laugh at the overwhelmed tourists who look like ants so far below.

Banks

- **Banco Popular** • 717 N Michigan Ave
- **Bank One** • 605 N Michigan Ave
- **Citibank** • 539 N Michigan Ave
- **Harris Trust & Savings Bank** • 455 N Cityfront Plaza Dr
- **North Bank** • 360 E Ohio St
- **Northern Trust Bank** • 201 E Huron St
- **US Bank** • 400 N Michigan Ave

Car Washes

- **River North Experts** • 161 E Chicago Ave

Hospitals

- **Northwestern Memorial Hospital** • 251 E Huron St

Landmarks

- **Navy Pier** • 600 E Grand Ave
- **Tribune Tower** • 435 N Michigan Ave

Pharmacies

- **Parkway Drugs** • 680 N Lake Shore Dr
- **Walgreens** • 430 N Michigan Ave
- **Walgreens** • 757 N Michigan Ave

Pizza

- **A Slice of Italy Pizzeria** • 435 E Illinois St

Post Offices

- 227 E Ontario St

Schools

- **Northwestern University** • 211 E Superior St

Supermarkets

- **Fox & Obel Food Store** • 401 E Illinois St
- **Market Place Food Store** • 393 E Illinois St
- **Treasue Island** • 680 N Lake Shore Dr (entrance on Huron)

Parking

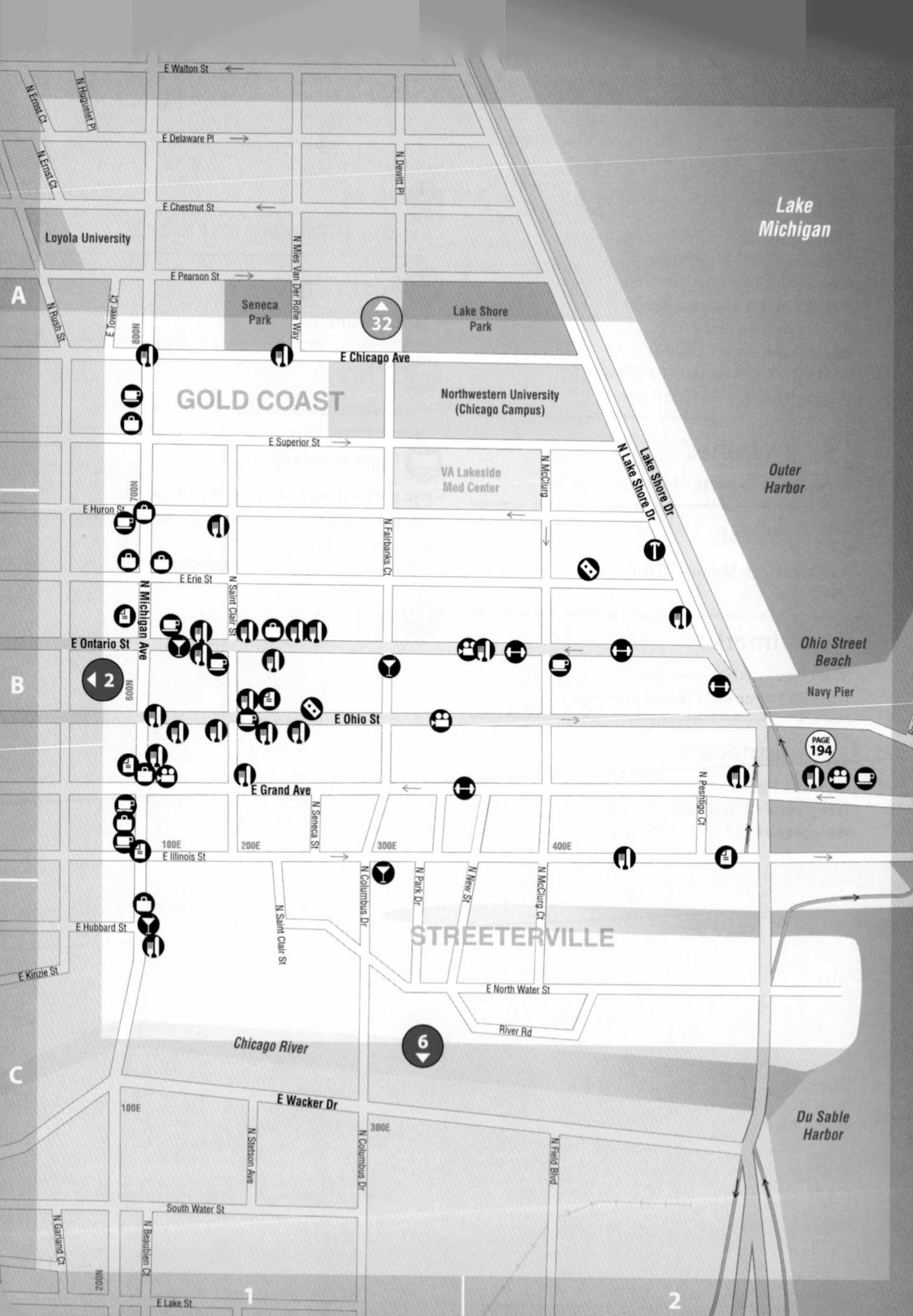
E Walton St
N Ernst Ct
N Huguelet Pl
E Delaware Pl
N Ernst Ct
N Dewitt Pl
E Chestnut St
Lake Michigan
Loyola University
N Mies Van Der Rohe Way
E Pearson St
A
N Rush St
E Tower Ct
800N
Seneca Park
32
Lake Shore Park
E Chicago Ave
GOLD COAST
Northwestern University (Chicago Campus)
E Superior St
VA Lakeside Med Center
N McClurg
N Lake Shore Dr
Lake Shore Dr
Outer Harbor
700N
E Huron St
N Fairbanks Ct
E Erie St
N Saint Clair St
N Michigan Ave
E Ontario St
Ohio Street Beach
B
2
600N
Navy Pier
E Ohio St
PAGE 194
N Peshtigo Ct
E Grand Ave
N Seneca St
100E
200E
300E
400E
E Illinois St
N Columbus Dr
N Park Dr
N New St
N McClurg Ct
N Saint Clair St
E Hubbard St
STREETERVILLE
E Kinzie St
E North Water St
River Rd
Chicago River
6
C
E Wacker Dr
100E
300E
Du Sable Harbor
N Stetson Ave
N Columbus Dr
N Field Blvd
South Water St
N Garland Ct
N Beaubien Ct
200N
E Lake St
1
2

Escape from the shopping bag-toting throngs at comfy Timothy O'Toole's Pub on Fairbanks or go underground on lower Michigan Ave. to Billy Goat Tavern, a Chicago institution. Indian Garden's lunch buffet is an office worker's fave. Bandera brings in the after-work ad. execs for roast chicken and also makes great takeout. If you've got bucks to blow and months to wait for a weekend reservation, Tru is for you.

Bars

- **Billy Goat Tavern** • 430 N Michigan Ave
- **Dick's Last Resort** • 435 E Illinois St
- **O'Neill's Bar & Grill** • 152 E Ontario St
- **Timothy O'Toole's Pub** • 622 N Fairbanks Ct

Copy Shops

- **AlphaGraphics** • 645 N Michigan Ave
- **Huey Reprographics** • 455 E Illinois St
- **Kinko's** • 540 N Michigan Ave, 2nd Fl
- **Kwik Kopy** • 500 N Michigan Ave
- **Mail Boxes Etc** • 207 E Ohio St

Coffee

- **Capra's Coffee** • 205 E Ohio St
- **Starbucks** • 401 E Ontario St
- **Starbucks** • 440 N Michigan Ave
- **Starbucks** • 600 E Grand Ave
- **Starbucks** • 670 N Michigan Ave
- **Torrefazione Italia** • 700 N Michigan Ave

Farmer's Markets

- **Museum of Contemporary Art/Streeterville** • E Chicago Ave and Mies Van der Rohe Way

Gyms

- **Holmes Place** • 355 E Grand Ave
- **Lakeshore Athletic Club** • 333 E Ontario St
- **North Pier Athletic Club** • 474 N Lake Shore Dr
- **Onterie Fitness Ctr** • 446 E Ontario St

Hardware Stores

- **Ace Hardware** • 680 N Lake Shore Dr

Movie Theaters

- **Cineplex Odeon** • 600 N Michigan Ave
- **McClurg Court Theatre** • 330 E Ohio St
- **Navy Pier Imax Theatre** • 700 E Grand Ave

Restaurants

- **Bandera** • 535 N Michigan Ave, 2nd fl
- **Bice Ristorante** • 158 E Ontario St
- **Billy Goat Tavern** • 430 N Michigan Ave
- **Cambridge House Grill** • 167 E Ohio St
- **Capital Grille** • 633 N St Clair St
- **Cite** • Lake Point Tower, 70th fl
  505 N Lake Shore Dr
- **Dick's Last Resort** • 435 E Illinois St
- **Eli's the Place for Steaks** • 215 E Chicago Ave
- **Emilio's Tapas Sol y Nieve** • 215 E Ohio St
- **Hatsuhana** • 160 E Ontario St
- **Heaven on Seven** • 600 N Michigan Ave
- **Hot Diggity Dogs** • 251 E Ohio St
- **Indian Garden** • 247 E Ontario St, 2nd fl
- **Kamehachi** • 240 E Ontario St
- **Les Nomades** • 222 E Ontario St
- **Nomi** • Park Hyatt Chicago, 800 N Michigan Ave
- **Riva** • Navy Pier, 700 E Grand Ave
- **Ron of Japan** • 230 E Ontario St
- **Sayat Nova** • 157 E Ohio St
- **Tru** • 676 N St Clair St
- **Volare** • 201 E Grand Ave
- **Wave** • 644 N Lake Shore Dr

Shopping

- **Chicago Place** • 700 N Michigan Ave
- **Crate & Barrel** • 646 N Michigan Ave
- **Decoro** • 224 E Ontario St
- **Eddie Bauer** • 600 N Michigan Ave
- **Garrett Popcorn Shop** • 670 N Michigan Ave
- **Niketown** • 669 N Michigan Ave
- **Rand McNally Store** • 444 N Michigan Ave
- **Virgin Megastore** • 540 N Michigan Ave

Video Rental

- **Chicago Video** • 230 E Ohio St
- **Hollywood Video** • 680 N Lake Shore Dr

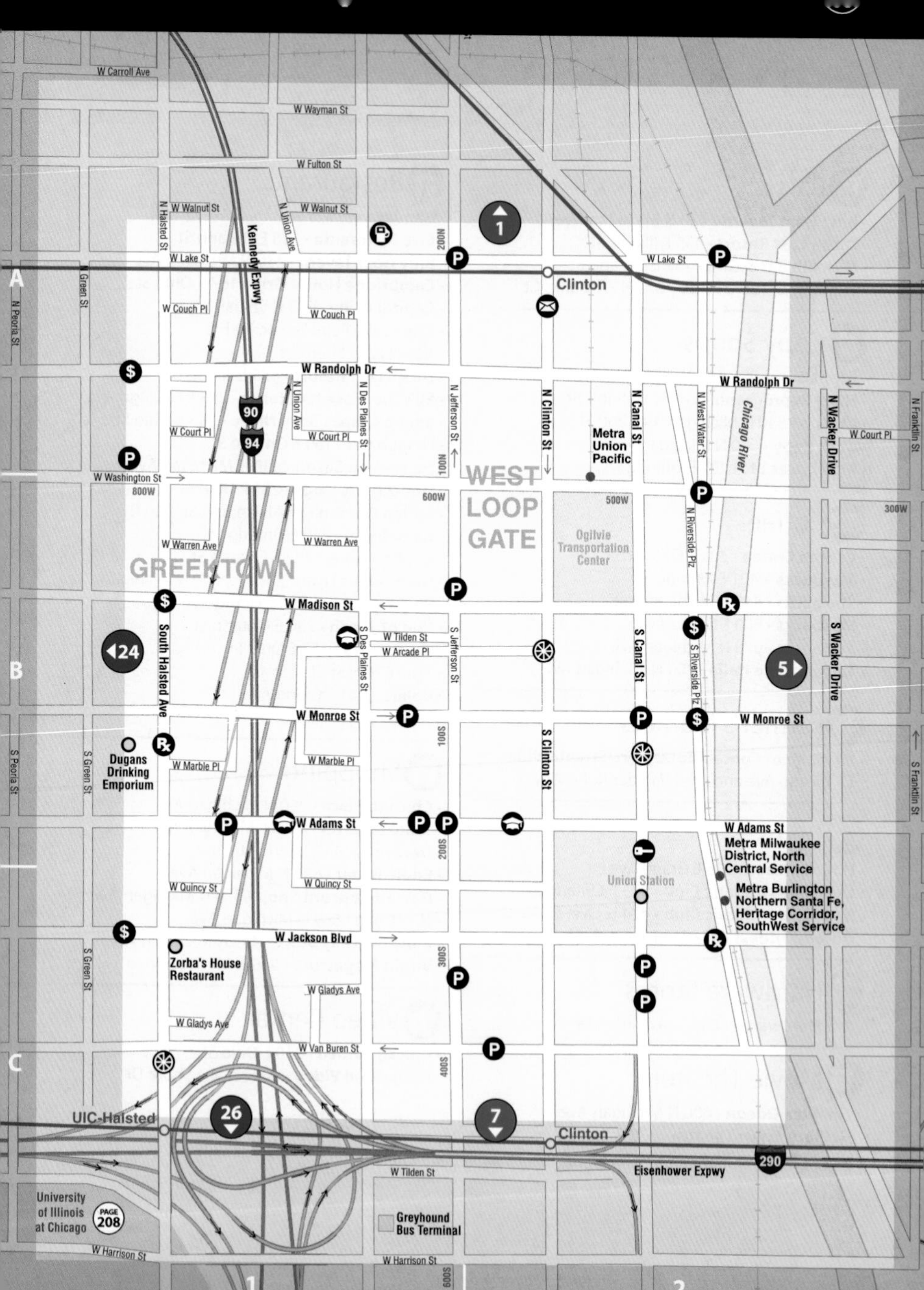

WEST LOOP GATE
GREEKTOWN
W Carroll Ave
W Wayman St
W Fulton St
W Walnut St
W Lake St
W Couch Pl
W Randolph Dr
W Court Pl
W Washington St
W Warren Ave
W Madison St
W Tilden St
W Arcade Pl
W Monroe St
W Marble Pl
W Adams St
W Quincy St
W Jackson Blvd
W Gladys Ave
W Van Buren St
W Harrison St
N Halsted St
N Green St
N Peoria St
N Union Ave
N Des Plaines St
N Jefferson St
N Clinton St
N Canal St
N West Water St
N Riverside Plz
N Wacker Drive
N Franklin St
South Halsted Ave
S Green St
S Peoria St
S Des Plaines St
S Jefferson St
S Clinton St
S Canal St
S Riverside Plz
S Wacker Drive
S Franklin St
Kennedy Expwy
Eisenhower Expwy
Chicago River
Clinton
UIC-Halsted
Metra Union Pacific
Ogilvie Transportation Center
Union Station
Metra Milwaukee District, North Central Service
Metra Burlington Northern Santa Fe, Heritage Corridor, SouthWest Service
Dugans Drinking Emporium
Zorba's House Restaurant
Greyhound Bus Terminal
University of Illinois at Chicago
PAGE 208
90
94
290
1
5
7
24
26
200N
100N
100S
200S
300S
400S
600S
800W
600W
500W
300W
A
B
C
1
2

Trains, buses, and gyros define this former warehouse district, which now contains loft residences and office spaces. The gateway for suburbanites into the city, West Loop is the address for the Richard B. Ogilvie Transportation Center (just call it Northwestern Train Station, please), grand Union Station, where Amtrak is based, and the downtown Greyhound Bus Terminal.

Map

Banks

- **American Chartered Bank** • 847 W Randolph St
- **Bank One** • 1 N Halsted St
- **Cole Taylor Bank** • 850 W Jackson Blvd
- **Corus Bank** • 10 S Riverside Plz
- **TCF Bank** • 120 S Riverside Plz

Car Rental

- **Enterprise** • 555 W Madison St • 312-906-8300
- **Hertz** • 210 S Canal St • 312-928-0538

Gas Stations

- **Fulton & Des Plaines Sinclair** • 225 N Des Plaines St

Landmarks

- **Dugans Drinking Emporium** • 128 S Halsted St
- **Union Station** • 200 S Canal St
- **Zorba's House Restaurant** • 301 S Halsted St

Pharmacies

- **Osco Drug** • 400 W Madison St
- **Walgreens** • 111 S Halsted St
- **Walgreens** • 300 S Riverside Plaza

Pizza

- **Bacino's** • 118 S Clinton St
- **Connie's Pizza** • 225 S Canal St
- **Giordano's** • 815 W Van Buren St

Post Offices

- 168 N Clinton St

Schools

- **Chicago-Kent College Law Ofc** • 565 W Adams St
- **Frances Xavier Ward School** • 700 W Adams St

Parking

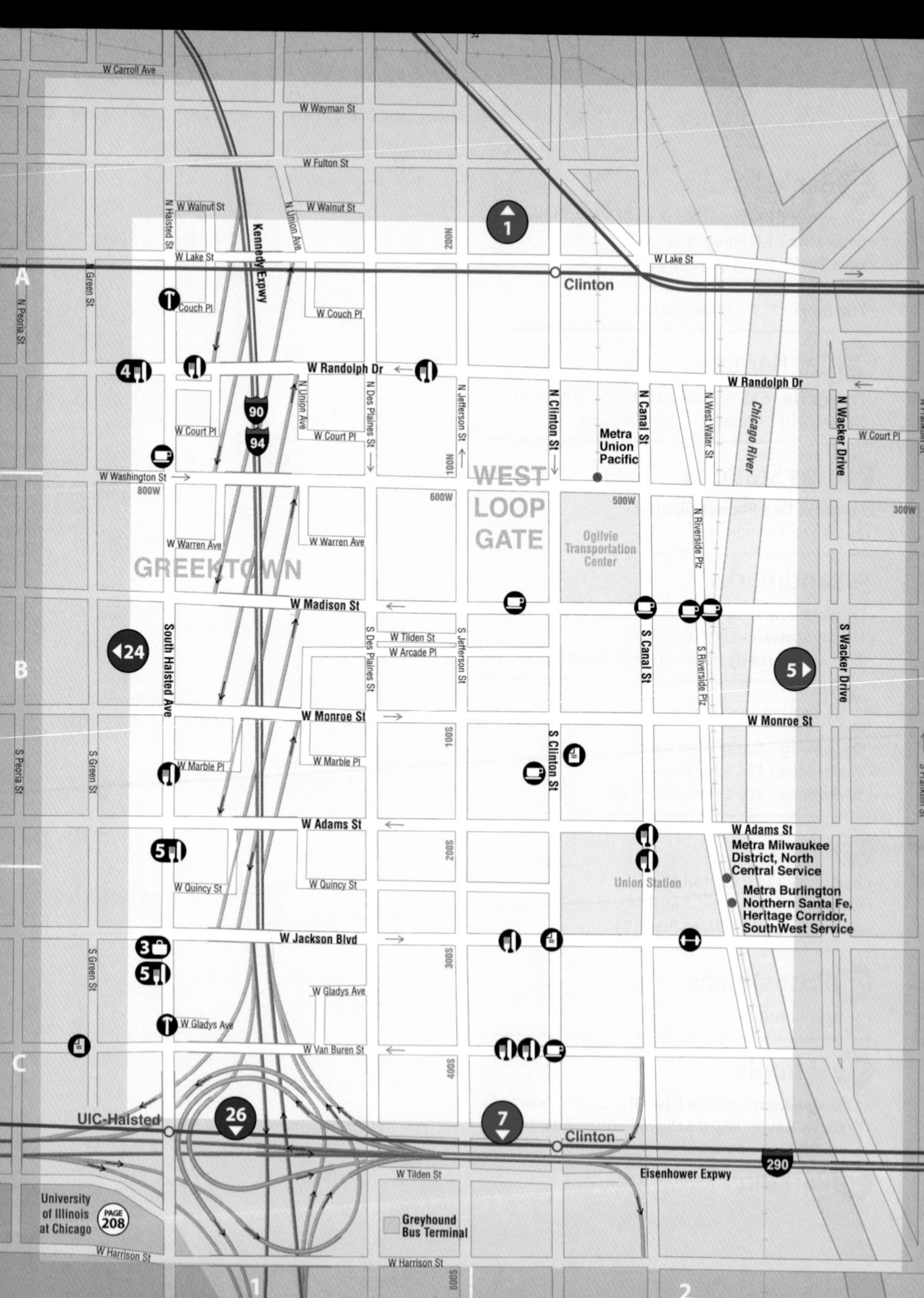

W Carroll Ave
W Wayman St
W Fulton St
W Walnut St
N Halsted St
N Union Ave
Kennedy Expwy
W Lake St
Clinton
N Green St
N Peoria St
W Couch Pl
W Randolph Dr
N Des Plaines St
N Jefferson St
N Clinton St
N Canal St
N West Water St
Chicago River
N Wacker Drive
W Court Pl
Metra Union Pacific
W Washington St
800W
600W
WEST LOOP GATE
500W
Ogilvie Transportation Center
N Riverside Plz
300W
W Warren Ave
GREEKTOWN
W Madison St
S Des Plaines St
W Tilden St
W Arcade Pl
S Jefferson St
S Canal St
S Riverside Plz
S Wacker Drive
South Halsted Ave
W Monroe St
S Clinton St
S Peoria St
S Green St
W Marble Pl
W Adams St
Metra Milwaukee District, North Central Service
Union Station
Metra Burlington Northern Santa Fe, Heritage Corridor, SouthWest Service
W Quincy St
W Jackson Blvd
W Gladys Ave
W Van Buren St
UIC-Halsted
Eisenhower Expwy
W Tilden St
University of Illinois at Chicago
PAGE 208
Greyhound Bus Terminal
W Harrison St
S Franklin St
N Franklin St

"Opaa!" rings through the streets, especially on summer evenings, when many of the fine Greek restaurants offer patio or rooftop dining. Grilled octopus is not to be missed at stylish Costa's, while Greek Islands is a sure-fire hit for birthday parties and other rowdy large-group outings. Seedy Zorba's was made famous in "My Big Fat Greek Wedding" and offers flaming cheese 24 hours a day. Athenian Candle company is not to be missed—where else can you purchase "Law be Gone" room spray, a 12-foot-tall gilded candle suitable for an Orthodox mass, a smiling Buddha statue, and a female icon allegedly dipped in dove's blood?

Copy Shops

- **Kinko's** • 127 S Clinton St
- **Kinko's** • 843 W Van Buren St
- **Sir Speedy** • 547 W Jackson Blvd

Coffee

- **Atruro Express** • 555 W Madison St
- **Cafe Apollo** • 800 W Washington Blvd
- **Seattle's Best** • 500 W Madison St
- **Starbucks** • 139 S Clinton St
- **Starbucks** • 2 N Riverside Plz
- **Starbucks** • 400 W Madison St
- **Starbucks** • 550 W Van Buren St

Gyms

- **Union Station Multiplex** • 444 W Jackson Blvd

Hardware Stores

- **Chicago Wholesale Hardware** • 171 N Halsted St
- **Turek & Sons** • 333 S Halsted St

Restaurants

- **Artopolis Bakery & Cafe** • 306 S Halsted St
- **Athena** • 212 S Halsted St
- **Azure** • 832 W Randolph St
- **Blackbird** • 619 W Randolph St
- **Bluepoint Oyster Bar** • 741 W Randolph St
- **Byzantium** • 232 S Halsted St
- **Costa's** • 340 S Halsted St
- **Gold Coast Dogs** • 2 N Riverside Plz
- **Gold Coast Dogs** • Union Station, 225 S Canal St
- **Greek Islands** • 200 S Halsted St
- **J and C Inn** • 558 W Van Buren St
- **Lou Mitchell's** • 565 W Jackson Blvd
- **Nine Muses** • 315 S Halsted St
- **Parthenon** • 314 S Halsted St
- **Pegasus Restaurant and Taverna** • 130 S Halsted St
- **Red Light** • 820 W Randolph St
- **Robinson's No 1 Ribs** • 225 S Canal St
- **Roditys** • 222 S Halsted St
- **Santorini** • 800 W Adams St
- **Sushi Wabi** • 842 W Randolph St
- **Vivo** • 838 W Randolph St

Shopping

- **Athenian Candle Co** • 300 S Halsted St
- **Athens Jewelry** • 310 S Halsted St
- **Greek Town Gifts** • 330 S Halsted St

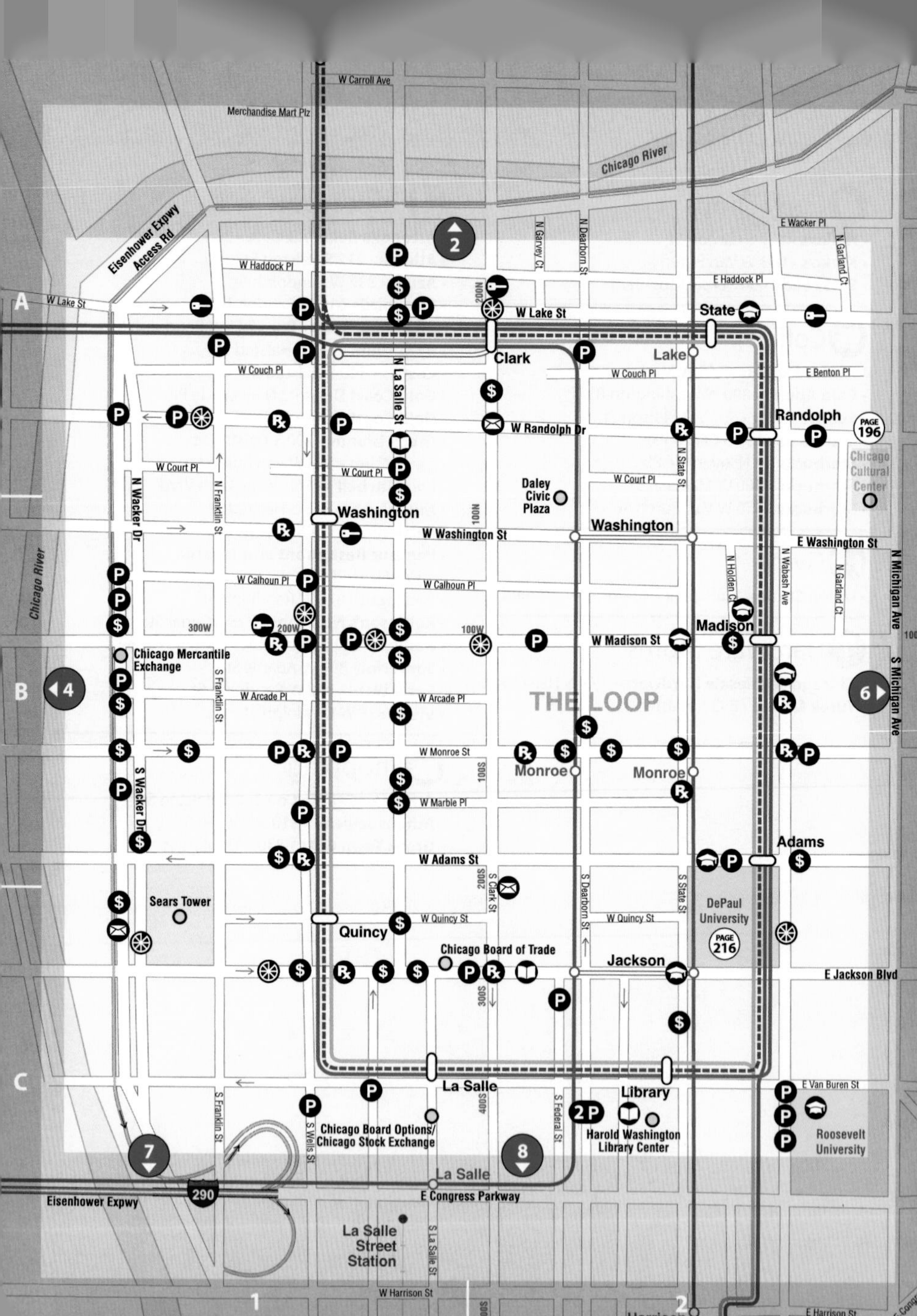
W Carroll Ave
Merchandise Mart Plz
Chicago River
Eisenhower Expwy Access Rd
E Wacker Pl
N Garvey Ct
N Dearborn St
N Garland Ct
W Haddock Pl
E Haddock Pl
A
W Lake St
200N
W Lake St
State
Clark
Lake
W Couch Pl
W Couch Pl
E Benton Pl
N La Salle St
Randolph
PAGE 196
W Randolph Dr
Chicago Cultural Center
W Court Pl
W Court Pl
W Court Pl
N State St
N Franklin St
N Wacker Dr
Daley Civic Plaza
Washington
100N
W Washington St
Washington
E Washington St
N Michigan Ave
Chicago River
W Calhoun Pl
W Calhoun Pl
N Holden Ct
N Wabash Ave
N Garland Ct
300W
200W
100W
W Madison St
Madison
Chicago Mercantile Exchange
B
4
S Franklin St
W Arcade Pl
W Arcade Pl
THE LOOP
6
S Michigan Ave
W Monroe St
Monroe
Monroe
100S
S Wacker Dr
W Marble Pl
Adams
W Adams St
200S
S Clark St
S Dearborn St
S State St
Sears Tower
DePaul University
W Quincy St
W Quincy St
Quincy
PAGE 216
Chicago Board of Trade
Jackson
E Jackson Blvd
300S
C
E Van Buren St
La Salle
Library
S Franklin St
S Federal St
400S
2P
Chicago Board Options/ Chicago Stock Exchange
S Wells St
Harold Washington Library Center
Roosevelt University
7
8
La Salle
290
Eisenhower Expwy
E Congress Parkway
La Salle Street Station
S La Salle St
W Harrison St
1
2
E Harrison St

It all starts here, where money changes hands at the CBOT, CBOE, CSE, and CME. The Loop, named after the El tracks lassoing Chicago's heart, is the bustling business and financial district. With all the banks, an ATM is much easier to find than a metered parking space, although pricey parking garages abound. The intersection of State and Madison Streets is the point from which Chicago's simple and efficient street number grid system starts making navigation pretty easy.

Banks

- **Amalgamated Bank Of Chicago** • 1 W Monroe St
- **Associated Bank** • 200 N La Salle St
- **Banco Popular** • 415 N La Salle St
- **Bank of America** • 231 S La Salle St
- **Bank of New York** • 209 W Jackson Blvd
- **Bank One** • 120 S La Salle St
- **Bank One** • 30 S Wacker Dr
- **Bank One** • 55 W Monroe St
- **Burling Bank** • 141 W Jackson Blvd
- **Charter One Bank** • 150 S Wacker Dr
- **Charter One Bank** • 400 S La Salle St
- **Citibank** • 11 S La Salle St
- **Citibank** • 222 W Adams St
- **CIB Bank** • 161 N Clark St
- **Cole Taylor Bank** • 111 W Washington St
- **Fifth Third Bank** • 233 S Wacker Dr
- **First American Bank** • 33 W Monroe St
- **First American Bank** • 50 E Adams St
- **First Bank** • 20 N Wacker Dr
- **Harris Trust & Savings Bank** • 311 W Monroe St
- **Harris Trust & Savings Bank** • 99 W Washington St
- **Harris Trust & Savings Bank** • 111 W Monroe St
- **International Commercial Bank of China** • 2 N La Salle St
- **LaSalle Bank** • 100 S Wacker Dr
- **LaSalle Bank** • 120 N La Salle St
- **LaSalle Bank** • 135 S La Salle St
- **LaSalle Bank** • 203 N La Salle St
- **LaSalle Bank** • 77 S Dearborn St
- **MB Financial Bank** • 1 S Wacker Dr
- **MB Financial Bank** • 2 S LaSalle St
- **Northern Trust Bank** • 50 S La Salle St
- **Shore Bank** • 333 S State St
- **TCF Bank** • 29 E Madison St

Car Rental

- **Avis** • 214 N Clark St • 312-782-6825
- **Budget** • 65 E Lake St • 773-686-6800
- **Enterprise** • 201 W Madison St • 312-553-5230
- **Enterprise** • 303 W Lake St • 312-332-7783
- **Enterprise** • 425 S Wells St • 312-939-6001
- **Hertz** • 181 W Washington Blvd • 312-726-1476
- **National/Alamo** • 203 N La Salle St • 312-236-2581

Landmarks

- **Chicago Board of Trade** • 141 W Jackson Blvd
- **Chicago Board Options Exchange** • 400 S La Salle St
- **Chicago Cultural Center** • 78 E Washington
- **Chicago Mercantile Exchange** • 20-30 S Wacker Dr
- **Chicago Stock Exchange** • 440 S La Salle St
- **Daley Civic Plaza** • 50 W Washington St
- **Harold Washington Library Center** • 400 S State St
- **Sears Tower** • 233 S Wacker Dr

Libraries

- **Chicago Public Library** • 400 S State St
- **Municipal Reference Library** • 121 N La Salle St
- **US Library** • 77 W Jackson Blvd

Pharmacies

- **CVS Pharmacy** • 105 S Wabash Ave
- **CVS Pharmacy** • 175 W Jackson Blvd
- **CVS Pharmacy** • 208 W Washington Blvd
- **Osco Drug** • 111 W Jackson Blvd
- **Osco Drug** • 137 S State St
- **Osco Drug** • 205 W Monroe St
- **Walgreens** • 151 N State St
- **Walgreens** • 200 W Adam St
- **Walgreens** • 201 W Madison St
- **Walgreens** • 240 W Randolph St
- **Walgreens** • 25 S Wabash Ave
- **Walgreens** • 79 W Monroe St

Pizza

- **Davino's Little Pompei** • 181 W Madison St
- **Davino's Little Pompei** • 218 W Washington St
- **Giordano's** • 310 W Randolph St
- **Giordano's** • 225 W Jackson Blvd
- **Giordano's** • 236 S Wabash Ave
- **Mama Falco's** • 5 N Wells St
- **Milano's Italian Eatery** • 201 N Clark St
- **Sbarro** • 105 W Madison St
- **Sbarro** • 253 S Wacker Dr

Post Offices

- 100 W Randolph St
- 211 S Clark St
- 233 S Wacker Dr

Schools

- **Burnham Park Prep School** • 421 S Wabash Ave
- **Career Colleges of Chicago** • 11 E Adams St
- **DePaul University** • 1 E Jackson Blvd
- **Harold Washington College** • 30 E Lake St
- **International Academy of Design and Technology-** • 1 N State St
- **Keller Graduate School of Mgmt** • 225 W Washington St
- **Loop Laboratory School** • 11 E Adams St
- **MacCormac College** • 29 E Madison St
- **School of the Art Institute** • 37 S Wabash Ave

Parking

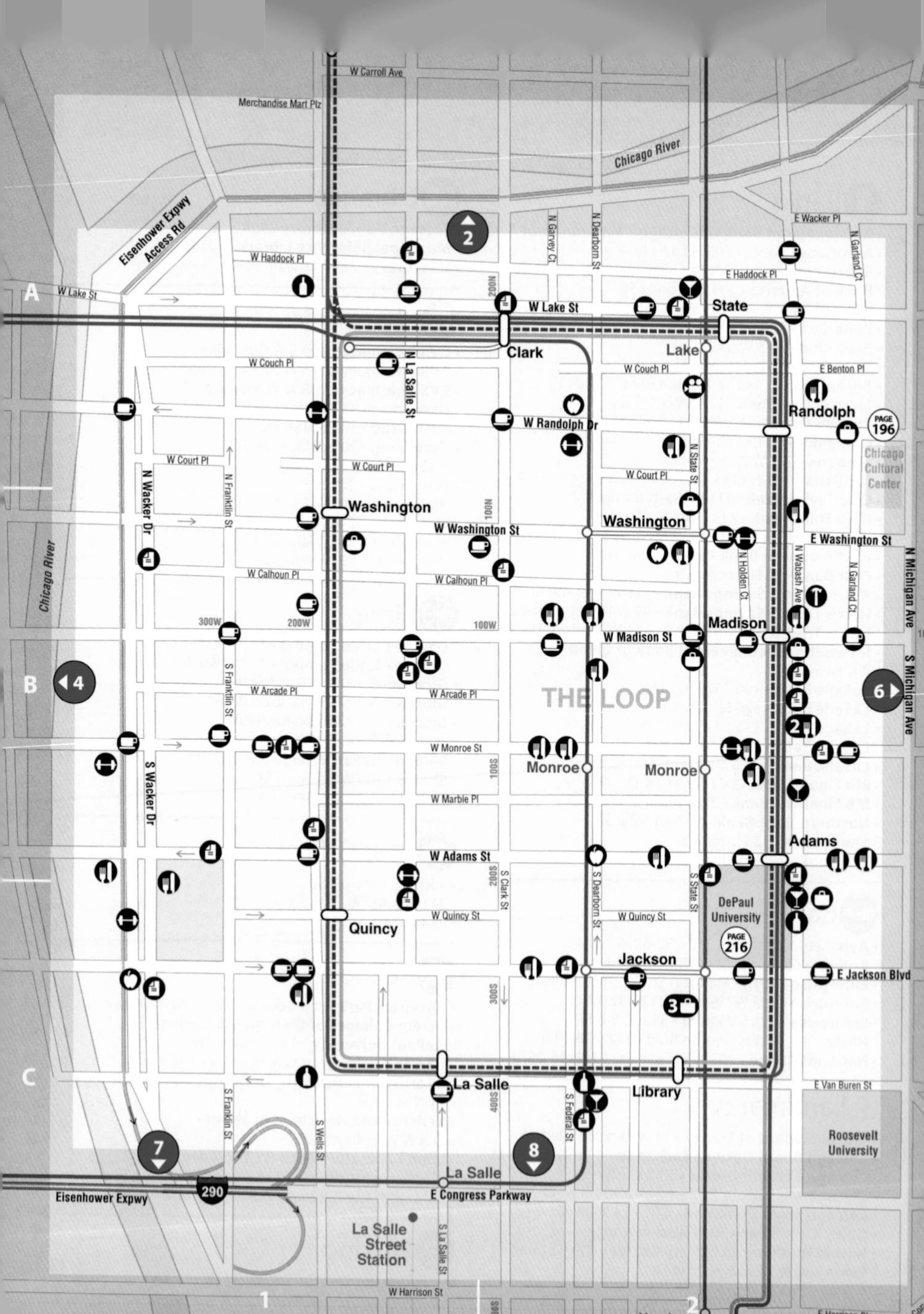

W Carroll Ave
Merchandise Mart Plz
Chicago River
Eisenhower Expwy Access Rd
W Haddock Pl
W Lake St
E Wacker Pl
N Garvey Ct
N Dearborn St
E Haddock Pl
N Garland Ct
State
Clark
Lake
W Couch Pl
E Benton Pl
N La Salle St
W Randolph Dr
Randolph
PAGE 196
Chicago Cultural Center
W Court Pl
N Wacker Dr
N Franklin St
Washington
W Washington St
N State St
E Washington St
Chicago River
W Calhoun Pl
N Holden Ct
N Wabash Ave
N Michigan Ave
300W
200W
100W
W Madison St
Madison
B
4
THE LOOP
6
W Arcade Pl
S Franklin St
S Michigan Ave
W Monroe St
S Wacker Dr
Monroe
W Marble Pl
W Adams St
Adams
S Clark St
S Dearborn St
S State St
DePaul University
PAGE 216
W Quincy St
Quincy
Jackson
E Jackson Blvd
C
La Salle
Library
E Van Buren St
S Federal St
S Wells St
Roosevelt University
7
8
Eisenhower Expwy
290
La Salle
E Congress Parkway
La Salle Street Station
S La Salle St
W Harrison St
1
2
E Harrison St

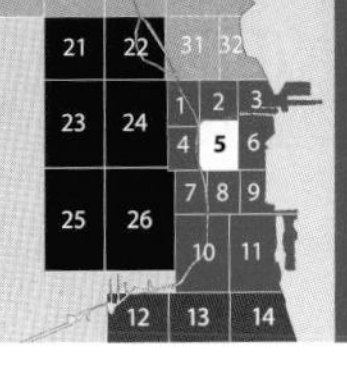

Retail giants Marshall Field's and Carson Pirie Scott anchor State St. Once a great street that went downhill, it's now making a comeback with new retail blood, renovated hotels, and revitalized theaters. Armies of lawyers and loyal civil servants march among dozens of government buildings located within blocks of each other. Everest Room is easily the biggest expense report restaurant in the Loop. For decades, spicy Heaven on Seven has drawn Loop workers for Creole home cookin'.

Bars

- **Exchequer Pub** • 226 S Wabash Ave
- **Govnor's Pub** • 207 N State St
- **Manhattans** • 415 S Dearborn St
- **Miller's Pub** • 134 S Wabash Ave

Copy Shops

- **24 Seven Copies** • 222 N La Salle St
- **Acme Copy** • 218 S Wabash Ave
- **Advance Instant Printing** • 5 S Wabash Ave
- **AlphaGraphics** • 208 S La Salle St
- **Aro Printing Services** • 200 W Adams St
- **Copy Box** • 417 S Dearborn St
- **Fastrac Copying** • 220 S State St
- **Huey Reprographics** • 19 S Wabash Ave
- **Instant Printing** • 200 S Clark St
- **Kinko's** • 227 W Monroe St
- **Kinko's** • 29 S La Salle St
- **Kinko's** • 55 E Monroe St
- **Kinko's** • 6 W Lake St
- **Kwik Kopy** • 11 S La Salle St
- **Loop Legal Copies** • 318 W Adams St
- **Mail Boxes Etc** • 27 N Wacker Dr
- **Record Copy Service** • 30 N La Salle St
- **Sir Speedy** • 311 S Wacker Dr
- **Viking Printing & Copying** • 53 W Jackson Blvd

Coffee

- **Caribou Coffee** • 10 S La Salle St
- **Caribou Coffee** • 311 W Monroe St
- **Caribou Coffee** • 55 W Monroe St
- **Cosi** • 203 N La Salle St
- **Cosi** • 230 W Monroe St
- **Cosi** • 230 W Washington St
- **Cosi** • 28 E Jackson Blvd
- **Dunkin' Donuts** • 100 W Randolph St
- **Dunkin' Donuts** • 19 N Wells St
- **Dunkin' Donuts** • 229 W Jackson Blvd
- **Dunkin' Donuts** • 31 E Adams St
- **Dunkin' Donuts** • 39 W Jackson Blvd
- **Dunkin' Donuts** • 6 N Wabash Ave
- **Java Java** • 2 N State St
- **Liberty Coffee and Tea** • 401 S La Salle St
- **Starbucks** • 100 S Wacker Dr
- **Starbucks** • 111 W Washington St
- **Starbucks** • 150 N Wacker Dr
- **Starbucks** • 180 N La Salle St
- **Starbucks** • 200 W Adams St
- **Starbucks** • 209 W Jackson Blvd
- **Starbucks** • 227 W Monroe St
- **Starbucks** • 25 E Washington Blvd
- **Starbucks** • 303 W Madison St
- **Starbucks** • 40 W Lake St
- **Starbucks** • 55 E Jackson Blvd
- **Starbucks** • 68 E Madison St
- **Starbucks** • 70 W Madison St
- **The Coffee Grounds** • 203 N Wabash Ave

Farmer's Markets

- **Daley Center Plaza** • 55 W Randolph St
- **Farmers Market** • 311 S Wacker Dr
- **Federal Plaza** • Adams St & Dearborn St
- **The Park at Jackson & Wacker** • 311 S Wacker Dr at Sears Tower

Gyms

- **Bally Total Fitness** • 230 W Monroe St
- **Bally Total Fitness** • 25 E Washington St
- **Executive Fitness Ctr** • 17 E Monroe St
- **Randolph Athletic Club** • 188 W Randolph St
- **Women's Workout World** • 208 S La Salle St
- **World Gym Fitness Center** • 150 S Wacker Dr

Hardware Stores

- **Ace Hardware** • 26 N Wabash Ave

Liquor Stores

- **Cal's Liquor Store** • 400 S Wells St
- **Lake & Wells Food & Liquor** • 201 W Lake St
- **Rothschild Liquor Marts** • 55 W Van Buren St
- **Wabash Food & Liquor** • 234 W Wabash Ave

Movie Theaters

- **Gene Siskel Film Center** • 164 N State St

Restaurants

- **Atwood Cafe** • 1 W Washington St
- **Berghoff Restaurant** • 17 W Adams St
- **Billy Goat Tavern** • 330 S Wells St
- **Everest** • 440 S LaSalle St
- **French Quarter/Palmer House Hilton** • 17 E Monroe St
- **Gold Coast Dogs** • 159 N Wabash Ave
- **Gold Coast Dogs** • 17 S Wabash Ave
- **Heaven on Seven** • 111 N Wabash Ave
- **Italian Village** • 71 W Monroe St
- **La Cantina Enoteca** • 71 W Monroe St
- **La Rosetta** • 70 W Madison St
- **Miller's Pub** • 134 S Wabash Ave
- **Mrs Levy's Delicatessen** • 233 S Wacker Dr
- **Oasis Restaurant** • 21 N Wabash Ave
- **Quincy Grille on the River** • 200 S Wacker Dr
- **Rhapsody** • Symphony Ctr, 65 E Adams St
- **Robinson's No 1 Ribs** • 77 W Jackson Blvd
- **Russian Tea Time** • 77 E Adams St
- **Taza** • 39 S Wabash Ave
- **Trattoria No 10** • 10 N Dearborn St
- **Vivere** • 71 W Monroe St

Shopping

- **Afrocentric Bookstore** • 333 S State St
- **American Music World** • 333 S State St
- **Carson Pirie Scott** • 1 S State St
- **Crows Nest Records** • 333 S State St
- **Gallery 37 Store** • 66 E Randolph St
- **Jeweler's Mall** • 7 S Wabash Ave
- **Marshall Field's** • 111 N State St
- **Ragstock** • 226 S Wabash Ave, 2nd fl
- **Rock Records** • 175 W Washington St
- **Sears** • 2 N State St

Map 6 • The Loop / Grant Park

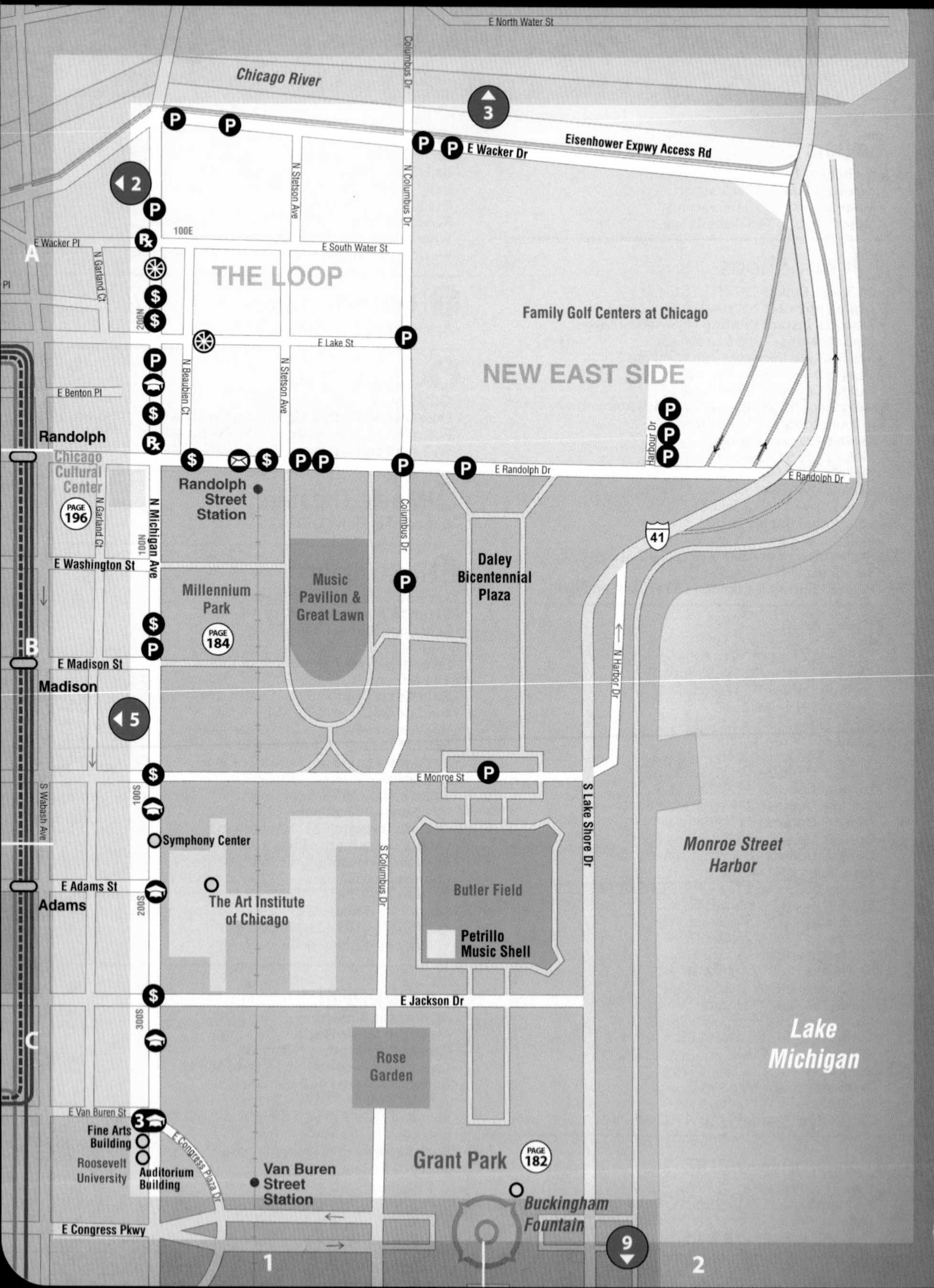

Essentials

Grant Park is Chicago's front lawn, where glass meets grass. The 319-acre park, designed by architect Daniel Burnham, is Chicagoans' favorite place to promenade, party, play, and protest. At Buckingham Fountain, turn back towards the city and survey the sparkling, stalwart stretch of skyscrapers representative of world renowned Chicago architectural styles. Millennium Park on the northwest corner promises to deliver more greenery and outdoor entertainment venues by the 21st Century's end.

Car Rental

- **Enterprise** • 151 E Wacker Dr • 312-565-6518

Banks

- **Associated Bank** • 130 E Randolph St
- **Associated Bank** • 200 E Randolph St
- **Associated Bank** • 225 N Michigan Ave
- **Chicago Community Bank** • 180 N Michigan Ave
- **Citibank** • 100 S Michigan Ave
- **Citibank** • 233 N Michigan Ave
- **Midwest Bank & Trust Company** • 300 S Michigan Ave
- **US Bank** • 30 N Michigan Ave

Landmarks

- **Art Institute of Chicago** • 111 S Michigan Ave
- **Auditorium Building** • 430 S Michigan Ave
- **Buckingham Fountain** • Grant Park, between Balbo & Columbus
- **Fine Arts Building** • 410 S Michigan Ave
- **Symphony Center** • 22 S Michigan Ave

Pharmacies

- **CVS Pharmacy** • 205 N Michigan Ave
- **Osco Drug** • 150 N Michigan Ave
- **Walgreens** • 300 N Michigan Ave

Pizza

- **Giordano's** • 135 E Lake St
- **Sbarro** • 233 N Michigan Ave

Post Offices

- 200 E Randolph St

Schools

- **American Academy of Art** • 332 S Michigan Ave
- **American English Academy** • 180 N Michigan Ave
- **Harrington Institute-Interior** • 410 S Michigan Ave
- **National-Louis University** • 122 S Michigan Ave
- **Roosevelt University** • 430 S Michigan Ave

Parking

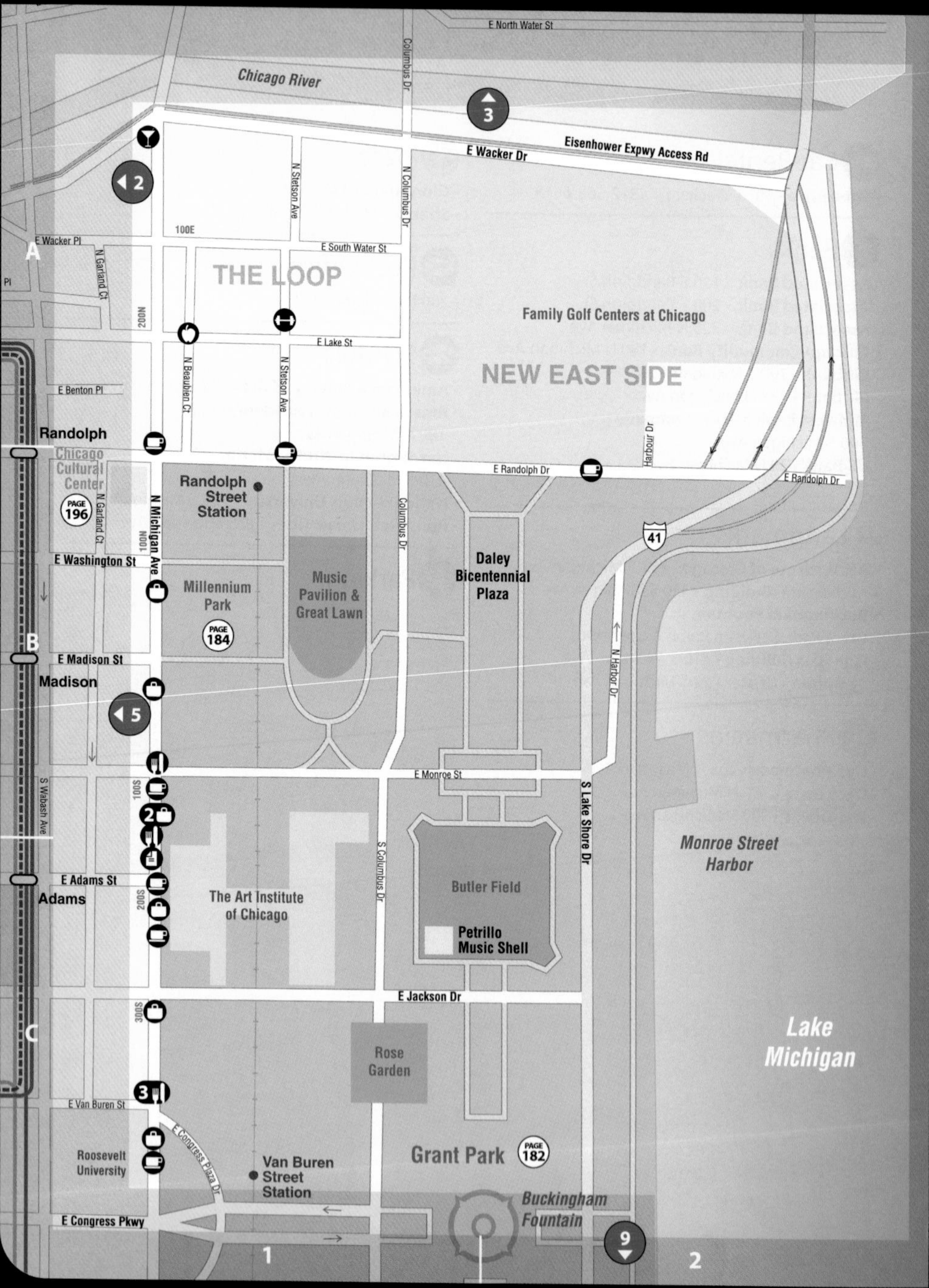

Map 6 • The Loop / Grant Park

Throngs pack belly-to-belly for the free summer festivals in Grant Park. Take in the finest collection of Impressionist paintings outside of Paris on Tuesdays at the Art Institute, when admission is free and it's open until 8pm. The Bennigan's across the street is the world's busiest—take that as you may. On non-festival days, the park is a lovely place to kill a few hours lounging on the lawn in the shadow of BuckinghamFountain—as long as you can avoid the occasional crazies who also enjoy the park's beautiful expanses.

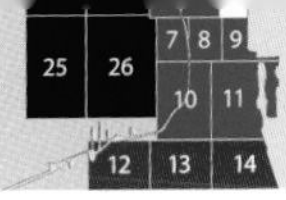

Bars

- **Houlihan's** • 111 E Wacker

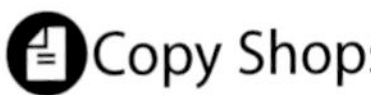

Copy Shops

- **AlphaGraphics** • 205 N Michigan Ave

Coffee

- **Cosi** • 116 S Michigan Ave
- **Dunkin' Donuts** • 233 N Michigan Ave
- **Rain Dog Books & Café** • 408 S Michigan Ave
- **Seattle's Best** • 150 N Michigan Ave
- **Starbucks** • 200 E Randolph St
- **Starbucks** • 200 N Michigan Ave
- **Starbucks** • 400 E Randolph St

Farmer's Markets

- **Prudential Plaza** • E Lake St & N Beaubien Ct

Gyms

- **Lakeshore Athletic Club** • 211 N Stetson Ave

Restaurants

- **Artist's Cafe** • 412 S Michigan Ave
- **Bennigan's** • 150 S Michigan Ave
- **Rain Dog Books & Café** • 408 S Michigan Ave
- **Restaurant on the Park** • The Art Institute of Chicago, 111 S Michigan Ave

Shopping

- **Art & Artisians** • 108 S Michigan Ave
- **Museum Shop of the Art Institute** • 111 S Michigan Ave
- **Poster Plus** • 200 S Michigan Ave
- **Precious Possessions** • 28 N Michigan Ave
- **Rain Dog Books and Café** • 408 S Michigan Ave
- **The Savvy Traveller** • 310 S Michigan Ave

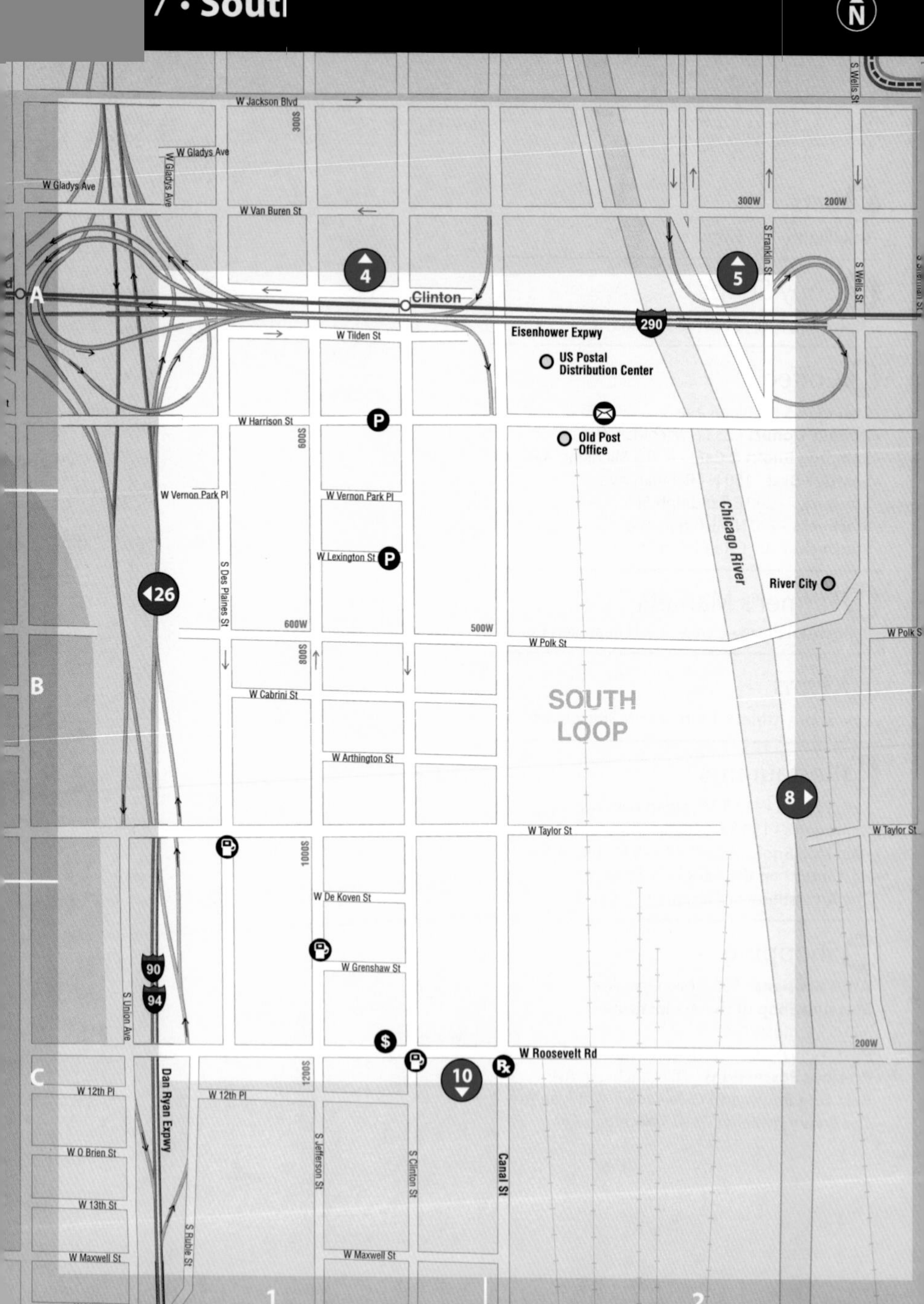
N
W Jackson Blvd
300S
W Gladys Ave
W Gladys Ave
W Gladys Ave
W Van Buren St
300W
200W
S Franklin St
S Wells St
S Wells St
4
5
A
Clinton
290
Eisenhower Expwy
W Tilden St
US Postal Distribution Center
W Harrison St
P
600S
Old Post Office
W Vernon Park Pl
W Vernon Park Pl
Chicago River
W Lexington St
P
26
S Des Plaines St
River City
600W
500W
W Polk St
W Polk St
800S
B
W Cabrini St
SOUTH LOOP
W Arthington St
8
W Taylor St
W Taylor St
1000S
W De Koven St
W Grenshaw St
90
94
S Union Ave
$
200W
W Roosevelt Rd
C
1200S
10
W 12th Pl
W 12th Pl
Dan Ryan Expwy
W O Brien St
S Jefferson St
S Clinton St
Canal St
W 13th St
S Ruble St
W Maxwell St
W Maxwell St
W Liberty St
1
2

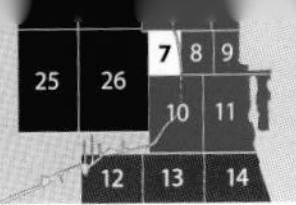

This stretch of South Loop is a tangle of train tracks and expressways, with a dirty river running through it. The old central Post Office could kiss the wrecking ball or go condo. Semis rumble around the giant mail distribution center on Harrison and get lost in the endless knot of the expressway interchange. So your check is on the road, not in the mail.

Banks

- **South Central Bank** • 525 W Roosevelt Rd

Gas Stations

- **BP** • 534 W Roosevelt Rd
- **Citgo** • 1004 S Des Plaines St
- **Marathon** • 1121 S Jefferson St

Landmarks

- **Old Post Office** • 404 W Harrison St
- **River City** • 800 S Wells St
- **US Postal Distribution Center** • 433 W Harrison St

Pharmacies

- **Walgreens** • 501 W Roosevelt St

Post Offices

- 433 W Harrison St

Parking

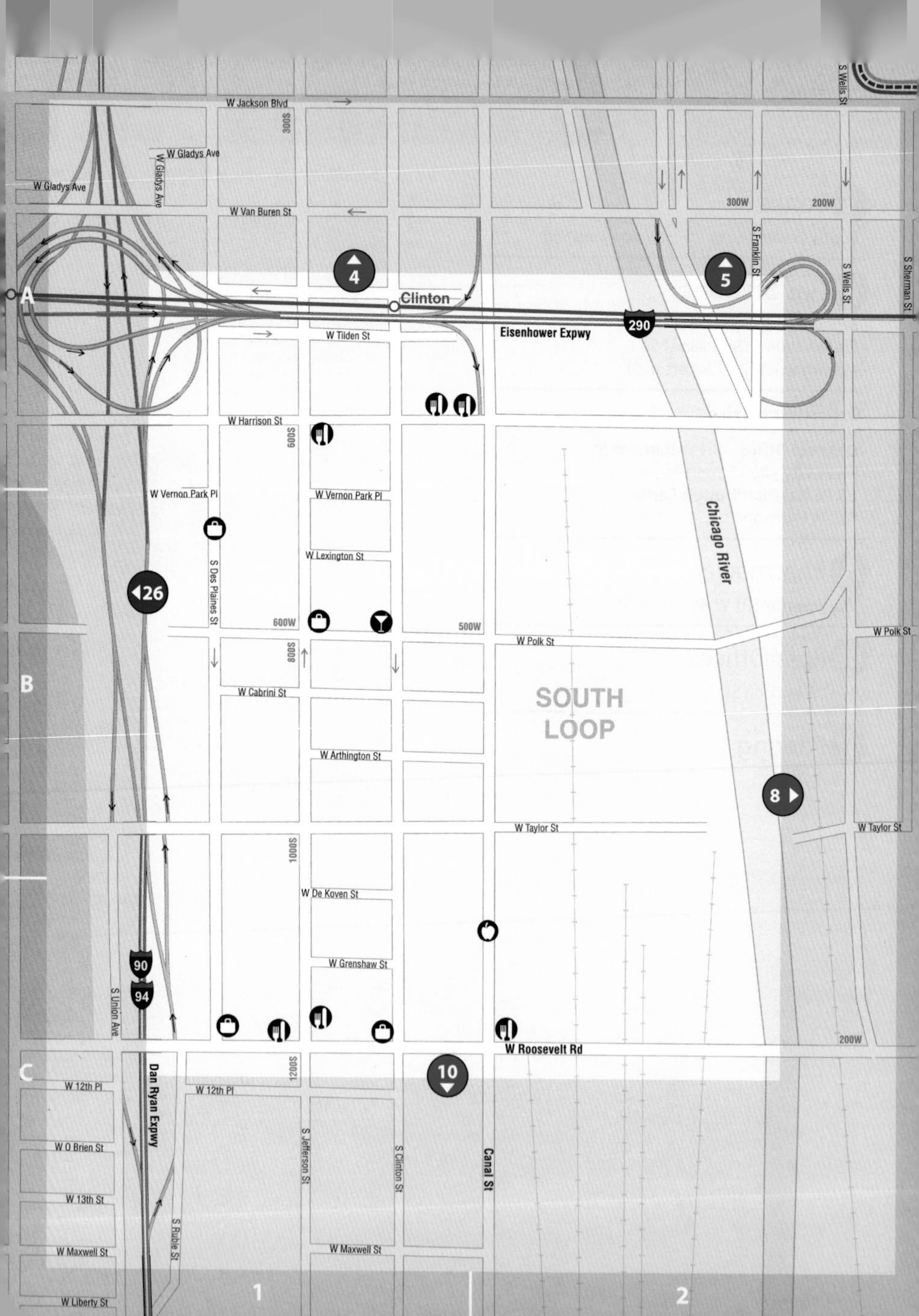

W Jackson Blvd
W Gladys Ave
W Gladys Ave
W Gladys Ave
W Van Buren St
300S
300W
200W
S Franklin St
S Wells St
S Wells St
S Sherman St
4
5
Clinton
W Tilden St
Eisenhower Expwy
290
A
W Harrison St
600S
W Vernon Park Pl
W Vernon Park Pl
W Lexington St
26
S Des Plaines St
600W
500W
W Polk St
W Polk St
800S
Chicago River
B
W Cabrini St
SOUTH LOOP
W Arthington St
8
W Taylor St
W Taylor St
1000S
W De Koven St
W Grenshaw St
90
94
S Union Ave
200W
W Roosevelt Rd
C
10
1200S
W 12th Pl
W 12th Pl
Dan Ryan Expwy
W O Brien St
S Jefferson St
S Clinton St
Canal St
W 13th St
S Ruble St
W Maxwell St
W Maxwell St
W Liberty St
1
2

The Maxwell Sunday Market is a shadow of its former self. Sadly, the colorful flea market lost its vibe in the move to Roosevelt Rd. to make way for UIC's expansion. The Chicago Fire Department Academy on De Koven St. sits on the spot where Mrs. O'Leary's lantern-booting bovine started the Great Chicago Fire of 1871. For kicks, see the fire exhibit and watch the recruits' rappelling exercises.

Bars

- **Scarlett's Gentleman's** • 750 S Clinton St

Farmer's Markets

- **Maxwell Sunday Market** • Canal St between Taylor St & Roosevelt Rd

Restaurants

- **Bake for Me** • 608 W Roosevelt Rd
- **Harrison Red Hot** • 565 W Harrison St
- **Harrison St Grill** • 506 W Harrison St
- **Manny's Coffee Shop** • 1141 S Jefferson St
- **Nick's Grill** • 518 W Harrison St
- **White Palace Grill** • 1159 S Canal St

Shopping

- **Chicago Vintage Motor Carriage** • 700 S Des Plaines St
- **Fishman's Fabrics** • 1101 S Des Plaines St
- **Joseph Adam's Hats** • 544 W Roosevelt Rd
- **Lee's Foreign Car Service** • 727 S Jefferson St

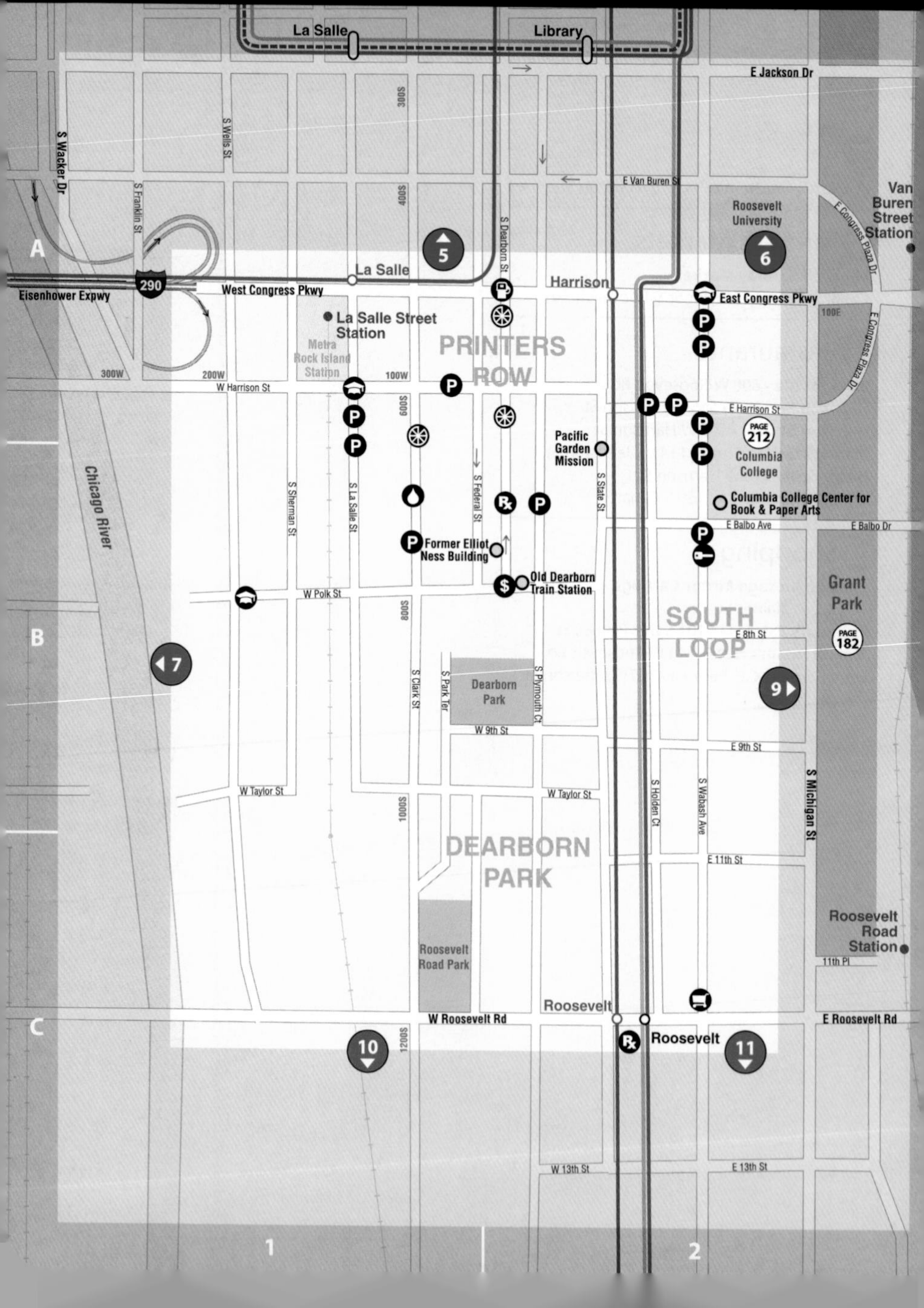
La Salle
Library
E Jackson Dr
S Wacker Dr
S Wells St
S Franklin St
300S
400S
E Van Buren St
Van Buren Street Station
Roosevelt University
E Congress Plaza Dr
A
5
6
La Salle
S Dearborn St
Harrison
290
Eisenhower Expwy
West Congress Pkwy
East Congress Pkwy
La Salle Street Station
Metra Rock Island Station
PRINTERS ROW
100E
300W
200W
100W
W Harrison St
E Harrison St
PAGE 212
Columbia College
Pacific Garden Mission
600S
S Federal St
S State St
S Sherman St
S La Salle St
Columbia College Center for Book & Paper Arts
E Balbo Ave
E Balbo Dr
Former Elliot Ness Building
Old Dearborn Train Station
Chicago River
W Polk St
800S
Grant Park
SOUTH LOOP
E 8th St
PAGE 182
B
7
9
S Clark St
S Park Ter
Dearborn Park
S Plymouth Ct
W 9th St
E 9th St
W Taylor St
W Taylor St
1000S
S Holden Ct
S Wabash Ave
S Michigan St
E 11th St
DEARBORN PARK
Roosevelt Road Park
Roosevelt Road Station
11th Pl
Roosevelt
W Roosevelt Rd
E Roosevelt Rd
C
10
1200S
Roosevelt
11
W 13th St
E 13th St
1
2

Essentials

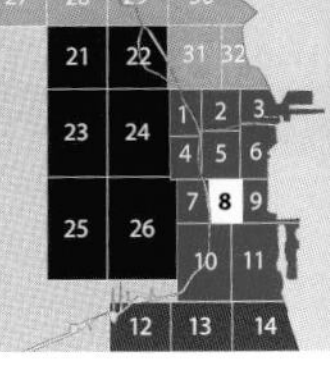

Despite the epidemic of single-family gated townhome communities popping up on its outskirts, the South Loop maintains the gritty urban feel long lost in the River West and Fulton Market districts. This is in no small part thanks to the presence of the Pacific Garden Mission—a true neighborhood landmark, love it or hate it, at State and Balbo. Now with Daley huffing about shuffling the mission off to less desireable digs, no doubt the door is open for this truly bluesy side of downtown to lose its mojo.

Car Rental

- **Budget** • 714 S Wabash Ave • 773-686-6800

Banks

- **Chicago Community Bank** • 47 W Polk St

Car Washes

- **Custom Hand Car Wash** • 700 S Clark St

Gas Stations

- **BP** • 50 W Congress Pkwy

Landmarks

- **Former Elliot Ness Building** • 618 S Dearborn St
- **Columbia College Center for Book & Paper Arts** • 1104 S Wabash Ave, 2nd Floor
- **Old Dearborn Train Station** • 47 W Polk St
- **Pacific Garden Mission** • 646 S State St

Pharmacies

- **Osco Drug** • 1224 S Wabash St
- **Printers Row Pharmacy** • 721 S Dearborn St

Pizza

- **Edwardo's Natural Pizza** • 521 S Dearborn St
- **Pat's Pizzeria** • 638 S Clark St
- **Trattoria Caterina** • 616 S Dearborn St

Schools

- **Chicago Hope Academy** • 601 S La Salle St
- **Daystar Education Assn** • 800 S Wells St
- **Jones Academic Magnetic College Prep** • 600 S State St

Supermarkets

- **Jewel** • 1224 S Wabash Ave

Parking

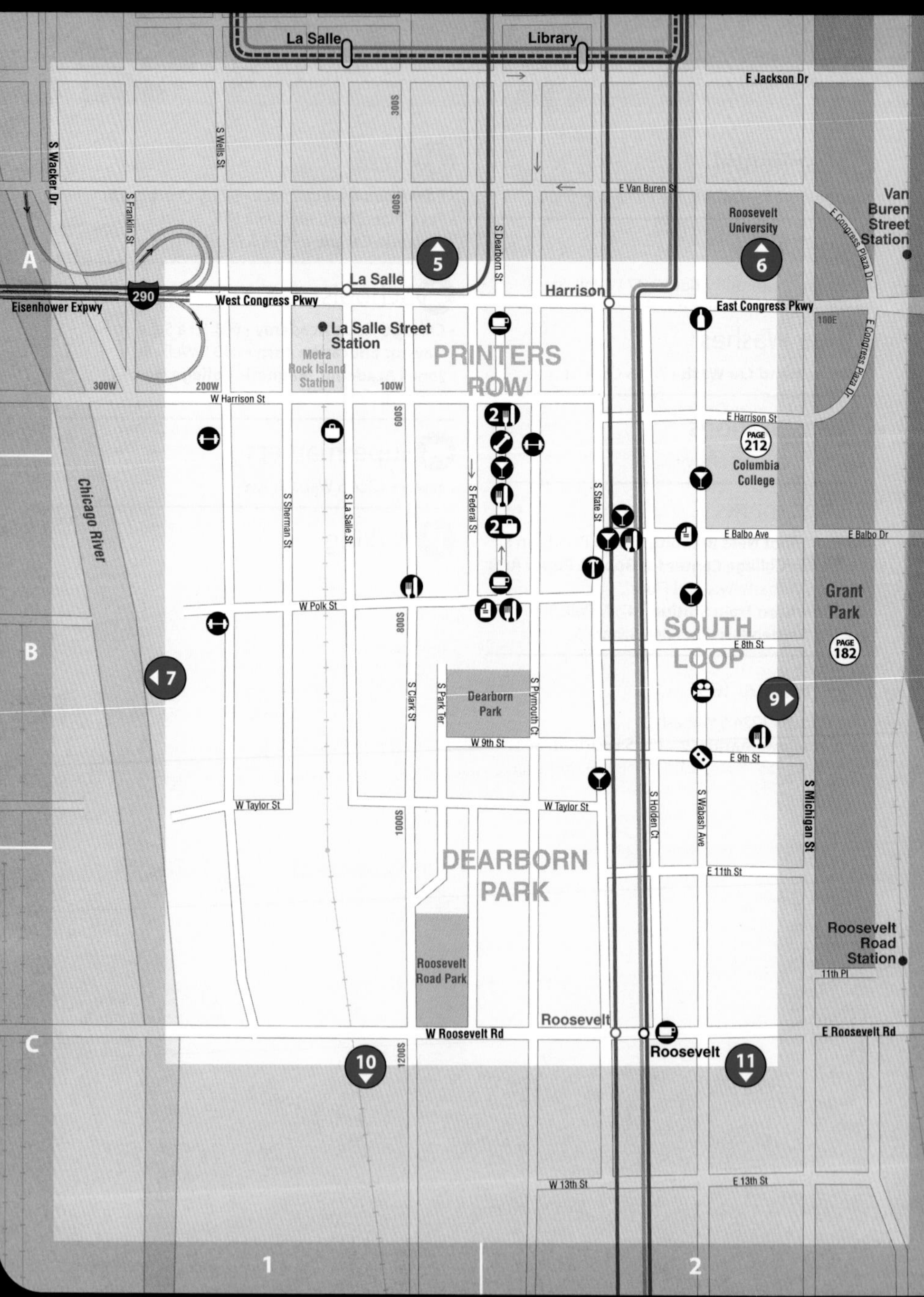

La Salle
Library
E Jackson Dr
S Wacker Dr
S Wells St
S Franklin St
E Van Buren St
Roosevelt University
Van Buren Street Station
E Congress Plaza Dr
5
6
A
La Salle
Harrison
290
Eisenhower Expwy
West Congress Pkwy
East Congress Pkwy
La Salle Street Station
Metra Rock Island Station
PRINTERS ROW
300W
200W
100W
100E
W Harrison St
E Harrison St
PAGE 212
Columbia College
Chicago River
S Sherman St
S La Salle St
S Federal St
S Dearborn St
S State St
E Balbo Ave
E Balbo Dr
W Polk St
Grant Park
SOUTH LOOP
E 8th St
PAGE 182
B
7
9
S Clark St
S Park Ter
Dearborn Park
S Plymouth Ct
W 9th St
E 9th St
W Taylor St
W Taylor St
S Holden Ct
S Wabash Ave
S Michigan St
DEARBORN PARK
E 11th St
Roosevelt Road Park
Roosevelt Road Station
11th Pl
Roosevelt
W Roosevelt Rd
E Roosevelt Rd
Roosevelt
C
10
11
W 13th St
E 13th St
1
2

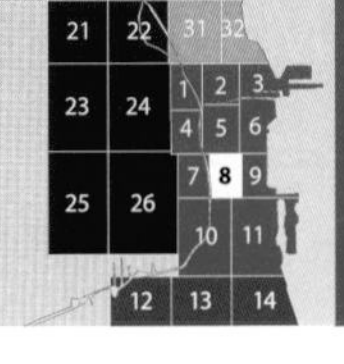

Columbia College students and faculty flock to dumpy George's after class—the artier types hang around to catch avant-garde jazz and world music at the Hot House. Buddy Guy's Legends boasts an authenticity lost to most of downtown and the Northside's more whitewashed and tourist-friendly blues joints. Business lunchers head to Prairie for elegant regional cuisine.

Bars

- **Buddy Guy's Legends** • 754 S Wabash Ave
- **George's Cocktail Lounge** • 646 S Wabash Ave
- **Hot House** • 31 E Balbo Ave
- **Kasey's Tavern** • 701 S Dearborn St
- **South Loop Club** • 701 S State St
- **Tantrum** • 1023 S State St

Copy Shops

- **Kinko's** • 700 S Wabash Ave
- **Mail Boxes Etc** • 47 W Polk St

Coffee

- **Gourmand** • 728 S Dearborn St
- **Starbucks** • 31 E Roosevelt Rd
- **Starbucks** • 555 S Dearborn St

Gyms

- **Bally Total Fitness** • 800 S Wells St
- **Chicago Training Club** • 641 S Plymouth Ct

Hardware Stores

- **South Loop Ace Hardeware** • 725 S State St

Liquor Stores

- **Warehouse Liquors** • 531 S Wabash Ave

Movie Theaters

- **Burnham Plaza Theater** • 826 S Wabash Ave
- **Village Theatres Burnham Plaza** • 826 S Wabash Ave

Pet Shops

- **Animal House** • 630 S Dearborn St

Restaurants

- **Bar Louie** • 47 W Polk
- **Blackie's** • 755 S Clark St
- **Hackney's** • 733 S Dearborn St
- **Prairie** • 500 S Dearborn St
- **South Loop Club** • 701 S State St
- **Trattoria Caterina** • 616 S Dearborn St

Shopping

- **Kozy's Bike Shop** • 600 S La Salle St
- **Printers Row Fine and Rare Books** • 715 S Dearborn St
- **Sandmeyer's Book Store** • 714 S Dearborn St

Video Rental

- **Movietime Home Video** • 900 S Wabash Ave

Map 9 • South Loop / South Michigan Ave

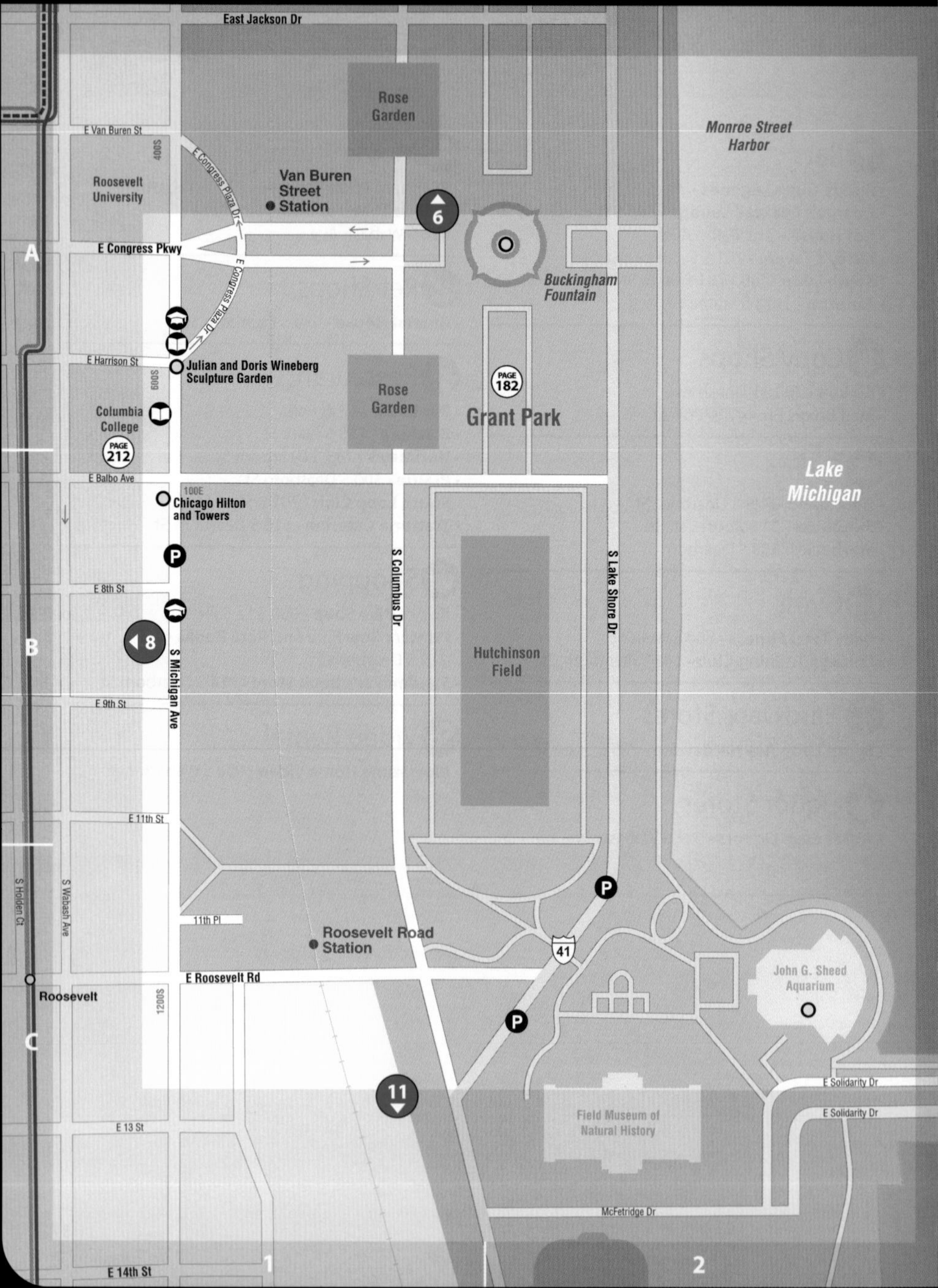

N

East Jackson Dr
Rose Garden
Monroe Street Harbor
E Van Buren St
400S
E Congress Plaza Dr
Roosevelt University
Van Buren Street Station
6
Buckingham Fountain
A
E Congress Pkwy
E Congress Plaza Dr
E Harrison St
600S
Julian and Doris Wineberg Sculpture Garden
Rose Garden
PAGE 182
Grant Park
Columbia College
PAGE 212
Lake Michigan
E Balbo Ave
100E
Chicago Hilton and Towers
S Columbus Dr
S Lake Shore Dr
E 8th St
B
8
Hutchinson Field
S Michigan Ave
E 9th St
E 11th St
S Holden Ct
S Wabash Ave
11th Pl
Roosevelt Road Station
41
E Roosevelt Rd
Roosevelt
John G. Shedd Aquarium
1200S
C
E Solidarity Dr
11
E Solidarity Dr
Field Museum of Natural History
E 13 St
McFetridge Dr
E 14th St
1
2

Green could describe this part of the city, from the gardens of Grant Park to the ecologically sensitive Shedd Aquarium on the Museum Campus. Beginning at dusk, Buckingham Fountain's skyrocketing water display, accompanied by lights and music, occurs every hour on the hour for twenty minutes until 11 p.m. This routine occurs daily from April to October.

Banks

- **Harris Trust & Savings Bank** • 1000 S Lake Shore Dr

Landmarks

- **Buckingham Fountain** • Columbus Dr and East Congress Pkwy
- **Chicago Hilton and Towers** • 720 S Michigan Ave
- **Julian and Doris Wineberg Sculpture Garden** • 681 S Michigan Ave
- **Shedd Aquarium** • 1200 S Lake Shore Drive

Libraries

- **Asher Library-Spertus Inst** • 618 S Michigan Ave
- **Library of Columbia College** • 600 S Michigan Ave

Schools

- **Columbia College** • 600 S Michigan Ave
- **East-West University** • 816 S Michigan Ave

Parking

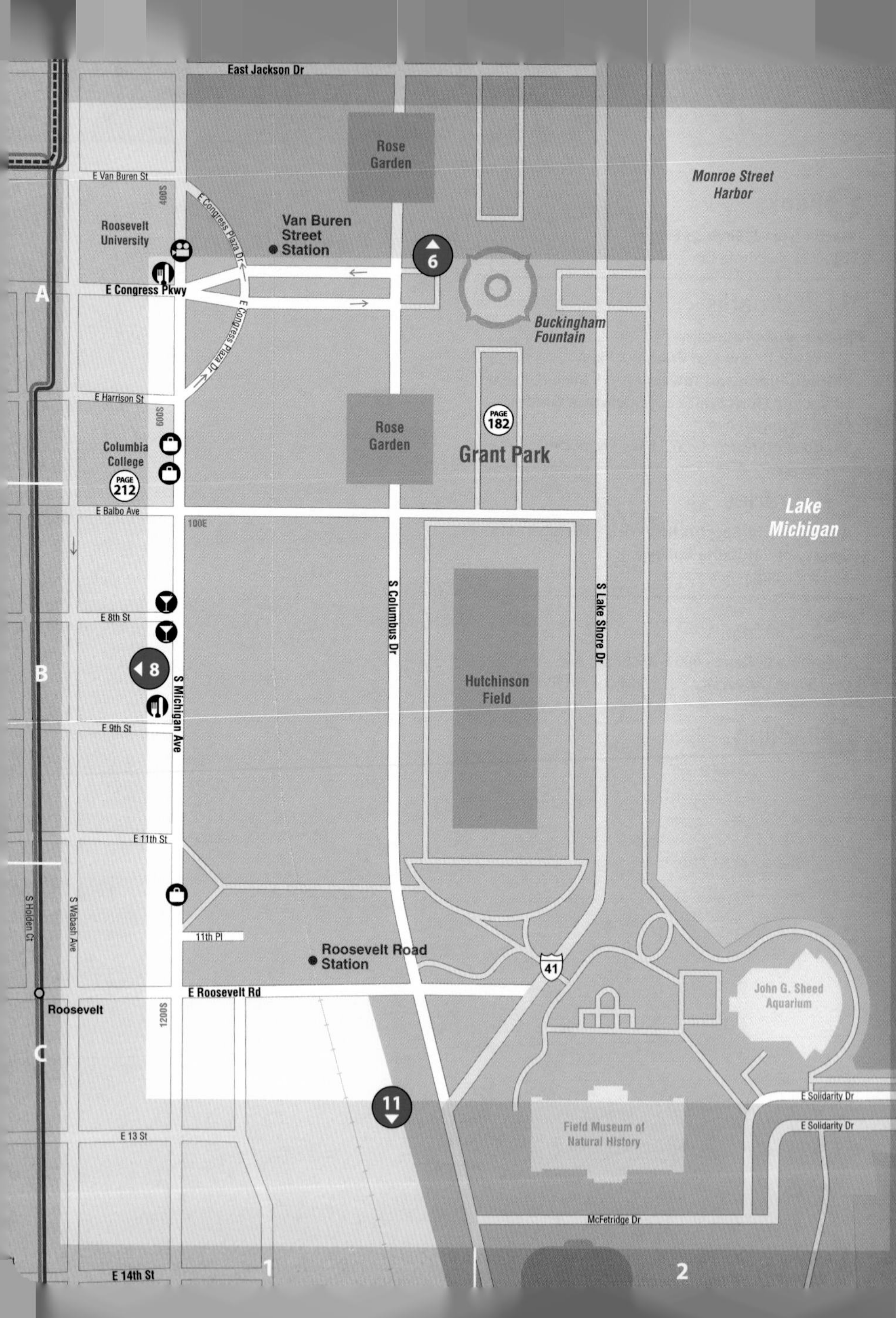

East Jackson Dr
Rose Garden
Monroe Street Harbor
E Van Buren St
400S
E Congress Plaza Dr
Roosevelt University
Van Buren Street Station
6
A
E Congress Pkwy
Buckingham Fountain
E Harrison St
600S
Rose Garden
PAGE 182
Columbia College
Grant Park
PAGE 212
E Balbo Ave
100E
Lake Michigan
S Columbus Dr
S Lake Shore Dr
E 8th St
8
B
Hutchinson Field
S Michigan Ave
E 9th St
E 11th St
S Holden Ct
S Wabash Ave
11th Pl
Roosevelt Road Station
41
John G. Shedd Aquarium
E Roosevelt Rd
Roosevelt
1200S
C
11
E Solidarity Dr
E Solidarity Dr
Field Museum of Natural History
E 13 St
McFetridge Dr
E 14th St
1
2

Sundries / Entertainment

The Chicago Hilton and Towers Hotel, at which the cops tossed Tom Hayden through a window during the 1968 Democratic Convention, anchors S. Michigan Ave.'s gentrification. After a few Killians at Kitty O'Shea's, sneak up to the spectacular 1927 Grand Ballroom for a twirl back in time. A flick at the Fine Arts Theater followed by a honking banana split is a fine way to spend a rainy day.

Bars

- **Kitty O'Shea's** • 720 S Michigan Ave
- **Savoy Bar and Grill** • 800 S Michigan Ave

Movie Theaters

- **Fine Arts Theater** • 418 S Michigan Ave

Restaurants

- **Artist's Cafe** • 412 S Michigan Ave
- **Oysy** • 888 S Michigan Ave

Shopping

- **Bariff Shop** • 618 S Michigan Ave
- **Clancy's Market** • 1130 S Michigan Ave

Map 10 • East Pilsen / Chinatown

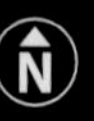

N
University of Illinois at Chicago
PAGE 208
W Taylor St
W De Koven St
W Grenshaw St
W Roosevelt Rd
Roosevelt
E 11th St
S Holden Ct
S Clark St
S Union Ave
S Ruble St
S Jefferson St
S Clinton St
1000S
1200S
1400S
1600S
1800S
2200S
2400S
2600S
W 12th Pl
W O' Brien St
W 13th St
W Maxwell St
W Liberty St
W 14th St
W Barber St
W 14thPl
W 15th St
W 15th Pl
W 15th St
W 16th St
W 17th St
W 17th Pl
W 18th Pl
W 18th St
W 19th St
W 19th Pl
W Cullerton St
W 20th Pl
W 21st St
W 21st Pl
W Cermak Rd
W 22nd Pl
W 23rd St
W 23rd Pl
W Alexander St
W 24th St
W 24th Pl
W 25th Pl
W 26th St
W 26th Pl
W 27th St
W 28th St
E 14th St
E 14th Pl
E 16th St
E 18th St
E Cullerton St
E 21st St
E 24th Pl
E 25th St
E 26th St
A
B
C
1
2
7
8
11
13
26
90
94
55
Dan Ryan Expwy
Stevenson Expressway
Connector
SOUTH LOOP
EAST PILSEN
CHINATOWN
South Branch Chicago River
Jefferson Park
Chinatown Square
Cermak-Chinatown
Halsted
S Halsted St
S Sangamon St
S Peoria St
S Newberry Ave
S Green St
S Desplaines St
S Normal Ave
S Canalport Ave
S Lumber St
S Grove Ave
S Stewart Ave
S Canal St
S Archer Ave
S China Pl
S Wentworth Ave
S Federal St
S Dearborn St
S Clark St
S La Salle St
S State St
S Wabash Ave
S Michigan Ave
S Ford Ave
S Emerald Ave
S Wallace St
S Princeton Ave
S Salle St
Todd St
W Lumber St
S Green St
800W
600W
500W
100E

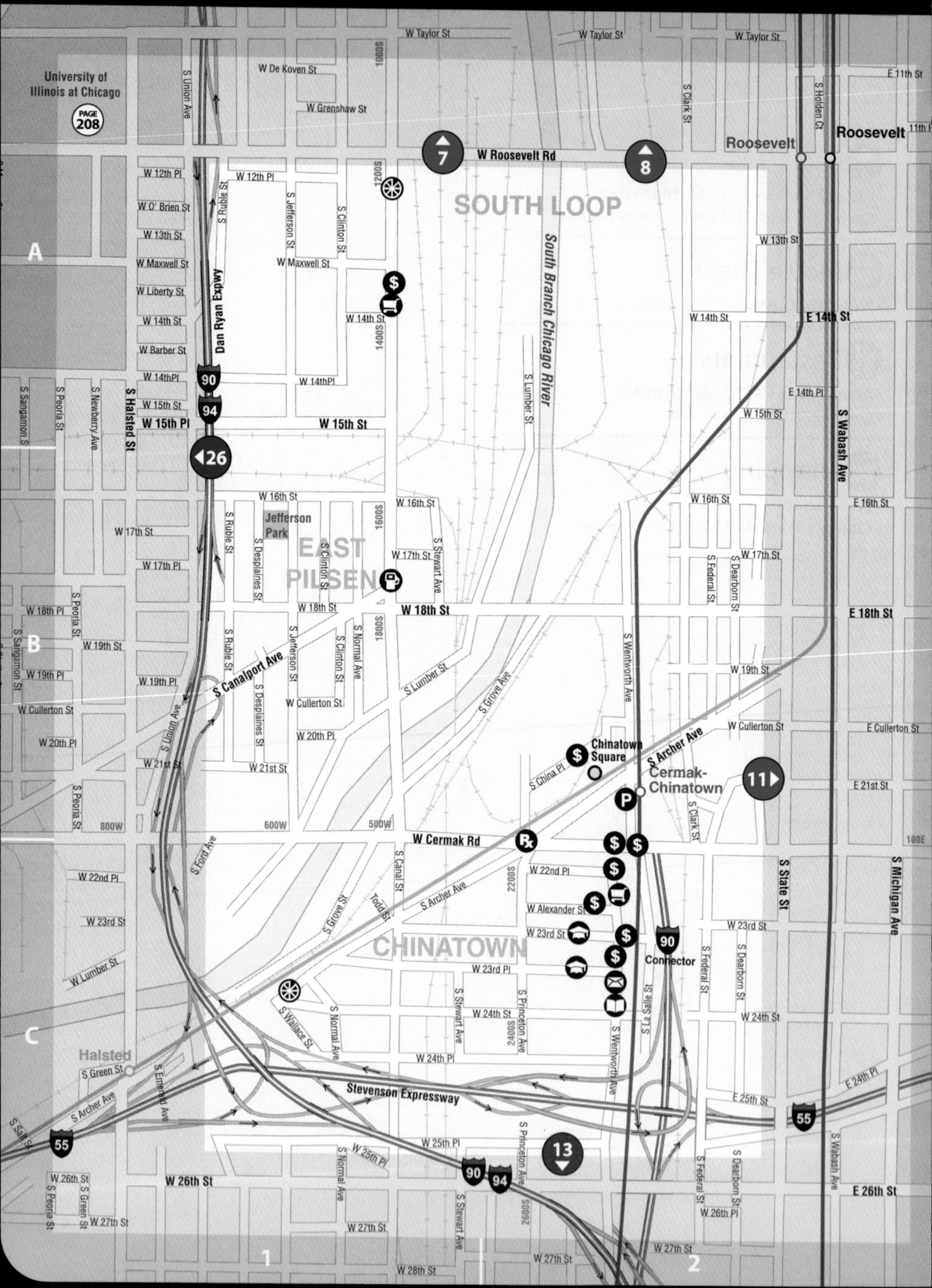

Urban artists still flock to affordable loft spaces in East Pilsen, despite occasional gang uprisings. Development around Chinatown is moving faster than the dim sum carts through the bustling expanse of Three Happiness during its popular Sunday brunch.

Banks

- **Bank One** • 1340 S Canal St
- **Charter One Bank** • 2131 S China Pl
- **Charter One Bank** • 2263 S Wentworth Ave
- **International Bank of Chicago** • 208 W Cermak Rd
- **New Asia Bank** • 222 W Cermak Rd
- **Pacific Global Bank** • 2323 S Wentworth Ave
- **South Central Bank** • 2335 S Wentworth Ave

Gas Stations

- **BP** • 1725 S Clark St

Landmarks

- **Chinatown Square** • S Archer Ave

Libraries

- **Chinatown Public Library** • 2353 S Wentworth Ave

Pharmacies

- **Walgreens** • 316 W Cermak Rd

Pizza

- **Connie's Pizza** • 2373 S Archer Ave
- **Domino's** • 1234 S Canal St

Post Offices

- 2345 S Wentworth Ave

Schools

- **John C Haines School** • 247 W 23rd Pl
- **South Loop Elementary School** • 1212 S Plymouth Ct
- **St Therese School** • 247 W 23rd St
- **Whittier Elementary School** • 1900 W 23rd St

Supermarkets

- **Dominick's** • 1340 S Canal St
- **Tai Wah Grocery** • 2226 S Wentworth Ave

Parking

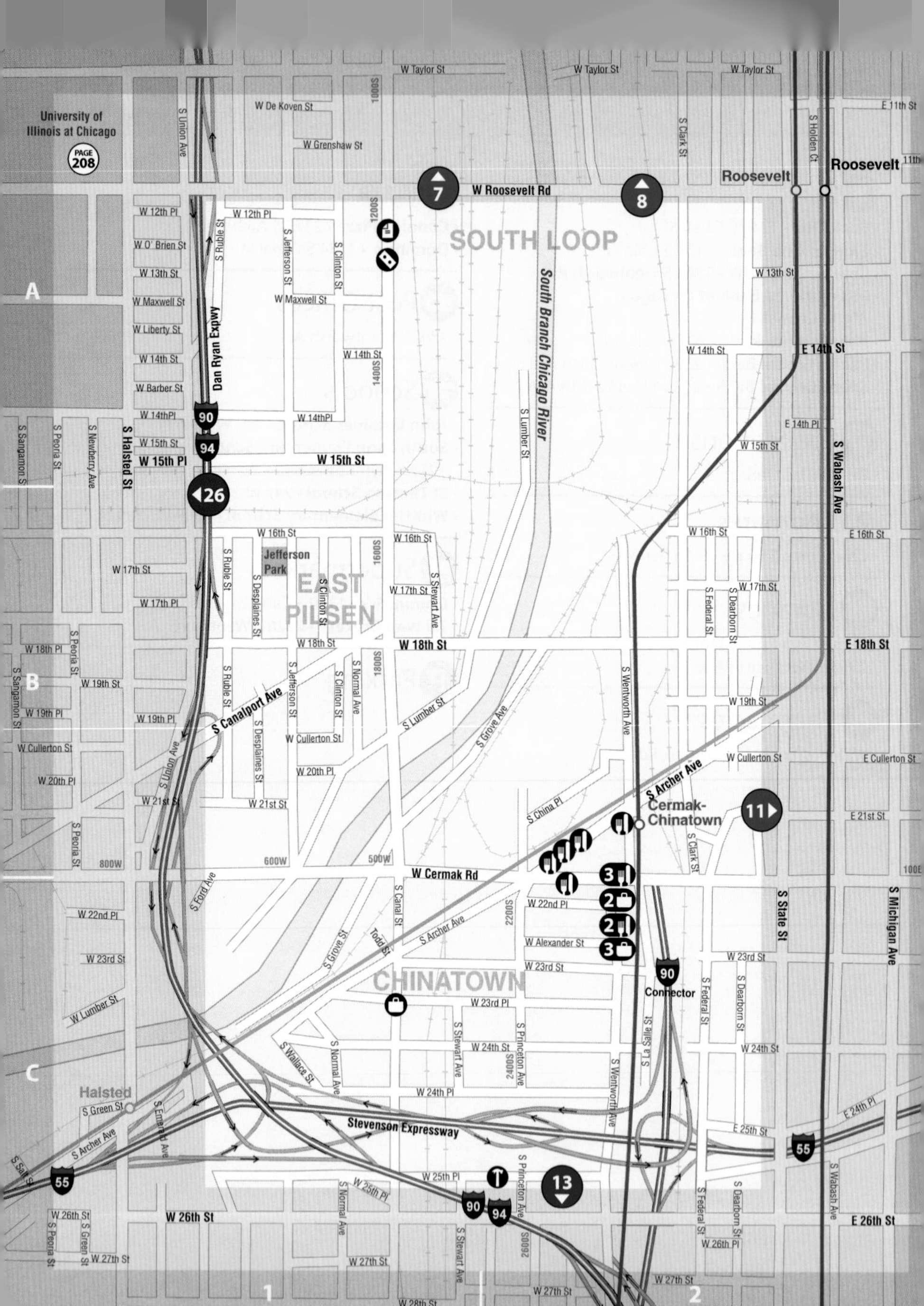
University of Illinois at Chicago
PAGE 208
SOUTH LOOP
EAST PILSEN
CHINATOWN
Roosevelt
Cermak-Chinatown
Halsted
South Branch Chicago River
Dan Ryan Expwy
Stevenson Expressway
Connector
Jefferson Park
W Taylor St
W Roosevelt Rd
W 15th St
W 18th St
W Cermak Rd
W 26th St
S Halsted St
S Canalport Ave
S Archer Ave
S Wabash Ave
S State St
S Michigan Ave
E 18th St
E 26th St
A
B
C
1
2

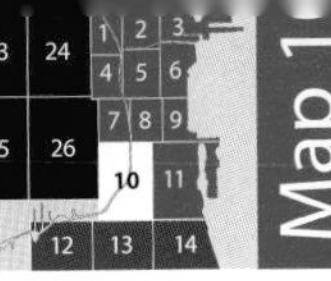

Skip Crate & Barrel and head to Chinatown for great cookware. Browse the shops along Wentworth Ave. for cooking utensils, Chinese furnishings, and imported wares. Woks 'n' Things gets our vote for best cookery. Ten Ren Tea & Ginseng Co. wins for exotic teas and accoutrements. If you haven't done dim sum at the Happy Chef, you should. The Phoenix Café is where the locals go out to eat.

Copy Shops

- **Kinko's** • 1242 S Canal St

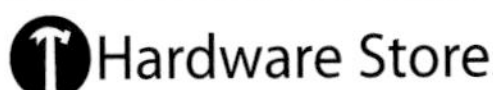

Hardware Stores

- **Zweifel True Value Hardware** • 345 W 25th Pl

Restaurants

- **Cugino's, The Original Cheesie Beef** • 300 W Cermak Rd
- **Emperor's Choice** • 2238 S Wentworth Ave
- **Happy Chef Dim Sum House** • 2164 S Archer Ave
- **Hong Min** • 221 W Cermak Rd
- **Lao Sze Chuan Spice City** • 2172 S Archer Ave
- **Penang** • 2201 S Wentworth Ave
- **Phoenix Café** • 2131 S Archer Ave
- **Three Happiness** • 209 W Cermak Rd
- **Won Kow** • 2237 S Wentworth Ave

Shopping

- **Chinatown Bazaar** • 2221 S Wentworth Ave
- **Chinatown Furniture** • 2326 S Canal St
- **Pacific Imports** • 2200 S Wentworth Ave
- **Sun Sun Tong** • 2260 S Wentworth Ave
- **Ten Ren Tea & Ginseng Co** • 2247 S Wentworth Ave
- **Woks 'n' Things** • 2234 S Wentworth Ave

Video Rental

- **Movie Gallery** • 1248 S Canal St
- **Video Update** • 1245 S Clinton St

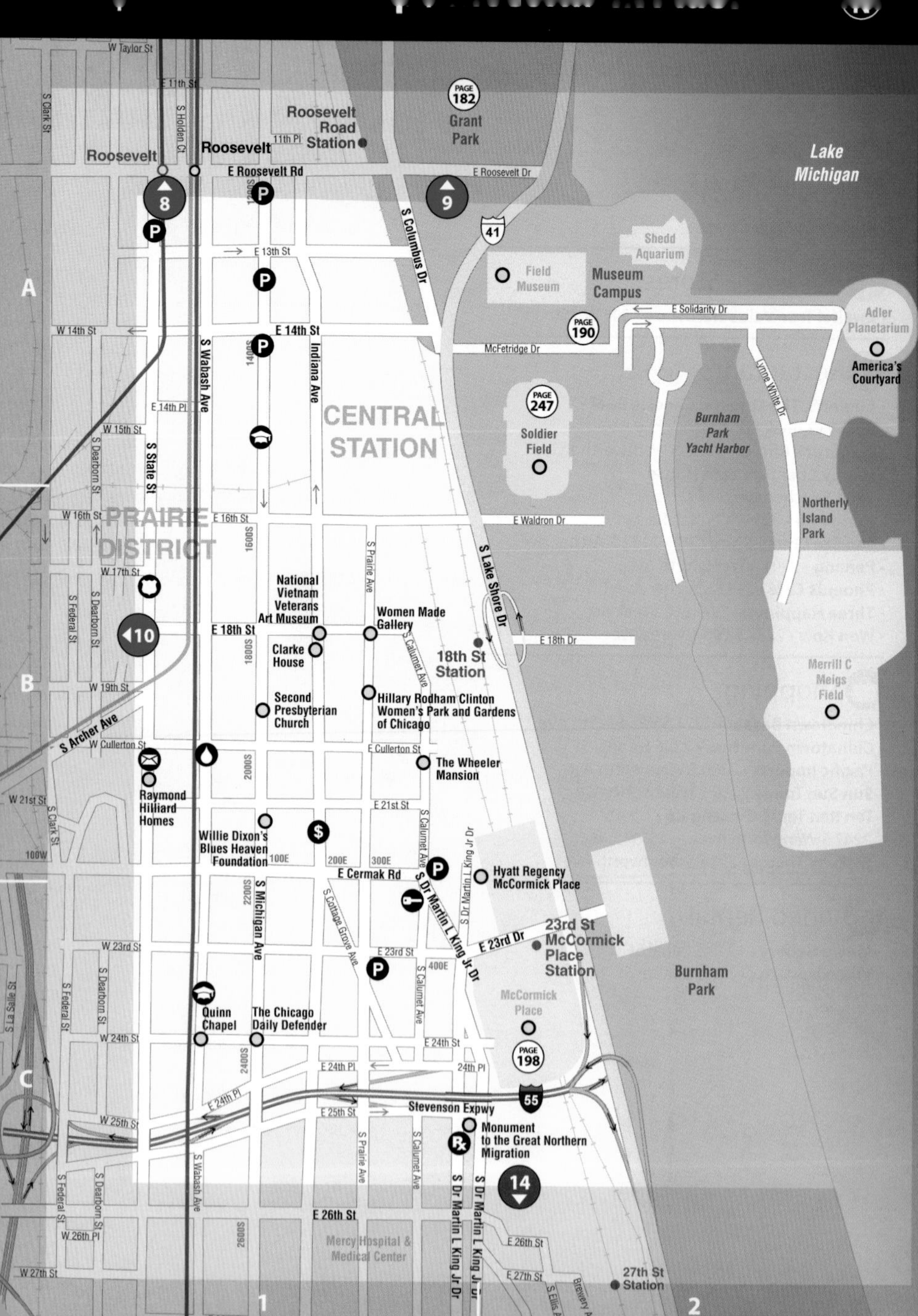

Roosevelt Road Station
Grant Park
Lake Michigan
Roosevelt
Roosevelt
E Roosevelt Rd
E Roosevelt Dr
S Columbus Dr
Shedd Aquarium
Field Museum
Museum Campus
E Solidarity Dr
Adler Planetarium
America's Courtyard
McFetridge Dr
E 13th St
E 14th St
W 14th St
S Wabash Ave
Indiana Ave
CENTRAL STATION
Soldier Field
Burnham Park Yacht Harbor
Lynne White Dr
Northerly Island Park
E Waldron Dr
PRAIRIE DISTRICT
S State St
S Lake Shore Dr
National Vietnam Veterans Art Museum
Women Made Gallery
E 18th St
E 18th Dr
Clarke House
18th St Station
Merrill C Meigs Field
Second Presbyterian Church
Hillary Rodham Clinton Women's Park and Gardens of Chicago
S Archer Ave
E Cullerton St
The Wheeler Mansion
Raymond Hilliard Homes
Willie Dixon's Blues Heaven Foundation
E Cermak Rd
Hyatt Regency McCormick Place
S Michigan Ave
S Dr Martin L King Jr Dr
E 23rd Dr
23rd St McCormick Place Station
Burnham Park
McCormick Place
Quinn Chapel
The Chicago Daily Defender
Stevenson Expwy
Monument to the Great Northern Migration
E 26th St
Mercy Hospital & Medical Center
27th St Station

The city's economic engine, McCormick Place, helps power the South Loop's steady gentrification. Construction has become a lifestyle here, including the new Soldier Field, an abundance of new housing development, and McCormick Place breaking ground in 2003 for yet another expansion. Museum Campus is the cultural anchor on the neighborhood's north end, while Burnham Park is its front yard.

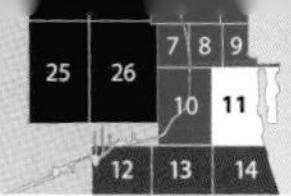

Car Rental

- **Hertz** • 2300 S Dr Martin L King Jr Dr • 312-567-0380

Banks

- **Lakeside Bank** • 2141 S Indiana Ave

Car Washes

- **Strictly By Hand** • 2007 S Wabash Ave

Hospitals

- **Mercy Hospital & Medical Ctr** • 2525 S Michigan Ave

Landmarks

- **America's Courtyard** • South of Adler Planetarium on the lakefront
- **Clarke House** • 1827 S Indiana Ave
- **Field Museum** • 1400 S Lake Shore Drive
- **Hillary Rodham Clinton Women's Park and Gardens of Chicago** • S Prairie Ave, between 18th and 19th
- **Hyatt Regency McCormick Place** • 2233 S Dr Martin L King Jr Dr
- **McCormick Place** • 2301 S Lake Shore Drive
- **Meigs Field Airport** • 1500 S Lake Shore Drive
- **Monument to the Great Northern Migration** • S Dr Martin L King Jr Dr, just before Stevenson Expressway
- **National Vietnam Veterans Art Museum** • 1801 S Indiana Ave
- **Quinn Chapel, African Methodist Episcopal Church** • 2401 S Wabash Ave
- **Raymond Hilliard Homes** • 2030 S State St
- **Second Presbyterian Church** • 1936 S Michigan Ave
- **Soldier Field** • 425 E McFetridge Dr
- **The Chicago Daily Defender** • 2400 S Michigan Ave
- **The Wheeler Mansion** • 2020 S Calumet Ave
- **Willie Dixon's Blues Heaven Foundation** • 2120 S Michigan Ave
- **Women Made Gallery** • 1900 S Prairie Ave

Pharmacies

- **Osco Drug** • 2545 S Dr Martin L King Jr Dr

Police

- **1st District (Central)** • 1718 S State St

Post Offices

- 2035 S State St

Schools

- **Perspectives Charter High School** • 1532 S Michigan Ave
- **Ray Graham Training Center** • 2347 S Wabash Ave

Parking

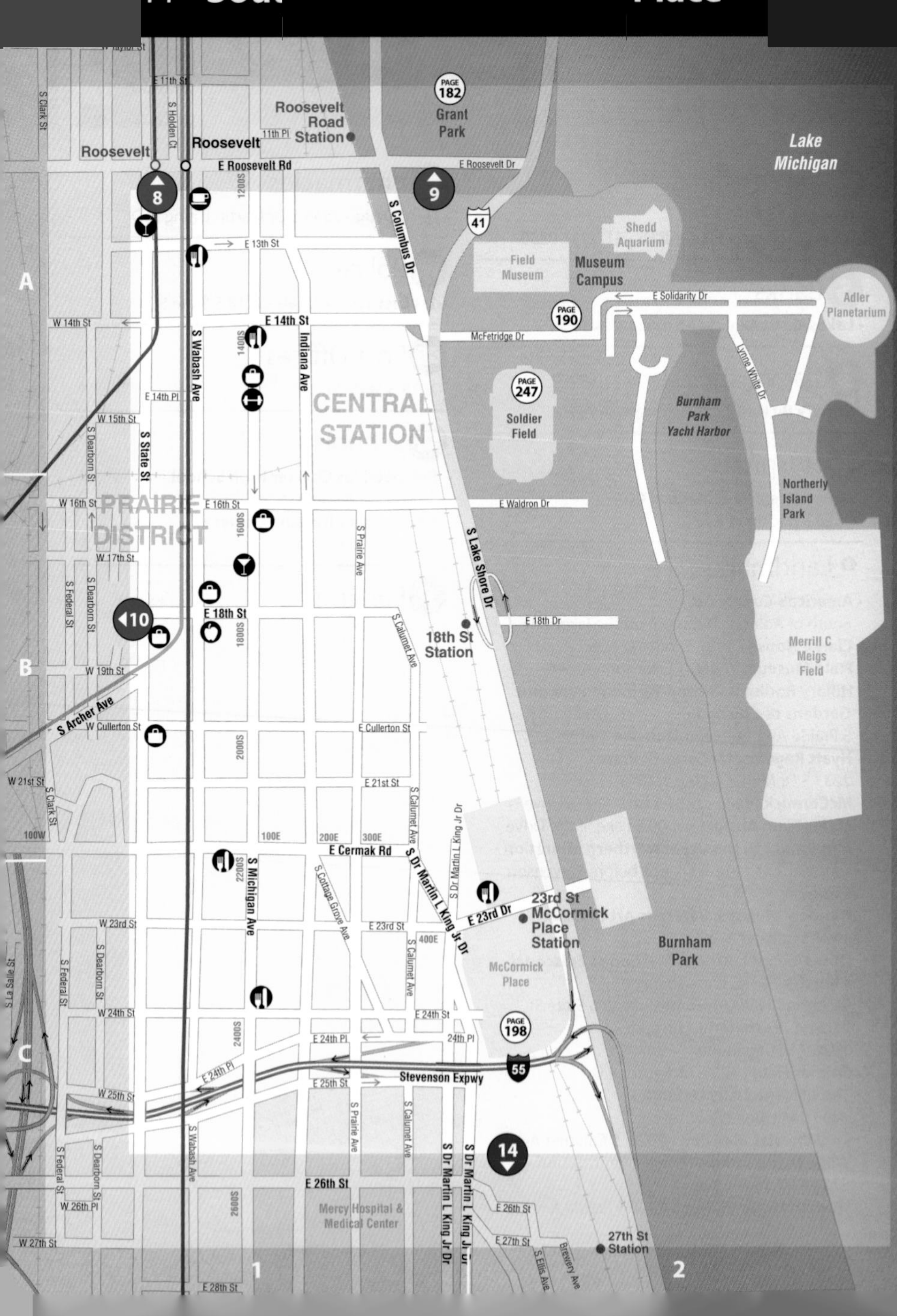
Roosevelt Road Station
Grant Park
PAGE 182
Lake Michigan
Roosevelt
E Roosevelt Rd
E Roosevelt Dr
S Columbus Dr
Shedd Aquarium
Field Museum
Museum Campus
Adler Planetarium
E Solidarity Dr
PAGE 190
McFetridge Dr
E 13th St
E 14th St
W 14th St
S Wabash Ave
Indiana Ave
CENTRAL STATION
PAGE 247
Soldier Field
Burnham Park Yacht Harbor
Lynne White Dr
E 14th Pl
W 15th St
S Dearborn St
S State St
W 16th St
E 16th St
PRAIRIE DISTRICT
E Waldron Dr
Northerly Island Park
S Prairie Ave
S Lake Shore Dr
W 17th St
S Federal St
E 18th St
E 18th Dr
S Calumet Ave
18th St Station
Merrill C Meigs Field
W 19th St
S Archer Ave
W Cullerton St
E Cullerton St
W 21st St
S Clark St
E 21st St
S Dr Martin L King Jr Dr
E Cermak Rd
S Michigan Ave
S Cottage Grove Ave
E 23rd Dr
23rd St McCormick Place Station
W 23rd St
E 23rd St
Burnham Park
McCormick Place
S La Salle St
W 24th St
E 24th St
E 24th Pl
24th Pl
PAGE 198
Stevenson Expwy
W 25th St
E 25th St
E 26th St
Mercy Hospital & Medical Center
W 26th Pl
E 27th St
27th St Station
W 27th St
S Ellis Ave
Brewery Ave
E 28th St
1
2
A
B
C

While the influx of businesses to service the pioneering residents is slow, the cultural scene is as diverse as the shows at McCormick Place. Take in the Prairie Avenue Historic District between 18th and E Cullerton Sts, where wealthy Chicagoans from the 1800s resided in swank, Victorian mansions. Go to the Chicago Firehouse for juicy steaks and fresh seafood. Famous 1940s juke joint, The Cotton Club, rocks with jazz and hip hop.

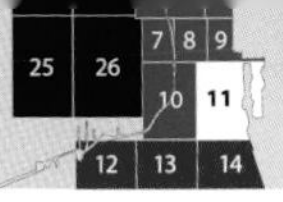

Bars

- **Bobby McGee's Sports Bar & Grill** • 1239 S State St
- **The Cotton Club** • 1710 S Michigan Ave

Coffee

- **Dunkin' Donuts** • 1231 S Wabash Ave

Farmer's Markets

- **South Loop Farmers Market** • 18th & Wabash Ave

Gyms

- **Phenomenal Fitness** • 1468 S Michigan Av e

Restaurants

- **Chef Luciano** • 49 E Cermak Rd
- **Chicago Firehouse Restaurant** • 1401 S Michigan Ave
- **Gioco** • 1312 S Wabash Ave
- **NetWorks** • Hyatt Regency McCormick Place, 2233 S Dr Martin L King Jr Dr

Shopping

- **Blossoms of Hawaii** • 1631 S Michigan Ave
- **Blue Star Auto Stores** • 2001 S State St
- **Re-Cycle Bicycle shop** • 1465 S Michigan Ave
- **Waterware** • 1829 S State St
- **Y'lonn Salon** • 1802 S Wabash Ave

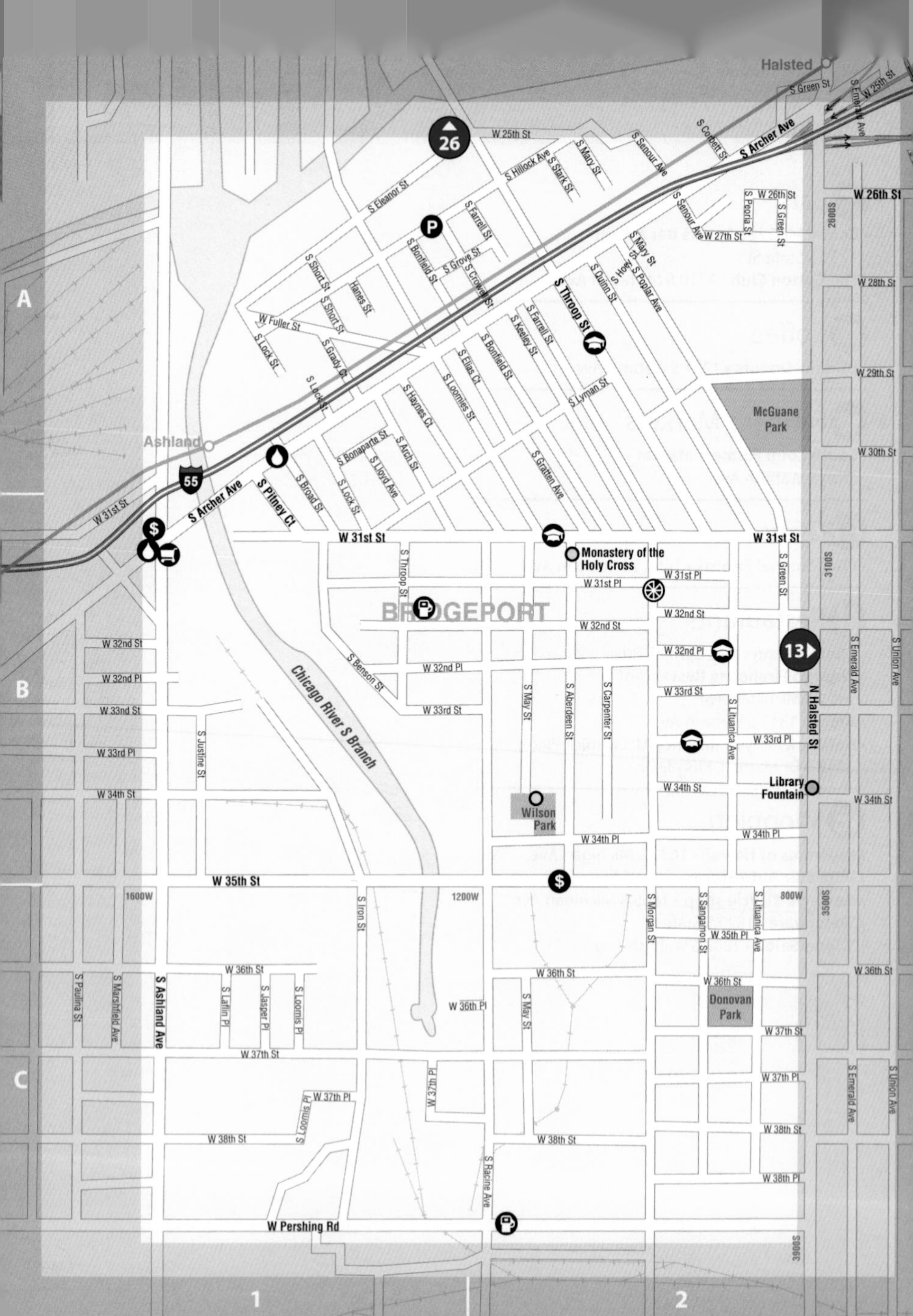
Halsted
S Green St
W 25th St
S Emerald Ave
26
W 25th St
S Corbett St
S Archer Ave
S Senour Ave
S Hillock Ave
S Stark St
S Mary St
S Eleanor St
P
S Farrell St
S Senour Ave
W 26th St
S Peoria St
S Green St
W 26th St
2600S
W 27th St
S Mary St
S Hoey St
S Poplar Ave
S Bonfield St
S Grove St
S Crowell St
S Short St
S Throop St
S Quinn St
W 28th St
A
Hanes St
S Short St
W Fuller St
S Lock St
S Grady Ct
S Farrell St
S Keeley St
S Bonfield St
S Elias Ct
S Loomies St
S Lock St
S Haynes Ct
S Lyman St
W 29th St
McGuane Park
Ashland
S Bonaparte St
S Arch St
S Lloyd Ave
S Gratten Ave
W 30th St
55
S Pitney Ct
S Broad St
S Lock St
S Archer Ave
W 31st St
$
W 31st St
W 31st St
S Throop St
Monastery of the Holy Cross
W 31st Pl
W 31st Pl
S Green St
3100S
BRIDGEPORT
W 32nd St
W 32nd St
W 32nd St
S Benson St
W 32nd Pl
13
S Emerald Ave
S Union Ave
W 32nd Pl
W 32nd Pl
B
Chicago River S Branch
W 33rd St
W 33nd St
S May St
S Aberdeen St
S Carpenter St
W 33rd St
S Lituanica Ave
N Halsted St
S Justine St
W 33rd Pl
W 33rd Pl
W 34th St
W 34th St
Library Fountain
W 34th St
Wilson Park
W 34th Pl
W 34th Pl
W 35th St
$
1600W
S Iron St
1200W
S Morgan St
S Sangamon St
S Lituanica Ave
800W
3500S
W 35th Pl
W 36th St
W 36th St
W 36th St
W 36th St
S Paulina St
S Marshfield Ave
S Ashland Ave
S Laflin Pl
S Jasper Pl
S Loomis Pl
W 36th Pl
S May St
Donovan Park
W 37th St
W 37th St
C
W 37th Pl
S Emerald Ave
S Union Ave
S Loomis Pl
W 37th Pl
W 37th Pl
W 38th St
W 38th St
W 38th St
S Racine Ave
W 38th Pl
W Pershing Rd
3900S
1
2

Essentials

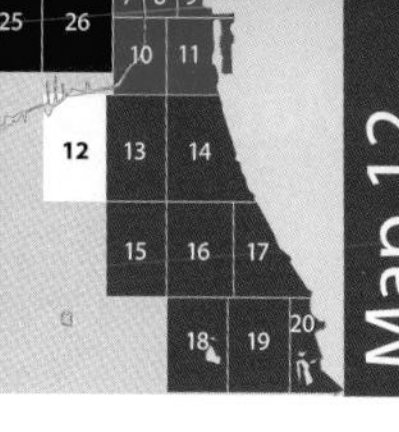

Old Style and Chicago fit cheek-to-jowl in Bridgeport. The Irish neighborhood's name is as working class in origin as the closely-knit residents. The neighborhood is home to the final port and bridge on the South Branch of the Chicago River, where boats unloaded cargo in the 1800s. Chinatown's and South Loop's building boom has initiated a Bridgeport revival. The city's largest new subdivision of single-family homes is being built east of the river and north of 35th St.

Banks

- **Bank One** • 3145 S Ashland Ave
- **Chicago Community Bank** • 1110 W 35th St

Car Washes

- **Windy City Car Wash & Detail** • 3117 S Archer Ave
- **Z Best Detailing Ctr** • 3033 S Archer Ave

Gas Stations

- **Citgo** • 970 W Pershing Rd
- **Marathon** • 3269 S Archer Ave

Landmarks

- **Library Fountain** • W 34th & Halsted
- **Monastery of the Holy Cross** • 3111 S Aberdeen
- **Wilson Park** • S May & W 34th Pl

Pharmacies

- **Osco Drug** • 3644 S Archer Ave

Pizza

- **Lina's Pizza** • 3132 S Morgan St

Schools

- **Armour Elementary School** • 950 W 33rd Pl
- **Bridgeport Catholic Academy** • 1040 W 32nd Pl
- **Holden Elementary School** • 1104 W 31st St
- **St Barbara Grammar & High School** • 2867 S Throop St

Supermarkets

- **Dominick's** • 3145 S Ashland Ave
- **Jewel-Osco** • 3644 S Archer Ave

Map 12 • Bridgeport (West)

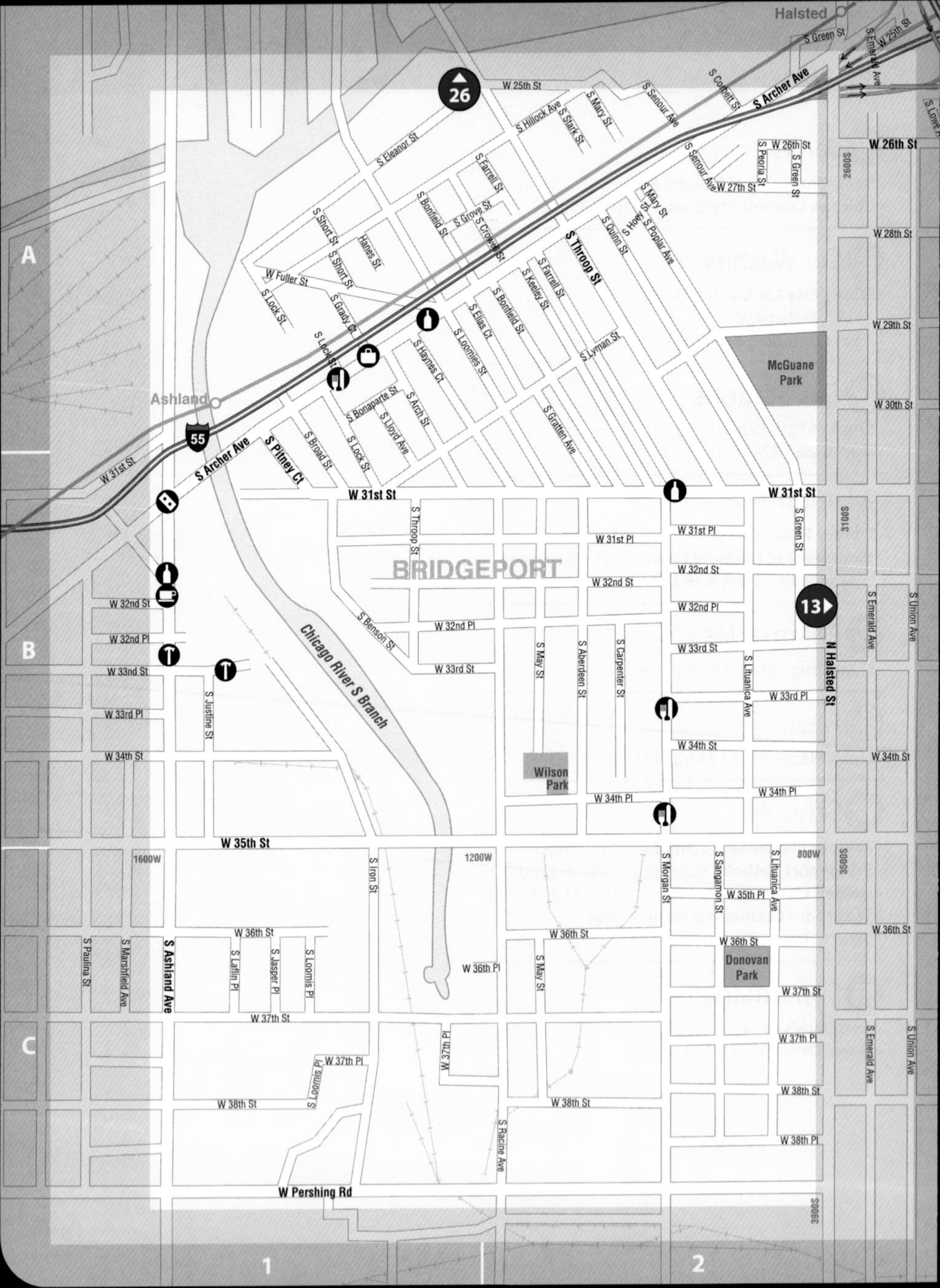

Hopefully Bridgeport's residential revival will eventually spur business and entertainment in the community. Right now, a big night out is watching a Sox game at a corner tavern or renting a video from Blockbuster.

Coffee

- **Dunkin' Donuts** • 3170 S Ashland Ave

Hardware Stores

- **Ace Hardware** • 1514 W 33rd St
- **Ace Hardware** • 3240 S Ashland Ave

Liquor Stores

- **All Star Food & Liquors** • 2911 S Archer Ave
- **Ashland S** • 3162 S Ashland Ave
- **J & Lee** • 960 W 31st St

Restaurants

- **Johnny O's** • 3465 S Morgan St
- **Mexico Steak House** • 2983 S Archer Ave
- **Polo's Nut & Candy Cafe** • 3322 S Morgan St

Shopping

- **Bridgeport Antiques** • 2963 S Archer Ave

Video Rental

- **Best Video** • 1637 W 35th St
- **Blockbuster Video** • 3145 S Ashland Ave

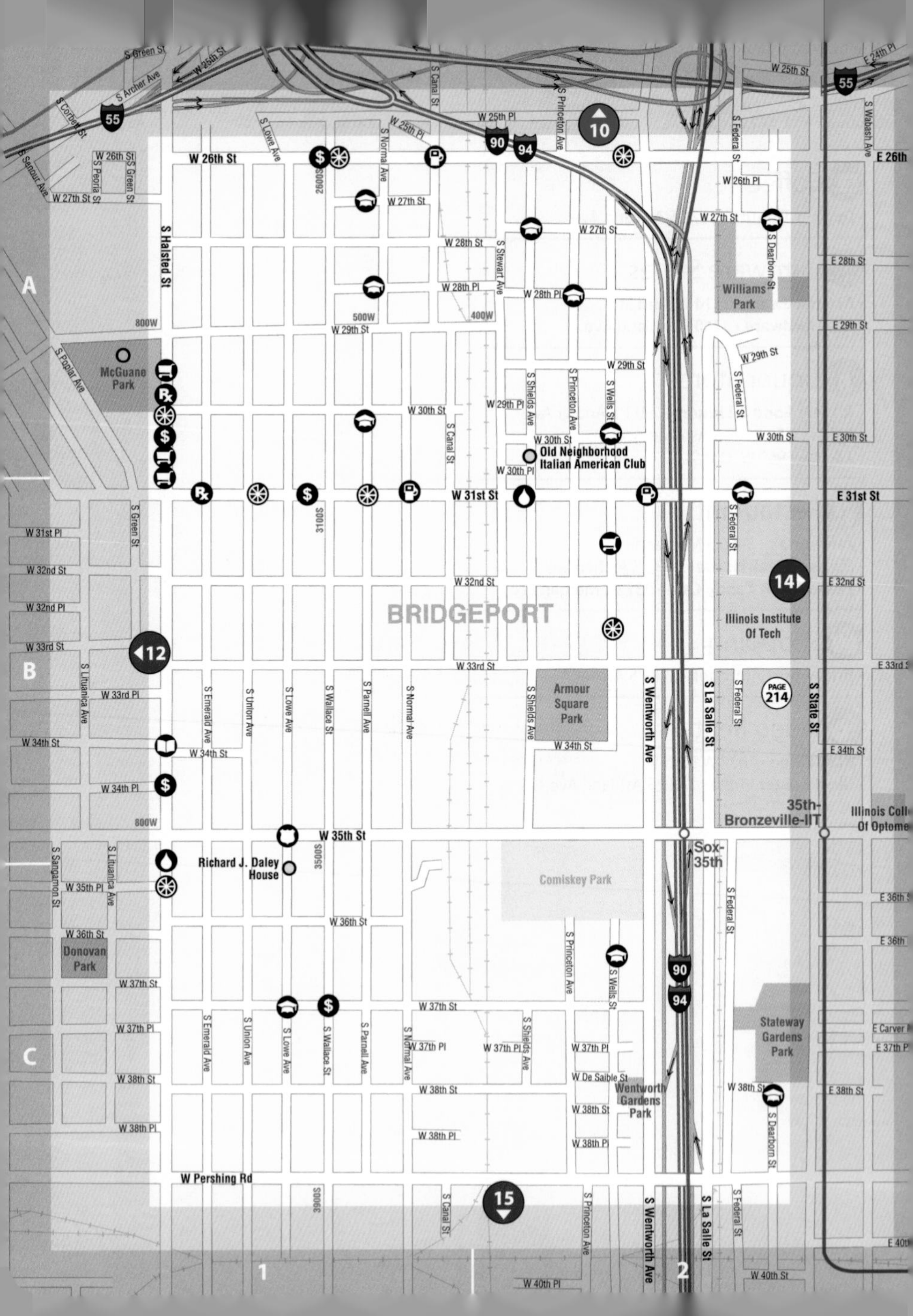

S Green St
W 25th St
S Archer Ave
S Corbett St
55
S Canal St
W 25th Pl
S Princeton Ave
W 24th Pl
E 24th Pl
W 25th St
55
S Lowe Ave
W 25th Pl
90
94
10
S Federal St
S Wabash Ave
W 26th St
W 26th St
S Peoria St
S Green St
S Normal Ave
600S
E 26th
S Sangamon Ave
W 27th St
W 27th St
W 26th Pl
W 27th St
W 27th St
S Halsted St
W 28th St
S Stewart Ave
S Dearborn St
E 28th St
A
W 28th Pl
W 28th Pl
Williams Park
800W
500W
400W
W 29th St
E 29th St
S Poplar Ave
McGuane Park
W 29th St
W 29th St
S Shields Ave
S Princeton Ave
S Wells St
S Federal St
W 29th Pl
W 30th St
S Canal St
W 30th St
W 30th St
E 30th St
Old Neighborhood
Italian American Club
W 30th Pl
W 31st St
E 31st St
S Green St
310S
W 31st Pl
W 32nd St
S Federal St
14
W 32nd St
E 32nd St
W 32nd Pl
BRIDGEPORT
Illinois Institute
Of Tech
W 33rd St
12
B
W 33rd St
E 33rd St
S Lituanica Ave
W 33rd Pl
S Emerald Ave
S Union Ave
S Lowe Ave
S Wallace St
S Parnell Ave
S Normal Ave
S Shields Ave
Armour Square Park
S Wentworth Ave
S La Salle St
S Federal St
PAGE 214
S State St
W 34th St
W 34th St
W 34th St
E 34th St
W 34th Pl
800W
35th-
Bronzeville-IIT
Illinois Coll
Of Optome
W 35th St
Sox-
35th
S Sangamon St
S Lituanica Ave
Richard J. Daley
House
350S
Comiskey Park
W 35th Pl
S Federal St
E 36th S
W 36th St
W 36th St
E 36th
Donovan Park
S Princeton Ave
S Wells St
90
W 37th St
94
W 37th St
Stateway
Gardens
Park
E Carver
C
W 37th Pl
S Emerald Ave
S Union Ave
S Lowe Ave
S Wallace St
S Parnell Ave
S Normal Ave
W 37th Pl
W 37th Pl
S Shields Ave
W 37th Pl
E 37th Pl
W De Saible St
W 38th St
W 38th St
Wentworth
Gardens
Park
W 38th St
E 38th St
W 38th St
S Dearborn St
W 38th Pl
W 38th Pl
W 38th Pl
W Pershing Rd
390S
S Canal St
15
S Princeton Ave
S Wentworth Ave
S La Salle St
S Federal St
E 40th
1
2
W 40th Pl
W 40th St

Bridgeport is the home turf of the Daley political dynasty and three other mayors. This part of Bridgeport is a gritty mix of urban styles and cultures: Irish, Italian, Chinese, and African-American. The Illinois Institute of Technology is in the throes of a multi-million-dollar rebuilding program to beautify its ugly campus, which will hopefully ignite more gentrification in these blocks, which are presently filled with Chicago-style brick bungalows.

Banks

- **Access Credit Union** • W 26th St & S Wallace St
- **Charter One Bank** • 600 W 37th St
- **Citibank** • 3430 S Halsted St
- **Marquette Bank** • 615 W 31st
- **South Central Bank** • 3032 S Halsted St

Car Washes

- **J & J Full Svc Car Wash** • 349 W 31st St
- **Looking Good Hand Car Wash** • 3540 S Halsted St

Gas Stations

- **Citgo** • 501 W 31st St
- **Marathon** • 444 W 26th St
- **Shell & Food Mart** • 215 W 31st St

Landmarks

- **McGuane Park** • W 29th St & S Halsted
- **Old Neighborhood Italian American Club** • 3031 S Shields Ave
- **Richard J Daley House** • 3536 S Lowe Ave

Libraries

- **Daley Public Library** • 3400 S Halsted St

Pharmacies

- **Osco Drug** • 741 W 31st St
- **Walgreens** • 3000 S Halsted

Pizza

- **Donnie's Pizza & Cafe** • 3258 S Wells St
- **Freddie's Pizza & Pasta Parlor** • 701 W 31st St
- **Little Caesar's Pizza** • 3010 S Halsted St
- **Nikko's Pizza** • 537 W 31st St
- **Paulie's Pizza & Itln Sndwchs** • 2600 S Wallace St
- **Phil's Pizza** • 3551 S Halsted St
- **Ricobene's Pizzeria** • 252 W 26th St

Police

- **9th District (Deering)** • 3501 S Lowe Ave

Schools

- **Attucks Elementary School** • 3813 S Dearborn St
- **Bridgeport Catholic Academy North** • 512 W 28th Pl
- **Bridgeport Catholic Academy South** • 3700 S Lowe Ave
- **Daniel H Williams School** • 2710 S Dearborn St
- **Healy Elementary School** • 3010 S Parnell Ave
- **Illinois Institute of Technology** • 3300 S Federal St
- **James Ward Elementary School** • 2701 S Shields Ave
- **M Sheridan Elementary School** • 533 W 27th St
- **Robert Abbott Elementary School** • 3630 S Wells St
- **Santa Lucia School** • 3017 S Wells St
- **St Jerome's Catholic School** • 2805 S Princeton Ave
- **Vandercook College Of Music** • 3140 S Federal St

Supermarkets

- **Chinese Fresh Food Market** • W 30th & S Halsted
- **Jewel-Osco** • 3033 S Halsted St
- **Russo's Deli** • 3160 S Wells St

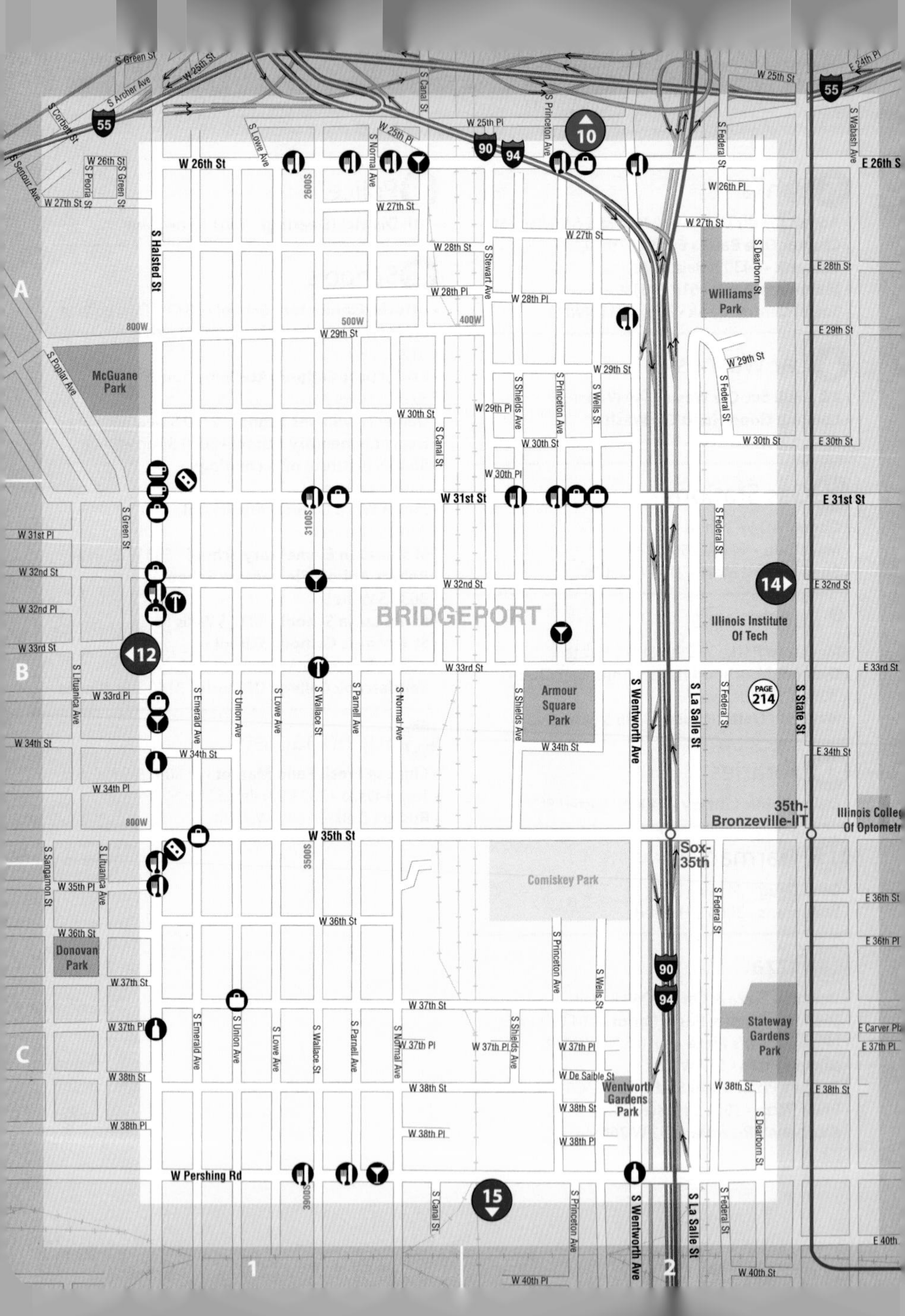

BRIDGEPORT
McGuane Park
Williams Park
Illinois Institute Of Tech
Armour Square Park
Comiskey Park
Donovan Park
Wentworth Gardens Park
Stateway Gardens Park
Illinois College Of Optometr
35th-Bronzeville-IIT
Sox-35th
PAGE 214
10
12
14
15
W 26th St
W 31st St
W 35th St
W Pershing Rd
E 26th St
E 31st St
S Halsted St
S Wentworth Ave
S La Salle St
S State St
A
B
C
1
2

There's nothing healthy about the large, artery-hardening portions at Healthy Foods Lithuanian, but if it's old-world comfort food you want, this is the place. Sox fans from the 'hood head to Jimbo's after a game at Old Comiskey a.k.a. US Cellular Field. There are some rough patches to this old Chicago neighborhood—outsiders are well advised to stick to well-lit streets after dark.

Bars

- **Boston Tavern** • 451 W 26th St
- **Cobblestone's Bar and Grill** • 514 E Pershing Rd
- **Jimbo's Lounge** • 3258 S Princeton Ave
- **Puffer's Bar** • 3356 S Halsted St
- **Redwood Lounge** • S Wallace St & W 32nd St

Coffee

- **Dunkin' Donuts** • 3100 S Halsted St
- **Dunkin' Donuts** • S Halsted & W 31 St

Hardware Stores

- **Joe Harris Paint & Hardware** • 3301 S Wallace St
- **Windy City Hardware** • 3262 S Halsted St

Liquor Stores

- **Brennan's Liquor Store** • 3738 S Halsted St
- **Bridgeport Liquors** • 3411 S Halsted St
- **Express Food & Liquor** • 3904 S Wentworth Ave

Restaurants

- **Bridgeport Restaurant** • 3500 S Halsted St
- **Dox's Place** • 600 W Pershing Rd
- **Ferro's Homemade Italian Lemonade** • 200 W 31 St
- **Franco's Ristorante** • 300 W 31st St
- **Furama** • 2828 S Wentworth Ave
- **Graziano's Ristorante** • 605 W 31st St
- **Healthy Food Restaurant** • 3236 S Halsted St
- **Kevin's Hamburger Heaven** • 554 W Pershing Rd
- **Offshore Steak House** • 480 W 26th St
- **Phil's Pizza** • 3551 S Halsted St
- **Sugar Shack** • 630 W 26th St
- **Wing Yip Chop Suey** • 537 W 26th

Shopping

- **Accutek Printing & Graphics** • 260 W 26th St
- **Ace Bakery** • 3200 S Halsted St
- **Antique Drugstore** • W 37th St & S Union Ave
- **Augustine's Spiritual Goods** • 3114 S Halsted St
- **Bridgeport News Travel & Tours** • 3252 S Halsted St
- **Chicago Technical Center** • 3500 S Emerald Ave
- **Computer Banana** • 547 W 31st St
- **Health King Enterprises Chinese Medicinals** • 238 W 31st St
- **Let's Boogie Records & Tapes** • 3321 S Halsted St
- **Modern Bookstore** • 3118 S Halsted St
- **Petals From Heaven Flowers** • 244 W 31st St

Video Rental

- **Bridgeport Video** • 742 W 31st St
- **Halsted Video** • 3515 S Halsted St

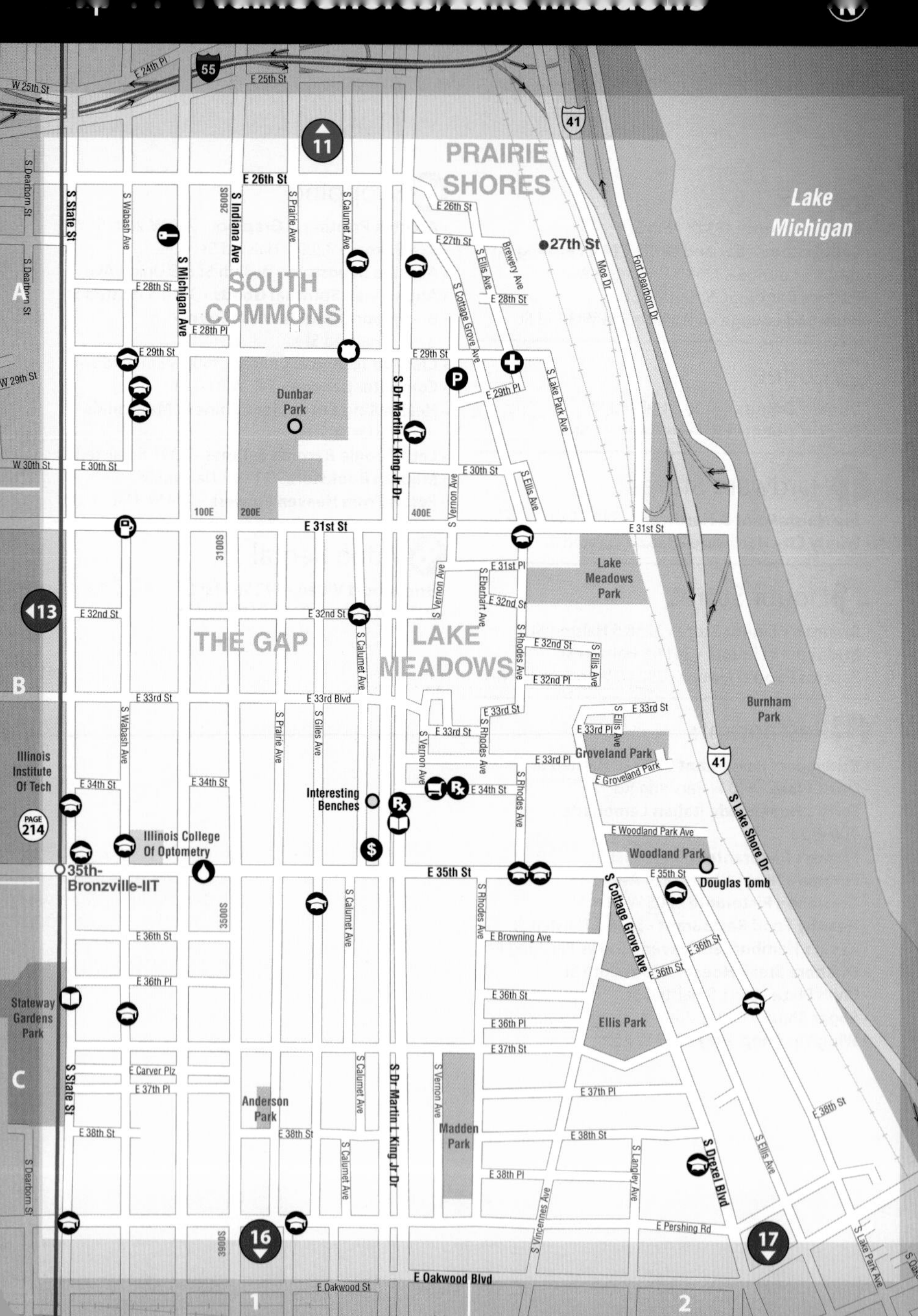

PRAIRIE SHORES
SOUTH COMMONS
THE GAP
LAKE MEADOWS
Lake Michigan
Dunbar Park
Lake Meadows Park
Groveland Park
Woodland Park
Douglas Tomb
Burnham Park
Ellis Park
Madden Park
Anderson Park
Stateway Gardens Park
Illinois Institute Of Tech
Illinois College Of Optometry
Interesting Benches
35th-Bronzville-IIT
27th St
E 26th St
E 31st St
E 35th St
S Dr Martin L King Jr Dr
S Michigan Ave
S Indiana Ave
S State St
S Cottage Grove Ave
S Lake Shore Dr
S Drexel Blvd
E Oakwood Blvd
E Pershing Rd
11
13
16
17
PAGE 214
A
B
C
1
2

Prairie Shores and Lake Meadows compose a residential high-rise neighborhood along the lakefront. The former Chicago Bee newspaper building, a restored 1929 Art Deco gem, is now the community's public library, housing an impressive African-American history collection. Although undergoing a resurgence, the neighborhood is still quite rough around the western edge on S State St., where the Robert Taylor Homes, a crime-riddled public housing complex, is located.

Banks

- **Shore Bank** • 3401 S Dr Martin L King Jr Dr

Car Rental

- **Enterprise Car Rental/Rogers Auto Group** • 2700 S Michigan Ave •

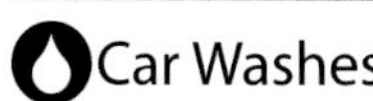

Car Washes

- **Starvin' Marvin Hand Car Wash** • 114 E 35th St

Gas Stations

- **BP** • 3101 S Wabash Ave

Hospitals

- **Michael Reese Hosp & Med Ctr** • 2929 S Ellis Ave

Landmarks

- **Interesting Benches** • S Dr Martin L King Jr Dr btn E 33rd-E 35th St
- **Douglas Tomb** • E 35th St & Lake Park
- **Dunbar Park** • S Indiana & E 31st St

Libraries

- **Chicago Bee Public Library** • 3647 S State St
- **King Public Library** • 3436 S Dr Martin L King Jr Dr

Pharmacies

- **Osco Drug** • 443 E 34th St
- **Walgreens** • 3405 S Dr Martin L King Jr Dr

Police

- **21st District (Prairie)** • 300 E 29th St

Schools

- **Benjamin W Raymond Elementary** • 3663 S Wabash Ave
- **Chicago Military Academy** • 3519 S Giles Ave
- **Christ the King Lutheran School** • 3701 S Lake Park Ave
- **Dawson Technical Institute** • 3901 S State St
- **De La Salle High School** • 3455 S Wabash Ave
- **Doolittle Middle School** • 535 E 35th St
- **Doolittle West Primary School** • 521 E 35th St
- **Douglas Community Academy** • 3200 S Calumet Ave
- **Drake Elementary School** • 2722 S Dr Martin L King Jr Dr
- **Dunbar Vocational Career Academy** • 3000 S Dr Martin L King Jr Dr
- **George T Donoghue School** • 707 E 37th St
- **Henry Booth House Head Start** • 2929 S Wabash Ave
- **Illinois College of Optometry** • 3241 S Michigan Ave
- **Pershing Elementary School** • 3113 S Rhodes Ave
- **Phillips Academy High School** • 244 E Pershing Rd
- **Senqstacke Academic Preparation** • 2641 S Calumet Ave
- **St James School** • 2920 S Wabash Ave
- **St Joseph's Carondelet** • 739 E 35th St
- **Young Women's Leadership Charter School** • 3410 S State St
- **Youth Connections Charter High School** • 10 W 35th St

Supermarkets

- **Jewel** • 443 E 34th St

Parking

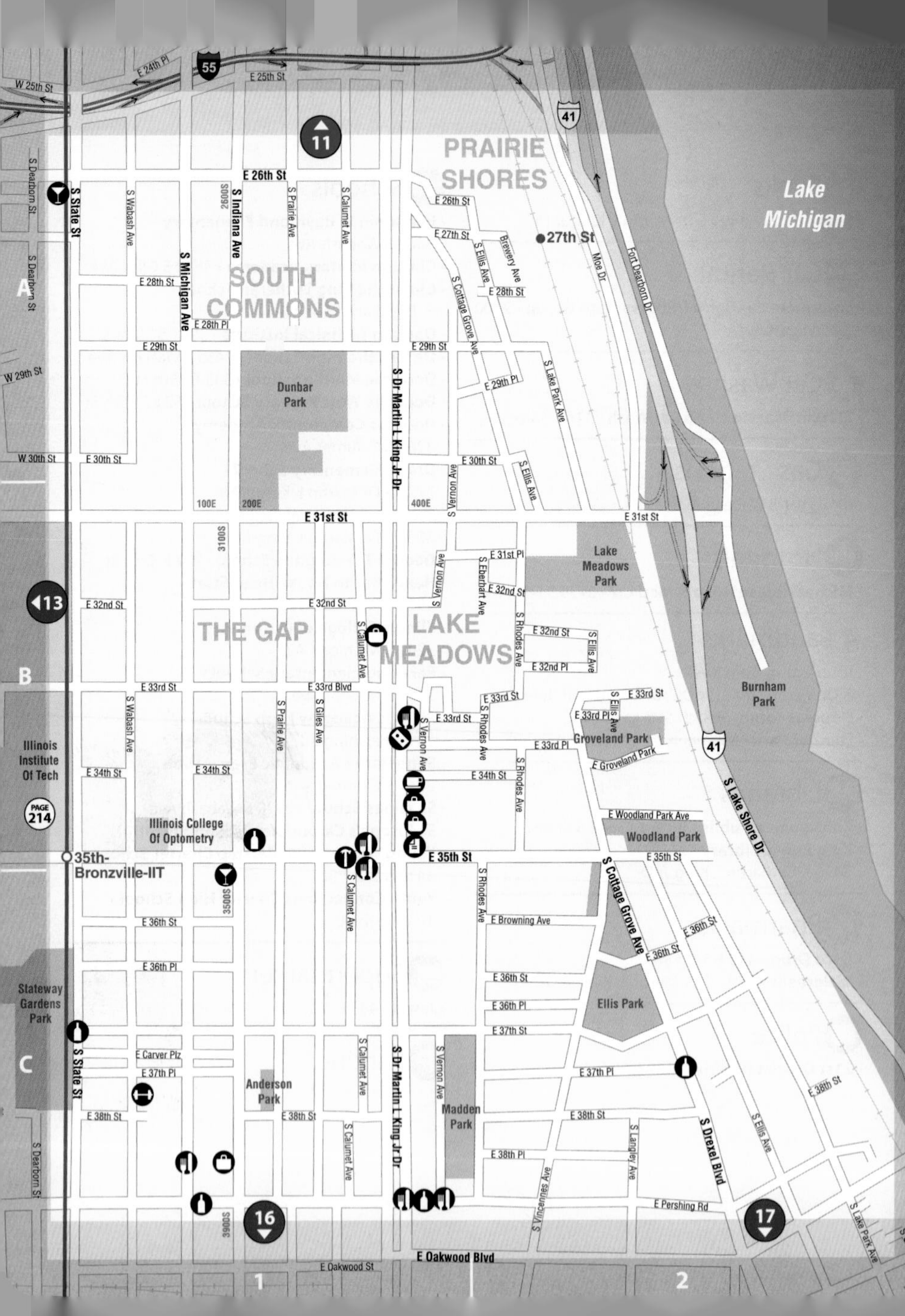

PRAIRIE SHORES
SOUTH COMMONS
THE GAP
LAKE MEADOWS
Lake Michigan
Dunbar Park
Lake Meadows Park
Groveland Park
Woodland Park
Ellis Park
Burnham Park
Madden Park
Anderson Park
Stateway Gardens Park
Illinois Institute Of Tech
Illinois College Of Optometry
35th-Bronzville-IIT
27th St
E 26th St
E 31st St
E 35th St
E Oakwood Blvd
S State St
S Indiana Ave
S Michigan Ave
S Dr Martin L King Jr Dr
S Cottage Grove Ave
S Drexel Blvd
S Lake Shore Dr
Fort Dearborn Dr
Moe Dr
E 25th St
E 24th Pl
W 25th St
W 29th St
W 30th St
E Pershing Rd
E Oakwood St
PAGE 214
11
13
16
17
55
41
A
B
C
1
2

Sundries / Entertainment

There are plenty of parks and several architecturally significant sites worth a visit. The Douglas Tomb State Historic Site at E 35th commemorates Illinois Senator Stephen A. Douglas, who faced off against Abe Lincoln in the 1858 debates. Historic Bronzeville starts around Douglas's Tomb. Restored mansions on S. 31st St. and further south date from the glitzy 1920s.

Bars

- **Darryl's Den** • 2600 S State St
- **Mr T's Lounge** • 3528 S Indiana Ave

Copy Shops

- **Mail Boxes Etc** • 3437 S Dr Martin L King Jr Dr

Coffee

- **Dunkin' Donuts** • 3481 S Dr Martin L King Jr Dr

Gyms

- **Wabash YMCA** • 3763 S Wabash Ave

Hardware Stores

- **Meyers Ace Hardware** • 315 E 35th St

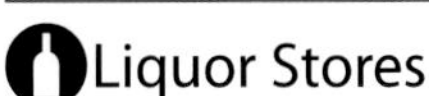

Liquor Stores

- **Grove Food & Liquors** • 3751 S Cottage Grove Ave
- **Midwest Food & Liquors** • 3701 S State St
- **Nevada & Dallas Liquor** • 419 E Pershing Rd
- **Poorwood Food & Liquors** • 200 E 35th St
- **Rothchild Liquor Marts** • 124 E Pershing Rd

Restaurants

- **Blue Sea Drive Inn** • 427 E Pershing Rd
- **Bronzville Market & Deli** • 339 E 35th St
- **Chicago Rib House** • 3851 S Michigan Ave
- **Fisher Fish & Chicken** • 3901 S Dr Martin L King Jr Dr
- **Hong Kong Delight** • 327 E 35th St
- **Mississippi Rick's** • 3351 S Dr Martin L King Jr Dr

Shopping

- **Ashley Stewart** • 3455 S Dr Martin L King Jr Dr
- **Avenue** • 3427 S Dr Martin L King Jr Dr
- **Living Word Book Store** • 3512 S Dr Martin L King Jr Dr
- **SMW Flea Market** • 3852 S Indiana Ave

Video Rental

- **Blockbuster Video** • 3349 S Dr Martin L King Jr Dr

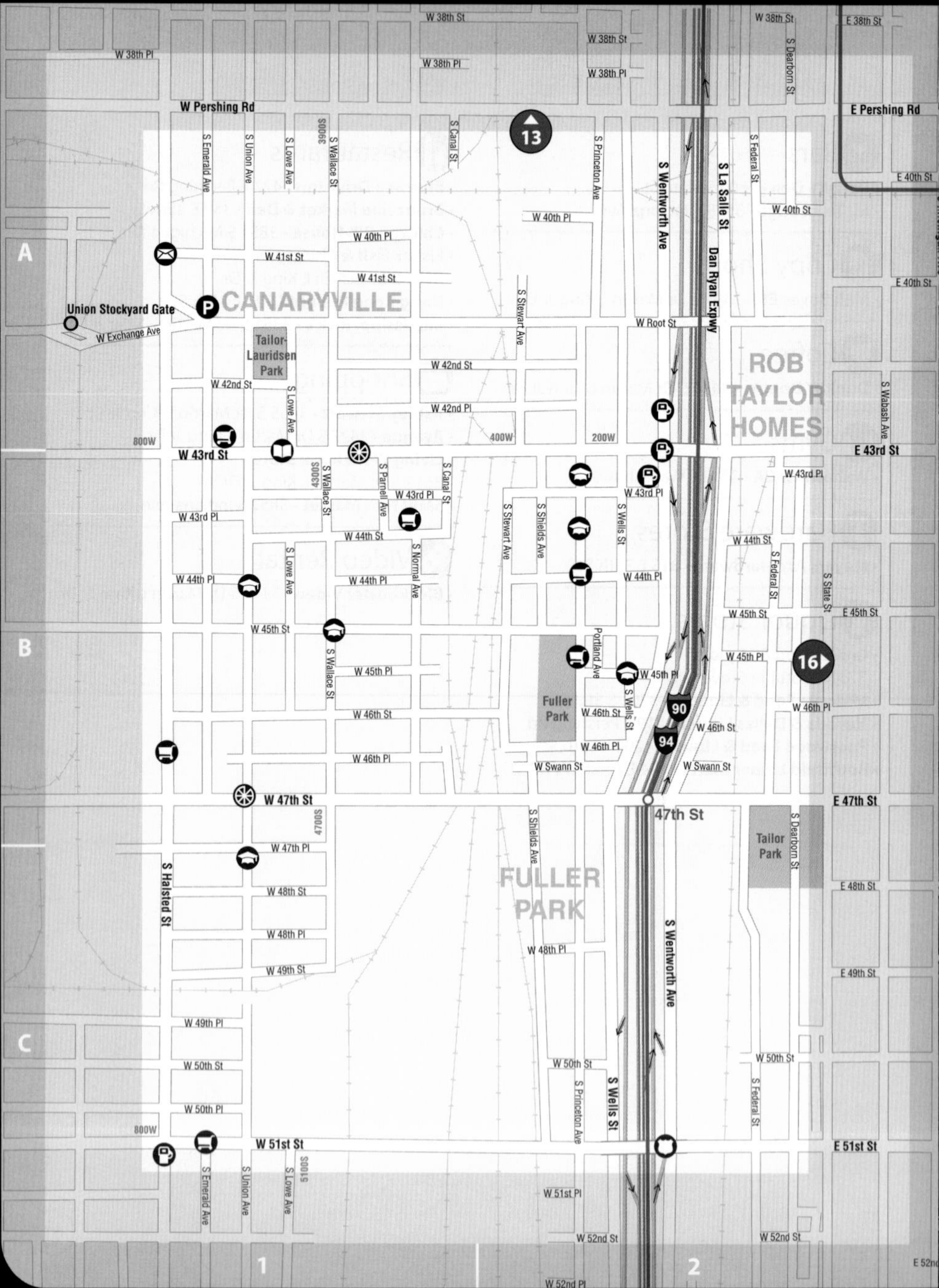

Map 15 • Canaryville / Fuller Park

CANARYVILLE
FULLER PARK
ROB TAYLOR HOMES
Union Stockyard Gate
Tailor-Lauridsen Park
Fuller Park
Tailor Park
13
16
90
94
A
B
C
1
2
W 38th St
W 38th Pl
W Pershing Rd
E Pershing Rd
E 38th St
E 40th St
W 40th St
W 40th Pl
W 41st St
W Exchange Ave
W Root St
W 42nd St
W 42nd Pl
W 43rd St
E 43rd St
W 43rd Pl
W 44th St
W 44th Pl
W 45th St
E 45th St
W 45th Pl
W 46th St
W 46th Pl
W Swann St
W 47th St
E 47th St
47th St
W 47th Pl
W 48th St
E 48th St
W 48th Pl
W 49th St
E 49th St
W 49th Pl
W 50th St
W 50th Pl
W 51st St
E 51st St
W 51st Pl
W 52nd St
W 52nd Pl
E 52nd
S Emerald Ave
S Union Ave
S Lowe Ave
S Wallace St
S Canal St
S Princeton Ave
S Wentworth Ave
S La Salle St
Dan Ryan Expwy
S Federal St
S Dearborn St
S Wabash Ave
S State St
S Stewart Ave
S Shields Ave
S Wells St
S Parnell Ave
S Normal Ave
Portland Ave
S Halsted St
800W
400W
200W
300S
4300S
4700S
5100S

This is a rough neighborhood that you should avoid unless jury duty demands you travel to the Cook County Criminal Court building on W 51st St. Public housing projects fraught with gang skirmishes dominate the streets. Here, the Union Stockyards, which earned Chicago's reputation as "hog butcher to the world," once stood. All that's left is the limestone entrance gate to the stockyards. Pass on the sightseeing and keep heading south to upbeat Bronzeville.

Gas Stations

- **BP** • 4248 S Wentworth Ave
- **BP** • 5101 S Halsted St
- **Citgo** • 4300 S Wentworth Ave

Landmarks

- **Union Stockyard Gate** • Exchange Ave & Peoria St

Libraries

- **Canaryville Public Library** • 642 W 43rd St

Pizza

- **Paisans III** • 704 W 47th St
- **Pizza Nova** • 558 W 43rd St

Police

- **2nd District (Wentworth)** • 5101 S Wentworth Ave

Post Offices

- 4101 S Halsted St

Schools

- **Garfield Alternative High School** • 220 W 45th Pl
- **Graham Elementary School** • 4436 S Union Ave
- **Milton Olive APC** • 5125 S Princeton Ave
- **Parkman Elementary School** • 245 W 51st St
- **St Gabriel's School** • 4500 S Wallace St
- **Thomas A Hendricks Community Academy** • 4316 S Princeton Ave
- **Tilden High School** • 4747 S Union Ave

Supermarkets

- **A&M Food Market** • 4425 S Princeton Ave
- **Canaryville Food Center** • 710 W 43rd St
- **Corner Store** • 501 W 44th St
- **Fairplay Finer Foods** • 4640 S Halsted St
- **Shamsan Food and Liquor** • 737 W 51st St

Parking

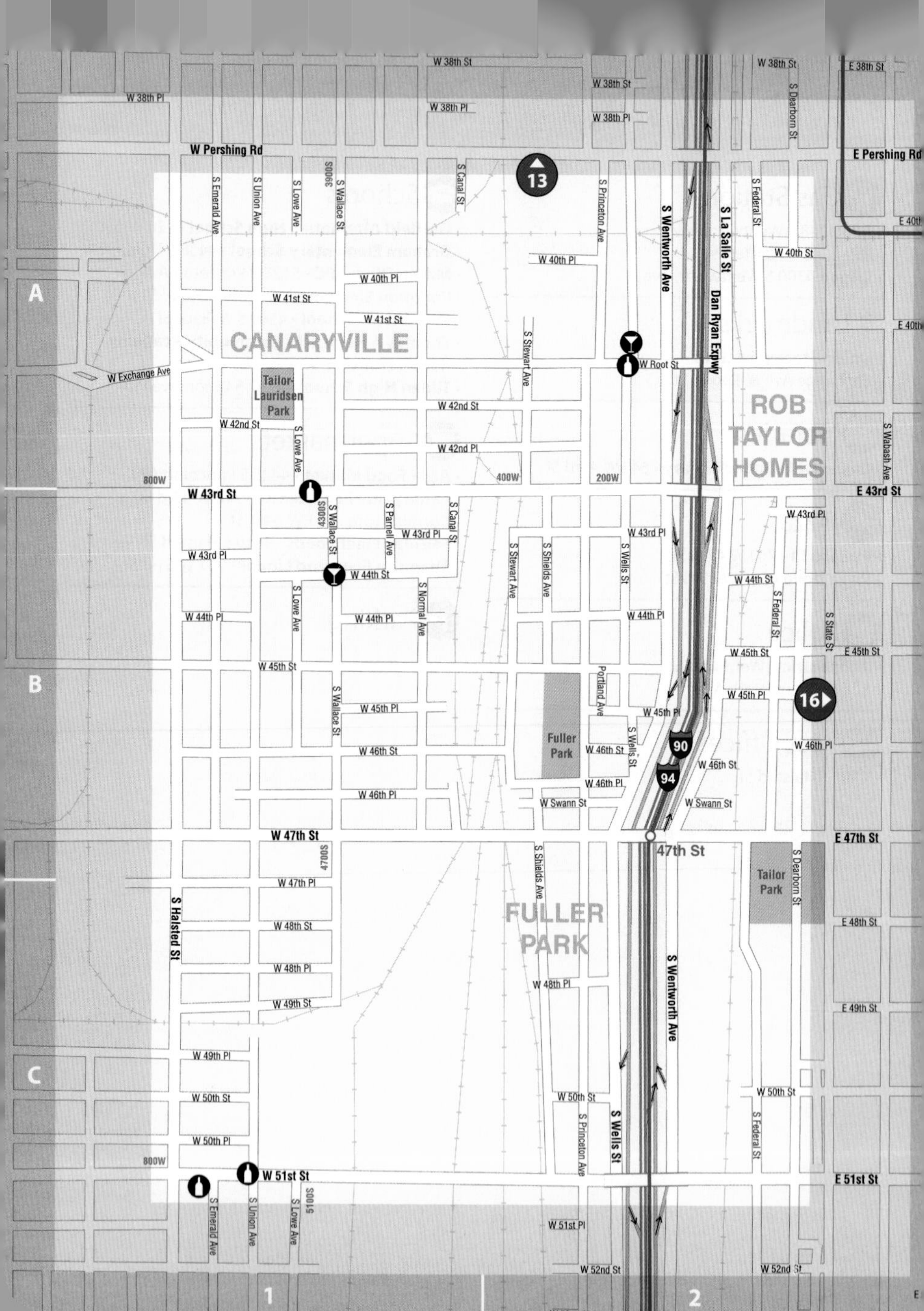

CANARYVILLE
ROB TAYLOR HOMES
FULLER PARK
Tailor-Lauridsen Park
Fuller Park
Tailor Park
W Pershing Rd
E Pershing Rd
W 38th St
W 38th Pl
W 40th Pl
W 40th St
W 41st St
W Exchange Ave
W Root St
W 42nd St
W 42nd Pl
W 43rd St
E 43rd St
W 43rd Pl
W 44th St
W 44th Pl
W 45th St
W 45th Pl
E 45th St
W 46th St
W 46th Pl
W Swann St
W 47th St
E 47th St
47th St
W 47th Pl
W 48th St
E 48th St
W 48th Pl
W 49th St
E 49th St
W 49th Pl
W 50th St
W 50th Pl
W 51st St
E 51st St
W 51st Pl
W 52nd St
S Halsted St
S Emerald Ave
S Union Ave
S Lowe Ave
S Wallace St
S Parnell Ave
S Normal Ave
S Canal St
S Stewart Ave
S Shields Ave
S Princeton Ave
S Wells St
Portland Ave
S Wentworth Ave
S La Salle St
Dan Ryan Expwy
S Federal St
S Dearborn St
S State St
S Wabash Ave
800W
400W
200W
3900S
4300S
4700S
5100S
90
94
13
16
A
B
C
1
2

If Chicago ever hosts the Olympics, this will be the perfect neighborhood to host the shooting event.

Bars

- **Kelley's Tavern** • 4403 S Wallace St
- **Root End Lounge** • 230 W Root St

Liquor Stores

- **Bravo Liquors** • 619 W 43rd St
- **Malkey Food & Liquor** • 737 W 51st St
- **Root Inn** • 234 W Root St
- **Shamsan Food and Liquor** • 737 W 51st st

Map 16 • Bronzeville

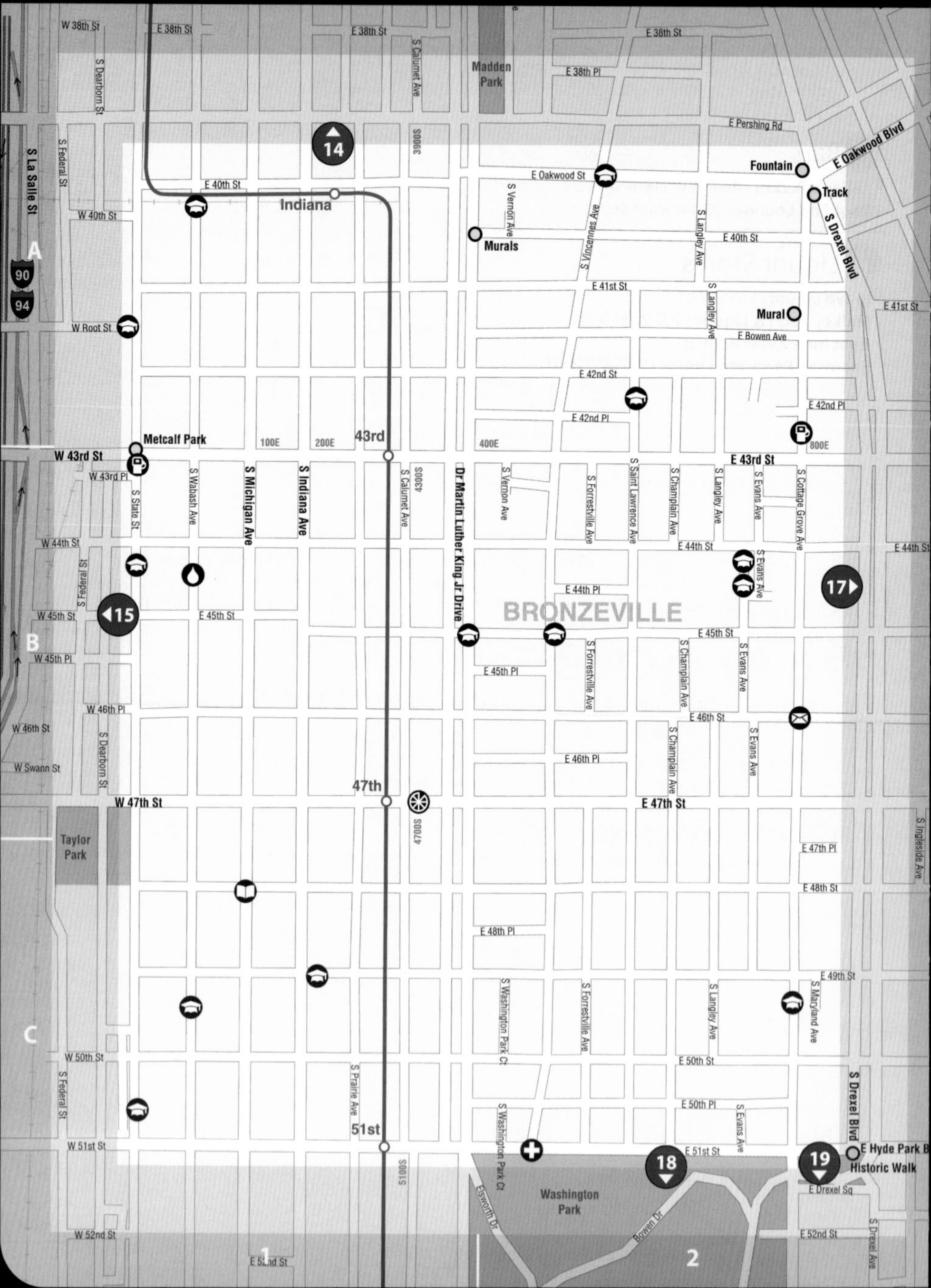

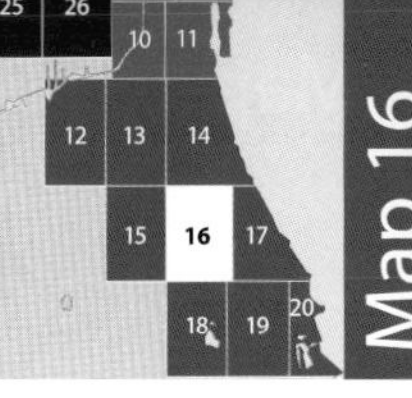

The once-thriving, African-American neighborhood of Bronzeville had the vibe of New York's Harlem, and now it's coming back. Bronzeville is experiencing a resurgence, thanks to community efforts to preserve its architecturally significant buildings dating from the 1920s. Neighborhood notables recognized on the Bronzeville Walk of Fame include horn blower Louis Armstrong, crooner Nat King Cole, astronaut Mae Jemison, choreographer Katherine Dunham (a graduate of the University of Chicago), and architect Walter T. Bailey.

Banks

- **Shore Bank** • 4658 S Drexel Blvd

Car Washes

- **Brown's Hand Car Wash** • 4451 S Wabash Ave

Gas Stations

- **BP** • 4300 S State St
- **Stop & Go 24-hr Towing** • 4257 S Cottage Grove Ave

Hospitals

- **Provident Hospital** • 500 E 51st St

Landmarks

- **Fountain** • S Drexel Blvd & E Oakwood Blvd
- **Historic Walk** • S Drexel Blvd & E Hyde Park Blvd
- **Metcalf Park** • S State St & E 43rd St
- **Mural** • S Cottage Grove Ave & E 41st St
- **Murals** • S Dr Martin L King Jr Dr & E 40th St
- **Track** • S Cottage Grove Ave & E Oakwood Blvd

Libraries

- **Hall Public Library** • 4801 S Michigan Ave

Pizza

- **Famous Magic Crust Pizza** • 345 E 47th St

Post Offices

- 4601 S Cottage Grove Ave

Schools

- **Beethoven Elementary School** • 25 W 47th St
- **Carter G Woodson School South** • 4444 S Evans Ave
- **Colman Elementary School** • 4655 S Dearborn St
- **Dyett Academy Center** • 555 E 51st St
- **Dyett Middle School** • 555 E 51st St
- **Fuller Elementary School** • 4214 S Saint Lawrence Ave
- **Hales Franciscan High School** • 4930 S Cottage Grove Ave
- **Hartigan Elementary School** • 8 W Root St
- **Helen J McCorkle Elementary** • 4421 S State St
- **Holy Angels' School** • 545 E Oakwood Blvd
- **Jean Baptiste Du Sable High** • 4934 S Wabash Ave
- **John Farren Elementary School** • 5055 S State St
- **Mollison Elementary School** • 4415 S Dr Martin L King Jr Dr
- **Overton Elementary School** • 221 E 49th St
- **St Elizabeth's School** • 4052 S Wabash Ave
- **William Reavis Elementary School** • 834 E 50th St
- **Woodson North Elementary Sch** • 4414 S Evans Ave

Supermarkets

- **Royal Food Center** • 4425 S Cottage Grove Ave

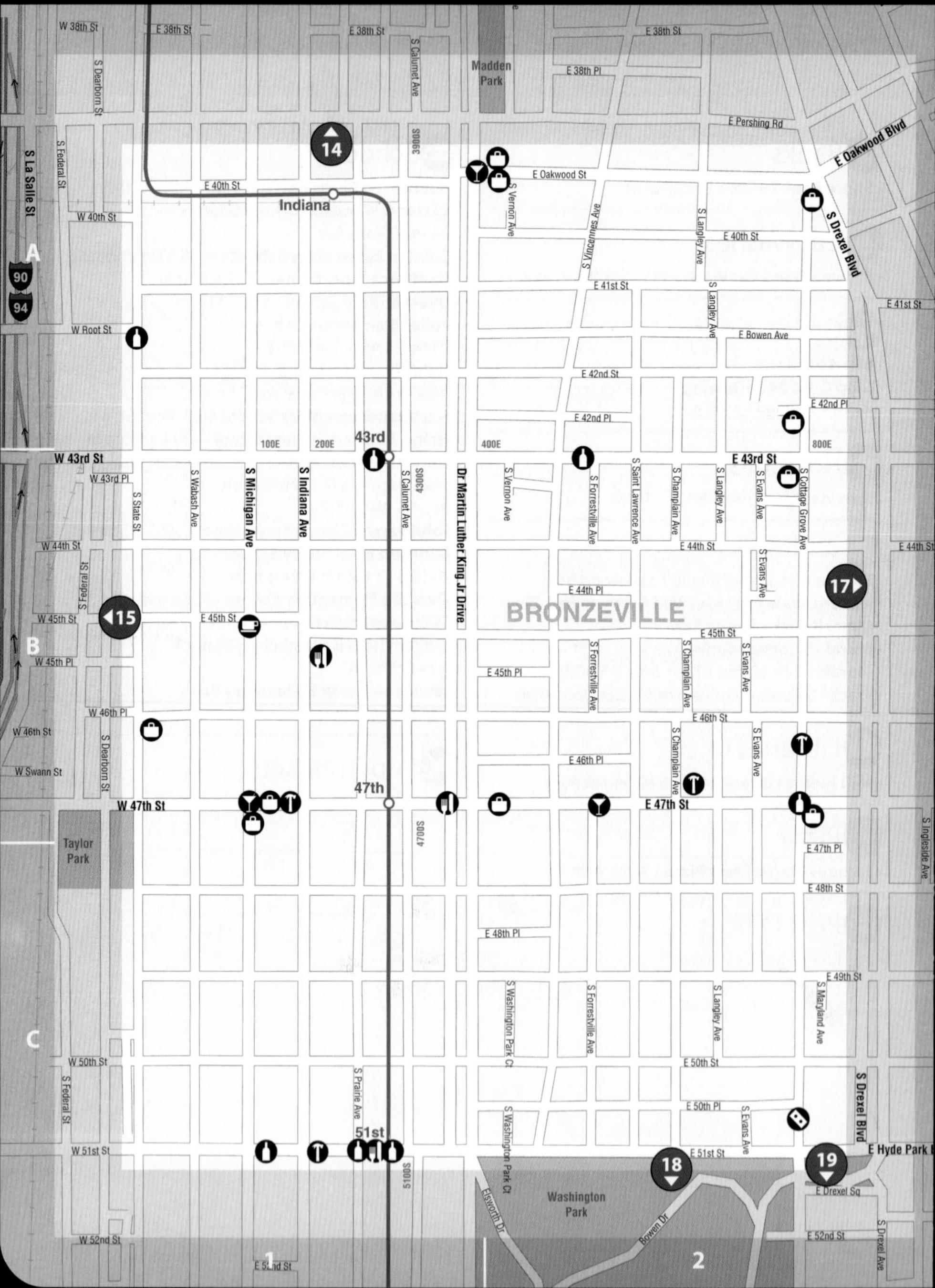

N
W 38th St
E 38th St
E 38th St
E 38th St
S Dearborn St
S Calumet Ave
Madden Park
E 38th Pl
E Pershing Rd
E Oakwood Blvd
S La Salle St
S Federal St
14
3900S
E Oakwood St
E 40th St
Indiana
W 40th St
S Vernon Ave
S Vincennes Ave
S Langley Ave
E 40th St
S Drexel Blvd
A
90
94
E 41st St
S Langley Ave
E 41st St
W Root St
E Bowen Ave
E 42nd St
E 42nd Pl
E 42nd Pl
43rd
100E
200E
400E
800E
W 43rd St
E 43rd St
W 43rd Pl
S Wabash Ave
S Michigan Ave
S Indiana Ave
S Calumet Ave
4300S
Dr Martin Luther King Jr Drive
S Vernon Ave
S Forrestville Ave
S Saint Lawrence Ave
S Champlain Ave
S Langley Ave
S Evans Ave
S Cottage Grove Ave
S State St
W 44th St
E 44th St
E 44th St
S Evans Ave
S Federal St
17
E 44th Pl
BRONZEVILLE
W 45th St
15
E 45th St
E 45th St
B
W 45th Pl
S Forrestville Ave
S Champlain Ave
S Evans Ave
E 45th Pl
W 46th Pl
E 46th St
W 46th St
S Dearborn St
S Champlain Ave
S Evans Ave
W Swann St
E 46th Pl
47th
W 47th St
E 47th St
4700S
Taylor Park
E 47th Pl
S Ingleside Ave
E 48th St
E 48th Pl
E 49th St
S Washington Park Ct
S Forrestville Ave
S Langley Ave
S Maryland Ave
C
W 50th St
E 50th St
S Federal St
S Prairie Ave
S Drexel Blvd
S Washington Park Ct
E 50th Pl
S Evans Ave
51st
W 51st St
E 51st St
5100S
18
19
E Hyde Park
Ellsworth Dr
Washington Park
E Drexel Sq
Bowen Dr
W 52nd St
E 52nd St
S Drexel Ave
1
2

Harold's Chicken Shack on 47th and 51st dishes the best fried bird in town, for sure. The African Hair & Weaving Center is Bronzeville's best beauty shack.

Bars

- **New Bonanza Lounge** • 552 E 47th St
- **Ritz Lounge** • 3947 S Dr Martin L King Jr Dr

Coffee

- **Some Like It Black Coffee Club** • 4500 S Michigan Ave

Hardware Stores

- **Brooks Hardware** • 110 E 47th St
- **Hyde Park Building Materials** • 4630 S Cottage Grove Ave
- **IR & R Hardware** • 642 E 47th St
- **Tarson Mastercraft Hardware** • 221 E 51st St

Liquor Stores

- **300 Cut Rate Liquor** • 300 E 51st St
- **Calumet Food & Liquor** • 315 E 43rd St
- **Joy Food & Liquors** • 526 E 43rd St
- **Lat's Food & Liquors** • 4121 S State St
- **Pappy's Liquors** • 4700 S Cottage Grove Ave
- **Petra** • 128 E 51st St
- **Red Apple Food & Liquor Store** • 317 E 51st St

Restaurants

- **Gladys' Luncheonette** • 4527 S Indiana Ave
- **Harold's Chicken Shack** • 307 E 51st St
- **Harold's Chicken Shack** • 364 E 47th St

Shopping

- **Alvin's Watch Repair** • 4317 S Cottage Grove Ave
- **Buddy's Shoe Shop** • 117 E 47th St
- **Chicago Furniture Co** • 4238 S Cottage Grove Ave
- **Dollar Junction** • 4701 S Cottage Grove Ave
- **Issues Barber & Beauty Salon** • 3958 S Cottage Grove Ave
- **Moone's Goodie Shop** • 413 E Oakwood Blvd
- **Parker House Sausage Co** • 4601 S State St
- **The African Hair & Weaving Center** • 428 E 47th St
- **The Dilo** • 111 E 47th St

Video Rental

- **Blockbuster Video** • 5052 S Cottage Grove Ave
- **Kat Video** • 360 E 47th St

Lake Michigan

OAKLAND

NORTH KENWOOD

KENWOOD

Burnham Park

Kenwood Park

Madison Park

South Kenwood Mansions

E Oakwood Blvd

S Drexel Blvd

S Oakenwald Ave

S Lake Park Ave

E 41st St

E 41st Pl

E 42nd St

E 42nd Pl

S Ellis Ave

E 43rd St

S Cottage Grove Ave

S Berkeley Ave

S Greenwood Ave

E 44th St

E 44th Pl Ext

S University Ave

E 46th St

E 47th St

47th

S Lake Shore Dr

E 47th Pl

S Ingleside Ave

S Woodlawn Ave

S Kimbark Ave

S Kenwood Ave

E 48th St

S Dorchester Ave

S East End Ave

E 49th St

S Chicago Beach Dr

S Maryland Ave

E 50th St

E 50th Pl

E Madison Park

E Hyde Park Blvd

S Hyde Park Blvd

E Drexel Sq

S Drexel Ave

S Blackstone Ave

S Cornell Ave

E 52nd St

3900S

4300S

4700S

5100S

800E

1200E

41

14

16

19

20

A

B

C

1

2

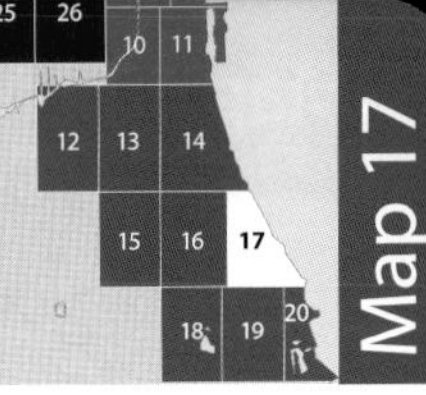

Essentials

Largely residential, Kenwood is the address for astounding, renovated Victorian mansions. Muhammad Ali once lived in the grand dame at 4944 S Woodlawn Ave and an 1897 Frank Lloyd Wright house is at 5132 S Woodlawn Ave. The graceful, tree-lined streets of South Kenwood are where the University of Chicago professors live, while students live on campus in neighboring Hyde Park just to the south.

Banks

- **Citibank** • 1310 E 47th St
- **Harris Trust & Savings Bank** • 901 E 47th St
- **United Credit Union** • 1300 E 47th St 2nd Fl

Gas Stations

- **BP** • 1158 E 47th St
- **BP** • 5048 S Cornell Ave

Hospitals

- **University of Chicago Physicians Group** • 1301 E 47th St

Landmarks

- **South Kenwood Mansions** • Between S Dorchester (east), S Ellis (west), S Hyde Park Blvd (south), and E 47th (north)

Libraries

- **Blackstone Public Library** • 4904 S Lake Park Ave

Pharmacies

- **Walgreens** • 1320 E 47th St

Pizza

- **Domino's** • 1453 E Hyde Park Blvd

Schools

- **Ancona Montessori School** • 4770 S Dorchester Ave
- **Ariel Community Academy** • 4434 S Lake Park Ave
- **Future Stomures High School** • 4071 S Lake Park Ave
- **Harvard School** • 4731 S Ellis Ave
- **Kenwood Academy School** • 5015 S Blackstone Ave
- **Martin Luther King Jr High School** • 4445 S Drexel Blvd
- **Price Elementary School** • 4351 S Drexel Ave
- **Robinson Elementary School** • 4225 S Lake Park Ave
- **Shoesmith Elementary School** • 1330 E 50th St
- **St Ambrose Catholic School** • 1014 E 47th St

Supermarkets

- **Co-op Market** • 1300 E 47th St
- **The Newport Mart** • 4800 S Chicago Beach Dr
- **Village Foods** • 1521 E Hyde Park Blvd
- **Whole Health at the Co-op** • 1300 E 47th St 2nd Fl

Parking

Map 17 • North Kenwood / Oakland

N

Lake Michigan
Burnham Park
OAKLAND
NORTH KENWOOD
KENWOOD
South Kenwood Mansions
Kenwood Park
Madison Park
E Oakwood Blvd
S Drexel Blvd
S Oakenwald Ave
S Lake Park Ave
E 41st St
E 41st Pl
S Ellis Ave
E 42nd St
E 42nd Pl
E 43rd St
S Cottage Grove Ave
4300S
S Berkeley Ave
S Greenwood Ave
E 44th St
E 44th Pl Ext
S University Ave
41
E 46th St
E 47th St
47th
S Lake Shore Dr
S Ingleside Ave
4700S
S Woodlawn Ave
S Kimbark Ave
S Kenwood Ave
E 47th Pl
E 48th St
800E
1200E
S Dorchester Ave
E 49th St
S East End Ave
S Chicago Beach Dr
S Maryland Ave
E 50th St
E 50th Pl
E Madison Park
E Hyde Park Blvd
E Drexel Sq
5100S
S Drexel Ave
S Blackstone Ave
S Cornell Ave
S Hyde Park Blvd
E 52nd St
3900S

14
16
19
20

A
B
C
1
2

When there are students nearby, count on good, cheap eats. Kenny's on E Hyde Park Blvd is the go-to place for cheap, finger-lickin'-good ribs. Get your music at Coop's Records and movies at Top Dollar Video and DVD, both on E 47th St.

Gyms

- **Bally Total Fitness** • 1301 E 47th St

Liquor Stores

- **Co-op Market** • 1300 E 47th St
- **One Stop Food & Liquors** • 4301 S Lake Park Ave

Restaurants

- **Kenny's Ribs & Chicken** • 1461 E Hyde Park Blvd
- **Lake Shore Cafe** • 4950 S Lake Shore Drive

Shopping

- **Coop's Records** • 1350 E 47th St
- **Footlocker** • 1340 E 47th St
- **South Shore Decor** • 1328 E 47th St
- **Top Dollar** • 1300 E 47th St

Video Rental

- **Top Dollar Video and DVD** • 1300 E 47th St

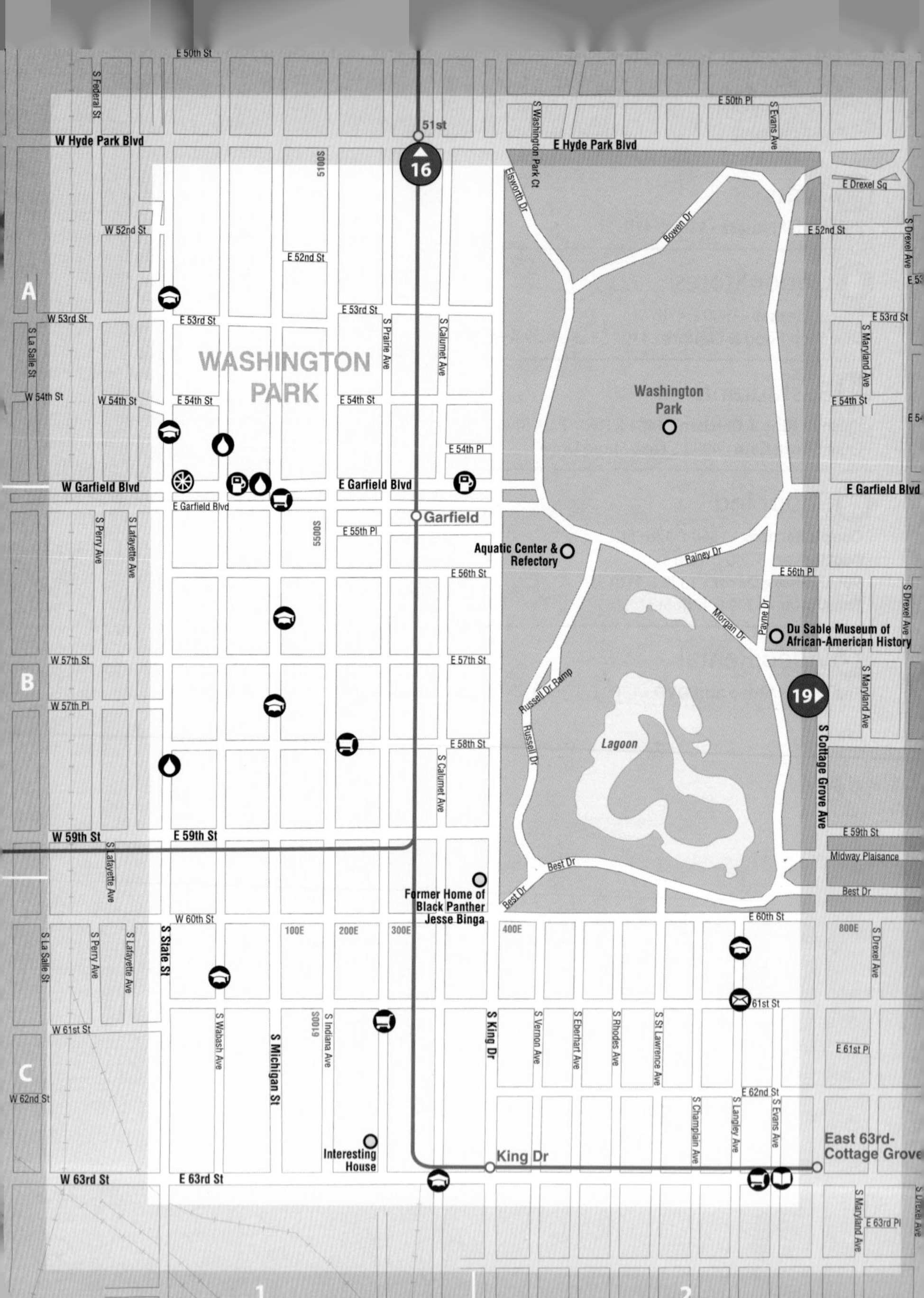

WASHINGTON PARK
Washington Park
Aquatic Center & Refectory
Du Sable Museum of African-American History
Lagoon
Former Home of Black Panther Jesse Binga
Interesting House
51st
Garfield
King Dr
East 63rd-Cottage Grove
16
19
W Hyde Park Blvd
E Hyde Park Blvd
W Garfield Blvd
E Garfield Blvd
W 59th St
E 59th St
W 63rd St
E 63rd St
S Cottage Grove Ave
S State St
S Michigan St
S King Dr
A
B
C
1
2

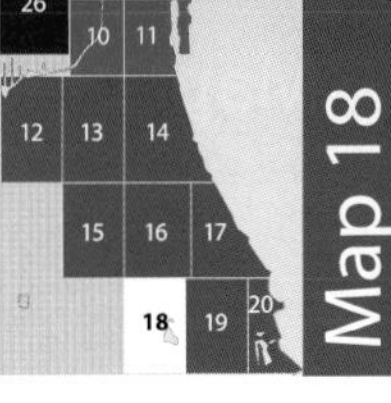

Designed in 1871 and one of the sites for the 1893 World Columbian Exposition, Washington Park dominates the neighborhood. Lorado Taft's depressing but impressive Fountain of Time stone sculpture portrays how life goes on while the clock tick-tocks. Within the 367-acre park's confines is the often overlooked DuSable Museum of African-American History. The museum's collections preserve and interpret the African-American experience.

Car Washes

- **Adam's Car Wash** • 48 E Garfield Blvd
- **Hand of Professional Car Wash** • 5812 S State St
- **Ricco's Car Wash** • 5437 S Wabash Ave

Gas Stations

- **2001** • 368 E Garfield Blvd
- **Marathon** • 48 E Garfield Blvd

Landmarks

- **DuSable Museum of African-American History** • 740 E 56th Pl
- **Former Home of Jesse Binga** • 5922 S Dr Martin L King Jr Dr
- **Interesting House** • 6215 S Prairie Ave
- **Washington Park** • E 60th St thru E 51st St, from S Cottage Grove Ave to S Dr Martin L King Jr Dr
- **Washington Park Aquatic Center & Refectory** • 5531 S Russell Dr

Libraries

- **Bessie Coleman Public Library** • 731 E 63rd St

Pizza

- **B & B Pizza King** • 4 W Garfield Blvd

Post Offices

- 700 E 61st St

Schools

- **A O Sexton School** • 6020 S Langley Ave
- **Beasley Academic Ctr** • 5255 S State St
- **Betsy Ross School** • 6059 S Wabash Ave
- **Coppin Memorial Head Start** • 5627 S Michigan Ave
- **John Foster Dulles School** • 6311 S Calumet Ave
- **Mary C Terrell School** • 5410 S State St
- **North Kenwood Charter School** • 1313 E 60th St
- **Sonia Sahnkman School** • 1365 E 60th St
- **William W Carter School** • 5740 S Michigan Ave

Supermarkets

- **Brothers Food Market** • 723 E 63rd St
- **Frank's Meat Market** • 230 E 58th St
- **John's Dairy Products** • 6115 S Prairie Ave
- **Twenty-One Grocery** • 5539 S Michigan Ave

N

WASHINGTON PARK
Washington Park
Lagoon
51st
16
19
Garfield
King Dr
East 63rd-Cottage Grove
E 50th St
E 50th Pl
S Federal St
W Hyde Park Blvd
E Hyde Park Blvd
5100S
S Washington Park Ct
S Evans Ave
Elsworth Dr
Bowen Dr
E Drexel Sq
W 52nd St
E 52nd St
E 52nd St
S Drexel Ave
W 53rd St
E 53rd St
E 53rd St
S Prairie Ave
S Calumet Ave
S Maryland Ave
S La Salle St
W 54th St
E 54th St
E 54th Pl
W Garfield Blvd
E Garfield Blvd
S Perry Ave
S Lafayette Ave
5500S
E 55th Pl
Rainey Dr
E 56th St
E 56th Pl
Payne Dr
Morgan Dr
W 57th St
E 57th St
W 57th Pl
Russell Dr Ramp
Russell Dr
E 58th St
S Cottage Grove Ave
W 59th St
E 59th St
Midway Plaisance
Best Dr
W 60th St
E 60th St
100E
200E
300E
400E
800E
S State St
E 61st St
S Wabash Ave
6100S
S Indiana Ave
S Michigan St
S King Dr
S Vernon Ave
S Eberhart Ave
S Rhodes Ave
S St Lawrence Ave
W 61st St
E 61st Pl
W 62nd St
E 62nd St
S Champlain Ave
S Langley Ave
W 63rd St
E 63rd St
E 63rd Pl
A
B
C
1
2

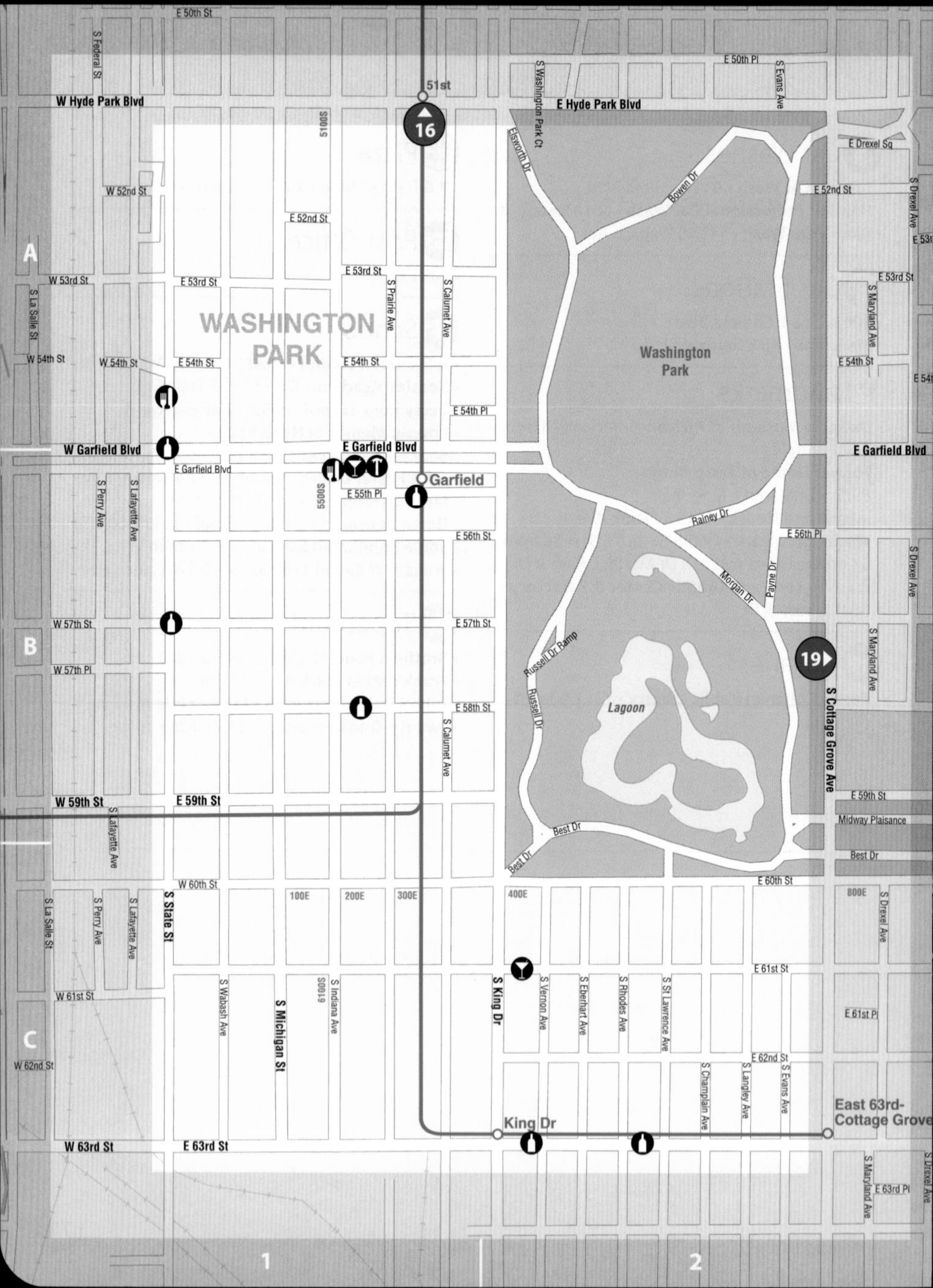

Washington Park exudes a relaxed attitude. Lots of great fried chicken joints can be found in this neighborhood, making it perfect for picnics. Look to the park for things to do. Its outdoor swimming pool, playing fields, fishing lagoons and, peaceful nature areas keep residents outdoors and active. The food at Rose's BBQ on S. State St. satisfies a hearty appetite.

Bars

- **Hank's Lounge** • 415 E 61st St
- **The Odyssey Cocktail Lounge** • 211 E Garfield Blvd

Hardware Stores

- **Boulevard Ace Hardware** • 227 E Garfield Blvd

Liquor Stores

- **Garden State Liquors** • 5701 S State St
- **Jordan Food & Liquor** • 315 E 55th St
- **Midway Food & Liquor** • 5500 S State St
- **Rothschild Liquor Marts** • 425 E 63rd St
- **S & J Food & Liquors** • 241 E 58th St
- **Steve's Liquors** • 558 E 63rd St

Restaurants

- **Ms Lee's Good Food** • 205 E Garfield Blvd
- **Rose's BBQ Chicken** • 5426 S State St

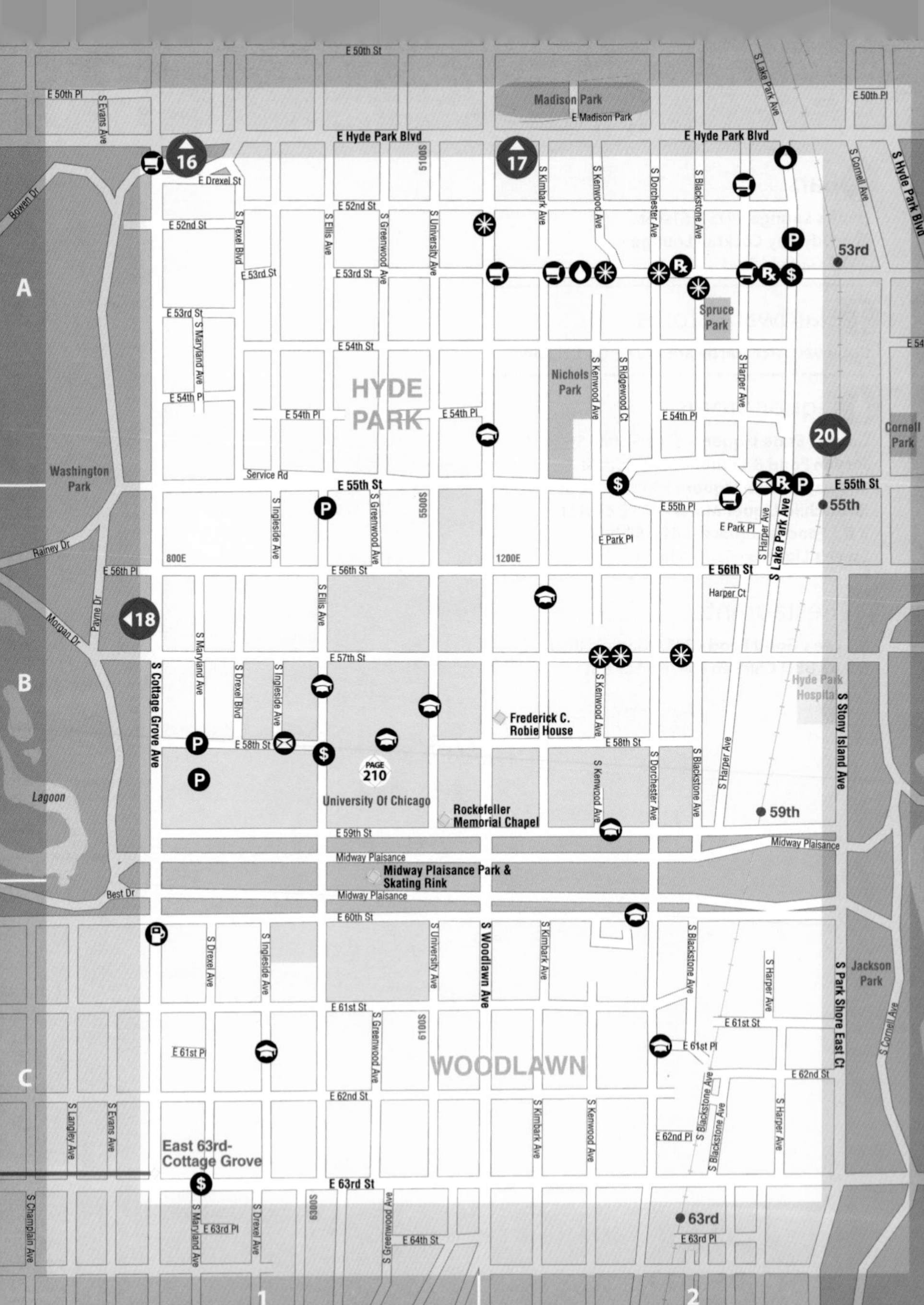

E 50th St
E 50th Pl
S Evans Ave
Madison Park
E Madison Park
E Hyde Park Blvd
S Lake Park Ave
S Hyde Park Blvd
S Cornell Ave
16
17
E Drexel St
Bowen Dr
E 52nd St
S Drexel Blvd
S Ellis Ave
S Greenwood Ave
S University Ave
S Kimbark Ave
S Kenwood Ave
S Dorchester Ave
S Blackstone Ave
53rd
E 53rd St
Spruce Park
E 54
S Maryland Ave
E 54th St
E 54th Pl
HYDE PARK
Nichols Park
S Ridgewood Ct
S Harper Ave
20
Cornell Park
Washington Park
Service Rd
E 55th St
E 55th Pl
55th
S Ingleside Ave
E Park Pl
Rainey Dr
800E
1200E
E 56th Pl
E 56th St
Harper Ct
Payne Dr
Morgan Dr
18
E 57th St
Hyde Park Hospital
S Stony Island Ave
S Cottage Grove Ave
Frederick C. Robie House
E 58th St
PAGE 210
Lagoon
University Of Chicago
Rockefeller Memorial Chapel
59th
E 59th St
Midway Plaisance
Midway Plaisance Park & Skating Rink
Best Dr
E 60th St
S Woodlawn Ave
Jackson Park
S Park Shore East Ct
E 61st St
E 61st Pl
WOODLAWN
E 62nd St
E 62nd Pl
S Langley Ave
East 63rd-Cottage Grove
E 63rd St
63rd
E 63rd Pl
E 64th St
S Champlain Ave
A
B
C
1
2

Essentials

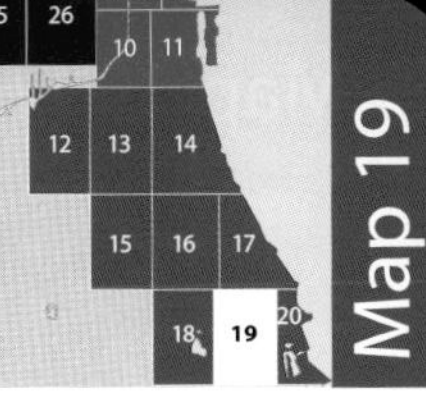

The brainy University of Chicago breeds culture like its scientists rack up Nobel Prizes. With concerts in the soaring Rockefeller Memorial Chapel, archeological wonders at the free Oriental Institute, the professional Court Theatre, Frank Lloyd Wright-designed Robie House, and the Smart Museum's moving contemporary artworks, U of C should be drawing more culturally-inclined Chicagoans south of the Stevenson Expressway.

Banks

- **Citibank** • 5812 S Ellis Ave
- **Cole Taylor Bank** • 824 E 63rd St
- **Hyde Park Bank** • 1525 E 53rd St
- **University National Bank** • 1354 E 55th St

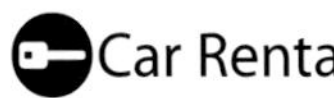

Car Rental

- **Enterprise** • 5508 S Lake Park Ave • 773-288-0500

Car Washes

- **BP** • 5130 S Lake Park Ave
- **Hyde Park Car Wash** • 1330 E 53rd St

Gas Stations

- **Lang's Standard Svc Station** • 6011 S Cottage Grove Ave
- **Shell** • 5200 S Lake Park Ave

Hospitals

- **Duchossois Center for Advanced Medicine (DCAM)** • 5758 S Maryland Ave
- **University of Chicago Children's Hospital** • 5839 S Maryland Ave
- **University Of Chicago Hospital** • 5841 S Maryland Ave

Landmarks

- **Frederick C Robie House** • 5757 S Woodlawn Ave
- **Midway Plaisance Park & Skating Rink** • S Ellis Ave & S University Ave, between E 59th St to E 60th St
- **Rockefeller Memorial Chapel** • 1156 E 59th Ave

Pharmacies

- **Katsaros Pharmacy** • 1521 E 53rd St
- **Osco Drug** • 1420 E 53rd St
- **Walgreens** • 1554 E 55th St

Pizza

- **Caffe Florian** • 1450 E 57th St
- **Edwardo's Natural Pizza** • 1321 E 57th St
- **Giordano's** • 5311 S Blackstone Ave
- **Medici on 57th** • 1327 E 57th St
- **Nicky's Chinese Food** • 5231 S Woodlawn Ave
- **Pizza Capri** • 1501 E 53rd St
- **Pizza Hut** • 1406 E 53rd St

Post Offices

- 1526 E 55th St
- 956 E 58th St

Schools

- **Andrew Carnegie School** • 1414 E 61st Pl
- **Charles Kozminski School** • 936 E 54th St
- **Chicago Theological Seminary** • 5757 S University Ave
- **John Fiske School** • 6145 S Ingleside Ave
- **Laboratory Schools** • 1362 E 59th St
- **McCormick Seminary** • 5460 S University Ave
- **Phillip Murray School** • 5335 S Kenwood Ave
- **St Thomas the Apostle Elementary** • 5467 S Woodlawn Ave
- **University of Chicago** • 5801 S Ellis Ave
- **William H Ray School** • 5631 S Kimbark Ave

Supermarkets

- **Bonne Sante Health Food** • 1512 E 53rd St
- **Co-op Market** • 1526 E 55th St
- **Co-op Market Express** • 1226 E 53rd St
- **Hyde Park Produce** • 1312 E 53rd St
- **Jimmy's Food Center** • 5131 S Cottage Grove Ave
- **Sunflower Seed Health Food** • 5210-C S Harper Ave

Parking

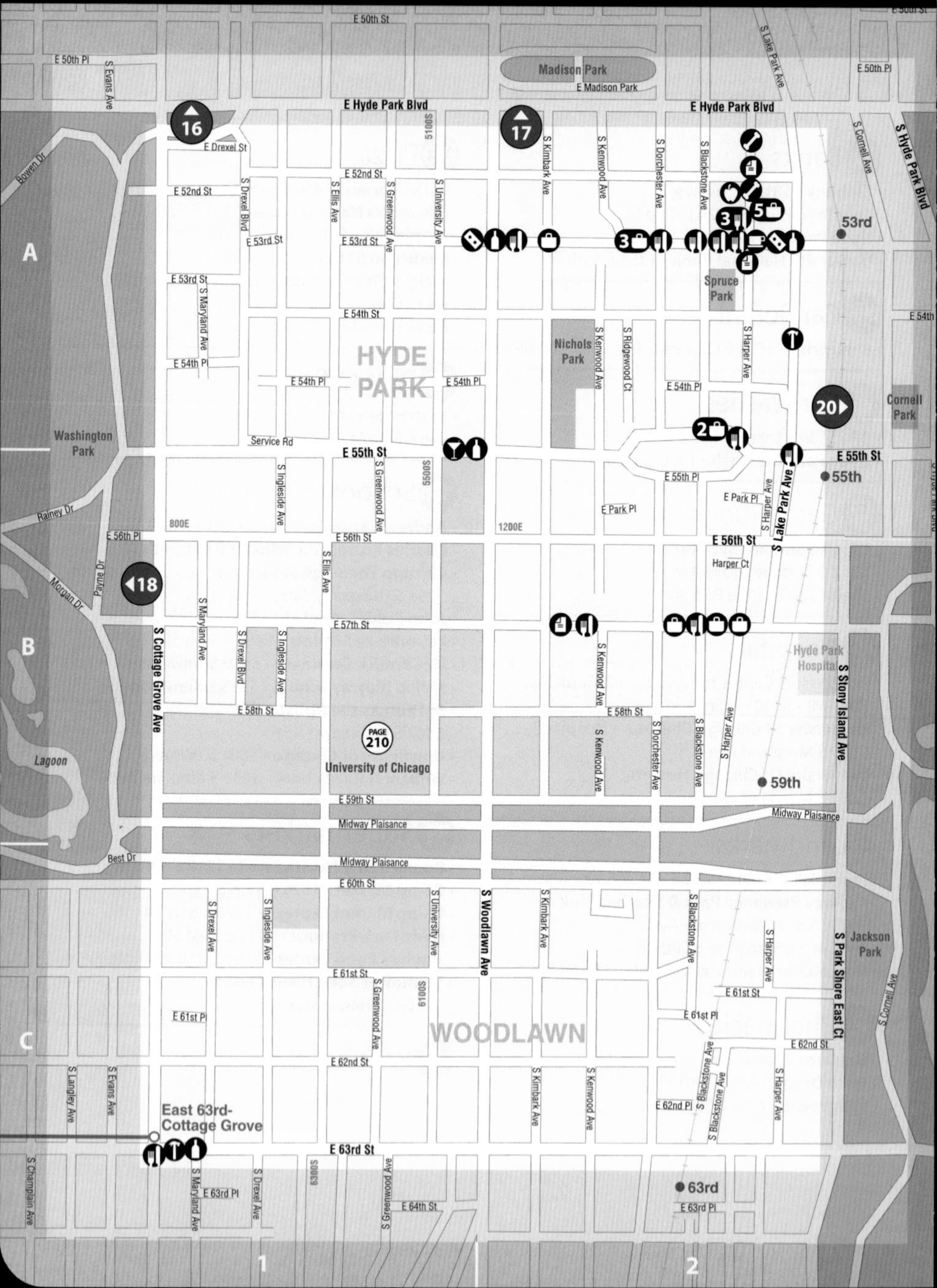

Map 19 • **Hyde Park / Woodlawn**

E 50th St
E 50th Pl
S Evans Ave
Madison Park
E Madison Park
S Lake Park Ave
E Hyde Park Blvd
S Cornell Ave
S Hyde Park Blvd
16
17
5100S
E Drexel St
Bowen Dr
S Kimbark Ave
S Kenwood Ave
S Dorchester Ave
S Blackstone Ave
E 52nd St
S Drexel Blvd
S Ellis Ave
S Greenwood Ave
S University Ave
E 53rd St
53rd
A
E 53rd St
Spruce Park
S Maryland Ave
E 54th St
E 54th St
HYDE PARK
Nichols Park
S Ridgewood Ct
S Harper Ave
E 54th Pl
E 54th Pl
E 54th Pl
E 54th Pl
20
Cornell Park
Washington Park
Service Rd
E 55th St
5500S
E 55th St
S Lake Park Ave
55th
S Ingleside Ave
E 55th Pl
E Park Pl
E Park Pl
Rainey Dr
800E
1200E
E 56th Pl
E 56th St
E 56th St
Harper Ct
Payne Dr
Morgan Dr
18
E 57th St
S Cottage Grove Ave
B
Hyde Park Hospital
S Stony Island Ave
E 58th St
E 58th St
PAGE 210
University of Chicago
Lagoon
59th
E 59th St
Midway Plaisance
Midway Plaisance
Midway Plaisance
Best Dr
E 60th St
S Woodlawn Ave
Jackson Park
S Park Shore East Ct
E 61st St
E 61st St
6100S
E 61st Pl
E 61st Pl
WOODLAWN
C
E 62nd St
E 62nd St
S Langley Ave
E 62nd Pl
East 63rd-Cottage Grove
E 63rd St
6300S
S Champlain Ave
E 63rd Pl
63rd
E 64th St
E 63rd Pl

1
2

Synonymous with the University of Chicago, Hyde Park is full of things to discover. The leafy, limestone campus oozes old money and intellectual achievements. Powell's Bookstore on 57th is a favorite haunt for serious page-turners.

Bars

- **Woodlawn Tap** • 1172 E 55th St

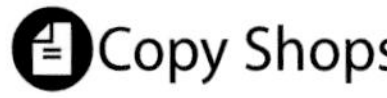

Copy Shops

- **Copy Works** • 5210 S Harper Ave
- **Kinko's** • 1315 E 57th St
- **Mail Boxes Etc** • 1507 E 53rd St

Coffee

- **Starbucks** • 1508 E 53rd St

Farmer's Markets

- **Hyde Park** • E 52nd Pl & Harper Ave

Hardware Stores

- **Elston Hardware** • 5422 S Lake Park Ave
- **Handy Hardware** • 6319 S Cottage Grove Ave

Liquor Stores

- **Chalet Wine & Cheese Shop** • 1531 E 53rd St
- **Fair Discount** • 801 E 63rd St
- **Kimbark Liquors & Wine Shop** • 1214 E 53rd St
- **Woodlawn Tap & Liquor Store** • 1172 E 55th St

Pet Shops

- **Hyde Park Pet** • 5210 S Harper Ct
- **Hyde Park Pet Spa** • 5226 Harper Ave

Restaurants

- **Calypso Cafe** • 5211-C S Harper Ave
- **Daley's Restaurant** • 805 E 63rd St
- **Dixie Kitchen and Bait Shop** • 5225-A S Harper Ave
- **Kikuya Japanese Restaurant** • 1601 E 55th St
- **La Petite Folie** • 1504 E 55th St
- **Leona's** • 1228 E 53rd St
- **Maravilla's Mexican Restaurant** • 5211 S Harper Ave
- **Medici on 57th** • 1327 E 57th St
- **Mellow Yellow** • 1508-10 E 53rd St
- **Noodles Etc** • 1460 E 53rd St
- **Rajun Cajun** • 1459 E 53rd St
- **Ribs N Bibs** • 5300 S Dorchester Ave
- **Salonica Restaurant** • 1438 E 57th St

Shopping

- **57th St Books** • 1301 E 57th St
- **Artisans 21** • 5225-J S Harper Ave
- **Artisans 21** • 5240 S Harper Ave
- **Brush Strokes** • 1369 E 53rd St
- **Calla Lily Gift Shop** • 5225 S Harper Ave
- **Cohn & Stern For Men** • 1500 E 55th St
- **Dr Wax Records and Tapes** • 5225-D S Harper Ave
- **Freehling Pot & Pan Co** • 1365 E 53rd St
- **Futons N More** • 1370 E 53rd St
- **O'Gara and Wilson** • 1448 E 57th St
- **Powell's Bookstore** • 1501 E 57th St
- **Tony's Sports** • 1308 E 53rd St
- **Wesley's Shoe Corral** • 1506 E 55th St
- **Wheels and Things** • 5210-E S Harper Ave

Video Rental

- **Hollywood Video** • 1530 E 53rd St
- **Video Connection** • 1204 E 53rd St

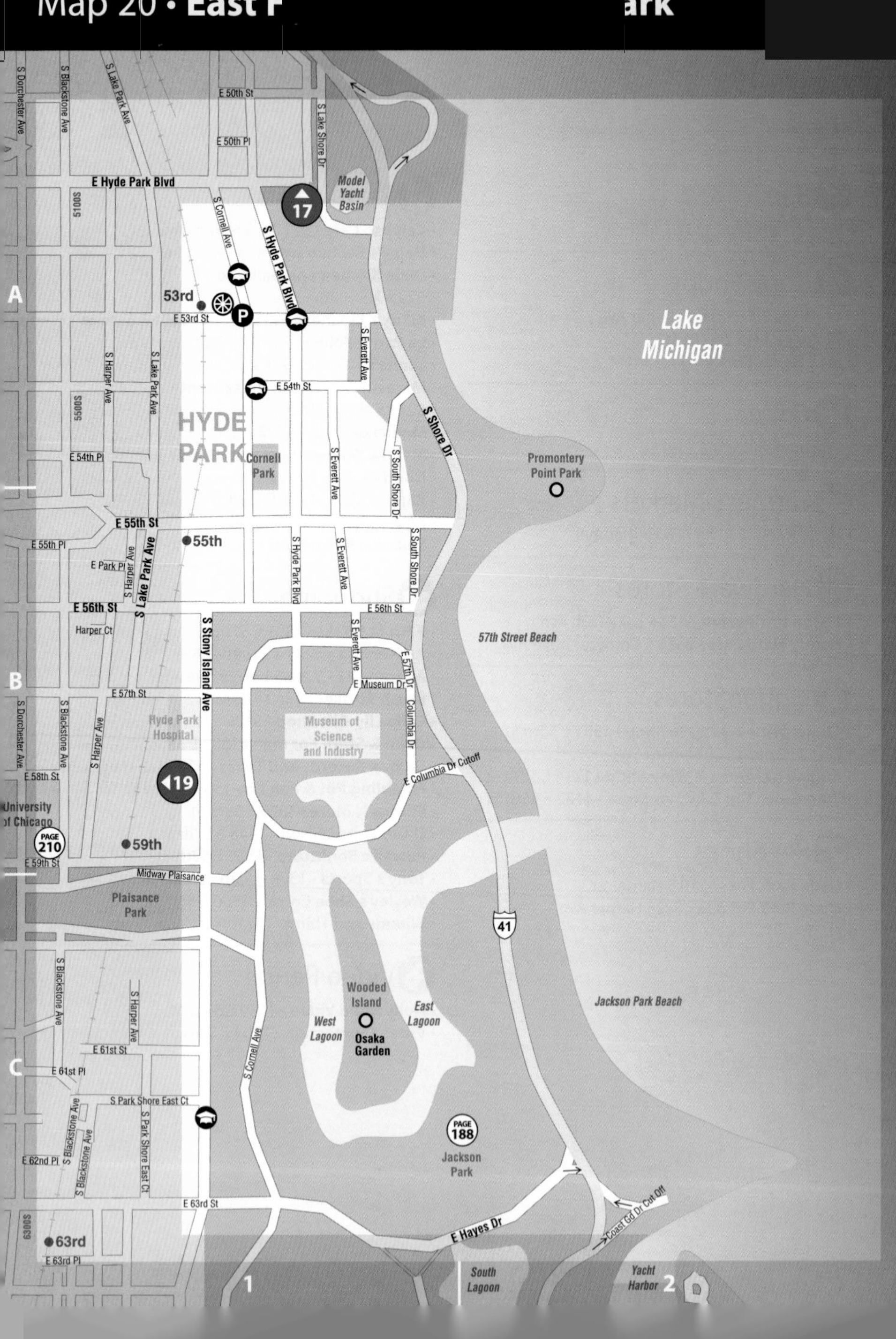

Lake Michigan
HYDE PARK
Cornell Park
Promontery Point Park
57th Street Beach
Museum of Science and Industry
Hyde Park Hospital
University of Chicago
Plaisance Park
Wooded Island
Osaka Garden
West Lagoon
East Lagoon
Jackson Park Beach
Jackson Park
Model Yacht Basin
South Lagoon
Yacht Harbor
53rd
55th
59th
63rd
17
19
PAGE 210
PAGE 188
41
E 50th St
E 50th Pl
E Hyde Park Blvd
S Hyde Park Blvd
S Cornell Ave
S Lake Shore Dr
S Lake Park Ave
S Dorchester Ave
S Blackstone Ave
S Harper Ave
5100S
5500S
6300S
E 53rd St
E 54th St
E 54th Pl
E 55th St
E 55th Pl
E Park Pl
E 56th St
S Stony Island Ave
S Everett Ave
S South Shore Dr
S Shore Dr
Harper Ct
E Museum Dr
E 57th Dr
E 57th St
Columbia Dr
E Columbia Dr Cutoff
E 58th St
E 59th St
Midway Plaisance
E 61st St
E 61st Pl
S Park Shore East Ct
E 62nd Pl
E 63rd St
E 63rd Pl
E Hayes Dr
Coast Gd Dr
Coast Gd Dr Cut Off
A
B
C
1
2

This is a great neighborhood in which to relax. Recently, the Chicago Park District dumped money into upgrading the neighborhood's lakefront. The 57th St. and 63rd St. beaches are less crowded than those on the North Side. The Museum of Science and Industry deserves multiple visits but beware, brain freeze sets in fast from all the information the institute presents. Osaka Garden on Wooded Island and Promontory Point Park are prime places to chill out.

Landmarks

- **Osaka Garden/Wooded Island** • Just south of the Museum of Science and Industry, between the West Lagoon and East Lagoon
- **Promontory Point Park** • 5491 S Shore Dr

Pizza

- **Cholie's Pizza** • 1601 E 53rd St

Schools

- **Akiba-Schechter Jewish Day School** • 5235 S Cornell Ave
- **Catholic Theological Union** • 5401 S Cornell Ave
- **Hyde Park Art Center & School** • 5307 S Hyde Park Blvd
- **Hyde Park Career Academy** • 6220 S Stony Island Ave

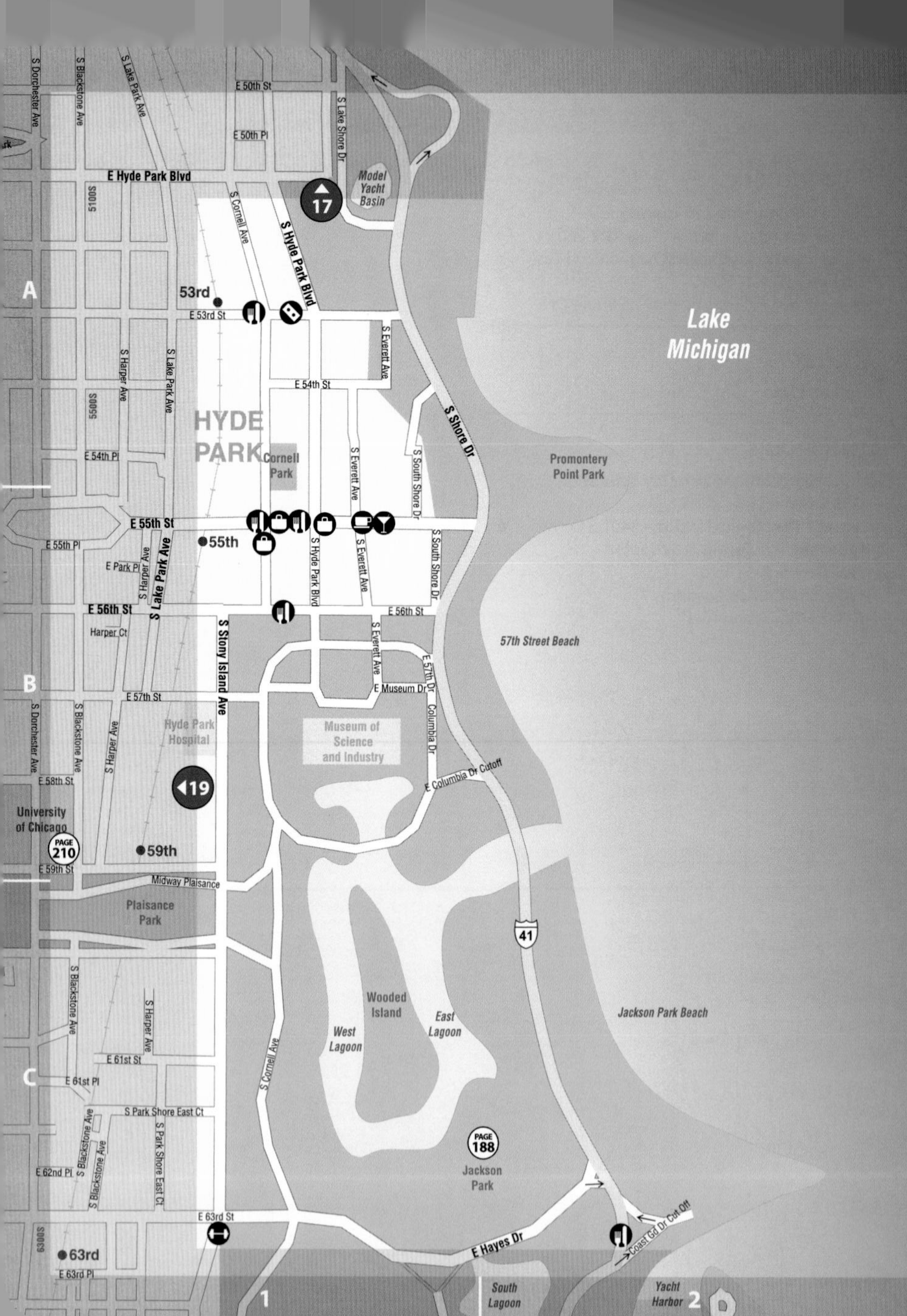
Lake Michigan
HYDE PARK
E 50th St
E 50th Pl
E Hyde Park Blvd
S Lake Shore Dr
Model Yacht Basin
17
S Hyde Park Blvd
S Cornell Ave
53rd
E 53rd St
S Everett Ave
E 54th St
S Shore Dr
S South Shore Dr
Promontery Point Park
Cornell Park
E 54th Pl
E 55th St
E 55th Pl
55th
E Park Pl
E 56th St
S Lake Park Ave
S Harper Ave
Harper Ct
S Stony Island Ave
57th Street Beach
E 57th St
E Museum Dr
E 57th Dr
Columbia Dr
Museum of Science and Industry
Hyde Park Hospital
E Columbia Dr Cutoff
19
E 58th St
University of Chicago
PAGE 210
59th
E 59th St
Midway Plaisance
Plaisance Park
41
S Blackstone Ave
S Dorchester Ave
5100S
5500S
Wooded Island
West Lagoon
East Lagoon
Jackson Park Beach
E 61st St
E 61st Pl
S Park Shore East Ct
S Cornell Ave
PAGE 188
Jackson Park
E 62nd Pl
E 63rd St
E Hayes Dr
Coast Gd Dr Cut Off
6300S
63rd
E 63rd Pl
A
B
C
1
2
South Lagoon
Yacht Harbor

Sundries / Entertainment

The bike path hugs the lake in these parts, and riding early in the peaceful morning will leave you in a Zen-like state. Rely on Art's Cycle on E 55th for your wheels. For good and cheap Middle Eastern eats, try Cedars of Lebanon on 53rd St. Boaters sway to live, smooth jazz Friday nights and Sundays at Jackson Harbor Grill by the yacht club, where lake views are amazing.

Bars

- **The Cove Cocktail Lounge** • 1750 E 55th St

Coffee

- **Future World** • 1744 E 55th St

Gyms

- **Southside YMCA** • 6330 S Stony Island Ave

Restaurants

- **Cedars of Lebanon** • 1618 E 53rd St
- **Jackson Harbor Grill** • 6401 S Coast Guard Dr
- **Morry's Deli** • 5500 S Cornell Ave
- **Nile Restaurant** • 1611 E 55th St
- **Orly's Cafe** • 1660 E 55th St
- **Piccolo Mondo** • 1642 E 56th St

Shopping

- **Art's Cycle Sales & Service** • 1636 E 55th St
- **Mothaland Books, Art and Culture** • 1635 E 55th St

Video Rental

- **Blockbuster Video** • 1644 E 53rd St

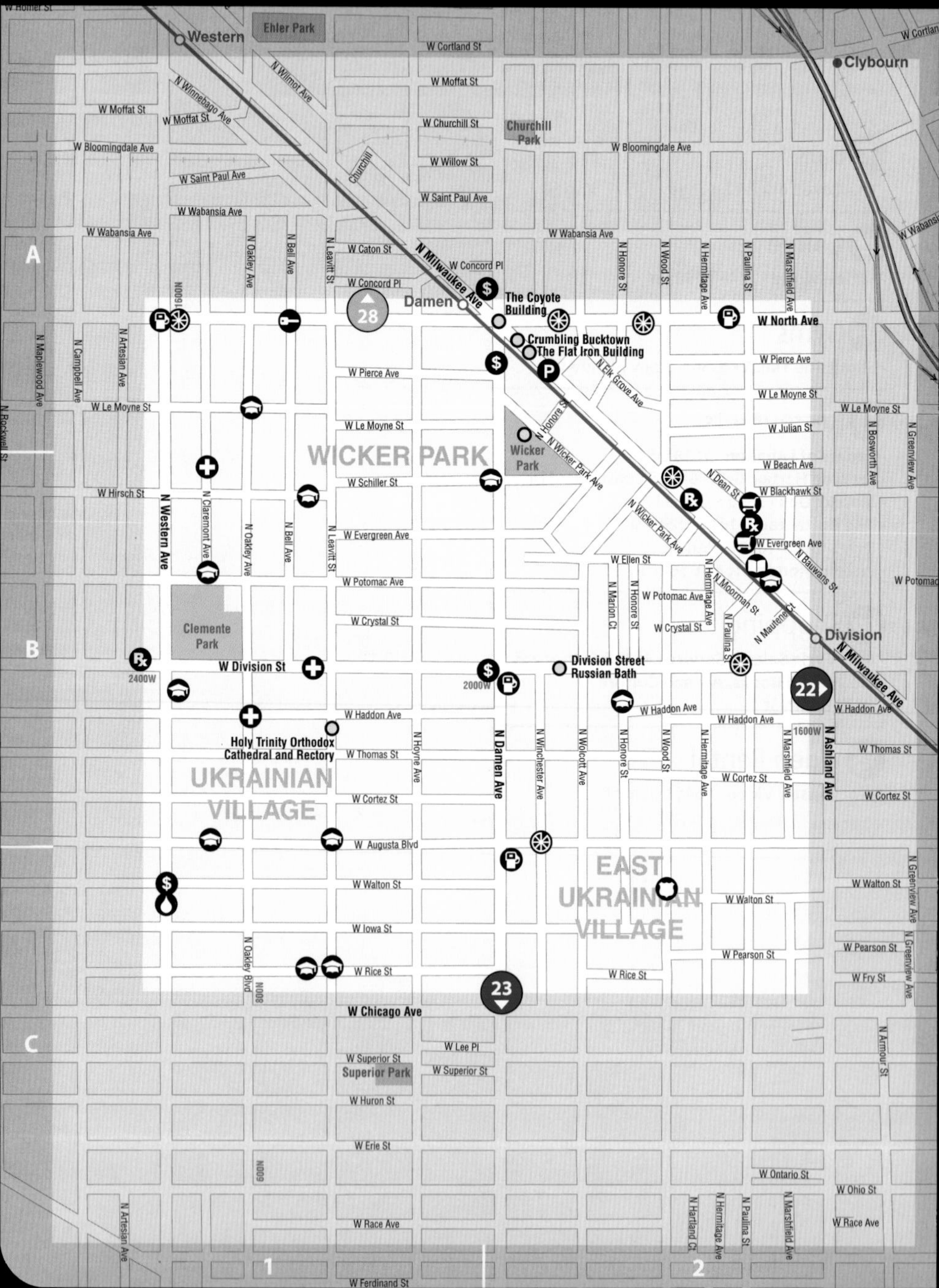

Map 21 • Wicker Park/Ukrainian Village

N

WICKER PARK

UKRAINIAN VILLAGE

EAST UKRAINIAN VILLAGE

The Coyote Building

Crumbling Bucktown

The Flat Iron Building

Division Street Russian Bath

Holy Trinity Orthodox Cathedral and Rectory

Ehler Park

Churchill Park

Wicker Park

Clemente Park

Superior Park

Western

Damen

Division

Clybourn

28

22

23

A

B

C

1

2

W Homer St
W Cortland St
W Moffat St
W Churchill St
W Bloomingdale Ave
W Willow St
W Saint Paul Ave
W Wabansia Ave
W Caton St
W Concord Pl
W North Ave
W Pierce Ave
W Le Moyne St
W Julian St
W Beach Ave
W Schiller St
W Blackhawk St
W Hirsch St
W Evergreen Ave
W Ellen St
W Potomac Ave
W Crystal St
W Division St
W Haddon Ave
W Thomas St
W Cortez St
W Augusta Blvd
W Walton St
W Iowa St
W Pearson St
W Rice St
W Fry St
W Chicago Ave
W Lee Pl
W Superior St
W Huron St
W Erie St
W Ontario St
W Ohio St
W Race Ave
W Ferdinand St

N Milwaukee Ave
N Wilmot Ave
N Winnebago Ave
Churchill
N Elk Grove Ave
N Wicker Park Ave
N Dean St
N Bauwans St
N Moorman St
N Mautene Ct
N Rockwell St
N Maplewood Ave
N Campbell Ave
N Artesian Ave
N Western Ave
N Claremont Ave
N Oakley Ave
N Oakley Blvd
N Bell Ave
N Leavitt St
N Hoyne Ave
N Damen Ave
N Winchester Ave
N Wolcott Ave
N Honore St
N Marion Ct
N Wood St
N Hermitage Ave
N Paulina St
N Marshfield Ave
N Ashland Ave
N Bosworth Ave
N Greenview Ave
N Armour St
N Hartland Ct

2400W
2000W
1600W
800N
1600N
600N

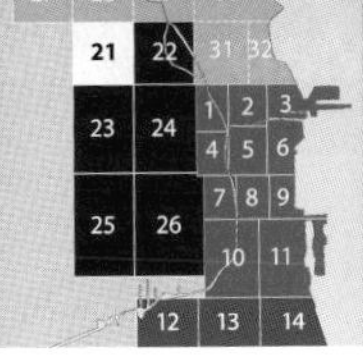

While yuppies rehab Victorians and developers strike for gold, the young arty community that paved the way is finding it harder and harder to stomach rising rents in this former ethnic enclave. Proximity to downtown and the expressway, as well as many cool boutiques, coffeeshops, and bakeries, still make this a desirable place to live, even if weekend parking and traffic rival those of Lincoln Park.

Banks

- **First Security Federal Savings** • 936 N Western Ave
- **Midwest Bank & Trust Company** • 1601 Milwaukee Ave
- **North Community Bank** • 1555 N Damen Ave
- **North Community Bank** • 2000 W Division St

Car Rental

- **Budget** • 2237 W North Ave • 773-686-6800

Gas Stations

- **BP** • 1600 N Western Ave
- **Citgo** • 1720 W North Ave
- **Clark Oil** • 1949 W Augusta Blvd
- **Shell** • 1950 W Division St

Hospitals

- **Nazareth Family Ctr** • 1127 N Oakley Blvd
- **St Elizabeth's Hospital** • 1431 N Claremont Ave
- **St Mary of Nazareth Hospital** • 2233 W Division St

Landmarks

- **Crumbling Bucktown** • 1579 N Milwaukee Ave
- **Division Street Russian Bath** • 1916 W Division St
- **Holy Trinity Orthodox Cathedral and Rectory** • 1121 N Leavitt St
- **The Coyote Building** • 1600 N Milwaukee Ave
- **The Flat Iron Building** • 1579 N Milwaukee Ave
- **Wicker Park** • Pierce and Hoyne Streets

Libraries

- **West Town Public Library** • 1271 N Milwaukee Ave

Pharmacies

- **Osco Drug** • 1343 N Paulina St
- **Osco Drug** • 2418 W Division St
- **Walgreens** • 1372 N Milwaukee Ave

Pizza

- **Big Tony's Pizza** • 1393 N Milwaukee Ave
- **Leona's** • 1936 W Augusta Blvd
- **Piece** • 1927 W North Ave
- **Pizza Hut** • 1601 N Western Ave
- **Pizza Metro** • 1707 W Division St
- **Zio Pino's Place** • 1814 W North Ave

Police

- **13th District (Wood)** • 937 N Wood St

Schools

- **A N Pritzker School** • 2009 W Schiller St
- **Christopher Columbus School** • 1003 N Leavitt St
- **Clemente High School** • 1147 N Western Ave
- **De Diego** • 1313 N Claremont Ave
- **Hans Christian Andersen School** • 1148 N Honore St
- **Josephinum High School** • 1501 N Oakley Blvd
- **Sabin Magnet School** • 2216 W Hirsch St
- **St Helen's School** • 2347 W Augusta Blvd
- **St Nicholas School** • 2200 W Rice St

Supermarkets

- **Jewel-Osco** • 1341 N Paulina St

Parking

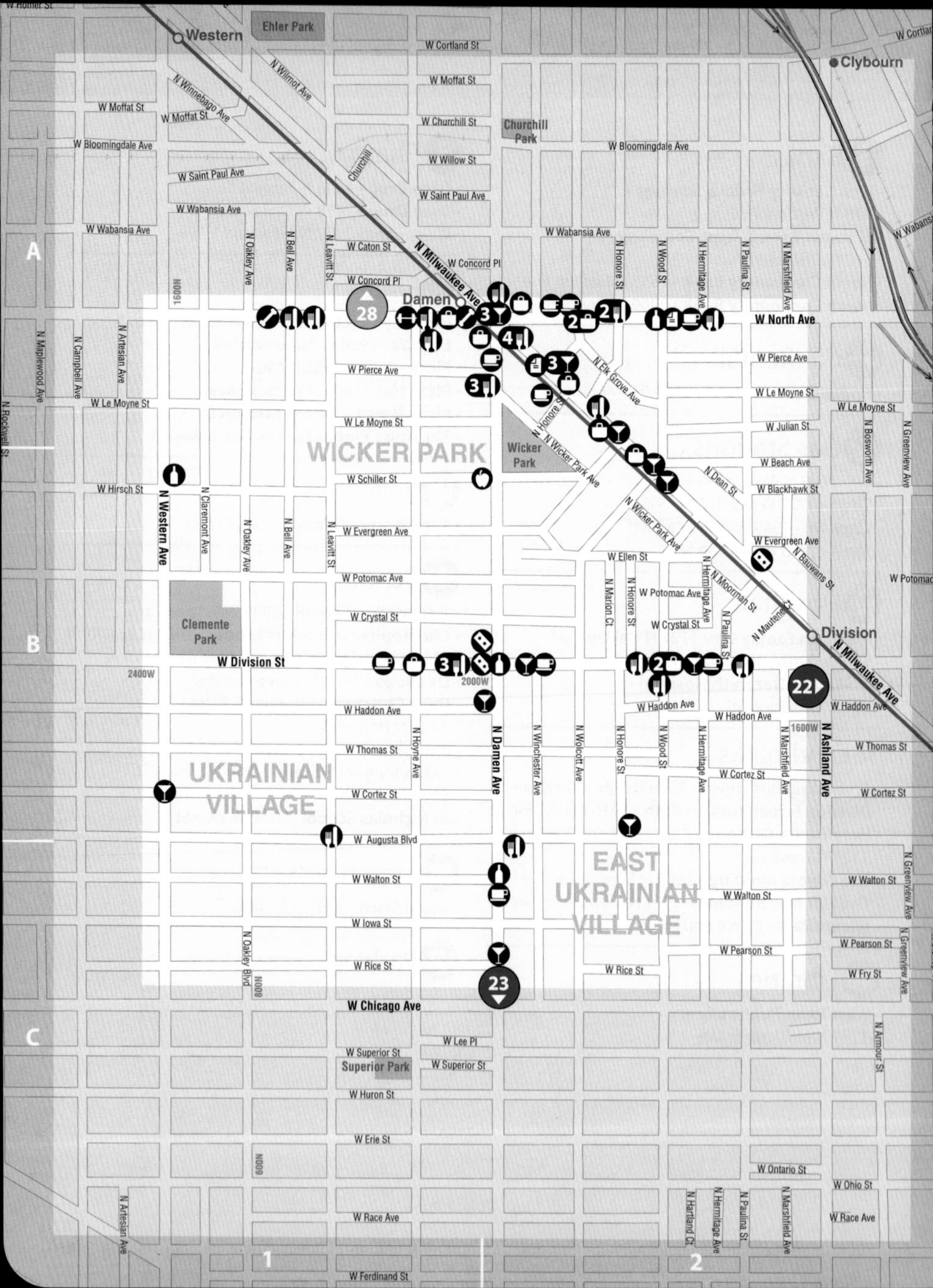

Map 21 • Wicker Park/Ukrainian Village

WICKER PARK

UKRAINIAN VILLAGE

EAST UKRAINIAN VILLAGE

Western
Damen
Division
Clybourn
Ehler Park
Churchill Park
Wicker Park
Clemente Park
Superior Park

N Milwaukee Ave
W North Ave
W Division St
W Chicago Ave
N Western Ave
N Damen Ave
N Ashland Ave
W Cortland St
W Moffat St
W Churchill St
W Bloomingdale Ave
W Willow St
W Saint Paul Ave
W Wabansia Ave
W Caton St
W Concord Pl
W Pierce Ave
W Le Moyne St
W Schiller St
W Evergreen Ave
W Potomac Ave
W Crystal St
W Haddon Ave
W Thomas St
W Cortez St
W Augusta Blvd
W Walton St
W Iowa St
W Rice St
W Superior St
W Lee Pl
W Huron St
W Erie St
W Ontario St
W Ohio St
W Race Ave
W Ferdinand St
W Hirsch St
W Julian St
W Beach Ave
W Blackhawk St
W Ellen St
W Pearson St
W Fry St
N Wicker Park Ave
N Elk Grove Ave
N Honore St
N Wood St
N Hermitage Ave
N Paulina St
N Marshfield Ave
N Bosworth Ave
N Greenview Ave
N Dean St
N Bauwans St
N Moorman St
N Mautene Ct
N Marion Ct
N Wolcott Ave
N Winchester Ave
N Hoyne Ave
N Leavitt St
N Bell Ave
N Oakley Ave
N Oakley Blvd
N Claremont Ave
N Artesian Ave
N Campbell Ave
N Maplewood Ave
N Rockwell St
N Winnebago Ave
N Wilmot Ave
N Hartland Ct
N Armour St
Churchill

2400W
2000W
1600W
1600N
800N
600N

28
22
23

A
B
C
1
2

The vibe is constant. Dance club Red Dog howls all night long. The Double Door on Milwaukee is a rock'n'roll place of worship where the Stones performed. The neighborhood's ornate Ukrainian Orthodox churches provide the perfect venue for atonement after a guaranteed raucous night out. On weekends, get to the Bongo Room for breakfast early and take a paper because you'll wait in line.

Bars

- **Bar Thirteen** • 1944 W Division St
- **Borderline** • 1958 W North Ave
- **Club Foot** • 1824 W Augusta Blvd
- **Davenport's** • 1383 N Milwaukee Ave
- **Double Door** • 1572 N Milwaukee Ave
- **Empty Bottle** • 1035 N Western Ave
- **Estelle's Cafe & Lounge** • 2013 W North Ave
- **Ezuli** • 1415 N Milwaukee Ave
- **Gold Star Bar** • 1755 W Division St
- **Holiday Club** • 1471 N Milwaukee Ave
- **Lava Lounge** • 859 N Damen Ave
- **Rainbo Club** • 1150 N Damen Ave
- **Red Dog** • 1958 W North Ave
- **Sinibar** • 1540 N Milwaukee Ave
- **Subterranean Cafe** • 2011 W North Ave
- **The Note** • 1565 N Milwaukee Ave

Copy Shops

- **Copy Max** • 1573 N Milwaukee Ave
- **Kinko's** • 1800 W North Ave

Coffee

- **Alliance Bakery** • 1736 W Division St
- **Earwax Cafe** • 1564 N Milwaukee Ave
- **Gallery Cafe** • 1760 W North Ave
- **Jinx** • 1928 W Division St
- **Letizia's Natural Bakery** • 2144 W Division St
- **Off the Wall Wireless Cafe** • 1904 W North Ave
- **Starbucks** • 1588 N Milwaukee Ave
- **Starbucks** • 1701 N Division St
- **Sweet Thang** • 1921 W North Ave
- **The Grasshopper** • 937 N Damen Ave

Farmer's Markets

- **Wicker Park/Bucktown** • W Schiller St & N Damen Ave

Gyms

- **Bucktown Fitness Club** • 2100 W North Ave

Liquor Stores

- **Carlos Food & Liquor** • 1401 N Western Ave
- **Ola's Liquor** • 947 N Damen Ave
- **Universal Food & Liquor** • 1803 W North Ave
- **Wicker Park Liquor** • 2006 W Division St

Pet Shops

- **For Dog's Sake** • 2257 W North Ave
- **Wicker Pet** • 2029 W North Ave

Restaurants

- **Bluefin** • 1952 W North Ave
- **Bongo Room** • 1470 N Milwaukee Ave
- **Cafe Absinthe** • 1958 W North Ave
- **Cold Comfort Cafe & Deli** • 2211 W North Ave
- **D'Vine Restaurant & Wine Bar** • 1950 W North Ave
- **Feast** • 1616 N Damen Ave
- **Half & Half** • 1560 N Damen Ave
- **Hi Ricky** • 1852 W North Ave
- **Las Palmas** • 1835 W North Ave
- **Leo's Lunchroom** • 1809 W Division St
- **Leona's** • 1936 W Augusta Blvd
- **Lulu's Hot Dogs** • 1000 S Leavitt St
- **Mas** • 1670 W Division St
- **Mirai Sushi** • 2020 W Division St
- **MOD** • 1520 N Damen Ave
- **Ohba** • 2049 W Division St
- **Pacific Cafe** • 1619 N Damen Ave
- **Piece** • 1927 W North Ave
- **Pontiac Cafe** • 1531 N Damen Ave
- **Settimana Cafe** • 2056 W Division St
- **Smoke Daddy** • 1804 W Division St
- **Soju** • 1745 W North Ave
- **Souk** • 1552 N Milwaukee Ave
- **Soul Kitchen** • 1576 N Milwaukee Ave
- **Spring** • 2039 W North Ave
- **Sultan's Market** • 2057 W North Ave
- **Thai Lagoon** • 2223 W North Ave

Shopping

- **Asian Essence** • 2025 1/2 W North Ave
- **Asrai Garden** • 1935 W North Ave
- **Chop Sooee Hair Salon** • 2109 W Division St
- **City Soles/Niche** • 2001 W North Ave
- **DeciBel Audio** • 1407 N Milwaukee Ave
- **Lille** • 1923 W North Ave
- **Noir** • 1746 W Division St
- **Paper Doll** • 1747 W Division St
- **Quimby's Bookstore** • 1854 W North Ave
- **Reckless Records** • 1532 N Milwaukee Ave
- **Sasabee** • 1849 W North Ave
- **The Silver Room** • 1410 N Milwaukee Ave

Video Rental

- **Blockbuster Video** • 1301 N Milwaukee Ave
- **Coconuts Music & Video** • 1520 N Damen Ave
- **Mass Video** • 2014 W Division St
- **North Coast Video** • 2014-16 W Division St
- **Star Video** • 2334 W North Ave

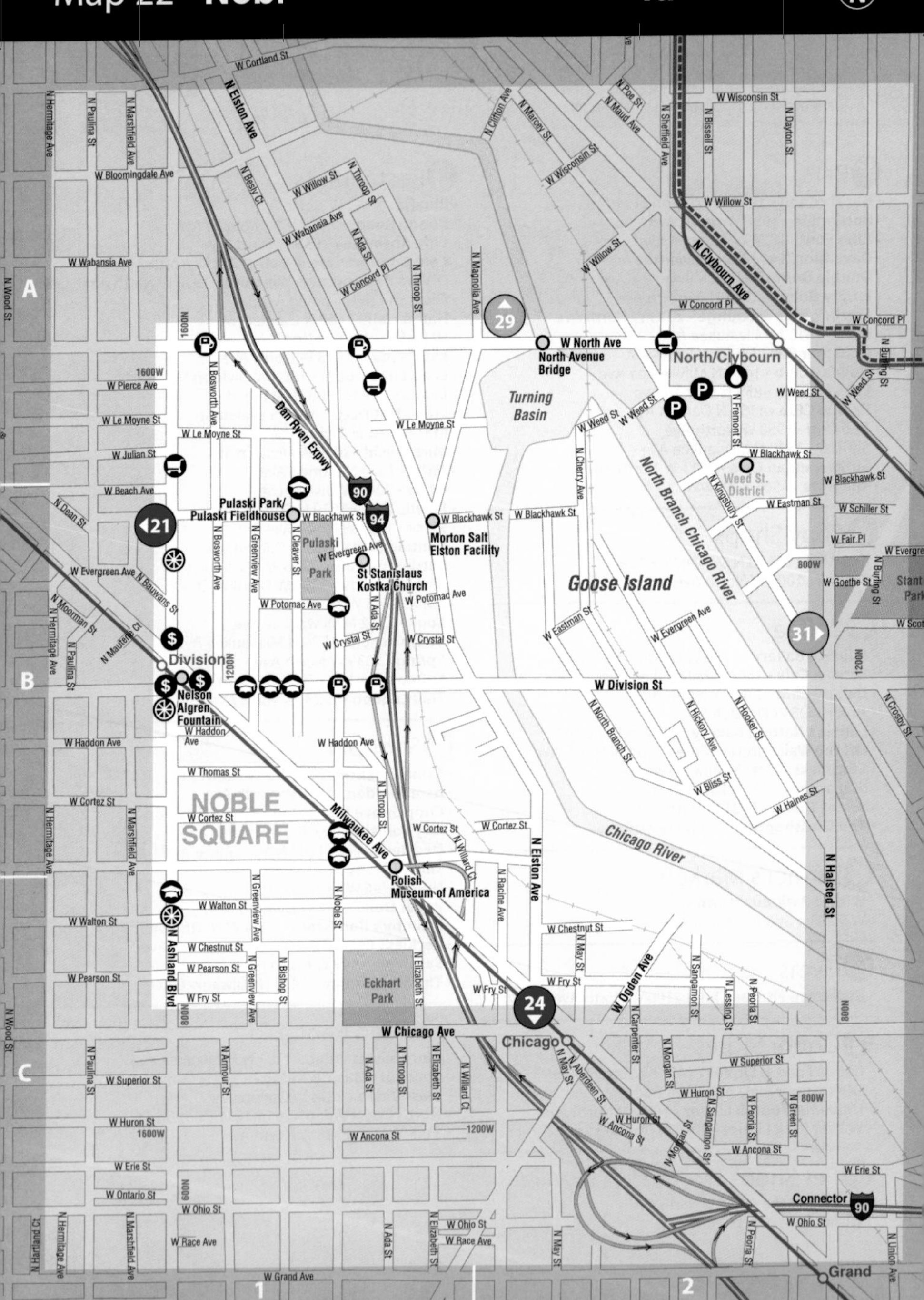
A
B
C
1
2
NOBLE SQUARE
Goose Island
Turning Basin
North Branch Chicago River
Chicago River
Division
North/Clybourn
Chicago
Grand
North Avenue Bridge
Weed St. District
Pulaski Park/ Pulaski Fieldhouse
Pulaski Park
St Stanislaus Kostka Church
Morton Salt Elston Facility
Nelson Algren Fountain
Polish Museum of America
Eckhart Park
Stanton Park
Dan Ryan Expwy
Connector
90
94
21
24
29
31
W Cortland St
N Elston Ave
W Bloomingdale Ave
W Wabansia Ave
W Willow St
W Concord Pl
W North Ave
W Pierce Ave
W Le Moyne St
W Julian St
W Beach Ave
W Blackhawk St
W Evergreen Ave
W Potomac Ave
W Crystal St
W Division St
W Haddon Ave
W Thomas St
W Cortez St
W Walton St
W Chestnut St
W Pearson St
W Fry St
W Chicago Ave
W Superior St
W Huron St
W Ancona St
W Erie St
W Ontario St
W Ohio St
W Race Ave
W Grand Ave
W Wisconsin St
W Weed St
W Eastman St
W Schiller St
W Fair Pl
W Goethe St
W Scott
W Bliss St
W Haines St
N Clybourn Ave
Milwaukee Ave
W Ogden Ave
N Ashland Blvd
N Halsted St
N Wood St
N Hermitage Ave
N Paulina St
N Marshfield Ave
N Bosworth Ave
N Greenview Ave
N Cleaver St
N Ada St
N Noble St
N Throop St
N Bishop St
N Elizabeth St
N Willard Ct
N Racine Ave
N Magnolia Ave
N Clifton Ave
N Marcey St
N Poe St
N Maud Ave
N Sheffield Ave
N Bissell St
N Dayton St
N Fremont St
N Kingsbury St
N Cherry Ave
N Burling St
N Crosby St
N Hooker St
N Hickory Ave
N North Branch St
N May St
N Aberdeen St
N Carpenter St
N Morgan St
N Sangamon St
N Lessing St
N Peoria St
N Green St
N Union Ave
N Armour St
N Besly Ct
N Dean St
N Moorman St
N Mautene Ct
N Bauwans St
N Hartland Ct
1600W
1200W
800W
1600N
1200N
800N
600N

Gritty industry, healthy retail, and alternative culture swirl together throughout this spicy neighborhood, which thrives on artistic ingenuity and Latin spirit. On Saturdays, it seems like the whole city drives here to fill up and go to Home Depot. Traffic on North Avenue Bridge is wretched.

Banks

- **Fifth Third Bank** • 1209 N Milwaukee Ave
- **Harris Trust & Savings Bank** • 1242 N Ashland Blvd
- **MB Financial Bank** • 1200 N Ashland Ave

Car Washes

- **Turtle Wax Car Wash** • 1550 N Fremont St

Gas Stations

- **BP** • 1334 W Division St
- **BP** • 1551 W North Ave
- **BP** • 1600 N Elston Ave
- **Shell** • 1400 W Division St

Landmarks

- **Morton Salt Elston Facility** • Elston Ave & Blackhawk St
- **Nelson Algren Fountain** • Division St & Ashland Blvd
- **North Avenue Bridge** •
- **Polish Museum of America** • 984 N Milwaukee Ave
- **Pulaski Park/Pulaski Fieldhouse** • Blackhawk St & Cleaver St
- **St Stanislaus Kostka Church** • 1351 W Evergreen Ave
- **Weed St District** • Between Chicago River & Halsted St

Pizza

- **Adorno's Restaurant** • 925 N Ashland Ave
- **Little Caesar's Pizza** • 1360 N Ashland Ave
- **Pizza Hut** • 1601 W Division St

Post Offices

- 1635 W Division St

Schools

- **Elizabeth P Peabody School** • 1444 W Augusta Blvd
- **Holy Trinity High** • 1443 W Division St
- **Montessori School-Near North** • 1434 W Division St
- **Noble Street Charter School** • 1010 N Noble St
- **Rudy Lozano Elementary School** • 1424 N Cleaver St
- **St Stanislaus Kostka Grade School** • 1255 N Noble St
- **The College of Office Technology** • 1520 W Division St
- **William H Wells Community High School** • 936 N Ashland Ave

Supermarkets

- **Guanajuato Grocery** • 1438 N Ashland Blvd
- **Stanley's Fresh Fruit & Vegetables** • 1558 N Elston Ave
- **Whole Foods Market** • 1000 W North Ave

Parking

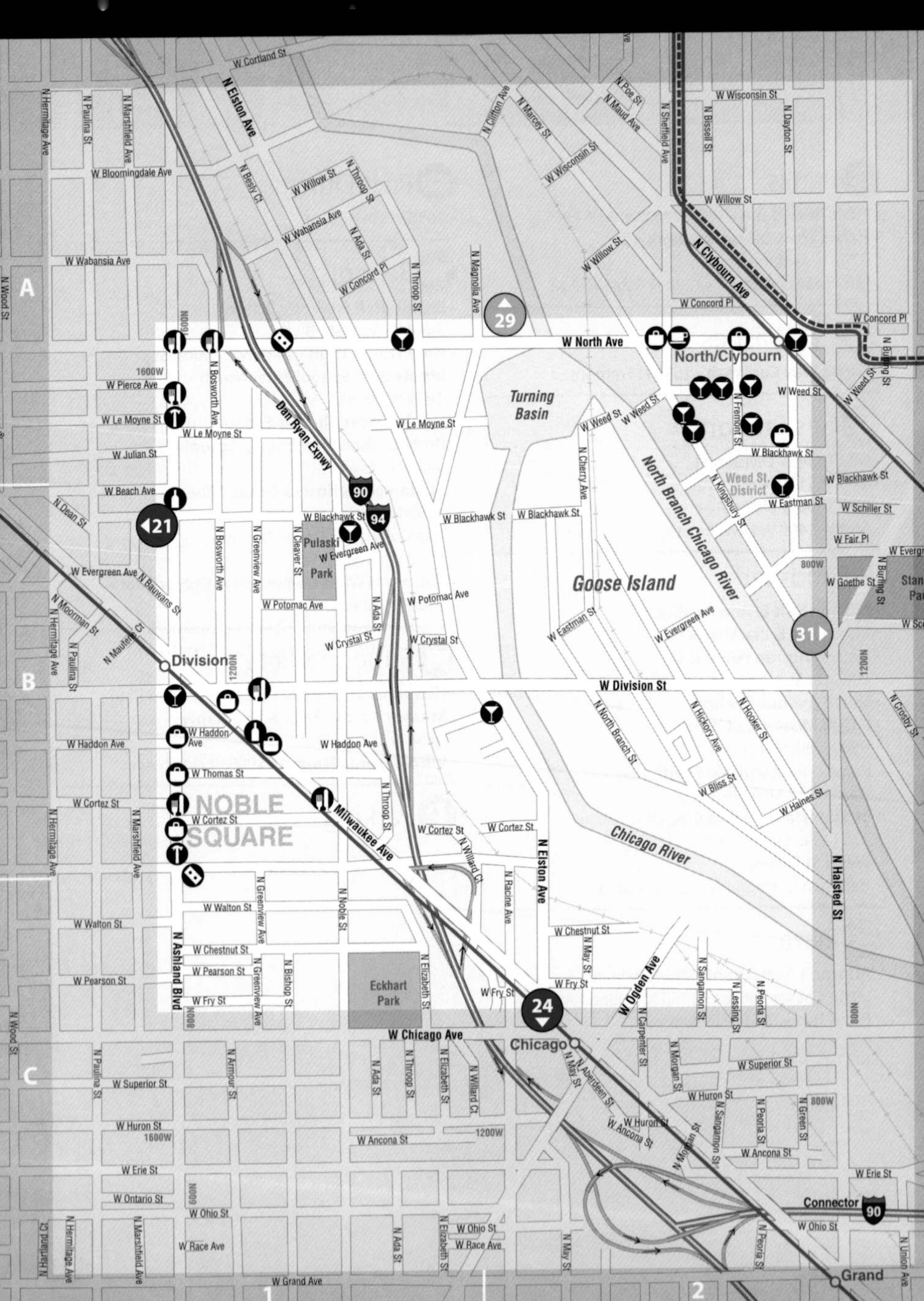

W Cortland St
N Elston Ave
N Hermitage Ave
N Paulina St
N Marshfield Ave
W Bloomingdale Ave
W Willow St
N Throop St
W Wabansia Ave
N Ada St
W Concord Pl
N Magnolia Ave
N Clifton Ave
N Marcey St
N Maud Ave
N Poe St
W Wisconsin St
N Sheffield Ave
N Bissell St
N Dayton St
W Willow St
N Clybourn Ave
W Concord Pl
W Concord Pl
29
W North Ave
North/Clybourn
1600W
W Pierce Ave
N Bosworth Ave
W Le Moyne St
W Le Moyne St
W Julian St
Dan Ryan Expwy
Turning Basin
W Weed St
W Weed St
W Weed St
N Fremont St
W Blackhawk St
N Cherry Ave
North Branch Chicago River
Weed St. District
N Kingsbury St
W Eastman St
W Blackhawk St
W Schiller St
W Beach Ave
90
94
N Dean St
21
W Blackhawk St
W Blackhawk St
W Blackhawk St
Pulaski Park
W Evergreen Ave
N Cleaver St
N Greenview Ave
W Fair Pl
W Evergreen Ave
N Bauwans St
800W
W Goethe St
N Burling St
Goose Island
W Potomac Ave
W Potomac Ave
N Moorman St
N Ada St
W Eastman St
W Evergreen Ave
31
W Crystal St
W Crystal St
N Mautene Ct
Division
1200W
1200N
W Division St
N North Branch St
N Hickory Ave
N Hooker St
N Crosby St
W Haddon Ave
W Haddon Ave
W Haddon Ave
W Thomas St
W Bliss St
W Haines St
W Cortez St
NOBLE SQUARE
W Cortez St
N Throop St
W Cortez St
W Cortez St
N Willard Ct
N Elston Ave
Chicago River
Milwaukee Ave
N Halsted St
N Racine Ave
N Noble St
W Walton St
W Walton St
N Greenview Ave
W Chestnut St
N May St
N Ashland Blvd
W Chestnut St
W Pearson St
N Bishop St
W Ogden Ave
N Sangamon St
Eckhart Park
N Elizabeth St
W Pearson St
W Fry St
W Fry St
W Fry St
N Lessing St
N Peoria St
N Carpenter St
800N
24
W Chicago Ave
Chicago
N Morgan St
N Wood St
W Superior St
N Armour St
N Ada St
N Willard Ct
N Aberdeen St
W Superior St
W Huron St
800W
W Huron St
1600W
W Ancona St
1200W
W Huron St
W Ancona St
N Sangamon St
N Peoria St
N Green St
W Ancona St
W Erie St
W Erie St
W Ontario St
900N
W Ohio St
Connector
90
N Harland Ct
N Hermitage Ave
N Marshfield Ave
W Ohio St
W Race Ave
N Elizabeth St
W Race Ave
N May St
W Ohio St
N Peoria St
N Union Ave
W Grand Ave
Grand
A
B
C
1
2

Division Street, only a short while ago the frontier of gentrification in these parts, is fast becoming the city's new restaurant row—stylish places sprout up like mushrooms seemingly overnight. Nightlife is still rich and boisterous with an enviable variety of neighborhood holes, live music venues, chi-chi see-and-be-seen joints, and pulsing clubs suitable to any taste.

Bars

- **Big Wig** • 1551 W Division St
- **Biology Bar** • 1520 N Fremont St
- **Circus** • 901 W Weed St
- **Crazy Horse Too** • 1531 N Kingsbury St
- **Crobar** • 1543 N Kingsbury St
- **Exit** • 1315 W North Ave
- **Glow** • 1615 N Clybourn Ave
- **Joe's** • 940 W Weed St
- **Mudbug/Trackside** • 901 W Weed St
- **Slow Down, Life's Too Short** • 1177 N Elston Ave

Coffee

- **Dunkin' Donuts** • 1244 N Ashland Ave
- **Hot Shots** • 1440 N Dayton St
- **Peet's Coffee and Tea** • 1000 W North Ave

Hardware Stores

- **Ace Hardware** • 1013 N Ashland Ave
- **Paragon Hardware & Mill Supply** • 1512 N Ashland Ave

Liquor Stores

- **Crater Food & Beer** • 1144 N Milwaukee Ave
- **D & D Liquors** • 1625 W North Ave
- **Rodriguez Grocery & Liquor** • 1415 N Ashland Blvd

Restaurants

- **Corosh** • 1072 N Milwaukee Ave
- **El Barco Mariscos Seafood** • 1035 N Ashland Blvd
- **Hilary's Urban Eatery** • 1500 W Division St
- **Hollywood Grill** • 1609 W North Ave
- **Luc Thang** • 1524 N Ashland Blvd
- **Watusi** • 1540 W North Ave

Shopping

- **Balloonz Special Event Décor** • 1121 N Ashland Blvd
- **Casa Loca Furniture** • 1130 N Milwaukee Ave
- **Dusty Groove Records** • 1120 N Ashland Blvd
- **Eastern Mountain Sports (EMS)** • 1000 W North Ave
- **Expo Design Center** • 1500 N Dayton St
- **Home Depot** • 1232 W North Ave
- **Old Navy** • 1569 N Kingsbury St
- **Olga's Flower Shop** • 1041 N Ashland Blvd
- **Restoration Hardware** • 938 W North Ave
- **Right-On Futon** • 1184 N Milwaukee Ave

Video Rental

- **Blockbuster Video** • 1500 W North Ave
- **Hi-Fi Video** • 957 N Ashland Ave

Map 23 • West
W Walton St
W Iowa St
W Rice St
W Chicago Ave
Ukrainian Cultural Center
Ukrainian National Museum
Superior Park
W Lee Pl
W Superior St
W Pearson St
W Pearson St
W Fry St
W Huron St
W Erie St
WEST TOWN
W Ohio St
W Ontario St
W Race Ave
W Grand Ave
W Ferdinand St
W Hubbard St
W Anson Pl
W Kinzie St.
Western Ave
W Carroll Ave
W Fulton St
W Walnut St
W Lake St
W Maypole Ave
Metropolitan Missionary Baptist Church
W Washington Blvd
W Warren Blvd
NEAR WEST SIDE
PAGE 250
United Center
First Baptist Congregational Church
W Madison St
W Arcade Pl
W Monroe St
W Adams St
W Quincy St
W Jackson Blvd
W Gladys Ave
W Kinzie St
Western
Medical Center
Eisenhower Expwy
290
W Congress Pkwy
W Harrison St
W Flournoy St
St Lukes Medical Center
Claremont Park
W Campbell Park Dr
Smith Park
Rockwell Park
Touhy Park
Union Park
Ashland
W Ogden Ave
S Marshfield Ave
N Western Ave
N Oakley Blvd
N Leavitt St
N Hoyne Ave
N Damen Ave
N Wolcott Ave
N Wood St
N Paulina St
N Ashland Ave
N Armour St
N Honore St
N Greenview Ave
N Harland Ct
N Hermitage Ave
N Marshfield Ave
N Artesian Ave
N Claremont Ave
N Bell Ave
N Jessie St
N Seeley Ave
N Winchester Ave
N Hart St
N Oswego St
N Justine St
S Western Ave
S Oakley Blvd
S Bell Ave
S Hamilton Ave
S Hoyne Ave
S Seeley Ave
S Winchester Ave
S Wolcott Ave
S Honore St
S Wood St
S Hermitage Ave
S Claremont Ave
S Leavitt St
S Laflin St
800N
600N
200N
100N
100S
300S
600S
2400W
2000W
1600W
21
24
25
A
B
C
1
2

United Center draws the faithful to Bulls and Blackhawks games. Hip Ukrainian Village seeps down into West Town's north end, making this area a mix of young professionals, working-class folk, and students from nearby University of Illinois at Chicago. Along Grand and Western are the city's best hand car washes and detailing outfits.

Banks

- **First Security Federal Savings** • 820 N Western Ave
- **Self Reliance Ukrainian Credit Union** • 2332 W Chicago Ave

Car Washes

- **G & L Car Wash** • 2213 W Grand Ave
- **G & L Car Wash & Detail** • 2215 W Grand Ave
- **Quiroga's Detail & Hand Car** • 2036 W Grand Ave

Gas Stations

- **Phillips** • 225 N Western Ave
- **Shell** • 45 N Western Ave

Landmarks

- **First Baptist Congregational Church** • 60 N Ashland Ave
- **Metropolitan Missionary Baptist Church** • 2151 W Washington Blvd
- **Ukrainian Cultural Center** • 2247 W Chicago Ave
- **Ukrainian National Museum** • 721 N Oakley Blvd
- **United Center** • 1901 W Madison St

Libraries

- **Mabel Manning Public Library** • 6 S Hoyne Ave
- **Malcolm X College Library** • 1900 W Van Buren St
- **Midwest Public Library** • 2335 W Chicago Ave

Pharmacies

- **Osco Drug** • 2427 W Chicago Ave
- **Walgreens** • 2340 W Madison St

Pizza

- **Angie's Restaurant** • 1715 W Chicago Ave
- **Bella's Pizza & Restaurant** • 1952 W Chicago Ave
- **Naty's Pizza 2** • 1757 W Chicago Ave

Post Offices

- 116 S Western Ave

Schools

- **Best Practice High School** • 2040 W Adams St
- **Crane Tech Prep Common School** • 2245 W Jackson Blvd
- **Ellen Mitchell School** • 2233 W Ohio St
- **Healy High School** • 100 N Western Ave
- **Henry Suder School** • 2022 W Washington Blvd
- **Malcolm X College** • 1900 W Van Buren St
- **Mancel Talcott School** • 1840 W Ohio St
- **Maryville Academy St Malachy** • 2252 W Washington Blvd
- **R Nathaniel Dett Elementary School** • 2306 W Maypole Ave
- **Ukrainian Catholic University** • 2247 W Chicago Ave
- **Victor Herbert Elementary School** • 2131 W Monroe St
- **William H Brown School** • 54 N Hermitage Ave

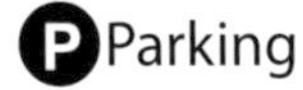

Supermarkets

- **Edmar Foods** • 2019 W Chicago Ave
- **Ukrainian Village Grocery** • 2105 W Chicago Ave

Parking

WEST TOWN
NEAR WEST SIDE
W Walton St
W Iowa St
W Rice St
W Chicago Ave
W Pearson St
W Fry St
W Lee Pl
W Superior St
W Huron St
Superior Park
N Western Ave
N Oakley Blvd
N Leavitt St
N Hoyne Ave
N Damen Ave
N Wolcott Ave
N Wood St
N Paulina St
N Ashland Ave
N Armour St
Smith Park
W Erie St
W Ontario St
W Ohio St
W Race Ave
W Grand Ave
N Hartland Ct
N Hermitage Ave
N Marshfield Ave
N Artesian Ave
W Ferdinand St
W Hubbard St
W Anson Pl
N Jessie St
N Seeley Ave
N Winchester Ave
N Hart St
N Oswego St
W Kinzie St
Western Ave
N Claremont Ave
N Bell Ave
W Carroll Ave
W Arbor
W Carrol
W Fulton St
W Fult
N Justine St
N Laflin St
W Walnut St
2000W
1600W
2400W
Ashland
W Lake St
W Maypole Ave
Union Park
W Washington Blvd
W Warren Blvd
PAGE 250
United Center
W Madison St
S Western Ave
S Oakley Blvd
S Hoyne Ave
S Seeley Ave
S Winchester Ave
S Wolcott Ave
S Honore St
S Wood St
W Arcade Pl
W Monroe St
W Ogden Ave
S Laflin St
Rockwell Park
S Bell Ave
S Hamilton Ave
Touhy Park
W Adams St
W Quincy St
W Jackson Blvd
S Hermitage Ave
S Marshfield Ave
W Gladys Ave
S Claremont Ave
S Leavitt St
N Damen Ave
Western
Medical Center
W Kinzie St
W Van Bu
Eisenhower Expwy
290
W Congress Pkwy
S Marshfield Ave
W Harrison St
St Lukes Medical Center
Claremont Park
W Flournoy St
W Campbell Park Dr
W Flourn
21
24
25
A
B
C
1
2

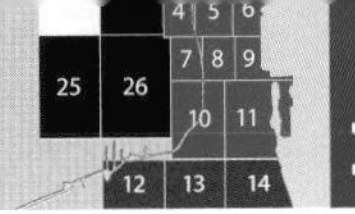

The warehouse commercial district around Damen Ave and Kinzie St is a burgeoning shopping district. If you're in the market for gargoyles or vintage marble fireplace mantles, go to Salvage One on Hubbard. For Cuban cigars, head to Donofrio's on Chicago. Ethnic eateries reflect the area's mish-mash of influences. Tiny, tasty, artsy Munch serves solid breakfasts.

Bars

- **Cleo's** • 1935 W Chicago Ave
- **Sak's Ukrainian Village Restaurant** • 2301 W Chicago Ave

Coffee

- **Atomix** • 1957 W Chicago Ave

Liquor Stores

- **DiCarlo's Armanetti Liquors** • 515 N Western Ave
- **J&L** • 1801 W Chicago Ave
- **Main Street Liquors** • 2000 W Madison St
- **S & F** • 2458 W Jackson Blvd
- **Trier's Liquors** • 2407 W Chicago Ave

Pet Shops

- **Liz's Bird Shop** • 2052 W Chicago Ave

Restaurants

- **China Dragon Restaurant** • 2008 W Madison St
- **Darkroom** • 2210 W Chicago Ave
- **Dionises Restaurant & Cafe** • 510 N Western Ave
- **Il Jack's Italian Restaurant** • 1758 W Grand Ave
- **Munch** • 1800 W Grand Ave
- **Old Lviv** • 2228 W Chicago Ave
- **Privata Cafe** • 1936 Chicago Ave
- **Tecalitlan Restaurant** • 1814 W Chicago Ave

Shopping

- **Alcala's** • 1733 W Chicago Ave
- **Decoro Studio** • 2000 W Carroll St
- **Donofrio's Double Corona Cigars** • 2058 W Chicago Ave
- **Edie's** • 1937 W Chicago Ave
- **H&R Sports** • 1741 W Chicago Ave
- **Salvage One Architectural Artifacts** • 1840 W Hubbard St
- **Through Maria's Eyes** • 1953 W Chicago Ave
- **Tomato Tattoo** • 1855 W Chicago Ave

Video Rental

- **Fredie's Video** • 1706 W Chicago Ave
- **Latin Video** • 1950 W Chicago Ave

Map 24 • Rive
N
W Walton St
W Walton St
N Greenview Ave
N Willard Ct
N Racine Ave
W Chestnut St
W Chestnut St
N Ogden Ave
W Pearson St
W Pearson St
Eckhart Park
W Milwaukee Ave
N May St
N Sangamon St
N Elizabeth St
W Fry St
W Fry St
W Fry St
N Lessing St
N Peoria St
22
800W
W Chicago Ave
Chicago
Goldblatt Bros Department Store
Eckhart Park/ Ida Crown Natatorium
W Superior St
W Superior St
N Carpenter St
N Morgan St
N Green St
N Ada St
N Throop St
N Aberdeen St
W Ancona St
W Huron St
W Huron St
W Huron St
A
N Paulina St
N Armour St
N Bishop St
1
W Ancona St
W Ancona St
W Erie St
W Erie St
W Ontario St
Connector
90
W Ohio St
W Ohio St
W Ohio St
W Race Ave
W Race Ave
N Hartland Ct
N Hermitage Ave
N Marshfield Ave
N Peoria St
W Grand Ave
Grand
N Union Ave
WEST TOWN
W Hubbard St
N Oswego St
N Hermitage Ave
94
W Kinzie St
N Aberdeen St
N Sangamon St
Dan Ryan Expwy
W Arbor Pl
N Ogden Ave
23
W Carroll Ave
W Carroll Ave
W Wayman St
N Justine St
B
W Fulton St
N Laflin St
W Walnut St
W Walnut St
W Walnut St
1600W
1200W
W Lake St
W Lake St
Ashland
W Randolph St
N Loomis St
N Hermitage Ave
Union Park
W Randolph St
W Couch Pl
N Ashland Ave
W Court Pl
100N
N Willard Ct
Harpo Studios
W Washington Blvd
N Halsted St
W Warren Ave
W Warren Blvd
NEAR WEST SIDE
N Bishop St
W Madison St
W Rundell Pl
4
S Laflin St
W Arcade Pl
W Arcade Pl
W Arcade Pl
W Monroe St
100S
S Aberdeen St
S Sangamon St
S Peoria St
S Green St
S Throop St
Skinner Park
S Racine Ave
W Marble Pl
W Adams St
W Quincy St
W Quincy St
W Quincy St
C
W Cottage Pl
W Jackson Blvd
S Morgan St
S Hermitage Ave
W Gladys Blvd
S Marshfield Ave
300S
S Carpenter St
W Van Buren St
26
Racine
S Tilden St
Dwight D Eisenhower Expwy
290
UIC-Halsted
W Congress Pkwy
W Congress Pky
W Congress Pky
S Throop St
S Marshfield Ave
S Ashland Ave
600S
W Harrison St
PAGE 208
S Halsted St
S Aberdeen St
S Miller St
W Westgate Ter
W Flournoy St
1
2
Univ of Illinois at Chicago
W Vernon

This neighborhood was once the heart of the city's produce and meat markets, and a few food supplier warehouses still exist, mixing in with loft conversions. Randolph St is Chicago's hottest restaurant row and a growing gallery district. The high priestess of talk, Oprah Winfrey, reigns over West Town from her broadcasting palace, Harpo Studios on Washington. D'Amato's Bakery supplies eateries all over the city with its crusty loaves.

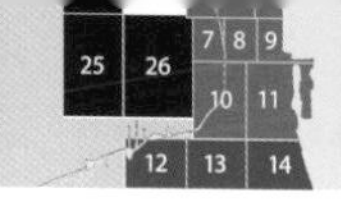

Car Rental

- **Victory Rent-A-Car** • 1352 W Lake St • 312-666-7728

Banks

- **Banco Popular** • 1445 W Chicago Ave
- **Broadway Bank** • 900 W Van Buren
- **MB Financial Bank** • 1420 W Madison St
- **RiverWest Bank** • 1650 W Adams St
- **US Bank** • 745 N Milwaukee Ave

Car Washes

- **Bert's Car Wash** • 1231 W Grand Ave
- **Red Carpet Car Wash** • 915 W Washington Blvd
- **Shell** • 1001 W Jackson Blvd
- **Ultimate Detail** • 1352 W Lake St

Gas Stations

- **BP** • 1600 W Van Buren St
- **Grand & Aberdeen Svc** • 1100 W Grand Ave
- **Shell** • 1001 W Jackson Blvd
- **Shell** • 1160 W Van Buren St
- **Shell & Food Mart** • 505 N Ashland Ave

Landmarks

- **Eckhart Park/Ida Crown Natatorium** • Noble St & Chicago Ave
- **Goldblatt Bros Department Store** • 1613-35 W Chicago Ave
- **Harpo Studios** • 1058 W Washington Blvd

Libraries

- **Chicago Eckhart Park Library** • 1371 W Chicago Ave

Pharmacies

- **Osco Drug** • 771 N Ogden Ave
- **Walgreens** • 1650 W Chicago Ave

Pizza

- **Di's Best** • 1521 W Grand Ave
- **Moretti's** • 1645 W Jackson Blvd
- **Penny's Pizza** • 234 S Ashland Ave
- **Salerno's Restaurant** • 1201 W Grand Ave
- **Via Bella Restaurant** • 1061 W Madison St

Police

- **12th District (Monroe)** • 100 S Racine Ave

Schools

- **Chicago Academy for the Arts** • 1010 W Chicago Ave
- **Esperenza Community Services** • 520 N Marshfield Ave
- **Holy Innocents School** • 1448 W Superior St
- **James Otis School** • 525 N Armour St
- **Jesse Spaulding School** • 1628 W Washington Blvd
- **Mark Skinner School** • 111 S Throop St
- **Midwest Apostolic Bible College** • 14 S Ashland Ave
- **Philo Carpenter School** • 1250 W Erie St
- **Santa Maria Addolorata School** • 1337 W Ohio St
- **St Gregory Episcopal School** • 201 S Ashland Ave
- **Whitney Young High School** • 211 S Laflin St

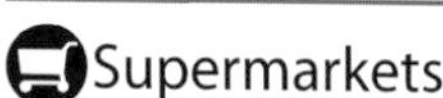

Supermarkets

- **Bari Italian Grocery** • 1120 W Grand Ave
- **Cyd & D'Pano** • 1325 W Randolph St

Parking

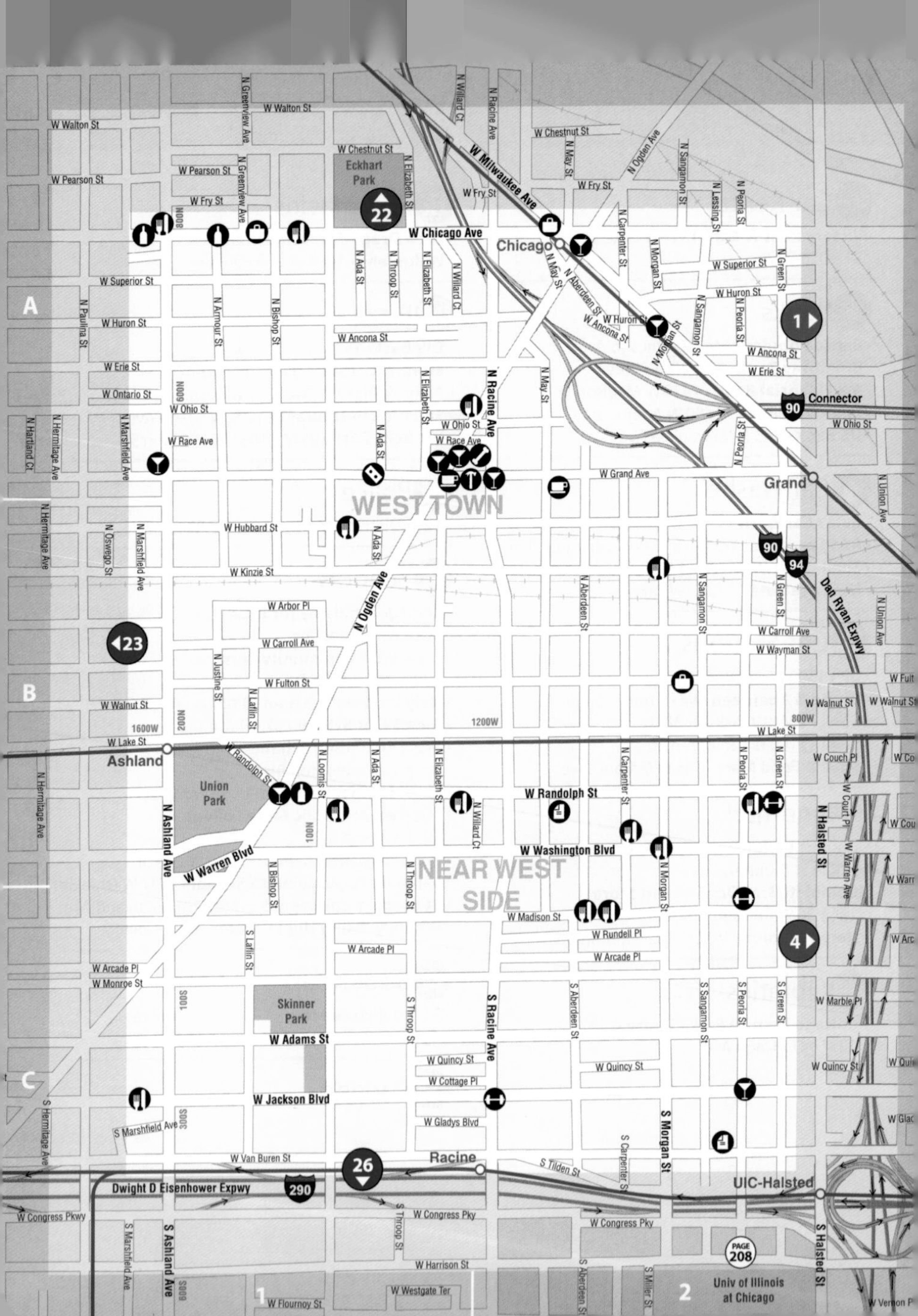
WEST TOWN
NEAR WEST SIDE
Eckhart Park
Union Park
Skinner Park
Univ of Illinois at Chicago
Chicago
Grand
Ashland
Racine
UIC-Halsted
W Chicago Ave
W Milwaukee Ave
N Racine Ave
N Ogden Ave
W Randolph St
W Washington Blvd
W Warren Blvd
W Adams St
W Jackson Blvd
Dwight D Eisenhower Expwy
Dan Ryan Expwy
Connector
N Ashland Ave
S Ashland Ave
N Halsted St
S Halsted St
S Racine Ave
S Morgan St
W Walton St
W Chestnut St
W Pearson St
W Fry St
W Superior St
W Huron St
W Ancona St
W Erie St
W Ontario St
W Ohio St
W Race Ave
W Grand Ave
W Hubbard St
W Kinzie St
W Arbor Pl
W Carroll Ave
W Wayman St
W Fulton St
W Walnut St
W Lake St
W Couch Pl
W Madison St
W Rundell Pl
W Arcade Pl
W Monroe St
W Marble Pl
W Quincy St
W Cottage Pl
W Gladys Blvd
W Van Buren St
S Tilden St
W Congress Pkwy
W Congress Pky
W Harrison St
W Westgate Ter
W Flournoy St
W Vernon Pl
N Paulina St
N Hartland Ct
N Hermitage Ave
N Marshfield Ave
N Oswego St
N Greenview Ave
N Armour St
N Bishop St
N Justine St
N Laflin St
N Loomis St
N Ada St
N Throop St
N Elizabeth St
N Willard Ct
N May St
N Aberdeen St
N Carpenter St
N Morgan St
N Sangamon St
N Lessing St
N Peoria St
N Green St
N Union Ave
N Ogden Ave
N Court Pl
N Warren Ave
S Hermitage Ave
S Marshfield Ave
S Laflin St
S Throop St
S Aberdeen St
S Carpenter St
S Sangamon St
S Peoria St
S Green St
S Miller St
800N
600N
200N
100N
100S
300S
600S
1600W
1200W
800W
90
94
290
22
23
26
1
4
PAGE 208
A
B
C
1
2

West Town has some great dining. We recommend breakfast at Wishbone, seafood at Crab Street Saloon and Marché for theatrical French. Matchbox is as trendy as Jack's Tap is basic. Construction booms on plenty of corners, but services have been slow to follow. Residents badly need a Dominick's.

Bars

- **Betty's Blue Star Lounge** • 1600 W Grand Ave
- **Bone Daddy** • 551 N Ogden Ave
- **Cafe Fresco** • 1202 W Grand Ave
- **Iggy's** • 700 N Milwaukee Ave
- **Jack's Tap** • 901 W Jackson Blvd
- **Matchbox** • 770 N Milwaukee Ave
- **The Tasting Room** • 1415 W Randolph St
- **Twisted Spoke** • 501 N Ogden Ave

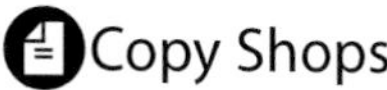

Copy Shops

- **AlphaGraphics** • 1017 W Washington Blvd
- **Mail Boxes Etc** • 910 W Van Buren St

Coffee

- **Bialy's Cafe** • South side of Chicago Ave
- **House of Coffee** • 1123 W Grand Ave
- **Sip Coffee House** • 1223 W Grand Ave

Gyms

- **Cutting Edge Fitness** • 849 W Randolph St
- **Eye Catchers Physique** • 14 N Peoria St
- **Naturally Fit** • 310 S Racine Ave

Hardware Stores

- **Imperial Hardware** • 1208 W Grand Ave

Liquor Stores

- **Loop Tavern** • 1610 W Chicago Ave
- **Randolph Wine Cellars** • SW corner Randolph & Ogden
- **Rothchild Liquor Marts** • 1532 W Chicago Ave

Pet Shops

- **Petcare Plus** • 1212 W Grand Ave

Restaurants

- **160 Blue** • 160 N Loomis St
- **Bone Daddy** • 551 Ogden Ave
- **Breakfast Club** • 1381 W Hubbard St
- **Crab Street Saloon** • 1061 W Madison
- **Flo** • 1434 W Chicago Ave
- **Hacienda Tecalitlan** • 820 N Ashland Blvd
- **Ina's** • 1235 W Randolph St
- **Jerry's Sandwiches** • 1045 W Madison
- **La Borsa** • 375 N Morgan St
- **La Sardine** • 111 N Carpenter St
- **Marche** • 833 W Randolph St
- **Moretti's** • 1645 W Jackson Blvd
- **Wishbone** • 1001 W Washington

Shopping

- **Arrow Vintage** • 1452 W Chicago Ave
- **Hollis Funk** • 949 W Fulton Market
- **Upgrade Cycle Works** • 1128 W Chicago Ave
- **Xyloform** • 1423 Chicago Ave

Video Rental

- **Erotic Warehouse** • 1246 W Randolph St
- **Grand Slam Video** • 1369 W Grand Ave

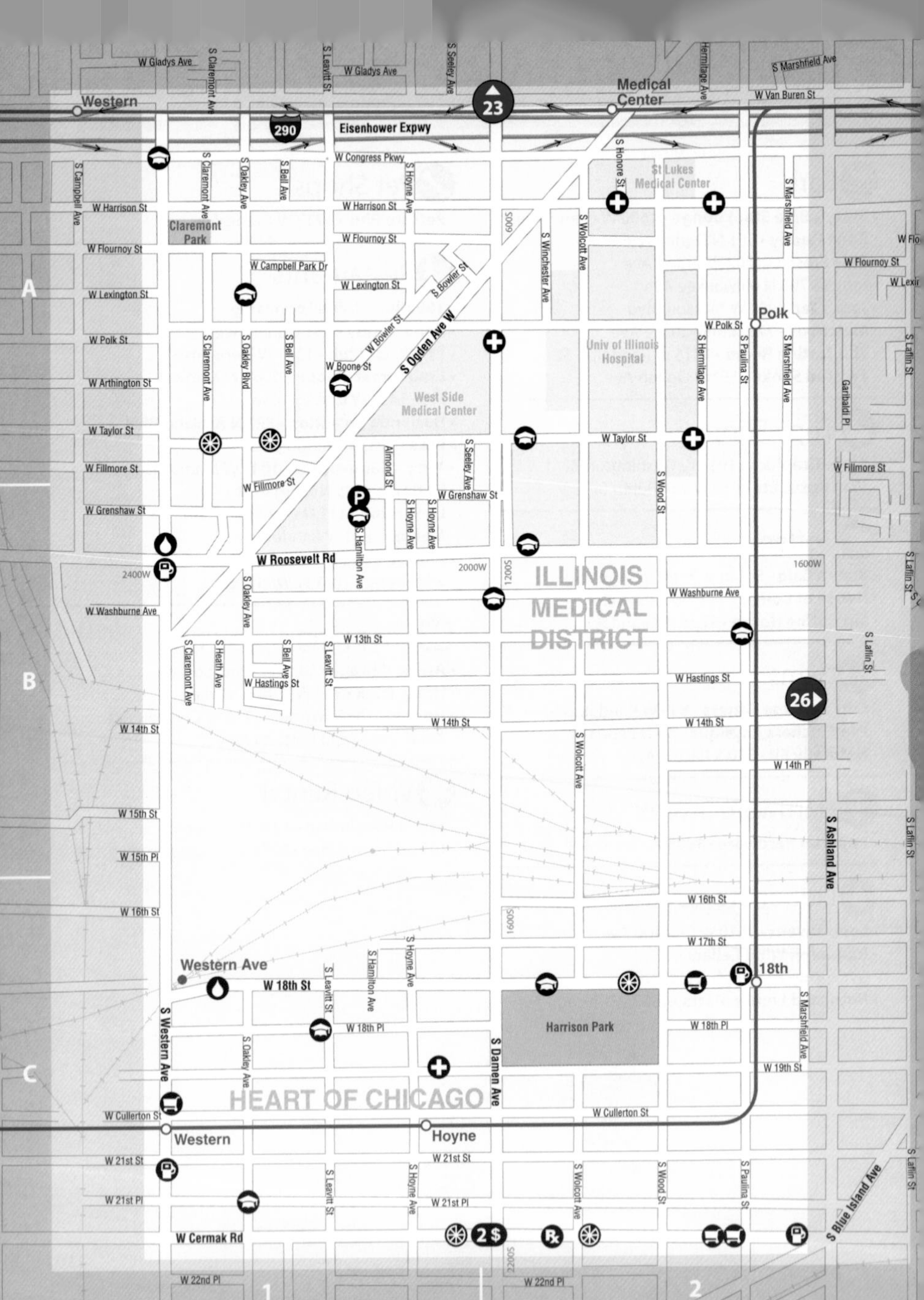

Western
23
Medical Center
290
Eisenhower Expwy
W Gladys Ave
W Van Buren St
S Marshfield Ave
W Congress Pkwy
St Lukes Medical Center
Claremont Park
W Harrison St
W Flournoy St
W Campbell Park Dr
W Lexington St
S Bowler St
W Bowler St
S Ogden Ave W
W Boone St
W Polk St
Polk
Univ of Illinois Hospital
West Side Medical Center
W Arthington St
W Taylor St
W Fillmore St
W Grenshaw St
W Roosevelt Rd
2400W
2000W
1600W
ILLINOIS MEDICAL DISTRICT
W Washburne Ave
W 13th St
W Hastings St
W 14th St
W 14th Pl
26
W 15th St
W 15th Pl
W 16th St
W 17th St
Western Ave
W 18th St
18th
W 18th Pl
Harrison Park
W 19th St
HEART OF CHICAGO
W Cullerton St
Western
Hoyne
W 21st St
W 21st Pl
W Cermak Rd
W 22nd Pl
S Western Ave
S Damen Ave
S Ashland Ave
S Blue Island Ave
S Campbell Ave
S Claremont Ave
S Oakley Ave
S Oakley Blvd
S Bell Ave
S Leavitt St
S Hoyne Ave
S Seeley Ave
S Hamilton Ave
Almond St
S Heath Ave
S Honore St
S Wolcott Ave
S Winchester Ave
S Wood St
S Hermitage Ave
S Paulina St
S Laflin St
Garibaldi Pl
600S
1200S
1600S
2200S
A
B
C
1
2

Health is at the heart of this neighborhood. Several hospitals and UIC's medical school are centered here, including publicly funded Cook County Hospital built in 1913. Doc-shock TV show ER was inspired by Cook's hectic emergency room treatment of some of Chicago's gang crime victims. If you get shot, this is where you want to go.

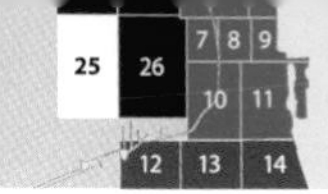

Banks

- **Bank One** • 2000 W Cermak Rd
- **Metropolitan Bank** • 2201 W Cermak Rd

Car Washes

- **G Express Hand Car Wash** • 2323 W 18th St
- **Shell** • 2401 W Roosevelt Rd

Gas Stations

- **BP** • 1955 W Cermak Rd
- **Citgo** • 2107 S Western Ave
- **Clark Oil** • 1721 S Paulina St
- **Shell** • 2401 W Roosevelt Rd

Hospitals

- **Cook County Hospital** • 1835 W Harrison St
- **Rush-Presbyterian St Luke's** • 1753 W Harrison St
- **St Anthony's Hospital** • 2075 W 19th St
- **University of Illinois at Chicago Hospital** • 1740 W Taylor St

Pharmacies

- **Walgreens** • 1931 W Cermak Rd

Pizza

- **Bacci Pizzeria** • 2248 W Taylor St
- **Damenzo's Pizza** • 2324 W Taylor St
- **Pisa Pizza** • 2057 W Cermak Rd
- **Pizza Nova** • 1842 W 18th St
- **Swordsmen Pizza** • 1900 W Cermak Rd

Police

- **11th District (Harrison)** • 3151 W Harrison St

Schools

- **Center for Rehab & Education** • 1950 W Roosevelt Rd
- **Children of Peace St Callistus** • 2187 W Bowler St
- **Cristo Rey High School** • 1851 W Cermak Rd
- **Holy Trinity School** • 1900 W Taylor St
- **Illinois College of Medicine** • 1853 W Polk St
- **Nancy Jefferson Schools** • 1100 S Hamilton Ave
- **Octavio Paz Charter School** • 2401 W Congress Pkwy
- **Orozco Community Academy** • 1940 W 18th St
- **Pickard Elementary School** • 2301 W 21st Pl
- **St Ann Grade School** • 2211 W 18th Pl
- **UIC University of Illinois** • 840 S Wood Ave
- **Washington Irving Schools** • 749 S Oakley Blvd
- **William E Gladstone School** • 1231 S Damen Ave

Supermarkets

- **Aldi Supermarket** • 1703 W Cermak Rd
- **DelRay Farms** • 1701 W Cermak Rd
- **Fairplay Finer Foods** • 2200 S Western Ave
- **Supermercado Guzman** • 1758 W 18th St

Parking

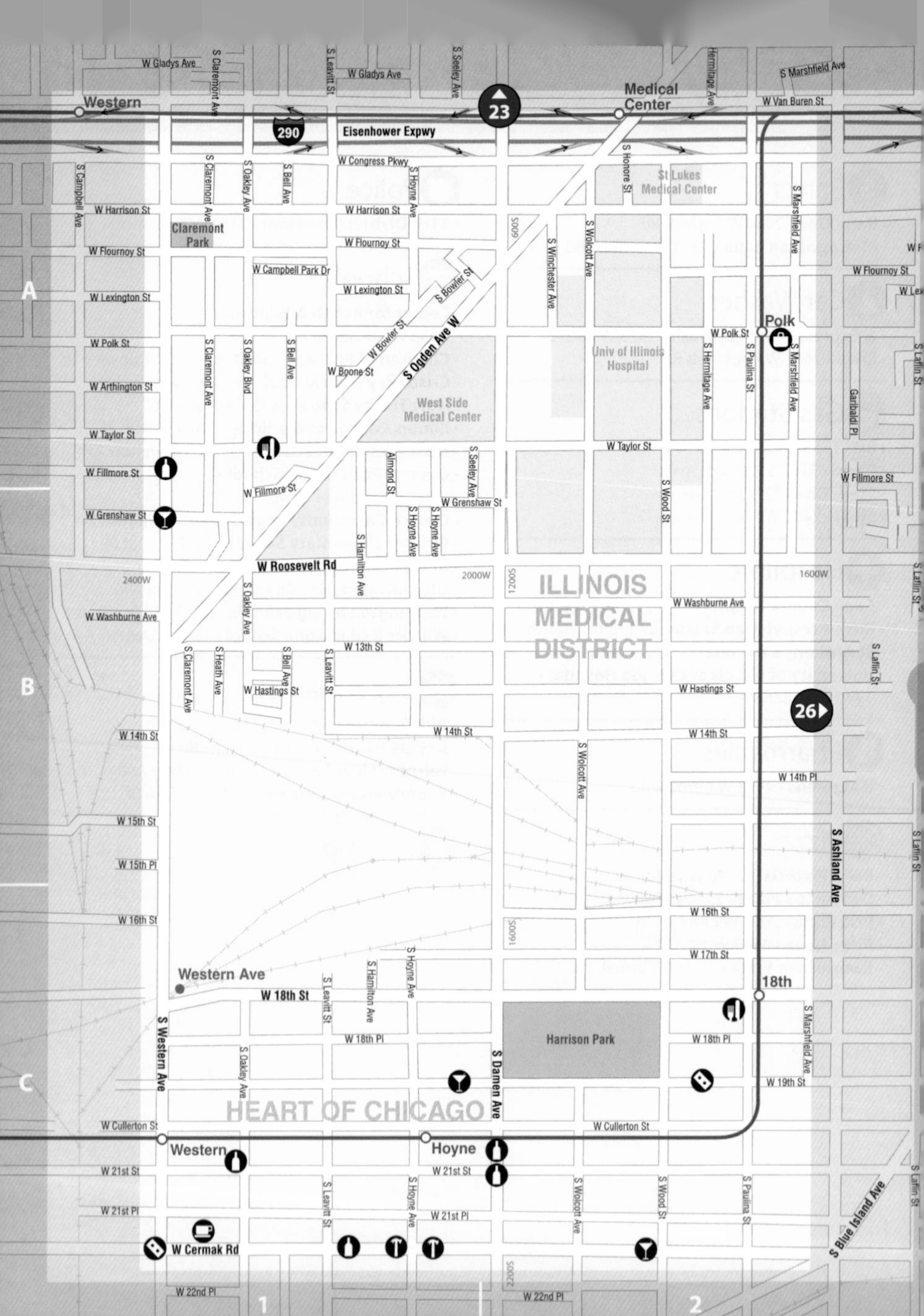

Western
Medical Center
23
290
Eisenhower Expwy
W Van Buren St
W Congress Pkwy
W Gladys Ave
S Marshfield Ave
St Lukes Medical Center
Claremont Park
W Harrison St
W Flournoy St
W Lexington St
W Campbell Park Dr
S Bowler St
W Bowler St
S Ogden Ave W
W Polk St
Polk
Univ of Illinois Hospital
W Boone St
W Arthington St
West Side Medical Center
W Taylor St
W Fillmore St
W Grenshaw St
W Roosevelt Rd
2400W
2000W
1200S
1600W
ILLINOIS MEDICAL DISTRICT
W Washburne Ave
W 13th St
W Hastings St
W 14th St
W 14th Pl
W 15th St
W 15th Pl
W 16th St
W 17th St
S Ashland Ave
26
Western Ave
W 18th St
18th
W 18th Pl
Harrison Park
S Damen Ave
W 19th St
HEART OF CHICAGO
W Cullerton St
Western
Hoyne
W 21st St
W 21st Pl
W Cermak Rd
W 22nd Pl
2200S
S Blue Island Ave
S Western Ave
S Campbell Ave
S Claremont Ave
S Oakley Ave
S Oakley Blvd
S Bell Ave
S Leavitt St
S Hoyne Ave
S Seeley Ave
S Hamilton Ave
Almond St
S Honore St
S Wolcott Ave
S Winchester Ave
S Wood St
S Hermitage Ave
S Paulina St
S Heath Ave
S Laflin St
Garibaldi Pl
A
B
C
1
2

Bars

- **Cerwood Inn** • 1759 W Cermak Rd
- **Simpson's** • Grenshaw & Western
- **White Horse Lounge** • 2059 W 19th St

Coffee

- **Dunkin' Donuts** • 2356 W Cermak Rd

Hardware Stores

- **Duran Hardware** • 2047 W Cermak Rd
- **Mitchell Hardware & Paints** • 2141 W Cermak Rd

Liquor Stores

- **El Valle Food & Liquors** • 2200? W 21st St
- **Helen's Grocery & Liquors** • W 21st St & S Oakley Ave
- **Three Star Liquor** • 2015 S Damen Ave
- **Topless Liquor** • 916 S Western Ave
- **Yo Yo's Liquor** • 2155 W Cermak Rd

Restaurants

- **Carnitas Uruapan Restaurant** • 1725 W 18th St
- **El Charco Verde** • 2253 W Taylor St

Shopping

- **RR#1 Chicago Apothecary** • 814 N Ashland Blvd

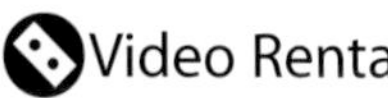

Video Rental

- **Blockbuster Video** • 2425 W Cermak Rd
- **Junior's Video** • 1810 W 18th St
- **Pedraza Video** • 1758 W 19th St
- **Taylor Video & VCR Repair** • 2234 W Taylor St

UNIVERSITY VILLAGE / LITTLE ITALY
PILSEN
University of Illinois Chicago
PAGE 208
Racine
UIC-Halsted
Polk
18th
Halsted
Arrigo Park
Sheridan Park
Plgd Park
Addams Park
Dvorak Park
W Van Buren St
W Congress Pkwy
W Harrison St
W Flournoy St
W Lexington St
W Polk St
W Taylor St
W Roosevelt Rd
W Washburne Ave
W 14th St
W 15th St
W 16th St
W 17th St
W 18th St
W 19th St
W 21st St
W Cermak Rd
W 22nd Pl
S Ashland Ave
S Blue Island Ave
S Racine Ave
S Morgan St
Halsted St
S Union Ave
Dan Ryan Expwy
S Canalport Ave
S Laflin St
S Loomis St
S Throop St
S Lytle St
S May St
S Aberdeen St
S Carpenter St
S Miller St
S Sangamon St
S Peoria St
S Paulina St
S Marshfield Ave

University of Illinois at Chicago is consuming blocks like the Great Chicago Fire of 1871, which started nearby. The campus expansion stretches south of Roosevelt Rd. What's left of Little Italy from the last UIC expansion centers around Taylor St., where Tuscan and Sicilian are spoken. Any pizza parlor is a good pick, but Pompeii's pies rule. The vibrant Latino Pilsen neighborhood starts here and spreads south.

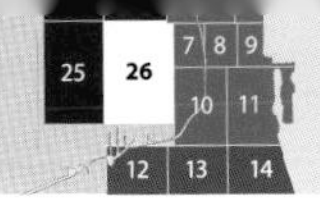

Banks

- **Bank One** • 2000 W Cermak Rd
- **MB Financial Bank** • 1618 W 18th St

Car Rental

- **Carmichael Lease** • 2200 S Loomis St • 312-666-8500
- **Enterprise** • 318 S Morgan St • 312-432-9780

Libraries

- **Douglass Public LIbrary** • 3353 W 13th St
- **Illinois Regional Library for the Blind** • 1055 W Roosevelt Rd
- **Lozano Public Library** • 1805 S Loomis St
- **Roosevelt Public Library** • 1101 W Taylor St
- **University of Chicago Library** • 801 S Morgan St

Pharmacies

- **Osco Drug** • 1220 S Ashland Ave
- **Osco Drug** • 1713 S Ashland Ave

Pizza

- **Benny's Pizza II** • 1236 W 18th St
- **Caire's Pizza** • 1165 W 18th St
- **Leona's Pizzeria** • 1419 W Taylor St
- **Pizza Tango** • 1013 W 18th St
- **Pompeii Bakery** • 1531 W Taylor St

Post Offices

- 1859 S Ashland Ave

Schools

- **Andrew Jackson Language Academy** • 1340 W Harrison St
- **Benito Juarez High School** • 2150 S Laflin St
- **Children of Peace School** • 1029 S May St
- **El Centro De La Causa School** • 731 W 17th St
- **Galileo School** • 820 S Carpenter St
- **Jacob A Riis Elementary School** • 1018 S Lytle St
- **John A Walsh School** • 2031 S Peoria St
- **John M Smyth School** • 1059 W 13th St
- **Joseph Jungman School** • 1746 S Miller St
- **Joseph Medill Primary School** • 1301 W 14th St
- **Montefiore Boys School** • 1300 S Ashland Ave
- **Perez School** • 1241 W 19th St
- **Peter Cooper School** • 1624 W 19th St
- **Pilsen Academy** • 1420 W 17th St
- **Ruben Salazar Bilingual Branch** • 1641 W 16th St
- **Simpson Alternative School** • 1321 S Paulina St
- **St Ignatius College Prep** • 1076 W Roosevelt Rd
- **St Pius School** • 1919 S Ashland Ave
- **St Procopius School** • 1625 S Allport St
- **Thomas Jefferson School** • 1522 W Fillmore St

Supermarkets

- **Jewel-Osco** • 1220 S Ashland Ave

Map 20 • University Village/Little Italy/Pilsen
N
24
4
290
Racine
UIC-Halsted
Polk
18th
Halsted
7
25
10
12
90
94
A
B
C
1
2
W Gladys Blvd
S Marshfield Ave
W Van Buren St
S Tilden St
S Carpenter St
W Congress Pkwy
W Harrison St
W Vernon Park
W Westgate Ter
W Flournoy St
W Lexington St
W Polk St
W Cabrini St
W Arthington St
W Taylor St
W Fillmore St
W Grenshaw St
W Roosevelt Rd
W Washburne Ave
W 12th Pl
W O'Brien St
W 13th St
W Maxwell St
W Hastings St
W Liberty St
W 14th St
W Barber St
W 14th Pl
W South Water Market
W 15th St
W 15th Pl
W 16th St
W 17th St
W 17th Pl
W 18th St
W 18th Pl
W 19th St
W 19th Pl
W Cullerton St
W 20th Pl
W 21st St
W 21st Pl
W Cermak Rd
W 22nd Pl
S Hermitage Ave
S Paulina St
S Marshfield Ave
S Ashland Ave
Garibaldi Pl
S Laflin St
S Laflin Cir
S Bishop St
S Loomis St
S Ada St
S Lytle St
S Throop St
S Racine Ave
S May St
S Aberdeen St
S Miller St
S Morgan St
S Blue Island Ave
S Sangamon St
S Peoria St
S Newbury Ave
S Shelby Ct
S Allport St
S Canalport Ave
Halsted St
S Union Ave
S Ruble St
S Desplaines St
S Ford Ave
Dan Ryan Expwy
1600W
1200W
800W
600S
1200S
1600S
2200S
Arrigo Park
Sheridan Park
Plgd Park
Addams Park
Dvorak Park
University of Illinois Chicago
PAGE 208
UNIVERSITY VILLAGE / LITTLE ITALY
PILSEN

Try Taylor St. for authentic Italian. Sports fans chow down here before games at the United Center. Just like mama, Gennaro's dishes up generous portions. Where's the beef? At Al's. Buy Scafuri Bakery's cannoli by the dozen. The murals in Pilsen, especially at the 18th St. El station, are outstanding. Come here for authentic Mexican tacos as restaurants and bodegas line the streets.

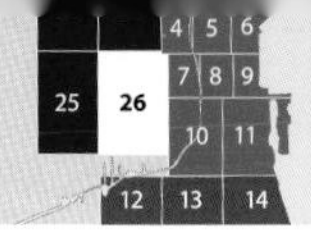

Coffee

- **Cafe Jumping Bean** • 1439 W 18th St
- **Jamoch's Caffe** • 1066 W Taylor St
- **Starbucks** • 1430 W Taylor St

Gyms

- **University of Illinois at Chicago** • 750 S Halsted St
- **YMCA** • 1608 W 21st Pl

Hardware Stores

- **A K Auto Supply** • 1535 W 18th St
- **Alvarez Hardware** • 1323 W 18th Pl
- **Chiarugi Hardware** • 1449 W Taylor St
- **La Brocha Gorda** • 974 W 18th St
- **Seigle's Lumber** • 977 W Cermak Rd
- **Torres Hardware** • 1836 S Ashland Ave

Liquor Stores

- **5th City Food & Liquor** • 1257 W Roosevelt Rd
- **Amador Liquors** • 1167 W 18th St
- **El Trebol Liquors** • 1135 W 18th St
- **F & R Liquor** • 2129 S Halsted St
- **Guadalajara Food & Liquors** • 1527 W 18th Pl
- **Mike & Sons Food & Liquor** • 1359 W Roosevelt Rd
- **Three Sons Food & Liquor** • 1311 W Taylor St

Restaurants

- **Al's Number 1 Italian Beef** • 1079 W Taylor St
- **Cafe Viaggio** • 1435 W Taylor St
- **Carm's Beef and Snack Shop** • 1057 W Polk St
- **Chez Joel** • 1119 W Taylor St
- **Francesca's** • 1400 W Taylor St
- **Genarro's** • 1352 W Taylor St
- **New Rosebud Cafe** • 1500 W Taylor St
- **Nuevo Leon** • 1515 W 18th St
- **Siam Pot** • 1509 Taylor St
- **Taj Mahal** • 1512 W Taylor St

Shopping

- **Scafuri Bakery** • 1337 W Taylor St

Video Rental

- **Central Video Mart** • 1354 W Taylor St
- **Manny's Video** • 1546 W 21st St
- **Manny's Video II** • 1943 S May St
- **Roly's Video** • 1448 W 18th St

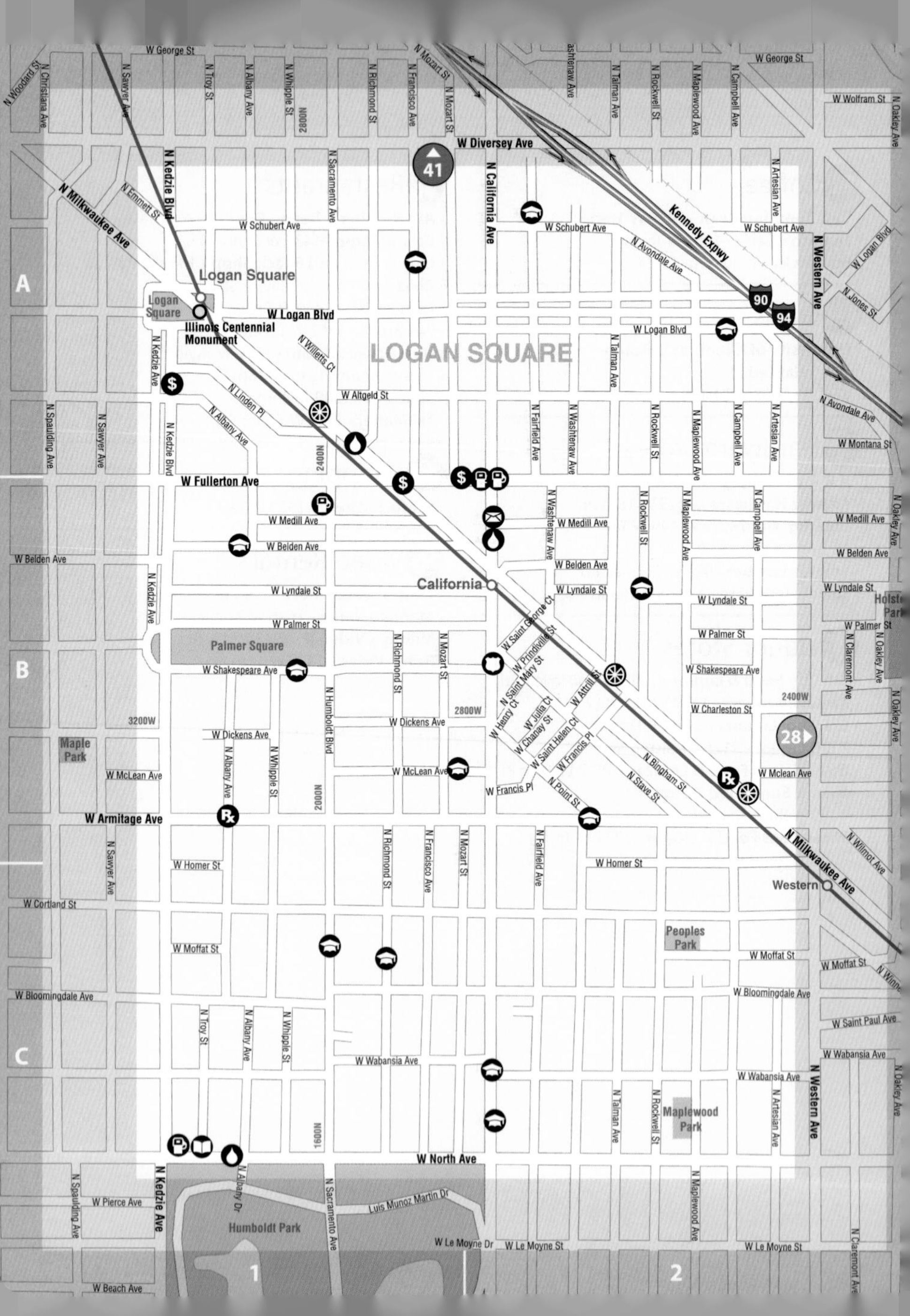
LOGAN SQUARE
Logan Square
Illinois Centennial Monument
California
Western
Palmer Square
Maple Park
Peoples Park
Maplewood Park
Humboldt Park
Kennedy Expwy
41
28
90
94
A
B
C
1
2
W George St
W Wolfram St
W Diversey Ave
W Schubert Ave
W Logan Blvd
W Altgeld St
W Fullerton Ave
W Medill Ave
W Belden Ave
W Lyndale St
W Palmer St
W Shakespeare Ave
W Dickens Ave
W Charleston St
W McLean Ave
W Francis Pl
W Armitage Ave
W Homer St
W Cortland St
W Moffat St
W Bloomingdale Ave
W Saint Paul Ave
W Wabansia Ave
W North Ave
W Pierce Ave
W Le Moyne Dr
W Le Moyne St
W Beach Ave
W Montana St
N Milwaukee Ave
N Kedzie Blvd
N Kedzie Ave
N California Ave
N Western Ave
N Sacramento Ave
N Humboldt Blvd
N Avondale Ave
N Logan Blvd
N Jones St
N Emmett St
N Willetts Ct
N Linden Pl
N Albany Ave
N Albany Dr
N Spaulding Ave
N Sawyer Ave
N Christiana Ave
N Woodard St
N Troy St
N Whipple St
N Richmond St
N Francisco Ave
N Mozart St
N Fairfield Ave
N Washtenaw Ave
N Talman Ave
N Rockwell St
N Maplewood Ave
N Campbell Ave
N Artesian Ave
N Oakley Ave
N Claremont Ave
N Saint George Ct
W Prindiville St
N Saint Mary St
N Henry Ct
W Julia Ct
W Chanay St
N Saint Helen Ct
W Attrill St
W Francis Pl
N Point St
N Bingham St
N Stave St
N Wilmot Ave
Luis Munoz Martin Dr
2800N
2400N
2000N
1600N
3200W
2800W
2400W

Logan Square still holds on to its Latin flavors—for now. The westward push for affordable conversion properties is heralded by the emergence of a Starbucks on Logan and California...a sure-fire indicator of what's in store for this rough-and-ready neighborhood.

Banks

- **Banco Popular** • 2525 N Kedzie Blvd
- **Liberty Bank for Savings** • 2392 N Milwaukee Ave
- **Northern Trust Bank** • 2814 W Fullerton Ave

Car Washes

- **California Car Wash** • 2340 N California Ave
- **Logan Square Car Wash II** • 2436 N Milwaukee Ave
- **Puerto Rico Car Wash** • 3110 W North Ave

Gas Stations

- **BP & Food Shop** • 2800 W Fullerton Ave
- **Citgo** • 2338 N Sacramento Ave
- **Citgo** • 3142 W North Ave
- **Shell** • 2811 W Fullerton Ave

Landmarks

- **Illinois Centennial Monument** • 3100 W Logan Blvd

Libraries

- **Humboldt Park Public Library** • 1605 N Troy St

Pharmacies

- **Osco Drug** • 2053 N Milwaukee Ave
- **Walgreens** • 3110 W Armitage Ave

Pizza

- **Congress Pizzeria** • 2033 N Milwaukee Ave
- **Father & Son Restaurant** • 2475 N Milwaukee Ave
- **Lucky Vito's Pizzeria** • 2171 N Milwaukee Ave

Police

- **14th District (Shakespeare)** • 2150 N California Ave

Post Offices

- 2339 N California Ave

Schools

- **Charles R Darwin School** • 3116 W Belden Ave
- **Humboldt Community Christian** • 1847 N Humboldt Blvd
- **J W Von Goethe School** • 2236 N Rockwell St
- **Lorenz Brentano School** • 2723 N Fairfield Ave
- **Moos Elementary School** • 1711 N California Ave
- **Prince of Peace Lutheran School** • 2649 N Francisco Ave
- **Richard Yates School** • 1839 N Richmond St
- **Salem Christian School** • 2845 W McLean Ave
- **Salomon P Chase School** • 2021 N Point St
- **St John Berchmans School** • 2511 W Logan Blvd
- **St Sylvesters School** • 3027 W Palmer Blvd
- **Wright College** • 1645 N California Ave

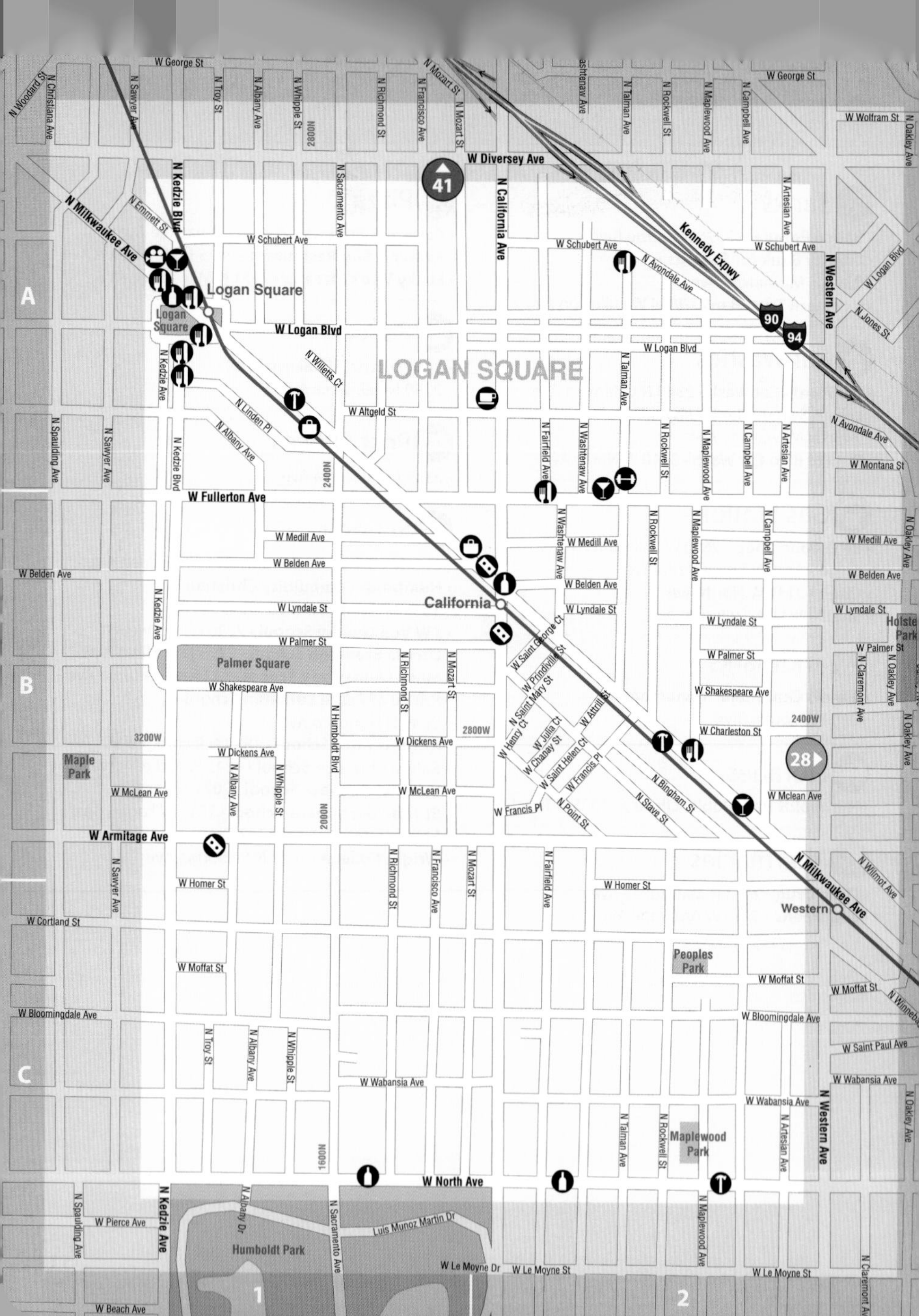

LOGAN SQUARE
Logan Square
Palmer Square
Maple Park
Peoples Park
Maplewood Park
Humboldt Park
California
Western
N Milwaukee Ave
Kennedy Expwy
W Diversey Ave
W Logan Blvd
W Fullerton Ave
W Armitage Ave
W North Ave
N Kedzie Blvd
N California Ave
N Western Ave
N Kedzie Ave
41
28
90
94
A
B
C
1
2

Come to Logan Square for the Latino food. El Nandu on Fullerton has live classical guitar music, Argentinean wine, and tasty empanadas for little cash. We like Abril's big burrito and mole enchiladas. Because lots of other people like Abril too, get there early or at off-peak hours. Ask for a booth near the window to watch this lively neighborhood's colorful street scene.

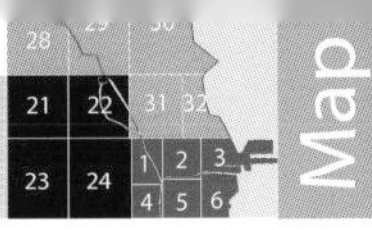

Bars

- **Fireside Bowl** • 2646 W Fullerton Ave
- **Palladium** • 2047 N Milwaukee Ave
- **The Winds Cafe** • 2657 N Kedzie Blvd

Coffee

- **No Friction Cafe** • 2502 N California Ave

Gyms

- **TLC Fitness Consulting** • 2419 N Talman Ave

Hardware Stores

- **Gillman's Hardware** • 2118 N Milwaukee Ave
- **Monroy's Hardware Store** • 2511 W North Ave
- **Tony's Tools** • 2500 N Milwaukee Ave

Liquor Stores

- **D & D Liquors** • 2958 W North Ave
- **Foremost Liquor Stores** • 2300 N Milwaukee Ave
- **Logan Liquors** • 2639 N Kedzie Ave
- **Yafa** • 2700 W North Ave

Movie Theaters

- **Logan Theater** • 2646 N Milwaukee Ave

Restaurants

- **Abril Mexican Restaurant** • 2607 N Milwaukee Ave
- **Boulevard Cafe** • 3137 W Logan Blvd
- **Cafe Bolero** • 2252 N Western Ave
- **Choi's Chinese Restaurant** • 2638 N Milwaukee Ave
- **El Cid** • 2116 N Milwaukee Ave
- **El Nandu** • 2731 N Fullerton Ave
- **Johnny's Grill** • 2545 N Kedzie Blvd
- **Lula Cafe** • 2537 N Kedzie Blvd

Shopping

- **MegaMall** • 2502 N Milwaukee Ave
- **Threads, Inc** • 2327 N Milwaukee Ave

Video Rental

- **Blockbuster Video** • 2251 N Milwaukee Ave
- **California Video** • 2208 N California Ave
- **Hi-Fi Video** • 3129 W Armitage Ave
- **Morelia Video** • 2381 N Milwaukee Ave

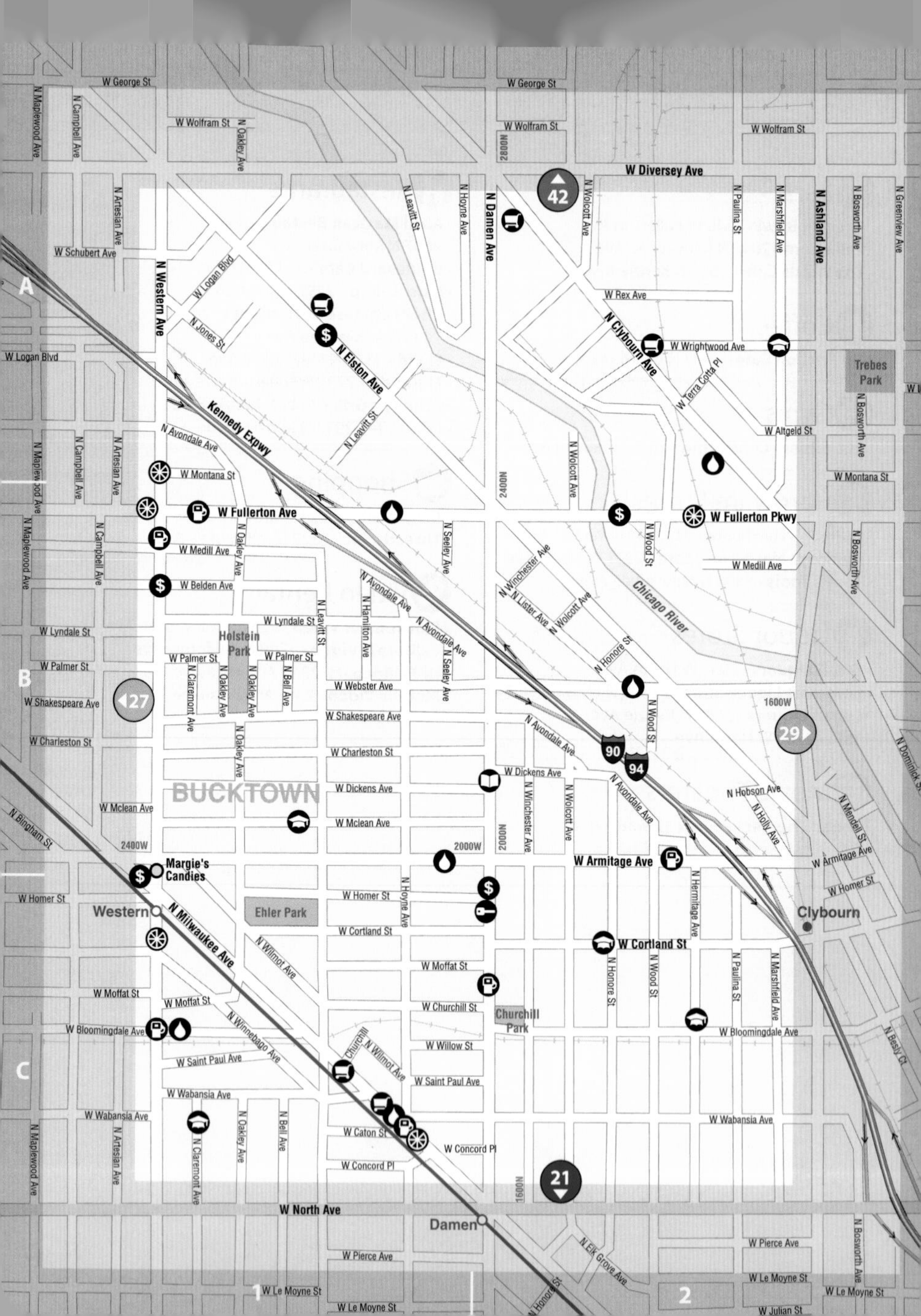

W George St
W Wolfram St
W Diversey Ave
42
N Maplewood Ave
N Campbell Ave
N Oakley Ave
N Artesian Ave
W Schubert Ave
N Western Ave
W Logan Blvd
N Jones St
N Elston Ave
N Leavitt St
N Hoyne Ave
N Damen Ave
N Wolcott Ave
N Paulina St
N Marshfield Ave
N Ashland Ave
N Bosworth Ave
N Greenview Ave
W Rex Ave
N Clybourn Ave
W Wrightwood Ave
W Terra Cotta Pl
Trebes Park
W Altgeld St
Kennedy Expwy
N Avondale Ave
W Montana St
W Fullerton Ave
W Fullerton Pkwy
N Seeley Ave
N Winchester Ave
N Lister Ave
N Wood St
W Medill Ave
W Belden Ave
Chicago River
W Lyndale St
Holstein Park
N Hamilton Ave
W Palmer St
N Claremont Ave
N Bell Ave
N Honore St
W Webster Ave
W Shakespeare Ave
27
1600W
29
W Charleston St
90
94
N Dominick St
W Dickens Ave
BUCKTOWN
N Hobson Ave
N Holly Ave
N Bingham St
W Mclean Ave
N Mendell St
2400W
2000W
2000N
2400N
2800N
W Armitage Ave
Margie's Candies
W Homer St
N Hermitage Ave
Western
N Milwaukee Ave
Ehler Park
W Cortland St
Clybourn
N Wilmot Ave
W Moffat St
W Churchill St
Churchill Park
W Bloomingdale Ave
N Winnebago Ave
W Willow St
N Besly Ct
W Saint Paul Ave
Churchill
W Wabansia Ave
W Caton St
W Concord Pl
1600N
21
W North Ave
Damen
N Elk Grove Ave
W Pierce Ave
W Le Moyne St
N Honore St
W Julian St
A
B
C
1
2

As Bucktown's once-thriving art scene fades further into oblivion, real estate becomes out of reach for all but the young executives who are attracted to the area's upscale boutiques, restaurants, and arty-urban reputation.

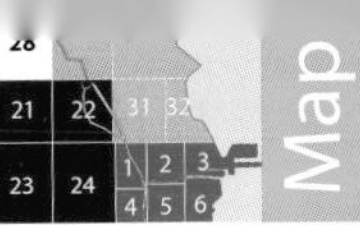

Banks

- **Cole Taylor Bank** • 1965 N Milwaukee Ave
- **MidAmerica Bank** • 1830 W Fullerton Ave
- **MidAmerica Bank** • 1955 N Damen Ave
- **MidAmerica Bank** • 2300 N Western Ave

Car Rental

- **Enterprise** • 1945 N Damen Ave • 773-862-4700

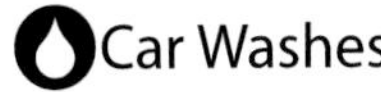

Car Washes

- **Bucktown Hand Car Wash** • 2036 W Armitage Ave
- **Celina's Hand Car Wash** • 1815 N Western Ave
- **Clybourn Express & Car Wash** • 2452 N Clybourn Ave
- **Express Car Wash** • 2111 W Fullerton Ave
- **Fast Eddie's Hand Car Wash** • 1828 W Webster Ave
- **Wash Express** • 1657 N Milwaukee Ave

Gas Stations

- **BP** • 2357 W Fullerton Ave
- **BP & Food Shop** • 1768 W Armitage Ave
- **Citgo** • 1750 N Western Ave
- **Larry's Service Ctr** • 1834 N Damen Ave
- **Marathon Svc Station** • 2346 N Western Ave

Landmarks

- **Margie's Candies** • 1960 N Western Ave

Libraries

- **Damen Avenue Library** • 2056 N Damen Ave

Pizza

- **Barcello's Pizzeria** • 1647 N Milwaukee Ave
- **Chuck E Cheese's** • 1730 W Fullerton Ave
- **Domino's** • 2455 W Fullerton Ave
- **John's Restaurant & Lounge** • 2104 N Western Ave
- **Plazzio's Pizza** • 1901 N Western Ave
- **Sonny's Pizza** • 2431 N Western Ave

Schools

- **Casimir Pulaski Academy** • 2230 W McLean Ave
- **Pedro Albizu Campos High School** • 1671 N Claremont Ave
- **St Mary of the Angels School** • 1810 N Hermitage Ave
- **Thomas Drummond School** • 1845 W Cortland St
- **William H Prescott School** • 1632 W Wrightwood Ave

Supermarkets

- **Aldi** • 1767 N Milwaukee Ave
- **Always Open** • 1704 N Milwaukee Ave
- **Costco** • 2746 N Clybourn Ave
- **Cub Foods** • 2627 N Elston Ave
- **Dominick's** • 2550 W Clybourn Ave

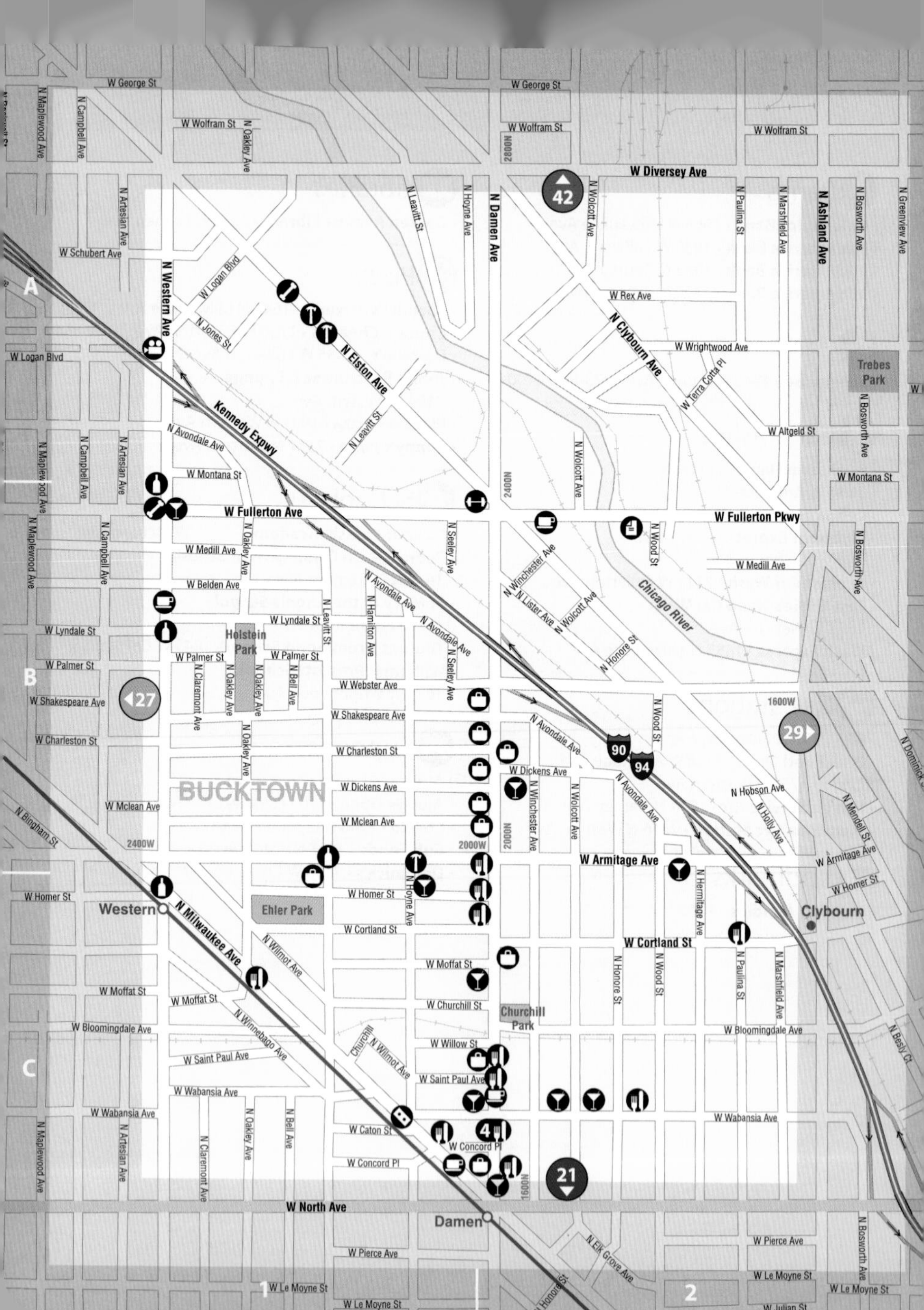

W George St
W Wolfram St
W Diversey Ave
W Schubert Ave
A
B
C
1
2
N Western Ave
N Elston Ave
N Damen Ave
N Ashland Ave
N Clybourn Ave
W Rex Ave
W Wrightwood Ave
N Terra Cotta Pl
W Altgeld St
Trebes Park
W Logan Blvd
N Logan Blvd
N Jones St
Kennedy Expwy
N Avondale Ave
W Montana St
W Fullerton Ave
W Fullerton Pkwy
W Medill Ave
W Belden Ave
W Lyndale St
W Palmer St
Holstein Park
W Webster Ave
W Shakespeare Ave
W Charleston St
W Dickens Ave
BUCKTOWN
W Mclean Ave
W Armitage Ave
W Homer St
W Cortland St
W Moffat St
W Churchill St
Churchill Park
W Bloomingdale Ave
W Willow St
W Saint Paul Ave
W Wabansia Ave
W Caton St
W Concord Pl
W North Ave
W Pierce Ave
W Le Moyne St
W Julian St
N Elk Grove Ave
N Honore St
Chicago River
N Winchester Ave
N Lister Ave
N Wolcott Ave
N Wood St
N Hobson Ave
N Holly Ave
N Hermitage Ave
N Paulina St
N Marshfield Ave
N Mendell St
N Besly Ct
N Dominick St
N Bosworth Ave
N Greenview Ave
Clybourn
Western
Damen
N Milwaukee Ave
N Wilmot Ave
N Winnebago Ave
Ehler Park
N Bingham St
N Maplewood Ave
N Campbell Ave
N Artesian Ave
N Oakley Ave
N Claremont Ave
N Bell Ave
N Leavitt St
N Hamilton Ave
N Hoyne Ave
N Seeley Ave
2800N
2400N
2000N
1600N
2400W
2000W
1600W
42
27
29
21
90
94
4

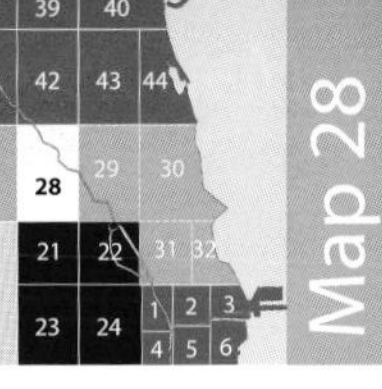

Café Matou is a hidden gem on Milwaukee Avenue. Punters still crowd the Northside Café, especially popular in the summer for its patios and fruity drink concoctions. Of all the upscale neighborhood taverns populating the streets, perhaps Lemmings has the most indicative name.

Bars

- **Artful Dodger Pub** • 1734 W Wabansia Ave
- **Bar Louie** • 1704 N Damen Ave
- **Charleston Tavern** • 2076 N Hoyne Ave
- **Danny's Tavern** • 1951 W Dickens Ave
- **Lemmings** • 1850 N Damen Ave
- **Lincoln Tavern** • 1858 W Wabansia Ave
- **Marie's Rip Tide Lounge** • 1745 W Armitage Ave
- **Northside Cafe** • 1635 N Damen Ave
- **Quencher Saloon** • 2401 N Western Ave
- **The Map Room** • 1949 N Hoyne Ave

Copy Shops

- **Copy Max** • 1829 W Fullerton Ave

Coffee

- **Caffe De Luca** • 1721 N Damen Ave
- **Dunkin' Donuts** • 1927 W Fullerton Ave
- **Red Hen Bread** • 1623 N Milwaukee Ave

Gyms

- **Mid-Town Tennis Club** • 2020 W Fullerton Ave

Hardware Stores

- **Great Ace Hardware** • 2639 N Elston Ave
- **Home Depot** • 2570 N Elston Ave
- **Novak's Paint & Hardware** • 2000 N Hoyne Ave

Liquor Stores

- **Bon Song Liquors** • 2000 N Leavitt St
- **Bucktown Food & Liquor** • 2422 W Fullerton Ave
- **Danny's Buy-Low Liquors** • 2220 N Western Ave
- **M W Food & Liquor** • 1950 N Milwaukee Ave

Movie Theaters

- **AMC City North** • 2600 N Western Ave

Pet Shops

- **And Feathers Bird Studio** • 2406 W Fullerton Ave
- **Petsmart** • 2665 N Elston Ave

Restaurants

- **Cafe Bolero** • 2252 W N Western
- **Cafe De Luca** • 1721 N Damen Ave
- **Cafe Matou** • 1848 N Milwaukee Ave
- **Club Lucky** • 1824 W Wabansia Ave
- **Glory** • 1952 N Damen Ave
- **Jambalaya's** • 1653 N Damen Ave
- **Jane's** • 1655 W Cortland St
- **Le Bouchon** • 1958 N Damen Ave
- **Northside Cafe** • 1635 N Damen Ave
- **Phlair** • 1935 N Damen Ave
- **Roong Thai Restaurant** • 1633 N Milwaukee Ave
- **Silver Cloud Club & Grill** • 1700 N Damen Ave
- **Zoom Kitchen** • 1646 N Damen Ave

Shopping

- **Bleeker Street Antiques** • 1946 N Leavitt St
- **Eclectic Junction** • 1630 N Damen Ave
- **Gypsy** • 2131 N Damen Ave
- **Jean Alan** • 2134 Damen Ave
- **Pagoda Red** • 1714 N Damen Ave
- **Pavilion Antiques** • 2055 N Damen Ave
- **Red Balloon Company** • 2060 N Damen Ave
- **Vagabond Books & Gear** • 2010 N Damen Ave
- **Viva La Femme** • 2115 N Damen Ave
- **Yardifacts** • 1864 N Damen Ave

Video Rental

- **Blockbuster Video** • 1704 N Milwaukee Ave
- **Video Corp of America** • 2525 N Elston Ave

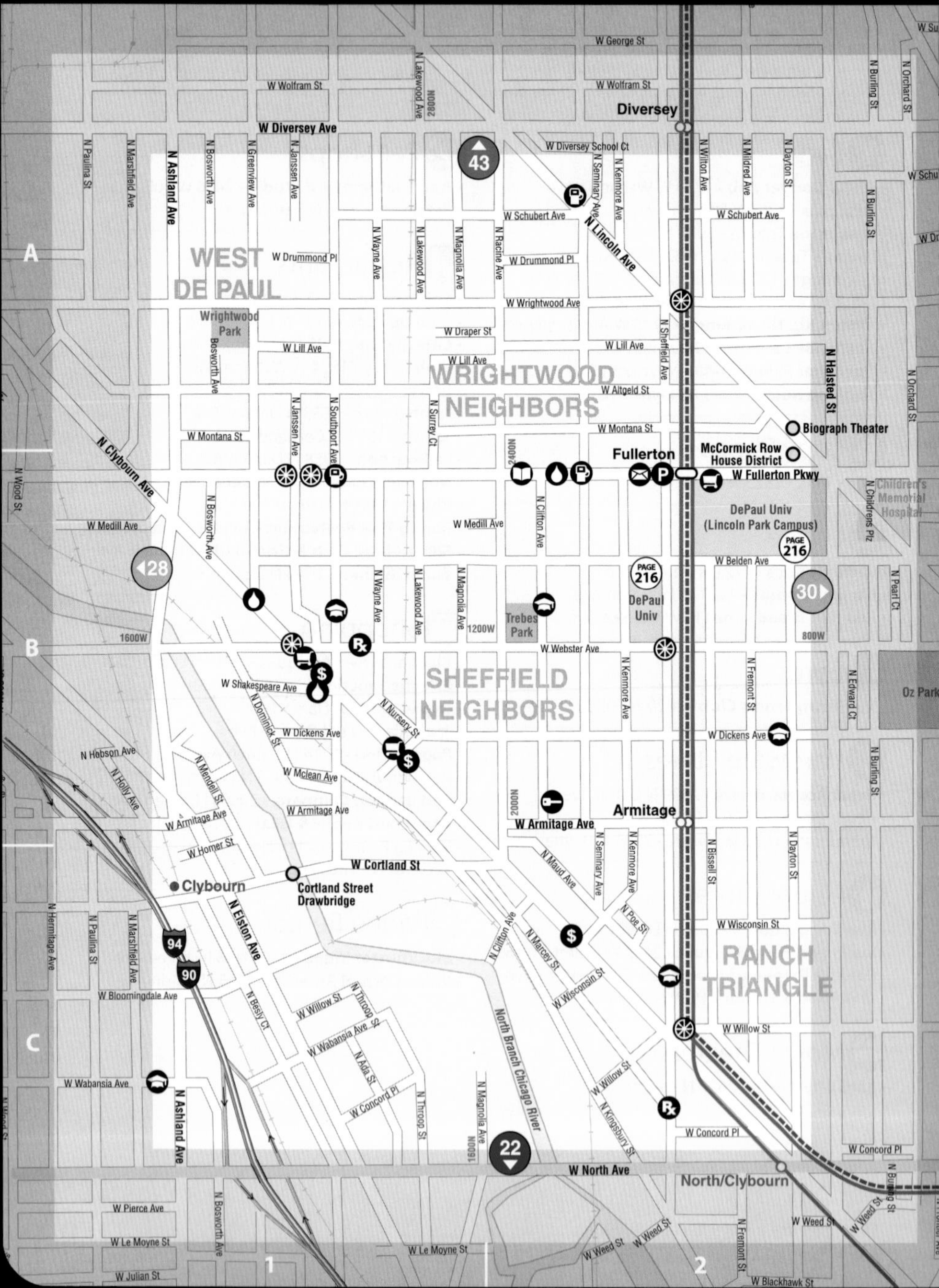

N

WEST DE PAUL
WRIGHTWOOD NEIGHBORS
SHEFFIELD NEIGHBORS
RANCH TRIANGLE

Diversey
Fullerton
Armitage
Clybourn
North/Clybourn

Biograph Theater
McCormick Row House District
DePaul Univ (Lincoln Park Campus)
DePaul Univ
Children's Memorial Hospital
Wrightwood Park
Trebes Park
Oz Park
Cortland Street Drawbridge
North Branch Chicago River

W Diversey Ave
W Fullerton Pkwy
W Armitage Ave
W Cortland St
W North Ave
N Ashland Ave
N Halsted St
N Lincoln Ave
N Clybourn Ave
N Elston Ave

PAGE 216
PAGE 216
43
28
30
22

Abodes on the quiet, shady streets around DePaul University and west of the El tracks command big mortgages and high rents. Always super-size when ordering Stefani's pizza because you'll want some for breakfast. The Clybourn Corrider's heavy traffic can be infuriating and narrow side streets crowded with parked cars and SUVs don't offer much relief. Around the area's eastern half, it's wiser to take the El and hoof it.

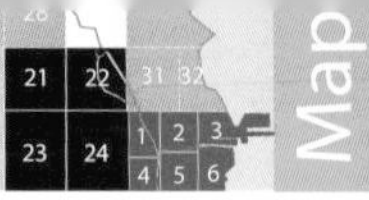

Banks

- **Bank One** • 2170 N Clybourn Ave
- **Harris Trust & Savings Bank** • 1011 W Armitage Ave
- **LaSalle Bank** • 2112 Clybourn Ave
- **US Bank** • 1953 N Clybourn Ave

Car Rental

- **Budget** • 1135 W Armitage Ave • 773-686-6800

Car Washes

- **Big Bear's Hand Car Wash** • 2261 N Clybourn Ave
- **R & S Car Wash** • 1142 W Fullerton Ave
- **White Glove Car Wash** • 1415 W Shakespeare Ave

Gas Stations

- **BP** • 2670 N Lincoln Ave
- **Fullerton-Seminary Standard** • 1106 W Fullerton Ave
- **Shell** • 1400 W Fullerton Ave

Landmarks

- **Biograph Theater** • 2433 N Lincoln Ave
- **Courtland Street Drawbridge** • 1440 W Cortland St
- **McCormick Row House District** •

Libraries

- **Lincoln Park Public Library** • 1150 W Fullerton Ave

Pharmacies

- **CVS Pharmacy** • 1714 N Sheffield Ave
- **Walgreens** • 1520 W Fullerton Ave

Pizza

- **Amato's Pizza** • 953 W Willow St
- **Lou Malnati's Pizzeria** • 958 W Wrightwood Ave
- **Pequod's Pizzeria** • 2207 N Clybourn Ave
- **Stefani's** • 1418 W Fullerton Ave
- **Tomato Head Pizza Kitchen** • 1001 W Webster Ave
- **Via-Carducci's Italian Eatery** • 1419 W Fullerton Ave

Post Offices

- 2405 N Sheffield Ave

Schools

- **Arts of Living School** • 1855 N Sheffield Ave
- **Jonathan Burr School** • 1621 W Wabansia Ave
- **Oscar F Mayer School** • 2250 N Clifton Ave
- **St James Lutheran School** • 2101 N Fremont St
- **St Josephat School** • 2245 N Southport Ave

Supermarkets

- **Always Open** • 2181 N Clybourn Ave
- **Dominick's** • 959 W Fullerton Ave
- **Treasure Island** • 2121 N Clybourn Ave

Parking

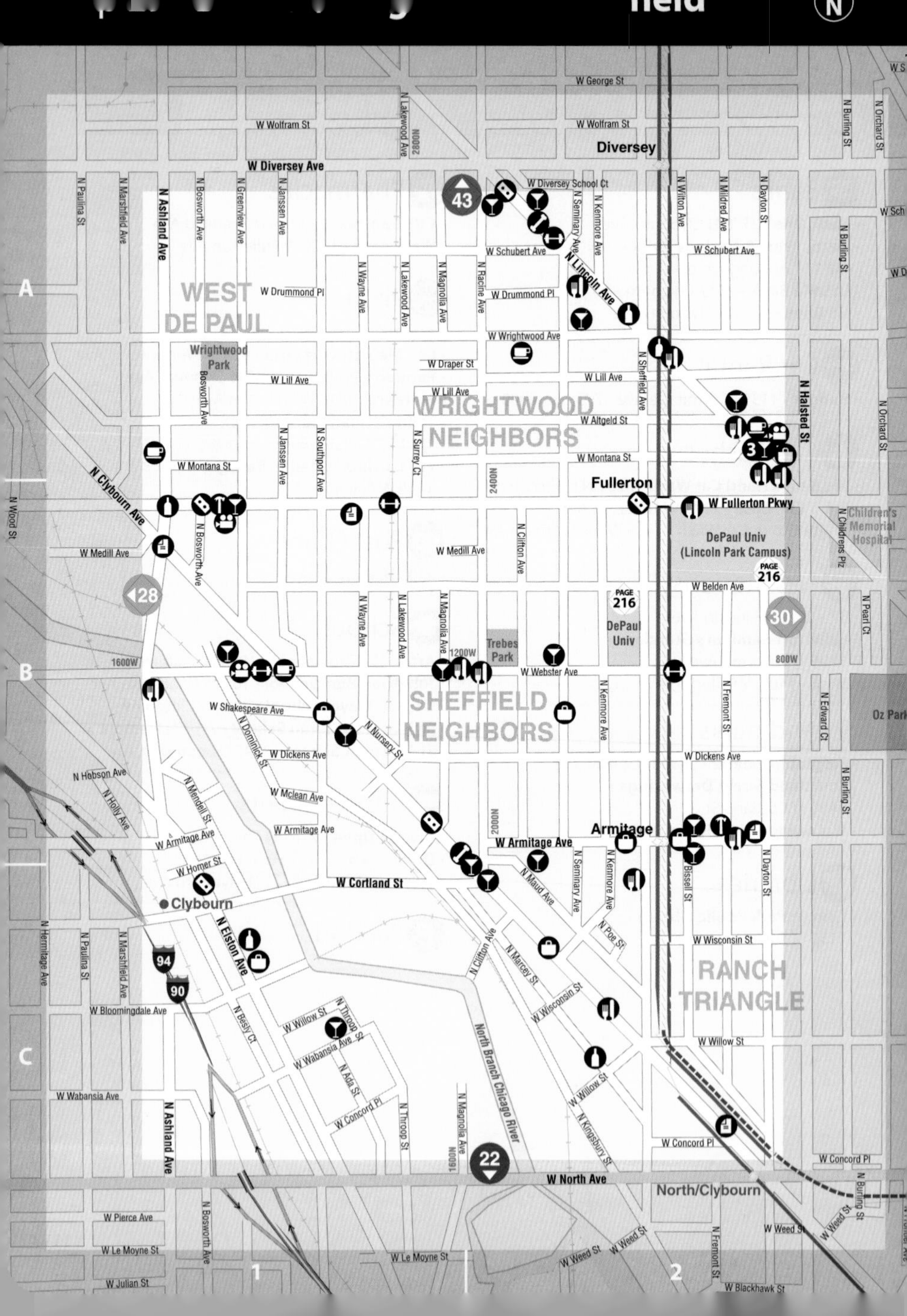

N
A
B
C
1
2
WEST DE PAUL
WRIGHTWOOD NEIGHBORS
SHEFFIELD NEIGHBORS
RANCH TRIANGLE
Wrightwood Park
Trebes Park
DePaul Univ (Lincoln Park Campus)
DePaul Univ
Children's Memorial Hospital
Oz Park
Diversey
Fullerton
Armitage
Clybourn
North/Clybourn
43
28
30
22
3
94
90
PAGE 216
PAGE 216
W George St
W Wolfram St
W Wolfram St
W Diversey Ave
W Diversey School Ct
W Schubert Ave
W Schubert Ave
W Drummond Pl
W Drummond Pl
W Wrightwood Ave
W Draper St
W Lill Ave
W Lill Ave
W Lill Ave
W Altgeld St
W Montana St
W Montana St
W Fullerton Pkwy
W Medill Ave
W Medill Ave
W Belden Ave
W Webster Ave
W Shakespeare Ave
W Dickens Ave
W Dickens Ave
W Mclean Ave
W Armitage Ave
W Armitage Ave
W Armitage Ave
W Homer St
W Cortland St
W Wisconsin St
W Wisconsin St
W Bloomingdale Ave
W Willow St
W Willow St
W Willow St
W Wabansia Ave
W Wabansia Ave
W Concord Pl
W Concord Pl
W Concord Pl
W North Ave
W Pierce Ave
W Le Moyne St
W Le Moyne St
W Julian St
W Weed St
W Weed St
W Weed St
W Weed St
W Blackhawk St
N Paulina St
N Marshfield Ave
N Ashland Ave
N Bosworth Ave
N Greenview Ave
N Janssen Ave
N Lakewood Ave
N Wayne Ave
N Magnolia Ave
N Racine Ave
N Seminary Ave
N Kenmore Ave
N Lincoln Ave
N Wilton Ave
N Mildred Ave
N Dayton St
N Burling St
N Orchard St
N Halsted St
N Sheffield Ave
N Southport Ave
N Surrey Ct
N Clybourn Ave
N Clifton Ave
N Childrens Plz
N Pearl Ct
N Fremont St
N Edward Ct
N Dominick St
N Nursery St
N Hobson Ave
N Holly Ave
N Mendell St
N Elston Ave
N Maud Ave
N Poe St
N Bissell St
N Marcey St
N Hermitage Ave
N Besly Ct
N Throop St
N Ada St
N Kingsbury St
North Branch Chicago River
N Wood St
2800N
2400N
2000N
1600N
1200W
1600W
800W

Sundries / Entertainment

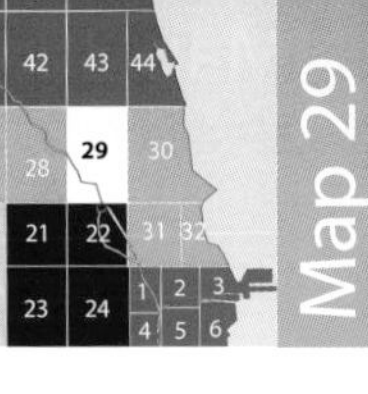

An afternoon is well spent swigging suds at one of the neighborhood's local taverns. Wrightwood Tap and Kincade's are our favorites. If you haven't had the fish 'n' chips at the Red Lion, you should—it's across from the Biograph Theater on Lincoln where notorious bank robber John Dillinger was gunned down by G-men. Be wary if your date wears red. Wine Discount Center on Elston is the ultimate bottle shop for wine enthusiasts.

Bars

- **Big John's** • 1147 W Armitage Ave
- **Charlie's Ale House** • 1224 W Webster Ave
- **Deliliah's** • 2771 N Lincoln Ave
- **Gin Mill** • 2462 N Lincoln Ave
- **Green Dolphin Street** • 2200 N Ashland Ave
- **Hog Head McDunna's** • 1505 W Fullerton Ave
- **Irish Eyes** • 2519 N Lincoln Ave
- **Jack Sullivan's** • 2142 N Clybourn Ave
- **Kincade's** • 950 W Armitage Ave
- **Kustom** • 1997 N Clybourn Ave
- **Local Option** • 1102 W Webster Ave
- **Lush** • 948 W Armitage Ave
- **Red Lion Pub** • 2446 N Lincoln Ave
- **The Hideout** • 1354 W Wabansia Ave
- **Webster Wine Bar** • 1480 Webster Ave
- **Wrightwood Tap** • 1059 W Wrightwood Ave
- **Zella** • 1983 N Clybourn Ave

Copy Shops

- **Kinko's** • 2300 N Clybourn Ave
- **Mail Boxes Etc** • 1341 W Fullerton Ave
- **Mail Boxes Etc** • 858 W Armitage Ave
- **Sir Speedy** • 1711 N Clybourn Ave

Coffee

- **Starbucks** • 1001 W Armitage Ave
- **Starbucks** • 1157 W Wrightwood Ave
- **Starbucks** • 2200 N Clybourn Ave
- **Starbucks** • 2454 N Ashland Ave
- **Starbucks** • 2475 N Lincoln Ave

Gyms

- **Bally Total Fitness** • 1455 W Webster Ave
- **Crunch Fitness** • 2727 N Lincoln Ave
- **Lakeshore Athletic Club** • 1320 W Fullerton Ave
- **Webster Fitness Club** • 957 W Webster Ave

Hardware Stores

- **Armitage Hardware & Bldg Supply** • 925 W Armitage Ave
- **Hollywood Industrial Supply** • 1524 W Fullerton Ave

Liquor Stores

- **J & R Liquor & Foods** • 2401 N Ashland Ave
- **Kegs To Go** • 2581 N Lincoln Ave
- **Sam's Wines & Spirits** • 1720 N Marcey St
- **Wine Discount Center** • 1826 1/2 N Elston Ave

Movie Theaters

- **Biograph Theater** • 2433 N Lincoln Ave
- **Facets Multimedia Theatre** • 1517 Fullerton Ave
- **Loews Cineplex** • 1471 W Webster Ave

Pet Shops

- **Galloping Gourmutts** • 2736 N Lincoln Ave
- **Petco** • 2000 N Clybourn Ave

Restaurants

- **Buffalo Wild Wings** • 2464 N Lincoln Ave
- **Charlie's Ale House** • 1224 W Webster Ave
- **Clarke's Pancake House & Restaurant** • 2441 N Lincoln Ave
- **Demon Dogs** • 944 W Fullerton Ave
- **Goose Island Wrigleyville** • 1800 N Clybourn Ave
- **Green Dolphin Street** • 2200 N Ashland Ave
- **John's Place** • 1202 W Webster Ave
- **Lindo Mexico** • 2642 N Lincoln Ave
- **Red Lion Pub** • 2446 N Lincoln Ave
- **Salt & Pepper Diner** • 2575 N Lincoln Ave
- **Shine & Morida** • 901 W Armitage Ave
- **Twisted Lizard** • 1964 N Sheffield Ave

Shopping

- **Active Endeavors** • 935 W Armitage Ave
- **Bed Bath & Beyond** • 1800 N Clybourn Ave
- **Best Buy** • 1700 N Marcey St
- **Gap** • 1740 N Sheffield Ave
- **Isabella Fine Lingerie** • 2150 N Seminary Ave
- **Jayson Home & Garden** • 1885 & 1911 N Clybourn Ave
- **Jolie Joli** • 2131 N Southport Ave
- **Tabula Tua** • 1015 W Armitage Ave
- **Uncle Dan's** • 2440 N Lincoln Ave
- **Wine Discount Center** • 1826 1/2 N Elston Ave

Video Rental

- **Blockbuster Video** • 2037 N Clybourn Ave
- **Blockbuster Video** • 2400 N Sheffield Ave
- **Facets Multimedia** • 1517 W Fullerton Ave
- **Hollywood Video** • 1940 N Elston Ave
- **Star Video** • 2781 N Lincoln Ave

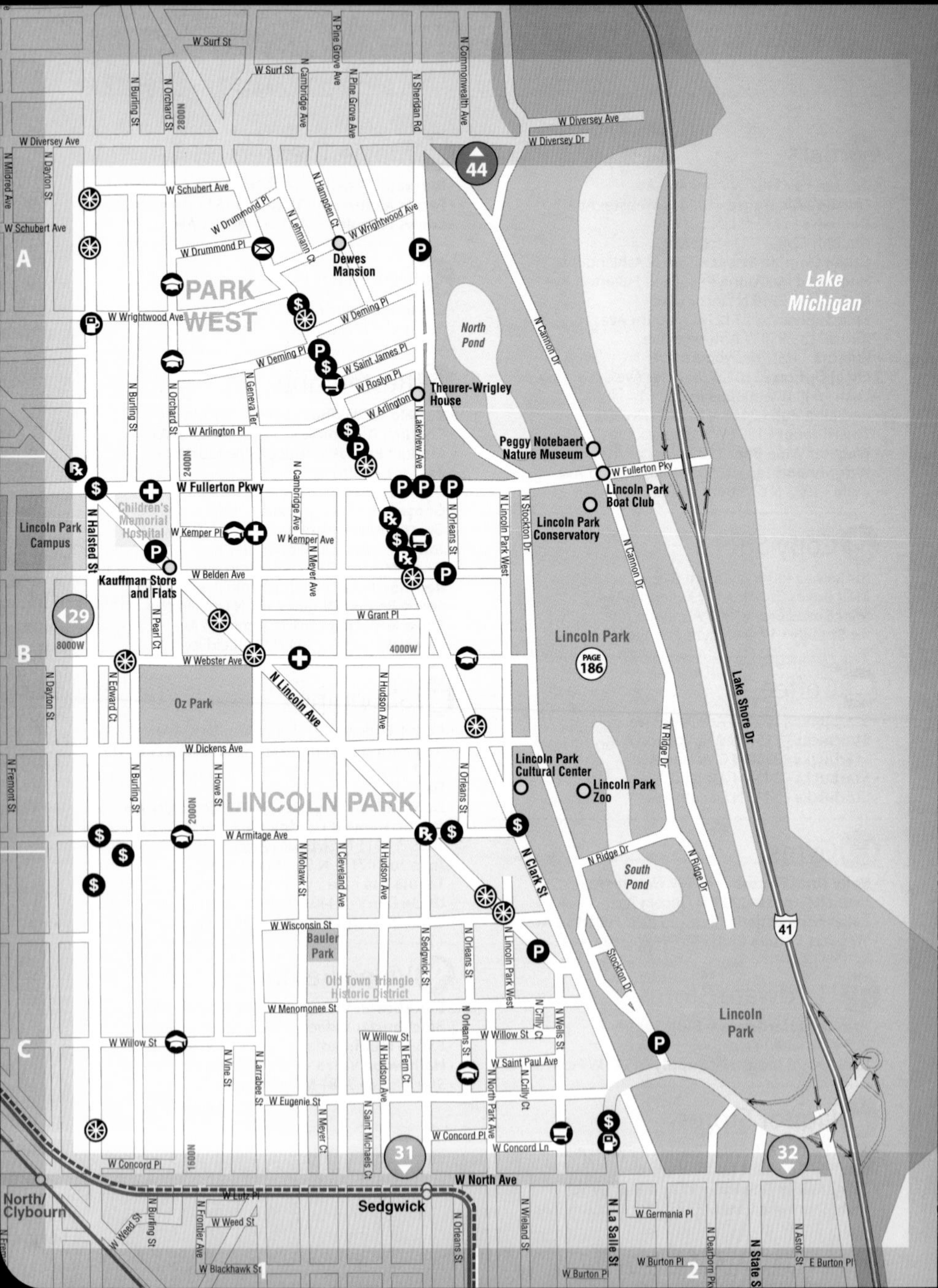

Map 30 • **Lincoln Park**

W Surf St
W Surf St
N Pine Grove Ave
N Cambridge Ave
N Pine Grove Ave
N Sheridan Rd
N Commonwealth Ave
N Burling St
N Orchard St
2800N
W Diversey Ave
W Diversey Dr
W Diversey Ave
44
N Mildred Ave
N Dayton St
W Schubert Ave
W Schubert Ave
W Drummond Pl
N Hampden Ct
N Lehmann Ct
W Wrightwood Ave
W Drummond Pl
Dewes Mansion
A
PARK WEST
Lake Michigan
W Wrightwood Ave
W Deming Pl
North Pond
N Cannon Dr
W Deming Pl
W Saint James Pl
W Roslyn Pl
N Geneva Ter
Theurer-Wrigley House
W Arlington Pl
N Burling St
N Orchard St
W Arlington Pl
N Lakeview Ave
Peggy Notebaert Nature Museum
2400N
N Cambridge Ave
W Fullerton Pkwy
W Fullerton Pkwy
Lincoln Park Boat Club
Children's Memorial Hospital
Lincoln Park Campus
N Halsted St
W Kemper Pl
W Kemper Pl
W Kemper Ave
N Meyer Ave
N Orleans St
N Lincoln Park West
N Stockton Dr
Lincoln Park Conservatory
N Cannon Dr
W Belden Ave
Kauffman Store and Flats
29
8000W
N Pearl Ct
W Grant Pl
4000W
Lincoln Park
PAGE 186
B
W Webster Ave
N Lincoln Ave
N Dayton St
N Edward Ct
Oz Park
N Hudson Ave
Lake Shore Dr
N Ridge Dr
N Fremont St
W Dickens Ave
N Burling St
2000N
N Howe St
LINCOLN PARK
N Orleans St
Lincoln Park Cultural Center
Lincoln Park Zoo
W Armitage Ave
N Mohawk St
N Cleveland Ave
N Hudson Ave
N Clark St
N Ridge Dr
South Pond
N Ridge Dr
W Wisconsin St
Bauler Park
N Sedgwick St
N Orleans St
N Lincoln Park West
41
Old Town Triangle Historic District
Stockton Dr
W Menomonee St
N Crilly Ct
N Wells St
Lincoln Park
C
W Willow St
W Willow St
W Willow St
N Orleans St
N Hudson Ave
N Fern Ct
W Saint Paul Ave
N Vine St
N Larrabee St
N North Park Ave
N Crilly Ct
W Eugenie St
N Meyer Ct
N Saint Michaels Ct
W Concord Pl
W Concord Ln
W Concord Pl
1600N
31
32
W North Ave
North/ Clybourn
W Lutz Pl
Sedgwick
N Burling St
N Frontier Ave
W Weed St
W Weed St
N Orleans St
N Wieland St
N La Salle St
W Germania Pl
N Dearborn Pkwy
N Astor St
N State St
W Blackhawk St
1
W Burton Pl
W Burton Pl
2
E Burton Pl

Lincoln Park is either heaven or hell, depending on your tolerance for yuppies, the fratboy mentalities of local students, and horrendous traffic congestion. On the upside, it IS awfully pretty and residents don't lack for upscale shopping and dinner options.

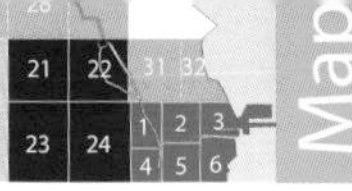

Banks

- **Bank Financial** • 2424 N Clark St
- **Bridgeview Bank** • 1970 N Halsted St
- **Builders Bank** • 1660 N La Salle St
- **Citibank** • 2001 N Halsted St
- **Citibank** • 2555 N Clark St
- **Corus Bank** • 2401 N Halsted St
- **First American Bank** • 356 W Armitage Ave
- **Mid Town Bank** • 2021 N Clark St
- **North Community Bank** • 2000 N Halsted St
- **North Community Bank** • 2335 N Clark St
- **North Community Bank** • 2500 N Clark St

Gas Stations

- **Archway Standard** • 1647 N La Salle Dr
- **Shell** • 2600 N Halsted St

Hospitals

- **Children's Memorial Hospital** • 707 W Fullerton Ave
- **Lincoln Park Hospital** • 550 W Webster Ave

Landmarks

- **Dewes Mansion** • 503 N Wrightwood Ave
- **Kauffman Store and Flats** • 2312-14 N Lincoln Ave
- **Lincoln Park Boat Club** • Cannon Dr/Fullerton Ave
- **Lincoln Park Conservatory** • 2400 N Stockton Dr
- **Lincoln Park Cultural Center** • 2045 N Lincoln Park W
- **Lincoln Park Zoo** • Cannon Dr @ Fullerton Pkwy
- **Peggy Notebaert Nature Museum** • 2430 N Cannon Dr
- **Theurer-Wrigley House** • 2466 N Lakeview Ave

Pharmacies

- **CVS Pharmacy** • 401 W Armitage Ave
- **Osco Drug** • 2414 N Lincoln Ave
- **Parkway Drugs** • 2342 N Clark St
- **Walgreens** • 2317 N Clark St

Pizza

- **Bacino's Pizza** • 2204 N Lincoln Ave
- **Bricks** • 1909 N Lincoln Ave
- **Cafe Luigi** • 2548 N Clark St
- **Chicago's Pizza & Oven Grinder Co** • 2121 N Clark St
- **Domino's** • 2231 N Lincoln Ave
- **Edwardo's Natural Pizza** • 2662 N Halsted St
- **My Pie Pizzeria** • 2417 N Clark St
- **O'Fame** • 750 W Webster Ave
- **Pane Pomodoro Restaurant** • 2703 N Halsted St
- **Pizza Capri** • 1733 N Halsted St
- **Ranalli's** • 2301 N Clark St
- **Ranalli's** • 1925 N Lincoln Ave

Post Offices

- 2643 N Clark St

Schools

- **Abraham Lincoln School** • 615 W Kemper Pl
- **Francis W Parker School** • 330 W Webster Ave
- **La Salle Language Academy** • 1734 N Orleans St
- **Lincoln Park High School** • 2001 N Orchard St
- **Louisa May Alcott School** • 2625 N Orchard St
- **Newberry Magnet School** • 700 W Willow St
- **St Clement School** • 2524 N Orchard St

Supermarkets

- **Big Apple Finer Foods** • 2345 N Clark St
- **Lincoln Park Super Market** • 2500 N Clark St
- **Treasure Island** • 1639 N Wells St

Parking

Map 30 • Lincoln Park

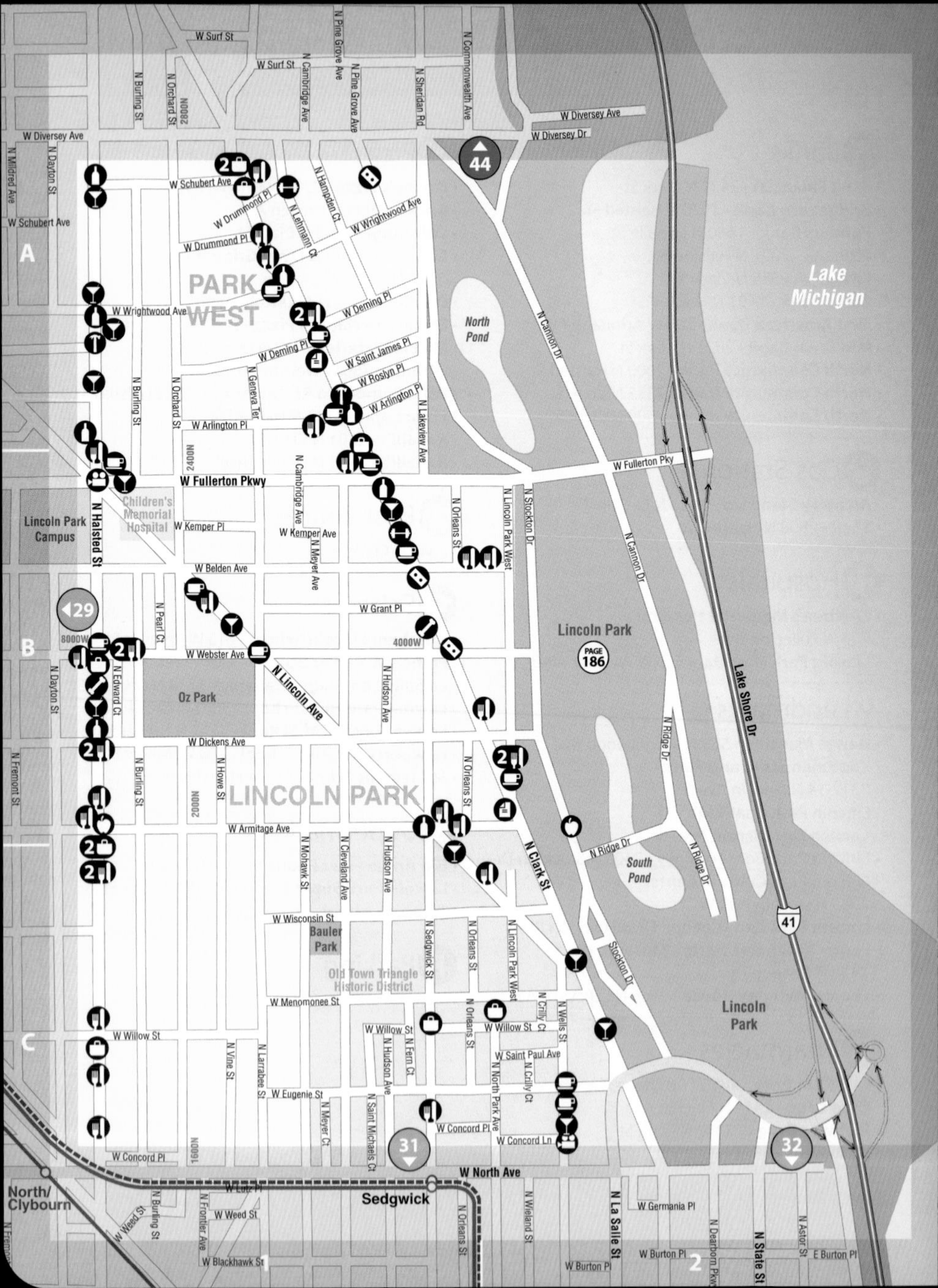

W Surf St
W Surf St
N Burling St
N Orchard St
2800N
N Cambridge Ave
N Pine Grove Ave
N Pine Grove Ave
N Sheridan Rd
N Commonwealth Ave
W Diversey Ave
W Diversey Dr
W Diversey Ave
N Mildred Ave
N Dayton St
W Schubert Ave
W Schubert Ave
W Drummond Pl
N Lehmann Ct
N Hampden Ct
W Wrightwood Ave
W Drummond Pl
44
A
PARK WEST
W Wrightwood Ave
W Deming Pl
W Deming Pl
W Saint James Pl
W Roslyn Pl
W Arlington Pl
N Burling St
N Orchard St
N Geneva Ter
W Arlington Pl
N Lakeview Ave
2400N
N Cambridge Ave
North Pond
N Cannon Dr
Lake Michigan
W Fullerton Pky
W Fullerton Pkwy
Children's Memorial Hospital
Lincoln Park Campus
N Halsted St
W Kemper Pl
W Kemper Pl
N Meyer Ave
N Orleans St
N Lincoln Park West
N Stockton Dr
N Cannon Dr
W Belden Ave
W Grant Pl
29
8000W
N Pearl Ct
4000W
Lincoln Park
PAGE 186
B
W Webster Ave
N Lincoln Ave
N Dayton St
N Edward Ct
Oz Park
N Hudson Ave
Lake Shore Dr
N Ridge Dr
W Dickens Ave
N Fremont St
N Burling St
2000N
N Howe St
LINCOLN PARK
N Orleans St
W Armitage Ave
N Mohawk St
N Cleveland Ave
N Hudson Ave
N Clark St
W Ridge Dr
South Pond
N Ridge Dr
W Wisconsin St
Bauler Park
N Sedgwick St
N Orleans St
N Lincoln Park West
Old Town Triangle Historic District
Stockton Dr
41
W Menomonee St
N Orleans St
N Crilly Ct
N Wells St
Lincoln Park
C
W Willow St
N Vine St
N Larrabee St
W Willow St
N Hudson Ave
N Fern Ct
W Willow St
W Saint Paul Ave
N North Park Ave
N Crilly Ct
W Eugenie St
N Meyer Ct
N Saint Michaels Ct
W Concord Pl
W Concord Ln
W Concord Pl
1600N
31
32
W North Ave
North/ Clybourn
W Lutz Pl
Sedgwick
N Burling St
N Frontier Ave
W Weed St
W Weed St
N Orleans St
N Wieland St
N La Salle St
W Germania Pl
N Dearborn Pkwy
N State St
N Astor St
W Blackhawk St
1
W Burton Pl
W Burton Pl
2
E Burton Pl

Sundries / Entertainment

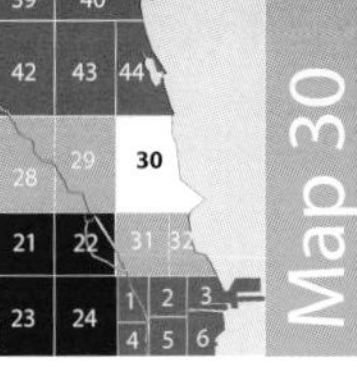

Lincoln Park provides the best outdoor entertainment in this high-rent district. Lincoln Park Zoo is the nation's oldest free zoo. Catch a live act at Park West. Post-show, settle in at Hidden Shamrock with a pint of Guinness. Lori's Designer Shoes is an institution among footwear fanatics. The French toast stuffed with mascarpone cheese and strawberry puree at Toast is worth the wait.

Bars

- **Bar Louie** • 1800 N Lincoln Ave
- **Blu** • 2247 N Lincoln Ave
- **Corner Pocket** • 2610 N Halsted St
- **Game Keepers** • 1971 N Lincoln Ave
- **Glascott's** • 2158 N Halsted
- **GoodBar** • 2512 N Halsted
- **Hidden Shamrock** • 2723 N Halsted
- **Kingston Mines** • 2548 N Halsted St
- **Neo** • 2350 N Clark St
- **Parkway Tavern** • 746 W Fullerton Ave
- **River Shannon** • 425 W Armitage Ave
- **Sauce** • 1750 N Clark St
- **Tequila Roadhouse** • 1653 N Wells St

Copy Shops

- **Mail Boxes Etc** • 2038 N Clark St
- **Mail Boxes Etc** • 2506 N Clark St

Coffee

- **Bourgeois Pig** • 738 W Fullerton Ave
- **Caribou Coffee** • 2453 N Clark St
- **Crescent City Beignets** • 2200 N Lincoln Ave
- **Monterotondo** • 612 W Wrightwood Ave
- **Savories** • 1651 N Wells St
- **Screenz Digital Universe** • 2717 N Clark St
- **Seattle's Best** • 1700 N Wells St
- **Siena Coffee** • 2308 N Clark St
- **Starbucks** • 2063 N Clark St
- **Starbucks** • 2200 N Halsted St
- **Starbucks** • 2273 N Lincoln Ave
- **Starbucks** • 2529 N Clark St

Farmer's Markets

- **Lincoln Park** • Armitage Ave & Halsted St
- **Lincoln Park Zoo** • 2001 N Stockton Dr

Gyms

- **Lehmann Sports Club** • 2700 N Lehmann Ct
- **Lincoln Park Fitness Center (LPFC)** • 2342 N Clark St

Hardware Stores

- **Arlington Hardware** • 2465 N Clark St
- **Wahler Brothers True Value** • 2551 N Halsted St

Liquor Stores

- **Chalet Wine & Cheese Shop** • 405 W Armitage Ave
- **Country Fresh Finer Foods** • 2583 N Clark St
- **Dynamic Liquors** • 2132 N Halsted St
- **Field House** • 2455 N Clark St
- **Miska's Wine Beer & Liquors** • 2353 N Clark St
- **Park West Food & Liquor** • 2733 N Halsted St
- **Park West Foods & Liquors** • 2427 N Lincoln Ave
- **R&A Grocery** • NE corner Halsted & Wrightwood

Movie Theaters

- **Sony Theatre** • 1616 N Wells St
- **Three Penny Theatre** • 2424 N Lincoln Ave

Pet Shops

- **Park View Pet Shop** • 2222 N Clark St
- **Three Dog Bakery** • 2142 N Halsted St

Restaurants

- **Aladdin Cafe** • 2269 N Lincoln Ave
- **Ambria** • 2300 N Lincoln Park W
- **Asiana** • 2546 N Clark St
- **Athenian Room** • 807 W Webster Ave
- **Aubriot** • 1962 N Halsted St
- **Cafe Ba-Ba-Reeba!** • 2024 N Halsted St
- **Cafe Bernard** • 2100 N Halsted St
- **Charlie Trotter's** • 816 W Armitage Ave
- **Dunlays** • 2600 N Clark St
- **Emilio's Tapas** • 444 Fullerton Pkwy
- **Escargot** • 1962 N Halsted St
- **Frances** • 2552 N Clark St
- **Geja's Cafe** • 340 W Armitage Ave
- **King Crab** • 1816 N Halsted St
- **L'Olive** • 1629 N Halsted St
- **Mon Ami Gabi** • 2300 N Lincoln Park W
- **Nookies, Too** • 2114 N Halsted St
- **O' Fame** • 750 W Webster Ave
- **Original Pancake House** • 2020 N Lincoln Park W
- **Piattini** • 934 W Webster
- **Ranalli's** • 1925 N Lincoln Ave
- **RJ Grunt's** • 2056 Lincoln Park W
- **Salvatore's Ristorante** • 525 W Arlington Pl
- **Sushi O Sushi** • 346 W Armitage Ave
- **Taco Burrito Palace #2** • 2441 N Halsted St
- **Tilli's** • 1952 N Halsted St
- **Toast** • 746 W Webster Ave
- **Twin Anchors** • 1655 N Sedgwick St
- **Via Emilia Ristorante** • 2119 N Clark St
- **Vinci** • 1732 N Halsted St
- **Wiener's Circle** • 2622 N Clark St
- **Zucco** • 543 W Diversey Pkwy

Shopping

- **Art & Science** • 1971 N Halsted St
- **Coconuts Music & Movies** • 2747 N Clark St
- **Cynthia Rowley** • 808 W Armitage Ave
- **Ethan Allen** • 1700 N Halsted St
- **Gallery 1756** • 1756 N Sedgwick St
- **GNC** • 2140 N Halsted St
- **GNC** • 2740 N Clark St
- **Kwik Mart** • 2427 N Clark St
- **Lori's Designer Shoes** • 824 W Armitage Ave
- **Sally Beauty Supply** • 2723 N Clark St
- **Triangle Gallery of Old Town** • 1763 N North Park Ave
- **Walgreens** • 2317 N Clark St

Video Rental

- **Blockbuster Video** • 2200 N Clark St
- **Blockbuster Video** • 2577 N Clark St
- **Emmy's & Oscar's** • 2619 N Halsted St
- **Tokyo Video of Chicago (Japanese)** • 2755 N Pine Grove Ave
- **Tower Records** • 2301 N Clark St

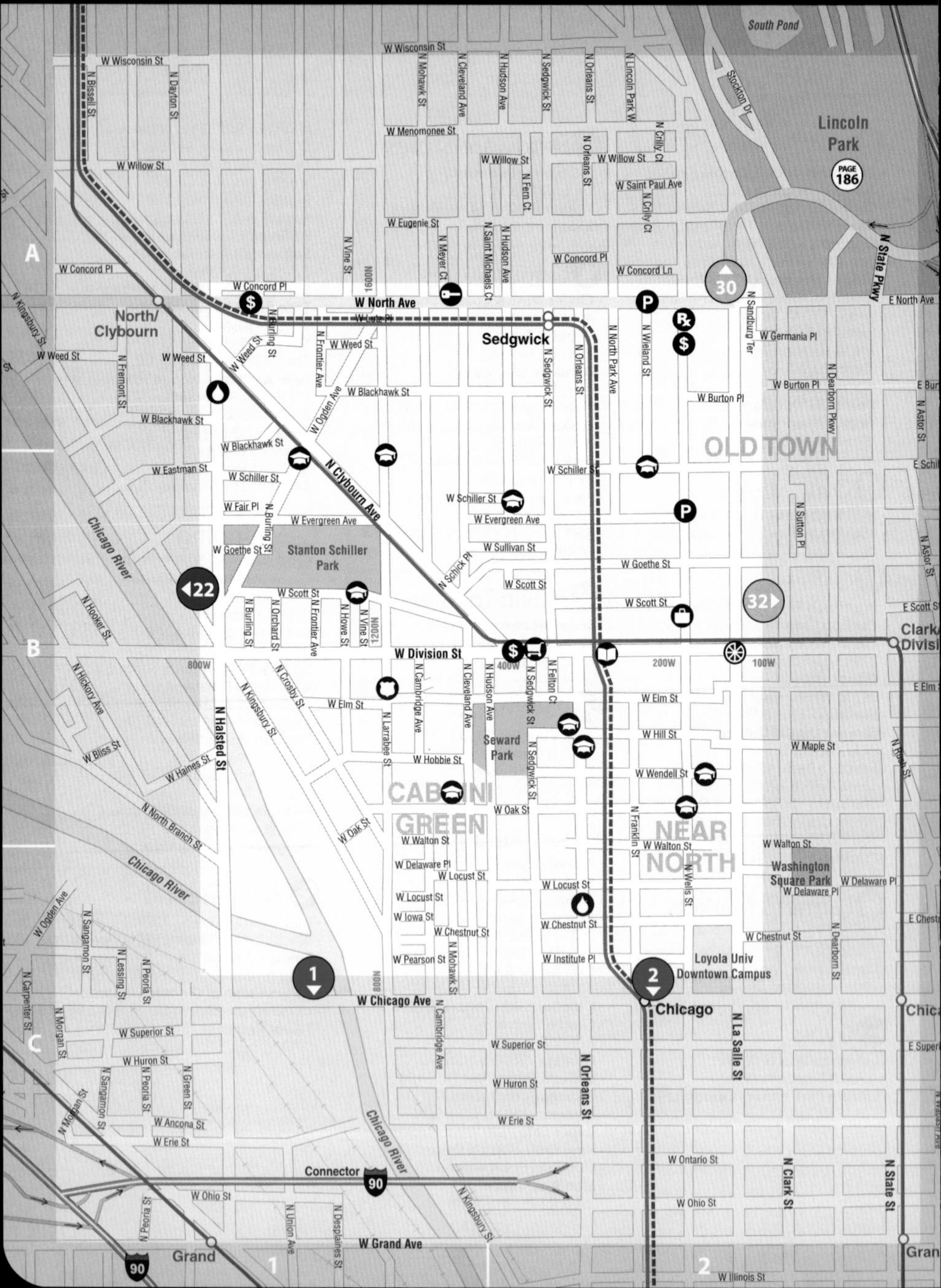

Map 31 • Old Town/Near North

South Pond
Lincoln Park
PAGE 186
OLD TOWN
NEAR NORTH
CABRINI GREEN
North/Clybourn
Sedgwick
Chicago
Grand
Clark/Division
Stanton Schiller Park
Seward Park
Washington Square Park
Loyola Univ Downtown Campus
Chicago River
30
32
22
1
2
A
B
C
W Wisconsin St
W Menomonee St
W Willow St
W Saint Paul Ave
W Eugenie St
W Concord Pl
W Concord Ln
W North Ave
E North Ave
W Lutz Pl
W Weed St
W Germania Pl
W Blackhawk St
W Burton Pl
W Eastman St
W Schiller St
W Fair Pl
W Evergreen Ave
W Sullivan St
W Goethe St
W Scott St
E Scott St
W Division St
W Elm St
E Elm St
W Hill St
W Maple St
W Hobbie St
W Wendell St
W Oak St
W Walton St
W Delaware Pl
W Locust St
W Iowa St
W Chestnut St
E Chestnut St
W Institute Pl
W Pearson St
W Chicago Ave
W Superior St
E Superior St
W Huron St
W Ancona St
W Erie St
W Ontario St
W Ohio St
W Grand Ave
W Illinois St
W Haines St
W Bliss St
Connector
90
N Bissell St
N Dayton St
N Mohawk St
N Cleveland Ave
N Hudson Ave
N Sedgwick St
N Orleans St
N Lincoln Park W
N Crilly Ct
N Fern Ct
N Vine St
N Meyer Ct
N Saint Michaels Ct
Stockton Dr
N State Pkwy
N Sandburg Ter
N Kingsbury St
N Fremont St
N Burling St
N Frontier Ave
N Ogden Ave
N Clybourn Ave
N North Park Ave
N Wieland St
N Dearborn Pkwy
N Astor St
N Sutton Pl
N Schick Pl
N Hooker St
N Orchard St
N Howe St
N Hickory Ave
N Halsted St
N Crosby St
N Larrabee St
N Cambridge Ave
N Felton Ct
N Franklin St
N Wells St
N Rush St
N North Branch St
N Dearborn St
N Ogden Ave
N Sangamon St
N Lessing St
N Peoria St
N Carpenter St
N Morgan St
N Green St
N La Salle St
N Clark St
N State St
N Union Ave
N Desplaines St
N Wabash Ave
1600N
1200N
800N
800W
400W
200W
100W

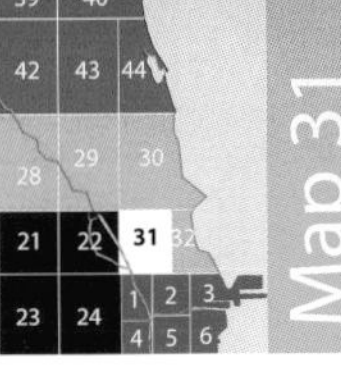

Close to all the action on Mag Mile and the lake front, this area is packed with people, history, and significant architecture. Old Town Triangle District is on the National Registry of Historic Places. The neighborhood's sophisticated, artsy flair is showcased during the annual Old Town Art Fair (June). The well-heeled live along State St. near the park in exquisite single-family homes.

Car Rental

- **Enterprise** • 523 W North Ave • 312-482-8322

Banks

- **Bank One** • 424 W Division St
- **LaSalle Bank** • 758 W North Ave
- **North Community Bank** • 1561 N Wells St

Car Washes

- **Gold Coast Car Wash** • 875 N Orleans St
- **We'll Clean** • 1520 N Halsted St

Gas Stations

- **BP** • 1560 N Halsted St

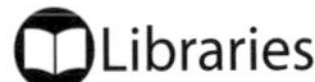

Libraries

- **Near North Public Library** • 310 W Division St

Pharmacies

- **Walgreens** • 1601 N Wells St

Pizza

- **Domino's** • 143 W Division St
- **Father & Son Pizza** • 645 W North Ave

Police

- **18th District (Near North)** • 1160 N Larrabee St

Schools

- **Catherine Cook School** • 226 W Schiller St
- **Edward Jenner School** • 1009 N Cleveland Ave
- **Franklin Fine Art Ctr** • 225 W Evergreen Ave
- **Manierre Elementary School** • 1420 N Hudson Ave
- **Near North Career Magnet High** • 1450 N Larrabee St
- **Richard E Byrd School** • 363 W Hill St
- **Ruben Salazar Bilingual Education** • 160 W Wendell St
- **Schiller Elementary School** • 640 W Scott St
- **Sojourner Truth School** • 1443 N Ogden Ave
- **St Joseph's School** • 1065 N Orleans St
- **Walter Payton College Prep High School** • 1034 N Wells St

Supermarkets

- **Dominick's** • 424 W Division St

Parking

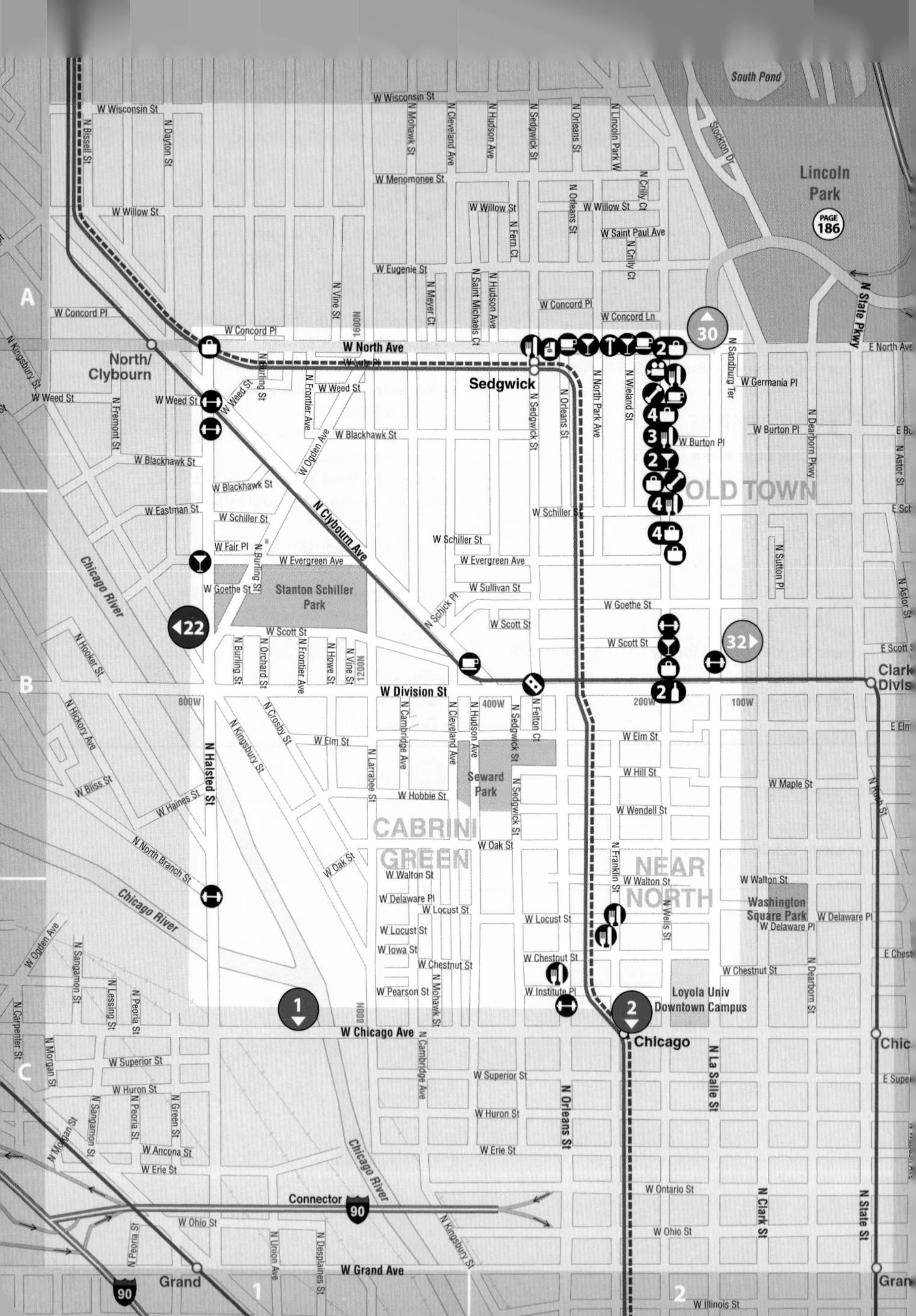

South Pond
Lincoln Park
PAGE 186
30
32
22
1
2
A
B
C
1
2
W Wisconsin St
N Bissell St
N Dayton St
N Mohawk St
N Cleveland Ave
N Hudson Ave
N Sedgwick St
N Orleans St
N Lincoln Park W
Stockton Dr
W Menomonee St
N Crilly Ct
W Willow St
N Fern Ct
W Saint Paul Ave
W Eugenie St
N Vine St
N Meyer Ct
N Saint Michaels Ct
W Concord Pl
W Concord Ln
N State Pkwy
W North Ave
E North Ave
North/ Clybourn
Sedgwick
N Kingsbury St
W Weed St
N Burling St
W Lutz Pl
N Frontier Ave
N Sandburg Ter
W Germania Pl
N Fremont St
W Blackhawk St
N Ogden Ave
N Park Ave
N Wieland St
W Burton Pl
N Dearborn Pkwy
N Astor St
OLD TOWN
W Eastman St
W Schiller St
N Clybourn Ave
W Fair Pl
W Evergreen Ave
W Sullivan St
N Sutton Pl
Chicago River
W Goethe St
Stanton Schiller Park
N Schick Pl
W Scott St
E Scott St
N Hooker St
N Orchard St
N Howe St
W Division St
Clark/Division
800W
400W
200W
100W
N Felton Ct
N Hickory Ave
N Halsted St
N Crosby St
W Elm St
E Elm St
N Cambridge Ave
N Larrabee St
W Hill St
Seward Park
W Bliss St
W Haines St
W Hobbie St
W Maple St
W Wendell St
CABRINI GREEN
W Oak St
N North Branch St
N Franklin St
NEAR NORTH
W Walton St
N Wells St
Washington Square Park
W Delaware Pl
W Locust St
W Iowa St
W Chestnut St
E Chestnut St
N Ogden Ave
N Sangamon St
N Lessing St
N Peoria St
W Pearson St
W Institute Pl
Loyola Univ Downtown Campus
N Carpenter St
W Chicago Ave
Chicago
N Morgan St
W Superior St
E Superior St
N La Salle St
W Huron St
N Green St
N Orleans St
W Ancona St
W Erie St
W Ontario St
N Clark St
N State St
Connector
90
W Ohio St
N Union Ave
N Desplaines St
W Grand Ave
Grand
W Illinois St

Sundries / Entertainment

You could be laughing with a rising star at Second City, Chicago's famed improv club, where John Belushi, Bill Murray, Gilda Radner, Rick Moranis, and Mike Myers got their starts. When in town, Minnie Driver and Gary Sinise browse for books at Barbara's. Topo Gigio's grilled calamari is never rubbery, and for sushi as fresh as fish can be out of water, go to Kamehachi.

Bars

- **Burton Place** • 1447 N Wells St
- **Dragon Room** • 809 W Evergreen St
- **Hobo's** • 1446 N Wells St
- **North Park Tap** • 313 W North Ave
- **Old Town Ale House** • 219 W North Ave
- **Spoon** • 1240 N Wells St
- **Weeds** • 1555 N Dayton St

Copy Shops

- **Mail Boxes Etc** • 333 W North Ave

Coffee

- **Dunkin' Donuts** • 333 W North Ave
- **Einstein Bagels** • 1549 N Wells St
- **Starbucks** • 1229 N Clybourn Ave
- **Starbucks** • 210 W North Ave

Gyms

- **Body Endeavors** • 1528 N Halsted St
- **Crunch Fitness** • 820 N Orleans St
- **Energy Training Center (ETC)** • 900 N North Branch St
- **Fitplex** • 1235 N La Salle Dr
- **Nautilus: A Women's Gym** • 1248 N Wells St
- **New City YMCA** • 1515 N Halsted St

Hardware Stores

- **Tipre Hardware** • 227 W North Ave

Liquor Stores

- **House of Glunz** • 1206 N Wells St
- **Old Town Liquors** • 1200 N Wells St

Movie Theaters

- **Piper's Alley Loews Cineplex** • 1608 N Wells St

Pet Shops

- **Collar & Leash** • 1435 N Wells St
- **Old Town Aquarium** • 1538 N Wells St

Restaurants

- **Bistrot Margot** • 1437 N Wells St
- **Chic Cafe** • 361 W Chestnut St
- **Cucina Bella Osteria & Wine Bar** • 1612 N Sedgwick St
- **Fireplace Inn** • 1448 N Wells St
- **Fresh Choice** • 1534 N Wells St
- **Kamehachi** • 1400 N Wells St
- **Kiki's Bistro** • 900 N Franklin St
- **Las Pinatas** • 1552 N Wells St
- **MK** • 868 N Franklin St
- **O'Brien's** • 1528 N Wells St
- **Old Jerusalem** • 1411 N Wells St
- **Topo Gigio Ristorante** • 1516 N Wells St

Shopping

- **Atom Antiques** • 1219 N Wells St
- **Barbara's Bookstore** • 1350 N Wells St
- **Chocolateer Confections** • 1212 N Wells St
- **Crate & Barrel Outlet Store** • 800 W North Ave
- **Etre** • 1361 N Wells St
- **Expo Design Center** • 1500 N Dayton St
- **Fleet Feet Sports** • 210 W North Ave
- **Fudge Pot** • 1532 N Wells St
- **Jumbalia** • 1427 N Wells St
- **Old Town Gardens** • 1555 N Wells St
- **See Hear Music** • 217 W North Ave
- **Sofie** • 1343 N Wells St
- **The Spice House** • 1512 N Wells St
- **Vagabonds Boutique** • 1357 N Wells St
- **Village Cycle** • 1337 N Wells St

Video Rental

- **Blockbuster Video** • 400 W Division St

Map 32 • **Gold Coast/Mag Mile**

PAGE 186

Lincoln Park

Lake Michigan

N Sedgwick St
N Orleans St
N Lincoln Park W
Stockton Dr
W Menomonee St
N Cirily Ct
W Willow St
W Saint Paul Ave
W Eugenie St
N Wells St
W Concord Pl
W Concord Ln
1800N
A
30
W North Ave
Sedgwick
W Germania Pl
N Sandburg Ter
N North Park Ave
N Wieland St
N Orleans St
W Burton Pl
N Dearborn Pkwy
N State St
E Burton Pl
N Astor St
N Lake Shore Dr
W Burton Pl
N La Salle St
W Schiller St
E Schiller St
N Ritchie Ct
E Banks St
W Evergreen Ave
31
N Sutton Pl
N Astor St
41
W Goethe St
N Stone St
N Felton Ct
W Scott St
E Scott St
1200N
Clark/Division
E Division St
B
GOLD COAST
E Elm St
W Elm St
E Cedar St
W Hill St
W Maple St
W Wendell St
Dr Scholl Coll of Podiatry
E Bellevue Pl
E Lake Shore Dr
W Oak St
200W
100W
100E
W Walton St
W Walton St
E Walton St
N Ernst Ct
N Huguelet Pl
N Dewitt Pl
W Delaware Pl
W Delaware Pl
W Delaware Pl
W Locust St
N Ernst Ct
N Miles Van Der Rohe Way
W Chestnut St
W Chestnut St
Water Tower and Park
E Chestnut St
W Institute Pl
Moody Bible Institute
E Pearson St
N Tower Ct
Seneca Park
N Rush St
Lake Shore Park
800N
2
3
Chicago
W Chicago Ave
Chicago
E Chicago Ave
41
C
W Superior St
N La Salle St
E Superior St
Lake Shore Dr
N Dearborn St
N Fairbanks Ct
W Huron St
E Huron St
N Orleans St
N Franklin St
N Wabash Ave
N Michigan Ave
N Mcclurg Ct
W Erie St
E Erie St
W Ontario St
E Ontario St
N Clark St
N State St
600N
N Saint Clair St
W Ohio St
E Ohio St
E Ohio St
Milton Lee Olive Park
N Miles Van Der Rohe Way
E Grand Ave
Grand
N Peshtigo Ct
W Illinois St
E Illinois St
1
2

Money, money, money equals location, location, location. The butter-yellow stone Water Tower, which survived the Great Chicago Fire of 1871, anchors the city's most expensive and exclusive place to live and play. You'll drop about $400 bucks for a bed at The Ritz, Park Hyatt, Peninsula, or Four Seasons. A high school education at the private, pricey Latin School of Chicago could buy a fleet of Mercedes.

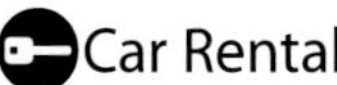

Car Rental

- **Enterprise** • 850 N State St • 312-951-6262
- **Hertz** • 1025 N Clark St • 312-951-2930

Banks

- **Bank One** • 1122 N Clark St
- **Bank One** • 875 N Michigan Ave
- **Charter One Bank** • 1201 N Clark St
- **Citibank** • 68 E Oak St
- **Cosmopolitan Bank and Trust** • 801 N Clark St
- **Delaware Place Bank** • 190 E Delaware Pl
- **LaSalle Bank** • 940 N Michigan Ave
- **North Community Bank** • 2 W Elm St
- **North Federal Savings Bank** • 100 W North Ave
- **Northern Trust Bank** • 120 E Oak St
- **Oak Bank** • 1000 N Rush St

Gas Stations

- **Shell** • 130 W North Ave

Landmarks

- **Water Tower Place and Park** • 845 N Michigan Ave

Libraries

- **Newberry Library** • 60 W Walton St

Pharmacies

- **Osco Drug** • 1165 N Clark St
- **Walgreens** • 1200 N Dearborn St

Pizza

- **California Pizza Kitchen** • 835 N Michigan Ave
- **Casa Del Pacci** • 941 N State St
- **Edwardo's Natural Pizza** • 1212 N Dearborn St
- **Gino's Pizzeria** • 930 N Rush St
- **Mama's Pizzeria** • 11 W Division St
- **Pizano's Pizza & Pasta** • 864 N State St

Schools

- **Dr Scholl School of Podiatry** • 1001 N Dearborn St
- **Moody Bible Institute** • 820 N La Salle St
- **Latin School of Chicago** • 59 W North Blvd
- **Quigley Preparatory Seminary** • 103 E Chestnut St
- **William B Ogden School** • 24 W Walton St

Supermarkets

- **Jewel** • 1210 N Clark St
- **Potash Brothers** • 1525 N Clark St
- **Treasure Island** • 75 W Elm St

Parking

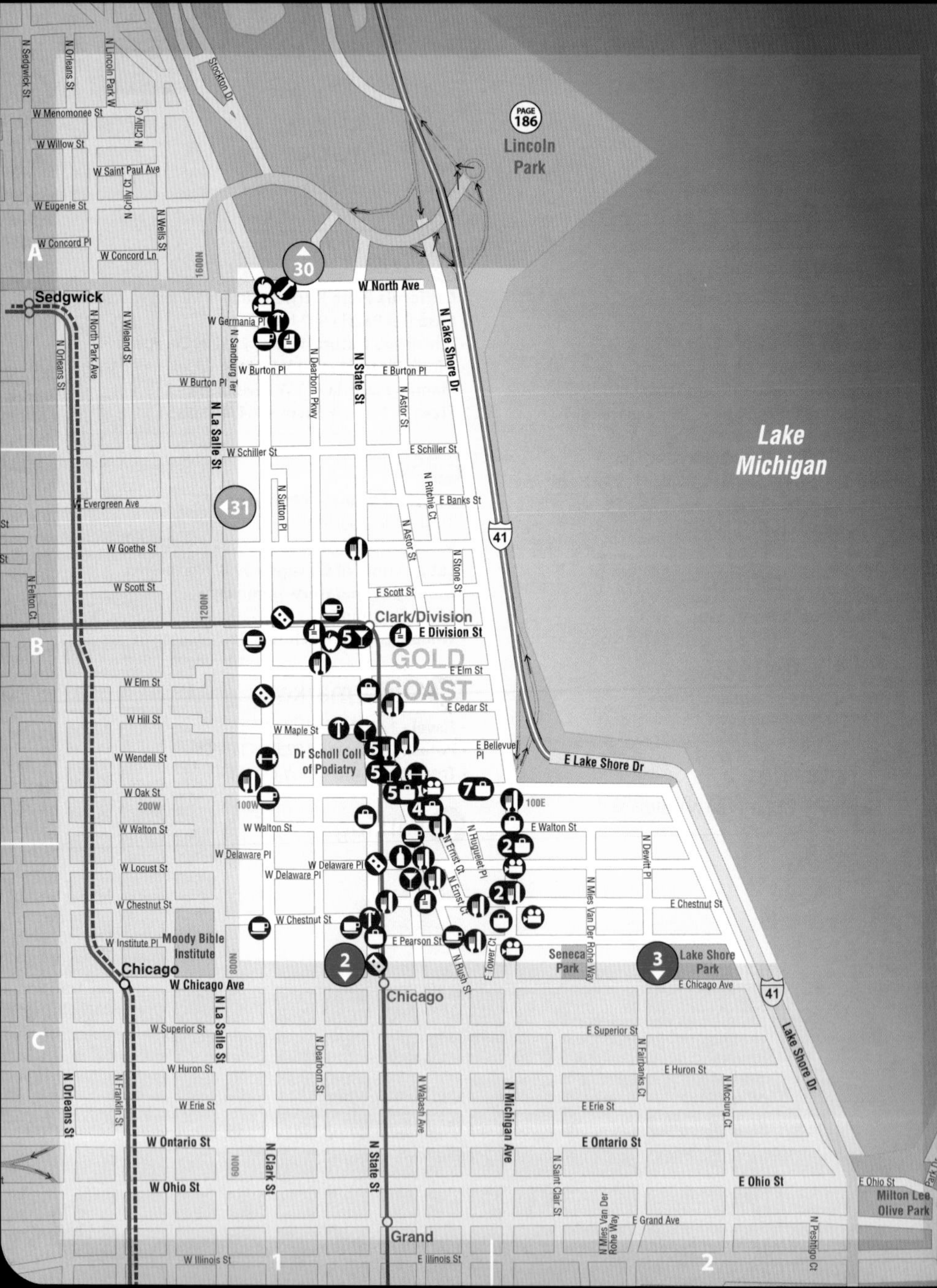

Lake Michigan
Lincoln Park
PAGE 186
GOLD COAST
30
31
2
3
Sedgwick
Clark/Division
Chicago
Grand
W North Ave
W Burton Pl
E Burton Pl
W Schiller St
E Schiller St
E Banks St
W Evergreen Ave
W Goethe St
W Scott St
E Scott St
E Division St
E Elm St
W Elm St
E Cedar St
W Hill St
W Maple St
W Wendell St
E Bellevue Pl
E Lake Shore Dr
W Oak St
W Walton St
E Walton St
W Delaware Pl
W Locust St
W Chestnut St
E Chestnut St
W Institute Pl
E Pearson St
W Chicago Ave
E Chicago Ave
W Superior St
E Superior St
W Huron St
E Huron St
W Erie St
E Erie St
W Ontario St
E Ontario St
W Ohio St
E Ohio St
E Grand Ave
W Illinois St
E Illinois St
N Lake Shore Dr
Lake Shore Dr
N State St
N Dearborn Pkwy
N Dearborn St
N La Salle St
N Clark St
N Michigan Ave
N Orleans St
N Franklin St
N Wabash Ave
N Rush St
Moody Bible Institute
Dr Scholl Coll of Podiatry
Seneca Park
Lake Shore Park
Milton Lee Olive Park
41
A
B
C
1
2

Shopping, shopping, shopping. Oak Street is Chicago's answer to L.A.'s Rodeo Dr—overpriced and unpractical fashion. For multiple pairs of cheap, stylish shades, shop at Urban Outfitters. Elements has cool home accessories and creative jewelry. The Downtown strip is sagging but the Rush and Division Street bars still pack 'em in. Bono hangs at Le Passage after U2's sell-out concerts at United Center.

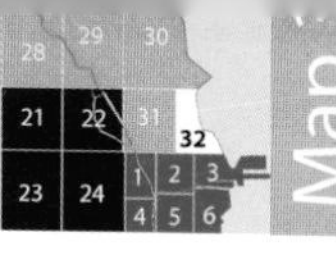

Bars

- **Bar Chicago** • 9 W Division St
- **Butch McGuire's** • 20 W Division St
- **Cactus** • 404 S Wells St
- **Cru Wine Bar** • 888 N Wabash Ave
- **Dublin's** • 1030 N State St
- **Le Passage** • 1 E Oak St
- **Leg Room** • 7 W Division St
- **Mothers** • 26 W Division St
- **She-nanigans** • 16 W Division St
- **The Hunt Club** • 1100 N State St
- **The Whisky** • 1015 N Rush St
- **Zebra Lounge** • 1220 N State St

Copy Shops

- **Kinko's** • 1201 N Dearborn St
- **Mail Boxes Etc** • 47 W Division St
- **Mail Boxes Etc** • 60 E Chestnut St

Coffee

- **Coffee Expressions** • 100 W Oak St
- **Dunkin' Donuts** • 101 W Division St
- **Starbucks** • 108 W Germania Pl
- **Starbucks** • 111 E Chestnut St
- **Starbucks** • 39 W Division St
- **Starbucks** • 828 N State St
- **Starbucks** • 932 Rush St
- **Wolf & Kettle** • 101 E Pearson St

Farmer's Markets

- **Chicago's Green City Market** • 1601 N Clark St
- **Near North** • 15 W Division St

Gyms

- **Body Balance** • 1011 N Rush St
- **Extreme Fitness Fitplex** • 1235 La Salle
- **Gold Coast Multiplex** • 1030 N Clark St

Hardware Stores

- **Gordon's Ace Hardware** • 24 W Maple St
- **Sandberg Ace Hardware** • 110 W Germania Pl
- **State Street True Value** • 845 N State St

Liquor Stores

- **Chalet Wine & Cheese Shop** • 40 E Delaware Pl

Movie Theaters

- **Esquire Theater** • 58 E Oak St
- **Village Theater** • 1548 N Clark St
- **Water Tower Theater** • 157 E Chestnut St

Pet Shops

- **Paws-a-Tively** • 109 W North Ave

Restaurants

- **Ashkenaz** • 12 E Cedar St
- **Bistro 110** • 110 E Pearson St
- **Cheesecake Factory** • 875 N Michigan Ave
- **Cru Wine Bar & Cafe** • 888 N Wabash Ave
- **Dave & Buster's** • 1030 N Clark St
- **Gibson's Steakhouse** • 1028 N Rush St
- **Johnny Rockets** • 901 N Rush St
- **Le Colonial** • 937 N Rush St
- **McCormick's & Schmick's** • 41 E Chestnut St
- **Mike Ditka's** • 100 E Chestnut St
- **Original Pancake House** • 22 E Bellevue Pl
- **Pane Caldo** • 72 E Walton St
- **Pump Room** • Omni Ambassador East Hotel, 1301 N State Pkwy
- **Signature Room at the 95th** • 875 N Michigan Ave
- **Spiaggia** • 940 N Michigan Ave
- **Tavern on Rush** • 1031 N Rush St
- **Tempo** • 6 E Chestnut St
- **Tsunami** • 1160 N Dearborn St
- **Whiskey Bar and Grill** • 1015 N Rush St

Shopping

- **Anthropologie** • 1120 N State St
- **Barney's New York** • 25 E Oak St
- **BCBG** • 103 E Oak St
- **Bloomingdale's** • 900 N Michigan Ave
- **Bravco Beauty Center** • 43 E Oak St
- **Chanel at the Drake Hotel** • 935 N Michigan Ave
- **Chelsea Passage** • 25 E Oak St
- **Diesel** • 923 N Rush St
- **Elements** • 102 E Oak St
- **Europa Books** • 832 N State St
- **Frette** • 41 E Oak St
- **G'bani** • 949 N State St
- **Gucci** • 900 N Michigan Ave
- **Hear Music** • 932 N Rush St
- **MAC** • 40 E Oak St
- **Nicole Miller** • 63 E Oak St
- **Portico** • 834 N Rush St
- **Prada** • 30 E Oak St
- **Pratesi** • 67 E Oak St
- **Tod's** • 121 E Oak St
- **Ultimate Bride** • 106 E Oak St, 2nd Fl
- **Ultimo** • 114 E Oak St
- **Urban Outfitters** • 935 N Rush St
- **Water Tower** • 845 N Michigan Ave

Video Rental

- **Blockbuster Video** • 1201 N Clark St
- **Video Shmideo** • 907 N State St

WEST ROGERS PARK
Rogers Park
Indian Boundary Park
Lerner Park
Chippewa Park
Warren Park
Bernard Horwich JCC
High Ridge YMCA
Thillen's Stadium
Croatian Cultural Center
India Town
Rogers Park/ West Ridge Historical Society
Dobson St
W Howard St
W Jerome St
W Birchwood Ave
W Fargo Ave
W Jarvis Ave
W Sherwin Ave
W Chase Ave
W Jarlath St
W Touhy Ave
W Fitch Ave
W Estes Ave
W Greenleaf Ave
W Lunt Ave
W Coyle Ave
W Morse Ave
W Farwell Ave
W Pratt Ave
W North Shore Ave
W Albion Ave
W Arthur Ave
W Devon Ave
W Highland Ave
W Rosemont Ave
N Albany Ave
N Scramento Ave
N Fairfield Ave
N Talman Ave
N Maplewood Ave
N Artesian Ave
N Campbell Ave
N Oakley Ave
N Bell Ave
N Ridge Blvd
N Claremont Ave
N Hamilton Ave
N Washtenaw Ave
N Rockwell St
N Western Ave
N Richmond St
N Franscisco Ave
N Mozart St
N California Ave
N Whipple St
N Kedzie Ave
N Leavitt St
7600N
7200N
6800N
6400N
2800W
2400W
A
B
C
1
2
34
35
36

Turbans, tandoori chicken, fedoras, kosher pizza, saris, live chickens, and chop suey. Devon Ave is a chaotic global marketplace where shopkeepers know how to make a buck in any language. Devon is a parking lot on weekends. Walking is the only way to negotiate this tempting and tasty international stretch. Side streets off Pratt and Touhy look like Skokie with modest single-family homes on compact lots lining the surprisingly bucolic streets.

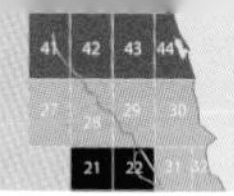

Car Rental

- **Avis** • 2250 W Devon Ave • 773-284-3640

Banks

- **Bank One** • 1763 W Howard
- **Bank One** • 7015 N Western Ave
- **Charter One Bank** • 1325 Howard St
- **Citibank** • 2801 W Devon Ave
- **Devon Bank** • 6445 N Western Ave
- **First Commercial Bank** • 2201 W Howard St
- **LaSalle Bank** • 2545 W Devon Ave
- **LaSalle Bank** • 2855 W Touhy Ave

Gas Stations

- **BP** • 7130 N Western Ave
- **Citgo Service Station** • Pratt and Western
- **Clark Oil & Refining** • 7050 N Western Ave
- **Marathon** • Touhy and Western

Landmarks

- **Bernard Horwich JCC** • 3003 W Touhy Ave
- **Croatian Cultural Center** • 2845 W Devon Ave
- **High Ridge YMCA** • 2430 W Touhy Ave
- **India Town** • Devon Street Indian strip
- **Indian Boundary Park** • 2500 W Lunt
- **Rogers Park / West Ridge Historical Society** • 6424 N Western Ave
- **Thillen's Stadium** • Devon & Kedzie
- **Warren Park** • 6601 N Western Ave

Libraries

- **Northtown Public Library** • 6435 N California Ave

Pharmacies

- **Osco Drug** • 2825 W Devon Ave
- **Walgreens** • 7510 N Western St

Pizza

- **Avraham's Ohel Pizza** • 2828 W Pratt Blvd
- **Barnaby's** • 2832 W Touhy Ave
- **Domino's** • 3144 W Devon Ave
- **Eastern Style Pizza** • 2911 W Touhy Ave
- **Gulliver's Pizzeria & Restaurant** • 2727 W Howard St
- **Pizza Hut** • 951 Howard St

Schools

- **Bethesda Lutheran School** • 6803 N Campbell Ave
- **Boone Elementary School** • 6710 N Washtenaw Ave
- **Brisk Rabbinical College** • 3000 W Devon Ave
- **Consolidated Hebrew High School** • 2828 W Pratt Blvd
- **Decatur Classical School** • 7030 N Sacramento Ave
- **George Armstrong Elementary School** • 2110 W Greenleaf Ave
- **Hanna Sacks Girls' High School** • 3021 W Devon Ave
- **Lubavitch Boys' High School** • 2756 W Morse Ave
- **Rogers Elementary School** • 7345 N Washtenaw Ave
- **St Margaret Mary School** • 7318 N Oakley Ave
- **St Scholastica High School** • 7416 N Ridge Blvd

Supermarkets

- **Dominick's** • 1763 W Howard St
- **Fresh Farms International Market** • 2626 W Devon Ave
- **Jewel Food Stores** • 2485 W Howard St
- **New York Kosher** • 2900 W Devon Ave

WEST ROGERS PARK
Rogers Park
Indian Boundary Park
Lerner Park
Chippewa Park
Warren Park
Dobson St
W Howard St
W Jerome St
W Birchwood Ave
W Fargo Ave
W Jarvis Ave
W Sherwin Ave
W Chase Ave
W Jarlath St
W Touhy Ave
W Fitch Ave
W Estes Ave
W Greenleaf Ave
W Lunt Ave
W Coyle Ave
W Morse Ave
W Farwell Ave
W Pratt Ave
W North Shore Ave
W Albion Ave
W Arthur Ave
W Devon Ave
W Highland Ave
W Rosemont Ave
N Albany Ave
N Scramento Ave
N Fairfield Ave
N Talman Ave
N Maplewood Ave
N Artesian Ave
N Oakley Ave
N Bell Ave
N Ridge Blvd
N Campbell Ave
N Claremont Ave
N Hamilton Ave
N Washtenaw Ave
N Rockwell St
N Western Ave
N Richmond St
N Francisco Ave
N Mozart St
N Whipple St
N California Ave
N Leavitt St
N Kedzie Ave
7600N
7200N
6800N
6400N
2800W
2400W
A
B
C
1
2
34
35
36

Just stand on a street corner and watch the world walk by. If you're feeling active, we recommend the batting cages at Indian Boundary Park. Warren Park's sledding hill makes for a great dog run. The fabrics at Taj Sari Palace on Devon are frameable art. See what's playing in India's theaters at Bombay Video. Inexpensive kebabs and tandoori are the fare of this 'hood.

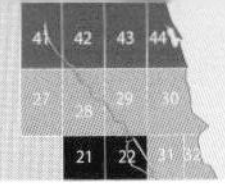

Bars

- **Cary's Lounge** • 2251 W Devon Ave
- **Mark II Chicago** • 7436 N Western Ave
- **McKellin's** • 2800 W Touhy Ave
- **Mullen's Sports Bar and Grill** • 7301 N Western Ave
- **Pinewood Inn** • 2310 W Touhy Ave

Hardware Stores

- **Basco Plumbing & True Value** • 2650 W Devon Ave
- **Coast To Coast Store** • 6942 N Western Ave

Liquor Stores

- **Adelphi Liquors** • 2351 W Devon Ave
- **Beatrice Liquor** • 2901 W Devon Ave
- **Extra Value Wine & Liquor** • 7300 N Western Ave
- **M & Y Liquor & Grocery Store** • 2252 W Devon Ave
- **Old City** • 2222 W Devon Ave
- **Western Liquor Store** • 6963 N Western Ave

Restaurants

- **Angus** • 7555 N Western Ave
- **Cafe Montenegro** • 6954 N Western Ave
- **Delhi Darbar Kabab House** • 6403 N California Ave
- **Desi Island** • 2401 W Devon Ave
- **Fluky's** • 6821 N Western Ave
- **Ghandi India Restaurant** • 2601 W Devon Ave
- **Gitel's Kosher Bakery** • 2745 W Devon Ave
- **Good Morgan Kosher Fish Market** • 2948 W Devon Ave
- **Hashalom** • 2905 W Devon Ave
- **Tiffin, The Indian Kitchen** • 2536 W Devon Ave
- **Udupi Palace** • 2543 W Devon Ave
- **Viceroy of India** • 2520 W Devon Ave

Shopping

- **Best Buy** • 2301 W Howard St
- **Cheesecakes by JR** • 2841 W Howard St
- **Chicago Harley Davidson** • 6868 N Western Ave
- **Office Mart** • 2801 W Touhy Ave
- **Office Max** • 2255 W Howard St
- **Snoop Shop Too** • 2742 W Touhy Ave
- **Taj Sari Palace** • 2553 W Devon Ave
- **Target** • 2209 W Howard St
- **Z'Afrique** • 7156 N California Ave

Video Rental

- **Atlantic Video Rentals (Indian)** • 2541 W Devon Ave
- **Blockbuster Video** • 7300 N Western Ave
- **Blockbuster Video** • 7574 N Western Ave
- **Bombay Video (Indian)** • 2634 W Devon Ave
- **Davika 5 Star Pan House (Indian)** • 2502 W Devon Ave
- **Elita Video (Russian)** • 2753 W Devon Ave
- **Golden Video** • 2761 W Devon Ave
- **Jai Hind Plaza** • 2658 W Devon Ave
- **New Devon Video** • 2304 W Devon Ave
- **New Jhankar Video (Indian)** • 2521 W Devon Ave
- **Super Star Video (Indian)** • 2538 W Devon Ave
- **Video Sonido** • 7117 N Ridge Blvd
- **Video Vision** • 2524 W Devon Ave
- **Western Video** • 7439 N Western Ave

ROGERS PARK
Rogers Ave Park & Beach
Howard St Park & Beach
Fargo Ave Park & Beach
Jarvis Ave Park & Beach
Sherwin Ave Park & Beach
Chase Ave Park & Beach
Leone Park & Beach
Loyola Beach
Loyola Park
Pratt Blvd Park & Beach
Columbia Ave Park & Beach
North Shore Ave Park & Beach
Hartigan Park & Beach
Loyola Univ
PAGE 220
Howard
Jarvis
Morse
Loyola
Rogers Park
Pottawattomie Park
Touhy Park
Paschen Park
Warren Park
Robert A Black Golf Course
W Howard St
N Rogers Ave
W Birchwood Ave
W Fargo Ave
W Jarvis Ave
W Sherwin Ave
W Chase Ave
W Touhy Ave
W Estes Ave
W Greenleaf Ave
W Lunt Ave
W Morse Ave
W Farwell Ave
W Pratt Blvd
W Columbia Ave
W North Shore Ave
W Wallen Ave
W Albion Ave
W Loyola Ave
W Arthur Ave
W Schreiber Ave
W Devon Ave
W Highland Ave
W Rosemont Ave
W Thorne Ave
W Sheridan R
N Ashland Ave
N Clark St
N Sheridan Rd
N Glenwood Ave
N Ridge Blvd
N Ridge Ave
N Ravenswood Ave
N Damen Ave
N Paulina St
N Hermitage Ave
N Marshfield Ave
N Greenview Ave
N Wolcott Ave
N Winchester Ave
N Seeley Ave
N Hoyne Ave
N Hamilton Ave
N Honore St
N Wayne Ave
N Lakewood Ave
N Magnolia Ave
N Winthrop Ave
N Bosworth Ave
N Newgard Ave
Elmwood Ave
Callan Ave
Clyde Ave
7600N
7200N
6800N
6400N
2000W
1600W
1200W
33
36
37
A
B
C
1
2

Students, seniors, liberals, and everyday urbanites mix in East Rogers Park. Loyola University anchors the southwest corner of the neighborhood. Renovated three-flats flank the tree-lined streets west of campus. A wall of ugly high-rises line the lake. Sheridan Rd. traffic heading into suburban Evanston is hellish during rush hours and on weekends.

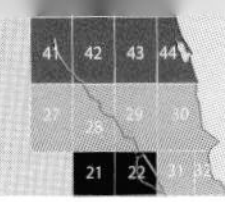

Banks

- **Bank One** • 6623 N Damen Ave
- **First Commercial Bank** • 6930 N Clark St
- **Harris Trust & Savings Bank** • 6538 N Sheridan Rd
- **LaSalle Bank** • 7516 N Clark St
- **MB Financial Bank** • 6443 N Sheridan Rd

Car Washes

- **Roger's Park Hand Car Wash** • 6828 N Clark St

Gas Stations

- **BP** • 1841 W Devon Ave
- **BP** • 7550 N Sheridan Rd
- **Citgo** • 1500 W Devon Ave
- **Citgo** • 7138 N Sheridan Rd
- **Marathon** • 555 Howard St
- **Sak's Service** • 7201 N Clark St
- **Shell** • 6346 N Clark St
- **Shell** • 6401 N Ridge Blvd

Landmarks

- **Robert A Black Golf Course** • 2045 W Pratt

Libraries

- **Rogers Park Public Library** • 6907 N Clark St

Pharmacies

- **Osco Drug** • 1425 W Morse St

Pizza

- **Alberto's Pizza** • 1324 W Morse Ave
- **Carmen's of Loyola Pizzeria** • 6568 N Sheridan Rd
- **Giordano's** • 6836 N Sheridan Rd
- **Hamilton's Pizza & Pub** • 6341 N Broadway St
- **J B Alberto's Pizza** • 1326 W Morse Ave
- **Leona's** • 6935 N Sheridan Rd
- **Riccardo's Pizza** • 6349 N Clark St
- **Vince's Pizzeria** • 1527 W Devon Ave

Police

- **24th District (Rogers Park)** • 6464 N Clark St

Post Offices

- 1723 W Devon Ave
- 7056 N Clark St
- 7617 N Paulina St

Schools

- **Field Elementary School** • 7019 N Ashland Blvd
- **Jordan Community School** • 7414 N Wolcott Ave
- **Joyce Kilmer School** • 6700 N Greenview Ave
- **Loyola University of Chicago** • 6525 N Sheridan Rd
- **North Shore School** • 1217 W Chase Ave
- **Sullivan High School** • 6631 N Bosworth Ave
- **Waldorf School of Chicago** • 1300 W Loyola Ave

Supermarkets

- **Art's Grocery** • 6333 N Clark St
- **Dominick's** • 1763 W Howard St
- **Dominick's** • 6623 N Damen Ave
- **Greenleaf Natural Grocery Company** • 1261 W Loyola Ave
- **Rogers Park Fruit Market** • 7401 N Clark St

Parking

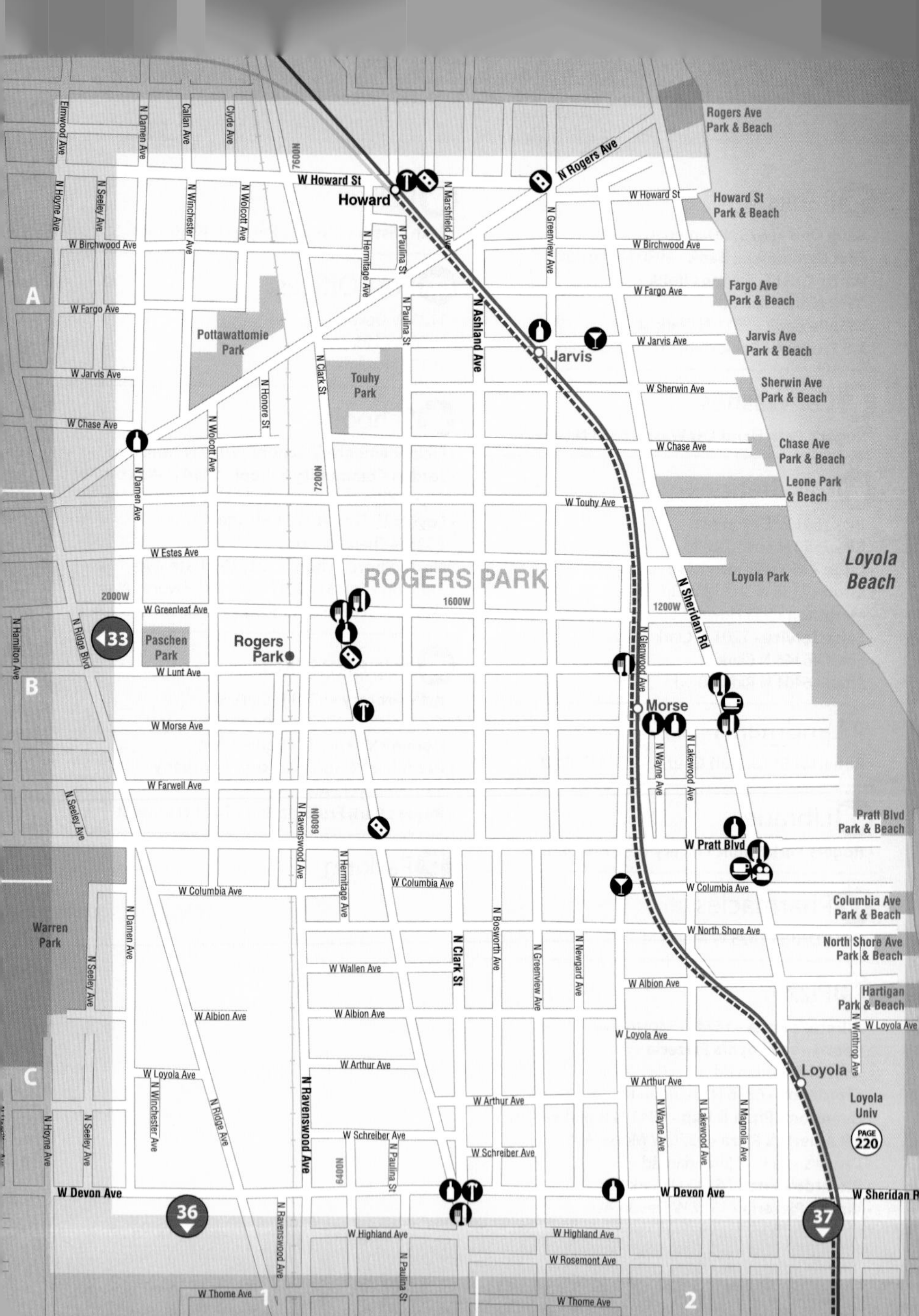
ROGERS PARK
Rogers Park
Howard
Jarvis
Morse
Loyola
Rogers Ave Park & Beach
Howard St Park & Beach
Fargo Ave Park & Beach
Jarvis Ave Park & Beach
Sherwin Ave Park & Beach
Chase Ave Park & Beach
Leone Park & Beach
Loyola Park
Loyola Beach
Pratt Blvd Park & Beach
Columbia Ave Park & Beach
North Shore Ave Park & Beach
Hartigan Park & Beach
Loyola Univ
Pottawattomie Park
Touhy Park
Paschen Park
Warren Park
W Howard St
N Rogers Ave
W Birchwood Ave
W Fargo Ave
W Jarvis Ave
W Sherwin Ave
W Chase Ave
W Touhy Ave
W Estes Ave
W Greenleaf Ave
W Lunt Ave
W Morse Ave
W Farwell Ave
W Pratt Blvd
W Columbia Ave
W North Shore Ave
W Wallen Ave
W Albion Ave
W Loyola Ave
W Arthur Ave
W Schreiber Ave
W Devon Ave
W Sheridan Rd
W Highland Ave
W Rosemont Ave
W Thome Ave
N Ashland Ave
N Clark St
N Sheridan Rd
N Ridge Blvd
N Ridge Ave
N Ravenswood Ave
N Damen Ave
N Paulina St
N Glenwood Ave
N Greenview Ave
N Wayne Ave
N Lakewood Ave
N Magnolia Ave
N Winthrop Ave
N Bosworth Ave
N Newgard Ave
N Hermitage Ave
N Marshfield Ave
N Honore St
N Wolcott Ave
N Winchester Ave
N Seeley Ave
N Hoyne Ave
N Hamilton Ave
Elmwood Ave
Callan Ave
Clyde Ave
7600N
7200N
6800N
6400N
2000W
1600W
1200W
33
36
37
PAGE 220
A
B
C
1
2

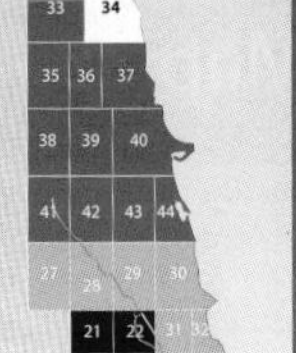

For a university neighborhood, the bar scene is barren. Lots of liquor stores supply the campus parties. Funky Heartland Café on Glenwood keeps flower power alive. Granola crunchers dig the vegetarian menu and health food store. Groove to live music including excellent folk and reggae. In summer, we recommend hanging out on the patio in your tie-dye T-shirt.

Bars

- **Don's Coffee Club** • 1439 W Jarvis Ave
- **No Exit** • 6730 N Glenwood Ave

Coffee

- **Ennui** • 6981 N Sheridan Rd
- **Light of the Moon** • 525 Howard St
- **Panini Cafe House** • 6764 N Sheridan Rd
- **Starbucks** • 6738 N Sheridan Rd

Hardware Stores

- **Ace Hardware** • 6955 N Clark St
- **Clark-Devon Hardware** • 6401 N Clark St
- **Northside Hardware** • 1640 W Howard St

Liquor Stores

- **Dino's Liquors** • 6400 N Clark St
- **Golden Valley Liquors** • 1339 W Morse Ave
- **Hahn Liquors** • 1410 W Devon Ave
- **Isam's Food & Liquor** • 6816 N Sheridan Rd
- **Jarvis Liquors** • 1508 W Jarvis Ave
- **Lunt-Liquors** • 7016 N Clark St
- **Morse Liquors** • 1400 W Morse Ave
- **Summit Grocery** • 7300 N Rogers Ave

Movie Theaters

- **Village North Theaters** • 6746 N Sheridan Rd

Restaurants

- **Deluxe Diner** • 6349 N Clark St
- **El Famous Burrito** • 7047 N Clark St
- **Ennui Cafe** • 6981 N Sheridan Rd
- **Heartland Café** • 7000 N Glenwood Ave
- **Panini Panini** • 6764 N Sheridan Rd
- **Tien Tsin** • 7018 N Clark St

Shopping

- **Mar-Jen Discount Furniture** • 1536 W Devon Ave

Video Rental

- **Blockbuster Video** • 7007 N Clark St
- **Hollywood Video** • 1751 W Howard St
- **Lakeside Mini Mart** • 6755 N Sheridan Rd
- **Syed Video** • 6808 N Clark St
- **United Video** • 1508 W Howard St

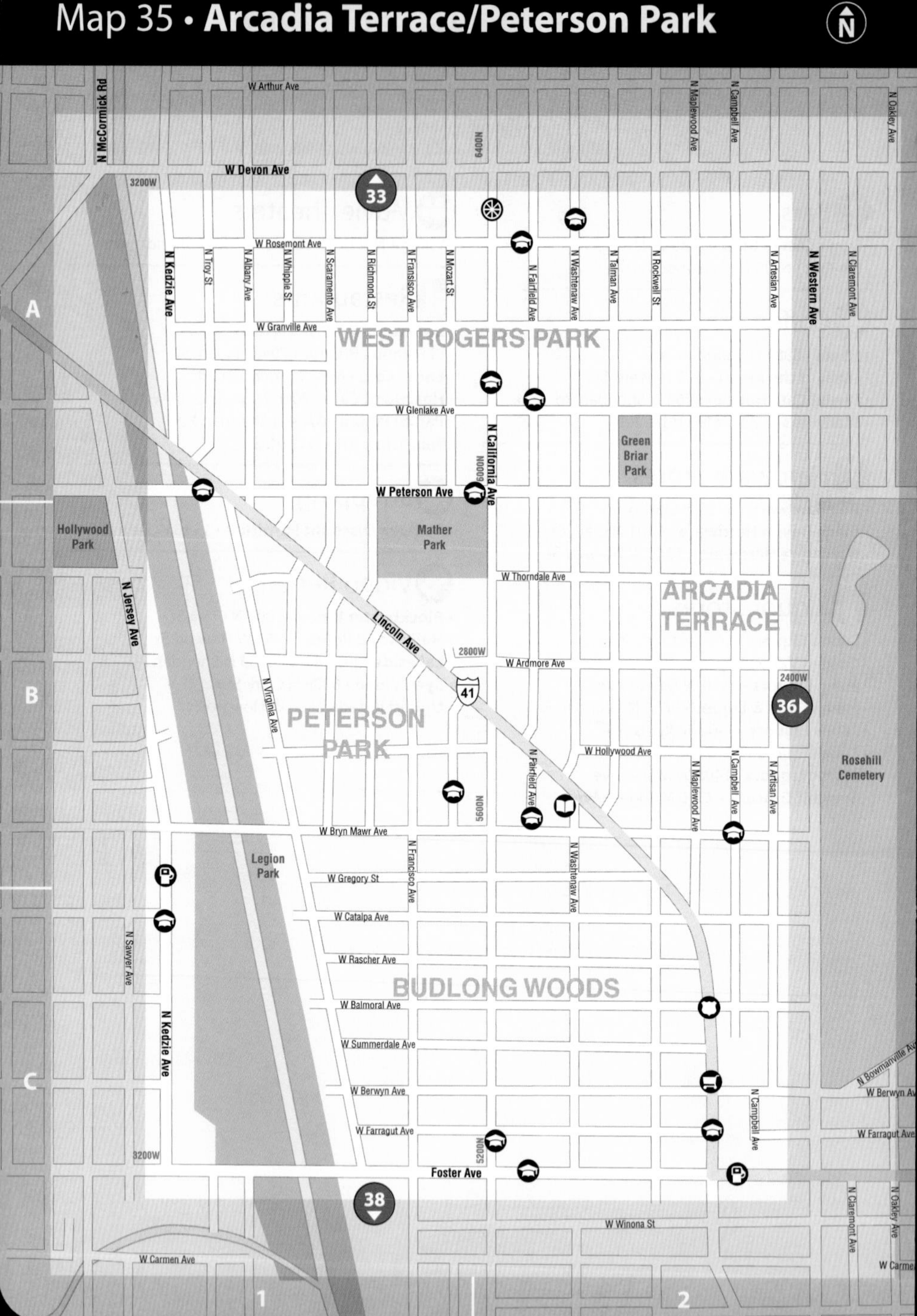
N
W Arthur Ave
N McCormick Rd
N Maplewood Ave
N Campbell Ave
N Oakley Ave
6400N
W Devon Ave
3200W
33
W Rosemont Ave
N Kedzie Ave
N Troy St
N Albany Ave
N Whipple St
N Scaramento Ave
N Richmond St
N Fransisco Ave
N Mozart St
N Fairfield Ave
N Washtenaw Ave
N Talman Ave
N Rockwell St
N Artesian Ave
N Western Ave
N Claremont Ave
A
W Granville Ave
WEST ROGERS PARK
W Glenlake Ave
N California Ave
6000N
Green Briar Park
W Peterson Ave
Hollywood Park
Mather Park
W Thorndale Ave
N Jersey Ave
ARCADIA TERRACE
Lincoln Ave
2800W
W Ardmore Ave
2400W
B
N Virginia Ave
41
PETERSON PARK
36
W Hollywood Ave
Rosehill Cemetery
N Maplewood Ave
N Campbell Ave
N Artisan Ave
5600N
W Bryn Mawr Ave
Legion Park
W Gregory St
N Francisco Ave
N Washtenaw Ave
W Catalpa Ave
N Sawyer Ave
W Rascher Ave
BUDLONG WOODS
W Balmoral Ave
N Kedzie Ave
W Summerdale Ave
N Bowmanville Ave
C
W Berwyn Ave
N Campbell Ave
W Berwyn Ave
W Farragut Ave
W Farragut Ave
3200W
5200N
Foster Ave
38
N Claremont Ave
N Oakley Ave
W Winona St
W Carmen Ave
W Carmen
1
2

Near, Middle, and Far East meet in Arcadia Terrace and Peterson Park.

Gas Stations

- **BP** • 5547 N Kedzie Ave
- **Citgo** • 2464 W Foster Ave

Libraries

- **Budlong Woods Public Library** • 5630 N Lincoln Ave

Pizza

- **Tel Aviv Kosher Pizza** • 6349 N California Ave

Police

- **20th District (Foster)** • 5400 N Lincoln Ave

Schools

- **Bais Yaakov School** • 6122 N California Ave
- **Budlong Elementary School** • 2701 W Foster Ave
- **Cheder Lubavitch Girls' High School** • 2754 W Rosemont Ave
- **Clinton Elementary School** • 6110 N Fairfield Ave
- **Jamieson Elementary School** • 5650 N Mozart St
- **Jewish Children's Bureau School** • 6014 N California Ave
- **Joan Dachs Bais Yaakov School** • 3200 W Peterson Ave
- **Northside College Prepatory** • 5501 N Kedzie Ave
- **Seventh-Day Adventist School** • 5220 N California Ave
- **St Hillary's School** • 5614 N Fairfield Ave
- **St Philip Evangelical Lutheran** • 2500 W Bryn Mawr Ave
- **St Timothy's School** • 6330 N Washtenaw Ave

Supermarkets

- **Dominick's** • 5233 N Lincoln Ave
- **Super Buy Farmer's Market and Deli** • 5300 N Lincoln Ave

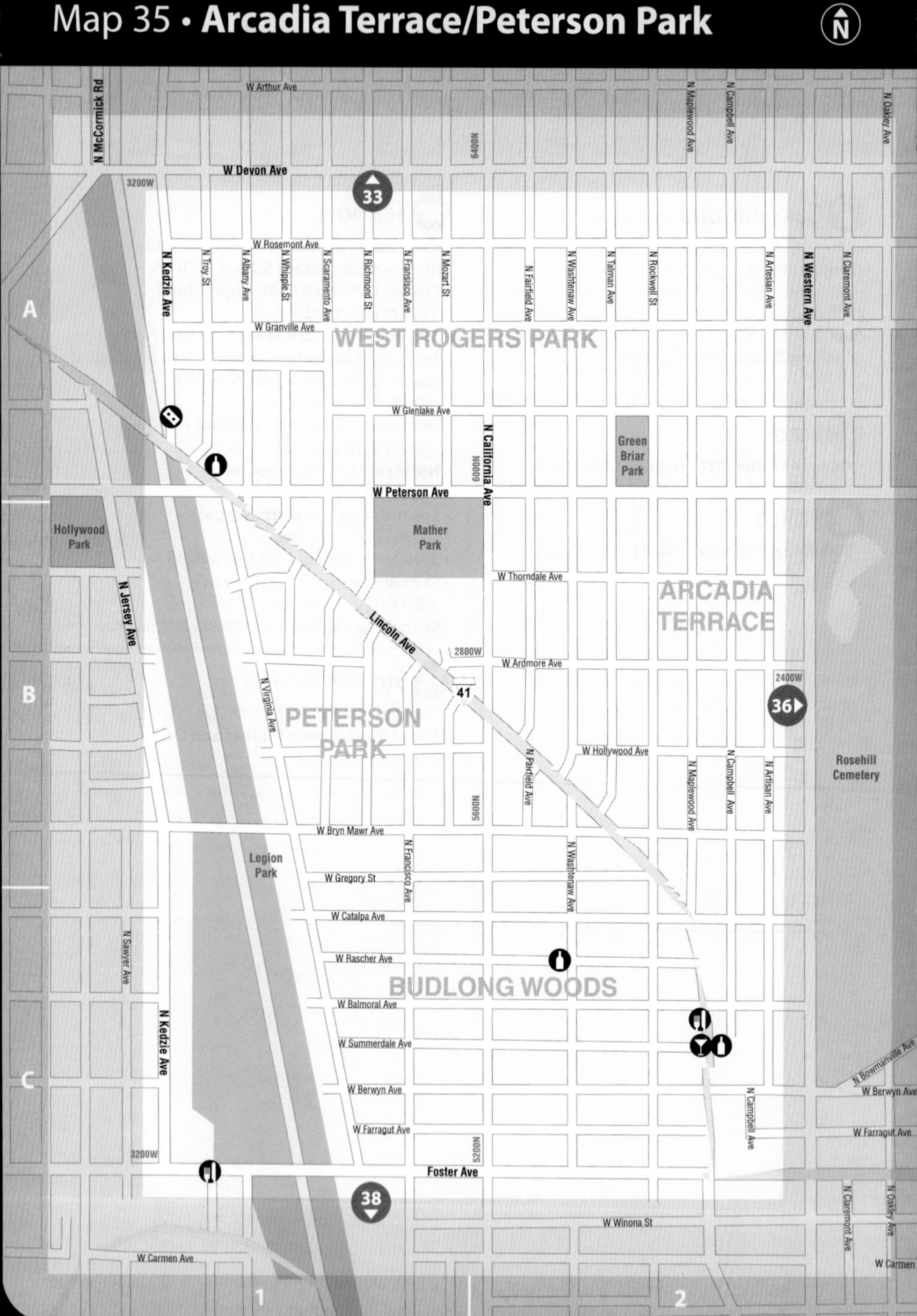
N
W Arthur Ave
N McCormick Rd
N Maplewood Ave
N Campbell Ave
N Oakley Ave
6400N
W Devon Ave
3200W
33
W Rosemont Ave
N Kedzie Ave
N Troy St
N Albany Ave
N Whipple St
N Sacramento Ave
N Richmond St
N Francisco Ave
N Mozart St
N Fairfield Ave
N Washtenaw Ave
N Talman Ave
N Rockwell St
N Artesian Ave
N Western Ave
N Claremont Ave
A
W Granville Ave
WEST ROGERS PARK
W Glenlake Ave
N California Ave
6000N
Green Briar Park
W Peterson Ave
Hollywood Park
Mather Park
W Thorndale Ave
N Jersey Ave
ARCADIA TERRACE
Lincoln Ave
2800W
W Ardmore Ave
2400W
41
B
N Virginia Ave
PETERSON PARK
36
W Hollywood Ave
Rosehill Cemetery
N Artisan Ave
5600N
W Bryn Mawr Ave
Legion Park
W Gregory St
W Catalpa Ave
N Sawyer Ave
W Rascher Ave
BUDLONG WOODS
W Balmoral Ave
W Summerdale Ave
N Bowmanville Ave
C
W Berwyn Ave
W Farragut Ave
5200N
Foster Ave
38
W Winona St
W Carmen Ave
W Carmen
1
2

Cruise Western Ave.'s car dealerships.

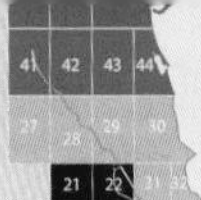

Bars

- **Hidden Cove** • 5336 N Lincoln Ave
- **Hollywood Lounge** • 3301 W Bryn Mawr Ave

Liquor Stores

- **Buy Low Liquors** • 6015 N Lincoln Ave
- **Eden Liquor Store & Foods** • 5359 N Lincoln Ave

Restaurants

- **Charcoal Delights** • 3139 W Foster Ave
- **Fondue Stube** • 2717 W Peterson Ave
- **Garden Buffet** • 5347 N Lincoln Ave

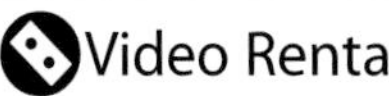

Video Rental

- **Lincoln Square Video II** • 6035 N Kedzie Ave

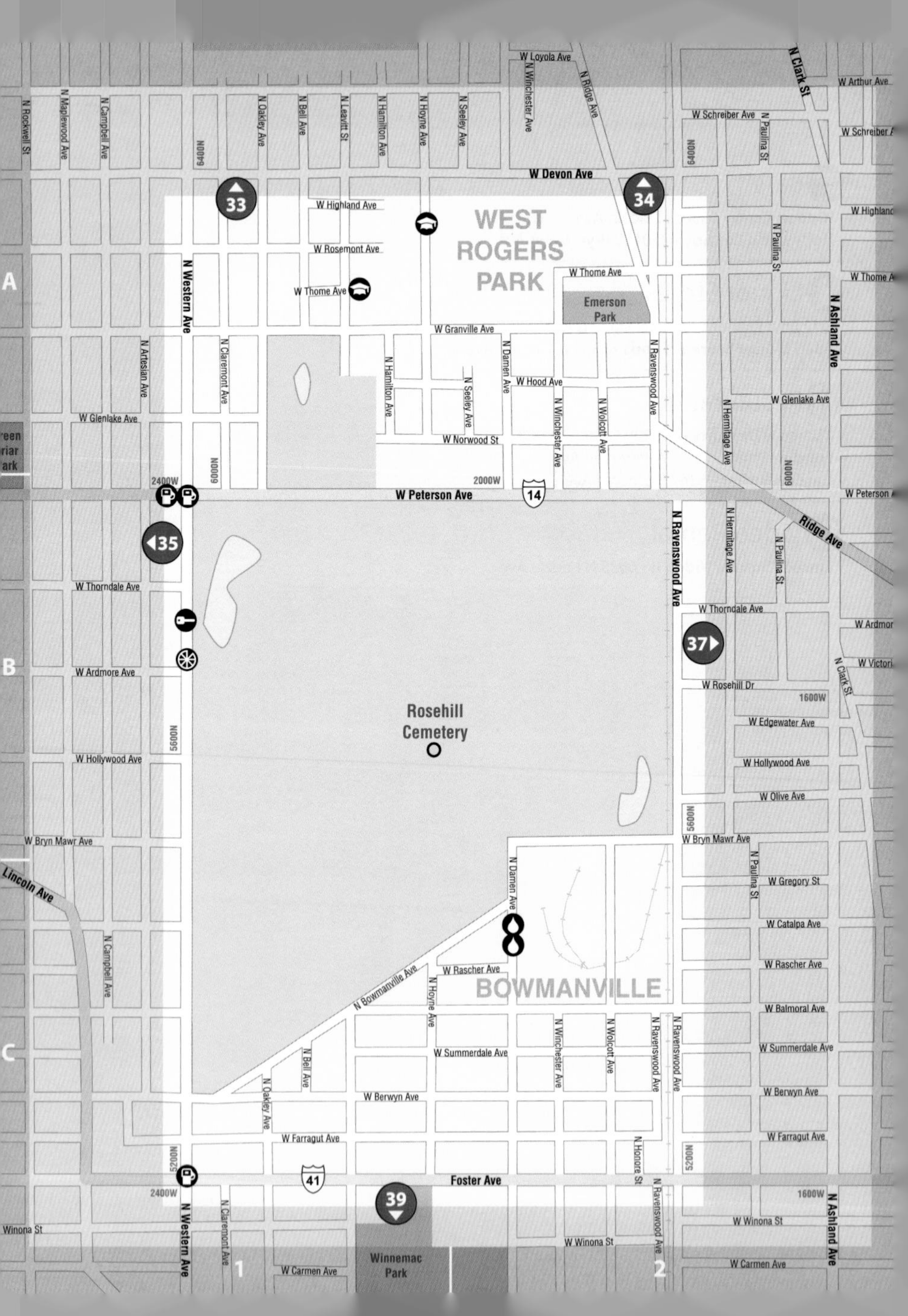

WEST ROGERS PARK
Emerson Park
Rosehill Cemetery
BOWMANVILLE
Winnemac Park
W Devon Ave
W Peterson Ave
Foster Ave
N Western Ave
N Ravenswood Ave
N Ashland Ave
N Clark St
Ridge Ave
Lincoln Ave
N Ridge Ave
W Loyola Ave
W Arthur Ave
W Schreiber Ave
W Highland Ave
W Rosemont Ave
W Thome Ave
W Granville Ave
W Hood Ave
W Glenlake Ave
W Norwood St
W Thorndale Ave
W Ardmore Ave
W Victoria
W Rosehill Dr
W Edgewater Ave
W Hollywood Ave
W Olive Ave
W Bryn Mawr Ave
W Gregory St
W Catalpa Ave
W Rascher Ave
W Balmoral Ave
W Summerdale Ave
W Berwyn Ave
W Farragut Ave
W Winona St
Winona St
W Carmen Ave
N Bowmanville Ave
N Rockwell St
N Maplewood Ave
N Campbell Ave
N Oakley Ave
N Bell Ave
N Leavitt St
N Hamilton Ave
N Hoyne Ave
N Seeley Ave
N Winchester Ave
N Paulina St
N Artesian Ave
N Claremont Ave
N Damen Ave
N Wolcott Ave
N Hermitage Ave
N Honore St
2400W
2000W
1600W
6400N
6000N
5600N
5200N
14
41
33
34
35
37
39
A
B
C
1
2

Bryn Mawr is residential—living and dead. Rosehill Cemetery takes up much of the neighborhood's real estate. The magnificent mausoleum houses mail-order magnates Montgomery Ward and Richard Warren Sears. Bryn Mawr has affordable homes, turn-of-the-century apartment buildings, and a burgeoning art scene.

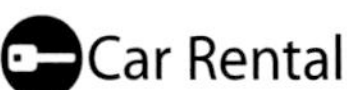

Car Rental

- **Enterprise** • 5844 N Western Ave • 773-989-3390

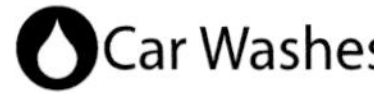

Car Washes

- **Norwood 2 Hand Carwash** • 5462 N Damen Ave
- **Superior Super Car Wash** • 5450 N Damen Ave

Gas Stations

- **Citgo** • 1840 W Peterson Ave
- **Shell** • 5201 N Western Ave
- **Shell** • 6000 N Western Ave

Landmarks

- **Rosehill Cemetery and Mausoleum** • 5800 N Ravenswood Ave

Pizza

- **Delisi's Pizzeria** • 5806 N Western Ave

Schools

- **Northside Catholic Academy** • 6325 N Hoyne Ave
- **Stone Scholastic Academy** • 6239 N Leavitt St

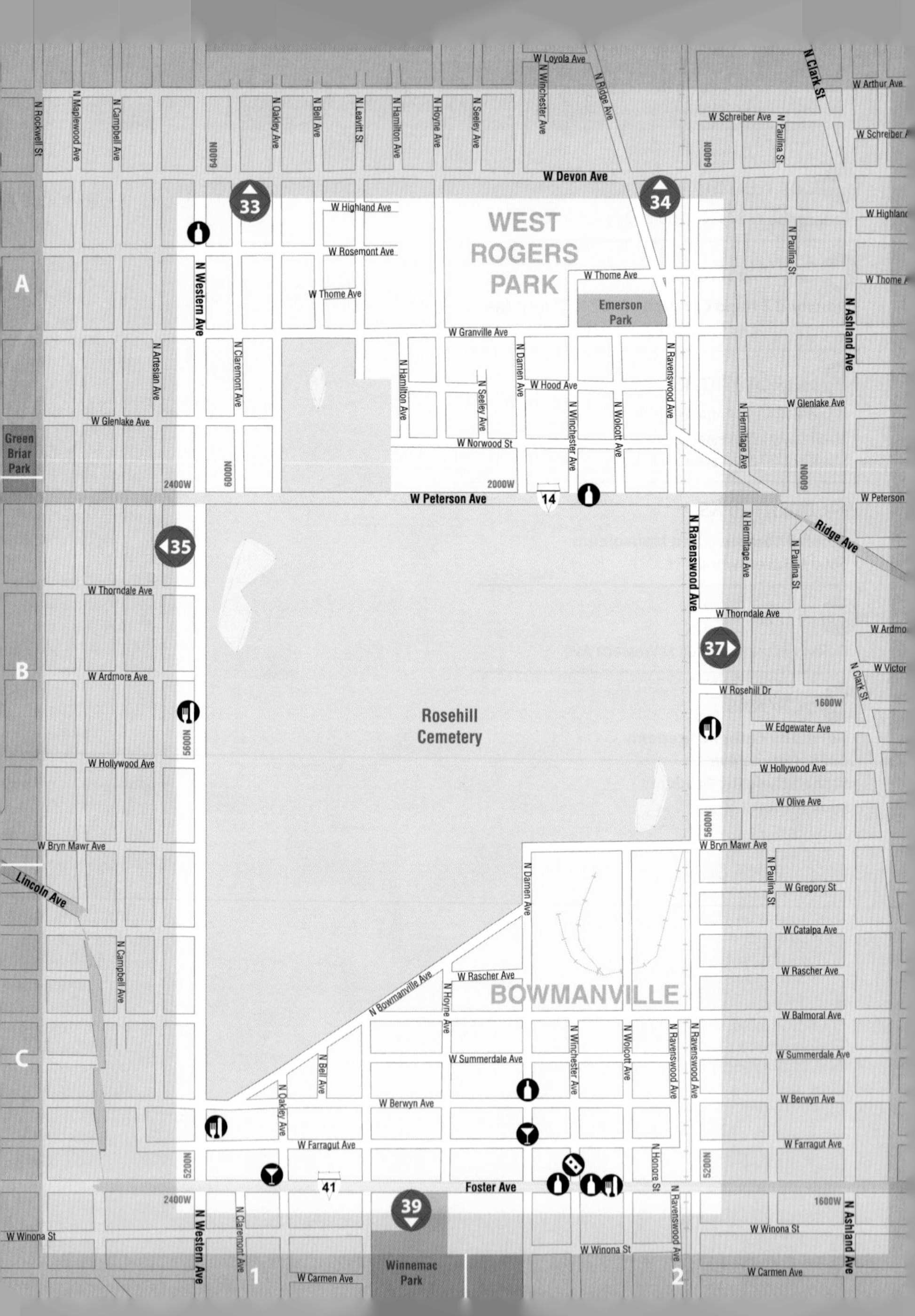
WEST ROGERS PARK
Emerson Park
Green Briar Park
Rosehill Cemetery
BOWMANVILLE
Winnemac Park
W Loyola Ave
N Clark St
W Arthur Ave
W Schreiber Ave
W Devon Ave
W Highland Ave
W Rosemont Ave
W Thome Ave
W Granville Ave
W Hood Ave
W Norwood St
W Glenlake Ave
W Peterson Ave
Ridge Ave
W Thorndale Ave
W Ardmore Ave
W Rosehill Dr
W Edgewater Ave
W Hollywood Ave
W Olive Ave
W Bryn Mawr Ave
Lincoln Ave
W Gregory St
W Catalpa Ave
W Rascher Ave
W Balmoral Ave
W Summerdale Ave
W Berwyn Ave
W Farragut Ave
Foster Ave
W Winona St
W Carmen Ave
N Bowmanville Ave
N Rockwell St
N Maplewood Ave
N Campbell Ave
N Western Ave
N Oakley Ave
N Bell Ave
N Leavitt St
N Hamilton Ave
N Hoyne Ave
N Seeley Ave
N Winchester Ave
N Ridge Ave
N Paulina St
N Ashland Ave
N Artesian Ave
N Claremont Ave
N Damen Ave
N Wolcott Ave
N Ravenswood Ave
N Hermitage Ave
N Honore St
6400N
6000N
5600N
5200N
2400W
2000W
1600W
33
34
35
37
39
14
41
A
B
C
1
2

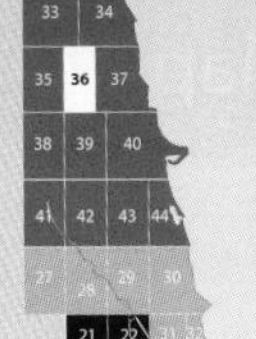

Bryn Mawr residents say that Rosehill Cemetery's mausoleum is haunted. Stop by local taverns where ghost stories might come up in the bar talk.

Bars

- **Claddagh Ring** • 2306 W Foster Ave
- **Leadway Bar & Cafe** • 5233 N Damen Ave

Liquor Stores

- **A & B Grocery & Liquors** • 6320 N Western Ave
- **Aces & Eights** • 5306 N Damen Ave
- **Diala Grocery & Liquor** • 1935 W Foster Ave
- **Foster Food & Liquor** • 1900 W Foster Ave
- **L & M Food & Liquor** • 1958 W Peterson Ave

Restaurants

- **El Tipico** • 1836 W Foster Ave
- **Fireside Restaurant & Lounge** • 5739 N Ravenswood Ave
- **Max's Italian Beef** • 5754 N Western Avenue
- **San Soo Gap San Korean Restaurant and Sushi House** • 5247 N Western Ave

Video Rental

- **Foster Video** • 1931 W Foster Ave

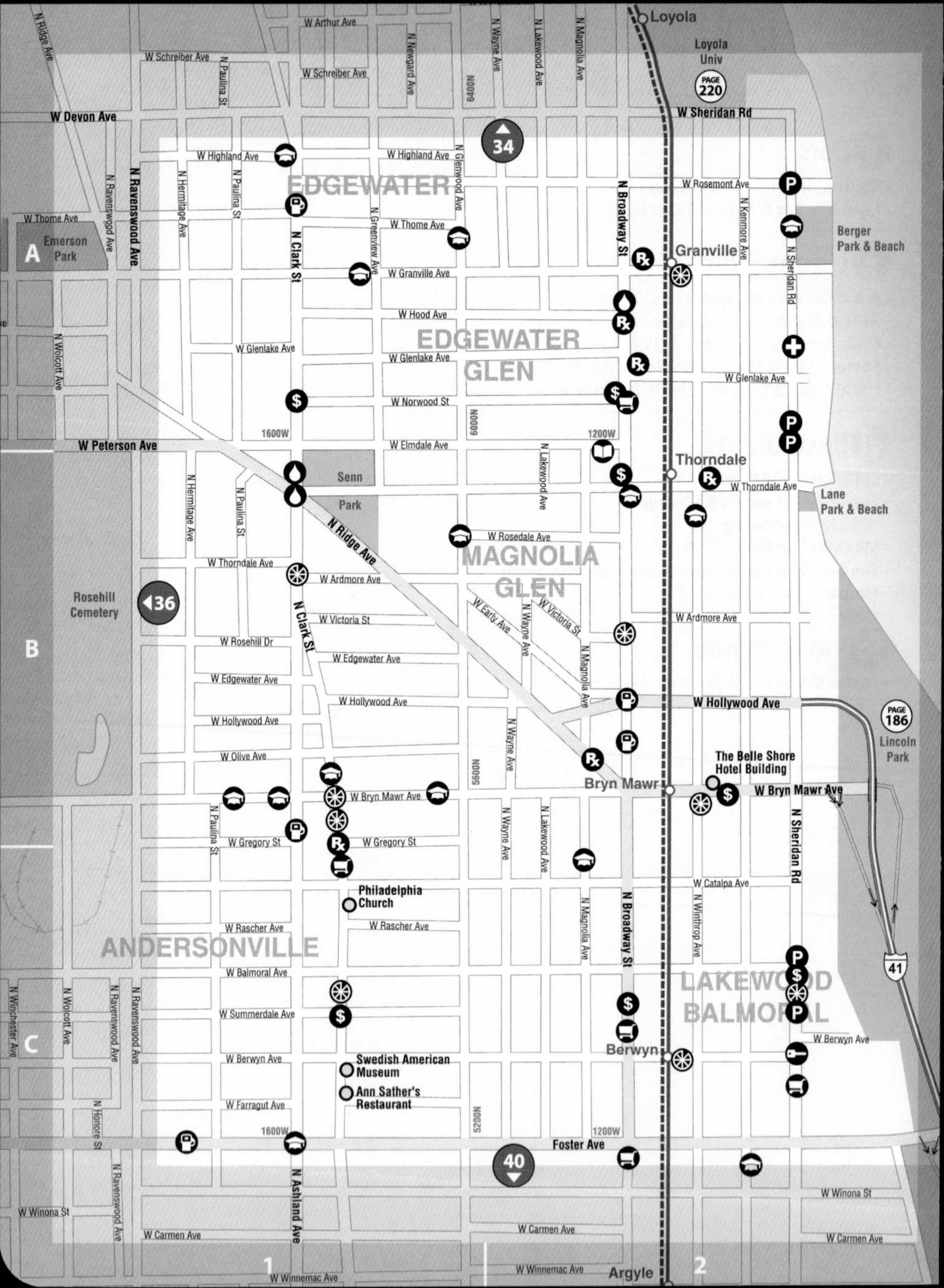

Map 37 • Edgewater/Andersonville

N Ridge Ave
W Arthur Ave
W Schreiber Ave
W Schreiber Ave
N Paulina St
N Newgard Ave
6400N
N Wayne Ave
N Lakewood Ave
N Magnolia Ave
Loyola
Loyola Univ
PAGE 220
W Devon Ave
W Sheridan Rd
34
W Highland Ave
W Highland Ave
EDGEWATER
N Glenwood Ave
N Ravenswood Ave
N Ravenswood Ave
N Hermitage Ave
N Paulina St
N Broadway St
W Rosemont Ave
W Thome Ave
Emerson Park
A
N Clark St
N Greenview Ave
W Thome Ave
N Kenmore Ave
Berger Park & Beach
Granville
N Sheridan Rd
W Granville Ave
W Hood Ave
EDGEWATER GLEN
N Wolcott Ave
W Glenlake Ave
W Glenlake Ave
W Glenlake Ave
W Norwood St
6000N
1600W
1200W
W Peterson Ave
W Elmdale Ave
N Lakewood Ave
Thorndale
Senn Park
W Thorndale Ave
Lane Park & Beach
N Hermitage Ave
N Paulina St
N Ridge Ave
W Rosedale Ave
W Thorndale Ave
MAGNOLIA GLEN
W Ardmore Ave
Rosehill Cemetery
36
N Clark St
W Victoria St
W Early Ave
N Wayne Ave
W Victoria St
W Ardmore Ave
B
W Rosehill Dr
W Edgewater Ave
N Magnolia Ave
W Edgewater Ave
W Hollywood Ave
W Hollywood Ave
PAGE 186
Lincoln Park
W Hollywood Ave
N Wayne Ave
W Olive Ave
5600N
The Belle Shore Hotel Building
Bryn Mawr
W Bryn Mawr Ave
W Bryn Mawr Ave
N Paulina St
N Wayne Ave
N Lakewood Ave
N Sheridan Rd
W Gregory St
W Gregory St
Philadelphia Church
W Catalpa Ave
N Magnolia Ave
N Broadway St
N Winthrop Ave
W Rascher Ave
W Rascher Ave
ANDERSONVILLE
41
W Balmoral Ave
LAKEWOOD BALMORAL
N Winchester Ave
N Wolcott Ave
N Ravenswood Ave
N Ravenswood Ave
W Summerdale Ave
C
W Berwyn Ave
Swedish American Museum
Berwyn
W Berwyn Ave
Ann Sather's Restaurant
W Farragut Ave
N Honore St
5200N
1600W
1200W
Foster Ave
40
N Ravenswood Ave
N Ashland Ave
W Winona St
W Winona St
W Carmen Ave
W Carmen Ave
W Carmen Ave
1
2
W Winnemac Ave
W Winnemac Ave
Argyle

Essentials

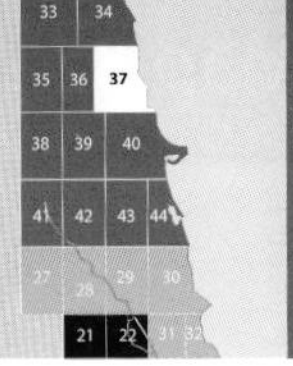

A range of housing types and small businesses (neighborhood groups start grumbling whenever the chains come knocking), along with cultural diversity make Andersonville and Edgewater bastions for lakefront. Besides beautiful residential areas and stroll-friendly commercial disctricts, Edgewater boasts the city's gay beach at Hollywood.

Banks

- **Bank One** • 6009 N Broadway St
- **Broadway Bank** • 5960 N Broadway St
- **North Community Bank** • 5342 N Broadway
- **Uptown National Bank** • 1058 W Bryn Mawr Ave
- **Uptown National Bank** • 5345 N Sheridan Rd
- **Uptown National Bank** • 6041 N Clark St
- **US Bank** • 5340 N Clark St

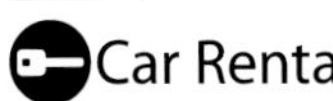

Car Rental

- **Enterprise** • 5313 N Sheridan Rd • 773-271-4500

Car Washes

- **Snappy Hand Car Wash** • 5961 N Ridge Ave
- **Super Spray Car Wash** • 5970 N Clark St
- **Superior Hand Car Wash** • 6147 N Broadway St

Gas Stations

- **BP** • 5657 N Broadway St
- **Clark Oil** • 1745 W Foster Ave
- **Marathon** • 5550 N Ashland Ave
- **Marathon** • 6262 N Clark St
- **Shell** • 5701 N Broadway St

Hospitals

- **Kindred Chicago Lakeshore** • 6130 N Sheridan Rd

Landmarks

- **Ann Sather's Restaurant** • 5207 N Clark St
- **Philadelphia Church** • 5437 N Clark St
- **Swedish American Museum** • 5211 N Clark St
- **The Belle Shore Hotel Building** • 1062 W Bryn Mawr Ave

Libraries

- **Edgewater Public Library** • 1210 W Elmdale Ave

Pharmacies

- **Granville Medical Pharmacy** • 1148 W Granville Ave
- **Osco Drug** • 5345 N Broadway St
- **Osco Drug** • 5516 N Clark St
- **Osco Drug** • 6150 N Broadway St
- **Thorndale Pharmacy** • 1104 W Thorndale Ave
- **Walgreens** • 5625 N Ridge Ave
- **Walgreens** • 6125 N Broadway St

Pizza

- **Barry's Spot Pizza** • 5759 N Broadway St
- **Calo Pizzeria Restaurant** • 5343 N Clark St
- **Domino's** • 5912 N Clark St
- **Franko's Pizza Express** • 1109 W Bryn Mawr Ave
- **Gino's North Pizzeria** • 1111 W Granville Ave
- **Monticello Pizzeria** • 5539 N Clark St
- **Pizzeria Aroma** • 1125 W Berwyn Ave
- **Primo Pizza** • 5600 N Clark St
- **Tedino's** • 5335 N Sheridan Rd

Schools

- **Hayt Elementary School** • 1518 W Granville Ave
- **Jose Marti Bilingual Education** • 5126 N Kenmore Ave
- **Lake Shore Schools** • 5611 N Clark St
- **Northside Catholic Academy** • 5525 N Magnolia Ave
- **Northside Catholic Academy** • 1643 W Bryn Mawr Ave
- **Northside Catholic Academy** • 6216 N Glenwood Ave
- **Peirce Elementary School** • 1423 W Bryn Mawr Ave
- **Rogers Park Montessori School** • 1244 W Thorndale Ave
- **Sacred Heart Schools Hardy** • 6250 N Sheridan Rd
- **Senn High School** • 5900 N Glenwood Ave
- **St Gregory's High School** • 1677 W Bryn Mawr Ave
- **Swift Elementary School** • 5900 N Winthrop Ave
- **Trumbull Elementary School** • 5200 N Ashland Ave

Supermarkets

- **DelRay Farms** • 5205 N Broadway St
- **Dominick's** • 5235 N Sheridan Rd
- **Dominick's** • 6009 N Broadway St
- **Jewel-Osco** • 5345 N Broadway St
- **Jewel-Osco** • 5516 N Clark St

Parking

N

Loyola
Loyola Univ
PAGE 220
W Sheridan Rd
W Devon Ave
W Arthur Ave
W Schreiber Ave
W Highland Ave
W Rosemont Ave
W Thome Ave
W Granville Ave
W Hood Ave
W Glenlake Ave
W Norwood St
W Peterson Ave
W Elmdale Ave
W Thorndale Ave
W Rosedale Ave
W Ardmore Ave
W Victoria St
W Rosehill Dr
W Edgewater Ave
W Hollywood Ave
W Olive Ave
W Bryn Mawr Ave
W Gregory St
W Catalpa Ave
W Rascher Ave
W Balmoral Ave
W Summerdale Ave
W Berwyn Ave
W Farragut Ave
Foster Ave
W Winona St
W Carmen Ave
W Winnemac Ave
W Early Ave
N Ridge Ave
N Clark St
N Ravenswood Ave
N Hermitage Ave
N Paulina St
N Wolcott Ave
N Winchester Ave
N Honore St
N Ashland Ave
N Greenview Ave
N Newgard Ave
N Glenwood Ave
N Wayne Ave
N Lakewood Ave
N Magnolia Ave
N Broadway St
N Kenmore Ave
N Winthrop Ave
N Sheridan Rd
6400N
6000N
5600N
5200N
1600W
1200W
EDGEWATER
EDGEWATER GLEN
MAGNOLIA GLEN
ANDERSONVILLE
LAKEWOOD BALMORAL
Emerson Park
Senn Park
Rosehill Cemetery
Berger Park & Beach
Lane Park & Beach
Lincoln Park
PAGE 186
Granville
Thorndale
Bryn Mawr
Berwyn
Argyle
34
36
40
41
A
B
C
1
2

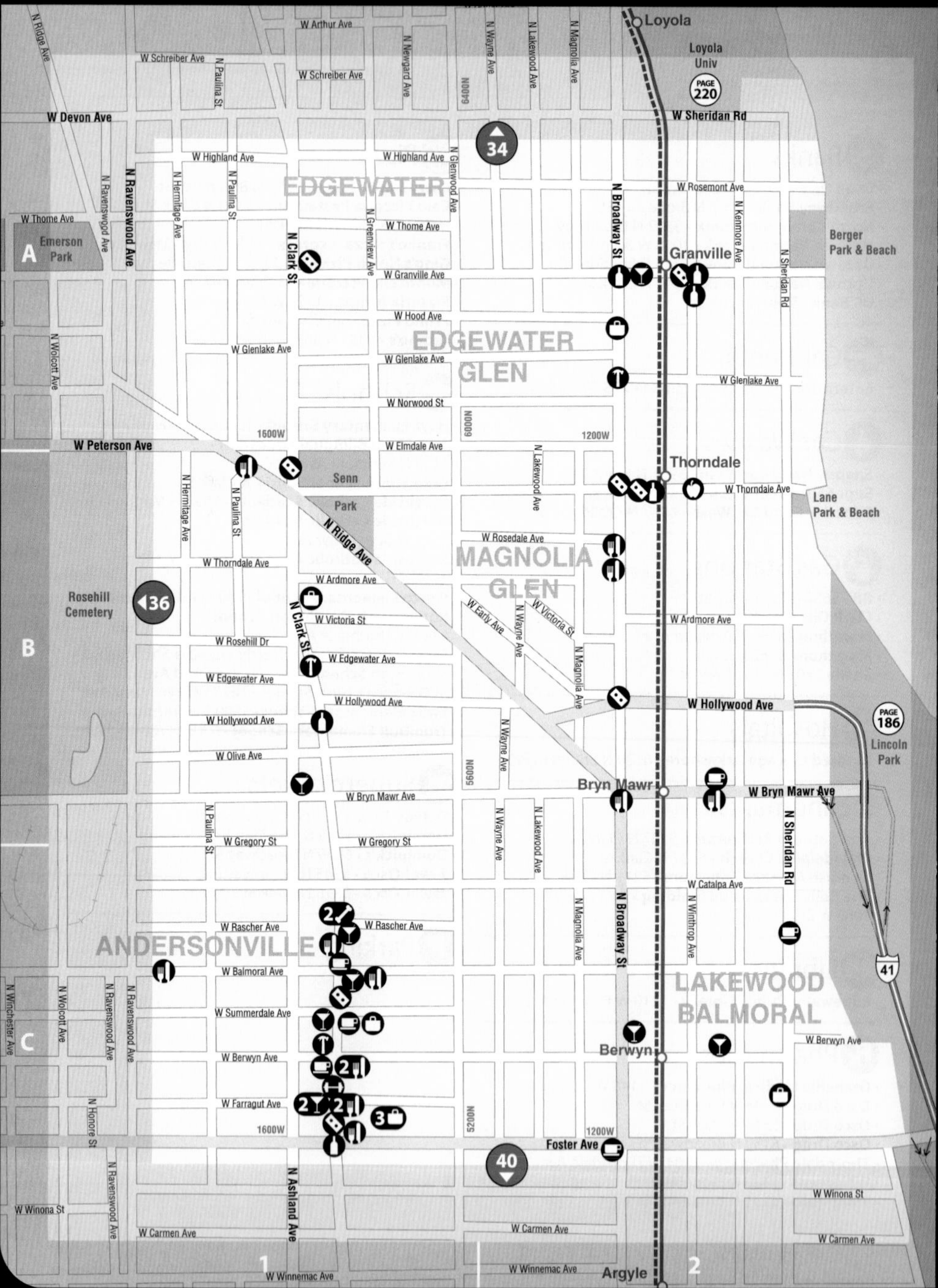

Sundries / Entertainment

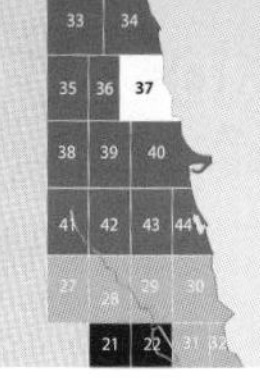

While there's Boystown with its bars and flamboyant parades, Andersonville is the real center of gay and lesbian life in Chicago. The liberal community around Clark and Foster has great depth. Pick up a read at Women & Children First bookstore and devour it at global Kopi Cafe. Edgewater entertainment consists of bingo and beach snoozing.

Bars

- **Atmosphere** • 5355 N Clark St
- **Charlie's Ale House** • 5308 N Clark St
- **Edgewater Lounge** • 5600 N Ashland Ave
- **Granville Anvil** • 1137 Granville Ave
- **Madrigals** • 5316 N Clark St
- **Moody's Pub** • 5910 N Broadway St
- **Ollie's** • 1064 W Berwyn Ave
- **Simon's** • 5210 N Clark St
- **StarGaze** • 5419 N Clark St

Coffee

- **Cafe Boost** • 5400 N Clark St
- **Chava Mocha Cafe** • 5440 N Sheridan Rd
- **Coffee Chicago** • 5256 N Broadway St
- **Kopi, A Traveler's Cafe** • 5317 N Clark St
- **Starbucks** • 1070 W Bryn Mawr Ave
- **Starbucks** • 5200 N Clark St

Farmer's Markets

- **Edgewater** • Broadway St & Thorndale Ave

Gyms

- **Cheetah Gym** • 5248 N Clark St

Hardware Stores

- **Ace Hardware** • 5820 N Clark St
- **Cas Hardware Store** • 5305 N Clark St
- **Clarendon Electric & Hardware** • 6050 N Broadway St

Liquor Stores

- **Buy Low Liquors** • 5201 N Clark St
- **Castle Wines & Spirits** • 1128 W Thorndale Ave
- **Granville Liquors** • 1100 W Granville Ave
- **M & D Food Liquors** • 5652 N Clark St
- **Sovereign Liquors** • 6202 N Broadway St
- **Sun Liquors** • 1101 W Granville Ave

Pet Shops

- **Fido Food Fair** • 5416 N Clark St
- **Ruff N'Stuff Dog Obedience** • 5430 N Clark St

Restaurants

- **Andie's** • 5253 N Clark St
- **Ann Sather** • 5207 N Clark St
- **Carson's Ribs** • 5970 N Ridge Ave
- **Francesca's Bryn Mawr** • 1039 W Bryn Mawr Ave
- **Jin Ju** • 5203 N Clark St
- **La Tache** • 1475 W Balmoral Ave
- **Moody's Pub** • 5910 N Broadway St
- **Pasteur** • 5525 N Broadway St
- **Pauline's** • 1754 W Balmoral Ave
- **Reza's** • 5255 N Clark St
- **Svea** • 5236 N Clark St
- **The Room** • 5900 N Broadway St
- **Tomboy** • 5402 N Clark St

Shopping

- **Broadway Antique Mart** • 6130 N Broadway St
- **Early to Bed** • 5232 N Sheridan Rd
- **Gethsemane Garden Center** • 5739 N Clark St
- **Paper Trail** • 5309 N Clark St
- **Surrender** • 5225 N Clark St
- **The Acorn Antiques & Uniques** • 5241 N Clark St
- **Women & Children First** • 5233 N Clark St

Video Rental

- **Broadway Grocery & Video** • 6322 N Broadway St
- **G-S Video Rental** • 5940 N Broadway St
- **Hollywood Video** • 6201 N Clark St
- **Lion Video** • 5218 N Sheridan Rd
- **Magic Video** • 5725 N Broadway St
- **National Video** • 1108 W Granville Ave
- **Select Video** • 5358 N Clark St
- **Specialty Video** • 5208 N Clark St
- **Specialty Video** • 5307 N Clark St
- **Top 40 Video** • 5977 N Clark St
- **Video Town** • 1127 W Thorndale Ave

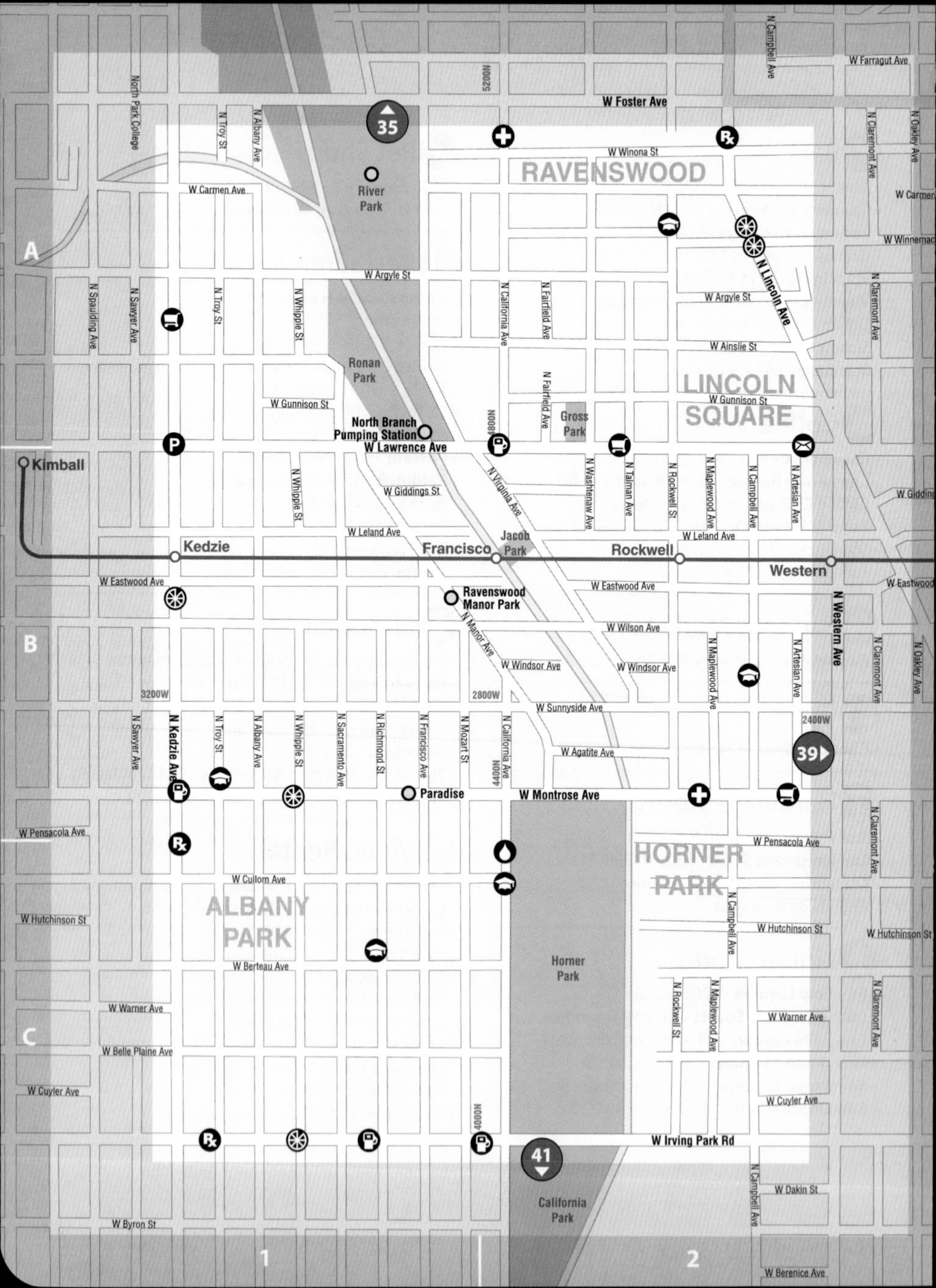

Map 38 • Ravenswood / Albany Park

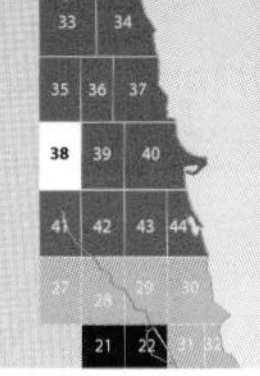

Within the Ravenswood neighborhood is The Manor, a small area of about a quarter of a mile that packs a lot of power and wealth. Generations of Chicago's elite live in this haven next to the river, where owls nest in trees and boat owners have private docks. Neighboring Albany Park residents are ethnic, working-class people living in tired flats and homes destined for gentrification. The mix of Persian, German, Latino, and Thai cultures make Albany Park worth a visit.

Car Washes

- **Ruby Hand Carwash** • 4334 N California Ave

Gas Stations

- **Bams** • 2816 W Irving Park Rd
- **BP** • 3201 W Montrose Ave
- **Clark Oil & Refining** • 2954 W Irving Park Rd
- **Shell** • 2800 W Lawrence Ave

Hospitals

- **Kindred Hospital** • 2544 W Montrose Ave
- **Swedish Covenant Hospital** • 5145 N California Ave

Landmarks

- **North Branch Pumping Station** • Lawrence and the River
- **Paradise** • 2910 W Montrose Ave
- **Ravenswood Manor Park** • 4626 N Manor Ave
- **River Park** • 5100 N Francisco Ave

Pharmacies

- **Osco Drug** • 5158 N Lincoln Ave
- **Walgreens** • 3153 W Irving Park Rd
- **Walgreens** • 4343 N Kedzie Ave

Pizza

- **Angelo's Pizza & Restaurant** • 3026 W Montrose Ave
- **Boomer's** • 5035 N Lincoln Ave
- **Golden Crust Pizzeria** • 4620 N Kedzie Ave
- **Paisano's Pizza** • 5047 N Lincoln Ave
- **Papa Giorgio's Pizzeria** • 2604 W Lawrence Ave

Post Offices

- 2522 W Lawrence Ave

Schools

- **Gospel Outreach Christian School** • 2800 W Cullom Ave
- **Newton Bateman School** • 4220 N Richmond St
- **Our Lady of Mercy** • 4416 N Troy St
- **Transfiguration School** • 5044 N Rockwell St
- **Waters Elementary School** • 4540 N Campbell Ave

Supermarkets

- **Aldi Foods** • 2431 W Montrose Ave
- **Harvestime Foods** • 2632 W Lawrence Ave
- **John's Food Mart** • 4947 N Kedzie Ave

Parking

N
RAVENSWOOD
LINCOLN SQUARE
ALBANY PARK
HORNER PARK
River Park
Ronan Park
Gross Park
Jacob Park
Horner Park
California Park
W Foster Ave
W Winona St
W Carmen Ave
W Argyle St
W Ainslie St
W Gunnison St
W Lawrence Ave
W Giddings St
W Leland Ave
W Eastwood Ave
W Wilson Ave
W Windsor Ave
W Sunnyside Ave
W Agatite Ave
W Montrose Ave
W Pensacola Ave
W Cullom Ave
W Hutchinson St
W Berteau Ave
W Warner Ave
W Belle Plaine Ave
W Cuyler Ave
W Irving Park Rd
W Dakin St
W Byron St
W Berenice Ave
W Farragut Ave
W Winnemac
W Gidding
N Lincoln Ave
N Western Ave
N Kedzie Ave
North Park College
N Troy St
N Albany Ave
N Spaulding Ave
N Sawyer Ave
N Whipple St
N Sacramento Ave
N Richmond St
N Francisco Ave
N Mozart St
N California Ave
N Fairfield Ave
N Virginia Ave
N Manor Ave
N Washtenaw Ave
N Talman Ave
N Rockwell St
N Maplewood Ave
N Campbell Ave
N Artesian Ave
N Claremont Ave
N Oakley Ave
Kimball
Kedzie
Francisco
Rockwell
Western
5200N
4800N
4400N
4000N
3200W
2800W
2400W
35
39
41
A
B
C
1
2

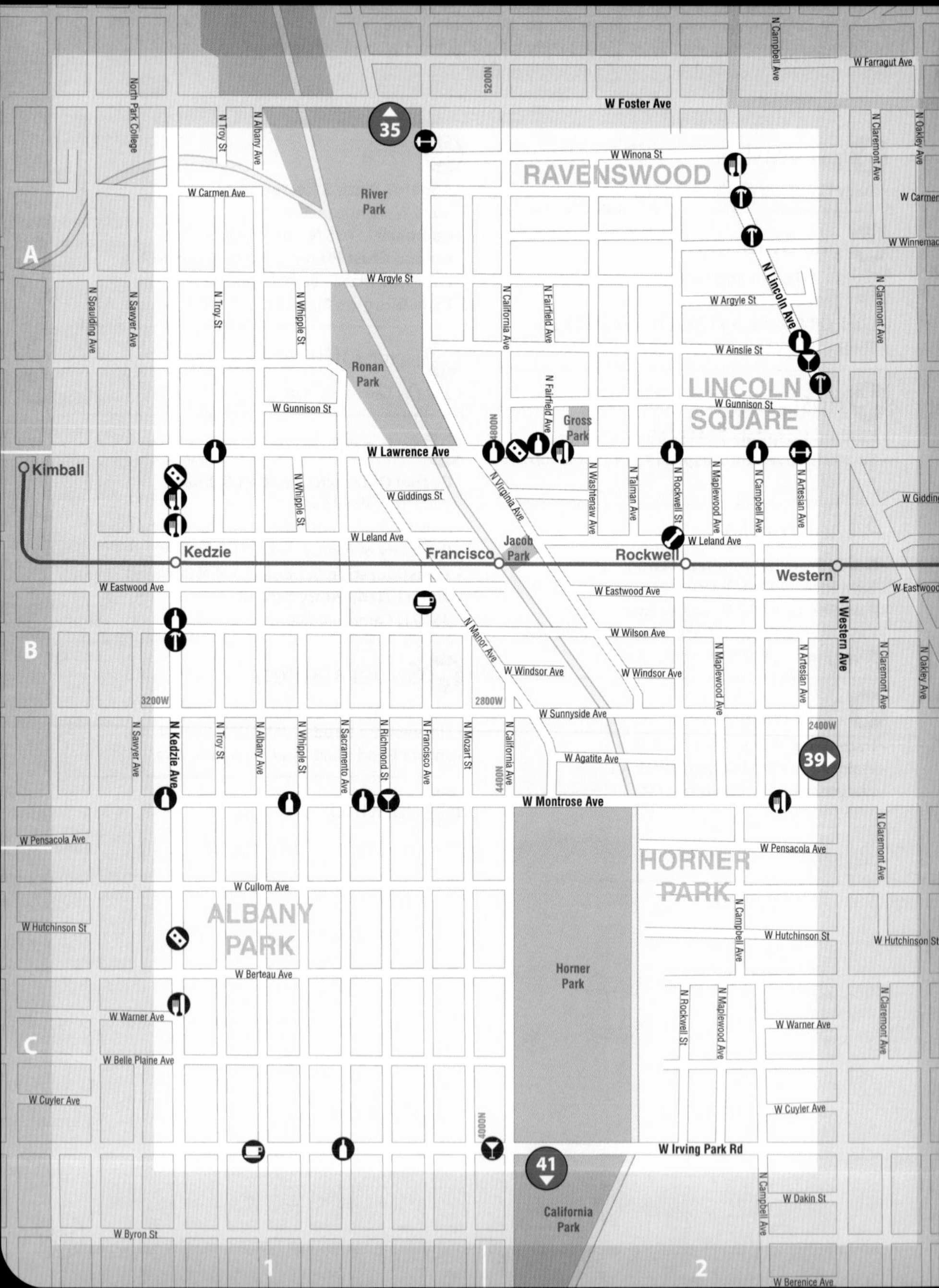

Here you'll find dollar stores for shopping and the world for dining. Go for bowling and brews at Lincoln Square Lanes. You won't hear a cell phone ring in Montrose Saloon. If your grandma was German, she served the same pastries as those made at Lutz Continental Café on Montrose. Eat cake in the old world tea room and on the green astroturf patio in summer.

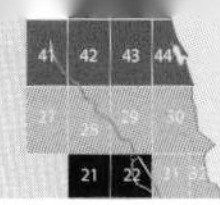

Bars

- **Lincoln Square Lanes** • 4874 N Lincoln Ave
- **Montrose Saloon** • 2933 W Montrose Ave
- **Peek Inn** • 2825 W Irving Park Rd

Coffee

- **Dunkin' Donuts** • 3101 W Irving Park Rd
- **Go! Coffee** • 4642 N Francisco Ave

Gyms

- **Galter Lifecenter** • 5157 N Francisco Ave
- **Women's Workout World** • 2540 W Lawrence Ave

Hardware Stores

- **Jay Hardware** • 4608 N Kedzie Ave
- **Just Ask Rental** • 5067 N Lincoln Ave
- **Lincoln Square Ace Hardware** • 4874 N Lincoln Ave
- **Singer's True Value Hardware** • 5075 N Lincoln Ave

Liquor Stores

- **AB Liquor** • 2807 W Lawrence Ave
- **C & K Food & Liquor** • 2941 W Montrose Ave
- **Cardinal Wine & Spirits** • 4905 N Lincoln Ave
- **Food & Liquors Express** • 2752 W Lawrence Ave
- **Foremost Liquor Stores** • 4616 N Kedzie Ave
- **Jerusalem Liquors** • 3135 W Lawrence Ave
- **Leader Liquors** • 3000 W Irving Park Rd
- **P & B Liquor & Food** • 2501 W Lawrence Ave
- **Peacock Liquors** • 3056 W Montrose Ave
- **Prestige Liquors** • 3210 W Montrose Ave

Pet Shops

- **Ruff Haus Pets** • 4652 N Rockwell Ave

Restaurants

- **Arun's** • 4156 N Kedzie Ave
- **Lutz Continental Cafe** • 2458 W Montrose Ave
- **Noon-O-Kabab** • 4661 N Kedzie Ave
- **Penguin** • 2723 W Lawrence Ave
- **Thai Little Home Cafe** • 4747 N Kedzie Ave

Video Rental

- **AV Video Center** • 5153 N Lincoln Ave
- **Hollywood Video** • 4246 N Kedzie Ave
- **V & K Video** • 4750 N Kedzie Ave
- **Video Hall Sales & Rental** • 2752 W Lawrence Ave

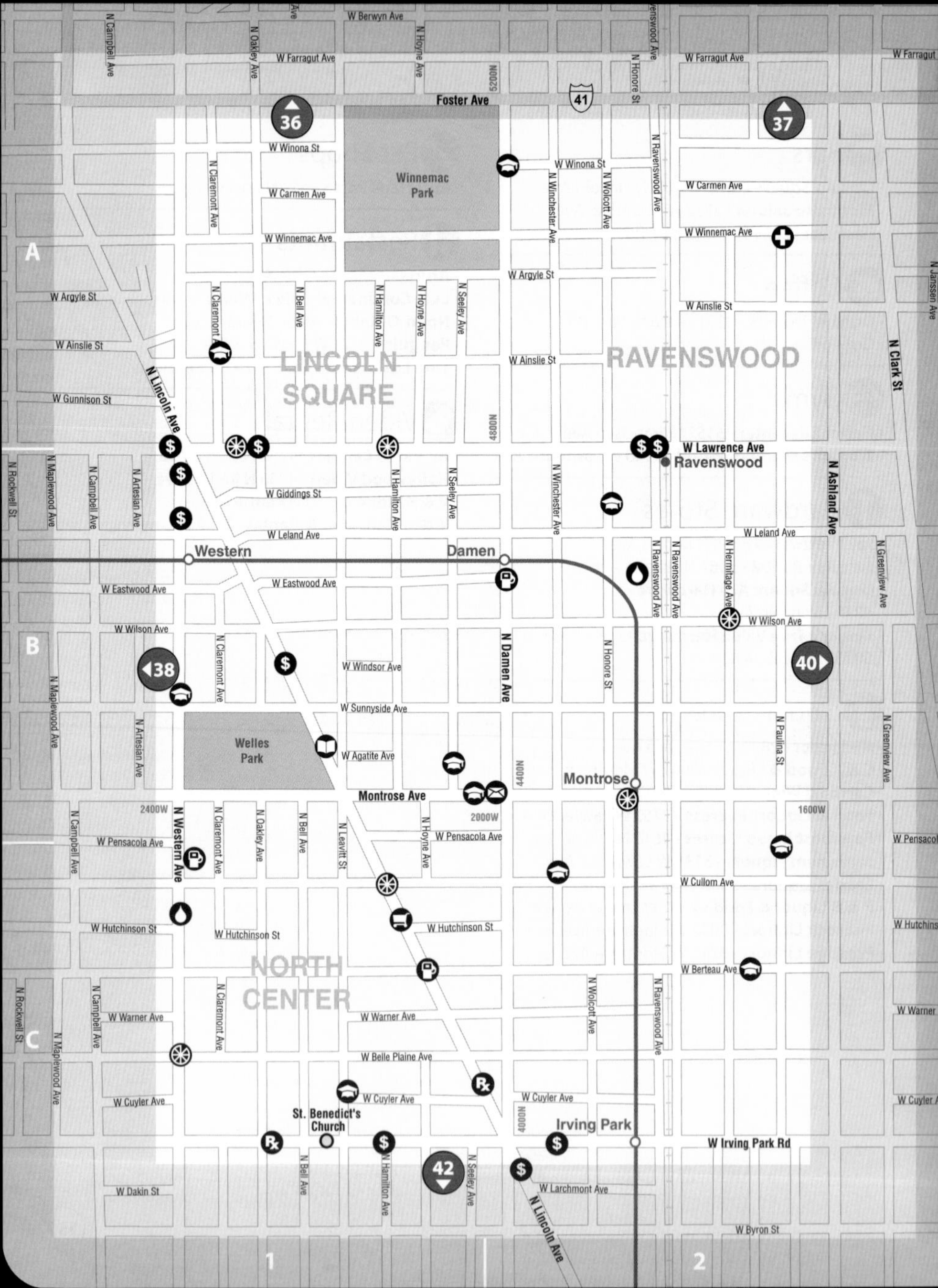

36
37
38
40
42

A
B
C
1
2

LINCOLN SQUARE
RAVENSWOOD
NORTH CENTER

Winnemac Park
Welles Park
St. Benedict's Church
Ravenswood
Western
Damen
Montrose
Irving Park

W Berwyn Ave
W Farragut Ave
Foster Ave
41
5200N
W Winona St
W Carmen Ave
W Winnemac Ave
W Argyle St
W Ainslie St
W Gunnison St
W Lawrence Ave
W Giddings St
W Leland Ave
W Eastwood Ave
W Wilson Ave
W Windsor Ave
W Sunnyside Ave
W Agatite Ave
Montrose Ave
W Pensacola Ave
W Cullom Ave
W Hutchinson St
W Berteau Ave
W Warner Ave
W Belle Plaine Ave
W Cuyler Ave
W Irving Park Rd
W Dakin St
W Larchmont Ave
W Byron St
4800N
4400N
4000N
2400W
2000W
1600W

N Rockwell St
N Maplewood Ave
N Campbell Ave
N Artesian Ave
N Western Ave
N Lincoln Ave
N Claremont Ave
N Oakley Ave
N Bell Ave
N Leavitt St
N Hamilton Ave
N Hoyne Ave
N Seeley Ave
N Damen Ave
N Winchester Ave
N Wolcott Ave
N Honore St
N Ravenswood Ave
N Hermitage Ave
N Paulina St
N Ashland Ave
N Greenview Ave
N Clark St
N Janssen Ave

Germans, Eastern Europeans, Latinos, and now yuppies who have discovered the comfortable housing share these increasingly popular neighborhoods. The heart of ethnically diverse Ravenswood is Lincoln Square, the locus of German life in Chicago. The closest you'll get to Munich for Octoberfest without boarding a plane is here. The blocks around St Benedict's Church have spawned a growing, family-friendly neighborhood that goes by "St Ben's".

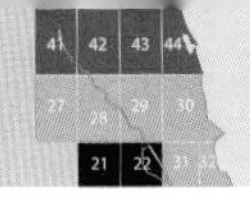

Map

Banks

- **Bank One** • 1825 W Lawrence Ave
- **Community Bank of Ravenswood** • 2300 W Lawrence Ave
- **Corus Bank** • 2420 W Lawrence Ave
- **Corus Bank** • 3959 N Lincoln Ave
- **Corus Bank** • 4800 N Western Ave
- **Great Bank of Lincoln Square** • 4725 N Western Ave
- **Lincoln Park Savings Bank** • 1946 W Irving Park Rd
- **Lincoln Park Savings Bank** • 2139 W Irving Park Rd
- **Uptown National Bank** • 4553 N Lincoln Ave

Car Washes

- **Ravenswood Hand Car Wash** • 4250 N Western Ave
- **Shurco** • 4638 N Ravenswood Ave

Gas Stations

- **J & L Oil** • 4638 N Damen Ave
- **Phil & Sons Gas For Less** • 4201 N Lincoln Ave
- **Shell** • 4346 N Western Ave

Hospitals

- **Methodist Hospital Of Chicago** • 5025 N Paulina St

Landmarks

- **St Benedict's Church** • 2215 W Irving Park Rd

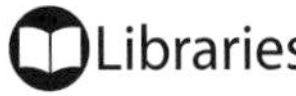

Libraries

- **Conrad Sullzer Public Library** • 4455 N Lincoln Ave

Pharmacies

- **Osco Drug** • 4051 N Lincoln Ave
- **Walgreens** • 2301 W Irving Park Rd

Pizza

- **Chicago's Pizza** • 1742 W Wilson Ave
- **Giordano's** • 2124 W Lawrence Ave
- **Jako's Pizza** • 4300 N Lincoln Ave
- **Pizza Hut** • 2309 W Lawrence Ave
- **Riggio's Caffe Pranzo** • 4100 N Western Ave
- **Villa May Pizza** • 1834 W Montrose Ave

Post Offices

- 2011 W Montrose Ave

Schools

- **Amundsen High School** • 5110 N Damen Ave
- **Coonley Elementary School** • 4046 N Leavitt St
- **Ethel Mary Courtenay School** • 1726 W Berteau Ave
- **McPherson Elementary School** • 4728 N Wolcott Ave
- **North Park Elementary School** • 2017 W Montrose Ave
- **Pilgrim Lutheran School** • 4300 N Winchester Ave
- **Queen of Angels** • 4520 N Western Ave
- **Ravenswood Baptist Christian** • 4437 N Seeley Ave
- **Ravenswood School** • 4332 N Paulina St
- **St Matthias School** • 4910 N Claremont Ave

Supermarkets

- **Jewel-Osco** • 4250 N Lincoln Ave

Map 39 • Ravenswood / North Center

This area has new restaurants opening as fast as the cost for housing is rising. On Lincoln, She She across from the Old Town School of Folk Music's state-of-the-art performance venue is getting good lip service from foodies. Chicago Brauhaus is where you go for pints.

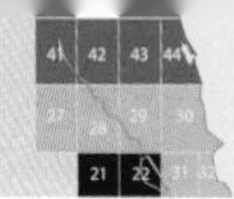

Bars

- **Chicago Brauhaus** • 4732 N Lincoln Ave
- **Daily Bar & Grill** • 4560 N Lincoln Ave
- **Lyon's Den** • 1934 W Irving Park Rd
- **Resi's Bierstube** • 2034 W Irving Park Rd
- **The Great Beer Palace** • 4128 N Lincoln Ave
- **The Long Room** • 1612 W Irving Park Rd

Copy Shops

- **AlphaGraphics** • 1611 W Irving Park Rd

Coffee

- **Beans & Bagels** • 1812 W Montrose Ave
- **Coffee Quest** • 4644 N Western Ave
- **Dunkin' Donuts** • 4010 N Western Ave
- **Katerina's** • 1920 W Irving Park Rd
- **Perfect Cup** • 4700 N Damen Ave
- **Starbucks** • 4015 N Lincoln Ave
- **Starbucks** • 4553 N Lincoln Ave

Farmer's Markets

- **Lincoln Square** • W Leland Ave & N Lincoln Ave
- **North Center** • W Belle Plaine Ave & N Damen Ave

Hardware Stores

- **Lincoln Square Ace Hardware** • 4250 N Lincoln Ave

Liquor Stores

- **Best Buy Food & Liquor** • 1832 W Montrose Ave
- **Bozic's Imports & Wholesale** • 1964 W Lawrence Ave
- **Bright** • 1628 W Lawrence Ave
- **Cotler's Liquors** • 4959 N Damen Ave
- **Fox Liquors** • 4707 N Damen Ave
- **Hank's Party Store** • 5029 N Western Ave
- **Leland Inn** • 4662 N Western Ave

Movie Theaters

- **Davis Theatre** • 4614 N Lincoln Ave

Pet Shops

- **Barking Lot** • 2442 W Irving Park Rd
- **Paws For Thought** • 1821 W Irving Park Rd
- **Vahle's Bird & Pet Shop** • 4710 N Damen Ave

Restaurants

- **Cafe 28** • 1800 W Irving Park Rd
- **Cafe Selmarie** • 4729 N Lincoln Ave
- **Chicago Brauhaus** • 4732 N Lincoln Ave
- **Daily Bar & Grill** • 4560 N Lincoln Ave
- **Garcia's** • 4749 N Western Ave
- **Grecian Taverna** • 4761 N Lincoln Ave
- **Jury's Food & Drink** • 4337 N Lincoln Ave
- **La Boca della Verita** • 4618 N Lincoln Ave
- **O'Donovan's** • 2100 W Irving Park Rd
- **Opart Thai House** • 4658 N Western Ave
- **Pangea** • 1935 W Irving Park Rd
- **She She** • 4539 N Lincoln Ave
- **Tartufo Restaurante** • 4601 Lincoln Ave
- **Woody's** • 4160 N Lincoln Ave

Shopping

- **Architectural Artifacts** • 4325 N Ravenswood Ave
- **Different Strummer** • 4544 N Lincoln Ave
- **Glass Art & Decorative Studio** • 4507 N Lincoln Ave
- **Laurie's Planet of Sound** • 4639 N Lincoln Ave
- **Play It Again Sports** • 2102 W Irving Park Rd
- **Sears** • 1900 W Lawrence Ave
- **Timeless Toys** • 4749 N Lincoln Ave

Video Rental

- **B P Video** • 4652 N Western Ave
- **Blockbuster Video** • 1958 W Irving Park Rd
- **Blockbuster Video** • 2301 W Lawrence Ave
- **Darkstar Video** • 4353 N Lincoln Ave
- **Lincoln Square Video** • 4725 N Lincoln Ave
- **Super Video** • 2055 W Irving Park Rd
- **Supermagic Video** • 1700 W Lawrence Ave
- **Tom's Video** • 1830 W Wilson Ave

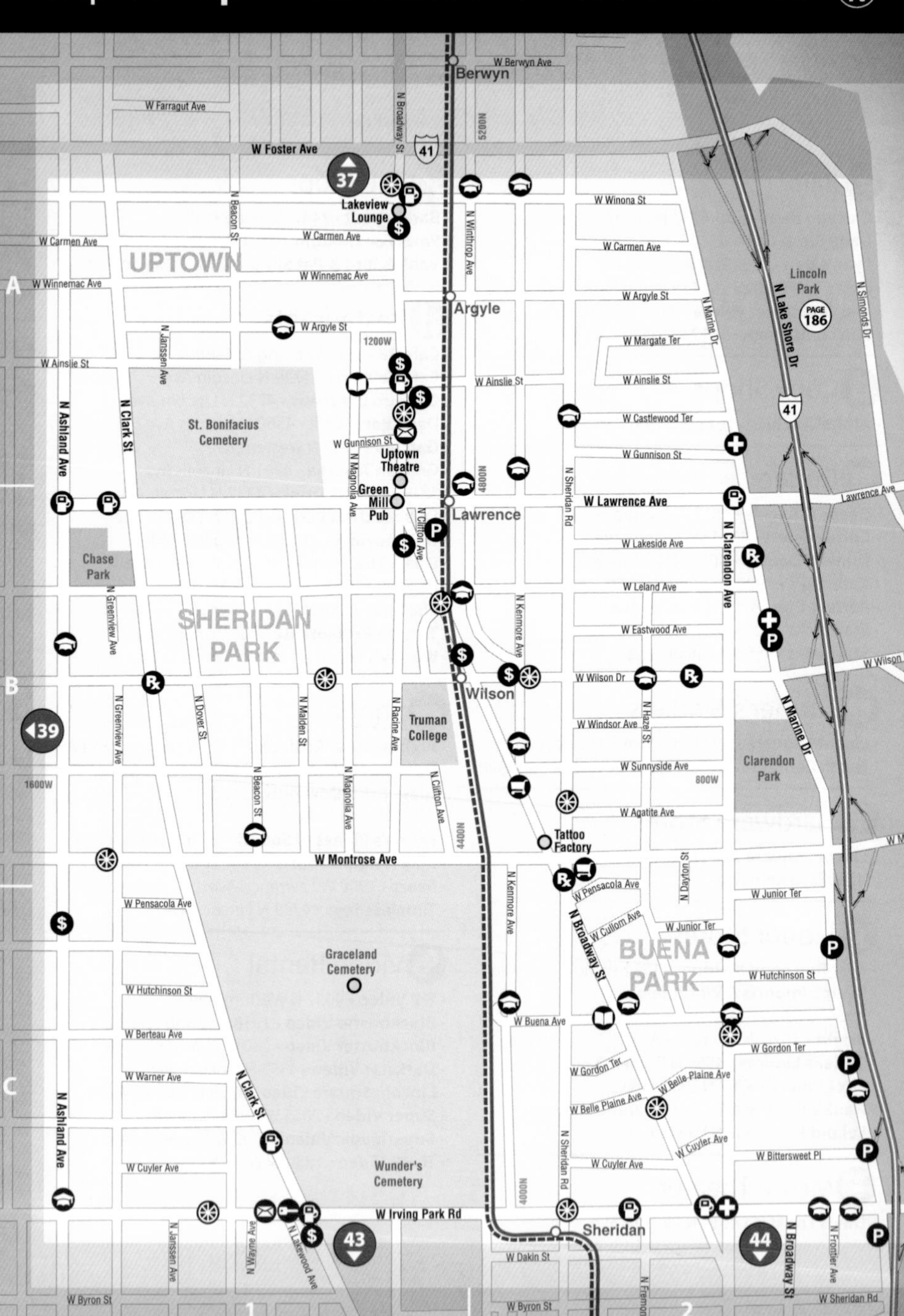

N
W Berwyn Ave
Berwyn
W Farragut Ave
N Broadway St
41
5200N
W Foster Ave
37
Lakeview Lounge
N Beacon St
W Winona St
W Carmen Ave
W Carmen Ave
W Carmen Ave
N Winthrop Ave
UPTOWN
W Winnemac Ave
A
W Winnemac Ave
Argyle
W Argyle St
Lincoln Park
N Lake Shore Dr
N Simonds Dr
PAGE 186
N Marine Dr
W Argyle St
1200W
W Margate Ter
N Janssen Ave
W Ainslie St
W Ainslie St
W Ainslie St
41
N Ashland Ave
N Clark St
St. Bonifacius Cemetery
W Castlewood Ter
W Gunnison St
W Gunnison St
Uptown Theatre
N Magnolia Ave
4800N
N Sheridan Rd
Green Mill Pub
Lawrence
W Lawrence Ave
Lawrence Ave
N Clifton Ave
W Lakeside Ave
N Clarendon Ave
Chase Park
W Leland Ave
N Greenview Ave
SHERIDAN PARK
N Kenmore Ave
W Eastwood Ave
W Wilson Dr
W Wilson Dr
B
Wilson
N Greenview Ave
N Dover St
N Malden St
N Racine Ave
Truman College
N Hazel St
W Windsor Ave
N Marine Dr
39
W Sunnyside Ave
Clarendon Park
1600W
N Beacon St
N Magnolia Ave
N Clifton Ave
800W
W Agatite Ave
4400N
Tattoo Factory
W Mon
W Montrose Ave
N Kenmore Ave
W Pensacola Ave
N Dayton St
W Junior Ter
W Pensacola Ave
W Cullom Ave
N Broadway St
W Junior Ter
BUENA PARK
Graceland Cemetery
W Hutchinson St
W Hutchinson St
W Buena Ave
W Berteau Ave
W Gordon Ter
W Gordon Ter
W Warner Ave
W Belle Plaine Ave
C
N Clark St
W Belle Plaine Ave
N Ashland Ave
W Cuyler Ave
N Sheridan Rd
W Bittersweet Pl
W Cuyler Ave
W Cuyler Ave
Wunder's Cemetery
4000N
W Irving Park Rd
Sheridan
43
44
N Janssen Ave
N Wayne Ave
N Lakewood Ave
W Dakin St
N Broadway St
N Frontier Ave
W Sheridan Rd
N Fremont St
W Byron St
W Byron St
1
2

Uptown is haunted by its past. The edgy neighborhood's glitzy history shows through the grit in the ornate but crumbling architecture of the Aragon Ballroom (now a rock venue) and the Uptown Theatre (quietly biding its time before the wrecking ball arrives). Politically, the neighborhood is divided between development-minded pro-gentrification guppies and grass-roots anti-gentrification hippies. Time will tell which group will prevail.

Banks

- **American Metro Bank** • 4878 N Broadway Ave
- **Charter One Bank** • 1301 Irving Park Rd
- **Harris Trust & Savings Bank** • 4531 N Broadway St
- **International Bank of Chicago** • 5069 N Broadway St
- **Marquette Bank** • 4322 Ashland Ave
- **New Asia Bank** • 4928 N Broadway St
- **TCF Bank** • 1050 W Wilson Ave
- **Uptown National Bank** • 4753 N Broadway St

Car Rental

- **Budget** • 1300 W Irving Park Rd • 773-686-6800

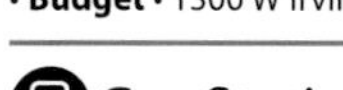

Gas Stations

- **BP** • 4000 N Clark St
- **BP** • 5156 N Broadway St
- **BP** • 841 W Irving Park Rd
- **Citgo** • 1530 W Lawrence Ave
- **Gas City** • 4070 N Clark St
- **Marine Drive Standard Svc** • 755 W Lawrence Ave
- **Shell** • 4800 N Ashland Ave
- **Shell** • 953 W Irving Park Rd
- **Uptown Svc Station** • 4900 N Broadway St

Hospitals

- **Columbia Chicago Lakeshore** • 4840 N Marine Dr
- **Louis A Weiss Memorial Hospital** • 4646 N Marine Dr
- **Thorek Hospital & Medical Ctr** • 850 W Irving Park Rd

Landmarks

- **Graceland Cemetery** • 4001 N Clark St
- **Green Mill Pub** • 4802 N Broadway St
- **Lakeview Lounge** • 5110 N Broadway St
- **Tattoo Factory** • 4408 N Broadway St
- **Uptown Theatre** • 4707 N Broadway St

Libraries

- **Bezazian Public Library** • 1226 W Ainslie St
- **Uptown Public Library** • 929 W Buena Ave

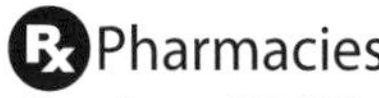

Pharmacies

- **Osco Drug** • 4355 N Sheridan Rd
- **Osco Drug** • 845 W Wilson Dr
- **Walgreens** • 1500 W Wilson Dr
- **Walgreens** • 4720 N Marine Dr

Pizza

- **Bo Jono's Pizzeria** • 4185 N Clarendon Ave
- **Domino's** • 1415 W Irving Park Rd
- **Fornello** • 1011 W Irving Park Rd
- **Gigio's Pizzeria** • 4643 N Broadway St
- **Godfather's Pizza** • 1265 W Wilson Ave
- **Laurie's Pizzeria & Liquors** • 5153 N Broadway St
- **Michael's Pizzeria & Sports** • 4091 N Broadway St
- **Pizza Factory** • 4443 N Sheridan Rd
- **Ranalli's Up North** • 1522 W Montrose Ave
- **Rosati's Pizza** • 4863 N Broadway St
- **Uptown Pizza** • 1031 W Wilson

Post Offices

- 1343 W Irving Park Rd
- 4850 N Broadway St

Schools

- **A Step Ahead Learning Center** • 4208 N Broadway St
- **American Islamic College** • 640 W Irving Park Rd
- **Arai Middle School** • 900 W Wilson Ave
- **Day School** • 800 W Buena Ave
- **Goudy Elementary School** • 5120 N Winthrop Ave
- **Joseph Brennemann School** • 4251 N Clarendon Ave
- **Lakeview High School** • 4015 N Ashland Ave
- **McCutcheon Elementary School** • 4865 N Sheridan Rd
- **Our Lady of Lourdes School** • 4641 N Ashland Ave
- **Prologue Alternative High School** • 1105 W Lawrence Ave
- **Rodriguez Academic Preparation** • 630 W Irving Park Rd
- **St Augustine College** • 1333 W Argyle St
- **St Mary of the Lake School** • 1026 W Buena Ave
- **St Thomas of Canterbury** • 4827 N Kenmore Ave
- **Stewart Elementary School** • 4525 N Kenmore Ave
- **Stockton Elementary School** • 4420 N Beacon St
- **Truman College** • 1145 W Wilson Ave
- **Van Nail School** • 1108 W Leland Ave
- **Walt Disney School** • 4140 N Marine Dr

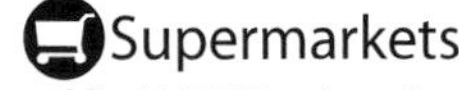

Supermarkets

- **Aldi** • 4440 N Broadway St
- **Jewel-Osco** • 4355 N Sheridan Rd
- **Jewel-Osco** • 4355 N Sheridan Rd

Parking

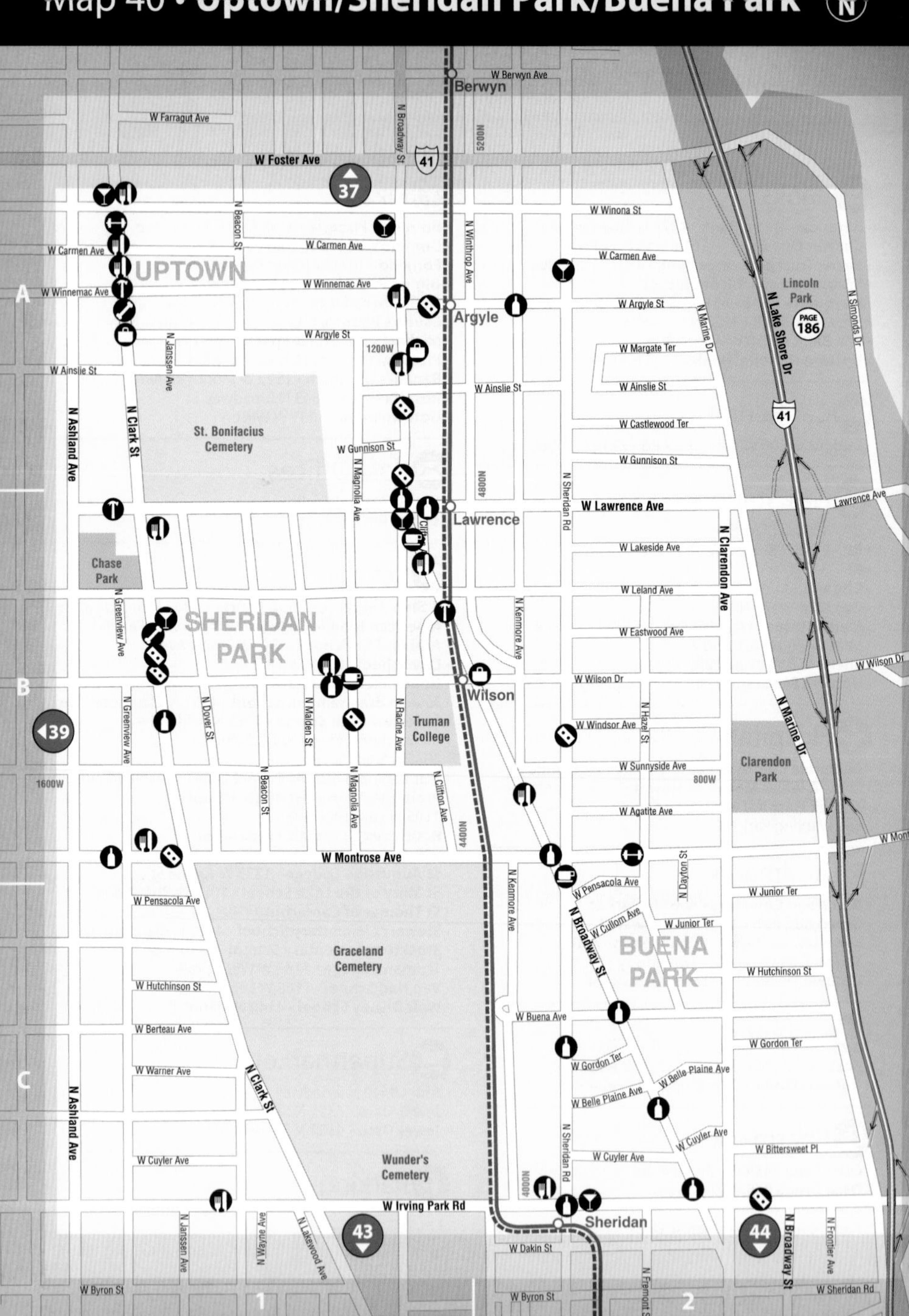
UPTOWN
SHERIDAN PARK
BUENA PARK
W Berwyn Ave
Berwyn
W Farragut Ave
W Foster Ave
N Broadway St
5200N
41
37
W Winona St
W Carmen Ave
W Carmen Ave
W Carmen Ave
N Beacon St
N Winthrop Ave
W Winnemac Ave
W Winnemac Ave
Argyle
W Argyle St
W Argyle St
N Marine Dr
Lincoln Park
PAGE 186
N Lake Shore Dr
N Simonds Dr
1200W
W Margate Ter
N Janssen Ave
W Ainslie St
W Ainslie St
W Ainslie St
N Clark St
N Ashland Ave
St. Bonifacius Cemetery
W Castlewood Ter
W Gunnison St
W Gunnison St
N Magnolia Ave
4800N
N Sheridan Rd
W Lawrence Ave
Lawrence Ave
Lawrence
N Clarendon Ave
W Lakeside Ave
Chase Park
W Leland Ave
N Greenview Ave
N Kenmore Ave
W Eastwood Ave
W Wilson Dr
W Wilson Dr
Wilson
39
N Dover St
N Malden St
N Racine Ave
Truman College
W Windsor Ave
N Hazel St
N Marine Dr
W Sunnyside Ave
Clarendon Park
1600W
800W
N Beacon St
N Magnolia Ave
N Clifton Ave
W Agatite Ave
4400N
W Montrose Ave
W Montrose
N Dayton St
W Pensacola Ave
W Pensacola Ave
W Junior Ter
N Broadway St
W Cullom Ave
W Junior Ter
Graceland Cemetery
W Hutchinson St
W Hutchinson St
W Buena Ave
W Berteau Ave
W Gordon Ter
W Gordon Ter
N Clark St
W Warner Ave
W Belle Plaine Ave
W Belle Plaine Ave
W Cuyler Ave
W Cuyler Ave
W Cuyler Ave
W Bittersweet Pl
Wunder's Cemetery
4000N
W Irving Park Rd
Sheridan
43
44
N Janssen Ave
N Wayne Ave
N Lakewood Ave
W Dakin St
N Broadway St
N Frontier Ave
W Byron St
W Byron St
N Fremont St
W Sheridan Rd
A
B
C
1
2

What do you expect in a neighborhood called the Psychiatric Ghetto? Thankfully, classic speakeasy Green Mill Pub, which opened in 1907, hasn't lost its vibe. Patronized by John Dillinger and Al Capone, this Chicago performance institution on Broadway specializes in live jazz and swing. If you haven't been to the Mill's Uptown Poetry Slam on Sundays, you must go.

Bars

- **Big Chicks** • 5024 N Sheridan Rd
- **Carol's Pub** • 4659 N Clark St
- **Green Mill Pub** • 4802 N Broadway St
- **Holiday Club** • 4000 N Sheridan Rd
- **Hopleaf** • 5148 N Clark St
- **Lakeview Lounge** • 5110 N Broadway St

Coffee

- **Starbucks** • 4355 N Sheridan Rd
- **Starbucks** • 4600 N Magnolia Ave
- **Starbucks** • 4753 N Broadway St

Gyms

- **Know No Limits** • 5121 N Clark St
- **World Gym Fitness Center** • 909 W Montrose Ave

Hardware Stores

- **Andersonville Hardware** • 5036 N Clark St
- **Crafty Beaver Home Center** • 1522 W Lawrence Ave
- **Uptown Ace Hardware** • 4654 N Broadway St

Liquor Stores

- **Able Food & Liquor** • 4808 N Broadway St
- **Foremost Liquor Stores** • 1040 W Argyle St
- **GNS Food & Liquor** • 4092 N Broadway St
- **H Heinze Cut Rate Liquor** • 1021 W Montrose Ave
- **Manhattan Food & Liquors** • 4200 N Broadway St
- **Rayan's Discount Liquors** • 1532 W Montrose Ave
- **Rayan's Liquor** • 4553 N Clark St
- **Saxony Liquor & Lounge** • 1136 W Lawrence Ave
- **Sheridan Park Food & Liquor** • 1255 W Wilson Ave
- **Sheridan-Irving Liquor** • 3944 N Sheridan Rd
- **Thomas Food & Liquor** • 4141 N Sheridan Rd
- **Wine Store** • 1040 W Argyle St

Pet Shops

- **Chicago Aquarium** • 5028 N Clark St
- **M & V Pet Shop** • 4623 N Clark St

Restaurants

- **Andie's** • 1467 W Montrose Ave
- **Atlantique** • 5101 N Clark St
- **Bale French Bakery** • 5018 N Broadway St
- **Don Quijote** • 4761 N Clark St
- **Frankie J's, An American Theatre and Grill** • 4437 N Broadway St
- **Furama** • 4936 N Broadway St
- **Golden House Restaurant** • 4744 N Broadway St
- **Holiday Club** • 4000 N Sheridan Rd
- **La Donna** • 5146 N Clark St
- **Magnolia Cafe** • 1224 W Wilson
- **Smoke Country House** • 1465 W Irving Park Rd
- **Tokyo Marina** • 5058 N Clark St

Shopping

- **Eagle Leathers** • 5005 N Clark St
- **Tai Nam Market Center** • 4925 N Broadway St
- **Wilson Broadway Mall** • 1114 W Wilson Dr

Video Rental

- **Albert Video** • 1435 W Montrose Ave
- **Bankok Video & Grocery (Foreign)** • 4617 N Clark St
- **Blockbuster Video** • 4620 N Clark St
- **Critic's Choice** • 655 W Irving Park Rd
- **Hollywood Video** • 4883 N Broadway St
- **Line Video** • 4554 N Magnolia Ave
- **Nationwide Video** • 736 W Irving Park Rd
- **Neehas Video Record Rental** • 1026 W Leland Ave
- **Power Video** • 4132 N Broadway St
- **United Video** • 4519 N Sheridan Rd
- **Video Express** • 1139 W Argyle St
- **Vietnam Video (Vietnamese/Chinese)** • 4820 N Broadway St
- **World of Video** • 4923 N Clark St

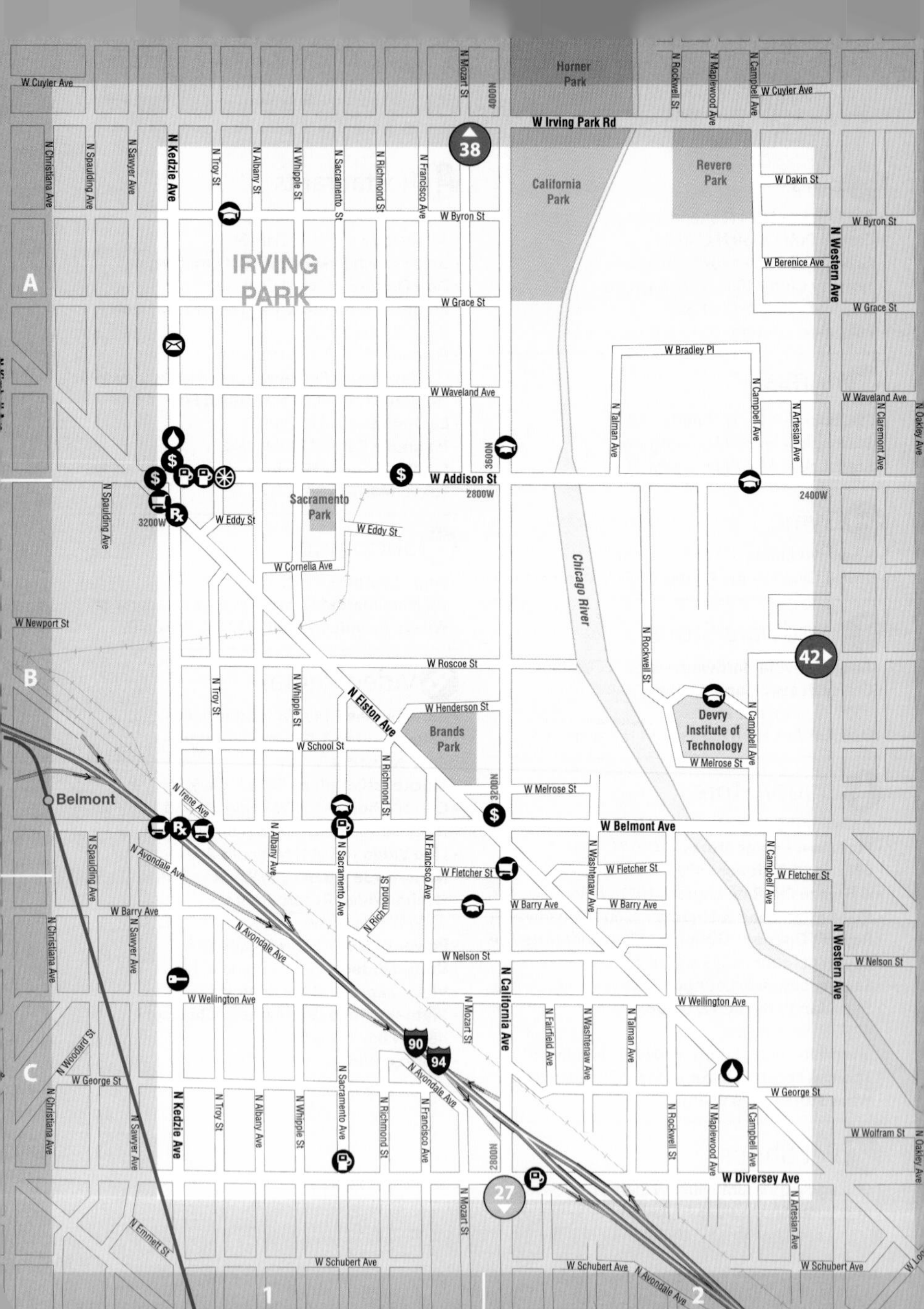

IRVING PARK
Horner Park
California Park
Revere Park
Sacramento Park
Brands Park
Devry Institute of Technology
Chicago River
Belmont
W Irving Park Rd
W Cuyler Ave
W Dakin St
W Byron St
W Berenice Ave
W Grace St
W Bradley Pl
W Waveland Ave
W Addison St
W Eddy St
W Cornelia Ave
W Newport St
W Roscoe St
W Henderson St
W School St
W Melrose St
W Belmont Ave
W Fletcher St
W Barry Ave
W Nelson St
W Wellington Ave
W George St
W Wolfram St
W Diversey Ave
W Schubert Ave
N Elston Ave
N Irene Ave
N Avondale Ave
N Woodard St
N Emmett St
N Christiana Ave
N Spaulding Ave
N Sawyer Ave
N Kedzie Ave
N Troy St
N Albany St
N Albany Ave
N Whipple St
N Sacramento St
N Sacramento Ave
N Richmond St
N Francisco Ave
N Mozart St
N California Ave
N Fairfield Ave
N Washtenaw Ave
N Talman Ave
N Rockwell St
N Maplewood Ave
N Campbell Ave
N Artesian Ave
N Western Ave
N Claremont Ave
N Oakley Ave
4000N
3600N
3200N
2800N
3200W
2800W
2400W
38
42
27
90
94
A
B
C
1
2

If hipster sightings are any indication, blue-collar Avondale is positioning itself as the new frontier in North Side urban gentrification. Roscoe Villagers and Logan Square residents branch ever outward, searching for that elusive street parking.

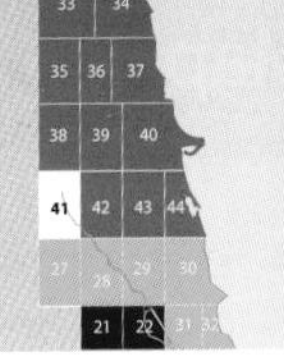

Banks

- **Bank One** • 3227 W Addison
- **Harris Trust & Savings Bank** • 2927 W Addison St
- **North Community Bank** • 2758 W Belmont Ave
- **US Bank** • 3611 N Kedzie Ave

Car Rental

- **Enterprise** • 3029 N Kedzie Ave • 773-478-3310

Car Washes

- **Gilbert's Carwash** • 3635 N Kedzie Ave
- **Tropical Car Wash** • 2933 N Elston Ave

Gas Stations

- **Citgo** • 3001 W Belmont Ave
- **Clark Station** • 2811 N Sacramento Ave
- **James Standard Svc** • 3201 W Addison St
- **Mobil** • 2801 W Diversey Ave
- **Shell** • 3159 W Addison St

Pharmacies

- **Osco Drug** • 3572 N Elston Ave
- **Walgreens** • 3302 W Belmont Ave

Pizza

- **Little Caesar's Pizza** • 3135 W Addison St

Post Offices

- 3750 N Kedzie Ave

Schools

- **DeVry Institute of Technology** • 3300 N Campbell Ave
- **Gordon Technical High School** • 3633 N California Ave
- **Grover Cleveland School** • 3121 W Byron St
- **Lane Tech High School** • 2501 W Addison St
- **Linne Elementary School** • 3221 N Sacramento Ave
- **Resurrection Catholic Academy** • 2845 W Barry Ave

Supermarkets

- **Carnicerias Guanajuato** • 3140 N California Ave
- **DelRay Farms** • 3239 W Belmont Ave
- **Dominick's** • 3300 W Belmont Ave
- **Jewel** • 3572 N Elston Ave

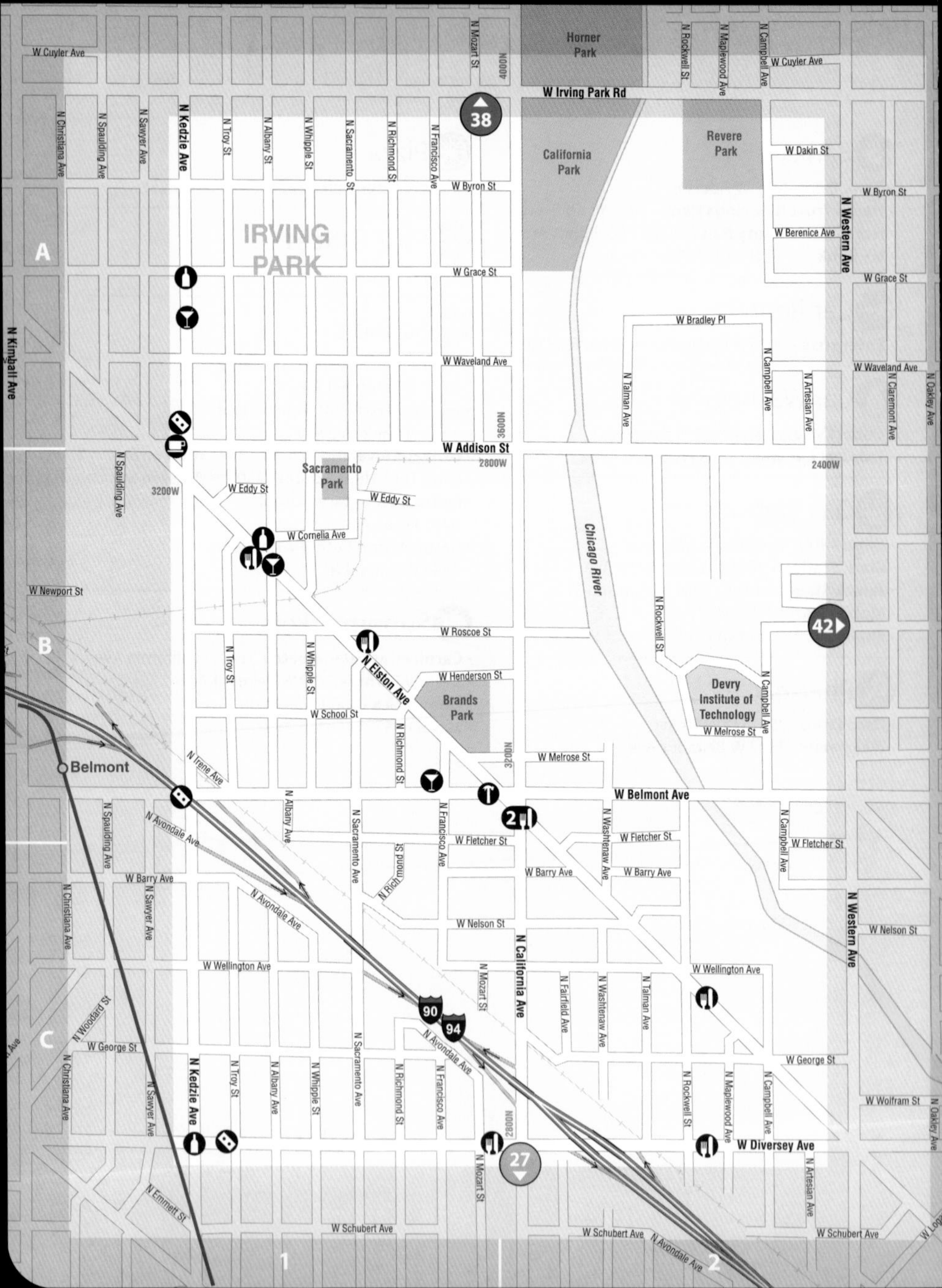

Horner Park
California Park
Revere Park
IRVING PARK
Sacramento Park
Brands Park
Devry Institute of Technology
Chicago River
Belmont

W Cuyler Ave
W Irving Park Rd
W Dakin St
W Byron St
W Berenice Ave
W Grace St
W Bradley Pl
W Waveland Ave
W Addison St
W Eddy St
W Cornelia Ave
W Newport St
W Roscoe St
W Henderson St
W School St
W Melrose St
W Belmont Ave
W Fletcher St
W Barry Ave
W Nelson St
W Wellington Ave
W George St
W Wolfram St
W Diversey Ave
W Schubert Ave

N Christiana Ave
N Spaulding Ave
N Sawyer Ave
N Kedzie Ave
N Troy St
N Albany St
N Whipple St
N Sacramento St
N Richmond St
N Francisco Ave
N Mozart St
N Rockwell St
N Maplewood Ave
N Campbell Ave
N Western Ave
N Talman Ave
N Artesian Ave
N Claremont Ave
N Oakley Ave
N Kimball Ave
N Elston Ave
N Irene Ave
N Avondale Ave
N California Ave
N Fairfield Ave
N Washtenaw Ave
N Woodard St
N Emmett St
W Logan

4000N
3600N
3200N
2800N
3200W
2800W
2400W

38
42
27
90
94
A
B
C
1
2

The community's Polish and Puerto Rican populations commingle in the local taverns dotting every corner. Younger crowds hang out at Chief O'Neill's, with its authentic Irish food and huge beer garden. Mycroft's is a friendly corner dive with a good jukebox. Local Mexican fave La Finca has recently undergone a facelift and price increases—what could it mean?

Bars

- **Abbey Pub** • 3420 W Grace St
- **Chief O'Neill's** • 3471 N Elston Ave
- **Christine's Place** • 3759 N Kedzie Ave
- **Mycroft's** • 2900 W Belmont Ave

Coffee

- **Dunkin' Donuts** • 3210 W Addison St

Hardware Stores

- **Elston Ace Hardware** • 2825 W Belmont Ave

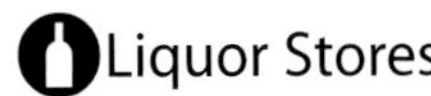

Liquor Stores

- **Discount Store** • 3457 N Albany Ave
- **JJ Peppers** • 3201 W Diversey Ave

Restaurants

- **Clara's** • 3159 N California Ave
- **Chief O'Neill's Pub** • 3471 N Elston Ave
- **IHOP** • 2818 W Diversey Ave
- **La Finca** • 3361 N Elston Ave
- **N** • 2977 N Elston Ave
- **Rancho Luna del Caribe** • 2554 W Diversey Ave
- **Taqueria Trespazada** • 3144 N California Ave

Video Rental

- **Blockbuster Video** • 3233 W Addison St
- **Blockbuster Video** • 3326 W Belmont Ave
- **Leo's Video** • 3151 W Diversey Ave

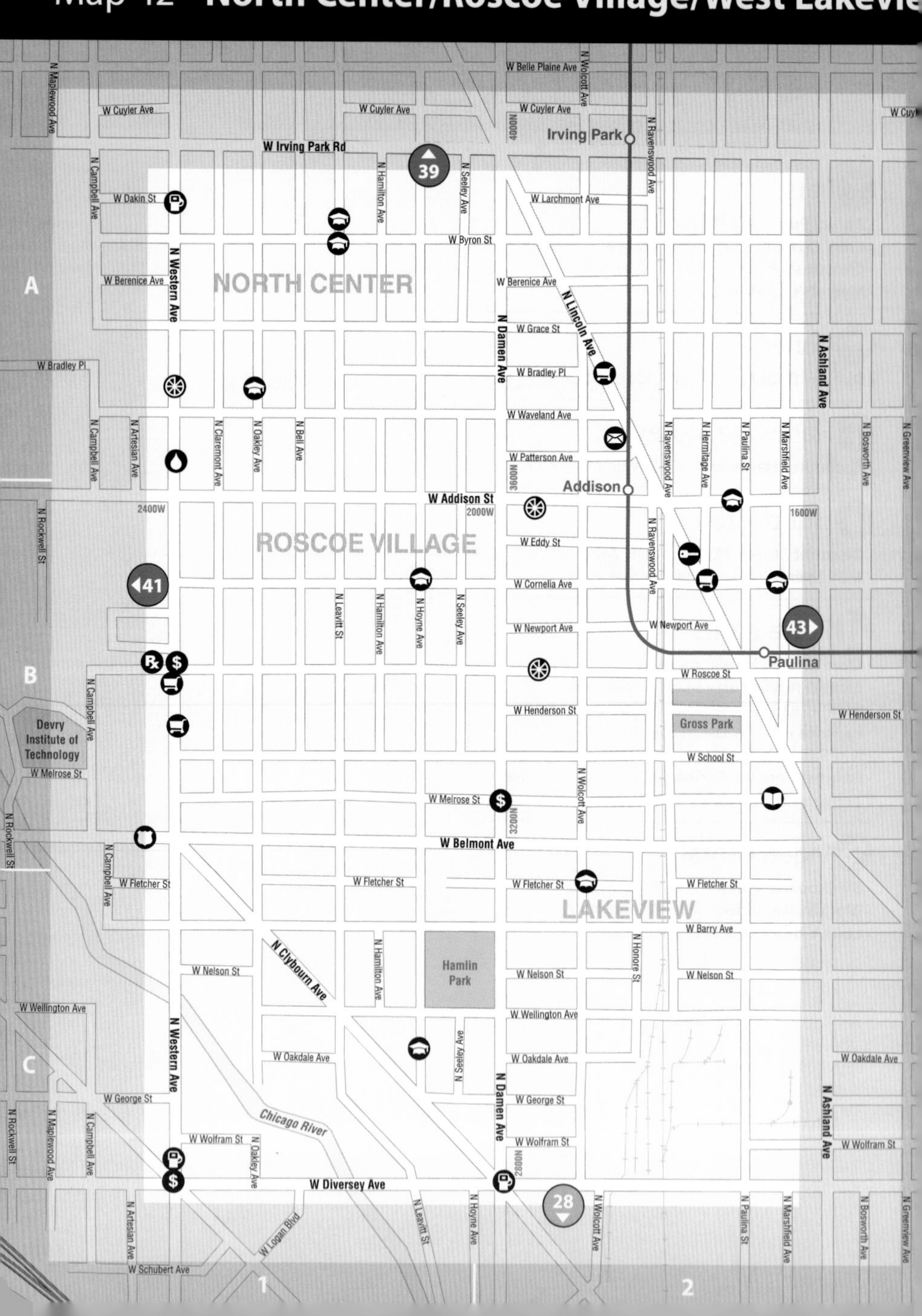
NORTH CENTER
ROSCOE VILLAGE
LAKEVIEW
Irving Park
Addison
Paulina
Devry Institute of Technology
Gross Park
Hamlin Park
Chicago River
39
41
43
28
A
B
C
1
2
2400W
2000W
1600W
4000N
3600N
3200N
2800N
W Belle Plaine Ave
W Cuyler Ave
W Irving Park Rd
W Dakin St
W Larchmont Ave
W Byron St
W Berenice Ave
W Grace St
W Bradley Pl
W Waveland Ave
W Patterson Ave
W Addison St
W Eddy St
W Cornelia Ave
W Newport Ave
W Roscoe St
W Henderson St
W School St
W Melrose St
W Belmont Ave
W Fletcher St
W Barry Ave
W Nelson St
W Wellington Ave
W Oakdale Ave
W George St
W Wolfram St
W Diversey Ave
W Schubert Ave
N Maplewood Ave
N Campbell Ave
N Western Ave
N Artesian Ave
N Claremont Ave
N Oakley Ave
N Bell Ave
N Rockwell St
N Leavitt St
N Hamilton Ave
N Hoyne Ave
N Seeley Ave
N Damen Ave
N Wolcott Ave
N Lincoln Ave
N Ravenswood Ave
N Hermitage Ave
N Paulina St
N Marshfield Ave
N Ashland Ave
N Bosworth Ave
N Greenview Ave
N Honore St
N Clybourn Ave
N Logan Blvd

The busy intersection of Western and Belmont was the grounds for Riverview Park, once the world's largest amusement park. Now it's a playground filled with funky bars, clubs, and trendy restaurants. Within this recently gentrified area is small but popular Roscoe Village.

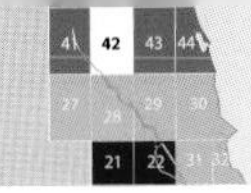

Banks

- **Lincoln Park Savings Bank** • 3234 N Damen Ave
- **North Community Bank** • 2800 N Western Ave
- **North Community Bank** • 3401 N Western Ave

Car Rental

- **Rent A Wreck** • 3535 N Lincoln Ave • 773-281-4242

Car Washes

- **Ultra Sonic Car Wash** • 3650 N Western Ave

Gas Stations

- **BP** • 2401 W Diversey Ave
- **BP** • 2801 N Damen Ave
- **BP** • 3955 N Western Ave

Libraries

- **Lincoln-Belmont Public Library** • 1659 W Melrose St

Pharmacies

- **Osco Drug** • 3400 N Western Ave

Pizza

- **Carreno's Pizza** • 1955 W Addison St
- **Pete's Pizza & Restaurant** • 3737 N Western Ave
- **Robey Pizza Co** • 1958 W Roscoe St

Police

- **19th District (Belmont)** • 2452 W Belmont Ave

Post Offices

- 3635 N Lincoln Ave

Schools

- **Alexander Hamilton Elementary School** • 1650 W Cornelia Ave
- **Bell Elementary School** • 3730 N Oakley Ave
- **Friedrich L Jahn School** • 3149 N Wolcott Ave
- **George Schneider School** • 2957 N Hoyne Ave
- **John L Audubon Elementary School** • 3500 N Hoyne Ave
- **St Andrew School** • 1710 W Addison St
- **St Benedict Grade School** • 3920 N Leavitt St
- **St Benedict High School** • 3900 N Leavitt St

Supermarkets

- **Dominick's** • 3350 N Western Ave
- **Jewel-Osco** • 3400 N Western Ave
- **Paulina Meat Market** • 3501 N Lincoln Ave
- **Trader Joe's** • 3745 N Lincoln Ave

W Belle Plaine Ave
N Wolcott Ave
N Maplewood Ave
W Cuyler Ave
W Cuyler Ave
W Cuyler Ave
4000N
W Cuy
Irving Park
N Ravenswood Ave
W Irving Park Rd
39
N Campbell Ave
W Dakin St
N Hamilton Ave
N Seeley Ave
W Larchmont Ave
W Byron St
A
W Berenice Ave
N Western Ave
NORTH CENTER
W Berenice Ave
N Lincoln Ave
W Grace St
N Damen Ave
N Ashland Ave
W Bradley Pl
W Bradley Pl
W Waveland Ave
N Campbell Ave
N Artesian Ave
N Claremont Ave
N Oakley Ave
N Bell Ave
W Patterson Ave
3600N
Addison
N Ravenswood Ave
N Hermitage Ave
N Paulina St
N Marshfield Ave
N Bosworth Ave
N Greenview Ave
N Rockwell St
2400W
W Addison St
2000W
1600W
ROSCOE VILLAGE
W Eddy St
41
W Cornelia Ave
N Leavitt St
N Hamilton Ave
N Hoyne Ave
N Seeley Ave
N Ravenswood Ave
W Newport Ave
W Newport Ave
43
Paulina
B
4
3
W Roscoe St
2
N Campbell Ave
W Henderson St
W Henderson St
Devry Institute of Technology
Gross Park
W Melrose St
W School St
N Rockwell St
N Wolcott Ave
W Melrose St
3200N
W Belmont Ave
N Campbell Ave
W Fletcher St
W Fletcher St
W Fletcher St
W Fletcher St
LAKEVIEW
W Barry Ave
N Clybourn Ave
N Hamilton Ave
Hamlin Park
N Honore St
W Nelson St
W Nelson St
W Nelson St
W Wellington Ave
W Wellington Ave
N Western Ave
N Seeley Ave
C
W Oakdale Ave
W Oakdale Ave
W Oakdale Ave
N Damen Ave
N Ashland Ave
W George St
W George St
N Rockwell St
N Maplewood Ave
N Campbell Ave
Chicago River
W Wolfram St
N Oakley Ave
W Wolfram St
W Wolfram St
2800N
W Diversey Ave
28
N Artesian Ave
W Logan Blvd
N Leavitt St
N Hoyne Ave
N Wolcott Ave
N Paulina St
N Marshfield Ave
N Bosworth Ave
N Greenview Ave
W Schubert Ave
1
2

Restaurant Row is Roscoe Ave. between Damen and Western. While there are lots of new eateries to choose from, we still like The Village Tap. Pull up a bar stool for good grease and cold beer and jaw a while. Belmont Ave. between Ashland and Western is lined with antique shops. Toy Town is our top pick.

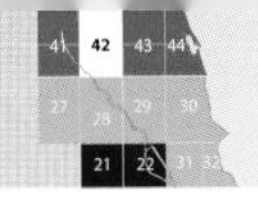

Bars

- **Art of Sports** • 2444 W Diversey Ave
- **Beat Kitchen** • 2100 W Belmont Ave
- **Benedict's** • 3937 N Lincoln Ave
- **Black Rock** • 3614 N Damen Ave
- **Cody's Public House** • 1658 W Barry Ave
- **Four Moon Tavern** • 1847 W Roscoe St
- **Four Treys** • 3333 N Damen Ave
- **G & L Fire Escape** • 2157 W Grace St
- **JT Collins** • 3358 N Lincoln Ave
- **Martyrs'** • 3855 N Lincoln Ave
- **Mulligan's Public House** • 2000 W Roscoe St
- **Riverview Tavern & Restaurant** • 1958 W Roscoe St
- **Seanchai Public House** • 2345 W Belmont Ave
- **Tavern 33** • 3328 N Lincoln Ave
- **The Hungry Brain** • 2319 W Belmont Ave
- **The Village Tap** • 2055 W Roscoe St
- **Tiny Lounge** • 1814 W Addison St
- **Xippo** • 3759 N Damen Ave

Copy Shops

- **Kinko's** • 3435 N Western Ave

Coffee

- **Dinkel's Bakery** • 3329 N Lincoln Ave
- **Dunkin' Donuts** • 1755 W Addison St
- **Dunkin' Donuts** • 3535 N Western Ave
- **Starbucks** • 1700 W Diversey Pkwy
- **Starbucks** • 2023 W Roscoe St
- **Starbucks** • 3350 N Lincoln Ave
- **Su Van's Cafe and Bake Shop** • 3405 N Paulina St

Farmer's Markets

- **Roscoe Village** • W Belmont Ave & N Wolcott Ave

Gyms

- **Know No Limits** • 3530 N Lincoln Ave
- **Lakeview YMCA** • 3333 N Marshfield Ave

Hardware Stores

- **Staubers Ace Hardware** • 3911 N Lincoln Ave

Liquor Stores

- **Damen Food & Liquor** • 1956 W School St
- **Grace & Leavitt Liquors** • 2157 W Grace St
- **J R Food & Liquors** • 3356 N Paulina St
- **Miller's Tap & Liquor Store** • 2204 W Roscoe St
- **Miska's Liquor Store** • 2156 W Belmont Ave
- **Pelly's Liquors** • 3444 N Lincoln Ave
- **R & S Liquor** • 2425 W Diversey Ave
- **West Lakeview Liquors** • 2156 W Addison St

Movie Theaters

- **Chicago Underground Film Festival** • 3109 N Western Ave

Restaurants

- **Brett's Cafe Americain** • 2011 W Roscoe St
- **Costello Sandwich & Sides** • 2015 W Roscoe St
- **El Tinajon** • 2054 W Roscoe St
- **Four Moon Tavern** • 1847 W Roscoe St
- **Hot Doug's** • 2314 W Roscoe St
- **Kitsch'n on Roscoe** • 2005 W Roscoe St
- **La Mora** • 2132 W Roscoe St
- **Lee's Chop Suey** • 2415 W Diversey Ave
- **Piazza Bella Trattoria** • 2116 W Roscoe St
- **Riverview Tavern & Grill** • 1958 W Roscoe St
- **Thai Linda Cafe** • 2022 W Roscoe St
- **Victory's Banner** • 2100 W Roscoe St
- **Wishbone** • 3300 N Lincoln Ave

Shopping

- **Antique Resources** • 1741 W Belmont Ave
- **Father Time Antiques** • 2108 W Belmont Ave
- **Glam to Go** • 2002 W Roscoe St
- **Good Old Days Antiques** • 2138 W Belmont Ave
- **Lynn's Hallmark** • 3353 N Lincoln Ave
- **Serendipity** • 2010 W Roscoe St
- **Toy Town** • 1903 W Belmont Ave

Video Rental

- **Blockbuster Video** • 1645 W School St
- **Blockbuster Video** • 3322 N Western Ave
- **Hard Boiled Records and Video** • 2008 W Roscoe St

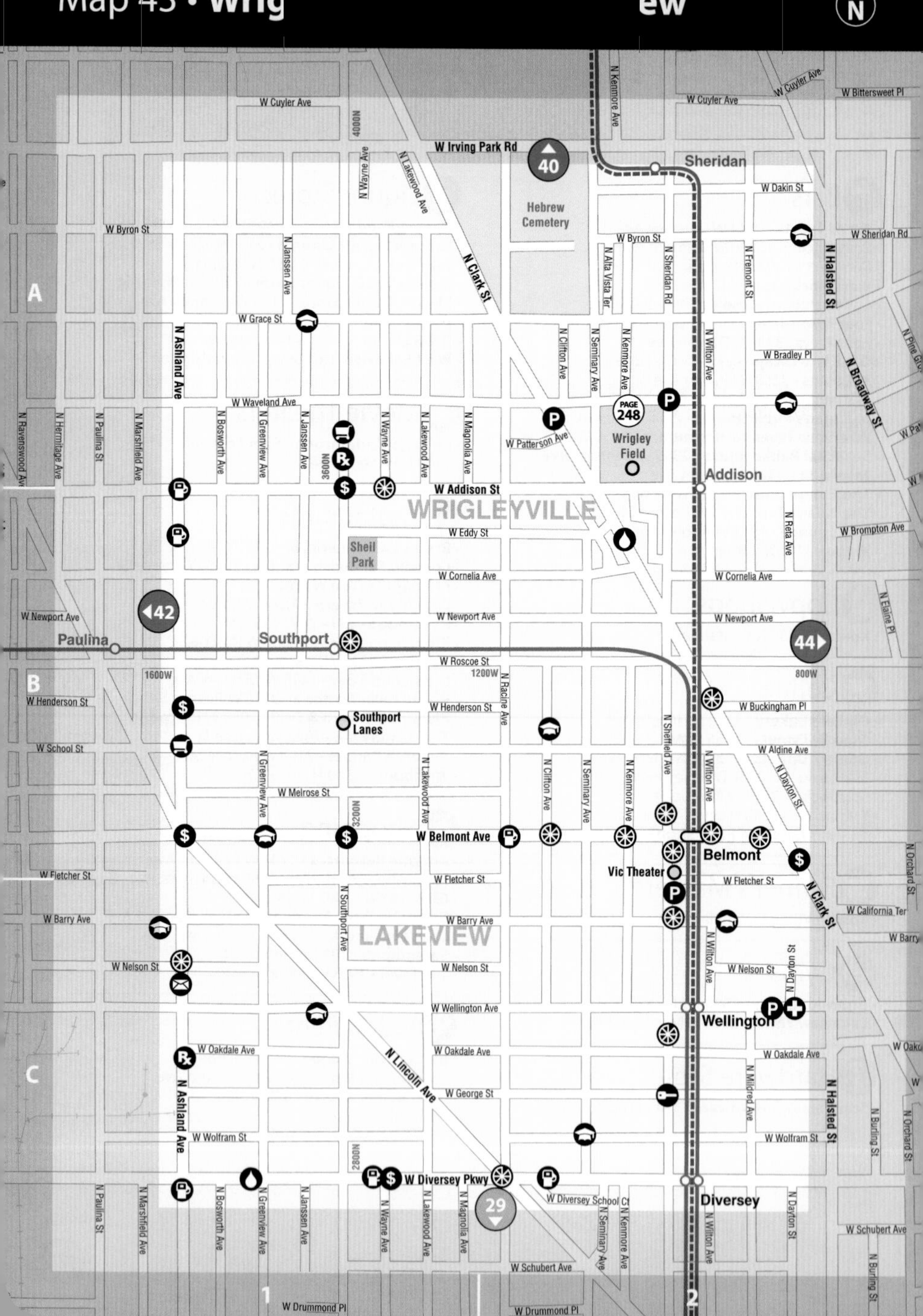

Map 43 • Wrig
ew
N
W Cuyler Ave
W Bittersweet Pl
4000N
W Irving Park Rd
40
N Wayne Ave
N Lakewood Ave
N Kenmore Ave
Sheridan
W Dakin St
Hebrew Cemetery
W Byron St
N Janssen Ave
N Clark St
N Alta Vista Ter
N Sheridan Rd
N Fremont St
W Sheridan Rd
N Halsted St
A
W Grace St
N Ashland Ave
N Clifton Ave
N Seminary Ave
N Wilton Ave
W Bradley Pl
N Broadway St
N Pine Grove
W Waveland Ave
PAGE 248
Wrigley Field
W Patterson Ave
N Ravenswood Ave
N Hermitage Ave
N Paulina St
N Marshfield Ave
N Bosworth Ave
N Greenview Ave
3600N
N Magnolia Ave
W Addison St
Addison
WRIGLEYVILLE
W Eddy St
Sheil Park
N Reta Ave
W Brompton Ave
W Cornelia Ave
N Elaine Pl
42
W Newport Ave
44
Paulina
Southport
W Roscoe St
B
1600W
1200W
800W
N Racine Ave
W Henderson St
Southport Lanes
W Buckingham Pl
W School St
N Sheffield Ave
W Aldine Ave
N Dayton St
W Melrose St
3200N
W Belmont Ave
Belmont
Vic Theater
W Fletcher St
N Orchard St
W Barry Ave
N Southport Ave
LAKEVIEW
W California Ter
W Nelson St
W Wellington Ave
Wellington
W Oakdale Ave
N Lincoln Ave
C
W George St
N Mildred Ave
N Burling St
W Wolfram St
2800N
W Diversey Pkwy
29
W Diversey School Ct
Diversey
W Schubert Ave
1
2
W Drummond Pl

Pleasant, pretty streets belie atrocious traffic and parking, as well as the constant summertime disturbance of drunken Cubs fans roaming the streets and urinating in alleys and doorways. On the plus side, residents don't have to travel far for anything—tons of good restaurants, a variety of nightlife, the lakefront, and loads of services from groceries to video rentals cram into this youthful 'hood.

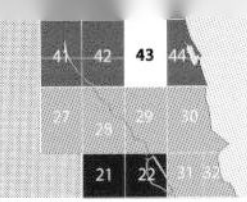

Banks

- **Bank One** • 3335 N Ashland Ave
- **Corus Bank** • 3179 N Clark St
- **Corus Bank** • 3604 N Southport Ave
- **First American Bank** • 1345 W Diversey Pkwy
- **LaSalle Bank** • 3201 N Ashland Ave
- **LaSalle Bank** • 3301 N Ashland Ave
- **North Community Bank** • 1401 W Belmont Ave

Car Rental

- **Enterprise** • 2900 N Sheffield Ave • 773-880-5001

Car Washes

- **Krystal's Hand Car Wash** • 3518 N Clark St
- **We'll Clean** • 1515 W Diversey Pkwy

Gas Stations

- **BP** • 1200 W Belmont Ave
- **BP** • 1355 W Diversey Pkwy
- **BP** • 3600 N Ashland Ave
- **Shell** • 1160 W Diversey Pkwy
- **Shell** • 2801 N Ashland Ave
- **Shell** • 3552 N Ashland Ave

Hospitals

- **Advocate Illinois Masonic Medical Ctr** • 836 W Wellington Ave

Landmarks

- **Southport Lanes** • 3325 N Southport Ave
- **Vic Theater** • 3145 N Sheffield Ave
- **Wrigley Field** • 1060 W Addison St

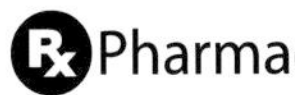

Pharmacies

- **Osco Drug** • 2940 N Ashland Ave
- **Osco Drug** • 3637 N Southport Ave

Pizza

- **Art of Pizza** • 3033 N Ashland Ave
- **Bacino's** • 3146 N Sheffield Ave
- **D'Agostino Pizzeria** • 1351 W Addison St
- **Gino's East of Chicago** • 2801 N Lincoln Ave
- **Giordano's** • 1040 W Belmont Ave
- **Homemade Pizza Co** • 1137 W Belmont Ave
- **Leona's Pizzeria** • 3215 N Sheffield Ave
- **Pat's Pizzeria** • 3114 N Sheffield Ave
- **Philly's Best** • 855 W Belmont Ave
- **Pizza Capri** • 964 W Belmont Ave
- **Pompei Bakery** • 2955 N Sheffield Ave
- **Red Tomato** • 3417 N Southport Ave

Post Offices

- 3024 N Ashland Ave

Schools

- **Augustus H Burley School** • 1630 W Barry Ave
- **Horace Greeley School** • 832 W Sheridan Rd
- **Inter-American Magnet School** • 919 W Barry Ave
- **James G Blaine School** • 1420 W Grace St
- **John V Le Moyne School** • 851 W Waveland Ave
- **Louis J Agassiz School** • 2851 N Seminary Ave
- **Nathaniel Hawthorne School** • 3319 N Clifton Ave
- **St Alphonsus School** • 1439 W Wellington Ave
- **St Luke Lutheran School** • 1500 W Belmont Ave

Supermarkets

- **Jewel-Osco** • 3630 N Southport Ave
- **Whole Foods Market** • 3300 N Ashland Ave

Parking

N
W Cuyler Ave
W Bittersweet Pl
4000N
W Irving Park Rd
40
Hebrew Cemetery
Sheridan
W Dakin St
W Byron St
W Sheridan Rd
N Halsted St
N Clark St
N Janssen Ave
N Wayne Ave
N Lakewood Ave
N Alta Vista Ter
N Sheridan Rd
N Fremont St
A
W Grace St
N Ashland Ave
N Clifton Ave
N Seminary Ave
N Kenmore Ave
N Wilton Ave
W Bradley Pl
N Broadway St
N Pine Grove Av
W Waveland Ave
PAGE 248
Wrigley Field
W Patterson Ave
N Ravenswood Ave
N Hermitage Ave
N Paulina St
N Marshfield Ave
N Bosworth Ave
N Greenview Ave
3600N
N Magnolia Ave
Addison
W Addison St
WRIGLEYVILLE
W Eddy St
Sheil Park
N Reta Ave
W Brompton Ave
W Cornelia Ave
N Elaine Pl
42
W Newport Ave
Paulina
Southport
44
W Roscoe St
1200W
1600W
800W
B
W Henderson St
N Racine Ave
W Buckingham Pl
N Sheffield Ave
W School St
W Aldine Ave
N Dayton St
W Melrose St
3200N
W Belmont Ave
Belmont
N Orchard St
W Fletcher St
N Southport Ave
W California Ter
W Barry Ave
LAKEVIEW
W Nelson St
W Wellington Ave
Wellington
W Oakdale Ave
N Lincoln Ave
C
W George St
N Mildred Ave
N Burling St
W Wolfram St
2800N
W Diversey Pkwy
Diversey
29
W Diversey School Ct
W Schubert Ave
W Drummond Pl
1
2

Live music venue Metro recently celebrated its 25th anniversary. The beautiful Music Box Theatre is the place to go for art house films—especially on weekends when they feature a live organist (their occasional sing-a-longs to musicals are also big hits). Spice lovers (and silverware haters) know to gnaw at Mama Desta's Red Sea Ethiopian restaurant. Touristy spots near the ballpark all cater to Cubs fans—caveat emptor. Further south at Clark and Belmont is the Punkin' Donuts—prime hang-out area for the city's pierced and pouty youth.

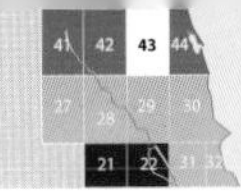

Bars

- **Bungalow Bar and Lounge** • 1622 W Belmont Ave
- **Cubby Bear** • 1059 W Addison St
- **Elbo Room** • 2871 N Lincoln Ave
- **Fizz Bar and Grill** • 3220 N Lincoln Ave
- **Fuel** • 3724 N Clark St
- **Ginger Man Tavern** • 3740 N Clark St
- **Gunther Murphy's** • 1638 W Belmont Ave
- **Higgin's Tavern** • 3259 N Racine Ave
- **Jack's Bar & Grill** • 2856 N Southport Ave
- **Justin's** • 3358 N Southport Ave
- **Lakeview Links** • 3206 N Wilton St
- **Lincoln Tap Room** • 3010 N Lincoln Ave
- **Metro** • 3730 N Clark St
- **Murphy's Bleachers** • 3655 N Sheffield Ave
- **Raw Bar** • 3720 N Clark St
- **Schuba's** • 3159 N Southport Ave
- **Sheffield's** • 3258 N Sheffield Ave
- **Slugger's** • 3540 N Clark St
- **Ten Cat Tavern** • 3931 N Ashland Ave
- **Y*k-zies-Clark** • 3710 N Clark St

Copy Shops

- **Kinko's** • 3524 N Southport Ave
- **Mail Boxes Etc** • 3540 N Southport Ave

Coffee

- **Cafe Avanti** • 3706 N Southport Ave
- **Caribou Coffee** • 3240 N Ashland Ave
- **Dunkin' Donuts** • 3000 N Ashland Ave
- **Dunkin' Donuts** • 3200 N Clark St
- **Emerald City Coffee** • 3928 N Sheridan Rd
- **Starbucks** • 1000 W Diversey Ave
- **Starbucks** • 1023 W Addison St
- **Starbucks** • 3045 N Greenview Ave
- **Starbucks** • 3184 N Clark St
- **Starbucks** • 3359 N Southport Ave

Gyms

- **Chicago Fitness Center** • 3131 N Lincoln Ave
- **Lincoln Park Athletic Club** • 1019 W Diversey Pkwy
- **Walk-a-Bye Baby Fitness** • 909 W Dakin St
- **Youthercise** • 3053 N Ashland Ave

Hardware Stores

- **Ace Hardware** • 3921 N Sheridan Rd
- **Klein True Value Hardware** • 3737 N Southport Ave
- **Tenenbaum Hardware & Paint** • 1138 W Belmont Ave

Liquor Stores

- **1000 Liquors** • 1000 W Belmont Ave
- **Ace Liquor Store** • 3949 N Ashland Ave
- **Addison Liquors** • 932 W Addison St
- **Bel-Port Food & Liquor** • 1362 W Belmont Ave
- **Courtesy Liquors** • 1622 W Belmont Ave
- **Fine Food & Liquor** • 3642 N Ashland Ave
- **Foremost Liquor Stores** • 3014 N Ashland Ave
- **Gilday Liquors** • 946 W Diversey Pkwy
- **Gold Crown Liquors Store** • 3425 N Clark St
- **Wrigleyville Food & Liquor** • 3515 N Clark St

Movie Theaters

- **Brew & View At the Vic** • 3145 N Sheffield Ave
- **Music Box Theatre** • 3733 N Southport Ave

Pet Shops

- **4 Legs** • 3809 N Clark St
- **Aquatic World** • 3039 N Lincoln Ave
- **Petco** • 3122 N Ashland Ave

Restaurants

- **Addis Abeba** • 3521 N Clark St
- **Ann Sather** • 929 W Belmont Ave
- **BD's Mongolian BBQ** • 3330 N Clark St
- **Bistrot Zinc** • 1131 N State St
- **Blue Bayou** • 3734 N Southport Ave
- **Cafe Le Loup** • 3348 N Sheffield Ave
- **Coobah** • 3423 N Southport Ave
- **Cy's Crab House** • 3819 N Ashland Ave
- **Heaven on Seven** • 3478 N Clark St
- **Leona's** • 3215 N Sheffield Ave
- **Little Bucharest** • 3001 N Ashland Ave
- **Mama Desta's Red Sea** • 3218 N Clark St
- **Menagerie** • 1232 W Belmont Ave
- **Matsuya** • 3469 N Clark St
- **Mia Francesca** • 3311 N Clark St
- **Moti Mahal** • 1031-35 W Belmont Ave
- **Orange** • 3231 N Clark St
- **Outpost** • 3438 N Clark St
- **Pepper Lounge** • 3441 N Sheffield Ave
- **PS Bangkok** • 3345 N Clark St
- **Shiroi Hana** • 3242 N Clark St
- **Standard India** • 917 W Belmont Ave
- **Technicolor Kitchen** • 3210 N Lincoln Ave
- **Tombo Kitchen** • 3244 N Lincoln Ave
- **Wrigleyville Dog** • 3737 N Clark St

Shopping

- **Bookworks** • 3444 N Clark St
- **Disc Revival** • 3182 N Clark St
- **Midwest Pro Stereo** • 1613 W Belmont Ave
- **Namascar** • 3946 N Southport Ave
- **Ragstock** • Belmont & Dayton 2nd fl
- **Uncle Fun** • 1338 W Belmont Ave

Video Rental

- **Blockbuster Video** • 2803 N Ashland Ave
- **Blockbuster Video** • 3753 N Clark St
- **City Lights Video** • 3761 N Racine Ave
- **Hollywood Video** • 3128 N Ashland Ave
- **Movie City** • 3456 N Clark St
- **Nationwide Video** • 843 W Belmont Ave
- **Southport Video** • 3408 N Southport Ave

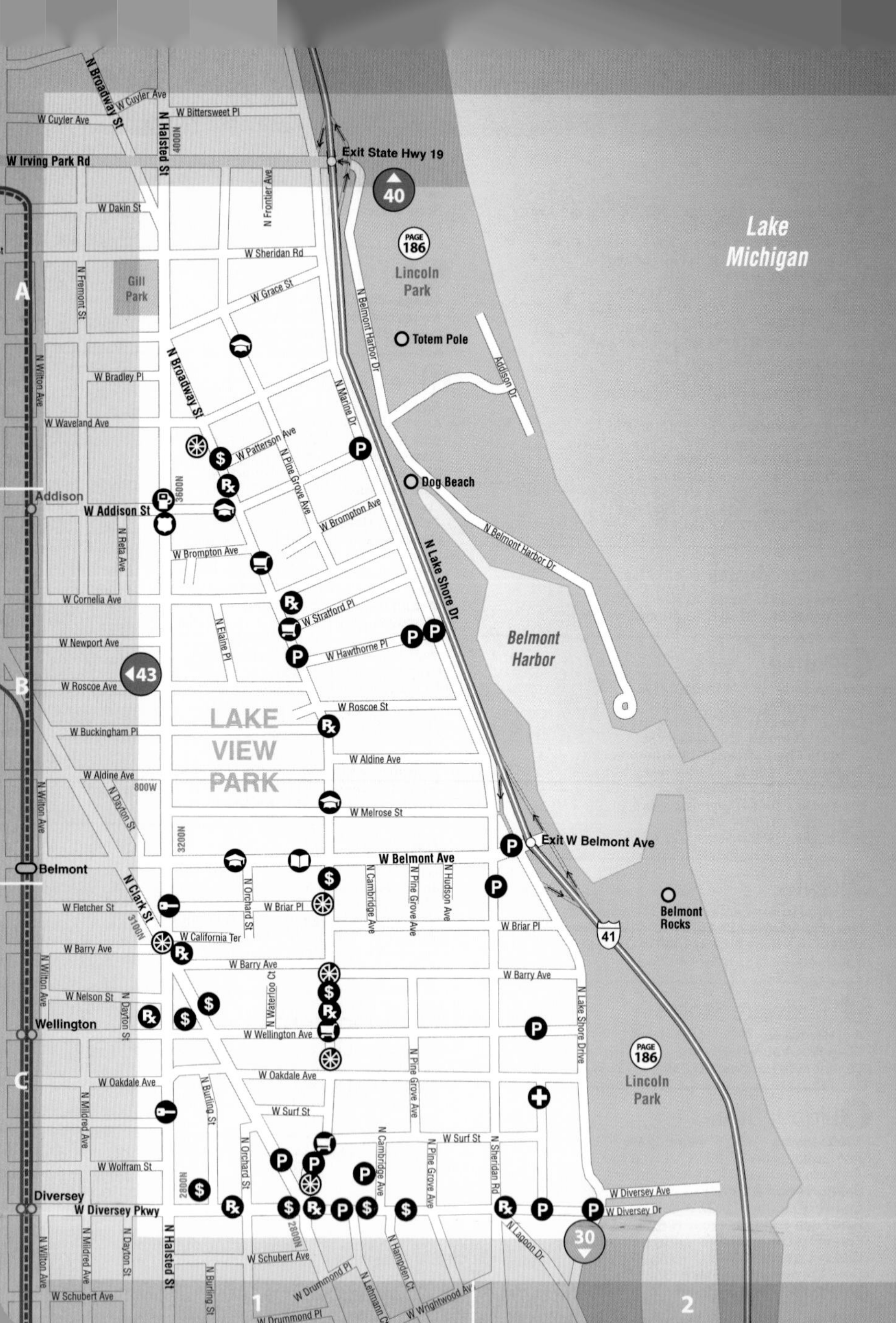

Lake Michigan
Lincoln Park
Totem Pole
Dog Beach
Belmont Harbor
Belmont Rocks
LAKE VIEW PARK
Gill Park
Exit State Hwy 19
Exit W Belmont Ave
N Lake Shore Dr
N Belmont Harbor Dr
Addison Dr
N Marine Dr
W Irving Park Rd
W Addison St
W Belmont Ave
W Diversey Pkwy
W Diversey Ave
W Diversey Dr
N Broadway St
N Halsted St
N Clark St
W Cuyler Ave
W Bittersweet Pl
W Dakin St
W Sheridan Rd
W Grace St
W Bradley Pl
W Waveland Ave
W Patterson Ave
N Pine Grove Ave
W Brompton Ave
W Cornelia Ave
W Stratford Pl
W Hawthorne Pl
W Newport Ave
W Roscoe Ave
W Roscoe St
W Buckingham Pl
W Aldine Ave
W Melrose St
W Fletcher St
W Briar Pl
W California Ter
W Barry Ave
W Nelson St
W Wellington Ave
W Oakdale Ave
W Surf St
W Wolfram St
W Schubert Ave
W Drummond Pl
W Wrightwood Ave
N Frontier Ave
N Fremont St
N Wilton Ave
N Reta Ave
N Elaine Pl
N Dayton St
N Orchard St
N Cambridge Ave
N Hudson Ave
N Waterloo Ct
N Burling St
N Mildred Ave
N Sheridan Rd
N Lagoon Dr
N Hampden Ct
N Lehmann Ct
N Lake Shore Drive
Addison
Belmont
Wellington
Diversey
4000N
3600N
3200N
3100N
2800N
800W
PAGE 186
40
43
30
41
A
B
C
1
2

Known equally as New Town, East Lakeview, and Boys Town (due to its highly visible gay community), East Lakeview is home to the city's annual gay pride parade (which attracts hundreds of thousands of participants and spectators every year), as well as the equally flamboyant Halsted Street Market Days. South of Belmont, things tone down a bit, as brownstones and greystone condos are occupied by young married couples. Active nightlife and residential zoning make parking in East Lakeview some of the worst in the city.

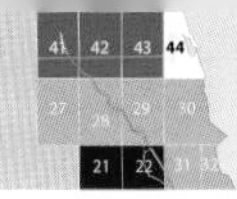

Car Rental

- **Budget** • 2901 N Halsted St • 773-528-1770
- **Hertz** • 3151 N Halsted St • 773-832-1912

Banks

- **Bank One** • 3032 N Clark St
- **Central Savings** • 2800 N Broadway St
- **Charter One Bank** • 664 W Diversey Pkwy
- **LaSalle Bank** • 3051 N Clark St
- **LaSalle Bank** • 538 W Diversey Pkwy
- **MidAmerica Bank** • 3020 N Broadway St
- **North Community Bank** • 3180 N Broadway St
- **North Community Bank** • 3639 N Broadway St
- **North Community Bank** • 742 W Diversey Pkwy

Gas Stations

- **Shell** • 801 W Addison St

Hospitals

- **St Joseph's Hospital** • 2900 Lake Shore Dr

Landmarks

- **Belmont Rocks** • Briar at the lake
- **Dog Beach** • Northern tip of Belmont Harbor
- **Totem Pole** • Waveland & Belmont Harbor Drive

Libraries

- **John Merlo Public Library** • 644 W Belmont Ave

Pharmacies

- **CVS Pharmacy** • 3033 N Broadway St
- **Osco Drug** • 3101 N Clark St
- **Osco Drug** • 3531 N Broadway St
- **Stone Medical Pharmacy** • 2800 N Sheridan Rd
- **Walgreens** • 2801 N Broadway St
- **Walgreens** • 3046 N Halsted St
- **Walgreens** • 3201 N Broadway St
- **Walgreens** • 3646 N Broadway St
- **Walgreens** • 740 W Diversey Pkwy

Pizza

- **Domino's** • 3103 N Clark St
- **Mac's Pizza** • 606 W Briar Pl
- **Nancy's Pizza** • 2930 N Broadway St
- **Pizza Hut** • 3034 N Broadway St
- **Pizza Primavera** • 3702 N Broadway St
- **Renaldi's Pizza Pub** • 2827 N Broadway St

Police

- **23rd District (Town Hall)** • 3600 N Halsted St

Schools

- **Bernard Zell Anshe Emet Day** • 3760 N Pine Grove Ave
- **Lake View Academy** • 716 W Addison St
- **Louis Nettelhorst School** • 3252 N Broadway St
- **Mt Carmel Academy** • 720 W Belmont Ave

Supermarkets

- **Dominick's** • 3012 N Broadway St
- **Jewel** • 3531 N Broadway St
- **Treasure Island** • 3460 N Broadway St

Parking

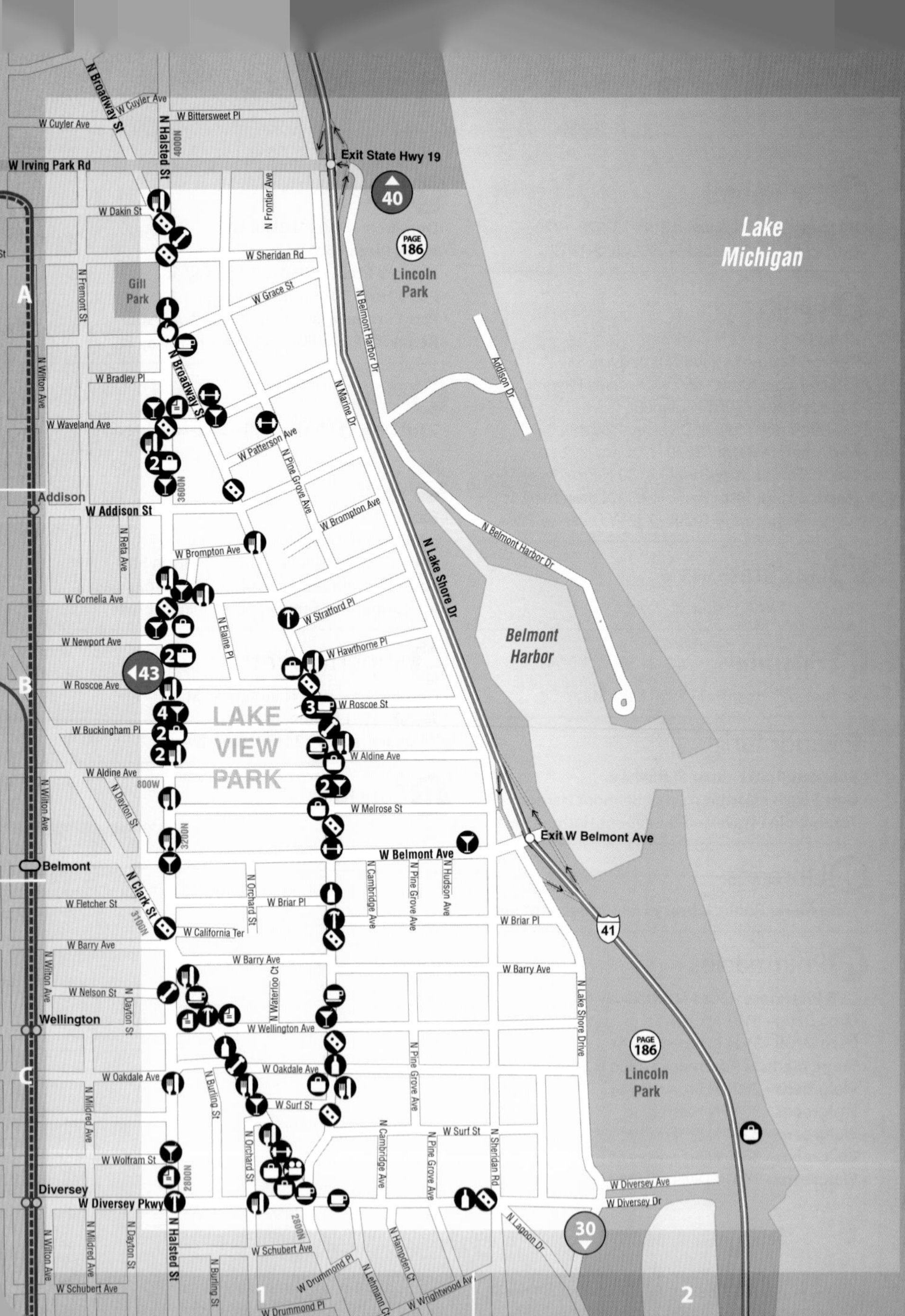

N Broadway St
W Cuyler Ave
W Bittersweet Pl
N Halsted St
4000N
W Irving Park Rd
Exit State Hwy 19
40
N Frontier Ave
W Dakin St
PAGE 186
Lincoln Park
Lake Michigan
W Sheridan Rd
Gill Park
A
W Grace St
N Fremont St
N Belmont Harbor Dr
Addison Dr
N Wilton Ave
W Bradley Pl
N Marine Dr
W Waveland Ave
W Patterson Ave
N Pine Grove Ave
3600N
Addison
W Addison St
W Brompton Ave
N Lake Shore Dr
N Reta Ave
W Brompton Ave
W Cornelia Ave
N Elaine Pl
W Stratford Pl
W Newport Ave
W Hawthorne Pl
Belmont Harbor
43
B
W Roscoe Ave
W Roscoe St
LAKE VIEW PARK
W Buckingham Pl
W Aldine Ave
W Aldine Ave
800W
N Dayton St
W Melrose St
3200N
Exit W Belmont Ave
W Belmont Ave
Belmont
N Clark St
N Orchard St
N Cambridge Ave
N Hudson Ave
W Fletcher St
W Briar Pl
3100N
W California Ter
W Briar Pl
41
W Barry Ave
W Barry Ave
W Barry Ave
N Waterloo Ct
W Nelson St
N Dayton St
Wellington
W Wellington Ave
N Lake Shore Drive
C
W Oakdale Ave
W Oakdale Ave
N Burling St
N Mildred Ave
W Surf St
W Surf St
N Sheridan Rd
W Wolfram St
2800N
Diversey
W Diversey Pkwy
W Diversey Ave
W Diversey Dr
N Lagoon Dr
30
W Schubert Ave
N Hampden Ct
W Drummond Pl
N Lehmann Ct
W Wrightwood Ave
W Schubert Ave
N Burling St
1
2

Heaps of good casual restaurants, a thriving bar scene (gay clubs mostly north of Belmont, Irish Pubs, south) and a first-rate cinema make East Lakeview a destination spot for night life. La Creperie is tiny and charming and frequently has live French music. Roscoe's and Sidetracks are two cavernous gay bars that really pack 'em in. Las Mananitas serves lethal margaritas on an outdoor patio great for people watching. Clark Street Dog is there to help you sop it up if you've had one too many. If you come to East Lakeview, do yourself a huge favor and cab it—taxis are abundant in these parts, and it's a cinch to hail one at any hour.

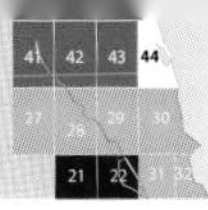

Bars

- **Charlie's Chicago** • 3726 N Broadway St
- **Circuit** • 3641 N Halsted St
- **Cocktail** • 3359 N Halsted St
- **Coyle's Tippling House** • 2843 N Halsted St
- **Duke of Perth** • 2913 N Clark St
- **Kit Kat Lounge** • 3700 N Halsted St
- **Little Jim's** • 3501 N Halsted St
- **Monsignor Murphy's** • 3019 N Broadway St
- **Roscoe's** • 3354-56 N Halsted St
- **Rose & Crown** • 420 W Belmont Ave
- **Sidetracks** • 3345-55 N Halsted St
- **Spin** • 800 W Belmont Ave
- **The Closet** • 3325 N Broadway St
- **Town Hall Pub** • 3340 N Halsted St

Copy Shops

- **Kinko's** • 3001 N Clark St
- **Mail Boxes Etc** • 3023 N Clark St
- **Mail Boxes Etc** • 3712 N Broadway St
- **Sir Speedy** • 2818 N Halsted St

Coffee

- **Borders Books & Music** • 2817 N Clark St
- **Caribou Coffee** • 3025 N Clark St
- **Caribou Coffee** • 3300 N Broadway St
- **Coffee & Tea Exchange** • 3311 N Broadway St
- **Intelligentsia Coffee Roasters** • 3123 N Broadway St
- **Seattle's Best** • 2951 N Broadway St
- **Starbucks** • 3358 N Broadway St
- **Starbucks** • 3845 N Broadway St
- **Starbucks** • 617 W Diversey St

Farmer's Markets

- **Halsted/Broadway/Grace Farmers Market** • On Halsted N of W Bradley Pl
- **North Halsted** • W Broadway St & N Halsted St

Gyms

- **Bally Total Fitness** • 2828 N Clark St
- **Chicago Sweat Shop** • 3215 N Broadway St
- **East Lakeview Multiplex** • 3657 N Pine Grove Ave
- **Quads Gym** • 3727 N Broadway St

Hardware Stores

- **Clark Street Ace Hardware** • 3011 N Clark St
- **Edwards True Value Hardware** • 2804 N Halsted St
- **Lehman's True Value Hardware** • 3473 N Broadway St
- **Midtown True Value Hardware** • 3130 N Broadway St

Liquor Stores

- **Binny's Beverage Depot** • 3000 N Clark St
- **Broadway Food & Liquor** • 3158 N Broadway St
- **Eastgate Wine & Spirits** • 446 W Diversey Pkwy
- **Gold Medal Liquors** • 3823 N Broadway St
- **Paradise Liquors** • 2934 N Broadway St

Movie Theaters

- **Landmark Century Cinema** • 2828 N Clark St

Pet Shops

- **Barker & Meowsky** • 3319 N Broadway St
- **Paradise Pet Salon** • 3920 N Broadway St
- **Petco** • 3046 N Halsted St
- **Scrub Your Pup** • 2935 N Clark St

Restaurants

- **Angelina** • 3561 N Broadway St
- **Ann Sather** • 3411 N Broadway St
- **Anna Maria Pasteria** • 3953 N Broadway St
- **Arco de Cuchilleros** • 3445 N Halsted St
- **Chicago Diner** • 3411 N Halsted St
- **Clark Street Dog** • 3040 N Clark St
- **Cornelia's Restaurant** • 750 W Cornelia Ave
- **Duke of Perth** • 2913 N Clark St
- **Erwin, An American Cafe & Bar** • 2925 N Halsted St
- **Half Shell** • 676 W Diversey Pkwy
- **Jack's on Halsted** • 3201 N Halsted St
- **Kit Kit Lounge & Supper Club** • 3700 N Halsted St
- **La Creperie** • 2845 N Clark St
- **Las Mananitas** • 3523 N Halsted St
- **Mark's Chop Suey** • 3343 N Halsted St
- **Melrose** • 3233 N Broadway St
- **Nancy's Original Stuffed Pizza** • 2930 N Broadway St
- **Nookie's Tree** • 3334 N Halsted
- **Yoshi's Cafe** • 3257 N Halsted

Shopping

- **Century Mall** • 2828 N Clark St
- **Equinox** • 3401 N Broadway St
- **Evil Clown Compact Discs** • 3418 N Halsted St
- **Gallimaufry Gallery** • 3345 N Halsted St
- **GayMart** • 3457 N Halsted St
- **The Brown Elephant Resale** • 3651 N Halsted St
- **Toyscape** • 2911 N Broadway St
- **Unabridged Bookstore** • 3251 N Broadway St

Video Rental

- **Adult Fantasy Book Store** • 2928 N Broadway St
- **Blockbuster Video** • 3120 N Clark St
- **Broadway Video** • 3916 N Broadway St
- **Golden Video** • 3619 N Broadway St
- **Hollywood Video** • 2868 N Broadway St
- **Mr Video** • 3356 N Broadway St
- **Nationwide Video** • 2827 N Broadway St
- **Nationwide Video** • 3936 N Clarendon Ave
- **R J's Video** • 3452 N Halsted St
- **Specialty Video** • 3221 N Broadway St
- **Video Island** • 440 W Diversey Pkwy
- **West Coast Video** • 3114 N Broadway St
- **Windy City Video** • 3701 N Halsted St

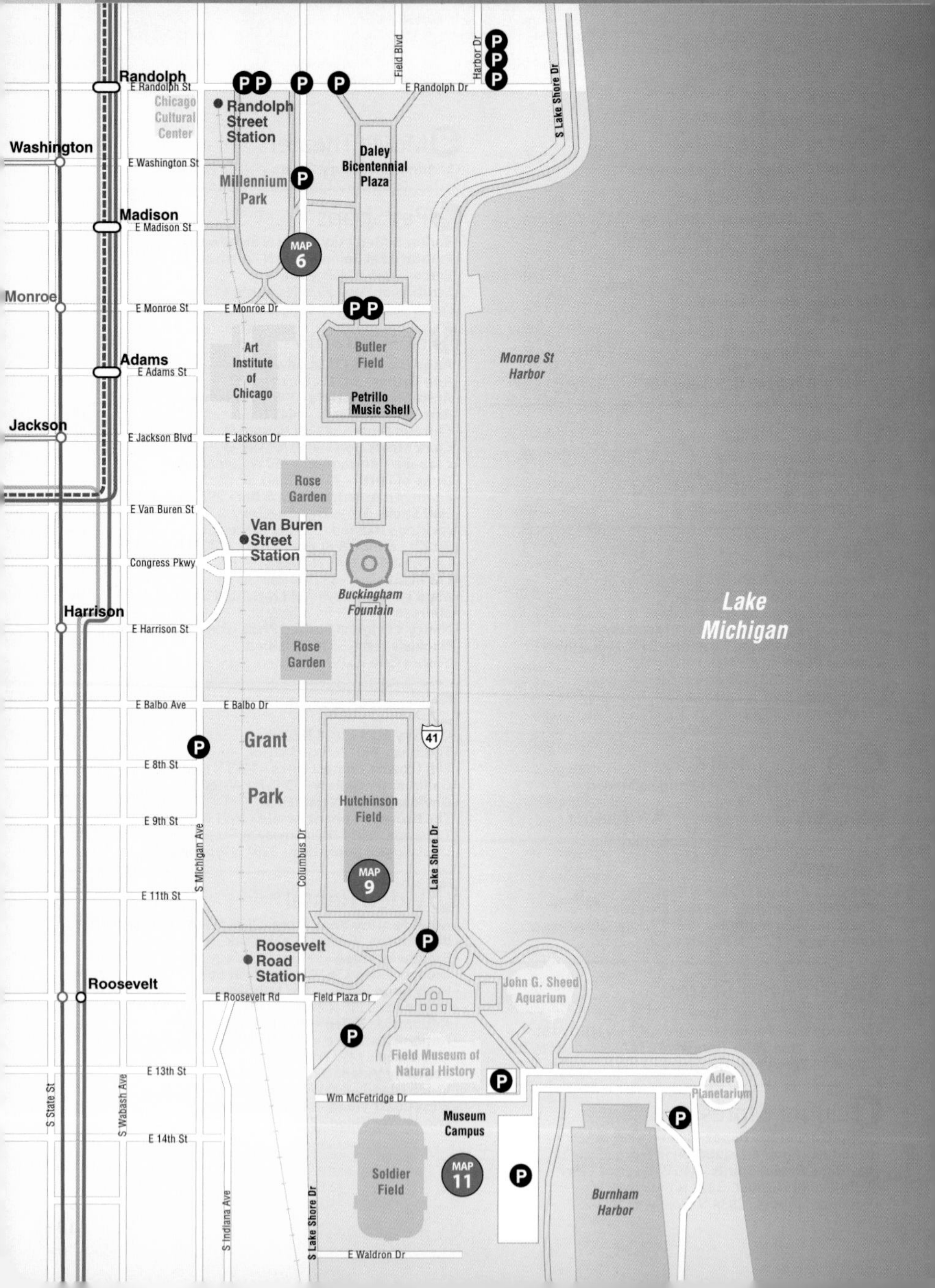

Randolph
E Randolph St
Chicago Cultural Center
Randolph Street Station
E Randolph Dr
Field Blvd
Harbor Dr
S Lake Shore Dr
Washington
E Washington St
Daley Bicentennial Plaza
Millennium Park
Madison
E Madison St
MAP 6
Monroe
E Monroe St
E Monroe Dr
Art Institute of Chicago
Butler Field
Petrillo Music Shell
Adams
E Adams St
Monroe St Harbor
Jackson
E Jackson Blvd
E Jackson Dr
Rose Garden
E Van Buren St
Van Buren Street Station
Congress Pkwy
Buckingham Fountain
Lake Michigan
Harrison
E Harrison St
Rose Garden
E Balbo Ave
E Balbo Dr
41
Grant Park
E 8th St
Hutchinson Field
E 9th St
S Michigan Ave
Columbus Dr
Lake Shore Dr
MAP 9
E 11th St
Roosevelt Road Station
Roosevelt
E Roosevelt Rd
Field Plaza Dr
John G. Shedd Aquarium
Field Museum of Natural History
E 13th St
Wm McFetridge Dr
Adler Planetarium
Museum Campus
S State St
S Wabash Ave
E 14th St
Soldier Field
MAP 11
Burnham Harbor
S Indiana Ave
S Lake Shore Dr
E Waldron Dr

Overview

Grant Park is Chicago's favorite place to promenade, picnic, protest, party, and play. Art permeates the park year-round from landscaped gardens, sculpture, and Buckingham Fountain to concerts, the Art Institute of Chicago, and Museum Campus—all on Grant Park's 319 acres.

Called Chicago's "front lawn," Grant Park stretches along the lakeshore from Randolph St. south to Roosevelt Rd. and west to Michigan Ave. where grass meets glass. Although the city's massive summer festivals turn the park into Chicago's doormat, Grant Park is usually a quiet place with open space to relax and play.

Architect Daniel Burnham laid the groundwork for the park. However, thank Chicago catalog king Aaron Montgomery Ward for pressuring the State of Illinois in 1911 to preserve the land as "public ground forever to remain vacant of buildings." Grant Park's development dragged on 'til 1934. History repeats itself. Traffic-traumatized Chicagoans pray that construction of the new Millennium Park complex at Grant Park's northwest corner will be complete by next century.

Nature

Grant Park's lawns, gardens, lakefront and, bench-lined paths attract office workers on break, as well as runners, bicyclists, readers, and thinkers (some disguised as snoozing homeless). South of Buckingham Fountain are the formal Music Garden and Rose Gardens. Near Daley Bicentennial Plaza is the riotously colorful Wildflower Garden recalling Illinois' prairies past. These gardens are butterfly and bird havens. Throughout the park are 18 sculptures created between 1893 and 1988.

Sports

Chicagoans play in Grant Park like kids in their back yards. After work, balls, kites, and Frisbees fly across Butler and Hutchinson Fields. Summer softball leagues fill baseball diamonds on the park's south end near the first-come-first-serve free tennis courts. Picnics for 50 or more people and tent set-up require permits from the Chicago Park District, 312-742-7529; www.chicagoparkdistrict.com.

On the park's north side is Daley Bicentennial Plaza, 337 E. Randolph St., 312-742-7648, with a fitness center, skating rink and 12 outdoor tennis courts. Year-round tennis hours are weekdays, 10 am to 9 pm; weekends, 8:30 am to 5 pm. Court time costs $7 an hour (2-hour limit); reservations recommended, 312-742-7650. The rink is open daily November to March for ice-skating ($2, skate rental available), and free in-line skating on off-ice months.

Buckingham Fountain

Buckingham Fountain is Grant Park's spouting centerpiece at the intersection of Congress Pkwy. and Columbus Dr. Designed by Edward Bennett and first operational in 1927, Buckingham Fountain showers onlookers with wind-blown spray April through October from 10 am to 11 pm daily. For 20 minutes every hour, on the hour the center basin jettisons water 150 feet. Beginning at dusk at the same times, the skyrocketing water display is accompanied by lights and music. Food concessions and restrooms are nearby.

Art Institute of Chicago

The Art Institute has 12 extensive, permanent collections and plenty of exhibitions, and also hosts interesting public programs daily, even on the free day—Tuesday. Other days, a $10 donation is recommended. The handy "Pocketguide" breaks collections down into hour-at-a-time visits, perfect and impressive for Loop lunch dates. Open June through September, the outdoor Garden Restaurant has live music some evenings. The museum is open weekdays 10:30 am to 4:30 pm (Tuesdays open 'til 8 pm), and weekends 10 am to 5 pm 111 S. Michigan Ave., 312-443-3600; www.artic.edu.

Festivals & Events

Chicagoans used to gather at the Petrillo Music Shell, Jackson Blvd. and Columbus Dr., for free Grant Park Orchestra and Chorus concerts during the summer, but now they will be going to the newly opened Millenium Park Music Pavilion. Concerts take place June through August on Wednesday and Friday evenings, (312-742-4763); www.grantparkmusicfestival.com. You can't always pass up a free headliner concert at Grant Park's monstrous Summer Festivals. Avoid the gut-to-gut, al fresco feeding frenzy at the 10-day Taste of Chicago by going, if you must, on a weekday. Contact the Mayor's Office of Special Events for a complete event schedule, 312-744-3315; www.cityofchicago.org/SpecialEvents.

How to Get There

By Car: Exits off Lake Shore Dr. west to Grant Park are Randolph St., Monroe Dr., Jackson Dr., Balbo Dr., and Roosevelt Rd. Also, enter the park from Michigan Ave. heading east on the same streets. The underground East Monroe Garage is off Monroe Dr. Columbus Dr. runs through Grant Park's center and has metered parking.

By Train: From the Richard B. Ogilvie Transportation Center, travel east to Michigan Ave. and Grant Park on CTA buses 56, 20, and 157 ($1.50 one-way). From Union Station board CTA buses 60, 157, 123, and 151.

Metra trains coming from the south stop at the Roosevelt Rd. station on the south end of Grant Park before terminating travel at the underground Randolph St. station below Millennium Park.

By El: Get off at any El stop in the Loop between Randolph St. and Van Buren St. ($1.50 one-way). Walk two blocks east to Grant Park.

By Bus: CTA buses 151, 145, 146, 147, 3, and 10 (weekends only) stop along Michigan Ave. in front of Grant Park ($1.50 one-way).

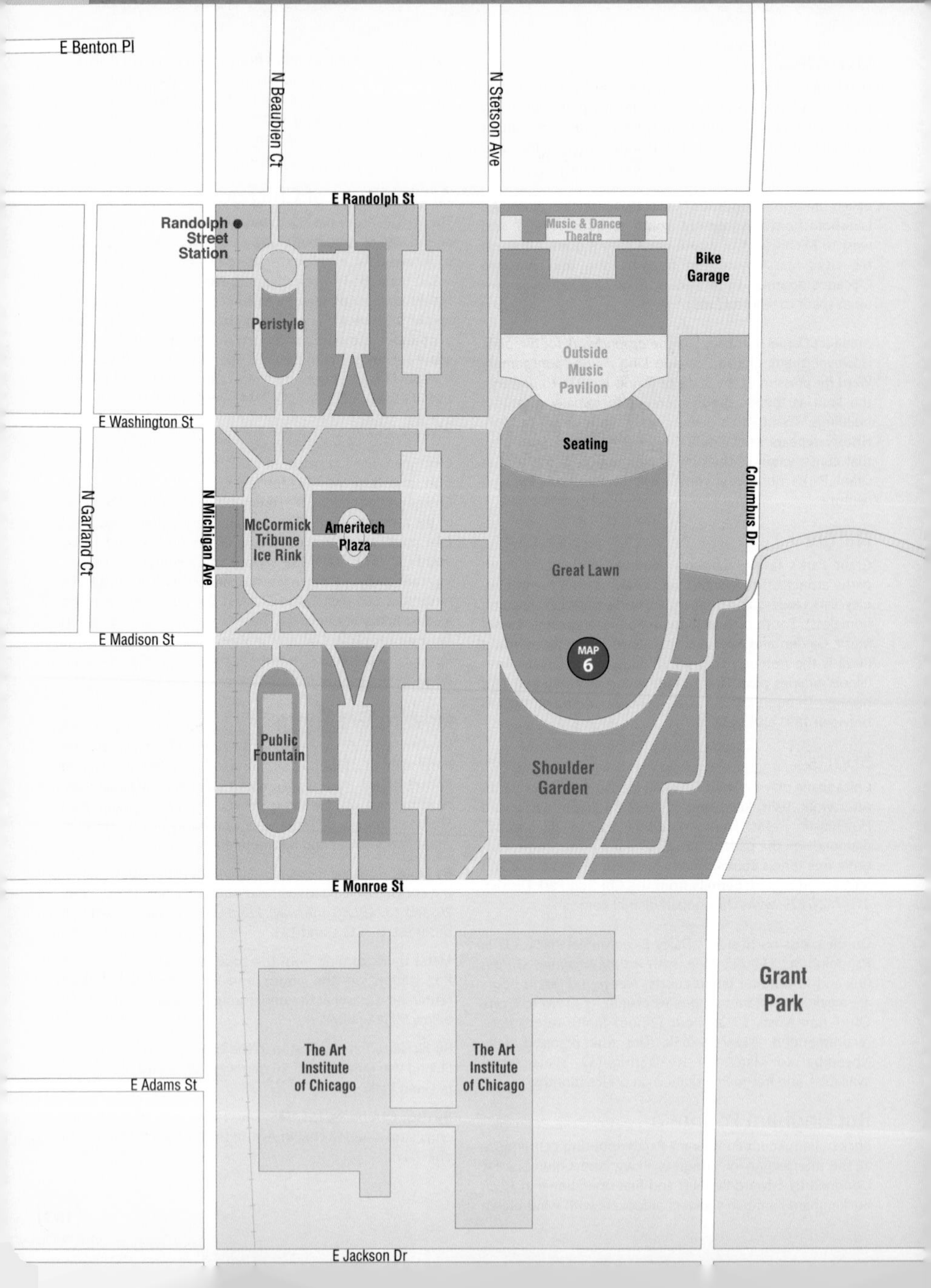

E Benton Pl
N Beaubien Ct
N Stetson Ave
E Randolph St
Randolph Street Station
Music & Dance Theatre
Bike Garage
Peristyle
Outside Music Pavilion
E Washington St
Seating
Columbus Dr
N Garland Ct
N Michigan Ave
McCormick Tribune Ice Rink
Ameritech Plaza
Great Lawn
E Madison St
MAP 6
Public Fountain
Shoulder Garden
E Monroe St
Grant Park
The Art Institute of Chicago
The Art Institute of Chicago
E Adams St
E Jackson Dr

Overview

It seems like centuries of construction since Mayor Daley unveiled the grandiose Millennium Park plan for Grant Park's northwest corner. The 24-acre cultural and recreational complex bounded by Michigan Ave., Columbus Dr., Randolph Dr., and Monroe St. will eventually include landscaped gardens, sculpture, performance venues, restaurants, and a 400-space indoor bicycle parking facility. The ice rink and underground garages are open now.

The park's master plan is as ambitious as it is behind schedule and over budget. The price tag has soared from $150 million to almost $400 million. Private donations exceeding $100 million will help pay for the project, whose target completion date was originally summer 2000. Now the goal is 2004.

Millennium Park officials keep promising it will be worth the pounding headaches construction has caused. But as the project drags on, we're asking the same question as Frank Gehry, architect of the park's music pavilion, did in a 2001 Chicago Tribune interview: "Why is it taking so [expletive] long?"

Music Pavilion

The park's 4,000-seat music pavilion, intended to replace the Petrillo Band Shell, was designed by renowned architect Frank Gehry. In keeping with his steely design for the Guggenheim Museum in Bilbao, Spain, the Millennium Park outdoor concert hall's roof is made of unfurling stainless steel bands curlicue-ing 40 feet into the sky. The stage faces south towards the 95,000-square foot Great Lawn that will seat up to 7,000. All pavilion events will be free.

Music & Dance Theatre

The underground 1,500-seat theatre is located behind the pavilion and will become home to nonprofit performing arts groups. A restaurant is on the drawing board. Two underground parking garages flank the theatre.

Nature & Sculpture

Gardens with sculpted hedges and flowing water designed by Kathyrn Gustafson are planned for the park's southeast corner bordered by Monroe St. Slated to open by 2006, the Art Institute's proposed, pricey addition by architect Renzo Piano will overlook them. A replica of Grant Park's original Peristyle of Greek Columns from 1917 anchors Millennium Park's northwest corner. A dramatic fountain will grace the southwest corner. On top of a proposed 300-seat restaurant next to the ice rink on Michigan Ave. will be Ameritech Plaza, featuring a 66-foot long, 100-ton, jelly bean-shaped sculpture of polished stainless steel by Anish Kapoor, his first public work installed in the United States. Mayor Daley's graffiti busters better be ready to blast that bean once it arrives.

Sports

While Millennium Park's construction moves at glacial speed, the McCormick Tribune Ice Rink has been operational since December 2001. The 15,910-square foot rink is open daily starting in November. Admission is free; skate rental available ($5 per session). In summer, the rink doubles as a dance floor and activity center. 55 N. Michigan Ave., 312-742-5222; www.chicagoparkdistrict.com.

How to Get There

No matter your mode of travel, approach the area around Millennium Park with patience and allow extra time. For train, El, and bus transportation recommendations see NFT's Grant Park section. Metra's Randolph St. train station servicing only south-bound trains is located under Millennium Park. Contact the RTA Information Center, 312-836-7000, www.rtachicago.com, for schedules and fares.

The park's garages are open. Access the Grant Park North Garage from Michigan Ave. Enter Millennium Park Garage from the lower levels of Randolph St. and mid-level of Columbus Dr. (12 hours or less, $10).

Additional Information

Public Building Commission Chicago, 312-744-3090; www.pbcchicago.com

Overview

The largest of Chicago's 552 parks, Lincoln Park stretches 1,208-acres along the lakefront from North Ave. to Hollywood Ave., which includes a substantial portion of one of the world's longest linked bike trails which, thanks to an ever-increasing abundance of headphone-wearing roller-bladers, proves treacherous for cyclists and normal pedestrians alike. Nonetheless, sports enthusiasts and culture seekers still find satisfaction indoors and out. Public buildings including animal houses at the Lincoln Park Zoo, Café Brauer, Peggy Notebaert Nature Museum, and vintage beach bath houses make the park as architecturally attractive as it is naturally beautiful.

Nature

Much of southern Lincoln Park is open green space popular for football, soccer, dog play, and barbeques. Paths shaded by mature trees lead to stoic statues. Until the 1860s, portions of this area were a municipal cemetery populated with cholera and small pox victims buried in shallow graves. Although the city attempted to relocate all the bodies in the cemetery-to-park conversion, digging doggies may unearth more than picnickers' chicken bones.

In spring, bird watchers flock to Lincoln Park's ponds and nature trails. Addison Bird Sanctuary Viewing Platform north of Belmont Harbor overlooks five fenced-in acres of wetlands and woods. Birding programs are held around Montrose Point, 312-742-7529; www.chicagoparkdistrict.com. The Chicago Ornithological Society, 312-409-9678, www.chicagobirder.org, leads walks around North Pond. The Fort Dearborn Chapter of the Illinois Audubon Society, 847-675-3622, hosts free park and zoo bird walks. Migratory birds gather around the revamped 1889 lily pond at Fullerton Ave. and N. Cannon Dr.

Sports

Baseball diamonds on the park's south end are bordered by La Salle Dr. and Lake Shore Dr. next to the newly renovated field house and NorthStar Eatery. Upgrades planned for the area include a running track, soccer field, and basketball and volleyball courts. Bicyclists and runners race along Lincoln Park Lagoon to the footbridge over Lake Shore Dr. to North Ave. Beach, Chicago's volleyball mecca. To reserve courts and rent equipment, go to the south end of the landmark, boat-shaped bath house, 312-742-3224. The upper deck of Chicago Beach Café rocks on weekends with live music. Just north of the bath house is a seasonal rollerblade rink and fitness club.

Nine-hole Sydney R. Marovitz Public Golf Course, 3600 N. Recreation Dr., 312-742-7930, hosts hackers year-round. Snail-slow play allows plenty of time to enjoy skyline views from this lakefront cow pasture, which is always crowded. (Greens fees are $14 Monday through Friday, $19 on weekends, and you can rent clubs for $10.) Reserve tee times, 312-245-0909, or show up at sunrise. The starter sits in the northeast corner of the clock tower field house.

Twenty first-come-first-served tennis courts are on Recreational Dr. north of Belmont Harbor beside baseball diamonds, playing fields, and a playground. Also, there are four courts next to the new Diversey Miniature Golf Course. These are the only clay courts left in Chicago and cost $12 per hour; tennis shoes are required. For reservations and further information, call 312-742-7821. Also nearby is the year-round Diversey Golf Range, 141 W. Diversey Pkwy, 312-742-7929. The Lincoln Park Tennis Association plays on six neighboring courts, 773-929-3671.

Members of the Lincoln Park Boat Club row in Lincoln Park Lagoon. Rowing classes for the public are offered May through September, 773-549-2628; www.lpbc.net.
Ply whimsical, swan-shaped paddleboats at South Pond next to Café Brauer, 2021 N. Stockton Dr., a restored Prairie School national landmark, housing, seasonal restaurants and an upstairs ballroom. Fishermen frequent South Pond and the lagoon. Belmont, Montrose and Diversey Harbors allow shore fishing. North of Montrose Harbor on lakefront N. Wilson Dr. is a new, free skateboard park.

Lincoln Park Zoo

Address: *2200 N. Cannon Dr.*
Phone: *312-742-2000*
Website: *www.lpzoo.com*
Hours: *Daily, 9-6 pm; animal buildings 10-5 pm*

Established in 1868, Lincoln Park Zoo is the nation's oldest free zoo. National television shows "Zoo Parade" and Ray Rayner's show "Ark in the Park" were filmed here. Supported by big corporate sponsorships and private funds, new zoo improvements "Farm in the Zoo" and "African Journey" (which included much needed ecological improvements to the primates habitat) opened in Spring 2003. The zoo's elephants, giraffes, hippos, and rhinos have returned and are joined in the new exhibit by other species native to the continent's natural habitats. Flanking the zoo's northwest side is the free Lincoln Park Conservatory, which is a fantastic source of oxygen renewal, particularly if you are suffering from a bit too much fun the night before..

Peggy Notebaert Nature Museum

Address: *2430 N. Cannon Dr.*
Phone: *773-755-5100*
Website: *www.naturemuseum.org*
Hours: *M-F 9-4:30 pm; S-S 10-5 pm*
Admission: *$7, Thursdays free*

The Peggy Notebaert Nature Museum succeeds at making Illinois' level landscape interesting. The contemporary version of the 1857 Chicago Academy of Sciences, this hands-on museum depicts the close connection between urban and natural environments. A flowing water lab and flitting butterfly haven invite return visits.

Chicago Historical Society

Address: *Clark St. & North Ave.*
Phone: *312-642-4600*
Website: *www.chicagohistory.org*
Hours: *Mon-Sat 9:30-4:30 pm; Sun 12-5 pm*
Admission: *$5, Mondays free*

The Chicago Historical Society preserves the life and times of Chicago's citizens. Exhibits on the city's pioneer roots, architecture, music, fashion, neighborhoods, and windy politics breathe life into otherwise dry history. Chicagoans access the excellent free research center (open Tuesday through Saturday) for genealogical information and housing history. Big Shoulders Café is a good, light lunch spot. Openings for 2004 include the groundbreaking Teen Chicago oral history project.

Performances

Lincoln Park Cultural Center, 2045 N. Lincoln Park West, 312-742-7726, produces plays, theater workshops, and family performances year-round. Theater on the Lake, Fullerton Ave. and Lake Shore Dr., 312-742-7994, performs nine weeks of alternative drama in summer ($15). Lincoln Park Zoo has outdoor summer concerts. Call events hotline, 312-742-2283.

How to Get There

By Car: Lake Shore Dr. exits to Lincoln Park are Bryn Mawr Ave., Foster Ave., Lawrence Ave., Wilson Dr., Montrose Dr., Irving Park Pkwy., Belmont Ave., Fullerton Ave., and North Ave.

Free parking lots are at Recreational Dr. near Belmont Harbor and Simonds Dr. near Montrose Harbor. Paid lots are at North Ave. Beach, Chicago Historical Society, Lincoln Park Zoo, and Grant Hospital Garage. Stockton Dr. and Cannon Dr. have free street parking. A metered lot is on Diversey Pkwy. next to the golf range.

By Bus: CTA buses 151, 156, 77, 146, and 147 travel through Lincoln Park ($1.50 one-way). For schedules and fares, contact the RTA Information Center, 312-836-7000; www.rtachicago.com.

By El: Get off the Red Line at any stop between Fullerton Ave. and Bryn Mawr Ave. ($1.50 one-way). Head one mile east.

E 55th St
55th St
S Harper Ave
S Lake Park Ave
S Cornell Ave
S Hyde Park Blvd
S South Shore Dr
57th St Beach
E 56th St
E 57th St
S Everett Ave
E 57th Dr
E 57th St
E Museum Dr
Museum of Science and Industry
Columbia Dr
E Columbia Dr Cutoff
S Harper Ave
Doctors Hospital of Hyde Park
Lake Michigan
59th St
E 59th St
Midway Plaisance
Plaisance Park
Osaka Garden
41
E 60th St
S Stony Island Ave
S Lake Shore Dr
Wooded Island
S Harper Ave
E 61st St
West Lagoon
East Lagoon
Jackson Park Beach
E 62nd St
MAP 20
S Harper Ave
Jackson Park
E 63rd St
Coast Guard Station
E Hayes Dr
Coast Gd Dr Cut Off
E 63rd Pl
E 64th St
S Dante Ave
S Harper Ave
S Stony Island Ave
S Cornell Ave
Jackson Park Golf Course
S Richards Dr
South Lagoon
S Promontory Dr
La Rabida Childrens Hospital & Research Center
Yatch Harbor
E 65th St
E 65th Pl
E Marquette Dr
E 66th St
S Coast Guard Dr
E 66th Pl
67th Bea
E 67th St
E 67th Pl
S Cornell Ave
S East End Ave
S Cregier Ave
S Bennett Ave
S Jeffery Ave
S Clyde Ave
S Crandon Ave
S South Shore Dr

Overview

The South Side's answer to Lincoln Park, historic Jackson Park forms the eastern edge of Hyde Park, the diverse neighborhood of the University of Chicago.

Jackson Park's history is rooted in humankind's quest for discovery. It was the site of the 1893 World's Columbian Exposition. Architect Daniel Burnham, chief of construction for the Exposition, transformed the windswept lakefront into a shimmering "White City" with lagoons, landscaped gardens, sculpture, harbors, and ornate, landmark buildings to house exhibits from around the world. Today, the Museum of Science and Industry and La Rabida Children's Hospital and Research Center occupy two former Fair structures.

Until recently, Jackson Park had gone to seed. But things are coming up roses again, thanks to clean and green Mayor Daley's passion for the city's parks. Major improvements to the area's lakefront, bike path, and beaches have Jackson Park shimmering again.

Museum of Science and Industry

Address:	*57th St. and Lake Shore Dr.*
Phone:	*773-684-1414*
Website:	*www.msichicago.org*
Hours:	*M-Sa 9:30 am–4 pm; Su 11am–4 pm*
Admission:	*Adults $9; Chicagoans $8*

The 1893 Exposition's original Arts Palace is now the 350,000-square foot Museum of Science and Industry—making it the largest science museum in a single building in the Western Hemisphere. Generations of Chicagoans have been wowed by the Human Body Slices, U-505 (the only World War II German submarine captured), 3,000-square foot Model Railroad, and Walk-Through Heart. "Genetics: Decoding Life", the museum's newest permanent exhibit, explores cloning, genetic engineering, and the human genome project. For relief from brain freeze, check out the fast food toy exhibit, early spacecrafts that look like toys, and the Fairy Castle.

Nature

The East and West Lagoons surround Wooded Island, also called Paul H. Douglas Nature Sanctuary. On the island's northern tip is Osaka Garden, a serene Japanese garden with an authentic tea house and entrance gate. The ceremonial garden, like the golden Statue of the Republic on Hayes Ave., recalls the park's 1893 Exposition origins. The Chicago Audubon Society, 773-539-6793, conducts bird walks here and in nearby Bob-O-Link Meadow. These sites and the Perennial Garden at 59th St. and Cornell Dr. are butterfly havens.

Sports

When Jackson Park Golf Course opened in 1899 it was the Midwest's first public course. Certified by the Audubon Cooperative Sanctuary, the 18-hole course has wilderness habitats—or are those scruffy fairways? Greens fees are $18 Monday through Friday and $21 on weekends. A driving range is adjacent to the course. 312-245-0909.

Jackson Park field house has a weight room and gymnasium. From Hayes Dr. north along Cornell Dr. are outdoor tennis courts, baseball diamonds, and a running track. Tennis courts are on the west side of Lakeshore Dr. at 63rd St. Jackson Park's beaches are at 57th St. and 63rd St. (water playground too). Inner and Outer Harbors allow shore fishing. 6401 S. Stony Island Ave., 312-747-6187.

Neighboring Parks

North of Jackson Park at 55th St. and Lake Shore Dr. is Promontory Point, a scenic lakeside picnic spot. Harold Washington Park, 51st St. and Lake Shore Dr., has a model yacht basin and eight tennis courts on 53rd St.

To the west, 460-acre Washington Park, 5531 S. Martin Luther King Dr., 312-747-6823, has an outdoor swimming pool, playing fields, nature areas, Lorado Taft's 1922 Fountain of Time sculpture, and the DuSable Museum of African American History, 740 E. 56th Pl., 773-947-0600; www.dusablemuseum.org.

At 71st St. and South Shore Dr. are South Shore Beach, a harbor, bird sanctuary, and South Shore Cultural Center, 7059 S. Shore Dr., 312-747-2536. South Shore Golf Course is a nine-hole, public course. Greens fees are $12 Monday through Friday and $13.50 on weekends. 312-245-0909.

How to Get There

By Car: From the Loop, drive south on Lake Shore Dr., exit west on 57th St. From the south, take I-94 west. Exit on Stony Island Ave. heading north to 57th Dr. The museum's parking garage entrance is on 57th Dr. The Music Court lot is behind the museum. A free parking lot is on Hayes Dr.

By Bus: From the Loop, CTA buses 6 and 10 (weekends and daily in summer) stop by the museum.

By El (the quickest way to get to Jackson Park): Take the Red or Green Lines to the Garfield Blvd. (55th St.) station stop ($1.50 one-way); walk two blocks east or transfer to the eastbound 55 bus ($1.80 one-way).

By Train: Sporadic service. From the Loop's Randolph St. and Van Buren St. stations, take Metra Electric service ($1.95 one-way). Trains stop at the 55th, 56th, and 57th St. station platform (may be under construction). Walk two blocks east. From Richard B. Ogilvie Transportation Center, walk two blocks south to Union Station on Canal St. and catch CTA bus 1.

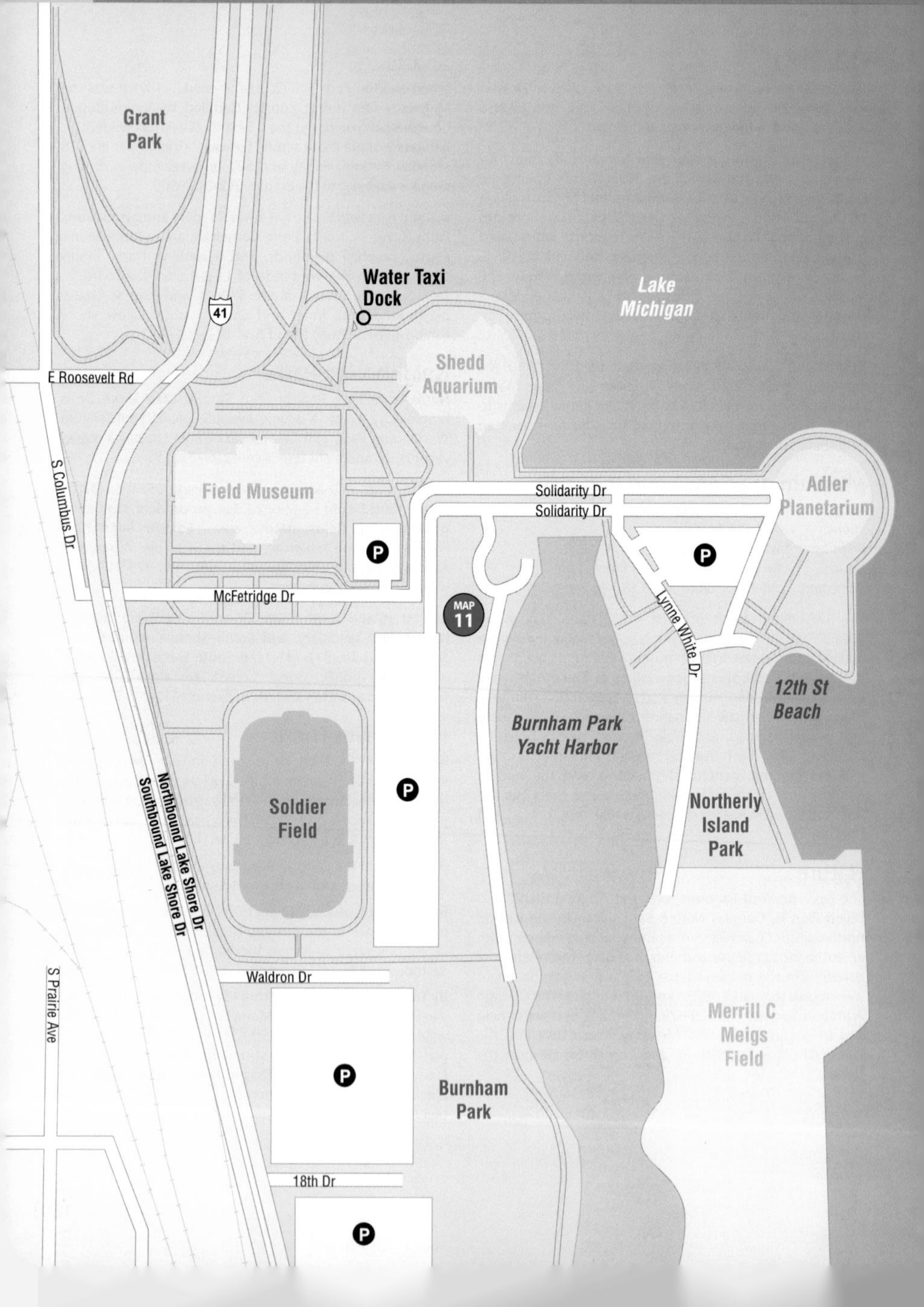

Grant Park

Water Taxi Dock

Lake Michigan

41

Shedd Aquarium

E Roosevelt Rd

S Columbus Dr

Field Museum

Solidarity Dr

Solidarity Dr

Adler Planetarium

P

P

McFetridge Dr

MAP 11

Lynne White Dr

12th St Beach

Burnham Park Yacht Harbor

Soldier Field

P

Northerly Island Park

Northbound Lake Shore Dr

Southbound Lake Shore Dr

Waldron Dr

S Prairie Ave

Merrill C Meigs Field

P

Burnham Park

18th Dr

P

Overview

The Museum Campus is the ultimate destination for an educational field trip. South of Grant Park at the intersection of Roosevelt Rd. and Lake Shore Dr., visitors can walk through uninterrupted lakefront parkland among three world-renowned institutions—Field Museum, Shedd Aquarium, and Adler Planetarium. However, it wasn't always a sprawling grassy peninsula on Burnham Park's northern edge. Mayor Daley championed the rerouting of Lake Shore Dr. to create the Museum Campus, which opened in 1998.

Field Museum of Natural History

Address: *1400 S. Lake Shore Dr.*
Phone: *312-922-9410*
Website: *www.fieldmuseum.org*
Hours: *Everyday except for Christmas 9-5 pm*
Admission: *$8*

Approach the Field Museum of Natural History as though it were a smorgasbord. The massive, classical Greek architectural-style museum constructed in 1921 houses over 20 million artifacts. From dinosaurs, diamonds, and earthworms to man-eating lions, totem poles, and mummies, there is just too much to savor in a single sitting. Some temporary exhibits and the Underground Adventure cost an additional $7. Free museum tours are weekdays at 11 am and 2 pm

John G. Shedd Aquarium

Address: *1200 S. Lake Shore Dr.*
Phone: *312-939-2438*
Website: *www.shedd.org*
Hours: *M-F 9-5 pm; Sa-Su 9-6 pm*
Admission: *$21 ($14 for Chicagoans)*

In Spring 2003, the John G. Shedd Aquarium will unveil an extremely cool underwater exhibit, Philippine Island, a coral reef shark habitat. Visitors walk through 385,000 gallons of water where sharks cruise. The ten-room, $45 million addition showcases Indo-Pacific animals, corals, and tropical fish. Opened in 1929, the Beaux Arts architectural-style aquarium's six wings radiate from a giant, circular coral reef tank.

Adler Planetarium

Address: *1300 S. Lake Shore Dr.*
Phone: *312-922-7827*
Website: *www.adlerplanetarium.org*
Hours: *M-F 9:30 am–4:30 pm; S-S 9 am-–4:30 pm*
Admission: *$13 ($11 for Chicagoans)*

Adler Planetarium & Astronomy Museum has interactive exhibits explaining space phenomena and intergalactic events. The museum's 2,000 historic astronomical and navigational instruments form the western hemisphere's largest collection. Chicago skyline views from planetarium grounds are out of this world.

Burnham Park

Burnham Park, the site of the 1933 Century of Progress exhibition, encompasses McCormick Place, Burnham Harbor, the former Merrill C. Meigs Airport (closed by political coup by Mayor Daley in 2003), and Soldier Field. At Lake Shore Dr. and 31st St. is a free skateboard park. The 12th St. Beach is on Northerly Island. Other beaches are at 31st St. and 49th St. Outdoor basketball courts are east of Lake Shore Dr. around 35th St. and 47th St. Along Solidarity Dr. and Burnham Harbor shore, fishing is welcome. The wilderness Nature Area at 47th St. attracts butterflies and birds.

How to Get There

By Car: From the Loop, take Columbus Dr. south; turn east on McFetridge Dr. From the south, take Lake Shore Dr. to McFetridge Dr. Area parking lots are near Soldier Field, Field Museum, Adler Planetarium, and McCormick Place. Metered parking lines Solidarity Dr.

By Bus: CTA buses 2, 6, 10, 12, 14, 127, 130, and 146 serve the area ($1.50 one-way). For schedules and fares, contact the RTA Information Center, 312-836-7000; www.rtachicago.com.

By El: Ride the Orange, Red, or Green Lines to the Roosevelt Rd. stop ($1.50). Walk east through the pedestrian underpass at Roosevelt Rd.

By Train: From Richard B. Ogilvie Transportation Center, travel east on CTA bus 20 to State St.; transfer to the 146 ($1.80 one-way). From Union Station take CTA bus 1, 151, or 126; transfer at State St. to the 146 or 10. From La Salle St. station, take the 146 ($1.50 one-way). South Shore and Metra trains stop at the Roosevelt Rd. station.

By Trolley: Free trolleys travel to the Museum Campus from public transportation stations and some parking lots. See www.cityofchicago.org/Transportation/trolleys/ or call 1-877-CHICAGO.

On Foot: Walk south through Grant Park past bobbing boats and Buckingham Fountain to the Museum Campus.

Water Taxis: Seasonally, water taxis operate between Navy Pier and the Museum Campus, 312-222-9328; www.shorelinesightseeing.com.

West Kinzie St
Carroll Dr
Carroll Ave
W Fulton St
Garfield Park Conservatory
N Avers Ave
North Central Park Ave
N St Louis Ave
N Homan Ave
W Fulton Blvd
Pulaski
Conservatory Dr
Gold Dome
Conservatory Central Park Drive
Walton St
N Pulaski Rd
N Harding Ave
West Lake St
North Hamilton Ave
W Schrader Dr
Ked
W Maypole Ave
North Central Park Ave
W Maypole Ave
W End St
Lagoon
W Washington Blvd
Garfield
W Washington Blvd
W Warren Ave
Park
W Madison St
S Pulaski Rd
S Springfield Ave
South Hamilton Blvd
Woodward Dr
South Central Park Ave
S St Louis Ave
S Homan Ave
S Spaulding Ave
W Monroa St
Music Court Dr
W Monroa St
Wilcox Ave
W Adams St
W Adams Ave
Baseball Field
W Jackson Blvd
W Jackson Blvd
Independence Blvd
S Christiana Ave
Baseball Field
Baseball Field
S Trumbull Ave
W Gladys Ave
W Van Buron St
Fifth Ave
W Glady Ave
S Millard Ave
Pulaski
W Congress St
290
Dwight D Eisenhower Expwy
W Harrison St

Overview

Until recently, the slowly gentrifying (read, sketchy) West Side had the city's best kept secret garden—Garfield Park Conservatory in Garfield Park. The Chicago Park District invested over $12 million to restore this national landmark. The 185-acre park's outdoor attractions include fishing lagoons, a swimming pool, an ice rink, baseball diamonds, and basketball and tennis courts. Garfield Park's landmark Gold Dome houses a fitness center, a basketball court, and the Peace Museum.

Garfield Park and its sister parks—Humboldt Park, 1400 N. Sacramento Ave., 312-742-7549, and Douglas Park, 1401 S. Sacramento Ave., 312-747-7670—compose a grand system of sprawling green spaces linked by broad boulevards designed in 1869 by William Le Baron Jenney. However, Jenney's plan didn't bear fruit until almost forty years later (after corrupt park officials were uprooted), when Danish immigrant and former park laborer Jens Jensen became chief landscape architect. In 1908, Jensen completed the parks and consolidated their three small conservatories under the 1.8-acre Garfield Park Conservatory's curvaceous glass dome, designed to resemble a "great Midwestern haystack."

Garfield Park Conservatory

Address: *300 N. Central Park Ave.*
Phone: *312-746-5100*
Website: *www.garfield-conservatory.org*
Hours: *Daily 9-5 pm*

One of the nation's largest conservatories, Garfield Park's has six thematic plant houses enclosing 1,000 species and over 10,000 individual plants from around the world. Plants Alive!, a 5,000-square foot children's garden, has touchable plants, a soil pool for digging, a Jurassic Park-sized bumble bee, and a two-story, twisting flower stem that doubles as a slide. School groups often book the garden, so call first to determine public access hours. Annual Conservatory events include the Spring Flower Show, Azalea/Camellia Show, Chocolate Festival, Summer Tropical Show, Chrysanthemum (Chicago's city flower) Show, and Holiday Garden Show. A snack-café cart operates weekends.

Peace Museum

Address: *100 N. Central Park Ave.*
Phone: *773-638-6450*
Website: *www.peacemuseum.org*
Hours: *Tues, Wed and Fri 11- 4 pm*

Located on the top floor of the landmark Garfield Park Gold Dome is the Peace Museum. The tiny museum's collection of 10,000 artworks, photographs, and artifacts promoting non-violence are displayed through rotating, thematic exhibits. Special exhibits include a John Lennon guitar, original U2 song sheet, and moving drawings by Nagasaki and Hiroshima survivors. Call for information on current and traveling exhibits.

Fishing

Garfield Park's two lagoons at Washington Blvd. and Central Park Ave. and those at Douglas and Humboldt Parks are favorite West Side fishing holes. Seasonally, they are stocked with bluegill, crappie, channel catfish, and largemouth bass, along with an occasional unfortunate gang member. Review your health insurance plan before eating what you hook. Weekdays June through August at park lagoons, the Chicago Park District sponsors free fishing instruction for all ages, 312-747-6067, as does the Illinois Department of Natural Resources' Urban Fishing Program, 847-294-4132.

Nature

The Chicago Park District hosts free nature walks and has created marked trails with information plaques at the city's bigger parks, Garfield and Humboldt Parks included. Seasonally, view as many as 100 species of colorful butterflies at the formal gardens of Garfield Park (Madison St. and Hamlin Ave.), Humboldt Park (Humboldt Ave. and Division St.), and Douglas Park (Ogden Ave. and S. Sacramento Ave.). The parks' lagoons are designated Chicago "birding parks." Free bird walks are offered by the Chicago Audubon Society, 773-539-6793; www.homepage.interaccess.com/~stephenc/index.html. Picnics for 50 people or more and tent set-up require permits issued by the Chicago Park District.

How to Get There

By Car: Garfield Park is ten minutes from the Loop. Take I-290 west; exit on Independence Blvd. and travel north. Turn east on Washington Blvd. to Central Park Ave. Go north on Central Park Ave. two blocks past the Golden Dome field house and Lake St. to the Conservatory. A free parking lot is on the building's south side just after Lake St. Street parking is available on Central Park Ave., Madison St., and Washington Blvd.

By El: From the Loop, take the Green Line west ($1.50 one-way) to the new Garfield Park Conservatory stop, a renovated Victorian train station at Lake St. and Central Park Ave.

By Bus: From the Loop, board CTA 20 Madison St. bus westbound ($1.50 one-way). Get off at Madison and Central Park Ave. Walk four blocks north to the Conservatory.

Additional Information

Chicago Park District, 312-742-7529;
www.chicagoparkdistrict.com
Nature Chicago Program - City of Chicago and Department of the Environment, 312-744-7606; www.cityofchicago.org
Chicago Ornithological Society, 312-409-9678;
www.chicagobirder.org

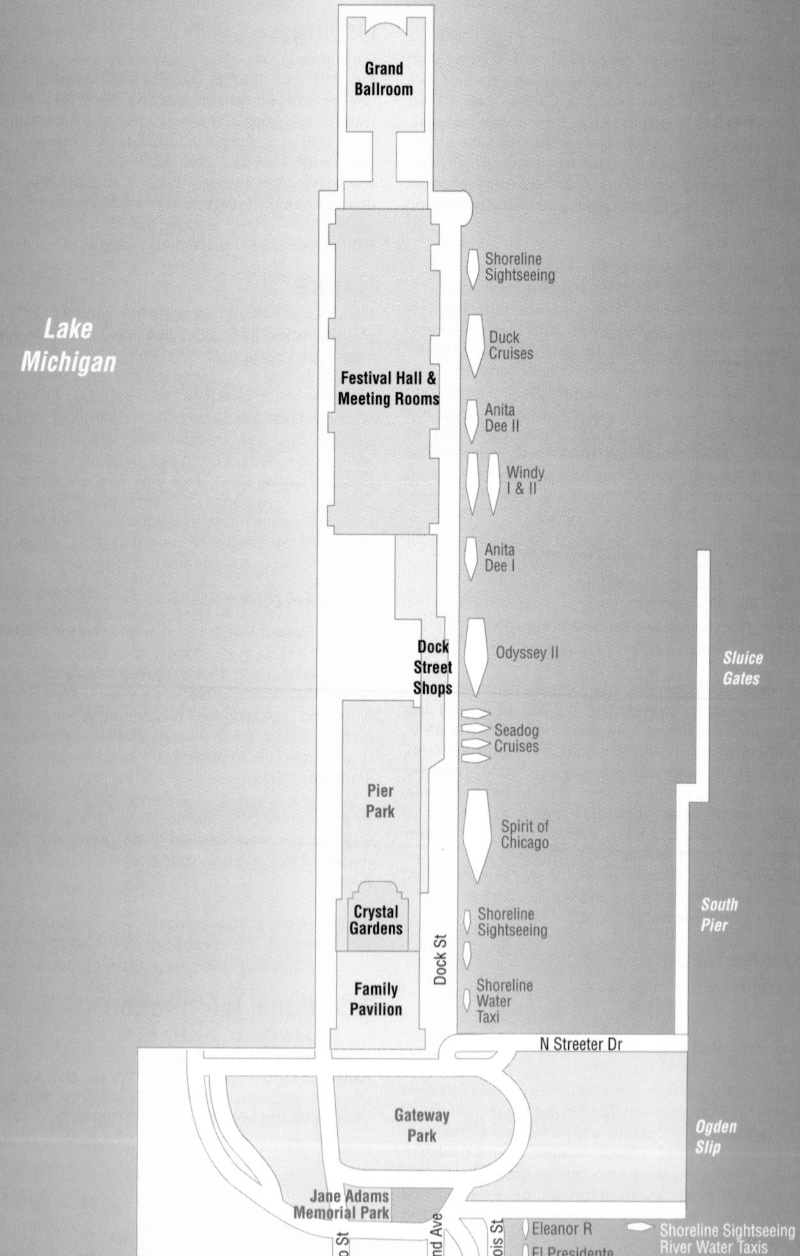
N
Grand Ballroom
Festival Hall & Meeting Rooms
Lake Michigan
Shoreline Sightseeing
Duck Cruises
Anita Dee II
Windy I & II
Anita Dee I
Dock Street Shops
Odyssey II
Sluice Gates
Seadog Cruises
Pier Park
Spirit of Chicago
Crystal Gardens
Shoreline Sightseeing
South Pier
Dock St
Family Pavilion
Shoreline Water Taxi
N Streeter Dr
Gateway Park
Ogden Slip
Jane Adams Memorial Park
Eleanor R
El Presidente
Musetts
Shoreline Sightseeing & River Water Taxis
E Ohio St
E Grand Ave
E Illinois St

Overview

A playground for the uninspired tourist, Navy Pier (a.k.a the mall on the lake) is often avoided by real Chicagoans, who scoff at its self-consciously inoffensive blandness. Save for an occasional Skyline Stage concert or high-end nosh at Reva, a trek to the pier is best reserved for those times when you have Grandma and a bevy of nieces and nephews in tow.

Built in 1916 as a municipal wharf, the pier has also done time as a) the University of Illinois at Chicago's campus, b) a hospital, c) a military training facility, d) a concert venue, and e) a white elephant. In 1989, the Metropolitan Pier and Exposition Authority invested $150 million to transform the crumbling pier into a peninsular entertainment-exhibition complex that attracts 8 million uninspired people a year. In addition to convention space, Navy Pier has two museums, the Shakespeare Theater, the Crystal Gardens, an ice rink, outdoor concert pavilion, vintage grand ballroom, 15-story Ferris wheel, IMAX Theatre, and, just for the hell of it, a radio station.

General Information

Location:	*600 E. Grand Ave.*
Phone:	*312-595-7437*
Website:	*www.navypier.com*
Pier Hours:	*Opens at 10 am daily. Pier closing times and hours of restaurants, shops, and attractions vary by season, holiday, and public exhibitions/events*
Skyline Stage:	*1,500-seat, outdoor performance pavilion in Pier Park; performances are May through September, 312-595-7437*
IMAX Theatre:	*312-595-5629*
Free Fireworks Displays:	*Memorial Day to Labor Day Evenings, Wednesdays (9:30 pm) and Saturdays (10:15 pm)*
Ice Rink:	*Open seasonally in Pier Park; free ($3.50 skate rental)*
WBEZ Radio:	*National Public Radio's local station, 312-948-4600; www.wbez.org.*
Exhibit Space:	*Festival Hall, Lakeview Terrace, Ballroom Lobby, Grand Ball Room; 36 meeting rooms*

Chicago Shakespeare Theater

The professional Chicago Shakespeare Theater has a 510-seat, courtyard-style theater and a 185-seat studio theater that are Chicago's sole venues dedicated to performing only wordsmith Willy's works. In addition to the season's plays, the theater produces Shakespeare "shorts" for younger patrons. A bookstore and Teacher Resource Center are on-site. 312-595-5600; www.chicagoshakes.com.

Chicago Children's Museum

The Chicago Children's Museum features daily activities, a creative crafts studio, and 15 interactive exhibits ranging from dinosaur digs and waterworks to a toddler tree house, safety town, and construction zone. Generally, hours are 10 am to 5 pm daily. Admission is $7; free Thursdays 5 pm to 8 pm 312-527-1000; www.chichildrensmuseum.org.

Smith Museum of Stained Glass Windows

This is the first stained glass-only museum in the country. The 150 windows installed in the lower level of Festival Hall are mostly from Chicago-area buildings and the City's renowned stained glass studios. Windows representing over a century of artistic styles include works by Louis Comfort Tiffany, Frank Lloyd Wright, Louis Sullivan, and John LaFarge. The free museum is open pier hours, 312-595-5024.

Getting There

By Car: From the north, exit Lake Shore Dr. at Grand Ave.; proceed east. From the southeast, exit Lake Shore Dr. at Illinois St.; go east. Three garages are on the pier's north side, and plenty of parking lots are just west of Lake Shore Dr. in Streeterville (Map 3).

By Bus: CTA busses 29, 56, 65, 66, and 120 serve Navy Pier.

By El: Take the Green or Red Line to Grand Ave. stop ($1.50 one-way). Board eastbound CTA Bus 29 (30¢ additional) or take the free trolley.

By Train: From Richard B. Ogilvie Transportation Center take CTA buses 56 or 120. From Union Station board bus 121.

By Trolley: Daily, free trolleys travel between Navy Pier and State St. and along Grand Ave. and Illinois St. See www.cityofchicago.org/Transportation/trolleys/.

By Boat: Seasonal water shuttles travel between Navy Pier and the Museum Campus and along the Chicago River to Sears Tower, 312-222-9328; www.shorelinesightseeing.com.

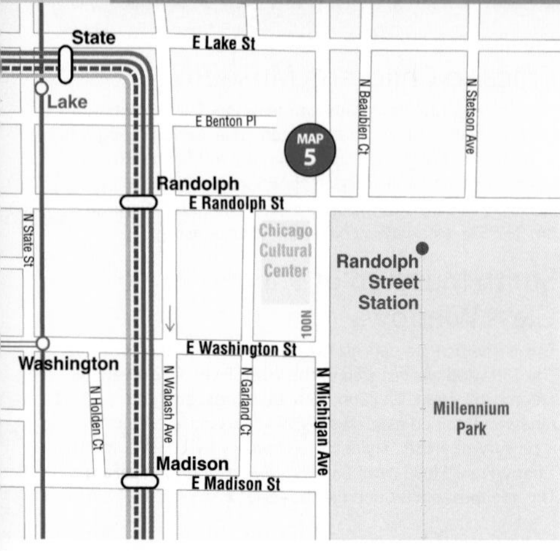

General Information

Address: *78 E. Washington St.*
Phone: *312-744-6630*
Website: *www.cityofchicago.org/Tour/CulturalCenter/*
Hours: *M-W:10-7; Th: 10-9; F: 10-6; Sa: 10-5, Su: 11-5.*

Overview

The Chicago Cultural Center is the Loop's public arts center. Free concerts, theatrical performances, films, lectures, and exhibits are offered daily. Admission to the Cultural Center, its art galleries, and Museum of Broadcast Communications are free too. Call for weekly event updates, 312-346-3278.

The building itself is a neoclassical landmark constructed in 1897. It features Carrara marble and intricate mosaics of glass and marble covering walls and grand stairways. Once the city's central public library, the Cultural Center boasts the world's largest Tiffany dome in Preston Bradley Hall and the Renaissance-style Grand Army of the Republic Exhibition Hall. Free architectural tours are Wednesdays, Fridays, and Saturdays at 1:15 pm

Performances

Weekday "LunchBreak" concerts are in the Randolph Cafe. Classical concerts and opera are performed Wednesdays at 12:15 pm in Preston Bradley Hall. Call for information on frequently scheduled special programs. Off-Loop theater productions appear regularly in the Studio Theater. The seasonal ShawChicago series features plays by Bernard Shaw on Saturdays, Sundays, and Mondays. Reservations recommended, 312-409-5605; www.shawchicago.org.

Art Galleries

A permanent exhibit in the Landmark Gallery, Chicago Landmarks Before the Lens is a stunning black-and-white photographic survey of Chicago architecture. Five additional galleries regularly rotate exhibits showcasing work in many media by renowned and local artists. Tours of current exhibits are Thursdays at 12:15 pm.

Museum of Broadcast Communications

Chicago's contributions to airwave history come alive at the free Museum of Broadcast Communications 312-629-6000; www.Museum.TV. Chicago television studios spawned national programs including Bozo's Circus and Kukla, Fran & Ollie. Footage and memorabilia are displayed. Visitors tape a play-by-play of historic sporting events, recreate radio shows, and produce television newscasts. Breakthrough advertising commercials are exhibited. The museum is home to America's only Radio Hall of Fame, www.radiohof.org, preserving 50,000 hours of broadcasts. Teachers can tap into museum resources, 312-629-6047, including the killer research center (closed Sundays). Museum hours: Monday through Saturday, 10 am to 4:30 pm; Sunday noon to 5 pm. Tours are weekdays from 10 am and 4:30 pm ($2).

How to Get There

By Car: Travel down Michigan Ave. to Randolph St. From Lake Shore Dr., exit at Randolph St. For parking garages in the area, see NFT Map 6.

By Train: From the Richard B. Ogilvie Transportation Center, travel east to Michigan Ave. on CTA buses 157, 20, 56, and 127. From Union Station, take CTA buses 60, 157, 151, and 123. From the Randolph St. station below Millennium Park, walk west across Michigan Ave. For schedules and fares, contact the RTA Information Center, 312-836-7000; www.rtachicago.com.

By El: Take the Green Line to the Randolph-Wabash stop. Walk east one block.

By Bus: CTA buses 151, 145, 146, 147, 3, and 10 (weekends only) stop on Michigan Ave. in front of the Cultural Center.

General Information

Address: *400 S. State St.*
Phone: *312-747-4999*
Website: *www.chipublib.org*

Overview

Harold Washington Library Center is the world's largest public library. Named after Chicago's first African American mayor, the 756,640-square foot architectural monstrosity has over 70 miles of shelves storing 9 million books, microforms, serials, and government documents. Over 50 works of notable sculpture, paintings, and mosaics adorn the free library visited by over 6,000 patrons daily.

Collections are on floors three through eight. Roam the outer walls for a windowed alcove to read, write, and snooze in blissful quiet. The Winter Garden, a welcome bad-weather escape, is on the ninth floor next to the Beyond Words Café (open for lunch and afternoon tea Monday through Saturday). A coffee shop and used bookstore are on the first floor. Frequent free public programs are held in the lower level's 385-seat auditorium, video theater, exhibit hall, and meeting rooms, 312-747-4649.

Library hours are Monday through Thursday 9 am to 7 pm; Friday and Saturday 9 am to 5 pm; Sunday 1 pm to 5 pm. Free library tours starting from the third floor Orientation Theater are Thursdays at 2 pm, 312-747-4136.

Research Services

To check availability or location of an item, call Catalog Information, 312-747-4340, or search the library's Online Catalog, www.chipublib.org. The Email Reference Service responds to information requests within a week. For quick answers to common research questions, check out the handy Virtual Library Service called "Reference Shelf."

Computer Services

The library's 32 computers with Internet access and 24 more with word processing, desktop publishing, graphic presentation, and spreadsheet applications are in the fifth floor Computer Connection Department. Computer use is free and available on a first-come-first-serve basis. Reserve computers for up to 2 hours per day based on walk-in availability. Limited time slots available via phone reservation, 312-747-4540. For downloads, bring your own formatted diskette or purchase one ($2). Free laser printing provided. Closed Sunday.

Thomas Hughes Children's Library

The 18,000-square foot Thomas Hughes Children's Library serves children through age 14. In addition to 120,000 books representing 40 foreign languages, there is a reference collection on children's literature for adults. Twenty free computers, two with internet connections, are available. Children's programs hosted weekly, 312-747-4647.

Special Collections

The library's Special Collections & Preservation Division's highlights include: Harold Washington Collection, Civil War & American History Research Collection, Chicago Authors & Publishing Collection, Chicago Blues Archives, Chicago Theater Collection, World's Columbian Exposition Collection, and Neighborhood History Research Collection. The reading room is closed Sundays.

How to Get There

By Car: The library is at the intersection of State St. and Congress Pkwy. in South Loop. Take I-290 east into the Loop. See NFT Map 5 for area parking garages.

By El: The Brown Line, Purple Line, and Orange Line stop at the Library station. Exit the Red Line and O'Hare Airport Blue Line at Van Buren Station; walk one block south. Change from the Harlem/Lake St. Green Line to the northbound Orange Line at Roosevelt Rd. station; get off at Library Station.

By Bus: CTA busses that stop on State St. in front of the library are the 2, 6, 29, 36, 62, 151, 145, 146, and 147.

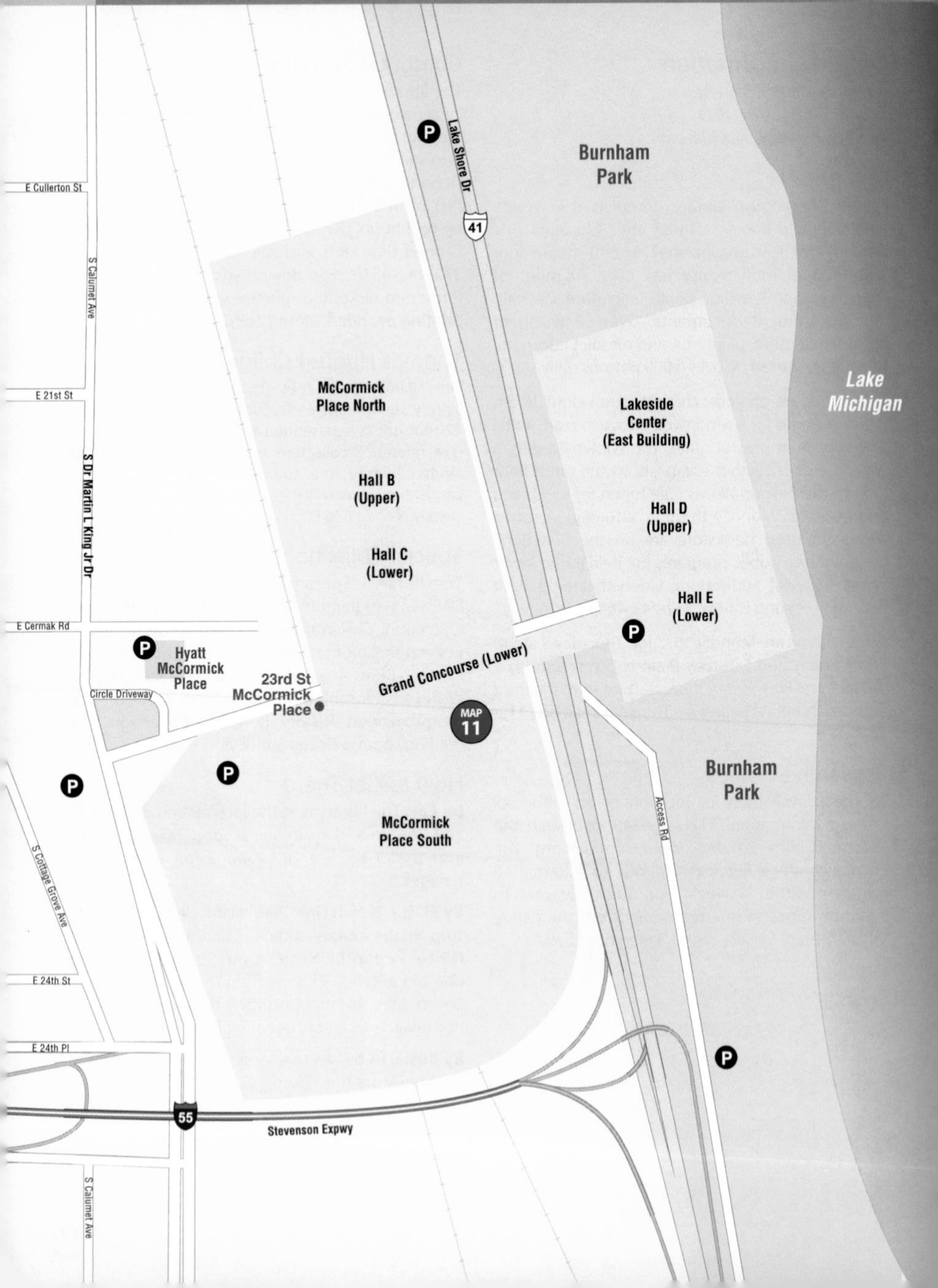

Lake Shore Dr
41
Burnham Park
E Cullerton St
S Calumet Ave
E 21st St
McCormick Place North
Lakeside Center (East Building)
Lake Michigan
S Dr Martin L King Jr Dr
Hall B (Upper)
Hall D (Upper)
Hall C (Lower)
Hall E (Lower)
E Cermak Rd
Hyatt McCormick Place
23rd St McCormick Place
Grand Concourse (Lower)
Circle Driveway
MAP 11
Burnham Park
Access Rd
McCormick Place South
S Cottage Grove Ave
E 24th St
E 24th Pl
55
Stevenson Expwy
S Calumet Ave

General Information

Mailing Address:	*McCormick Place* *2301 S. Lake Shore Dr.* *Chicago, IL 60616*
Phone:	*312-791-7000*
Website:	*www.mccormickplace.com*
South Building:	*Exhibit Hall A; charter bus stop*
North Building:	*Exhibit Halls B and C; Metra train station*
Lakeside Center:	*Exhibit Halls D and E; 4,249-seat Arie Crown Theater (Level 2); underground parking garage*

Overview

When it comes to the convention business, size does matter. With 2.2 million square feet of exhibit space spread among three buildings, McCormick Place is the largest convention center in North America. Annually, over three million visitors attend its trade shows and public exhibitions in the South Building, North Building, and Lakeside Center (East Building). Apparently, the city's colossal cash cow is about to get even bigger with the addition of a new $800 million West Building. Slated for completion in 2007, the expansion will add 600,000 square feet of exhibit space and 200,000 square feet of meeting rooms.

McCormick Place's growth continues to bolster the rapid gentrification of South Loop, and with each expansion, the complex's overall aesthetic appeal steadily improves. However, despite major renovations to Lakeside Center, Chicagoans still call it "the mistake on the lake." Wedged between the water and Lake Shore Dr. in Burnham Park, Mayor Daley refers to the black boxy behemoth as the "Berlin Wall" separating Chicagoans from their beloved lakefront.

Finding Your Way Around

Getting to McCormick Place is easy compared to finding your way around inside. The main entrance is off Martin Luther King Dr. next to the Hyatt Hotel. Here's how to crack the code names for meeting rooms and exhibit halls:

All meeting room locations start with E (Lakeside Center/East Building), N (North Building), or S (South Building). The first numeral is the floor level. The last two digits specify which room. Room numbers are not duplicated among the complex's three buildings.

Exhibit halls are named by consecutive letters starting with the South Building where Hall A (Level 3) is located. North Building houses Halls B (Level 3) and C (Level 1). Exhibit Halls D (Level 3) and E (Level 2) are in Lakeside Center.

Restaurants & Services

In addition to the complex's concessions, Connie's Pizza and McDonald's Express are in the North Building (Level 2). The Plate Room food court can be found in the South Building (west side of Level 2.5) where Starbucks, shops, a shoe shine, and massage services are also located. Business centers and ATMs are in the Grand Concourse (Level 2.5), North Building (Level 2), and Lakeside Center (Level 2).

How to Get There

By Car: From the Loop, take Lake Shore Dr. south; from the southeast, travel north on Lake Shore Dr. Signage to McCormick Place on the Drive is frequent and clear. Parking garages are in Lakeside Center and the Hyatt. Lots are at 31st St. and Lake Shore Dr. and at Martin Luther King Dr. across from the South Building. Additional lots are north of McCormick Place at Burnham Harbor and Soldier Field.

By Bus: From the Loop, CTA buses 3 and 4 stop in front of the South Building. From Richard B. Ogilvie Transportation Center, take buses 122, 125, or 157 to Michigan Ave.; transfer to a southbound 3 or 4 ($1.80 with transfer one-way). From Union Station, board eastbound bus 1 to Michigan Ave.; transfer to a southbound 3 or 4.

During major shows, countless charter buses circle downtown hotels transporting conventioneers to McCormick Place for free. With the new express busway, charter buses travel from Randolph St. to the South Building in less than 10 minutes. For schedules, check with the hotels and at McCormick Place information desks. A 2003 expansion of the busway connects it to 18th St., providing closer access to the North Building and Lakeside Center.

By Train: Metra electric trains from the Loop's Randolph St. and Van Buren St. stations to the 23rd St. stop under the North Building take 9 minutes ($1.85 one-way). The escalators to the train platform are on the west side of the Grand Concourse (Level 2.5).

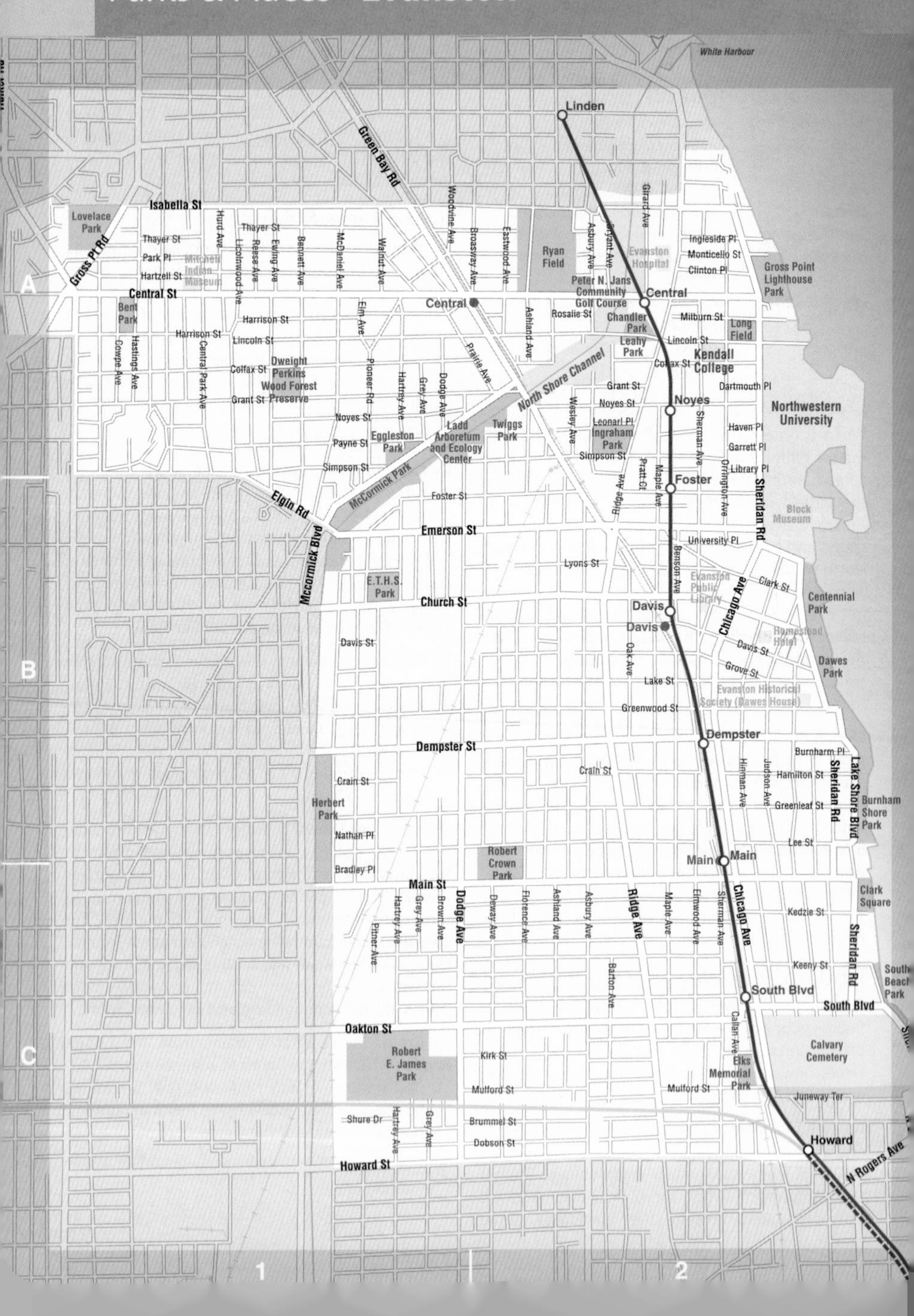
White Harbour
Linden
Green Bay Rd
Isabella St
Lovelace Park
Gross Pt Rd
Thayer St
Park Pl
Hartzell St
Mitchell Indian Museum
Central St
Bent Park
Harrison St
Lincoln St
Colfax St
Grant St
Dweight Perkins Wood Forest Preserve
Central
Ryan Field
Peter N. Jans Community Golf Course
Evanston Hospital
Ingleside Pl
Monticello St
Clinton Pl
Gross Point Lighthouse Park
Milburn St
Long Field
Chandler Park
Leahy Park
Kendall College
North Shore Channel
Noyes
Northwestern University
Dartmouth Pl
Haven Pl
Garrett Pl
Library Pl
Ladd Arboretum and Ecology Center
Twiggs Park
Eggleston Park
Ingraham Park
Foster
Sheridan Rd
Block Museum
McCormick Park
Elgin Rd
Mccormick Blvd
Emerson St
University Pl
Lyons St
E.T.H.S. Park
Evanston Public Library
Clark St
Centennial Park
Church St
Davis
Chicago Ave
Homestead Hotel
Davis St
Grove St
Dawes Park
Lake St
Greenwood St
Evanston Historical Society (Dawes House)
Dempster
Dempster St
Burnham Pl
Hamilton St
Greenleaf St
Lake Shore Blvd
Burnham Shore Park
Lee St
Herbert Park
Crain St
Nathan Pl
Bradley Pl
Robert Crown Park
Main
Main St
Dodge Ave
Ridge Ave
Clark Square
Kedzie St
Keeny St
South Blvd
South Beach Park
Oakton St
Robert E. James Park
Kirk St
Mulford St
Elks Memorial Park
Calvary Cemetery
Juneway Ter
Shure Dr
Brummel St
Dobson St
Howard
Howard St
N Rogers Ave
A
B
C
1
2

Overview

Just 13 miles from Chicago's bustling Loop, Evanston seems a world away. Spacious Victorian and Prairie Style homes with mini-vans and Mercedes parked on tree-lined streets overlook Lake Michigan and surround the quaint college town's downtown.

Evanston was founded in 1850 by a group of Methodists. They established prestigious Northwestern University five years later on the lake's shores, once home to Potawatami Indians. Today, residents are as devoted to cultural and intellectual pursuits as the morally minded patriarchs were to enforcing prohibition. The sophisticated, racially diverse suburb of over 74,000 packs a lot of business and entertainment into its 8.5 square miles. Superb museums, many national historic landmarks, parks, artistic events, eclectic shops, and theaters make up for the poor sports performances by Northwestern University's Wildcats in recent Big Ten football and basketball seasons.

Culture

Evanston has several museums and some interesting festivals that definitely warrant investigation. Besides Northwestern's Block Museum of Art (see Northwestern University pages), the impressive Mitchell Museum of the American Indian at Kendall College, 2600 Central Park Ave., 847-475-1030, showcases life of the Midwest's Native Americans. The 1865 home of Frances E. Willard, founder of the Women's Christian Temperance Union and women's suffrage leader, is at 1730 Chicago Ave., 847-328-7500.

Festivals & Events

December: First Night, a city-wide arts celebration, rings in the New Year, 847-328-5864; May: Evanston goes Baroque during Bach Week, 847-236-0452; June: Fountain Square Arts Festival, 847-328-1500, and free Starlight Concerts hosted in many of the city's 80 parks through August, 847-448-8058; July: Ethnic Arts Festival, 847-448-8058; September: Town architectural walking tour, 312-922-3432.

Nature

Evanston is blessed with six public beaches open June 10th through Labor Day. For hours, fees, and boating information, contact the City of Evanston's Recreation Division, 847-866-2910; www.cityofevanston.org. The town's most popular parks encircle its beaches: Grosse Point Lighthouse Park, Centennial Park, Burnham Shores Park, Dawes Park, and South Blvd. Beach Park. All are connected by a bike path and fitness trail. On clear days, Chicago's skyline is visible from Northwestern's Lakefill Park. West of downtown, McCormick, Twiggs, and Herbert Parks flank the North Shore Channel. Bicycle trails thread along the shore from Green Bay Rd. south to Main St. North of Green Bay Rd. is Peter N. Jans Community Golf Course, a short 18-hole, par 60 public links at 1031 Central St., 847-475-9173, and the Ladd Memorial Arboretum and Ecology Center, 2024 McCormick Blvd., 847-864-5181.

Where to Eat

- **Trio**, 1625 Hinman Ave. in the Homestead Hotel, 847-733-8746. French. Deep-pocketed regulars gush about the daring food combinations. A favorite for foodies.
- **Blind Faith Café**, 525 Dempster St., 847-328-6875. Vegetarian. Healthy, fiber-filled fare for the Birkenstock set. Food so earthy, you need to floss dirt from your teeth.
- **Va Pensiero**, 1566 Oak Ave. in the Margarita Inn, 847-475-7779. Italian. Classy, romantic supper club offering over 250 Italian wines. A "pop the question" kind of place.
- **The Dining Room at Kendall College Culinary Institute**, 2408 Orrington Ave. , 847-866-1399. Eclectic. Charlie Trotter hopefuls dish up lunch and dinner. Four-star dining hall eats.
- **Pet Miller's Original Steakhouse**, 1557 Sherman Ave., 847-328-0399. American. Beef bubbas stake out this joint as one of Chicago's best for red meat served in a cozy dining room; fist-thick burgers slung in live jazz lounge.
- **Tapas Barcelona**, 1615 Chicago Ave., 847-866-9900. Spanish. Lick your fingers with friends over tasty tapas and sangria.

How to Get There

By Car: Lake Shore Dr. to Sheridan Rd. is the most direct and scenic route. Drive north on LSD, which ends at Hollywood; jog west to Sheridan and continue north. Near downtown, Sheridan becomes Burnham Pl. briefly, then Forest Ave. Go north on Forest, which turns into Sheridan again by lakefront Centennial Park.

By Train: Metra's Union Pacific North Line departing from the Richard B. Ogilvie Transportation Center in West Loop stops at the downtown Davis Street CTA Center station, 25 minutes from the Loop ($2.90 one-way). This station is the town transportation hub where Metra and El trains and buses interconnect. For all Metra, El, and CTA bus schedules contact the RTA Travel Information Center, 312-836-7000; www.rtachicago.com.

By El: The CTA Purple Line Express El train travels direct to and from the Loop during rush hours ($1.50 one-way). Other hours, ride the Howard-Dan Ryan Red Line to Howard St., transfer (additional 30¢) to Purple Line.

By Bus: From Chicago's Howard St. Station, CTA and Pace Suburban buses service Evanston ($1.50 rush hours one-way; other, $1.25).

Additional Information

Evanston Convention & Visitors Bureau, 847-328-1500; Chicago's North Shore Convention & Visitors Bureau, 847-763-0011; www. visitchicagonorthshore.com
Evanston Public Library, 1703 Orrington Avenue, 847-866-0300; www.epl.org

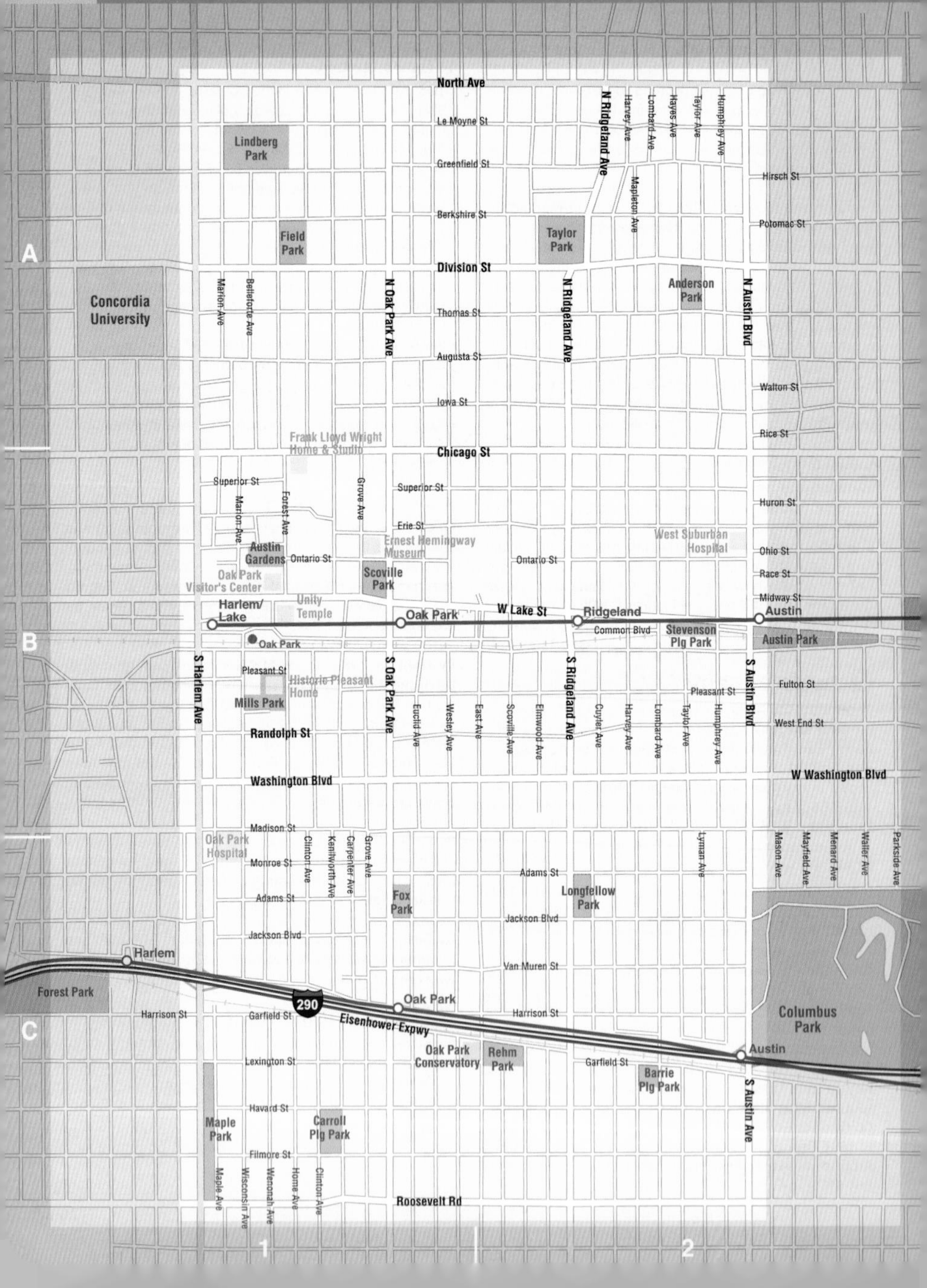

North Ave
Le Moyne St
Greenfield St
Berkshire St
Division St
Thomas St
Augusta St
Iowa St
Chicago St
Superior St
Erie St
Ontario St
W Lake St
Common Blvd
Pleasant St
Randolph St
Washington Blvd
W Washington Blvd
Madison St
Monroe St
Adams St
Jackson Blvd
Van Muren St
Harrison St
Garfield St
Lexington St
Havard St
Filmore St
Roosevelt Rd
Hirsch St
Potomac St
Walton St
Rice St
Huron St
Ohio St
Race St
Midway St
Fulton St
West End St
N Ridgeland Ave
S Ridgeland Ave
N Oak Park Ave
S Oak Park Ave
N Austin Blvd
S Austin Blvd
S Austin Ave
S Harlem Ave
Harvey Ave
Lombard Ave
Hayes Ave
Taylor Ave
Humphrey Ave
Mapleton Ave
Marion Ave
Belleforte Ave
Forest Ave
Grove Ave
Euclid Ave
Wesley Ave
East Ave
Scoville Ave
Elmwood Ave
Cuyler Ave
Lyman Ave
Clinton Ave
Kenilworth Ave
Carpenter Ave
Mason Ave
Mayfield Ave
Menard Ave
Waller Ave
Parkside Ave
Maple Ave
Wisconsin Ave
Wenonah Ave
Home Ave
Lindberg Park
Field Park
Taylor Park
Anderson Park
Concordia University
Frank Lloyd Wright Home & Studio
Ernest Hemingway Museum
West Suburban Hospital
Austin Gardens
Oak Park Visitor's Center
Scoville Park
Unity Temple
Harlem/Lake
Oak Park
Ridgeland
Austin
Stevenson Plg Park
Austin Park
Historic Pleasant Home
Mills Park
Oak Park Hospital
Fox Park
Longfellow Park
Columbus Park
Harlem
Forest Park
290
Eisenhower Expwy
Oak Park Conservatory
Rehm Park
Barrie Plg Park
Maple Park
Carroll Plg Park
A
B
C
1
2

General Information

Oak Park Visitors Bureau, 708-524-7800; visitoakpark.com
Oak Park Tourist, www.oprf.com

Overview

Thank Oak Park for McDonald's, Tarzan, A Moveable Feast, and Prairie Style architecture. Their creators called the charming suburb their home: Ray Kroc, Edgar Rice Burroughs, Ernest Hemingway, and Frank Lloyd Wright.

Best known for its architectural gems and strong public schools, Oak Park is a happy hunting ground for home buyers seeking an upscale, integrated suburb 10 miles from the Loop. Less impressed than most with his picture-perfect hometown of 52,500, Hemingway described Oak Park as "a village of wide lawns and narrow minds."

Village trustees must still be smarting from Hemingway's crack because they publicize an official policy on maintaining diversity. The "diversity statement" sounds like a disclaimer or zealot's vision for heaven on Earth: "Ours is a community that encourages contributions of all citizens regardless of race, gender, ethnicity, sexual orientation, disability, religion . . ."

Architecture

Oak Park harbors the nation's largest concentration of Frank Lloyd Wright buildings, 25 in the village and another six in neighboring River Forest. The village's must-see sites are located in a compact area bordered by Division St., Lake St., Forest Ave., and Ridgeland Ave. Designs by Wright, William Drummond, George W. Maher, John Van Bergen, and E.E. Roberts are represented.

Ground yourself in Prairie Style architectural principles at the Frank Lloyd Wright Home and Studio, 951 Chicago Ave., 708-848-1976, daily at 11 am, 1 pm, and 3 pm ($9). Only 15 people are allowed per tour and tickets are bought on-site; early arrival recommended. Worthwhile walking tours of surrounding streets are offered ($9). A combined ticket covers the home-studio site and a walking tour ($16).

Unity Temple, 875 Lake St., 708-383-8873, was Wright's first public building. Open daily for self-directed tours and on weekends for guided tours ($6). Designed by George W. Maher, Historic Pleasant Home, 217 S. Home Ave., 708-383-2654, aptly illustrates the architectural evolution from Victorian design to early Prairie Style. Tours: Thursday through Sunday at 12:30 pm, 1:30 pm, and 2:30 pm ($5, Fridays free).

Oak Park Visitors Center, 158 N. Forest Ave., 708-848-1500; www.visitoakpark.org, offers maps and an audio walking tour of the Ridgeland Historic District featuring 15 Victorian painted ladies ($6).

Culture & Events

Once a year in May, the public gets to snoop inside Wright-designed homes that are private residences during the popular Wright Plus Tour ($85). His home-studio and Robie House in Hyde Park (shuttle provided) are included, 708-848-9518; www.wrightplus.org.

Get your fill of he-man author Hemingway at the Ernest Hemingway Museum, 200 N. Oak Park Ave., 708-848-2222; www.hemingway.org, open daily ($7). His birthplace is at 339 N. Oak Park Ave.

Summer evenings, see Shakespeare's works performed outdoors in Austin Gardens by Festival Theatre, 708-524-2050. The lush Oak Park Conservatory, built in 1929, is at 615 Garfield St., 708-386-4700; free admission.

Where to Eat

- **Petersen Ice Cream**, 1100 Chicago Ave., 708-386-6131. American. Comfort food and silky ice cream make this diner a popular destination.
- **Cucina Paradiso**, 814 North Blvd., 708-848-3434. Italian. Fork-twirling Oak Parkers patronize this friendly pasta place.
- **Khyber Pass**, 1031 Lake St., 708-445-9032. Indian. Taxi drivers and curry-loving locals fill up on lunch and dinner buffets.
- **Philander's Oak Park** in the Carleton Hotel, 1120 Pleasant St., 708-848-4250. Seafood. Marine cuisine served in handsome atmosphere; nightly, fishtail to live jazz.

How to Get There

By Car: From Loop, drive west on I-90; exit Harlem Ave. Travel north to Lake St. and head east to historic sites and downtown. Close to architectural sites is inexpensive garage parking: Lake & Forest Garage, 938 W. Lake St. (above the Oak Park Visitors' Center); Holly Court Garage, 1125 Ontario St.

By Train: Metra's Union Pacific West Line travels to Oak Park in 15 minutes from Chicago's Richard B. Ogilvie Transportation Center ($1.95 one-way). From the Oak Park stop, walk north up Oak Park Ave. to Lake St. For schedules, contact the RTA Travel Information Center, 312-836-7000; www.rtachicago.com.

By El: CTA Green Line service is frequent ($1.50 one-way). From the Oak Park station walk north up Oak Park Ave. to Lake St.

By Bus: From Chicago's Union Station take the 60 Blue Island bus west to 24th St. and Cicero Ave. Pick up 312 Pace Suburban west to Ogden Ave. and Oak Park Ave. Transfer to 311. Off at Lake St. and Oak Park Ave. ($1.80 including all transfers).

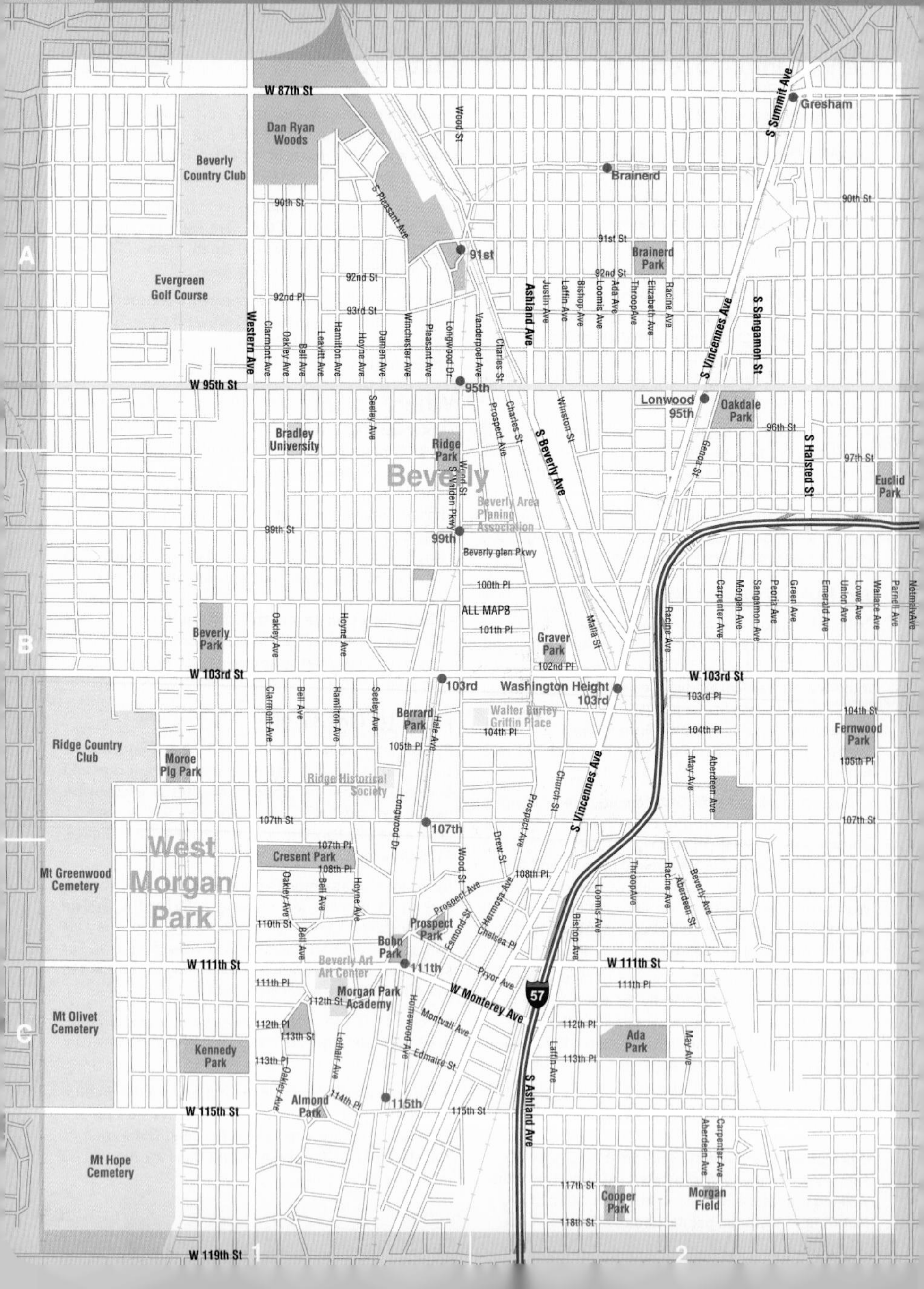

W 87th St
Dan Ryan Woods
Beverly Country Club
Wood St
S Summit Ave
Gresham
Brainerd
90th St
90th St
S Pleasant Ave
A
91st
91st St
Brainerd Park
Evergreen Golf Course
92nd St
92nd St
92nd Pl
93rd St
Western Ave
Claremont Ave
Oakley Ave
Bell Ave
Leavitt Ave
Hamilton Ave
Hoyne Ave
Damen Ave
Winchester Ave
Pleasant Ave
Longwood Dr.
Vanderpoel Ave
Charles St
Ashland Ave
Justin Ave
Laflin Ave
Bishop Ave
Loomis Ave
Ada Ave
ThroopAve
Elizabeth Ave
Racine Ave
S Vincennes Ave
S Sangamon St
W 95th St
95th
Seeley Ave
Prospect Ave
Charles St
Winston St
Lonwood 95th
Oakdale Park
96th St
Bradley University
Ridge Park
S Beverly Ave
Genoa St
S Halsted St
97th St
Beverly
Wood St
S Walden Pkwy
Beverly Area Planing Association
Euclid Park
99th St
99th
Beverly glen Pkwy
100th Pl
ALL MAP8
Oakley Ave
Hoyne Ave
101th Pl
Graver Park
Malta St
Racine Ave
Carpenter Ave
Morgan Ave
Sangamon Ave
Peoria Ave
Green Ave
Emerald Ave
Union Ave
Lowe Ave
Wallace Ave
Parnell Ave
Normal Ave
B
Beverly Park
102nd Pl
W 103rd St
103rd
Washington Height 103rd
W 103rd St
103rd Pl
Claremont Ave
Bell Ave
Hamilton Ave
Seeley Ave
Berrard Park
Hale Ave
Walter Burley Griffin Place
104th Pl
104th St
104th Pl
Fernwood Park
Ridge Country Club
Moroe Pig Park
105th Pl
105th Pl
May Ave
Aberdeen Ave
Ridge Historical Society
Church St
Prospect Ave
S Vincennes Ave
107th St
107th
107th St
Longwood Dr
West Morgan Park
107th Pl
Cresent Park
Drew St
Wood St
108th Pl
108th Pl
Mt Greenwood Cemetery
Oakley Ave
Bell Ave
Hoyne Ave
Prospect Ave
Hermosa Ave
ThroopAve
Racine Ave
Aberdeen St
Beverly Ave
110th St
Bell Ave
Prospect Park
Esmond St
Chelsea Pl
Bishop Ave
Loomis Ave
Bohn Park
W 111th St
Beverly Art Art Center
111th
Pryor Ave
W 111th St
111th Pl
111th Pl
Morgan Park Academy
112th St
W Monterey Ave
57
Mt Olivet Cemetery
C
112th Pl
113th St
Lothair Ave
Homewood Ave
Montvail Ave
112th Pl
Ada Park
May Ave
Kennedy Park
113th Pl
Edmaire St
113th Pl
Laflin Ave
Oakley Ave
S Ashland Ave
Almond Park
114th Pl
115th
W 115th St
115th St
Carpenter Ave
Aberdeen Ave
Mt Hope Cemetery
117th St
Cooper Park
Morgan Field
118th St
W 119th St
1
2

Overview

Beverly Hills, best known simply as Beverly, is the stronghold of Chicago's heralded "South Side Irish" community. An authentic medieval castle, baronial mansions, rolling hills, and plenty of pubs compose Chicago's Emerald Isle of 39,000 residents.

Once populated by Illinois and Potawatomi Indian tribes, Beverly is now home to clans of Irish-American families who moved here after the Great Chicago Fire. Famous residents: Andrew Greeley, Brian Piccolo, George Wendt, the Schwinn Bicycle family, and decades of loyal Chicago civil servants.

Proud and protective of their turf, these close-knit South Siders call Beverly and its sister community Morgan Park "the Ridge." The somewhat integrated neighborhood occupies the highest ground in Chicago, 30 to 60 feet above the rest of the city atop Blue Island Ridge.

Although the Ridge is just 15 miles from the Loop, most North Siders never venture south of Cermak Rd except to invade Beverly on St. Patrick's Day weekend to see the parade and guzzle green beer at pubs lining Western Ave. Chicago playwright Mike Houlihan called the strip the "South Side Irish Death March."

But there are better than a six-pack of reasons to visit Beverly. The Ridge Historic District is one of the country's largest urban areas on the National Register of Historic Places. Surprised, huh?

Architecture

Sadly, many Chicagoans are unaware of the rich architectural legacy on the city's far South Side. Beverly and Morgan Park encompass four landmark districts including the Ridge Historic District, three Chicago Landmark Districts, and over 30 Prairie Style structures.

Within approximately a nine-mile radius, from 87th St. to 115th St. and Prospect. Ave. to Hoyne Ave., view a vast collection of homes and public buildings representing American architectural styles developed between 1844 and World War II. Like an outdoor museum, designs by Chicago's prominent residential architects, including Frank Lloyd Wright, stand side-by-side.

The 109th block of Prospect Ave., every inch of Longwood Dr., and Victorian train stations at 91st St., 95th St., 99th St., 107th St., 111th St., and 115th St. are Chicago landmarks. Walter Burley Griffin Place on W. 104th has Chicago's largest concentration of Prairie School houses built between 1909 and 1913 by Griffin, a student of Frank Lloyd Wright and designer of the city of Canberra in Australia.

Beverly Area Planning Association (BAPA), 10233 S. Wood St., 773-233-3100; www.bapa.org, provides a good architectural site map plus events and shopping information. The Ridge Historical Society and museum is open Sundays and Thursdays, 2 pm to 5 pm. 10621 S. Seeley Ave., 773-881-1675; www.ridgehistoricalsociety.org.

Culture & Events

The new Beverly Art Center is the epicenter of Ridge culture. The $8 million facility hosts Chicago's only contemporary Irish film festival the first week of March. 2407 W. 111th St., 773-445-3838; www.beverlyartcenter.org.

Historic Ridge homes open their doors to the public every May during the annual Home Tour, Chicago's oldest such tour. Sites represent diverse architectural styles. Tour hours: 11 am to 5 pm; guided trolley tours offered. Purchase tickets through BAPA or Beverly Art Center ($25 advance; $30 day-of).

A Chicago must-see, the justly famous South Side Irish Parade marches down Western Ave. from 103rd to 112th St. on the Sunday nearest St. Patrick's Day. Contact BAPA, 773-233-3100.

Where to Eat

- **Franconello's**, 10222 S. Western Ave. at 103rd St., 773-881-4100. Italian. Perhaps the only pure Italians in Beverly make pasta dishes at this authentic Roma restaurant.
- **Rainbow Cone**, 9233 S. Western Ave., 773-238-7075. Ice Cream. On summer nights more than 50 folks line up for sweet treats at this 76-year old soda fountain.
- **Café Luna**, 1742 W. 99th St., 773-239-8990. Eclectic. Sink your teeth into heart-healthy sandwiches and sinful desserts.

How to Get There

By Car: From Loop, take Lake Shore Dr. south to I-55 and follow signs "To Indiana" that lead to I-90/94. Travel south on I-90/94 to I-57; exit Halsted St. Head south on frontage road to 99th St. Turn west on 99th St. to Beverly.

By Train: Metra's Rock Island Line departs from the Loop's La Salle St. Station, 414 S. La Salle St. The 20-minute ride runs through Ridge historic districts stopping at seven stations in Beverly and Morgan Park ($3.30 one-way).

By Bus: From the Loop, board the El Red Line heading south to the end at 95th St. CTA busses 119 and 114 and 96 Pace suburban bus serve the Ridge ($1.80 one-way fare including transfer).

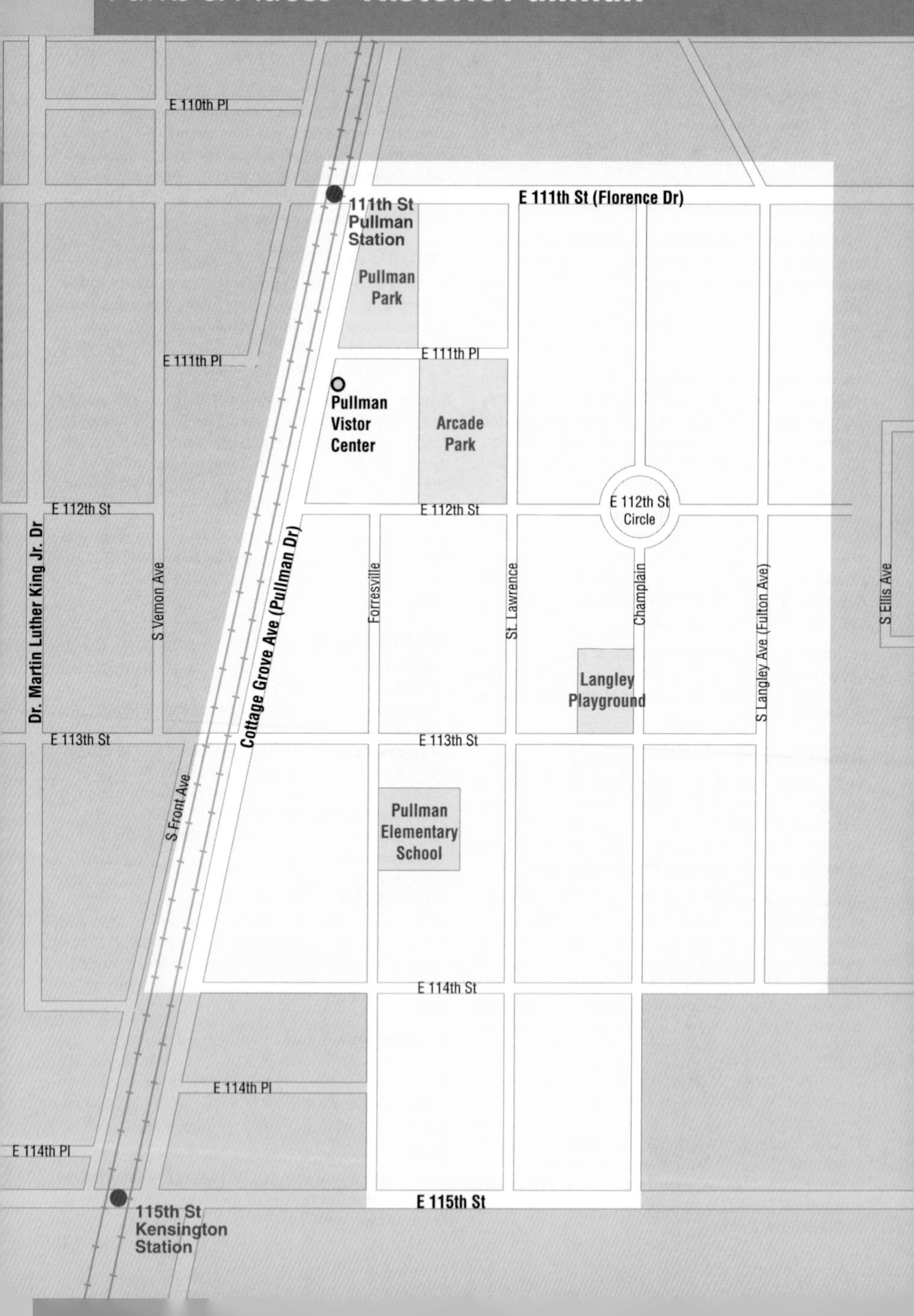
E 110th Pl
E 111th St (Florence Dr)
111th St
Pullman
Station
Pullman
Park
E 111th Pl
E 111th Pl
Pullman
Vistor
Center
Arcade
Park
E 112th St
E 112th St
E 112th St
Circle
Dr. Martin Luther King Jr. Dr
S Vernon Ave
Cottage Grove Ave (Pullman Dr)
Forresville
St. Lawrence
Champlain
S Langley Ave (Fulton Ave)
S Ellis Ave
Langley
Playground
E 113th St
E 113th St
S Front Ave
Pullman
Elementary
School
E 114th St
E 114th Pl
E 114th Pl
E 115th St
115th St
Kensington
Station

Overview

Although railroad magnate George Pullman's utopian community went belly-up, the Town of Pullman he founded 14 miles south of the Loop survives as a National Landmark Historic District. Built between 1880 and 1885, Pullman is one of America's first planned, model industrial communities.

The "workers' paradise" earned Pullman humanitarian hoorahs, as well as a 6 percent return on his investment. Pullman believed that if laborers and their families lived in comfortable housing with gas, plumbing, and ventilation, in other words, livable conditions, their productivity would increase, as would his profits. Pullman was voted "the world's most perfect town" at the Prague International Hygienic and Pharmaceutical Exposition of 1896.

All was perfect on the plantation until a depression incited workers to strike in 1894. The idealistic industrialist refused to negotiate with his ungrateful workers. While George Pullman's dream of a model community of indentured servitude died with him in 1897, hatred for him lived on. Pullman's tomb at Graceland Cemetery is more like a bomb shelter. To protect his corpse from irate labor leaders, Pullman was buried under a forest of railroad ties and concrete.

Architecture & Events

Architect Solon Beman and landscape architect Nathan Barrett based Pullman's design on French urban plans. Pullman had mostly brick rowhouses (95 percent still in use) and several parks, shops, schools, churches, and a library, plus health, recreational, and cultural facilities.

The compact community's borders are 111th St. (Florence Dr.), 115th St., Cottage Grove Ave. (Pullman Dr.), and S. Langley Ave. (Fulton Ave.). For sightseeing, start at the Pullman Visitor Center, 11141 S. Cottage Grove Ave. (773-785-8901); www.pullmanil.org. The 20-minute film provides a good historical overview. Free self-guided walking tour brochures are available. Call the center for lecture and additional specialty tour information.

The annual House Tour on the second weekend in October is a popular Pullman event. Eight private residences open their doors from 11 am to 5 pm ($12). May through October, the center offers a two-hour First Sunday Guided Walking Tour, 12:30 and 1:30 pm ($4). Key tour sites: Hotel Florence, Greenstone Church (interior), Market Square, the stables, and the fire station. Hotel Florence's interior is being restored, as well as the fire-damaged Clock Tower Administration Building.

How to Get There

By Car: Take I-94 south to the 111th St. exit. Go west to Cottage Grove Ave. and turn south driving one block to 112th St. to the Visitor Center surrounded by a large, free parking lot.

By Train: The Illinois Central Metra Electric Line departs from Randolph St. Station (underground) at Michigan Ave. between S. Water St. and Randolph St. Ride 30 minutes to Pullman Station at 111th St. ($3.30 one-way). Walk east to Cottage Grove Ave. and head south one block to 112th and the Visitor Center.

By El: From the Loop, take the Red Line to the 95th St. station. Board CTA 111 Pullman bus going south ($1.80 with transfer).

By Bus: CTA 4 bus from the Randolph St. Station travels south to the 95th St. and Cottage Grove stop. Transfer to 111 Pullman bus heading south ($1.80 with transfer).

University of Illinois at Chicago

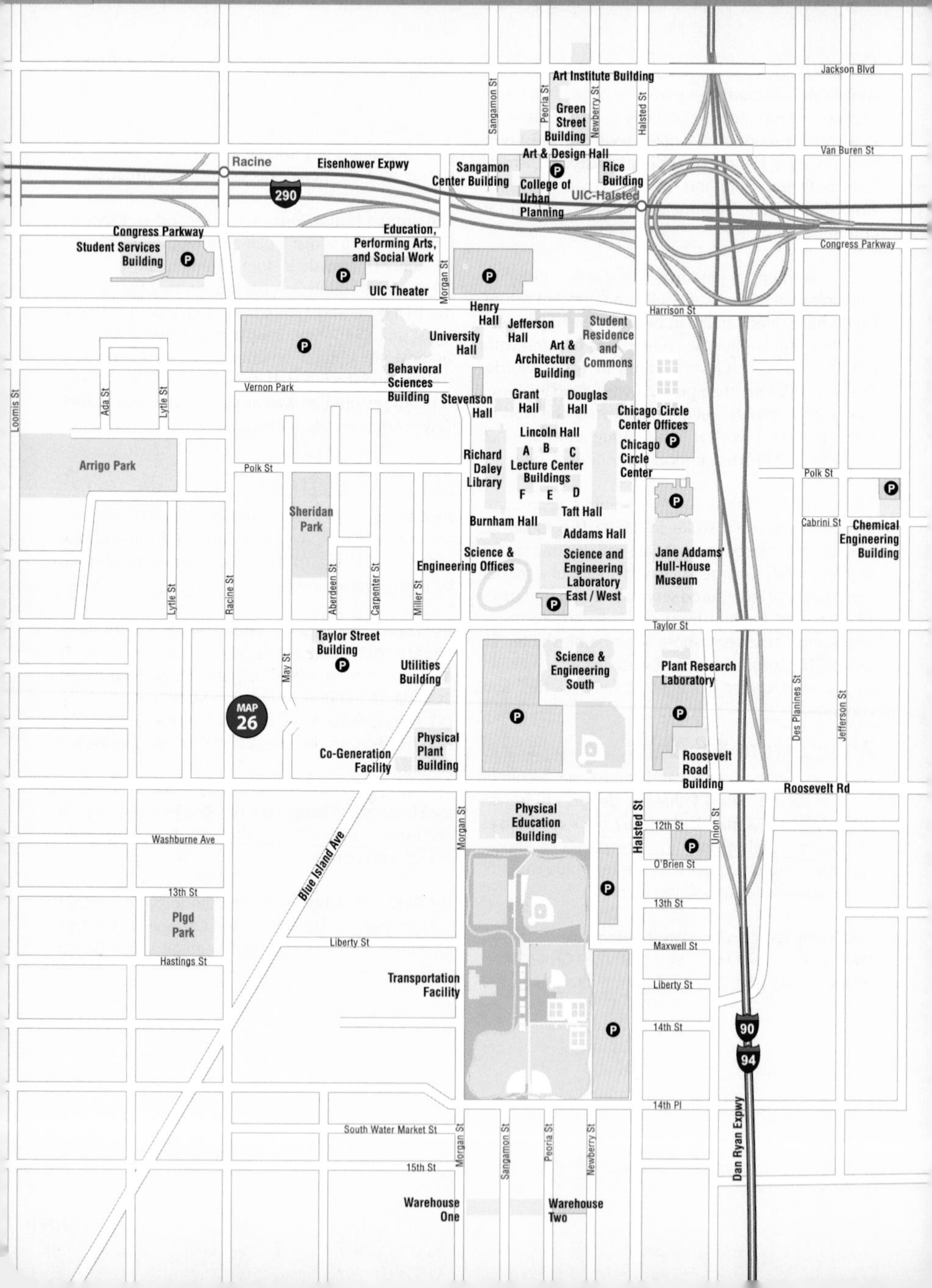

Jackson Blvd
Art Institute Building
Sangamon St
Peoria St
Green Street Building
Newberry St
Halsted St
Van Buren St
Racine
Eisenhower Expwy
290
Sangamon Center Building
Art & Design Hall
P
Rice Building
College of Urban Planning
UIC-Halsted
Congress Parkway
Student Services Building
P
Education, Performing Arts, and Social Work
P
UIC Theater
Morgan St
P
Congress Parkway
Harrison St
P
Henry Hall
University Hall
Jefferson Hall
Student Residence and Commons
Art & Architecture Building
Behavioral Sciences Building
Vernon Park
Loomis St
Ada St
Lytle St
Stevenson Hall
Grant Hall
Douglas Hall
Chicago Circle Center Offices
P
Lincoln Hall
Chicago Circle Center
Arrigo Park
Richard Daley Library
A B C
Lecture Center Buildings
F E D
Polk St
Polk St
P
P
Sheridan Park
Taft Hall
Burnham Hall
Addams Hall
Cabrini St
Chemical Engineering Building
Science & Engineering Offices
Science and Engineering Laboratory East / West
P
Jane Addams' Hull-House Museum
Lytle St
Racine St
Aberdeen St
Carpenter St
Miller St
Taylor St
Taylor Street Building
P
May St
Utilities Building
Science & Engineering South
Plant Research Laboratory
P
P
Des Plaines St
Jefferson St
MAP 26
Physical Plant Building
Co-Generation Facility
Roosevelt Road Building
Roosevelt Rd
Physical Education Building
Morgan St
Halsted St
12th St
Union St
P
Washburne Ave
O'Brien St
Blue Island Ave
13th St
P
13th St
Plgd Park
Liberty St
Maxwell St
Hastings St
Transportation Facility
Liberty St
14th St
P
90
94
14th Pl
South Water Market St
Morgan St
Sangamon St
Peoria St
Newberry St
Dan Ryan Expwy
15th St
Warehouse One
Warehouse Two

University of Illinois at Chicago

General Information

Mailing Address: *University of Illinois at Chicago, 601 S. Morgan St., Chicago, IL 60607*
Phone: *312-996-7000*
Website: *www.uic.edu*

Overview

With 25,000 students, the University of Illinois at Chicago (UIC) is the largest university in Chicago. Located on the city's Near West Side, UIC is ethnically diverse and urban to the core. It is a leading public research university and home to the nation's largest medical school.

However, its legacy as a builder in Chicago is a bit spotty. In the mid-1960s, the school leveled most of what was left of a vibrant Italian-American neighborhood to build its campus next to the Eisenhower. During current development of the South Campus, UIC is consuming city blocks south of Roosevelt Rd. UIC's expansion all but erased the colorful, landmark Maxwell Street flea market area. The saving grace of UIC's construction craze is that many of the original campus's ugly, cement slab structures designed by Walter Netsch are kissing the wrecking ball and being replaced with more inspired buildings. But even with the multi-million dollar improvements, the campus still doesn't ignite a desire to visit. Other than going to class or the doctor, a lone trip to UIC to see the Jane Addams Hull House Museum is sufficient.

Tuition

In the 2003-2004 academic year, an Illinois resident, undergraduate student's tuition and fees will be $6,520; room and board will cost between $6,620 and $8,638. These figures do not include books, supplies, lab fees, or personal expenses.

Sports

In recent years, the Division I Flames have been hot. The men's basketball team's first appearance in the NCAA Tournament was 1997. They returned in 2002 after winning their first-ever Horizon League Tournament. Additionally, recently the Flames women's gymnastics, tennis squad, and softball teams all advanced to NCAA Tournament play.

Other Flames men's and women's teams are swimming & diving and cross-country/track & field. UIC also has men's tennis, gymnastics, baseball, and soccer, plus women's basketball and volleyball. Basketball games and women's volleyball matches are played at the recently renovated UIC Pavilion at the corner of Racine Ave. and Harrison St. For tickets, call 312-413-8421; www.uicflames.com.

Too bad the NCAA doesn't have a bowling tournament because UIC would be a strong contender. The campus has two alleys. The public is welcome to sling balls and swig beers with students. The larger alley is at 750 S. Halsted St., 312-413-5170; the other is at 828 S. Walcott St., 312-413-5268.

Culture on Campus

Jane Addams Hull House, 800 S. Halsted St., 312-413-5353, www.uic.edu/jaddams/hull, was America's first settlement house opened in 1889. The free museum documents the pioneering organization's social welfare programs supporting the community's destitute immigrant workers. Museum hours are 10 am to 4 pm Tuesday through Friday and noon to 5 pm on Sunday.

Department Contact Information

All area codes are 312 unless otherwise noted

Admissions and Records 996-4350
Graduate College 413-2550
College of Architecture & the Arts 996-3337
College of Applied Health Sciences 996-6695
College of Dentistry 996-7555
College of Business Administration 996-2700
College of Education 996-4532
College of Engineering 996-3463
College of Liberal Arts and Sciences 996-3366
College of Medicine 996-5635
College of Nursing 996-7800
College of Pharmacy 996-7240
College of Public Health 996-6620
College of Social Work 996-7096
College of Urban Planning & Public Affairs 413-8088
Office of Continuing Education 355-0423
University of Illinois Medical Center 996-3900

University of Chicago

1. Laboratory for Astrophysics and Space Research
2. Astronomy and Astrophysics Center
3. Research Institutes
4. Biopsychological Research Center
5. Disciples Divinity House
6. Kovler Viral Oncology Laboratories
7. Ingleside Hall
8. Searle Chemical Laboratory
9. Jones Laboratory
10. Zoology
11. Hutchinson Commons
12. Reynolds Club
13. Statistics and Mathematics
14. Development Office-5733 South University
15 Calvert House
16. Student Counseling and Resource Service
17. Human Development
18. Development Office-5736 South Woodlawn
19. Nursery School-5740 South Woodlawn
20. Nursery School-5750 South Woodlawn
21. Abbott Memorial Hall
22. Goldblatt Pavillion
23. Armour Clincial Research
24. Goldblatt Memorial Building
25. McElwee Building
26. Gates-Blake Hall
27. Goodspeed Hall
28. Wieboldt Hall
29. Harper Memorial Library
30. Beecher Hall
31. Green Hall
32. Kelly Hall
33. Foster Hall
34. University High School
35. Orthogenic School

General Information

Mailing Address: *University of Chicago Administration Building, 5801 S. Ellis Ave., Chicago, IL 60637*
Phone: *773-702-1234*
Website: *www.uchicago.edu*
Campus Visitors Center: *Ida Noyes Hall, 1st Floor, 1212 E. 59th St.,*
Phone: *773-702-9739*
Guest Parking: *Lot located between 58th and 59th Sts. Enter off Woodlawn Ave. Meters are north of Ida Noyes Hall*

Overview

University of Chicago is a world-renowned research institution with a winning tradition in Nobel Prizes. Seventy-three Nobel laureates have been associated with the university as faculty, students or researchers. More importantly (for some people) is the fact that University of Chicago helped found the Big ten Conference and created "the world's first controlled release of nuclear energy"—uh, for us regular folks, that's the atomic bomb.

Besides hordes of brainy gurus of economics, business, law, and medicine, University of Chicago graduates include artists, writers, politicians, film directors, and actors. To name a few: Studs Terkel, Sara Paretsky, Carol Mosely-Braun, Kurt Vonnegut, Susan Sontag, John Ashcroft, Ed Asner, Saul Bellow, Katharine Graham, Philip Glass, Sherry Lansing, Martin Marty, and co-creators of Chicago's Second City comedy troupe, Bernard Sahlins and Mike Nichols.

Established in 1890, University of Chicago was founded and funded by John D. Rockefeller. Built on 200 acres donated by Marshall Field and designed by architect Henry Ives Cobb, the university's English Gothic buildings of ivy-clad limestone ooze old money and intellectual achievements. Rockefeller described the university as "the best investment I ever made." We just hope parents footing the bill for their kids' education feel the same.

Tuition

University of Chicago's academic year is three quarters. In the 2003-2004 academic year, an undergraduate student will pay approximately $29,238 for tuition and fees, and an additional $9,165 for room and board. Add on costs for books, lab fees, and personal expenses. Costs for graduate students vary based on the school. Chicago has 13,000 students, 4,000 of them undergraduate students. About 2,000 of the graduate students attend classes at the downtown riverfront campus's Gleacher Center, 450 N. Cityfront Plaza Dr., 312-464-8740, where the popular Graham School of General Studies holds most of its continuing education classes.

Sports

At one time, University of Chicago racked up football trophies as well as Nobel Prizes. In 1935, the first Heisman Trophy winner was senior Jay Berwanger. The Maroons won seven Big Ten football championships between 1899 and 1924, followed by a steady losing streak. In 1946, the university threw in the proverbial towel, resigning from the Big Ten in favor of developing students' brains instead of brawn.

But the school hasn't totally abandoned sports. A member of the University Athletic Association, Chicago has women's volleyball and softball teams and men's baseball, football, and wrestling squads. There are men's and women's basketball, cross-country, soccer, swimming, tennis, and track & field teams. And, hey, the Maroons must have a killer College Bowl team because a university contestant was the 1999 Jeopardy College Champion.

Culture on Campus

Located at 5757 S. Woodlawn Ave., Robie House, 773-834-1847, Frank Lloyd Wright's Prairie Style residential masterpiece, is a must-see for architecture fans, although it will be much more impressive once renovations are completed. Two must-see but often overlooked free museums on campus are the Oriental Institute, 1155 E. 58th St., 773-702-9514, www.oi.uchicago.edu, and Smart Museum of Art, 5550 S. Greenwood Ave., 773-702-0200, smartmuseum.uchicago.edu. Showcasing archeological finds from university digs since the 1900s, the Oriental Institute has treasures from the ancient Near East dating from 9000 BC to 900 AD. The Smart Museum displays 8,000 fine arts items with strong collections in painting and sculpture spanning centuries and continents.

Now in its 48th season, the university's professional Court Theatre presents fresh interpretations of classic dramas, 773-753-4472. For information on additional professional arts organizations' performances, including Contemporary Chamber Players, Pacifica String Quartet, and University of Chicago Presents, go to the school website.

University of Chicago's campus is considered a botanic garden. Grand plans are underway to revitalize the Midway Plaisance parkway. In addition to a permanent ice-skating rink, the plan envisions an urban horticultural center, children's garden, canals, and a healing garden.

Department Contact Information

Log onto www.uchicago.edu/uchi/directories/ for a university directory and links to division and department web pages. The area code for the following numbers is 773, unless otherwise noted.

Undergraduate Student Admissions	702-8650
Biological Sciences	702-9000
Humanities	702-8030
Physical Sciences	702-7950
Social Sciences	702-8415
Divinity School	702-8217
Graduate School of Business	702-7743
Graduate Affairs	702-7813
Graham School of General Studies	702-0539
Harris Graduate School of Public Policy Studies	702-8401
Law School	702-9494
Pritzker School of Medicine	702-1939
School of Social Service Administration	702-1250

Columbia College

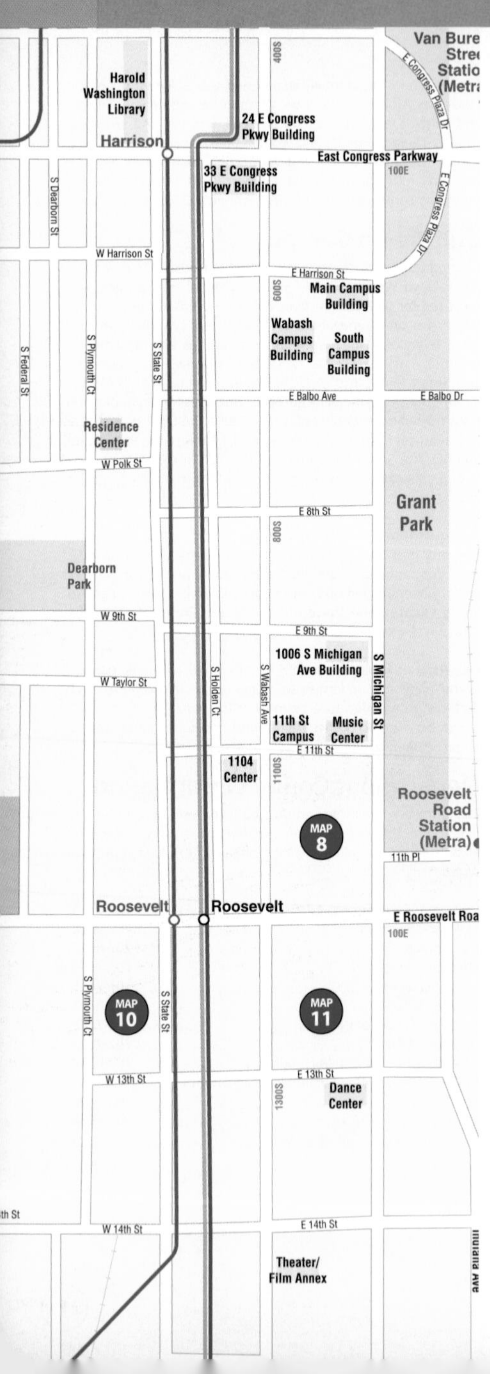

General Information

Main Office:	*600 S. Michigan Ave.* *Chicago, Il 60605*
Phone:	*312-663-1600*
Website:	*www.colum.edu*

Overview

Named in honor of the Columbia Exposition World Fair, Columbia College first opened its doors in 1890, as a women's college of speech. Over the years the private college has evolved into the nation's largest Media Arts school, although psychologically staff and students grin and bear second fiddle status to the more highly acclaimed school of the Art Institute of Chicago. Columbia's image is looking up, however, thanks in part to the successes of alumni from their reputable film and fiction departments, which have sprouted, in recent years, a bountiful harvest of novels and feature films (including the successful indie films *Barbershop* and *Real Women Have Curves* and the critically acclaimed novels of alums Joe Meno and Don DeGrazia, both now Fiction Department faculty).

Tuition

Tuition hikes for the 2004 school year now have full time students shelling out $14,880 per year not including various lab, activity, and amenity fees.

Culture

The Dance Center of Columbia brings the DanceAfrica! exposition to Chicago every fall. The Museum of Contemporary Photography at the main campus building is one of only two fully accredited photography museums in the United States. The theater department's Getz Theater (62 E. 11th St) and New Studio Theater (72 E. 11th) mount productions regularly.

Department Contact Information

Undergraduate Admissions	312-344-7129
Graduate Admissions	312-344-7260
Continuing Education	312-344-8190
Art & Design	312-344-7380
Dance	312-344-8300
Educational Studies	312-344-8140
Fiction Writing	312-344-7611
Film and Video	312-344-6700
ASL – English Interpretation	312-344-7837
Marketing Communications	312-344-7600
Television	312-344-7410
Library	312-344-7906

Illinois Institute of Technology

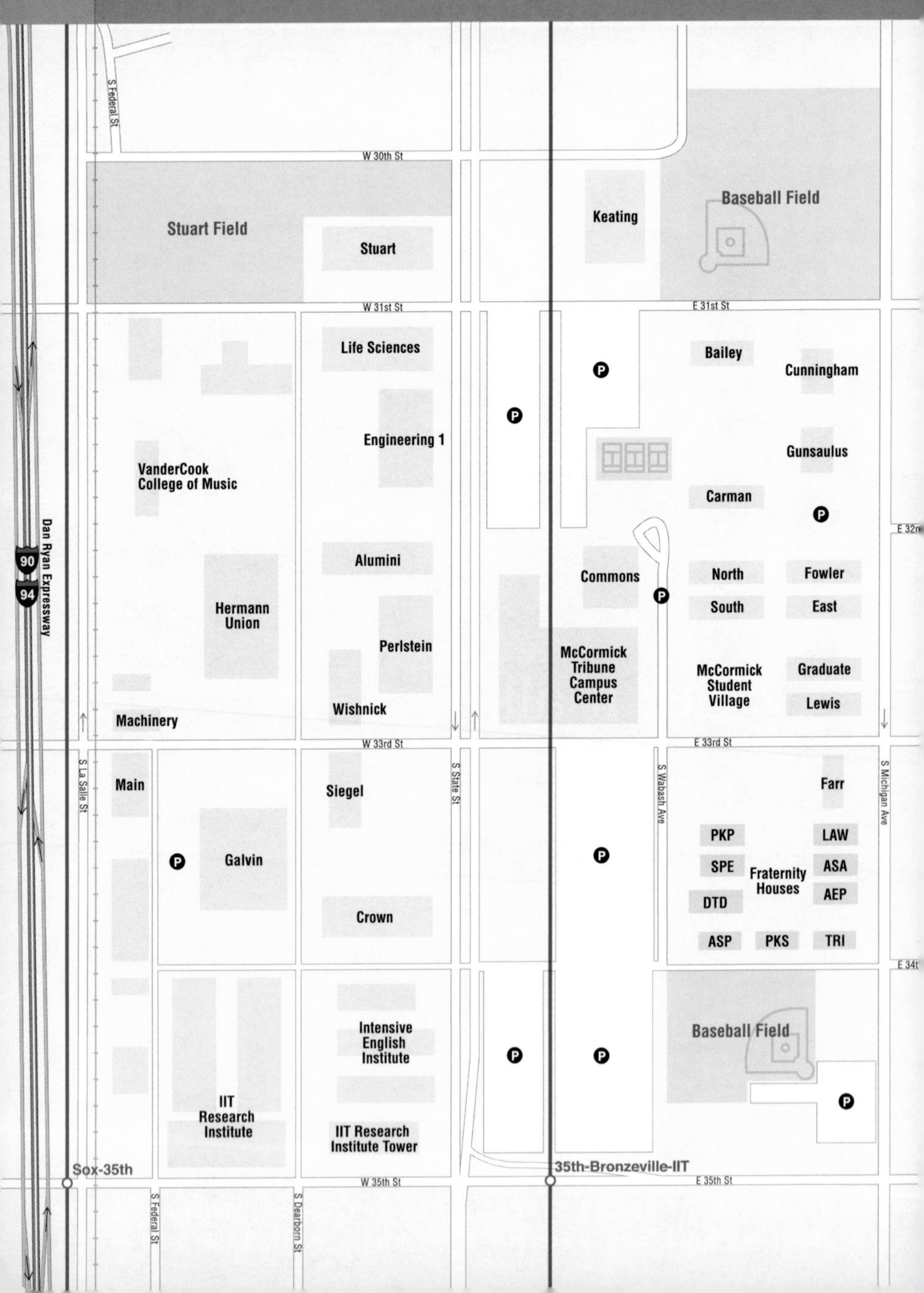

General Information

Main Campus: *3300 S Federal St.*
Chicago, IL 60616
Phone: *312-567-3000*
Website: *www.iit.edu*

Overview

IIT opened its doors as the Armour Institute in 1893, funded by a million-dollar grant by meat magnate Philip Danforth Armour. A merger with the engineering school in 1940 saw the name change to Illinois Institute of Technology, and over the next 40 years, the college continued to merge with other small technical colleges, resulting in the IIT of today. Nowadays, the school is as notable for its Mies Van Der Rohe designed campus as for its ground-breaking work in aeronautics research, and the architectural legacy continues. The new student center, designed by Dutch architect Rem Koolhaas, will include a space-aged metallic tube through which the local El-train will travel.

Tuition

Current full time tuition is $19,200 per year, more for the design institute and law school, and not including lab and activity fees.

Sports

IIT is affiliated with the National Association of Intercollegiate Athletics. Students can compete with other schools in baseball, basketball, cross-country, swimming, and volleyball. The IIT team name is the Scarlet Hawks.

Department Contact Information

Armour College of Engineering
and Science 312-567-3163
Center for Law and Financial Markets 312-906-6506
Center for Professional Development 312-906-6506
Kent College of Law 312-906-5000
College of Architecture 312-567-3230
Institute of Design 312-595-4900
Institute of Psychology 312-567-3500
Stuart School of Business 312-906-6500
Undergraduate Admissions 312-567-3025

W Altgeld St
W Montana St
Book Store
Seton Hall
1150 W Fullerton Building
990 W Fullerton Building
Fullerton
Fullerton Ave
Student Residence Hall
University Hall
Richardson Library
Centennial Hall
Maintenance Building
School of Music
Lincoln Ave
Sanctuary Hall
Sheffield Parking Garage
Corcoran Hall
Schmitt Academic Center
Levan Center
Sheffield Square
Hayes-Healy Athletic Center
Cortelyou Commons
McGaw Hall
McGowan Biological & Environmental Sciences Center
Office of Admissions
IND. Living
Athletic Training Center
Wish Field
McCabe Hall
Student Residence Hall
Muroe Hall
Stuart Center
Parking Services
O'Connell Hall
IND. Living
Belden APT.
Concert Hall
W Belden Ave
Racine Ave
Clifton Ave
Seminary Ave
Kenmore Ave
Student Center
Sheffield Ave
Bissell St
Fremont St
Dayton St
Halsted St
Ray Meyer Fitness & Recreation Center
Vincentian Residence
MAP 5
Byrne Hall
St. Vincent De Paul Church
Trebes Park
W Webster Ave
Theatre School Annex
Theatre School
W Dickens Ave

General Information

Loop Campus:	*DePaul University - Loop Campus* *1 E. Jackson Blvd.* *Chicago, IL 60604*
Phone:	*312-362-8000*
Lincoln Park Campus:	*DePaul University* *Schmitt Academic Center* *2320 N. Kenmore Ave.* *Chicago, IL 60614-3298*
Phone:	*773-325-7000*
Website:	*www.depaul.edu*
Suburban Campuses:	*Barat College, 847-234-3000; Lake Forest, 312 362-6400/847-604-8220; Naperville, 312 476-4500/630-548-9378; Oak Forest, 312 476-3000/708-633-9091; O'Hare 312 476-3600/847-296-5348; Rolling Meadows, 312 476-4800/847-437-9522*

Overview

Established in 1898 by the Vincentian Fathers, DePaul is the largest Catholic university in the country and biggest private educational institution in Chicago. Total enrollment last year was approximately 21,400 students. According to The Princeton Review's recent survey of college students nationwide, "DePaul students were the happiest in the nation." It must be all the bars near campus on Halsted St. and Lincoln Ave.

DePaul has eight campuses in the Chicago area, but the Lincoln Park and Loop campuses are the university's core locations. The highly acclaimed Theatre School, College of Liberal Arts and Sciences, School of Music, and School of Education are on the 36-acre Lincoln Park campus amidst renovated, vintage homes on tree-lined streets. Prominent DePaul alumni include Chicago father-son mayors Richard M. Daley and his dad, late Richard J. Daley; McDonald's Corporation's CEO Jack Greenberg; Pulitzer Prize-winning composer George Perle; and actress Gillian Anderson.

DePaul's Loop Campus at Jackson Blvd. and State St. is where the College of Commerce, College of Law, and School of Computer Science, Telecommunications, and Information Systems are located. So are the nationally respected Kellstadt Graduate School of Business and DePaul's thriving continuing education program, the "School of New Learning." The heart of the Loop campus is DePaul Center, located in the old Goldblatt Brothers Department Store.

Tuition

Each college has its own tuition; room and board costs depend on the residence facility and meal plan chosen by the student. In the 2002-2003 academic year, undergraduate tuition and fees were approximately $17,880 plus an average room and board cost of $7,455. Add on books, lab fees, and personal expenses. Graduate student tuition, fees, and expenses vary by college.

Sports

DePaul's Blue Demons men's basketball team teased Chicago with an NCAA Division I Championship in 2000 when the team appeared in its first tournament since 1992. Newly appointed in 2002, Coach Dave Leitao plans to reinstate the Demons' winning record. The Blue Demons play at United Center, 1901 W. Madison St., www.unitedcenter.com, and Allstate Arena, 6920 N. Mannheim Rd. in Rosemont, www.allstatearena.com. For tickets, call Ticketmaster, 312-559-1212; www.ticketmaster.com; go to the stadiums' box offices; or visit the DePaul Athletic Center box office, 2323 N. Sheffield Ave., 773-325-7526; www.depaulbluedemons.com.

Blue Demons men's and women's teams include basketball, cross-country, soccer, tennis, and track & field. DePaul also has a men's golf team, as well as women's softball and volleyball squads. For stats and schedules, visit the Blue Demons' website.

Culture on Campus

DePaul's vibrant Theatre School is the oldest in the Midwest. Founded in 1925 as the Goodman School of Drama, the respected school produces over 200 performances during its Showcase, Chicago Playworks, New Directors Series, and School Workshop seasons. The Theatre School Showcase performs contemporary and classic plays at its 1,325-seat Merle Reskin Theatre, 60 E. Balbo Dr. in South Loop. The Chicago Playworks for Families and Young Audiences and the School of Music's annual opera are also performed at the Merle Reskin Theatre, a French Renaissance-style theatre built in 1910. For tickets ($8-$12), directions, and parking garage locations call 312-922-1999; www.theatreschool.depaul.edu. Take the Red Line to the Harrison St. or Jackson St. stops just southwest of the theatre. CTA buses 29, 62, and 146 stop near the theatre. Check the Theatre School website for New Directors Series and School Workshop productions, theater locations, and ticket prices.

DePaul University Art Gallery is located in the John T. Richardson Library, 2350 N. Kenmore Ave. (773-325-7506). Permanent collections of sculpture and oils from local and international artists adorn the free gallery. A pay parking lot is one block east of the library on Sheffield Ave. DePaul's John T. Richardson Library and Loop campus library in DePaul Center are open to the public year-round. Take plenty of change for the copy machines as check-out privileges are reserved for students and faculty.

Department Contact Information

Log onto www.directory.depaul.edu/index.asp for a full university directory.

Lincoln Park Campus Admissions Office	773-325-7500
Loop Campus Admissions Office	312-362-8300
College of Commerce	312-362-6783
College of Law	312-362-8701
College of Liberal Arts and Sciences	773-325-7300
John T. Richardson Library	773-325-7862
Kellstadt Graduate School of Business	312-362-8810
Loop Campus Library	312-362-8432
School for New Learning	312-362-8001
School of Computer Science, Telecommunications and Information Systems	312-362-8381
School of Music	773-325-7260
Theatre School	773-325-7917

Northwestern University (Evanston Campus)

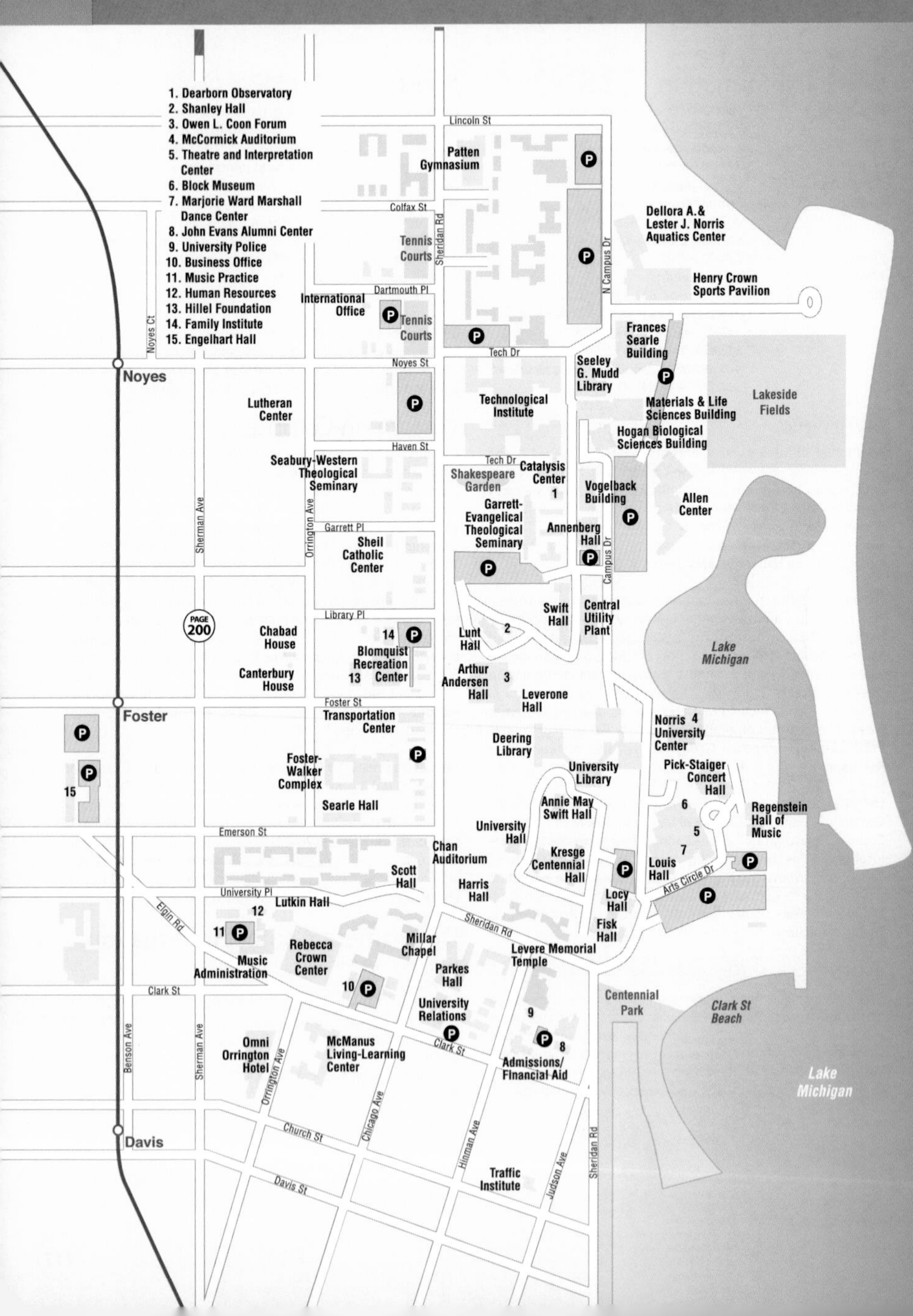

1. Dearborn Observatory
2. Shanley Hall
3. Owen L. Coon Forum
4. McCormick Auditorium
5. Theatre and Interpretation Center
6. Block Museum
7. Marjorie Ward Marshall Dance Center
8. John Evans Alumni Center
9. University Police
10. Business Office
11. Music Practice
12. Human Resources
13. Hillel Foundation
14. Family Institute
15. Engelhart Hall
Lincoln St
Patten Gymnasium
Colfax St
Tennis Courts
Sheridan Rd
Dellora A. & Lester J. Norris Aquatics Center
N Campus Dr
Henry Crown Sports Pavilion
Dartmouth Pl
International Office
Tennis Courts
Noyes Ct
Tech Dr
Frances Searle Building
Noyes St
Seeley G. Mudd Library
Noyes
Lakeside Fields
Lutheran Center
Technological Institute
Materials & Life Sciences Building
Hogan Biological Sciences Building
Haven St
Seabury-Western Theological Seminary
Tech Dr
Shakespeare Garden
Catalysis Center
Vogelback Building
Allen Center
Garrett-Evangelical Theological Seminary
Annenberg Hall
Sherman Ave
Orrington Ave
Garrett Pl
Sheil Catholic Center
Campus Dr
Swift Hall
Central Utility Plant
Library Pl
PAGE 200
Chabad House
Blomquist Recreation Center
Lunt Hall
Lake Michigan
Canterbury House
Arthur Andersen Hall
Leverone Hall
Foster St
Foster
Transportation Center
Norris University Center
Deering Library
Foster-Walker Complex
University Library
Pick-Staiger Concert Hall
Searle Hall
Annie May Swift Hall
Regenstein Hall of Music
University Hall
Emerson St
Chan Auditorium
Kresge Centennial Hall
Louis Hall
Scott Hall
Arts Circle Dr
University Pl
Harris Hall
Locy Hall
Lutkin Hall
Elgin Rd
Sheridan Rd
Fisk Hall
Millar Chapel
Rebecca Crown Center
Levere Memorial Temple
Music Administration
Parkes Hall
Clark St
Centennial Park
Clark St Beach
University Relations
Benson Ave
Omni Orrington Hotel
McManus Living-Learning Center
Clark St
Admissions/ Financial Aid
Lake Michigan
Church St
Chicago Ave
Davis
Hinman Ave
Sheridan Rd
Judson Ave
Traffic Institute
Davis St

Northwestern University (Evanston Campus)

General Information

Evanston Campus

Administrative Offices:	*Northwestern University* *633 Clark St.* *Evanston, IL 60208*
Phone:	*847-491-3741*

Chicago Campus

Administrative Offices:	*Abbot Hall* *710 N. Lake Shore Dr.* *Chicago, IL 60611*
Phone:	*312-503-8649*
Website:	*www.northwestern.edu*

Northwestern University's wealth and influence is evident in its lakefront campuses in Evanston and downtown Chicago. About 15,800 full and part-time students attend Northwestern's 11 colleges and schools. The private research university is known nationally for its strong liberal arts undergraduate program and for its highly ranked graduate schools in law, medicine, journalism, and business.

Opened in 1855, Northwestern University was established in Evanston by many of the same Methodist founding fathers of the town itself. The 380-acre lakefront campus is bordered roughly by Central Ave. on the north and Sheridan Rd. to the south and west. The Evanston campus houses the College of Arts and Sciences; Schools of Engineering, Music, Speech, Education and Social Policy; the Graduate School; Medill School of Journalism; and J.L. Kellogg School of Management.

Northwestern's Chicago campus opened in 1920. Located between the Lake and Michigan Ave. in the Streeterville neighborhood, it houses the Schools of Law, Medicine, and Continuing Studies. Graduate school and Kellogg courses are offered here as well. Several excellent hospitals and medical research institutions affiliated with the university dominate the northern edge of Streeterville. In 2004, construction of the Robert H. Lurie Medical Research Center at Fairbanks Ct. and Superior St. will be completed. The new women's hospital across from it will be finished in 2007.

Tuition

The tuition and fees for an undergraduate to attend Northwestern University during the 2003-2004 school year is $28,404 and $8,967 for room and board. Books, lab fees, and personal expenses are additional. Graduate school expenses vary by school.

Sports

Like all Big Ten Conference schools, Northwestern has football and basketball teams—but that's all we can really say of the Wildcats lately. There was more to talk about in the 1990s with back-to-back bowl appearances in the 1996 Rose Bowl (their first bowl appearance and only bowl win since 1949) and the1997 Citrus Bowl. After Nebraska de-clawed, skinned, and gutted the Wildcats at the 2001 Alamo Bowl, it seems the team has been licking its wounds. (The trouncing is conveniently not listed on the university's sports website in the bowl games summary.)

The Wildcat's home field is Ryan Field at 1501 Central Ave., about three blocks east of the Central Ave. stop on the Purple El Line ($1.50 one-way). Basketball games are at Welsh-Ryan Arena behind the stadium. For football and basketball tickets, call 847-491-2287. All sports contests are listed at www.nusports.com where you can also purchase tickets online.

Northwestern also has men's wrestling and baseball teams, plus men's and women's basketball, golf, soccer, tennis, field hockey, and swimming and diving teams. Additional sports Wildcat women compete in are cross-country, fencing, softball, lacrosse, and volleyball. Purchase tickets at the door for volleyball, baseball, and wrestling events.

Culture on Campus

The Mary and Leigh Block Museum of Art on the Evanston campus, 40 Arts Circle Dr., 847-491-4000; www.blockmuseum.northwestern.edu, has 4,000 items in its permanent collection, including Old Masters' prints, architectural drawings, and contemporary photographic images. The Block also has a 1,000-seat concert hall and other performance spaces. The free museum is open to the public Tuesday, 10 am to 5 pm; Wednesday through Friday, 10 am to 8 pm; and on weekends from noon to 5 pm.

The Pick-Staiger Concert Hall, 1977 50 Arts Circle Dr., 847-491-5441, www.northwestern.edu/pick-staiger, is not only the stage for the university's musical and theatrical performances, but is also home to several professional performance organizations: Chicago Chamber Musicians, Symphony of the Shores, Chicago String Ensemble, Performing Arts Chicago, and others. Call 847-467-4000 to purchase tickets.

Department Contact Information

Undergraduate Admissions 847-491-7271
Graduate School 847-491-7264
College of Arts and Sciences 847-491-7561
Kellogg Graduate School of Management ... 847-491-3300
Medill School of Journalism 847-491-1882
School of Communication 847-491-7023
School of Continuing Studies 312-503-6950
or 847-491-5612
School of Education and Social Policy: 847-491-8193
School of Engineering and Applied Sciences 847-491-5220
School of Law 312-503-3100
School of Medicine 312-503-8206
School of Music 847-491-3141
School of Speech 847-491-7241

Loyola University (Rogers Park Campus)

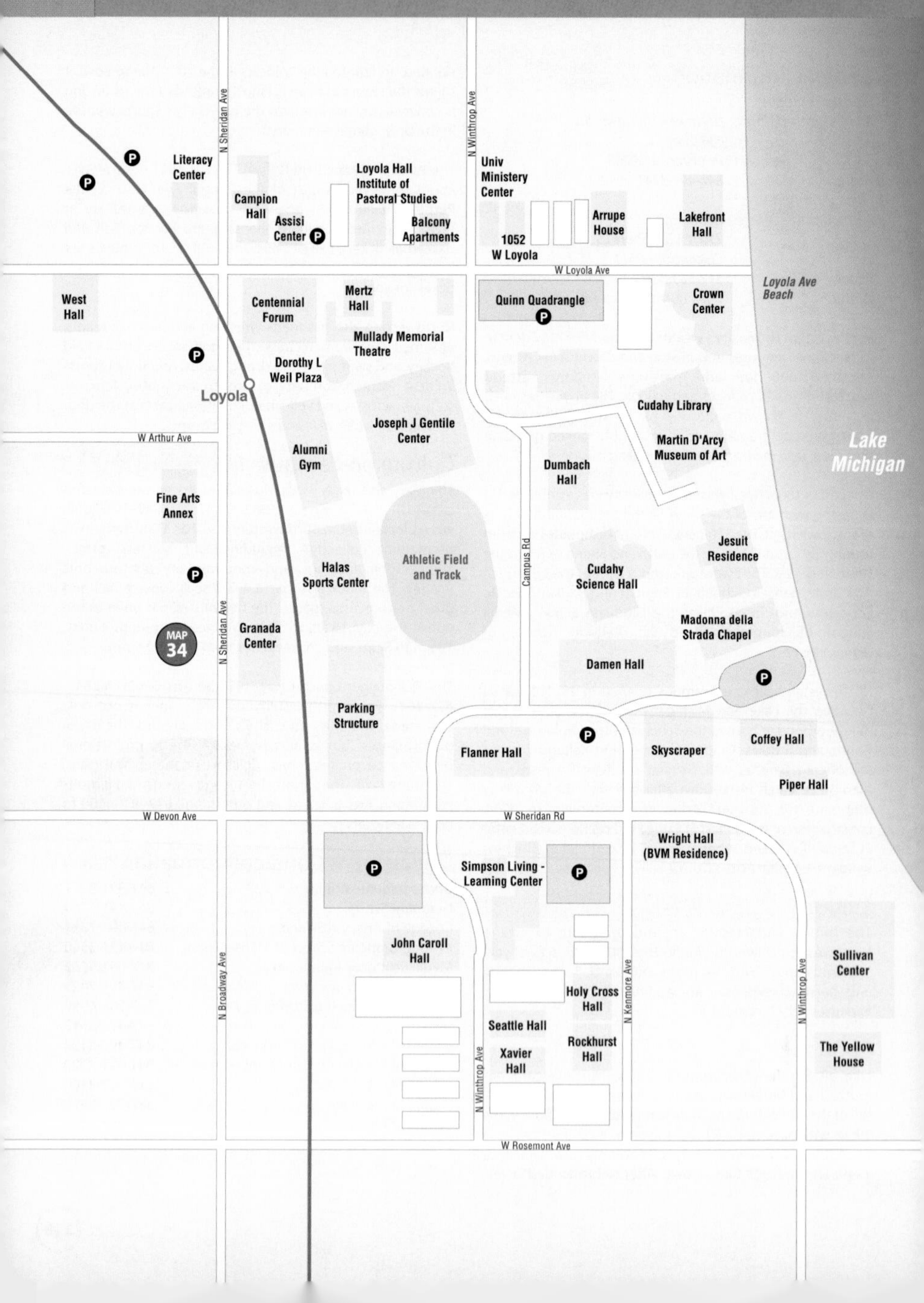

N Sheridan Ave
N Winthrop Ave
Literacy Center
Loyola Hall Institute of Pastoral Studies
Univ Ministery Center
Campion Hall
Assisi Center
Balcony Apartments
Arrupe House
Lakefront Hall
1052 W Loyola
W Loyola Ave
West Hall
Centennial Forum
Mertz Hall
Quinn Quadrangle
Crown Center
Loyola Ave Beach
Mullady Memorial Theatre
Dorothy L Weil Plaza
Loyola
Cudahy Library
W Arthur Ave
Joseph J Gentile Center
Martin D'Arcy Museum of Art
Lake Michigan
Alumni Gym
Dumbach Hall
Fine Arts Annex
Athletic Field and Track
Campus Rd
Jesuit Residence
Halas Sports Center
Cudahy Science Hall
Madonna della Strada Chapel
MAP 34
Granada Center
Damen Hall
Parking Structure
Flanner Hall
Skyscraper
Coffey Hall
Piper Hall
W Devon Ave
W Sheridan Rd
Wright Hall (BVM Residence)
Simpson Living - Leaming Center
John Caroll Hall
N Broadway Ave
Sullivan Center
Holy Cross Hall
N Kenmore Ave
Seattle Hall
Rockhurst Hall
Xavier Hall
The Yellow House
W Rosemont Ave

Loyola University (Rogers Park Campus)

General Information

Lake Shore Campus:	*Loyola University* *6525 N. Sheridan Rd.* *Chicago 60626*
Phone:	*773-274-3000*
Water Tower Campus:	*Loyola University - Lewis Towers* *820 N. Michigan Ave.* *Chicago 60611*
Phone:	*312-915-6000*
Medical Center Campus:	*Loyola University Medical Center* *2160 S. First Ave.* *Maywood, IL 60153*
Phone:	*708-216-9000*
Website:	*www.luc.edu*

Overview

Loyola University, one of the largest Jesuit universities in the United States, is known throughout the Midwest for its undergraduate and graduate Schools of Business, School of Law, and the University of Loyola Medical Center, a respected medical research institution. Approximately 13,400 students attend the university.

Lake Shore Campus, the largest campus of Loyola's four campuses, is on the lake in Rogers Park and houses the College of Arts and Sciences, the Graduate School, Niehoff School of Nursing, Mundelein College Adult Education Program, and Cudahy Library. The university's Water Tower campus downtown on Michigan Ave. is home to the Schools of Business, Education, Law, and Social Work and some College of Arts and Sciences courses. Loyola operates the Stritch School of Medicine and the master's degree programs through the Niehoff School of Nursing at its suburban Maywood campus. The university also has a campus in Rome, one of the largest American campuses in Western Europe.

Tuition

In the 2003-2004 academic year, undergraduate tuition and fees amounted to $20,544 plus an average room and board cost of $7,500. Add on books, lab fees, and personal expenses. Graduate student tuition, fees, and expenses vary by college.

Sports

Loyola is the only Illinois school to win a Division I National Championship basketball tournament. The year 2003 marked the fortieth anniversary of the Loyola Ramblers' 1963 NCAA men's basketball championship. The Ramblers' most recent tournament appearance was in 1985. They play at the Joseph J. Gentile Center on the Lake Shore Campus. For tickets, visit the box office or call 773-508-2569; www.ramblermania.com.

Loyola University has men's and women's basketball, cross-country, track, soccer, and volleyball teams. The women also have a softball squad. Last year, the men's volleyball team was ranked as one of the top 10 in the nation.

Culture on Campus

The Martin D'Arcy Museum of Art at the Cudahy Library, 773-508-2679, on Lake Shore Campus is Chicago's only museum specializing in Medieval, Renaissance, and Baroque art. Paintings by Masters Tintoretto, Guercino, Bassano, and Stomer, plus sculpture, furniture, jewelry, decorative arts, and liturgical vessels are part of the over 500-piece collection dating from 1150 to 1750. Admission is free. Museum hours are Tuesday through Saturday 12 pm to 4 pm during the school year. Call for summer hours. Take the Red Line El to the Loyola stop. CTA buses 151 and 147 travel to campus from downtown. The Cudahy Library, the Lewis Library at the Water Tower Campus, Science Library, Health Sciences Library, and Graduate Business School Library welcome the public to use their resources; however, checkout privileges are for students and faculty only.

The Loyola University Theatre performs four classic dramas a season at the Kathleen Mullady Theatre, 1125 W. Loyola Ave., 773-508-3847, in the Centennial Forum/Mertz Hall building on the Lake Shore campus. Tickets are $15 for the general public and available for purchase through the box office open Monday through Friday 2:30 pm to 5:30 pm.

Department Contact Information

Undergraduate Admissions 773-508-3075
Adult Continuing Education,
Mundelein College 312-915-6501
College of Arts and Sciences 773-508-3500
School of Business Administration 312-915-6113
School of Education 847-853-3000
School of Law 312-915-7120
Stritch School of Medicine 708-216-3223
Niehoff School of Nursing 773-508-3249
Rome Center of Liberal Arts 773-508-2760
School of Social Work 312-915-7005
Graduate School of Business 312-915-6120
The Graduate School 773-508-3396
University Libraries 773-508-2632

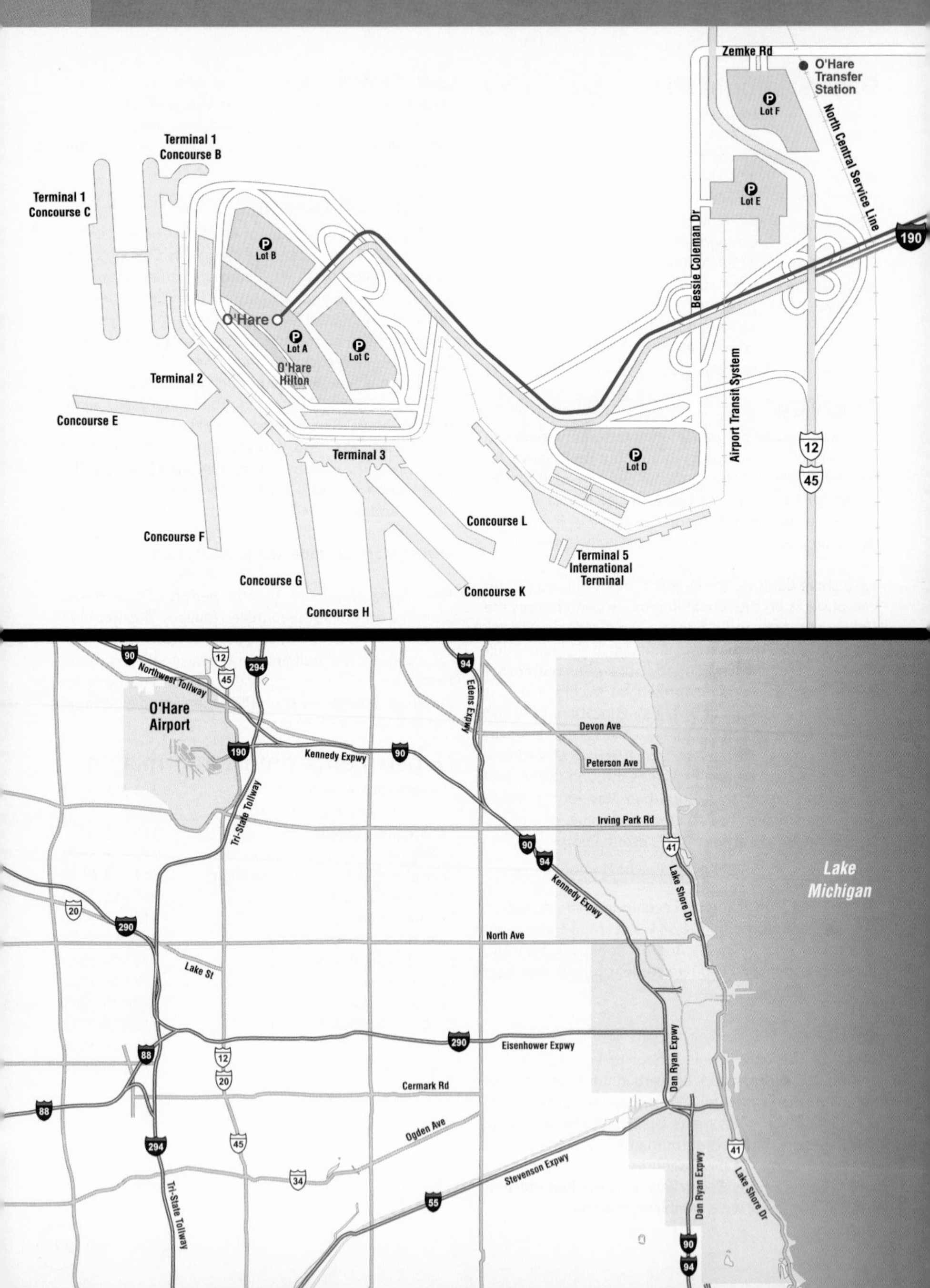

Zemke Rd
O'Hare Transfer Station
Lot F
North Central Service Line
Terminal 1 Concourse B
Terminal 1 Concourse C
Lot E
Bessie Coleman Dr
190
Lot B
O'Hare
Lot A
Lot C
O'Hare Hilton
Terminal 2
Airport Transit System
Concourse E
12
Terminal 3
Lot D
45
Concourse L
Concourse F
Terminal 5 International Terminal
Concourse G
Concourse K
Concourse H
90
Northwest Tollway
12
45
294
94
Edens Expwy
O'Hare Airport
Devon Ave
190
Kennedy Expwy
90
Peterson Ave
Tri-State Tollway
Irving Park Rd
90
41
94
Kennedy Expwy
Lake Shore Dr
Lake Michigan
20
290
North Ave
Lake St
Dan Ryan Expwy
290
Eisenhower Expwy
88
12
20
Cermark Rd
88
Ogden Ave
294
45
41
Stevenson Expwy
34
Dan Ryan Expwy
Lake Shore Dr
55
Tri-State Tollway
90
94

General Information

Location:	*10000 W. O'Hare Chicago, IL 60666*
Phone:	*773-686-2200; 800-832-6352*
Website:	*www.ohare.com*
Ground Transportation:	*773-686-8040*
Lost and Found:	*773-686-2201*
Parking:	*773-686-7530*
Traveler's Aid:	*773-894-2427*
Police:	*773-686-2385*
Customs Information:	*773-894-2900*

Overview

O'Delay might be a better name for O'Hare. What else can we say about the nation's busiest airport? To its credit, O'Hare serves 190,000 travelers daily in one of the most unpredictable weather zones in the country. Although located just 17 miles northwest of the Loop, sometimes it can take the better part of a day to get to your departure gate. Commuter traffic, airline snafus, parking, security checks, snowstorms, airport construction, and roadwork can make the O'Hare leg of your journey as pleasurable as a migraine.

Expansion spells relief, according to Mayor Daley and Governor Ryan, who have joined forces to push through a controversial $6.6 billion plan designed to double O'Hare's capacity and secure its "busiest" title for the duration of the 21st century. The plan calls for building another runway, reconfiguring the other seven, building an additional entrance on the airport's west side, and spending millions in soundproofing area homes and schools. In addition, O'Hare's World Gateway Program proposes development of two new passenger terminals, renovation of existing ones, and adding two new federal customs inspection facilities. Recently, political opposition has thrown up hefty lawsuits to block legislation that would cement the Daley-Ryan deal into federal law.

Meanwhile, the rest of us are stuck in traffic, in line, on the runway, etc…

How to Get There

By Car: If you must drive, pack aspirin in your glove compartment along with favorite CDs, because the crawl down the Kennedy can often equate to a grueling road trip. To be safe, allow over an hour just for the drive, more during rush hours between 6 am to 9 am and 3 pm to 7 pm. From the Loop to O'Hare, take the I-90 west. From the north suburbs, take I-294 south. From the south suburbs, take I-294 north. From the west suburbs, take I-88 east to I-294 north. Get off all of the above highways at I-190, which will lead you directly to the airport. All of the major routes have clear signage easily legible at a snail's pace.

Parking: O'Hare Airport's parking garage reflects its hometown's passion for sports. All levels are "helpfully" labeled with Chicago sports teams' colors and larger-than-life logos (Wolves, Bulls, Blackhawks, White Sox, Bears, Cubs). From floor to floor, annoying elevator musak whines each team's fight song. If this isn't enough to guide you to your car, we can't help you, because the garage's numbering-alphabetical system is more frustrating than the tinny elevator tunes.

If parking for less than three hours, go to Level 1. It costs $3 for the first hour, $21 for up to 4 hours, and a deterring $50 per day. Overnight parking close to Terminals 1, 2, and 3 on Levels 2 through 6 of the garage or in outside lots B and C costs $25 a day. For flyers with cash to burn, valet parking is available on Level 1 of the garage for $10 per hour or $32 per day. Parking in the International Terminal 5's designated Lot D costs $3 for the first hour; the daily rate is $30. Know that incoming international passengers always disembark in Terminal 5 (even if the airline departs from another terminal) because passengers must clear customs.

Long-term parking lots are Economy Lots E and G costing $2 for the first hour; $13 per day. From Lot E, walk or take the free shuttle to the free Airport Transit System (ATS) train station servicing all terminals. From Lot G, the shuttle will take you to the ATS stop in Lot E. Frequent flyers who are budget-conscious may want to purchase a prepaid Lot E "ExpressLane Parking" windshield tag for hassle-free, speedy departure from the airport. Lot F is currently closed until further notice.

By Bus: CTA buses 220 and 330 stop at the airport. If you're not near either of those bus lines, your best bet is to take your nearest bus line north or south to one of the O'Hare Blue Line train stations. The CTA also offers a special door-to-door service to and from the airport for Chicago-area residents and out-of-towners needing extra assistance. Call 312-917-4357 or 312-917-1338 (TTY) for additional information. All shuttles to airport hotels depart from the Bus Shuttle Center in front of the O'Hare Hilton Hotel in the center of the airport.

By Train: Take the Metra train only if you seek a transportation challenge above and beyond what your airline will provide. The Wisconsin North Central Line departs Union Station for Antioch with a stop at the

O'Hare Transfer station five times a day starting in the afternoons on weekdays only ($3.15 one-way). Travel time is 30 minutes. Then add time to hop on the free Airport Transit System (ATS) to get to your terminal. Needless to say, the odds of the Metra's schedule conveniently coinciding with your flight schedule are only slightly better than those of the Bulls winning the championship this year.

By El: We recommend the Blue Line as the best transportation method if you don't have several large bags or dependents in tow. The train runs between downtown Chicago and O'Hare 24 hours a day every 8 to 10 minutes ($1.50 one-way). Travel time from the Loop is 45 minutes. The train station is on the lowest level of the airport's main parking garage. Walk through the underground pedestrian tunnels to Terminals 1, 2 and 3. If you're headed for the International Terminal 5, walk to Terminal 3 and board the free Airport Transit System (ATS) train.

By Cab: Join the cab queue at the lower level curb-front of all terminals. Metered cab fares from O'Hare to downtown run up to $40. Some cab companies servicing O'Hare include American United, 773-248-7600, Flash Cab Co., 773-561-1444, Jiffy Cab, 773-487-9000, and Yellow Cab, 312-829-4222. Share-ride fares are a flat $15 a head to the Loop. Check with the cab starter to confirm current pricing.

By Kiss 'n' Fly: The Kiss 'n' Fly is a convenient drop-off and pick-up point for "chauffeurs" who wisely want to avoid the terminal curb-side chaos. But the flyer needs to build in more time for the ATS transfer to his or her terminal. The Kiss 'n' Fly zone is off Bessie Coleman Dr. Take I-190 to the International Exit, and then to Bessie Coleman Dr. Turn left at the light and follow Bessie Coleman Dr. north to the Kiss 'n' Fly entrance and ATS stop.

By Shuttle: Continental Airport Express, 312-454-7800 or 800-654-787, provides a shuttle service between O'Hare and downtown Chicago from 6 am until 11:30 pm with departures approximately every 15 minutes. Shuttles stop at all major downtown hotels. Tickets are $20 one-way ($36 return) for individuals, $15 per person for pairs going to the same destination, and $12 per person for three or more going to the same downtown destination. Shuttle ticket counters are located in the baggage claim areas of Terminal 1 by Door 1E and Terminal 3 at Door 3E; however, shuttles pick up passengers at Terminals 1, 2, 3, and 5. Look for the shuttle stop identification signage curb-side. If you haven't pre-purchased a ticket at a counter, have cash ready for the driver. To calculate a shuttle fare to north suburb locations, go to www.airportexpress.com and use their online fare calculator.

Omega Airport Shuttle offers service between O'Hare and Midway every 45 minutes beginning around 6:40 am each day 'til about 11:45 pm. The shuttle leaves from the International Terminal's outside curb by Door 5E and from the airport's Bus Shuttle Center in front of the O'Hare Hilton Hotel by Door 4. Allow at least an hour for travel time between the airports. Expect to pay $20 for a one-way fare. Omega also has over 20 pickup and drop-off locations on the South Side serving O'Hare and Midway Airports. Contact Omega for information on current schedules, to make reservations, and to prearrange home pickups, 773-483-6634; www.omegashuttle.com.

By Limousine: Sounds pricey, but depending on where you're going and how many people you are traveling with, it may be cheaper to travel by limo than by cab or shuttle. Advance reservations recommended. Limo services include O'Hare-Midway Limousine Service, 312-558-1111, www.ohare-midway.com; My Chauffeur/American Limo, 630-920-8888, www.americanlimousine.com; and Sundling Limousine, 800-999-7552, www.limousineservicecorp.com.

How to Get There—Really

Taking surface roads is an option, but you can relieve yourself of any O'Hare hassles by spending the night before your flight at one of the airport hotels. Otherwise get to O'Hare in plenty of time to work out at the O'Hare Hilton Hotel fitness center ($9) and pray for the expansion to get approved at the airport's Interfaith Chapel (free).

O'Hare International Airport (ORD)

Airline	*Terminal*	*Phone*
Aer Lingus	5	888-474-7424
Aeromexico	5	800-237-6639
Air Canada	2	888-247-2262
Air France	5	800-237-2747
Air Jamaica	2 dep/5 arr	800-523-5585
Alaska Airlines	3	800-426-0333
Alitalia	5	800-223-5730
America West Airlines	2	800-235-9292
American Airlines domestic	3	800-443-7300
Americal Airlines international	3/5 int arr	800-443-7300
American Eagle	3	800-443-7300
British Airways	5	800-247-9297
BMI British Midland	5	800-241-6522
Continental Airlines	2	800-525-0280
Delta Airlines	3	800-221-1212
El Al	5	800-223-6700
Iberia Airlines	3 dep/5 arr	800-772-4642
Japan Air Lines	5	800-525-3663
KLM Royal Dutch Airlines	5	800-374-7747
Korean Airlines	5	800-438-5000
Kuwait Airways	5	800-458-9248
LOT Polish Airlines	5	800-223-0593
Lufthansa German Airlines	1/5 int arr	800-645-3880
Mexicana Airlines	5	800-531-7921
National Airlines	2	888-757-5378
Northwest Airlines	2	800-225-2525
Royal Jordanian	5	800-223-0470
Ryan Air	3/5 int arr	800-942-6735
Scandinavian Airlines SAS	5	800-221-2350
Singapore Airlines	5	800-742-3333
Spirit Airlines	5	800-772-7117
Swissair	5	800-221-4750
TACA Airlines	5	888-337-8466
Trans World Airlines TWA	3	800-221-1980
Turkish Airlines	5	800-874-8875
United Airlines	1 int dep/2/5 int arr	800-241-6522
United Express	1,2	800-241-6522
US Airways	2	800-428-4322
USA 3000	5	877-872-3000

Car Rental

On-site

Alamo	800-327-9633	Dollar	800-800-4000
Avis	800-331-1212	Hertz	800-654-3131
Budget	800-527-0700	National	800-227-7368

Off-site

Enterprise • 4025 Mannheim Rd • 847-928-3320
Payless • 3950 N Mannheim Rd • 800-PAY-LESS
Thrifty • 3902 N Mannheim Rd • 847-928-2000

Hotels

Amerisuites • 8101 W Higgins Rd	773-867-0000
Best Western at O'Hare • 10300 W Higgins Rd	847-296-4471
Clarion Barcelo' Hotel • 5615 N Cumberland Ave	847-693-5800
Comfort Inn O'Hare • 2175 E Touhy Ave	847-635-1300
Courtyard by Marriott • 2950 S River Rd	847-824-7000
Days Inn O'Hare International • 1920 E Higgins Rd	847-437-1650
DoubleTree Club Chicago O'Hare • 5460 N River Rd	847-292-9100
Embassy Suites • 5500 N River Rd	847-678-4000
Four Points Hotel Sheraton • 10249 Irving Park Rd	847-671-6000
Hampton Inn O'Hare • 3939 N Mannheim Rd	847-671-1700
Hampton Suites North Shore • 5201 Old Orchard Rd	847-583-1111
Hawthorn Hotel & Suites • 1251 E American Ln	847-954-8600
Hilton Chicago O'Hare • at the airport	773-686-8000
Holiday Inn O'Hare International • 5440 N River Rd	847-671-6350
Hotel Sofitel Chicago • 5550 N River Rd	847-678-4488
Hyatt Regency O'Hare • 9300 W Bryn Mawr Ave	847-696-1234
Hyatt Rosemont • 6350 N River Rd	847-518-1234
LaQuinta Inn • 1900 E Oakton Ave	847-439-6767
Marriott Suites O'Hare • 6155 North River Rd	847-696-4400
O'Hare Marriott Hotel • 8535 W Higgins Rd	773-693-4444
Radisson Hotel O'Hare • 6810 N Mannheim Rd	847-297-1234
Ramada Hotel O'Hare • 6600 N Mannheim Rd	847-827-5131
Residence Inn by Marriott • 7101 Chestnut St	847-725-2210
Rosemont Suites Hotel O'Hare	847-678-4000
Sheraton Gateway Suites • 6501 N Mannheim Rd	847-699-6300
Suburban Lodge • 2411 Landmeier Rd	847-228-5500
Super 8 • 2951 Touhy Ave	708-456-3600
Travelodge Chicago O'Hare • 3003 Mannheim Rd	847-296-5541
Westin Hotel, O'Hare • 6100 N River Rd	847-698-6000

Midway Airport (MDW)

Airline	*Concourse*	*Phone*
Air Tran	F	800-825-8538
American Airlines	C	800-433-7300
ATA	A, B	800-225-2995
ATA Connections/Chicago Express	A	800-264-3929
ComAir	C	800-927-0927
Continental Airlines	C	800-525-0280
Delta Airlines	C	800-221-1212
Frontier Airlines	C	800-432-1359
Indigo Aviation		773-585-5155
Mexicana Airlines	A	800-531-7921
National Airlines	B	888-757-5387
Northwest Airlines	B	800-225-2525
Southwest Airlines	F	800-435-9792
US Airways	F	800-245-2966

Car Rental

Alamo	800-327-9633	Enterprise	800-566-9249
Avis	800-831-2847	Hertz	800-654-3131
Budget	800-517-0700	National	800-227-7368
Dollar	800-800-4000	Thrifty	800-527-7075

Hotels

Best Western Inn • 8220 S Cicero Ave	708-497-3000
Fairfield Inn • 6630 S Cicero Ave	708-594-0090
Four Points Sheraton • 7353 SCicero Ave	773-581-5300
Hampton Inn • 6540 S Cicero Ave	708-496-1900
Hampton Inn • 13330 S Cicero Ave	708-597-3330
Hampton Suites N Shore • 5201 Old Orchard Rd	847-583-1111
Hilton • 9333 S Cicero Ave	708-425-7800
Holiday Inn Express • 6500 S Cicero Ave	708-458-0202
Holiday Inn • 4140 W 95th St	708-425-7900
Holiday Inn Select • 6520 S Cicero Ave	708-594-5500
Marriott Courtyard • 6610 S Cicero Ave	708-563-0200
Radisson • 5000 W 127th St	708-371-7300
Sleep Inn • 6650 S Cicero Ave	708-594-0001

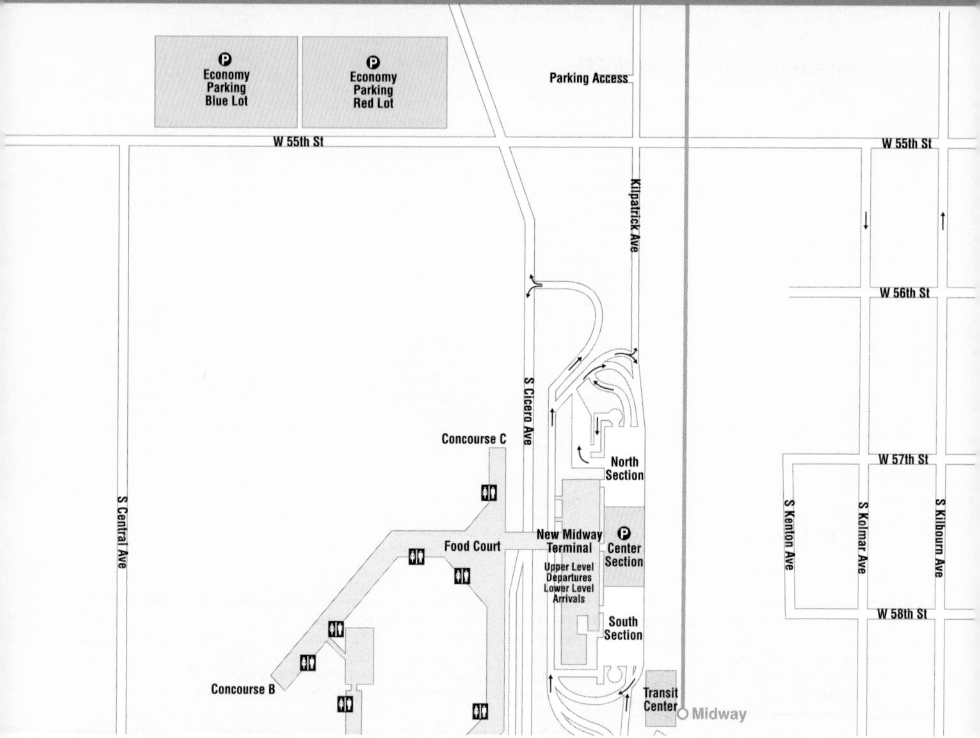

Transit • **Midway Airport**

Economy Parking Blue Lot
Economy Parking Red Lot
Parking Access
W 55th St
Kilpatrick Ave
W 56th St
S Cicero Ave
Concourse C
North Section
W 57th St
S Central Ave
New Midway Terminal
Upper Level Departures
Lower Level Arrivals
Center Section
Food Court
S Kenton Ave
S Kolmar Ave
S Kilbourn Ave
W 58th St
South Section
Concourse B
Transit Center
Midway

General Information

Address:	*5700 S. Cicero Ave.* *Chicago, IL 60638*
Phone:	*773-838-0600*
Website:	*www.ohare.com/midway*
Police:	*773-838-3003*
Parking:	*773-838-0756*

Overview

Just ten miles southwest of downtown Chicago, Midway is one of the fastest growing airports in the country, serving 47,000 passengers daily. Considered Chicago's outlet mall of airports, Midway primarily provides service from budget carriers, especially Southwest Airlines.

However, expect Midway to gain altitude in national airport rankings in 2004 when the $793 million Terminal Development Plan is completed. Plans include a swank new Terminal Building, new concourses, a 3,000-space parking facility, food court, retail corridor, and a customs facility to facilitate international jumbo jet arrivals and departures. In 2003, Concourses G and H were demolished to allow for the expansion of Concourse B. When all the dust settles, Midway will have upped its jet gate count from 29 to 41. Anticipating increased passenger traffic, several prominent hotel chains have built new properties close to Midway.

How to Get There

By Car: From downtown, take I-55 south. From the northern suburbs, take I-290 south to I-55 north. From the southern suburbs, take I-294 north to I-55 north. From the western suburbs, take I-88 east to I-294 south to I-55 north. Whether you're traveling north or south along I-55, look for the Cicero Ave./South/Midway Airport exit. Passenger drop-off is on the upper level and pick-up on the bottom level of the new terminal building.

By Bus: CTA buses 55, 59, and 63 all run from points east to the airport. Take the Green Line or the Red Line to the Garfield station and transfer to bus 55 heading west ($1.80 one-way including transfer). If you're coming from the south on the Red Line, get off at the 63rd St. stop and take bus 63 westbound ($1.80 one-way). Other buses that terminate at the airport include 54B, 379, 382, 383, 384, 385, 386, 831, and 63W.

By El: The Orange Line is the most convenient and cost-effective method for travel between the Loop and Midway Airport, especially since the train's operational hours were extended ($1.50 one-way). The Orange Line's first train of the day departs from Midway Station (last stop on the line's southern end) for the Loop at 3:55 am daily and 5:35 am on Sundays and holidays. The trip to the Loop is 30 minutes. The first train of the day departing south from the Loop's Adams/Wabash station at 4:29 am arrives at Midway at 4:54 am, well in advance of the airport's first early bird flight. The Orange Line's Loop-bound owl service ends at 12:56 am when the last train leaves Midway arriving at the Library Station stop at 1:23 am. The final Midway-bound owl train departs from the Adams/Wabash stop southbound around 1:29 am arriving at Midway by 1:53 am. Trains run every 5 to 7 minutes during rush hours, 10 minutes most other times, and 15 minutes late evenings. We recommend that wee hours travelers stay alert at all times.

By Cab: Cabs depart from the lower level of the main terminal and are available on a first-come, first-served basis. You can expect to pay around $20 to the Loop. Some cab companies servicing Midway include American United, 773-248-7600, Flash Cab Co., 773-561-1444, Jiffy Cab Co., 773-487-9000, and Yellow Cab, 312-829-4222. Share-ride fares are a flat $15 a head to the Loop. Check with the cab starter to confirm current pricing.

By Shuttle: Continental Airport Express, 312-454-7800, 800-654-7871, travels between Midway and downtown and some northern suburbs locations from 6 am until 11:30 pm. Departures are approximately every 15 minutes. Shuttles stop at all major downtown hotels. Tickets are $15 one-way ($27 return) for individuals, $12 per person for pairs going to the same destination, and $10 per person for three or more going to the same downtown destination. The ticket counter and loading zone are in the terminal's lower level across from the baggage claim area by door D3. To calculate a shuttle fare to north suburb locations, go to www.airportexpress.com and use their online fare calculator.

Omega Airport Shuttle, 773-483-6634; www.omegashuttle.com, offers service leaving every 45 minutes or so between Midway and O'Hare beginning around 7 am each day with the final shuttle departing around 11:45 pm. The shuttle's information desk and boarding area is on the terminal's lower level across from baggage claim. Allow at least an hour for travel time between the airports, and expect to pay $20 one-way. Contact Omega for information on over 20 pickup locations on the South Side, to confirm schedules, make reservations, and to prearrange home pickups.

By Limousine: Sounds pricey, but depending on where you're going and how many people you are traveling with, it may be cheaper to travel by limo than by cab or shuttle. Advance reservations recommended. Limo services include O'Hare-Midway Limousine Service, 847-948-8050, www.ohare-midway.com; My Chauffeur/American Limo, 630-920-8888, www.americanlimousine.com; and Sundling Limousine, 800-999-7552, www.limousineservicecorp.com.

Parking

Short-term parking in the new garage is on the 3rd floor. It costs $3 for the first hour and $2 for every hour thereafter, up to $50 for 24 hours. Overnight parking is $23 in the daily parking sections on Levels 1, 4, 5 and 6 (Level 2 is for rental car pick-up and drop-off). The economy lot for $10 a day is located on Cicero Ave. at 55th St., a quarter mile away. Allow extra time to take the free shuttle between the lot and the terminal.

General Information

RTA Mailing Address:	*Regional Transportation Authority 175 W. Jackson Blvd., Ste. 250 Chicago, IL 60604*
Phone:	*312-913-3110*
RTA Information Center:	*312-836-7000*
RTA Website:	*www.rtachicago.com*
CTA Phone:	*1-888-YOUR-CTA (968-7282)*
CTA Website:	*www.transitchicago.com*
Pace Phone:	*847-364-7223*
Pace Website:	*www.pacebus.com*
Greyhound Phone:	*1-800-229-9424*
Greyhound Website:	*www.greyhound.com*

Overview

Three major bus networks contribute to the mobility of Chicagoans, and are the perfect complement to the rail system—CTA, Pace, and Greyhound. The RTA oversees the Chicago Transit Authority (CTA) that operates Chicago's buses, as well as Pace, the suburban bus service. The RTA's website (www.ratchicago.com) has great point-to-point directions for anywhere in the city or suburbs that you want to go.

CTA Buses

The CTA's buses cart 1 million sweaty, crabby passengers around Chicago daily. CTA's 134 bus routes mirror Chicago's efficient grid system. The majority of CTA routes run north-south or east-west and, in areas where the streets are numbered, the bus route is usually the same as the street.

Bus Stops: CTA stops are clearly marked with blue and white signs displaying the name and number of the route, as well as the final destination. Most routes operate from the early morning until 10:30 pm. Night routes called "Night Owls" are identified on bus stop signage by an owl picture. Owl service runs approximately every half-hour through the night.

Fares: Exact fare is required for individual bus rides. A regular one-way fare is $1.50. A transfer slip, good for two additional rides on either different CTA buses or CTA El/Subway trains within two hours of issuance, costs an additional 30¢, making the total fare $1.80 for up to three legs of a single journey. Transfers must be purchased with the base fare on the first leg of your journey. An "express surcharge" of 25¢ is required (in addition to a valid transfer card) when you board buses 2, 14, 16, and 147 downtown in designated pickup zones.

Reduced fares of 75¢ per individual trip and 15¢ for a transfer are available for riders who qualify. These include children 7-11, seniors aged 65+ with an RTA Reduced Fare Riding Permit, and riders with disabilities showing a permit and their companion. Grade and high school students with a CTA Student Riding Permit ($5 per semester, $2 summer school) pay reduced fares on weekdays from 5:30 am to 8:00 pm. Children aged six and under ride free with a fare-paying customer, as do "other uniformed or ID-bearing categories authorized by the Chicago Transit Board."

The CTA offers a number of different fare packages. These include:

- For the convenience of not having to fish for exact change, purchase Ten Packs of one-way tickets for $15.
- Unlimited Ride Passes: 1-Day ($5), 2-Day ($9), 3-Day ($12), and 5-Day ($18).

Frequent CTA riders prefer Monthly Passes with unlimited rides for $75 or Transit Cards sold through vending machines at all CTA rail stations. Transit Cards are available in various increments up to $100. For every $10 you put on your card, the CTA will contribute an extra $1 free. Transit Cards are sold in $10 and $20 increments at currency exchanges, Jewel and Dominick's stores, via the Internet, and at many other City locations.

Bicycles Onboard: Designated CTA buses are equipped with bike racks to carry a maximum of two bikes. Bike racks are mounted on the buses' front grills. Generally speaking, CTA bike buses are those that travel to lakefront beaches. They include the 63rd St. and 72 North Ave. buses. Others with bike racks are the 75th St. and 65 Grand buses. During the summer season and special events downtown, additional buses with bike racks may be added. Check the website for an update on bike buses as the service may be expanding.

Here is how to load your bike on a CTA bus:

- If your bike is the first to be loaded, lower the rack and place it in position with the front wheel facing the curb.
- If there is already a bike on the rack, place your bike's rear wheel toward the curb.
- If two bikes are already, loaded the rack is full: wait for the next bus.

Pace Suburban—Chicago Buses

Pace buses serve over 37 million passengers in the Chicago suburbs and some parts of the City. With 248 routes covering 3,446 square miles, Pace provides a vital transportation service to commuters traveling between suburbs, within their suburbs, to Metra train stations, and into the city. Buses usually run every 20-30 minutes. Generally, service stops by mid-evening. Special express service is offered to Chicago-area entertainment and cultural venues. Contact Pace for specific bus route and schedule information.

Park-n-Ride Stations: Pace has 11 Park-n-Ride stations located throughout Pace's six-county coverage area. Check the Pace website for addresses.

Fares: Pace fares vary according to the route: $1.25 for local service and $1.50 for expanded service. The one-way fare on express routes 210, 355, 737, 855, and 1018 is $3.00. CTA transit cards may be used on Pace buses. Pace offers qualified discounts and several bus pass package purchase options. Contact Pace for a full menu of choices; however, here is a sampling of what's available for purchase:

Pace offers discounts for students, seniors, children, and disabled riders. Passengers must display an RTA Reduced Fare Card Permit to enjoy discounts.

Pass options include the Pace 30-Day Commuter Club Cards (CCC), allowing unlimited Pace rides for $50.00. A combined Pace/CTA 30-day unlimited pass is $75 and can be used on all Pace buses and CTA trains and buses. The PlusBus Sticker (sold by Metra with a Metra Monthly Train Pass) is $30 and allows unlimited Pace bus use.

Greyhound Buses

Greyhound is the rock-bottom travelers' best friend. Called "the Dog" by its patrons, Greyhound offers dirt cheap fares, the flexibility drifters prefer, basic station amenities (toilets and vending machines), and the gritty, butt-busting experience of traveling America's scenic blue-line highways and rural byways along with some very colorful characters.

Here are some tips on taking "the Dog" out of town:

- Even though bathrooms are onboard, pack your own toilet paper and Wet Ones.
- Air freshener, deodorant, a pillow, and earplugs make being bused more bearable.
- Pack a cooler. Then padlock it.
- Wear padded bicycle shorts or bring a cushion.
- Get your shots.

Stations: Greyhound's main train station is south of Union Station at 630 W. Harrison St. at S. Desplaines Ave. in West Loop, 312-408-5800. CTA buses 60, 125, 156, and 157 stop near the terminal. The closest El stop is on the Blue Line's Forest Park Branch at the Clinton St. Station on Congress Pkwy. Additional Chicago-area Greyhound stations are located within El train stations: 14 W. 95th St. in the Red Line's 95th St./Dan Ryan station, 312-408-5999, and 5800 N. Cumberland Ave. on the Blue Line's O'Hare Branch in the Cumberland station, 773-693-2474. Contact Greyhound to determine which routes best suit your regional and national travel requirements. Like most urban bus stations, the Chicago Greyhound Station has a palpable seedy element. Keep your belongings with you at all times.

Shipping Services: Greyhound Package Express offers commercial and personal shipping services and is available at all three Chicago bus stations. Packages are held at the station for pick-up. The main terminal in South Loop also houses a UPS shipping office that provides door-to-door package delivery. Call the stations for shipping office hours and rates.

Fares: To purchase tickets, call the toll-free number and pay by credit card, book online with a credit card through Greyhound's website, or visit a station where cash, travelers checks, and major credit cards are accepted.

Regular fare pricing applies for both individual advance ticket sales and minutes-before-departure sales as Greyhound does not reserve seats. Tickets can be used for travel to the designated destination on any day or at any departure time. Boarding is first-come-first-served, so get in line at the boarding zone for a choice seat. However, Greyhound's bark is bigger than its bite—if a significant number of passengers are abandoned, Greyhound rolls another bus, or two, or three, out on the spot. Good dog.

Discounts are given for children under 12 (40%), seniors 62 and older (10%), military (10%), and patients of Veteran's Administration Hospitals (25%). The cost for an individual return ticket is deeply discounted if it is purchased at the same time as a departure ticket.

Traveling companions can save money. Purchase a ticket three days in advance and earn a free ticket for your companion (no age restrictions). Passengers accompanying someone with a disability always ride free.

Super Friendly Fares offer the greatest savings for travelers who can purchase seven days in advance of travel. For example, a regular one-way ticket from Chicago to New York City is $90 and a regular fare round-trip ticket costs $159. However, if you book a round-trip Super Friendly Fare the ticket costs only $89. You do the math.

Transit • Metra Train Lines

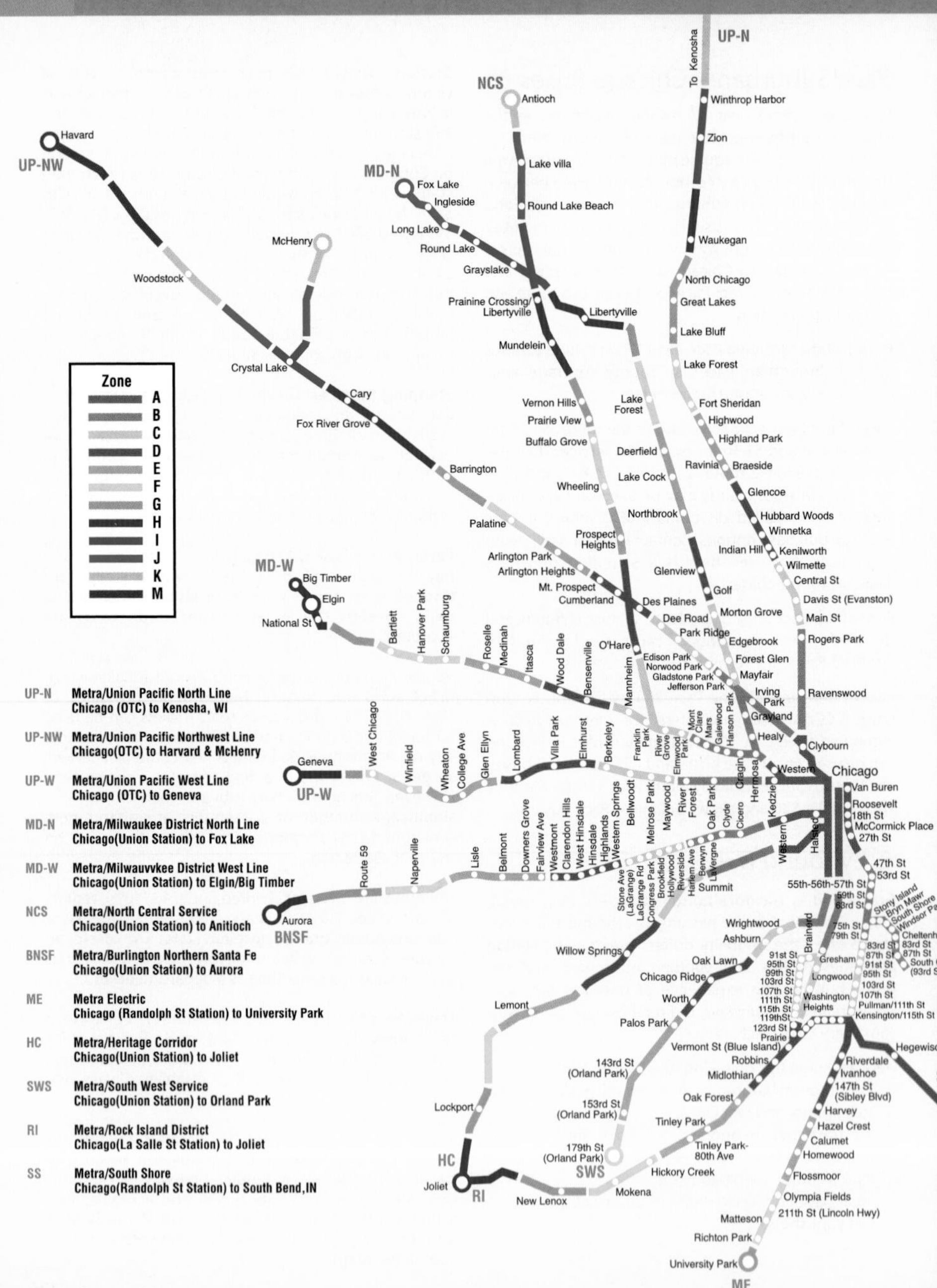

General Information

Metra Address:	*Metra Passenger Services* *547 W. Jackson Blvd., 14th Fl.* *Chicago, IL 60661*
Phone:	*312-322-6777*
Website:	*www.metrarail.com*
Metra Passenger Service:	*312-322-6777*
South Shore Metra Lines:	*800-356-2079*
RTA Information Center:	*836-7000; www.rtachicago.com*

Overview

With a dozen lines and roughly 495 miles of track, Metra does its best to service Cook, DuPage, Lake, Will, McHenry, and Kane counties with 230 stations scattered throughout the city and 'burbs. The rails emanating from four major downtown stations are lifelines for commuters traveling to and from the Loop.

The good news for Metra is that ridership is strong. The bad news for the riders is trying to find station parking. In an attempt to resolve its parking issues, Metra is purchasing land surrounding many suburban stations and constructing new parking facilities. See Metra's website for development plans.

Loop Stations

There are four major Metra train stations in the Loop from which twelve train lines emanate. To try and make everyone slightly less confused, here's a chart:

Station	*Line*
Richard B. Ogilvie Transportation Center	Union Pacific North Union Pacific West Union Pacific Northwest
Union Station	Milwaukee District North Milwaukee District West North Central Service Southwest Service Burlington Northern Heritage Corridor Amtrak
La Salle St. Station	Rock Island Line
Randolph St. Station	South Shore Railroad Metra Electric—3 Branches: • Main Line • South Chicago • Blue Island

Fares

Fares are calculated according to the number of Metra zones traversed during your journey. one-way, full-fare tickets range in price from $1.85 to $6.95. To calculate a base one-way fare, visit http://metrarail.com/Data/farechk.html. Tickets may be purchased through a ticket agent or onboard the train ($2 more if the ticket windows were open at the time you boarded the train). There is no reserved seating.

Metra offers a number of reasonably-priced ticket packages, including a 10-Ride Ticket (which saves 15% off one-way fares) and a Monthly Unlimited Ride Ticket (the most economical choice for commuters who use Metra service daily). If your commute includes CTA and/or Pace bus services, consider purchasing the Link-Up Sticker ($36) for unlimited connecting travel on CTA and Pace buses. If you only use the Pace suburban buses, purchase the Metra/Pace PlusBus Pass ($30) for unlimited travel on all Pace suburban buses. Metra's Weekend Pass is ideal for urbanites to visit the 'burbs on the weekend or suburbanites to spend the weekend in the city. It's only $5 and includes unlimited rides on both Saturday and Sunday. Metra's South Shore route is not included. You can buy all the aforementioned tickets in person, through the mail or online at http://metrarail.com/TBI/index.html.

Metra makes travel by rail attractive through discounted fares, which include children under 7 riding free. On weekdays, children 7-11 ride for half-price, while on weekends they ride free. On weekends, children 12-17 ride the rails for half-price on a regular one-way fare. Full time students enrolled in an accredited grade school or high school enjoy Student Fares that are approximately 50% off the cost of regular one-way fares.

Additionally, Senior Citizens/Disability Fares are approximately half of the regular fare. To qualify, riders must present an RTA Reduced Fare Riding Permit ID card. U.S. Military Personnel in uniform ride Metra for approximately half the regular one-way fare.

CTA Rush Shuttles and Wendella RiverBuses

If you're traveling to the downtown stations on CTA buses at rush hours, CTA offers $1 cash shuttle fares on many of its routes. Check the Metra website for a comprehensive list of participating buses and the latest on road construction that may affect those routes.

Spring through fall, commuters can get to N. Michigan Ave. quickly on a RiverBus plying the Chicago River during rush hours. Operated by Wendella, boats leave from Transportation Center at the dock on the northwest corner of Madison St. RiverBuses run daily from April 1 through November 29. The trip takes 9 minutes one-way. The first boat leaves the train station dock at 7 am; the last boat departs from the 400 N. Michigan Ave. dock at the base of the Wrigley Building at 7 pm. The fare is $2 one-way. Discounted Monthly and Ten-Ride fares are available. 312-337-1446; www.wendellariverbus.com.

Baggage & Pets

While Metra may be "the way to really fly," your carry-on train baggage is more limited than on an aircraft. Bicycles, skis, golf clubs, non-folding carts, and other large luggage items cannot be transported on trains at any time. This is one more reason, besides the limited schedules, not to take Metra to O'Hare. The pet rules are as prohibitive as the baggage rules. No pets are allowed unless they are trained guide animals assisting the disabled.

General Information

Loop Station Address:	*Randolph St. Station 151 E. Randolph St. Underground at N. Michigan Ave. and E. Randolph St. Chicago, IL 60601*
Phone:	*312-782-0676*
Website:	*www.nictd.com*
Lost and Found:	*219-874-4221 x205*

Overview

Although the historic South Shore train lines were built in 1903, they still get you from the Loop to Indiana's South Bend Airport in just 2.5 hours. The Northern Indiana Commuter Transportation District (NICTD) oversees the line and its modern electric trains, which serve as a vital transportation link for many northwest Indiana residents working in the Loop.

The South Shore's commuter service reflects its Indiana ridership. Outbound heading from the Loop, there are limited stops before the Hegewisch station, close to the Indiana state line. If traveling by train to Chicago's South Side, you're better off on an outbound Metra Electric Line train departing from the Randolph St. Station (see Metra page).

The underground Randolph St. Station at the corner of N. Michigan Ave. and E. Randolph St. is feeling the jackhammers of Millennium Park's construction overhead as well as within its own confines. Currently the station is undergoing massive construction improvements, slated for completion sometime before 2004.

Fares

Regular one-way fares can be purchased at the stations or on the train. Ticket prices vary with the distance traveled. Tickets purchased onboard the train cost $1 more if the station's ticket windows were open at the time of departure.

Special South Shore fares and packages include commuter favorites: 10-Ride and 25-Ride Tickets and the Monthly Pass, which is good for unlimited travel. These can be purchased in person at stations staffed with ticket agents, station vending machines, and via the mail. Senior Citizens/Disability Fares offer savings for persons aged 65 and older with valid identification and for disabled passengers. Students with school identification qualify for Student Fares, including reduced one-way tickets and discounted 25-Ride Tickets good for travel during weekdays. Youth Fares range from free passage for infants under two (who must sit in a paying passenger's lap) and half off a regular fare for children aged two to 13 years. On weekends and holidays Family Fares are available. Each fare-paying adult (minimum age 21) may take two children (age 13 and under) with them free of charge. Additional children will be charged the youth fare. There are no published fare discounts for military personnel.

Baggage & Pets

Any accompanying baggage must be placed in the overhead racks. No bicycles are permitted onboard. Apart from small animals in carry-on cages, the only other pets allowed onboard are service dogs accompanied by handlers or passengers with disabilities. Animals must not occupy seats.

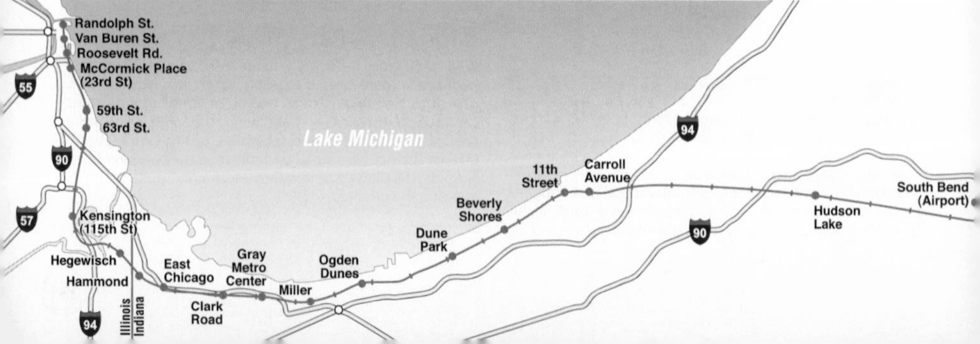

General Information

Amtrak Reservations: *1-800-USA-Rail (872-7245)*
Website: *www.amtrak.com*
Union Station: *210 S. Canal St.*
Chicago, IL 60661
Phone: *312-322-6900*

Overview

Chicago is the nucleus for Amtrak's national rail network comprising over 500 stations in 46 states (not including Alaska, Hawaii, South Dakota, and Wyoming). Departing from Chicago's Union Station, Amtrak trains head west to Seattle and Portland, east to New York City and Boston, north to Ontario, and south to New Orleans, San Francisco, and San Antonio.

Fares

Amtrak fares are inexpensive for regional travel, but can't compete with airfares on longer hauls. But, just as airlines deeply discount, so does Amtrak. And like booking an airline ticket, you have to ask Amtrak's sales agents about special fares and search Amtrak's website for the best deals (booking in advance does present some savings). We recommend the website route as you could be on hold longer than it takes to get from Chicago to Los Angeles on Amtrak. At the time of this writing, financial troubles threaten to eliminate several of Amtrak's long-haul routes. Check the status ahead of time before making plans.

Amtrak offers special promotional fares year-round targeting seniors, veterans, students, children under 16, and two or more persons traveling together. The "Rail SALE" page on Amtrak's website lists discounted fares between certain city pairs. Amtrak has hooked its sleeper cars up with plenty of travel partners to create interesting packages. The Air-Rail deals whereby you rail it one-way and fly back the other are attractive for long distance destinations. Call 1-877-937-7245 and surf the "Amtrak Partners" website page for more partner promotional fares.

Service

No one we know can claim to have ever arrived on time travelling Amtrak, so tell whoever is picking you up you'll just call them on your cell phone when you're close. And here's another tip: pack food because dining car fare is just fair, and pricey. But Amtrak's seats are comfortably roomy, some have electric sockets for computer hookup, and bathrooms are in every car.

Within Illinois: Four main Amtrak lines travel south through Illinois on a daily basis: the "State House" travels to St. Louis, MO; the "Illinois Zephyr" travels to Quincy, IL; the "Illini Service" travels daily between Chicago and Carbondale, IL; and the Ann Rutledge travels daily to Kansas City, MO.

Going to New York City or Boston: If you're heading east, the "Lake Shore Limited" breaks off at Albany and goes to New York (21 hours) and Boston (24 hours). One-way tickets range from $90 to $110.

Going to Seattle or Portland: The "Empire Builder" takes passengers to Seattle and Portland and everywhere in between. With the journey to Seattle taking around 44 hours, we definitely recommend dropping some additional dollars on a sleeper car. A one-way fare costs between $130 and $195.

Going to San Francisco: You'll spend two solid days and then some riding the rails during the 52-hour journey on the "California Zephyr" to San Francisco (Emeryville). The fare is approximately $165 one-way. "Zephyr" passes through Lincoln, Denver, and Salt Lake City and makes a whole host of small town America stops along the way.

Going to New Orleans: The "City of New Orleans" line goes from Chicago via Memphis to New Orleans in roughly 20 hours. The fare is approximately $125 one-way.

Going to San Antonio: The mighty "Texas Eagle" shoots across the Alamo and stops at 40 cities on its way from the Midwest to the South. The 32-hour trip will cost approximately $130 each way.

Going to Milwaukee: "Hiawatha" runs six times daily to Milwaukee: 8:25 am, 10:20 am, 1 pm, 3:15 pm, 5:08 pm, and 8:05 pm. The 90-minute trip costs $20 each way. This is a viable alternative to driving from Chicago on busy weekends and rush hours.

Going to Kansas City: The "Missouri Routes" line terminates in Kansas City while the "Southwest Chief" passes through it on the way to Los Angeles. "Missouri" departs daily at 8:30 am and travels via St. Louis to Kansas City in just over 12 hours. The fare is $50 one-way; $95 return. "Southwest Chief" departs daily at 3:15 pm and reaches Kansas City in just over seven hours. The fare is $63 one-way.

Going to Los Angeles: The "Southwest Chief" departs for Los Angeles, travels via Albuquerque, takes almost 42 hours, and costs $165 one-way.

Union Station

210 S. Canal St. at E. Adams St. and E. Jackson Blvd.
312-322-4269

Designed by the architects Graham, Anderson, Probst and White, monumental and massive Union Station is a national railroad hub. In its peak in the 1940s, 100,000 passengers passed through the terminal daily, while today's volume is half that. Despite the number of times you rush through Union Station, the magnificent, light-swathed Great Hall is impressive. It is the surviving half of the original 1925 station and a favorite site for black-tie soirees.

Both Metra's and Amtrak's train services are on the ground floor (or "Concourse Level") of the station. This level is then further divided into the North Concourse and South Concourse. An information booth is between the concourses on this level, although not always staffed. While there is signage throughout Union Station, the many escalators can make navigating the block-long building with multiple entrances and exits a challenge.

Ticket Windows: The easiest way to get to Metra ticket agents is to enter Union Station at the Clinton St. entrance near E. Jackson Blvd. and go down into and through the Grand Hall. Metra's ticket agents will be on your left in the North Concourse. Metra's ticket office is open from 6 am to 11:30 pm weekdays, 6:30 am to 11:30 pm on Saturday, and 7 am to 11:30 pm on Sunday. Metra Lines that terminate at Union Station are Milwaukee District East and West Lines, North Central Service, Burlington Northern Santa Fe, Heritage Corridor, and South West Service.

To get to the Amtrak action, enter Union Station off Canal St., take the escalator down into the Grand Hall, and turn left. Amtrak's attractive, vintage ticket agent desk straddles the two concourses and is open daily from 6:30 am to 9 pm. Amtrak's waiting rooms and baggage claim are in the South Concourse. For more detail on Amtrak service, call 1-800-872-7245.

Services: On the Mezzanine/Street Level, there is a plethora of convenience stores, newsstands, and eateries including Connie's Pizza, Snuggery, Corner Bakery, and Kelly's Cajun Grill. ATMs are in both concourses on this level.

Public Transportation: The closest El station to Union Station is the Blue Line, which stops two blocks south of the station at the Clinton St. stop on Congress Parkway. The Orange, Brown, and Purple Lines stop three blocks east of the station at the Quincy stop on Wells St. CTA buses 1, 51, and 60 all stop at Union Station. Most commuters heading to work in the Loop enter and exit the station from the Madison St., Adams St., and Jackson Blvd. doorways where cabs line up.

Richard B. Ogilvie Transportation Center

500 W. Madison St. at S. Canal St.
312-496-4777

Metra's Union Pacific Lines emanate from the Richard B. Ogilvie Transportation Center, which Chicagoans commonly call Northwestern Station, its former name. Sterile by comparison to Union Station, the tall, smoky glass-and-green-steel-girder building replaced a classic, grand train station. Oh well. Roughly 40,000 passengers pass through the Richard B. Ogilvie Transportation Center daily.

Ticket Windows: Metra's ticket office is on the Upper Level, across from the entrance to the train platform, and is open from 5:30 am until 12:40 am. Monday to Saturday, and 7:00 am to 12:40 am on Sundays. ATMs can be found on the Upper Level at Citibank and next to the currency exchange. Public phones are also by the currency exchange in the southeast corner of the Upper Level. Trains depart from this level, and the smoking waiting room looks out onto the platform.

Services: There are a lot of fast junky options on the Street Level food court, which also serves as a de facto waiting room. If you want healthier fare, try the Rice Market and Boudin Sourdough Bakery on the east side of the building. There is a selection of stores to wander through if you're killing time or to pick up a last-minute gift. These include several women's career clothing and shoe shops, Bath and Body Works, Waldenbooks, Dakota Watch Company, Claire's Accessories, Petite Sophisticate, and Carlton Cards. Annoyingly enough, the only restrooms in the station are on the Street Level, which is a long escalator ride from the train platform.

Public Transportation: The closest El station is the Green Line's Clinton St. stop at Lake St. several blocks north of the station. CTA buses 14, 20, 56, and 157 board at Washington and Canal Sts. and travel to N. Michigan Ave. and the Loop. Coming from the Loop, take the same bus lines west across Madison St. If you're after a cab, you'll find other like-minded commuters lining up in front of the main entrance on Madison St. between Canal and Clinton Sts.

Randolph St. Station

151 E Randolph St. at N. Michigan Ave.
312-322-7819

The underground Randolph St. Station is the Loop station from which Metra Electric's three branches of service to Chicago's South Side and the South Shore Line to South Bend, Indiana depart. Schedules are somewhat sporadic for both except during weekday rush hours. The Van Buren St. Station also serves both the Metra Electric and South Shore lines and is located at E. Jackson Blvd. and Van Buren St., 312-322-6777. When planning train travel from the Randolph St. and Van Buren St. Stations, it is wise to double-check schedules and stops with the RTA Information Center, 312-836-7000; www.rtachicago.com.

Ticket Windows: Enter the Randolph St. Station at E. Randolph St. and N. Michigan Ave. or from Metra's South Water St. Station via the Randolph St. platform. The ticket office is immediately visible upon descending the steps off Michigan Ave. or entering via the Pedway which tunnels around the Loop and east under Michigan Ave., ending at the station. Ticket office hours are 6 am to 10:20 am daily. The waiting room is open 5 am to 12:50 am daily.

Services: As the Randolph St. Station undergoes a massive reconstruction effort, the best way to describe amenities is "self-serve." There is no end date for construction in sight as the station's final configuration and appearance is influenced by the seemingly never-ending Millennium Park development overhead.

Public Transportation: Randolph St. Station is served by CTA buses 56, 151, 157 and, on days when there are events at the United Center, Express bus 19. A little over one block west of the train station in the Loop is the Randolph St. El station, which the Orange, Green, Purple, and Brown Lines service.

La Salle St. Station

414 S. LaSalle St. at E. Congress Pkwy.
312-322-6509

The La Salle St. Station located underneath the Chicago Stock Exchange serves the Metra Rock Island District Line's 15,000 commuters daily. The service has 11 mainline stops and 10 south suburban stops on its way to Joliet.

Ticket Windows: Enter the station off La Salle St., take the escalator one floor up, walk through the lobby past the bar to an open area where there are tracks and the ticket office. Agents are on duty from 7 am to 8 pm weekdays and 10:30 am to 6:30 pm on Saturday.

Services: There are no shops to speak of, but at least there's a bar. During the week, the small waiting room is less crowded than the bar (duh), especially after the markets close. The waiting room is open daily from 6 am to midnight.

Public Transportation: The Blue Line's La Salle St. stop at Congress Pkwy. and the Orange, Purple, and Brown Lines' La Salle St. stop at Van Buren St. all drop El riders right in front of the train station. CTA buses 145 and 147 stop in front of the station as well.

Transit • The "El"

General Information

CTA Mailing Address:	*Chicago Transit Authority* *Merchandise Mart Plaza, 7th Fl.* *P.O. Box 3555, Chicago, IL 60654*
Phone:	*312-664-7200*
CTA Information:	*1-888-YOUR-CTA (968-7282)*
Website:	*www.transitchicago.com*
Email:	*ctahelp@transitchicago.com*

Overview

Whether traveling underground, street level, or above the sidewalk, Chicagoans call their rapid transit system the "El." (Some prefer to call it the "Smell.") No matter which one you choose, either name says Chicago as loud and clear as the high-pitched whine, guttural grumble, and steely grind of the train itself. El tracks lasso Chicago's heart creating The Loop, where six of the seven El lines ride side-by-side above the pulsating business and financial district.

CTA riders herd onto the El trains and buses roaming about the city. CTA trains make 1,452 trips each day and serve 143 stations in the Chicago Metropolitan Area. Daily, thousands of Chicagoans rely on the system to transport them to and from work, home, and entertainment, making summer and winter (when you're bundled up for the weather) nearly unbearable, especially in light of the numerous track delays and stalls in service. Nonetheless, due to the general directness of the El routes, easy station-to-station transfers, and the difficulties of parking (especially near popular destinations like Grant Park and Wrigley Field), the benefits of El transportation usually outweigh the occasional discomforts and inconveniences.

Fares

The standard full fare on CTA trains is $1.50. A 30¢ transfer allows two additional rides within two hours of issuance and can be used for transferring from rail to bus (or vice versa), and also between buses. Transfers must be purchased with the base fare on the first leg of the journey. Transferring within the rail network is free.

Avoid fishing for exact change by purchasing a Transit Card at vending machines located in all El stations. Cards are available in various increments up to $100. For every $10 you put on your card, the CTA will contribute an extra $1 free. Transit Cards are also sold for $10 and $20 at currency exchanges, Jewel and Dominick's stores, online, and at many other city locations. CTA also offers a 10-Pack of one-way tickets for $15, no savings but no change hassle either. A $75 Monthly Pass is good for unlimited rides. Day Passes are 1-Day ($5), 2-Day ($9), 3-Day ($12), and 5-Day ($18).

Reduced Fares cost 75¢ for the base trip and 15¢ for a transfer for riders who qualify: children ages seven to 11 years, seniors age 65+ with an RTA Reduced Fare Riding Permit, and riders with disabilities (with an RTA permit) and their companion. Grade school students with CTA Student Riding Permits ($5 per semester; $2 summer school) pay reduced fares on weekdays from 5:30 pm to 8:00 pm. Free Rides are reserved for children aged six and under. Riders that are in "other uniformed or ID-bearing categories authorized by the Chicago Transit Board" (whatever that means) also enjoy free rides. You might want that stinking badge after all…

Frequency of Service

CTA publishes schedules that say trains run every 3 to 12 minutes during weekday rush hours and every 6 to 20 minutes at other times. But service can be irregular, especially during non-rush hours, after hours, and in bad weather. While the system is relatively safe late at night, stick to stations in populated areas as much as possible. Buses with owl service may be better options in the wee hours.

El Lines

For ease of navigation, the El's seven lines are color-coded: Blue, Red, Brown, Orange, Green, Purple, and Yellow. While we provide general schedule information for each line, contact the RTA Information Center for detailed schedule information.

Blue Line: Comprising the O'Hare, Forest Park, and Cermak branches traveling west, O'Hare and Forest Park run 24-hours while Cermak is operational only on weekdays.

Red Line: Runs north-south from the Howard St. station down to the 95th St./Dan Ryan station; operates 24-hours.

Brown Line: Starts from the Kimball St. station and heads south with service to the Loop and sometimes just to Belmont Ave. On weekdays and Saturdays, the first Loop-bound train leaves Kimball St. at 4:01 am; the last train to leave the Loop is at 12:18 am. Sunday service begins at 6:46 am and ends at 11:40 pm. After that, take the Red Line to Belmont Ave. and transfer to the Brown Line where the last train leaves at 2:25 am (12:55 am on Sundays). The Brown Line also runs between Kimball St. and Belmont Ave. from 4:00 am to 2:04 am weekdays and Saturdays; and from 5:01 am to 2:04 am on Sundays.

Orange Line: Travels from Midway Airport to the Loop and back. Trains depart from Midway beginning at 3:55 am weekdays and Saturdays and at 7 am on Sundays; the last train leaves the Loop for the airport at 1:29 am daily.

Green Line: Covers portions of west and south Chicago. The Harlem/Lake St. branch travels straight west. The Ashland Ave./63rd St. and E. 63rd St./Cottage Grove branches go south and split east and west. Depending on the branch, service begins around 4 am weekdays with the last trains running around 1 am. Weekend schedules vary.

Purple Line: Shuttles north-south between Linden Pl. in suburban Evanston and Howard St., Chicago's northernmost station. Service starts at 4:35 am and ends at 12:55 am weeknights, 1:45 am on weekends and 12:55 am. Sundays. Weekdays, an express train runs between Linden Pl. and the Loop between 6:25 am and 10:10 am and then again between 2:55 pm and 6:15 pm. At all other times, take the Purple Line Shuttle to the Howard St. station and transfer to the Red Line to reach the Loop.

Yellow Line: Runs between the north suburban Skokie station and Chicago's Howard St. station on weekdays from 4:50 am to 10:18 pm. On weekends, take CTA bus 97 from the Skokie station to Howard St. and catch the Red Line to the Loop.

Bicycles

Bicycles ride free and are permitted onboard at all times except weekdays from 7 am to 9 am and 4 pm to 6 pm. Only two bikes are allowed per car, so survey the platform for other bikes and check out the cars as they pull into the station for two-wheelers already onboard. When entering a station, either use the turnstile or ask an attendant to open the gate. Don't try to take your bike through the tall steel gates—it WILL get stuck!

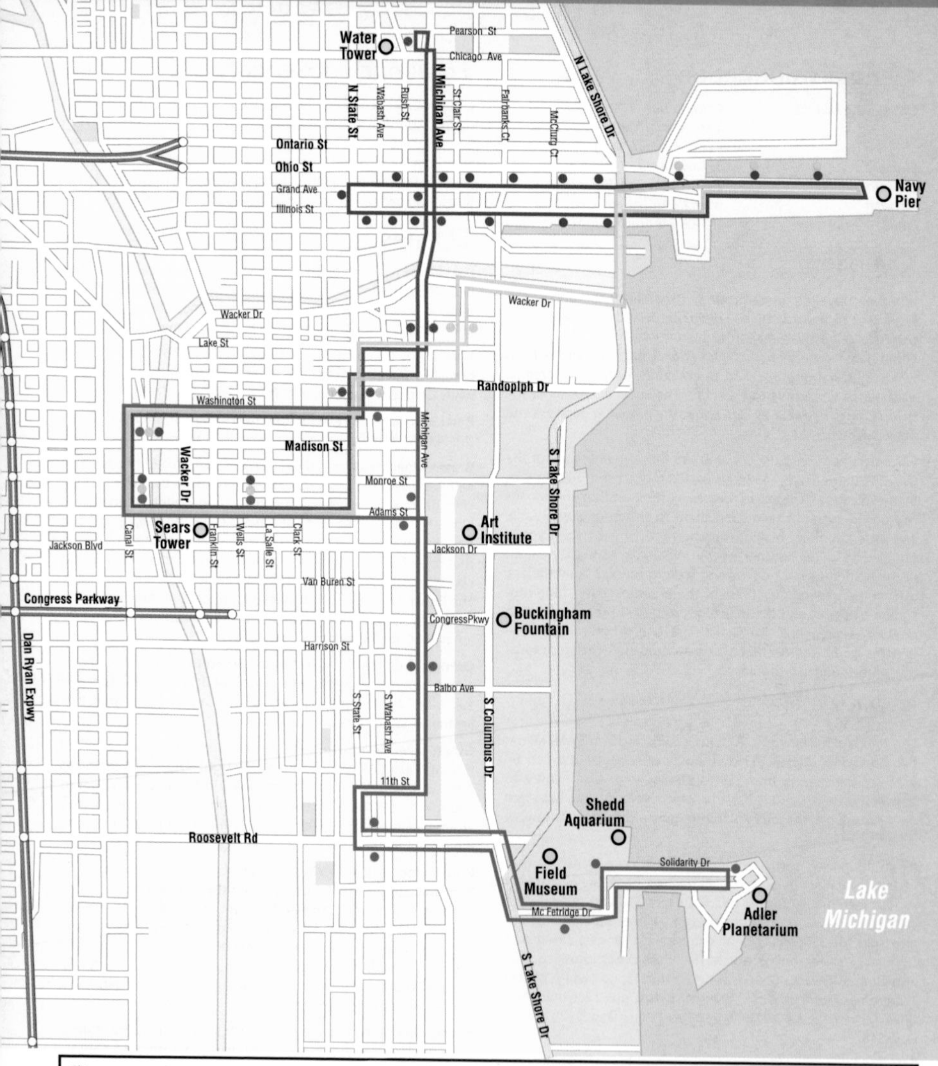

Chicago recently expanded its free trolley service by adding more lines and offering service daily from Memorial Day through Labor Day and on weekends year-round. Daily service is also scheduled during heavy travel periods throughout the year including school breaks, holidays, and special city events.

- **Shopping** Daily 10am-6pm
- **Metra/Navy Pier** Daily 10am-6pm
- **Metra/Museums** Daily 10am-6pm
- **Navy Pier** Sun-Thurs 10am-11pm Fri-Sat 10am-1am

Trolleys run every 20 minutes. The four color-coded trolley routes dovetail with CTA bus routes, make stops at major Loop El stations and Metra stations, and travel to and from Chicago's most popular attractions. Trolley stops are identifiable by graphic, color-coded signage. Because fare-based trolley companies also roam the streets, be sure to look for the "Free Trolley" sign in the front window. You don't need a ticket to ride; just hop on and off as you please.

For more information, contact 1-877-244-2246; www.cityofchicago.org/Transportation/trolleys.

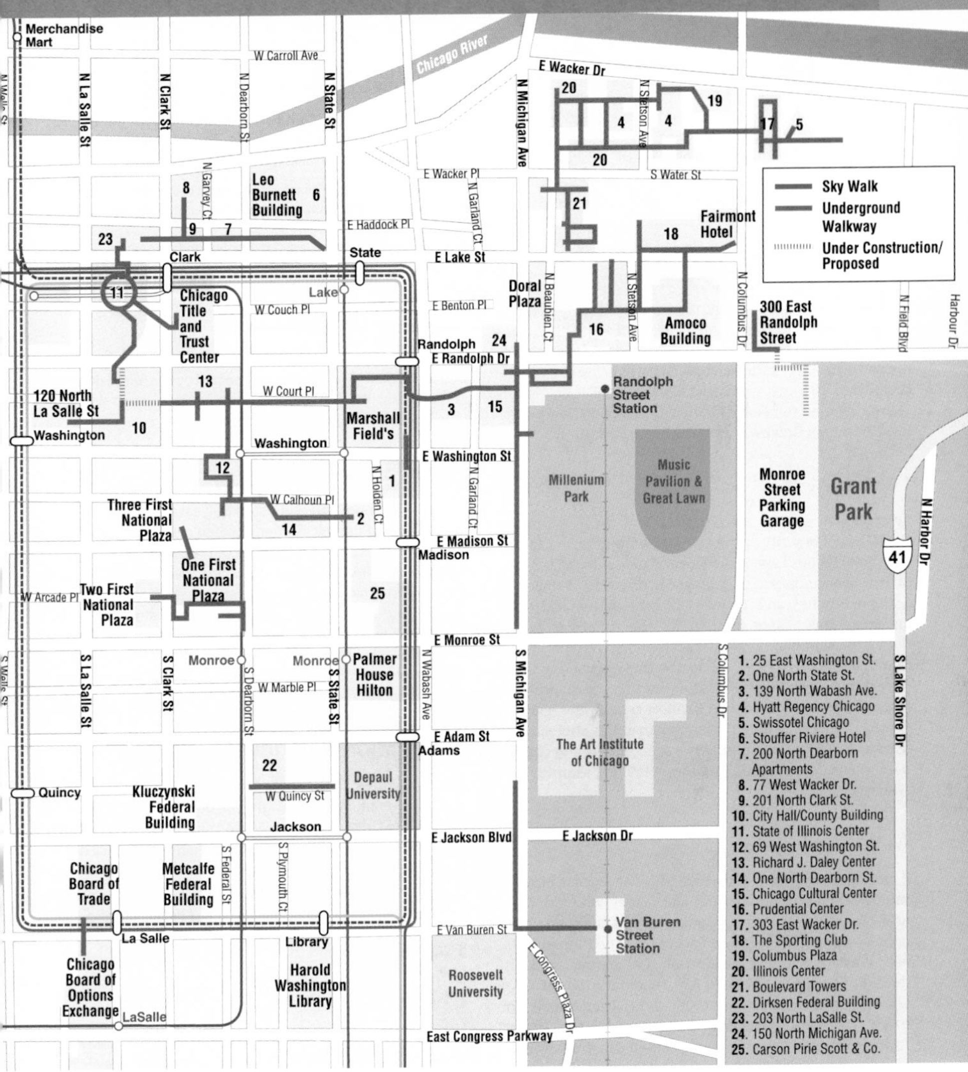

The downtown underground Pedway keeps Chicagoans moving throughout the central business district. An over 40-block network of tunnels and overhead bridges connects important public, government, and private sector buildings with retail stores, major hotels, rapid transit stations, and commuter rail stations. A subterranean city with shops, restaurants, services, and public art works, the Pedway is a welcome alternative to navigating trafficked intersections on foot and walking outdoors in Chicago's below wind-chill winters. The underground walkway system is open 24-hours; however access to a number of the buildings is limited after standard business hours. The first Pedway links were built in 1951 to connect the State St. and Dearborn St. subways at Washington St. and Jackson Blvd. Today, Chicago's Pedway continues to grow as city government and the private sector cooperate to expand it.

General Information

Chicago Park District:	*www.chicagoparkdistrict.com* *312-742-PLAY*
Chicagoland Bicycle Federation:	*www.chibikefed.org* *312-42-PEDAL*
Chicago Area Runner's Association:	*www.cararuns.org* *312-666-9836*

Overview

Greater Chicago offers dozens of recreational off-road paths that allow users to bike, skate, walk, and jog without the worry of vehicular traffic—now if only we could get dogs off the paths! In addition to recreational paths in the city's parks, designated off-street trails exist along the Lakefront, North Shore Channel, the North Branch Trail along the Chicago River, Burnham Greenway, and the Major Taylor Trail.

Lakefront Trail

Chicago has one of the prettiest and most accessible shorelines of any city in the U.S. (aside from having to first cross treacherous Lake Shore Drive to get to there). Use one of the over/underpasses and you'll discover 15 miles of bathing beaches and 18 miles of bike paths—just don't anticipate being able to train for the Athens Olympics during the summer months, when the sheer numbers make it impossible to advance along the path beyond a snail's pace during peak times. Thankfully for Chicagoans, in 1909, Daniel Burnham and Edward Bennett created the "Plan for Chicago," which included deeming that the shoreline be used as a public, non-commercial space where the city has paid plans for cycling, jogging, blading, skating, and swimming.

Major Taylor Trail

If you've ever wanted to take in a slice of Chicago's southwesternmost corner (and let's face it, who hasn't?), a new bike route, which incorporates an abandoned railroad right-of-way begins at Dawes Park at 81st and Hamilton Sts., near Western Ave. The 6-mile trail runs to the southeast through Beverly and Morgan Park, ending up at the Cook County Forest Preserve near 130th and Halsted Streets. The trail was named in honor of cycling legend Marshall "Major" Taylor, an African-American who competed in the early years of cycle-racing and lived out the final years of his life in a YMCA in Chicago.

Burnham Greenway

The following information was present in a Trust For Public Land report on the state of the proposed route of the Burnham Greenway Trail before it was paved:

Site History: Five-mile Conrail right-of-way between Chicago and the south suburbs, running through both industrial and natural areas.
Contamination: Phase II indicated pollution from adjacent uses, including fly dumping, railroad pollutants, and some unnatural coloration in adjacent water. Assessment determined no risk as long as the soil remains undisturbed.
REMEDIATION: Corridor will be paved.

So, as long as you stick to the paved trail and don't feel the desire to go digging around off the path, you should remain in good health! The path is suitable for riding, skating, rollerblading, and pedestrian activity.

North Branch Trail

To access the northern end of the trail, take Lake Cook Road to the Chicago Botanic Garden, located east of I-94. Starting from any of the forest preserves as the path winds southward is also an option. To access the southern end of the trail in Chicago, take Milwaukee Avenue to Devon Avenue and head a short way east to the Caldwell Woods Preserve. The North Branch winds along the Chicago River and the Skokie Lagoons but, unlike most of the other trails, this one crosses streets, so be careful and look out for cars as you approach.

North Shore Channel Trail

This trail follows North Shore Channel of the Chicago River from Lawrence Ave. through Lincolnwood, Skokie, and Evanston to Green Bay Rd. at McCormick Blvd. Not all of the seven miles of the trail are paved bike paths, and you'll have to endure the hassle of switching between path and street. Skokie recently paved the trail segment between Oakton and Howard Sts., but there are still many missing links in the route, much to the chagrin of Friends of the Chicago River (FOCR), who are trying to extend and improve the Channel Trail.

Chicago Park District

Many of the parks under the jurisdiction of the Chicago Park District have paths dedicated to cycling, jogging, walking, rollerblading, and skating. The Chicago Area Runner's Association is so committed to lobbying for runners' rights that it successfully petitioned to have the Lincoln Park running paths plowed through the winter so they could continue their running activities. This calls into question the sanity of such masochistic dedication, but we can only assume that the entire year is needed to prepare for the Chicago Marathon, held annually on the last Sunday in October. Check out the chart on the pacing page to determine Chicago Parks that designate jogging/walking and cycling/skating paths.

Park District—North Region	*Address*	*Phone*	*Jog/Walk*	*Bike/Skate*	*Map*
Brooks Park	7100 N Harlem Ave	312-742-7855	■		
Emmerson Park	1820 N Granville Ave	312-742-7877	■		36
Eugene Field Park	5100 N Ridgeway Ave	312-742-7591		■	
Indian Boundary Park	2500 W Lunt Ave	312-742-7887	■		33
Oz Park	2021 N Burling St	312-742-7898	■		30
Peterson Park	5801 N Pulaski Ave	312-742-7584	■		
Portage Park	4100 N Long Ave	312-742-7634	■		
River Park	5100 N Francisco Ave	312-742-7516		■	38
Shabbona Park	6935 W Addison St	312-742-7608	■		
Warren Park	6601 N Western Ave	312-742-7888	■	■	33
Frank J. Wilson Park	4630 N Milwaukee Ave	312-742-7616	■		
Winnemac Park	5100 N Leavitt St	312-742-5101	■		39

Park District—Central Region	*Address*	*Phone*	*Jog/Walk*	*Bike/Skate*	*Map*
Columbus Park	500 S Central Ave	312-746-5046	■	■	
Douglas Park	1401 S Sacramento Blvd	312-747-7670	■	■	
Dvorak Park	1119 W Cullerton St	312-746-5083	■		26
Humboldt Park	1400 N Sacramento Blvd	312-742-7549	■	■	
Pietrowski Park	4247 W 31st St	312-745-4801	■	■	
Riis Park	6100 W Fullerton Ave	312-746-5363	■	■	
Rutherford Sayre Park	6871 W Belden Ave	312-746-5368	■		
Union Park	1501 W Randolph St	312-746-5494	■		24

Park District—Southwest Region	*Address*	*Phone*	*Jog/Walk*	*Bike/Skate*	*Map*
Bogan Park	3939 W 79th St	312-747-6025	■		
Cornell Square Park	1809 W 50th St	312-747-6097	■		
Hayes Park	2936 W 85th St	312-747-6177	■		
LeClaire Courts/Hearst Community	5120 W 44th St	312-747-6438	■		
Mount Greenwood Park	3724 W 111th St	312-747-6564	■		
Rainey Park	4350 W 79th St	312-747-6630	■		
Senka Park	5656 S St. Louis Ave	312-747-7632	■		
Sherman Park	1301 W 52nd St	312-747-6672	■		
Avalon Park	1215 E 83rd St	312-747-6015	■		
Bradley Park	9729 S Yates Ave	312-747-6022	■		
Gately Park/Wendell Smith School Park	810 E 103rd St	312-747-6155	■		
Hamilton Park	513 W 72nd St	312-747-6174	■		
Lake Meadows Park	3117 S Rhodes Ave	312-747-6287	■	■	14
Meyering Park	7140 S Martin Luther King Dr	312-747-6545	■		
Palmer Park	301 E 111th St	312-747-6576	■		
Rosenblum Park	7547 S Euclid Ave	312-747-6649	■		
Washington Park	5531 S Martin Luther King Dr	312-747-6823	■	■	

Park District—Lakefront Region	*Address*	*Phone*	*Jog/Walk*	*Bike/Skate*	*Map*
Calumet Park	9801 S Avenue G	312-747-6039		■	
Jackson Park	6401 S Stony Island Ave	312-747-6187	■	■	
Lincoln Park	2045 N Lincoln Park West	312-742-7726	■	■	
Loyola Park	1230 W Greenleaf Ave	312-742-7857	■	■	34
Rainbow Park & Beach	3111 E 77th St	312-745-1479		■	
South Shore Cultural Center	7059 S South Shore Dr	312-747-2536		■	

General Information

Chicagoland Bicycle Federation: 650 S. Clark St., #300, 312-427-3325, www.biketraffic.org
Chicago Park District: www.chicagoparkdistrict.com, 312-742-PLAY
Chicago Cycling Club: www.chicagocyclingclub.org, 773-509-8093 (Organized rides April through October)
Chicago Transit Authority: www.transitchicago.com
DOT Bikes Page: http://www.ci.chi.il.us/Transportation/Bikes/

Despite the environmental and physical benefits, and Mayor Daley's efforts to make Chicago streets more hospitable to pedallers, bike riders are still seen by most drivers as a road nuisance, and the designated bike lanes on streets such as Milwaukee, King Drive, and Elston are a joke—illegal passing lanes are more like it. Furthermore, designated lakefront bike paths are more often than not crowded with headphone-wearing roller bladers, leashless dogs, and shoulder-to-shoulder stroller pushers. Nonetheless, every year thousands of Chicagoans choose to take their lives into their hands by taking it to the street in a demonstration of the type of urban perseverance by which great cities were built. Or is it simple foolhardiness?

If you are a cyclist bear in mind that in Chicago, bicycles, like any other vehicle of the road, are subject to the same laws and rights as drivers—but good luck enforcing this. This includes the right to take a lane, and the obligation to hand signal for turns. Helmets are still optional, but you'd have to have a pretty thick head to tempt fate without one. The same goes for an adequate assortment of chains and u-locks. Bike thievery is rampant in every neighborhood in the city.

Bikes Onboard Mass Transit

Bicycles are permitted (free) on all El trains at all times except 7 am–9 am and 4 pm–7 pm weekdays. Use the accessible turnstile or ask an attendant to open an access gate. Don't try to take your bike through the tall steel gates—it will get stuck! Only two bikes per carriage are allowed, so check for other bikes before you get on. The following CTA Buses are equipped with bike racks: 63rd St., 72 North Ave., 75th St., and 65 Grand buses. If your bike is the first to be loaded, lower the rack and place it in position with the front wheel facing the curb. If there is already a bike on the rack, place your bike's rear wheel toward the curb. If two bikes are already loaded, wait for the next bus. Plan on taking the Metra? Leave your bike at home! Items larger than a briefcase are not permitted on Metra Trains.

Bike Shops	*Address*	*Phone*	*Map*
Art's Cycle	1646 E 55th St	773-363-7524	20
Atlantic Cyclery Inc	3001 N Broadway St	773-244-1079	44
Bicycle Garage	11 E Jackson Blvd	800-300-1993	5
Bike Chicago	600 E Grand Ave	800-915-BIKE	3
Bike Stop Cycles	1034 W Belmont Ave	773-868-6800	43
Chicagoland Bicycle	10355 S Kedzie	773-445-081	
Cycle Smithyone Sports	2468 N Clark St	773-281-0444	30
Edgebrook Cycle & Sport	6450 N Central Ave	773-792-1669	
Higher Gear	1435 W Fullerton Ave	773-472-7433	29
Irv's Bike Shop	1725 S Racine Ave	312-226-6330	26
Johnny Sprocket's	1052 W Bryn Mawr	773-293-1695	
Johnny Sprocket's	3001 N Broadway	773-244-1079	
Kozy Cyclery	1451 W Webster Ave	773-528-2700	29
Kozy Cyclery	3712 N Halstead St	773-281-2263	44
Kozy Cyclery	601 La Salle St	312-360-0020	8
Mission Bay Multi Sports	738 W Randolph St	312-466-9111	4
On The Route Bicycles	3146 N Lincoln Ave	773-477-5066	43
Oscar Wastyn Cycles	2634 W Fullerton Ave	773-384-8999	27
Performance Bicycle Shop	2720 N Halsted St	773-248-0107	30
Quick Release Bike Shop	1623 N Halsted St	773-871-3110	31
Rapid Transit Cycle Shop	1900 W North Ave	773-227-2288	21
Recycle Bike Shop	1465 S Michigan Ave	312-987-1080	11
Roberts Cycle	7054 N Clark St	773-274-9281	34
Sportmart Inc	3134 N Clark St	773-871-8500	44
Sportmart Inc	620 N La Salle Dr	312-337-6151	2
Upgrade Cycle Works	1130 W Chicago Ave	312-226-8650	24
Urban Bikes	4653 N Broadway St	773-728-5212	40
Village Cycle Center	1337 N Wells St	312-726-2453	31
Wheels & Things	5210 S Harper Ave	773-493-4326	19

General Information

Chicago Park District: *www.chicagoparkdistrict.com*
312-742-PLAY (7529)

Overview

Due to the temperature extremes that Chicago experiences, its residents can enjoy both ice-skating and inline skating at various times of the year. Ice-skating can be a fun, free winter activity if you have your own skates, and if you don't, many rinks rent them. Skateboarding is also a popular pastime and a number of parks throughout the city are equipped with skating facilities.

Inline Skating

Similar to bike riding, inline skating in Chicago serves dual purposes. If you plan on strapping on the blades to get you from A to B, be super-careful navigating the streets. As it is, Chicago drivers tend to have difficulty seeing bicycle riders and, chances are, they won't notice you until you've slammed into the inside of their car door. Wear protective gear whenever possible, especially a helmet, and learn to shout loudly so that people can anticipate your approach. If recreational skating is more your speed, check out the Recreational Paths page for cool places to skate. If you'd like to join the hundreds of skaters on the paths in summer and you don't have your own gear, the following places offer skate rental: Londo Mondo, 1100 N Dearborn St. at W Maple St., 312-751-2794; Bike Chicago at Navy Pier, 800-915-BIKE; City Sweats, 2467 N Clark St. at Fullerton Ave., 773-348-2489. Hourly rates range from $7-$10, while daily rates are from $20-$30.

Skate Parks

If what you're after is a phat jam session, grab your blades or board and a couple of buddies and head down to the magnificent Burnham Skate Park (East of Lake Shore Drive at 31st St.). With amazing grinding walls and rails, vert walls and banks, Burnham Park presents hours of fun and falls. Less intense, but equally fun, are the two skate parks with ramps, quarter pipes, and grind rails. One can be found at West Lawn Park, 4233 W 65th St., 312-747-7032, the other at Oriole Park, 5430 N Olcott Ave., 312-742-7852.

Ice-Skating

The long-running and popular Skate on State was canceled due to the opening of two new ice rinks: the McCormick-Tribune Ice Rink at Millennium Park and the Midway Plaisance ice rink.

The Millennium Park rink is a beautiful place to skate during the day or evening, with Chicago's glorious skyline in the background. In summer months, the area becomes home to al fresco dining and entertainment. Located at 55 N. Michigan Ave., enter on the east side of Michigan Ave. between Monroe Dr. and Randolph St. Parking is available for $10 at the Grant Park North Garage (enter from Michigan Ave. median at Washington or Madison Sts.). Skate rental is $3 for adults and children and, if you have your own and want them sharpened, it's $5, 312-742-7529.

The new Olympic-sized skating rink and warming house complex at Midway Plaisance is the alternative to to Millennium Park. The construction of the permanent skating rink was a joint effort by the University of Chicago, the City of Chicago, and the Chicago Park District. Located at 59th and Woodlawn Ave., entry costs $3-$5. During summer the facility is used for roller-skating and entertainment, 312-747-0233.

Other ice-skating rinks are located seasonally at:
McFetridge Sports Complex (year-round),
3843 N. California Ave., 312-742-7585
($1.50-$2.50 admission + rental)
Daley Bicentennial Plaza Rink,
337 E. Randolph St., 312-742-7650
($1-$2 admission + rental)
McKinley Park,
2210 W. Pershing Rd., 312-747-5992 ($3-$5 rental)
Mt. Greenwood Park,
3721 W. 111th St., 312-747-2200 ($2-$3 rental)
Navy Pier Ice Rink,
600 E Grand Ave., 312-595-5100 ($3-$4 rental)
Riis Park,
6100 W. Fullerton Ave., 312-746-5735 ($2-$3 rental)
Rowan Park,
11546 S. Avenue Ln., 312-747-2200 ($2-$3 rental)
Warren Park, 6601 N. Western Ave., 312-742-6600
West Lawn Park, 4233 W. 65th St., 312-747-8500
The Rink (rollerskating), 1122 E 87th St, 773-221-2600 ($1)

Gear

If you're after skateboard gear, check out Air Time Skate Boards at 3317 N Clark St.,773-248-4970, and Uprise Skateboard Shop at 1820 N Milwaukee Ave.,773-342-7763.

For skating equipment, Air Time (above) also does inline skates as does Londo Mondo which has two locations: 1100 N Dearborn St. at W Maple St.,312-751-2794.

For all your ice-skating needs, try the Skater's Edge store in the McFetridge Sports Complex. They deal in hockey skates and equipment as well as inline skates and accessories such as sequined dresses! (3843 N. California, 773-463-1505)

Chicago is blessed with a number of golf courses within the city limits. Many courses offer discounts for residents and seniors, so be sure to ask. We couldn't possibly list all the great links in the surrounding suburbs, so we picked a few close to NFT's coverage area. Our Chicago favorites include: Jackson Park for being the closest 18 holes to the Loop; Sydney R. Marovitz executive course for beautiful lake views; Harborside International for a challenging Scottish-links experience; and Family Golf Center for a lunchtime 9.

Golf Courses

	Phone	Map	Holes	Fees
Robert A. Black Golf Course 2045 West Pratt Ave	312-245-0909	34	9	$11.50 weekdays/ $13 weekends
Sydney R Marovitz Golf Course 3600 N Recreation Dr	312-742-7930	43	9	$16 weekdays/ $19 weekends
Columbus Park Golf Course 5700 W Jackson Blvd	312-245-0909		9	$12 weekdays/ $13.50 weekends
Edgebrook Golf Course 5900 N. Central Ave	773-763-8320		18	$13 weekdays/ $16 weekends
Glencoe Park District Course 621 Westley Rd., Glencoe	847-835-0250		18	$38 weekdays/ $46 weekends
Harborside International Golf Center 11001 S Doty Ave	312-STARTER		18	$76 weekdays/ $87 weekends
Indian Boundary Golf Course 8600 W Forest Preserve Ave	773-625-9630		18	$23 weekdays/ $26 weekends
Jackson Park Golf Course 6400 Richards Dr	312-245-0909		18	$10 weekdays/ $20 weekends
Marquette Park Golf Course 6700 S Kedzie Ave	312-747-2761		9	$10.75 weekdays/ $12 weekends
Peter N. Jans Community Golf Course 1019 Central Ave, Evanston	847-475-9173		18	$15 weekdays/ $17 weekends
Riverside Golf Club 2320 Desplaines Ave	708-447-1049		18	$65 weekdays/ $75 weekends
South Shore Country Club 7059 South Shore Dr	312-245-0909		9	$10 weekdays/ $11.50 weekends
The Glen Club 2901 West Lake Ave, Glenview	847-724-7272		18	$105 weekdays/ $130 weekends
Winnetka Park District Course 1300 Oak St, Winnetka	847-501-2050		18	$40 weekdays/ $46 weekends

Driving Ranges

	Phone	Map	Fees
Diversey Driving Range 455 N Cityfront Plaza Dr	312-742-7929	3	$7/65 balls, $2 clubs
Harborside International Golf Center 11001 S Doty Ave	312-STARTER	18	$10/100, $3 clubs
Jackson Park Golf Course 6400 Richards Dr	312-245-0909	18	$6-50/65 balls, $2 clubs

Volleyball Courts

Hoops The Gym 312-850-HOOP
2 locations: 1380 W Randolph St, 1001 W Washington Blvd. State-of-the-art court rentals. 24/7.

Lincoln Park/North Avenue Beach 312-74-BEACH (reservations and price info.)
101 courts—12 are always open to the public. Much league play and reserved courts.
Office hours: 1pm-9pm Mon-Fri; 8am-5pm weekends.

Lincoln Park/Montrose Beach 312-742-1976 (reservations and price info.)
45 courts—first-come, first-served. League play in the evening.

Jackson Park/63rd Street Beach
4 courts—first-come, first-served. Free.

312-742-PLAY (general info); 312-747-2474 (Lake Front Region Office). All tennis courts (except Daley Bicentennial Plaza in Grant Park, Diversey Park, and Waveland Park) are free to the public and first-come, first-served. Courts are open daily, check each park for individual hours.

Tennis Courts	*Address*	*Phone*	*Map*
Armour Square Park	3309 S Shields Ave	312-747-6012	13
Ashe Beach Park	2701 E 74th St		N/A
Athletic Field Park	3546 W Addison St		N/A
Brands Park	3259 N Elston Ave	312-742-7582	41
California Park	3843 N California Ave	312-742-7585	41
Chase Park	4701 N Ashland Ave	312-742-7518	40
Clemente Park	2334 W Division St	312-742-7538	21
Cornell Square Park	1809 W 50th St	312-747-6097	N/A
Daley Bicentennial Plaza $7/hr; reservations must be made in person, 7am-10pm	337 E Randolph St	312-742-7650	6
David Square Park	4430 S Marshfield Ave	312-747-6107	N/A
Douglas Park Cultural & Community Center	1401 S Sacramento Ave	312-747-7670	N/A
Dunham Park	4638 N Melvina Ave	312-742-7603	N/A
Ellis Park	648 E 37th St	312-747-6122	14
Emmerson Playground Park	1820 W Granville Ave	312-742-7877	36
Eugene Field Park	5100 N Ridgeway Ave	312-742-7877	N/A
Fuller Park	331 W 45th St	312-747-6144	15
Gompers Park	4222 W Foster Ave	312-742-7628	N/A
Grant Park	331 E Randolph St	312-742-7648	6
Green Briar Park	2650 W Peterson Ave	312-742-7886	N/A
Hamilton Park	513 W 72nd St	312-747-6174	N/A
Hamlin Park	3035 N Hoyne Ave	312-742-7785	42
Harrison Park	1824 S Wood St	312-746-5491	25
Hollywood Park	3312 W Thorndale Ave	312-742-7578	N/A
Horner Park	2741 W Montrose Ave	312-742-7572	38
Humboldt Park	1400 N Sacramento Ave	312-742-7549	N/A
Independence Park	3945 N Springfield Ave	312-742-7590	N/A
Indian Boundary Park	2500 W Lunt Ave	312-742-7887	33
Jackson Park	6401 S Stony Island Ave	312-747-2763	N/A
Jefferson Park	4822 N Long Ave	312-742-7609	N/A
Jensen Playground Park	4600 N Lawndale Ave	312-742-7580	N/A
Jonquil Park	1023 W Wrightwood Ave		29
Kenwood Community Park	1330 E 50th St	312-747-6285	17
Kosciuszko Park	2732 N Avers Ave	312-742-7546	N/A
Lake Shore Park	808 N Lake Shore Dr	312-742-7891	N/A
Legion Park	W Peterson Ave to W Foster Ave at the Chicago River		N/A
Lerner Park	7000 N Sacramento Ave		33
Loyola Park	1230 W Greenleaf Ave	312-742-7857	34
Mandrake Park	900 E Pershing Rd		12
Mather Park	5941 N Richmond St	312-742-7501	35
McFetridge Sports Center (California Park)	3843 N California Ave	312-742-7585	41
McGuane Park	2901 S Poplar Ave	312-747-6497	12
McKinley Park	2210 W Pershing Rd	312-747-6527	N/A
Metcalfe Park	4134 S State St		16
Nichols Park	1300 E 55th St		19
Oz Park	2021 N Burling St	312-742-7898	30
Piotrowski Park	4247 W 31st St	312-747-6608	N/A
Pottawattomie Park	7340 N Rogers Ave	312-742-7878	34
Rainbow Park & Beach	2873 E 76th St		N/A
Revere Park	2509 W Irving Park Rd	312-742-7594	38
River Park	5100 N Francisco Ave	312-742-7516	38
Rogers Park	7345 N Washtenaw Ave	312-742-7859	33
Roosevelt Park	62 W Roosevelt Rd		8
Senn Park	1550 W Thorndale Ave		37
Sheridan Park	910 S Aberdeen St	312-746-5369	26
Sherman Park	1307 W 52nd St	312-747-6672	N/A
Smith (Joseph Higgins) Park	2526 W Grand Ave	312-742-7534	N/A
South Shore Culture Center	7059 S Shore Dr	312-747-2536	N/A
Taylor Park	41 W 47th St	312-747-6728	N/A
Touhy Park	7348 N Paulina St	312-742-7870	34
Union Park	1501 W Randolph St	312-746-5494	24
Warren Park	6601 N Western Ave	312-742-7879	33
Washington Park	5531 S Martin Luther King Dr	312-747-6823	N/A
Welles Park	2333 W Sunnyside Ave	312-742-7511	39
Frank J. Wilson Park	4630 N Milwaukee Ave	312-742-7616	N/A
Lincoln Park-Diversey Tennis Center $12/hr; reservations must be made in person. Clay courts.		312-742-7821	N/A
Lincoln Park-Waveland Tennis Center $12/hr; reservations must be made in person; 7:30am-8pm		312-742-7674	N/A

312-742-PLAY (general park info number); 312-742-5121 (Department of Beaches and Pools). All outdoor pools are free for the summer (Memorial Day-Labor Day). During the year, all lap swim fees are for 10-week sessions. $20 before 9 am; $10 after 9 am.

Outdoor Pools

Avondale Park	3516 W School St	312-742-7581
Chase Park	500 N Ashland Ave	312-742-7518
Douglas Park Cultural & Community Center	1401 S Sacramento Ave	312-747-7670
Dvorak Park	1119 W Cullerton St	312-746-5083
Franklin Park	4320 W 15th St	312-747-7676
Gompers Park	4222 W Foster Ave	312-742-7628
Hamlin Park	3035 N Hoyne Ave	312-742-7785
Humbolt Park	1400 N Sacramento Ave	312-742-7549
Jefferson Park	4822 N Long Ave	312-742-7609
McFetridge Sports Center (California Park)	3843 N California Ave	312-742-7585
Piotrowski Park	4247 W 31st St	312-747-6608
Pulaski Park	1419 W Blackhawk St	312-742-7559
River Park	5100 N Francisco Ave	312-742-7516
Sherman Park	1307 W 52nd St	312-747-6672
Sherwood Park	5705 S Shields Ave	
Smith (Joseph Higgins) Park	2526 W Grand Ave	312-742-7534
Taylor Park	41 W 47th St	312-747-6728
Union Park	1501 W Randolph St	312-746-5494
Washington Park	5531 S Martin Luther King Dr	312-747-2490
Wentworth Gardens Park	3770 S Wentworth Ave	312-747-6996
Wrightwood Park	2534 N Greenview Ave	312-742-7816

Indoor Pools

Altgeld Park	515 S Washtenaw Ave	312-746-5001
Clemente Park	2334 W Division St	312-742-7466
Eckhart Park	1330 W Chicago Ave	312-746-5553
Gill Park	825 W Sheridan Rd	312-742-5807
Harrison Park	1824 S Wood St	312-421-8572
Independence Park	3945 N Springfield Ave	312-742-7530
Kosciuszko Park	2732 N Avers Ave	312-742-7556
Leone Park & Beach	1222 W Touhy Ave	
Mather Park	5941 N Richmond St	312-742-7513
McGuane Park	2901 S Poplar Ave	312-747-7463
Sheridan Park	910 S Aberdeen St	312-746-5370
Stanton Park	618 W Scott St	312-742-9553
Washington Park	5531 S Martin Luther King Dr	
Welles Park	2333 W Sunnyside Ave	312-742-7515

Bowling Alleys

Diversey-River Bowl Inc	2211 W Diversey Ave	773-227-5800	Sun-Thurs: $19/hr per lane, $3 for shoes; Fri-Sat: $26/hr per lane, $3 for shoes
Drake Bowl	3550 W Montrose Ave	773-463-1377	$1.50-2 per game; $2 for shoes
Habetler Bowl Inc	5250 N Northwest Hwy	773-774-0500	$4 per game, $2.50 for shoes; Tuesdays $1 per game
Lucky Strike	2747 N Lincoln Ave	773-549-2695	$15/hr per lane, $2 for shoes
Marigold Bowl	828 W Grace St	773-935-8183	$1.75-3.25 per game; $2 for shoes
Southport Lanes & Billiards	3325 N Southport Ave	773-472-6600	$16/hr per lane, $2 for shoes
Timber Lanes Inc	1851 W Irving Park Rd	773-549-9770	$2.50 per game, $2 for shoes
Waveland Bowl Inc	3700 N Western Ave	773-472-5900	$3-6 per game, $4 for shoes

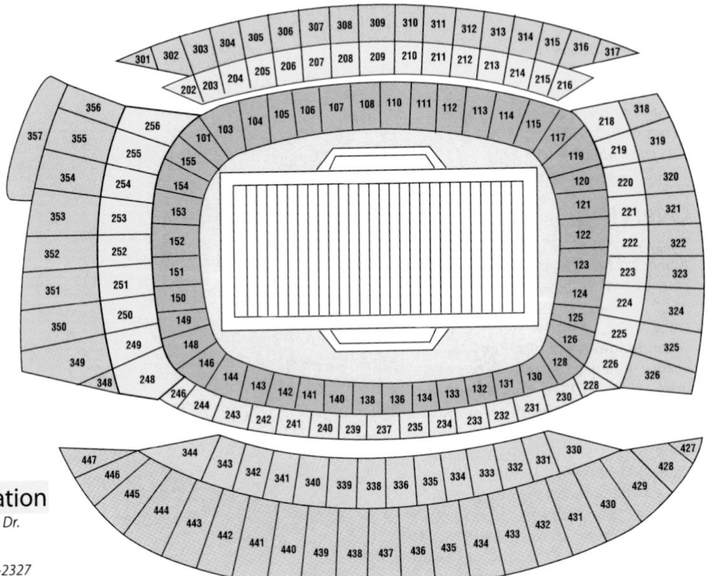

General Information

Location: 425 E. McFetridge Dr.
Chicago, IL 60605
Phone: 312-747-1285
Bears Sales Office: 847-615-2327
Bears Box Office: 847-295-BEAR (2327)
Re-opens for the 2003 season.
Bears website: www.chicagobears.com
Bears email: stadiumsales@bears.nfl.com
Ticketmaster: 312-559-1212; www.ticketmaster.com

Overview

Construction of the new Soldier Field in 2002 is best described as the ultimate political football. When the final buzzer rang, Soldier Field stayed put and all but the signature colonnade from the original stadium built in 1924 met the wrecking ball. In 2003, when the new stadium (we hope) opens in time for the regular season, fierce Chicago Bears fans will judge whether harangue and traffic hang-ups on Lake Shore Dr. not only delivers a better den for their beloved Bears, but helps stir them from hibernation since their only Super Bowl win in 1985.

The new Soldier Field is a key player in a $587 million Lakefront Improvement Plan for the shoreline between Navy Pier and McCormick Place. An estimated $365 million went towards the 61,000-seat stadium. The new underground garage cost $75 million and another $147 million was spent on outside parking facilities, infrastructure, road improvements, and 17 acres of parkland with memorials to war veterans and Chicago's Finest. Tree-hugger victories include a winter garden, children's park, and sledding hill.

How to Get Tickets

Contact Ticketmaster to purchase individual game tickets. Season tickets in the new stadium are already sold out. So, your best bet to get good seats is to get top billing on somebody's will or work with a licensed ticket broker. Fans marked their territory early by purchasing a one-time Permanent Seat License (PSL). In exchange for paying big premiums to help cover construction expenses, PSL holders were promised first choice of ticket seating each year. Of the stadium's 61,000 seats, 27,500 are PSL zones and the remaining 33,500 are non-licensed seats in the stadium's higher altitudes. Call the Bears sales office to get on the season ticket wait list.

How to Get There

By Car: From the north or south, take Lake Shore Dr.; follow the signs to Soldier Field. For parking lots, exit at E. McFetridge, E. Waldron, E. 14th Blvd., and E. 18th Dr. From the west, take I-55 east to Lake Shore Dr., turn north and follow the signs. Travel east on I-290, then south on I-90/94 to I-55; get on I-55 heading east to Lake Shore Dr.

Parking lots surrounding Soldier Field cost between $6 and $12, including the new underground North Parking Garage. Two parking and game-day tailgating lots are south of Waldron Dr. There are lots on the Museum Campus off McFetridge Dr. and near McCormick Place off 31st St. and E. 18th St.

By Train: On game days, CTA Soldier Field Express bus 128 runs non-stop between the Ogilvie Transportation Center and Union Station to Soldier Field ($1 one-way). Service starts two hours before the game, runs up to 45 minutes before kickoff, and up to 45 minutes post-game.

By El: Take the Red, Orange or Green Lines to the Roosevelt Rd. station stop ($1.50 one-way; 30¢ additional for bus transfer). Either board eastbound CTA bus 12 or the free green trolley to the Museum Campus. Walk south to Soldier Field.

By Bus: CTA buses 12, 127, and 146 stop on McFetridge Dr. near Soldier Field. Contact the RTA Information Center for routes and schedules, 312-836-7000; www.rtachicago.com.

By Trolley: The Green Trolley travels along Michigan Ave., Washington St., Canal St., and Adams St. to the Museum Campus. From there, walk south to the field. For routes and schedules, visit www.cityofchicago.org/Transportation/trolleys/.

General Information

Location:
1060 West Addison St.
Chicago, IL 60613-4397
Cubs Box Office Phone:
773-404-CUBS (2827)
Tickets.com: 800-THE-CUBS (843-2827)
Lost and Found: 773-404-4185
Website: www.cubs.com

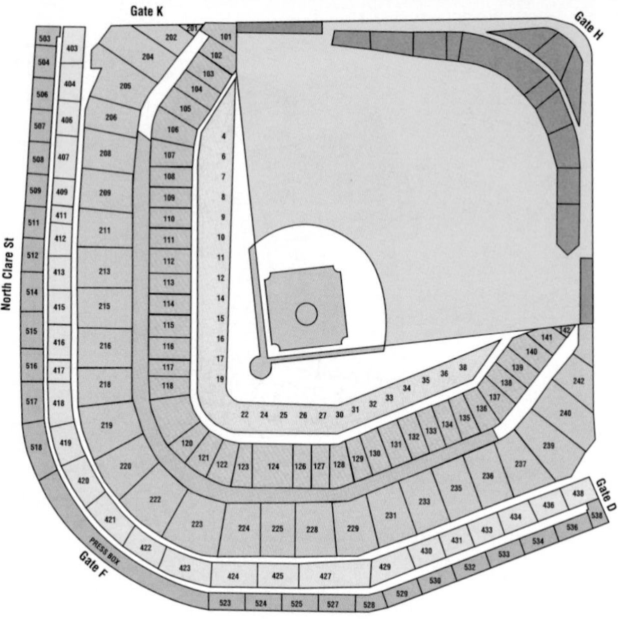

Overview

Wrigley Field draws worshipers of America's favorite pastime like St. Peter's draws Catholics to Rome. Built in 1914, and the Cubs' home field since 1916, Wrigley Field is the second-oldest ball park in Major League Baseball (Boston's Fenway is from 1912). Called the "Friendly Confines," Wrigley Field's ivy-strewn walls, classic grass-field design, and hand-turned scoreboard transcend time and technology. Lights for night games were not installed until 1988 when the League threatened to force the Cubbies into playing their post-season games in St. Louis, nesting grounds of the arch-rival Cardinals. You can't please everyone—since then neighborhood activists have lobbied heavily to limit the glaring lights effects on their evening tranquility.

Today, nostalgia for the cherished, landmark ballpark limits the number of night games and is leading the charge against recent proposals to expand the bleachers. A sacred section of Wrigley Field, the bleachers are fiercely protected by park denizens who defiantly toss opposing teams' homerun balls back onto the field. And just like God-fearing folk, fervent Cubs fans believe in a Second Coming. Although the Cubbies haven't won a World Series since their back-to-back wins over Detroit in 1907 and 1908, the loveable losing team has one of the most impressive attendance records in league history. Perhaps in 2003, the Cubs' 90th season at Wrigley Field, faithful fans' prayers will be answered…then again, perhaps not.

How to Get Tickets

Individual game tickets can be purchased from the Cubs' website, by calling Tickets.com or in person at some Chicagoland Sears and Sears Hardware stores. Also, buy tickets at the Wrigley Field Box Office, which is open weekdays from 8 am to 6 pm; weekends from 9 am to 4 pm. Generally, seats are discounted April, May, and September for Monday through Thursday afternoon games. A purchase of 20 or more tickets is a group sale; purchase them at the box office, by phone, or mail order. Children age 2 years and over require tickets. Call Tickets.com Customer Service (1-800-955-5566) to change previously purchased tickets.

How to Get There

By Car: If you must…Traffic on game days is horrendous and parking prices are sky-high. Aftergame spill-out from local bars freezes traffic as police do their best to prevent drunken revelers from stumbling into the streets. From the Loop or south, take Lake Shore Dr. north; exit at Irving Park Rd. and head west to Clark St.; turn south on Clark St. to Wrigley Field. From the north, take Lake Shore Dr. to Irving Park Rd.; head west to Clark St. and turn south. From Chicago's West Side, take I-290 east or I-55 north to Lake Shore Dr. Follow directions above. From the northwest, take I-90 east exiting at Addison St.; travel east three miles. From the southwest side, take I-55 north to I-90/94 north. Exit at Addison St.; head east to the park.

Street parking around Wrigley Field is heavily restricted. The Cubs operate a garage at 1126 W. Grace St. Purchase parking passes through the mail or at the Wrigley Field Box Office. On game nights, tow trucks cruise Wrigleyville's streets nabbing cars without a resident permit sticker. So park smart at the DeVry Institute, 2600 W. Rockwell, because CTA bus 154 Wrigley Express shuttles patrons to and from the park (just $5 covers parking and roundtrip shuttle per carload).

By El: Riding the Howard/Dan Ryan Red Line is the fastest and easiest way to get to Wrigley Field ($1.50 one-way). Get off at the Addison St. stop one block east of the field.

By Bus: CTA buses 22, 8, and 152 stop closest to Wrigley Field ($1.50 one-way). For schedules, contact the RTA Information Center, 312-836-7000; www.rtachicago.com.

General Information

Location:
333 W. 35th St.
Chicago, IL 60616
Chicago White Sox:
312-674-1000; tickets@chisox.com
Tickets.com:
1-866-SOX-GAME (769-4263)
Lost and Found:
312-674-1000
Website: www.whitesox.com

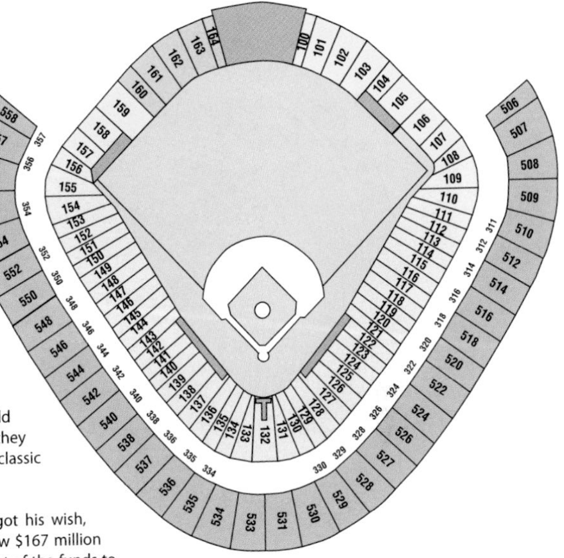

Overview

It was a sad day for baseball when "Old Comiskey Park" became a deal-breaker. In 1988, Chicago White Sox owner Jerry Reinsdorf (also owner of the Bulls) threatened that the ChiSox would abandon the South Side for Florida if they didn't get a new stadium to replace their classic but crumbling 1910 ballpark.

Notoriously stingy Reinsdorf not only got his wish, but got someone else to pay for the new $167 million US Cellular Field. The state collected most of the funds to build the sleek, stylish, sterile stadium from an additional hotel tax. Guess where the rest of the money came from. The new park opened in 1991. In anticipation of hosting the All-Star Game in July, 2003, "new" Comiskey Park was recently renovated.

But there is one thing new construction and team ownership just can't change—tradition. Raunch and paunch still go together like a beer and hotdog no matter what you call the venue. Bawdy bards of baseball, White Sox fans shout creative strings of expletives between beer guzzles and finger flip-offs. Nothing and no one is spared their gritty, expressive slurs—their beloved players and their mothers, the team's cretin owner, the opponent, the park, its burritos, or the weather. But under all the crass commentary burns a fierce love for a tough ball club that has given their passionate fans plenty to cheer about since their last World Series win in 1917.

How to Get Tickets

Purchase tickets over the website or at the US Cellular Field Box Office, open weekdays 10 am to 6 pm and 'til 4 pm on weekends. Tickets.com also sells seats over the phone and at their retails outlets in Chicagoland Sears and Sears Hardware stores. Children shorter than the park's turnstile arm (approximately 36 inches so let 'em slouch for once!) are admitted free, but share your seat. Ballpark bargains include Half-Price Mondays for all regular seats, and Willy Wonka's Kids Days on select Sundays when children 14 and under get in for $1. Wonka tickets must be purchased at park ticket windows on game day. Check the website for Wonka schedules.

How to Get There

By Car: US Cellular Field is located at the 35th St. exit off the Dan Ryan Expressway. From the north or south, take I-90/94, stay in the local lanes and exit at 35th St. If you possess a green parking coupon or plan on paying cash for parking ($13), exit at 35th St. Follow signs to "Sox Parking" at lots E, F and L on the stadium's south side. Fans with red, prepaid season parking coupons exit at 31st St. and follow signs for "Red Coupons" to lots A, B, and C just north of the stadium. If the 35th St. exit is closed due to heavy traffic, which is often the case on game days, proceed to the 39th St. exit; turn right for "Sox Parking" and left for "Red Coupons." The handicapped parking and stadium drop-off area is in Lot D, west of the field and accessible via 37th St. All lots open two hours prior to the opening pitch and close right after the game. Additional public parking lots with shuttle service to and from US Cellular Field are at the Illinois Institute of Technology, 3300 S. Federal St.

By Bus: CTA buses 24 and 35 stop closest to the park. Others stopping in the vicinity are the 29, 44, and 39. Armies of cops surround US Cellular Field on game days because the neighborhood is rough, especially at night.

By El: Ride the Red Line to the Sox-35th St. stop just west of the ballpark. If taking the Green Line, get off at the 35th-Bronzeville-IIT station.

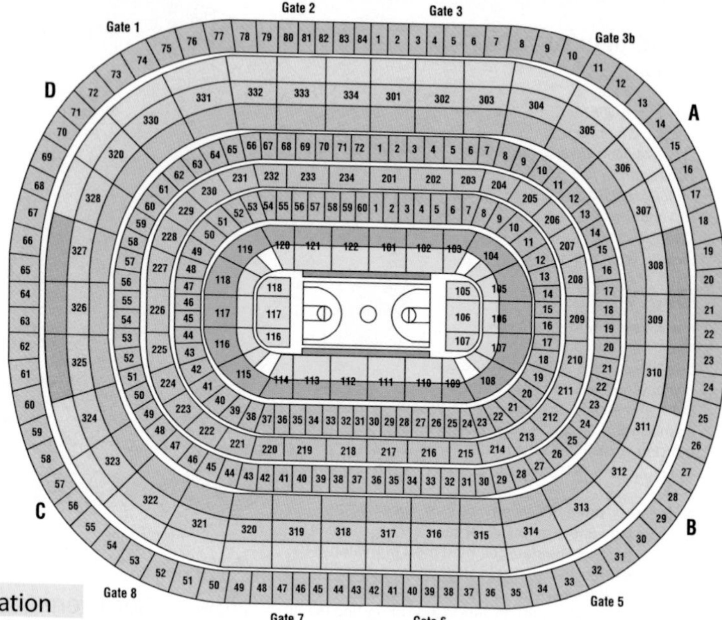

General Information

Location: 1901 W. Madison St., Chicago, IL 60612
Phone: 312-455-4500
Website: www.unitedcenter.com
Ticketmaster: 312-559-1212; www.ticketmaster.com
Chicago Bulls: 312-455-4000
Bulls website: www.bulls.com
Chicago Blackhawks: 312-455-7000
Blackhawks website: www.chicagoblackhawks.com

Overview

Looming over the West Side, United Center is home to the NHL's Blackhawks and the NBA's Chicago Bulls. The glitzy stadium is also a premier concert arena. Opened in 1994, the $175 million stadium was privately funded by deep-pocketed Blackhawks owner William Wirtz and penny-pinching Bulls majority owner Jerry Reinsdorf.

The Bulls still sell out even though the team with the six-pack of NBA championship trophies is history. It must be the ingenious half-time antics drawing the crowds because, despite Coach Bill Cartwright's efforts in the 2001-2002 season, the Bulls finished last in the Central Division.

Although it's been an ice age since the Blackhawks won the Stanley Cup (1961), the team enjoys unwavering support by boisterous fans. Last season showed signs of thaw when the Blackhawks made it to the playoffs. Coach Brian Sutter hopes to heat things up in the 2002-2003 season.

How to Get Tickets

Book tickets over the phone or online with Ticketmaster, by United Center mail order, or visit the United Center box office at Gate 4 next to the soaring, tongue-wagging statue of Michael Jordan. Box office hours are Monday to Saturday, 11 am to 6 pm. For Bulls and Blackhawks season tickets and group bookings call the phone numbers above.

How to Get There

By Car: From the Loop, drive west on Madison St. to United Center. From the north, take I-90/94 exit at Madison St; head west to the stadium. From the southwest, take I-55 north to the Damen/Ashland exit; head north to Madison St. From the west, take I-290 east to the Damen Ave. exit; go north to Madison St.

Parking lots surround United Center, as do countless cops. General public parking is in Lot B on Warren Blvd. (cars, $13-16; limo, R.V. and bus parking, $21). Lot H on Wood St. is closest to the stadium and is reserved for VIPs. Disabled parking is in Lots G and H on Damen Ave. Additional lots within easy walking distance of the stadium are on Damen Ave., Madison St., Adams St. Wood St., Paulina St., and Warren Blvd.

By El: Take the Forest Park Branch of the Blue Line to the Medical Center-Damen Ave. station. Walk two blocks north to the United Center.

By Bus: CTA bus 19 United Center Express is the most intelligent and safest choice. In service only on event and game days, this express bus travels from Chicago Ave. south down Michigan Ave., then west along Madison St. to the United Center. Michigan Ave. stops are at Chicago Ave., Illinois St., and Randolph St. On Madison St., stops are at State St., Wells St., and Clinton St. ($1.50 one-way). Service starts two hours before an event and runs up to 30 minutes before it ends. After events, bus service continues for 45 minutes. CTA bus 20 also travels Madison St. beginning at Wabash Ave. and has "owl service" but travel is slow, schedules sometimes erratic, and even with cops circling the stadium, the neighborhood's level of safety is questionable. Contact the RTA Information Center for schedules, 312-836-7000; www.rtachicago.com.

Television

	CLTV	(Cable)
2	WBBM	(CBS)
5	WMAQ	(NBC)
7	WLS	(ABC)
9	WGN	
11	WTTW	(PBS)
20	WYCC	(PBS)
23	WFBT	(Brokered—ethnic)
26	WCIU	(Independent)
32	WFLD	(Fox)
38	WCPX	(PAX)
44	WSNS	(Telemundo)
50	WPWR	(UPN)
60	WEHS	(Home shopping)
66	WGBO	(Univision)

Radio

AM

560	WIND	Spanish
620	WTMJ	News/Talk
670	WMAQ	Sports
720	WGN	Talk
780	WBBM	Talk
820	WCSN	Sports
850	WAIT	Standards
890	WLS	News/Talk
1000	WLUP	Sports
1110	WMBI	Religious
1200	WLXX	Spanish
1280	WBIG	Talk
1390	WGCI	Gospel
1450	WVON	Talk (Black oriented)
1490	WPNA	Polish
1510	WWHN	Gospel
1570	WBEE	Jazz

FM

88.1	WCRX	Columbia College
88.5	WHPK	U of Chicago
88.7	WLUW	Loyola U
89.3	WNUR	Northwestern
90.1	WMBI	Christian
90.0	WDCB	Jazz
91.5	WBEZ	National Public Radio
93.1	WXRT	Rock
93.5	WJTW	Adult Contemporary
93.9	WLIT	Adult Contemporary
94.7	WZZN	Modern Rock
95.1	WIIL	Rock
95.5	WNUA	New Age
95.9	WKKD	Oldies
96.3	WBBM	Dance
97.9	WLUP	Rock
98.7	WFMT	Classical
99.5	WUSN	Country
100.3	WNND	Adult Contemporary
101.1	WKQX	Modern Rock
101.9	WTMX	Adult Contemporary
102.7	WVAZ	Urban Contemporary
103.1	WXXY	Latin Pop
103.5	WKSC	Top 40
104.3	WJMK	Oldies
105.1	WOJO	Spanish
105.9	WCKG	Rock
106.7	WYLL	Christian
107.5	WGCI	Urban Contemporary

Print

Chicago Defender	2400 S Michigan Ave, 60616	(312) 225-2400	Black community newspaper.
Chicago Free Press	3714 N Broadway St, 60613	(773) 325-0005	Gay community news.
Chicago Magazine	500 N Dearborn, 60610	(312) 222-8999	Upscale glossy mag.
Chicago Reader	11 E Illinois St, 60611	(312) 828-0350	Free weekly with listings.
Chicago Sun-Times	401 N Wabash, 60611	(312) 321-3000	One of the big dailies.
Chicago Tribune	435 N Michigan Ave, 60611	(312) 222-3232	The other big daily.
Crain's Chicago Business	740 N Rush, 60611	(312) 649-5200	Business news.
Ebony	820 S Michigan Ave, 60605	(312) 322-9200	National glossy about African Americans.
Hyde Park Herald	5240 S Harper, 60615	(773) 643-8533	Local for Hyde Parkers.
La Raza	3909 N Ashland Ave, 60613	(773) 525-9400	Hispanic Community Paper.
Lerner-Booster-Skyline	7331 N Lincoln, Lincolnwood 60646	(847) 329-2000	Conglomeration of neighborhood papers.
N'Digo	401 N Wabash, 60611	(312) 822-0202	Black community weekly.
New City	770 N Halsted Ave, #208	(312) 243-8786	Alternative free weekly.
Playboy	680 N Lake Shore Dr, 60611	(312) 751-8000	The classic men's mag.
Today's Chicago Woman	233 E Ontario St, 60611	(312) 951-7600	Weekly for working women.
Windy City Times	1115 W Belmont, 60657	(773) 871-7610	Gay-targeted news weekly.

12 Essential Chicago Books

Native Son, by Richard Wright. Gripping novel about a young black man on the South Side in the 30s.

Neon Wilderness, by Nelson Algren. Short story collection set in Ukranian Village and Wicker Park.

One More Time, by Mike Royko. Collection of Royko'sTribune columns.

The Boss: Richard M. Daley, by Mike Royko. Biography of the former Mayor.

The Jungle, by Upton Sinclair. Gritty look at the life in the meat-packing plants.

Adventures of Augie March, by Saul Bellow. More Chicago in the 30s.

V.I. Warshawsky mystery series, by Sara Paretsky. Series firmly rooted in Chicago landscape.

50 Years at Hull House, by Jane Addams. Story of the Near West Side.

Secret Chicago, by Sam Weller. Off-the-beaten path guidebook.

Ethnic Chicago, by Melvin Holli & Peter D'A. Jones. Insider's guide to Chicago's ethnic neighborhoods

House on Mango Street, by Sandra Cisneros. Short story collection about a Latina childhood in Chicago.

Our America: Life and Death on the South Side of Chicago, by Lealan Jones, et al. Life in the Chicago Projects as told by two schoolchildren.

General Information • 2004 Calendar of Events

From May to June, every corner of the city is hopping with all manner of block parties, church carnivals, neighborhood festivals, and all-out hootenany. Contact the Mayor's Office of Special Events for a complete list of the city's 100+ festivals.

Event	When / Where	Description
Around the Coyote	February and September, Throughout Wicker Park	The edgier version of the Old Town Art Fair.
St Patrick's Day Parade	Saturday closest to 3/17, Columbus Dr., Balbo to Monroe	The Disney version of the real deal (see below).
South Side St Patrick's Day Parade	Sunday closest to 3/17, Western Ave, 103rd to 113th	The real deal, with oversized leprechauns and green beer flowing.
Gospel Music Festival	June 4-6, Grant Park	As much about the soul food as the music.
Chicago Blues Festival	June 10-13, Grant Park	Drawing the top names in blues for 21 years.
Printers Row	2nd weekend in June, Dearborn, between Harrison & Balbo	Watch for "Booksellers Gone Wild" coming soon to pay-per-view.
Andersonville Midsommer Fest	2nd weekend in June, Clark St, between Foster & Balmoral	Ain't it Swede?
Old Town Art Fair	Mid-June, 1800 N Orleans, Menominee, Lincoln	Arts AND crafts.
Taste of Chicago	June 25-July 4, Grant Park	Why go to a restaurant when you can eat standing up in the hot sun in a crowd?
Country Music Fest	June 26-27, Grant Park	Annual Lakeside hoe-down.
Gay Pride Parade	June 27, Halsted/Broadway between Halsted & Grace	200,000 of the city's gay community and their fans take it to the streets.
Independence Eve Fireworks	July 3, Grant Park	Real fireworks occur when a million spectators try to leave Grant Park.
Outdoor Film Festival	Tuesdays, July 13-Aug 24, Grant Park	Classic movies, a carafe of vino and KFC. Life is good.
Venetian Night	July 24, Chicago River Basin	Wow! Decked out boats!
Fiesta Del Sol	Last weekend in July, Cermak, between Throop & Morgan	One of the most festive of the fests.
Bud Billiken Parade	2nd Saturday in August, King Drive	World's biggest African-American parade!
North Halsted Market Days	August 14-15, Halsted between Belmont & Addison	See Gay Pride Parade. Add beer and live music.
Air and Water Show	August 21-22, lakefront	The Stealth Bombers never fail to thrill.
Viva Chicago Latin Music Fest	August 28-29, Grant Park	Salsa under the stars.
Taste of Polonia	Last weekend in August, 5200 W Lawrence	Polka and keilbasa! Heaven! Pierogis! Paradise!
Celtic Fest	September 18-19, Grant Park	Clog dance in the bonny heath.
Tree Lighting	November 26, Daley Plaza	Decking the halls by City Hall.

*All dates subject to change. For more up to date info. and a schedule of neighborhood festivals, contact the Mayor's Office of Special Events at www.cityofchicago.org/specialevents

Address	Phone	Zip
Map 2		
222 Merchandise Mart Plz	312-321-0233	60654
540 N Dearborn St	312-644-0233	60610
Map 3		
227 E Ontario St	312-642-3576	60611
Map 4		
168 N Clinton St	312-906-8557	60661
Map 5		
100 W Randolph St	312-263-2686	60601
211 S Clark St	312-427-0016	60604
233 S Wacker Dr	312-876-1024	60606
Map 6		
200 E Randolph St	312-861-0473	60601
Map 7		
433 W Harrison St	312-983-8182	60607
Map 10		
2345 S Wentworth Ave	312-326-6440	60616
Map 11		
2035 S State St	312-225-0218	60616
Map 15		
4101 S Halsted St	773-247-7491	60609
Map 16		
4601 S Cottage Grove Ave	773-924-6658	60653
Map 18		
700 E 61st St	773-493-0731	60637
Map 19		
1526 E 55th St	773-324-1822	60615
956 E 58th St	773-324-1822	60637
Map 22		
1635 W Division St	773-278-2069	60622
Map 23		
116 S Western Ave	312-243-2560	60612
Map 26		
1859 S Ashland Ave	312-733-4750	60608
Map 27		
2339 N California Ave	773-489-2855	60647
Map 29		
2405 N Sheffield Ave	773-929-7041	60614
Map 30		
2643 N Clark St	773-525-4350	60614
Map 34		
1723 W Devon Ave	773-743-2650	60660
7056 N Clark St	773-274-9430	60626
7617 N Paulina St	773-743-2830	60626
Map 38		
2522 W Lawrence Ave	773-561-8633	60625
Map 39		
2011 W Montrose Ave	773-472-1314	60618
Map 40		
1343 W Irving Park Rd	773-327-0345	60613
4850 N Broadway St	773-561-5216	60640
Map 41		
3750 N Kedzie Ave	773-539-6210	60618
Map 42		
3635 N Lincoln Ave	773-404-0980	60657
Map 43		
3024 N Ashland Ave	773-248-2875	60657

Chicago is home to some of the nation's leading research and teaching hospitals. Encompassing several hospitals and medical institutions, the Illinois Medical District is one of the largest health-care centers in the world. Cook County Hospital established the nation's first emergency trauma unit in 1966.

Hospitals

	Address	*Phone*	*Map*
Advocate Illinois Masonic Medical Ctr	836 W Wellington Ave	773-878-4300	43
Children's Memorial Hospital	707 W Fullerton Ave	773-880-4000	30
Columbia Chicago Lakeshore	4840 N Marine Dr	773-878-9700	40
Cook County Hospital	1835 W Harrison St	312-633-6000	25
Duchossois Center for Advanced Medicine (DCAM)	5758 S Maryland Ave		19
Kindred Chicago Lakeshore	6130 N Sheridan Rd	773-381-1222	37
Kindred Hospital	2544 W Montrose Ave	773-267-2622	38
La Rabida Children's Hospital and Research Center	E 65th St at Lake Michigan	773-363-6700	20
Lincoln Park Hospital	550 W Webster Ave	773-883-2000	30
Louis A Weiss Memorial Hosp	4646 N Marine Dr	773-878-8700	40
Mercy Hospital & Medical Ctr	2525 S Michigan Ave	312-567-2000	11
Methodist Hospital Of Chicago	5025 N Paulina St	773-271-9040	39
Michael Reese Hosp & Med Ctr	2929 S Ellis Ave	312-791-2000	14
Nazareth Family Ctr	1127 N Oakley Blvd	312-770-2391	21
Northwestern Memorial Hospital	251 E Huron St	312-926-2000	3
Provident Hospital	500 E 51st St	312-572-1200	16
Rush-Presbyterian St Luke's	1725 W Harrison St	312-942-5000	25
St Anthony's Hospital	2075 W 19th St	773-484-1000	25
St Elizabeth's Hospital	1431 N Claremont Ave	773-278-2000	21
St Josephs Hospital	2900 Lake Shore Dr	773-665-3000	44
St Mary Of Nazareth Hospital	2233 W Division St	312-770-2000	21
Swedish Covenant Hospital	5145 N California Ave	773-878-8200	38
Thorek Hospital & Medical Ctr	850 W Irving Park Rd	773-525-6780	40
Univ of Chicago Children's Hospital	5839 S Maryland Ave		19
University Of Chicago Hospital	5841 S Maryland Ave	773-702-1000	19
University of Chicago Physicians Group	1301 E 47th St		17
University Of Illinois at Chicago Hospital	1740 W Taylor St	312-996-7000	25

Police Departments

	Address	*Phone*	*Map*
1st District (Central)	1718 S State St	312-745-4290	11
2nd District (Wentworth)	5101 S Wentworth Ave	312-747-8366	15
9th District (Deering)	3501 S Lowe Ave	312-747-8227	13
11th District (Harrison)	3151 W Harrison St	312-746-8386	25
12th District (Monroe)	100 S Racine Ave	312-746-8396	24
13th District (Wood)	937 N Wood St	312-746-8350	21
14th District (Shakespeare)	2150 N California Ave	312-744-8290	27
18th District (Near North)	1160 N Larrabee St	312-742-5870	31
19th District (Belmont)	2452 W Belmont Ave	312-744-5983	42
20th District (Foster)	5400 N Lincoln Ave	312-742-8714	35
21st District (Prairie)	300 E 29th St	312-747-8340	14
23rd District (Town Hall)	3600 N Halsted St	312-744-8320	44
24th District (Rogers Park)	6464 N Clark St	312-744-5907	34

The Chicago Public Library System has 75 branches and two regional libraries serving Chicago citizens. In the midst of a huge capital improvement program, the city expects to have built or renovated 55 neighborhood branch libraries by the end of 2004.

Families and schools should take advantage of the Chicago Public Library System's "Imagination on Loan" pass, which is available to library cardholders who are Chicago residents. You can check out the free Pass using your library card, just like you would any other item, and the loan is good for two weeks. The Pass entitles entry for up to 8 people to the Chicago Children's Museum at Navy Pier. For more information, call your local library or the Museum on 312-527-1000.

Chicago has many excellent research libraries and university libraries, one of which is the independent Newberry Library, established in 1887. It shelves rare books, manuscripts, and maps. Generally, Chicago's universities and colleges welcome the public to their libraries during specified hours, but it's best to call first and check.

Libraries	*Address*	*Phone*	*Map*
Asher Library-Spertus Institute	618 S Michigan Ave	312-922-8248	9
Bessie Coleman Public Library	731 E 63rd St	312-747-7760	18
Bezazian Public Library	1226 W Ainslie St	312-744-0019	40
Blackstone Public Library	4904 S Lake Park Ave	312-747-0511	17
Budlong Woods Public Library	5630 N Lincoln Ave	312-742-9590	35
Canaryville Public Library	642 W 43rd St	312-747-0644	15
Chicago Bee Public Library	3647 S State St	312-747-6872	14
Chicago Eckhart Park Library	1371 W Chicago Ave	312-746-6069	24
Chicago Public Library	400 S State St	312-747-4999	5
Chinatown Public Library	2353 S Wentworth Ave	312-747-8013	10
Conrad Sullzer Public Library	4455 N Lincoln Ave	312-744-7616	39
Daley Public Library	3400 S Halsted St	312-747-8990	13
Damen Avenue Library	2056 N Damen Ave	312-744-6022	28
Douglass Public LIbrary	3353 W 13th St	312-747-3725	26
Edgewater Public Library	1210 W Elmdale Ave	312-744-0718	37
Hall Public Library	4801 S Michigan Ave	312-747-2541	16
Humboldt Park Public Library	1605 N Troy St	312-744-2244	27
Illinois Regional Library for the Blind	1055 W Roosevelt Rd	312-746-9210	26
John Merlo Public Library	644 W Belmont Ave	312-744-1139	44
King Public Library	3436 S Dr Martin L King Jr Dr	312-747-7543	14
Library of Columbia College	600 S Michigan Ave	312-344-7906	9
Lincoln Park Public Library	1150 W Fullerton Ave	312-744-1926	29
Lincoln-Belmont Public Library	1659 W Melrose St	312-744-0166	42
Lozano Public Library	1805 S Loomis St	312-746-4329	26
Mabel Manning Public Library	6 S Hoyne Ave	312-746-6800	23
Malcolm X College Library	1900 W Van Buren St	312-850-7244	23
Midwest Public Library	2335 W Chicago Ave	312-744-7788	23
Municipal Reference Library	121 N La Salle St	312-744-4992	5
Near North Public Library	310 W Division St	312-744-0992	31
Newberry Library	60 W Walton St	312-943-9090	32
Northtown Public Library	6435 N California Ave	312-744-2292	33
Rogers Park Public Library	6907 N Clark St	312-744-0156	34
Roosevelt Public Library	1101 W Taylor St	312-746-5656	26
University Of Chicago Library	801 S Morgan St	312-996-2724	26
Uptown Public Library	929 W Buena Ave	312-744-8400	40
US Library	77 W Jackson Blvd	312-353-2022	5
West Town Public Library	1271 N Milwaukee Ave	312-744-1473	21

General Information • **FedEx Locations**

The last FedEx drop in Chicago is at 10 p.m. at O'Hare Airport. Get off the Kennedy at Manheim Road South. Go to Irving Park Rd. and head west to the first light. Make a right on O'Hare Cargo Area Rd. FedEx's address is Building 611, O'Hare Cargo Area Rd., 800-463-3339; www.fedex.com. *=Pick-up time, p.m. WSC=World Service Center.

Map 1

		*
Drop Box	700 N Green St	7:00
Drop Box	770 N Halsted St	7:00
Drop Box	727 N Hudson Ave	6:00
Drop Box	600 W Chicago Ave	7:30
Drop Box	400 W Erie St	7:30
Drop Box	430 W Erie St	7:30
Drop Box	445 W Erie St	7:00
Drop Box	600 W Fulton St	7:45
Drop Box	401 W Superior St	7:00

Map 2

		*
Drop Box	1 E Erie St	7:00
Drop Box	100 E Huron St	7:00
Drop Box	1 E Wacker Dr	6:30
Drop Box	35 E Wacker Dr	7:00
WSC	222 Merch Mart Plz	9:00
WSC	350 N Clark St	9:00
Drop Box	540 N Dearborn St	6:30
Drop Box	730 N Franklin St	7:30
Drop Box	414 N Orleans St	7:30
Drop Box	515 N State St	7:30
Drop Box	300 N State St	7:00
Drop Box	330 N Wabash Ave	8:30
Drop Box	401 N Wabash Ave	7:30
Drop Box	405 N Wabash Ave	7:30
Drop Box	420 N Wabash Ave	8:00
Drop Box	444 N Wabash Ave	7:00
Kinko's	444 N Wells St	8:00
Drop Box	71 W Chicago Ave	4:00
Drop Box	223 W Erie St	7:45
Drop Box	308 W Erie St	8:00
Drop Box	343 W Erie St	7:30
Drop Box	54 W Hubbard St	8:00
Drop Box	56 W Illinois St	8:00
Drop Box	20 W Kinzie St	7:00
Drop Box	225 W Ohio St	7:00
Drop Box	320 W Ohio St	8:00
Drop Box	1 W Superior St	7:30
Drop Box	311 W Superior St	7:30
Drop Box	205 W Wacker Dr	8:00
Drop Box	225 W Wacker Dr	7:00
Drop Box	55 W Wacker Dr	6:30
Drop Box	77 W Wacker Dr	8:00
Image Direct	211 W Wacker Dr	4:30
Drop Box	68 Wacker Place	4:15

Map 3

		*
Drop Box	211 E Chicago Ave	7:30
Drop Box	233 E Erie St	8:00
Drop Box	251 E Huron St	7:30
Drop Box	9 E Huron St	5:00
Drop Box	150 E Huron St	7:30
Drop Box	401 E Illinois St	7:00
Drop Box	455 E Illinois St	7:00
Drop Box	303 E Ohio St	7:30
Drop Box	142 E Ontario St	7:00
Drop Box	211 E Ontario St	7:30
Drop Box	240 E Ontario St	7:30
Drop Box	333 E Ontario St	7:30
Drop Box	474 N LSD	7:00
Drop Box	505 N LSD	8:00
Drop Box	680 N LSD	7:00
Drop Box	400 N McClurg Ct	7:30
Drop Box	440 N McClurg Ct	7:00
Drop Box	400 N Michigan Ave	8:00
Drop Box	401 N Michigan Ave	8:00
Drop Box	430 N Michigan Ave	7:15
Drop Box	435 N Michigan Ave	7:00
Drop Box	444 N Michigan Ave	7:30
Drop Box	625 N Michigan Ave	7:30
Drop Box	645 N Michigan Ave	7:30
Drop Box	676 N Michigan Ave	7:00
Drop Box	737 N Michigan Ave	8:00
WSC	500 N Michigan Ave	9:00
Kinko's	540 N Michigan Ave	6:00
Drop Box	360 N Michigan Ave	7:00
Drop Box	701 N Michigan Ave	7:30
Drop Box	676 N Saint Clair St	7:30
Drop Box	633 N Saint Clair St	7:30

Map 4

		*
Drop Box	100 N Riverside Plz	7:00
Drop Box	2 N Riverside Plz	7:00
Drop Box	118 S Clinton St	6:00
Kinko's	127 S Clinton St	7:00
Drop Box	322 S Green St	7:00
Drop Box	130 S Jefferson St	6:00
Drop Box	216 S Jefferson St	5:30
Drop Box	10 S Riverside Plz	7:00
Drop Box	120 S Riverside Plz	7:00
Drop Box	222 S Riverside Plz	8:00
Drop Box	300 S Riverside Plz	7:35
Drop Box	547 W Jackson Blvd	7:00
Drop Box	600 W Jackson Blvd	6:30
Drop Box	820 W Jackson Blvd	7:00
Drop Box	833 W Jackson Blvd	7:30
Drop Box	850 W Jackson Blvd	7:00
Drop Box	641 W Lake St	6:00
Drop Box	555 W Madison St	7:30
Drop Box	500 W Madison St	7:00
WSC	500 W Madison St	9:00
Drop Box	500 W Monroe St	7:00
Kinko's	843 W Van Buren St	7:45
Drop Box	550 W Washington	7:00
Drop Box	651 W Washington	6:00

Map 5

		*
Drop Box	11 E Adams St	7:00
Drop Box	1 E Jackson Blvd	6:30
Drop Box	55 E Jackson Blvd	6:30
Drop Box	70 E Lake St	7:00
Drop Box	29 E Madison St	8:00
Kinko's	55 E Monroe St	6:00
Drop Box	35 E Wacker Dr	7:00
Drop Box	25 E Washington St	6:30
Drop Box	171 N Clark St	7:00
Drop Box	33 N Dearborn St	7:00
Drop Box	1 N Franklin St	8:00
Drop Box	100 N La Salle St	7:00
Drop Box	120 N La Salle St	7:30
Drop Box	134 N La Salle St	8:00
Drop Box	200 N La Salle St	8:00
Drop Box	222 N La Salle St	8:00
Drop Box	30 N La Salle St	6:30
WSC	2 N La Salle St	9:00
WSC	203 N La Salle St	9:00
Drop Box	1 N State St	7:00
Drop Box	180 N Wabash Ave	7:30
Drop Box	203 N Wabash Ave	6:30
Drop Box	123 N Wacker Dr	7:30
Drop Box	150 N Wacker Dr	7:00
Drop Box	155 N Wacker Dr	7:00
Drop Box	20 N Wacker Dr	7:00
Drop Box	29 N Wacker Dr	7:00
WSC	101 N Wacker Dr	8:00
Drop Box	191 N Wacker Dr	7:00
Drop Box	210 S Clark St	8:00
Drop Box	20 S Clark St	7:00
WSC	136 S Dearborn	9:00
Drop Box	2 S Dearborn St	7:30
Drop Box	219 S Dearborn St	5:00
Drop Box	230 S Dearborn St	5:00
Drop Box	407 S Dearborn St	7:30
WSC	400 S La Salle	7:00
Drop Box	135 S La Salle St	7:30
Drop Box	115 S La Salle St	8:00
Drop Box	190 S La Salle St	8:00
Drop Box	208 S La Salle St	7:45
Drop Box	209 S La Salle St	6:00
Drop Box	29 S La Salle St	7:00
Drop Box	247 S State St	7:00
Drop Box	401 S State St	7:00
Drop Box	243 S Wabash Ave	6:30
Drop Box	36 S Wabash Ave	7:30
Drop Box	36 S Wabash Ave	7:30
Drop Box	1 S Wacker Dr	7:00
Drop Box	125 S Wacker Dr	8:00
Drop Box	150 S Wacker Dr	8:00
Drop Box	200 S Wacker Dr	7:00
Drop Box	250 S Wacker Dr	7:30
Drop Box	30 S Wacker Dr	7:00
Drop Box	300 S Wacker Dr	7:00
Drop Box	311 S Wacker Dr	7:45
WSC	233 S Wacker Dr	6:30
Drop Box	200 W Adams St	7:00
Drop Box	111 W Jackson Blvd	7:00
Drop Box	175 W Jackson Blvd	7:30
WSC	200 W Jackson Blvd	9:00
Drop Box	53 W Jackson Blvd	7:00
Kinko's	6 W Lake St	8:00
Drop Box	105 W Madison St	7:30
Drop Box	200 W Madison St	7:45
Drop Box	303 W Madison St	7:00
Drop Box	100 W Monroe St	8:00
Drop Box	200 W Monroe St	8:00
Drop Box	230 W Monroe St	7:00
Drop Box	30 W Monroe St	7:00
WSC	227 W Monroe St	9:00
Drop Box	100 W Randolph St	6:00
Drop Box	188 W Randolph St	6:30
Drop Box	205 W Randolph St	8:00
Drop Box	333 W Wacker Dr	9:00
Drop Box	309 W Washington	7:00
Drop Box	225 W Washington	7:00
WSC	111 W Washington	7:00
Drop Box	65 Wacker Dr	6:30

Map 6

		*
Drop Box	200 E Randolph St	8:00
Drop Box	300 E Randolph St	8:00
WSC	130 E Randolph St	9:00
Drop Box	200 E Randolph St	4:30
Sullivan's	111 E Wacker Dr	5:00
Drop Box	155 N Michigan Ave	7:00
Drop Box	20 N Michigan Ave	7:00
Drop Box	30 N Michigan Ave	8:00
Drop Box	307 N Michigan Ave	7:00
Drop Box	333 N Michigan Ave	7:00
WSC	150 N Michigan Ave	8:30
WSC	180 N Michigan Ave	8:30
Drop Box	233 N Michigan Ave	6:00
WSC	225 N Michigan Ave	9:00
Drop Box	200 S Michigan Ave	7:00
Drop Box	224 S Michigan Ave	7:00
Drop Box	310 S Michigan Ave	7:00
Drop Box	332 S Michigan Ave	7:45
Drop Box	430 S Michigan Ave	7:00
Drop Box	8 S Michigan Ave	7:30
WSC	34 S Michigan Ave	9:00

Map 8 *

Drop Box	33 E Congress Pkwy	6:00
Drop Box	640 N La Salle St	7:00
Drop Box	734 N La Salle St	4:30
Drop Box	536 S Clark St	7:30
Drop Box	542 S Dearborn St	7:00
Drop Box	600 S Federal St	7:00
Drop Box	819 S Wabash Ave	5:30
Drop Box	700 S Wabash Ave	7:00
Drop Box	800 S Wells St	7:30
Drop Box	47 W Polk St	7:00

Map 9 *

Drop Box	1000 N LSD	7:00

Map 10 *

Kinko's	1242 S Canal St	8:00
Drop Box	2345 S Wentworth	6:30
Drop Box	329 W 18th St	7:30

Map 11 *

Drop Box	1211 S Michigan	7:00
Drop Box	1347 S State St	7:30
Drop Box	2035 S State St	5:00

Map 12 *

Drop Box	3757 S Ashland Ave	6:30
Drop Box	3737 S Ashland Ave	6:30

Map 13 *

Drop Box	3300 S Federal St	6:00

Map 14 *

Drop Box	3200 S Wabash Ave	6:30
Drop Box	10 W 35th St	6:00

Map 17 *

Co-op Mkts	1300 E 47th St	5:00

Map 19 *

Drop Box	1525 E 53rd St	7:00
Drop Box	1554 E 55th St	7:00
Kinko's	1315 E 57th St	7:00
Drop Box	956 E 58th St	6:30
Drop Box	1126 E 59th St	6:30
Drop Box	1155 E 60th St	7:00
Drop Box	59th & Kimbark	6:30
Drop Box	5801 S Ellis Ave	7:00
Drop Box	5841 S Maryland	6:30
Drop Box	57th & University	6:30

Map 20 *

Post Link	1634 E 53rd St	5:30

Map 21 *

CopyMax	1573 N Milwaukee	6:00
Drop Box	1608 N Milwaukee	7:00
Drop Box	2233 W Division St	6:30
Kinko's	1800 W North Ave	8:00

Map 22 *

Drop Box	935 W Chestnut St	7:30
WSC	875 W Division St	9:45
WSC	875 W Division St	9:45
Drop Box	848 W Eastman St	7:30
Box Shoppe	1001 W North Ave	7:00

Map 23 *

Drop Box	2023 W Carroll Ave	5:30
Packaging& Shipping Specialists	2002 W Chicago Ave	6:00
Drop Box	1700 W Van Buren	7:00

Map 24 *

Drop Box	216 N May St	7:00
Drop Box	400 N Noble St	7:00
Drop Box	1550 W Carroll Ave	6:30
Drop Box	1030 W Chicago	5:00
Drop Box	901 W Jackson Blvd	7:00
WSC	1260 W Madison	9:00
Drop Box	1260 W Madison St	8:00
Drop Box	1436 W Randolph	6:30
Drop Box	1017 W Washington	8:30
Drop Box	1327 W Washington	7:30

Map 25 *

Drop Box	820 S Damen Ave	6:00
Drop Box	715 S Wood St	7:00
Drop Box	840 S Wood St	7:00
Drop Box	1725 W Harrison St	6:30

Map 26 *

Drop Box	851 S Morgan St	5:30
Drop Box	1100 W Cermak Rd	6:30
Drop Box	1201 W Harrison St	6:30

Map 27 *

Post Net	2820 W North Ave	5:00

Map 28 *

Drop Box	2355 N Damen Ave	7:00
Drop Box	2525 N Elston Ave	7:30
Drop Box	1644 N Honore St	6:30
Drop Box	1965 N Milwaukee	4:00
Drop Box	1735 N Paulina St	6:30
CopyMax	1829 W Fullerton	7:00

Map 29 *

Drop Box	1870 N Clybourn	7:00
Drop Box	1925 N Clybourn	7:00
Kinko's	2300 N Clybourn	8:00
Drop Box	2000 N Racine Ave	7:00
Drop Box	2323 N Seminary	7:00
Drop Box	990 W Fullerton	7:15

Map 30 *

Drop Box	1749 N Wells St	7:00
Drop Box	802 W Belden Ave	7:15

Map 31 *

Drop Box	900 N Franklin St	8:00
Drop Box	1332 N Halsted St	7:45
Drop Box	1010 N Hooker St	4:00
Drop Box	900 N Kingsbury St	5:30
Drop Box	820 N Orleans St	7:30
Drop Box	1350 N Wells St	6:00
Drop Box	1030 W Chicago	8:00
Drop Box	213 W Institute Pl	7:30
Drop Box	393 W North Ave	6:00

Map 32 *

Drop Box	1 E Delaware Pl	7:30
Drop Box	100 E Walton St	7:30
Drop Box	163 E Walton St	7:30
Drop Box	1165 N Clark St	6:30
Kinko's	1201 N Dearborn St	8:00
Drop Box	875 N Michigan Ave	6:30
Drop Box	900 N Michigan Ave	7:00
Drop Box	919 N Michigan Ave	7:00
Drop Box	980 N Michigan Ave	7:30
WSC	875 N Michigan Ave	9:00
Drop Box	844 N Rush St	6:00
Drop Box	884 N Rush St	6:00
Postal Plus	1151 N State St	6:00

Map 33 *

Drop Box	7555 N California	7:15
Unik Business	2337 W Devon Ave	7:15

Map 34 *

Drop Box	7056 N Clark St	6:00
Drop Box	1723 W Devon Ave	7:00

Map 37 *

Drop Box	5419 N Sheridan Rd	7:30

Map 38 *

Drop Box	2522 W Lawrence	7:00

Map 39 *

Drop Box	2011 W Montrose	3:30
Remesas	1924 W Montrose	6:00
Drop Box	1807 W Sunnyside	7:30

Map 40 *

Drop Box	4850 Broadway	6:30
Drop Box	4753 N Broadway	6:30
Drop Box	4600 N Clarendon	7:30
Mailstop & More	1338 W Irving Park Rd	5:30

Map 41 *

Drop Box	3401 N California	7:00
Drop Box	3611 N Kedzie Ave	7:00
Drop Box	2630 W Bradley Pl	6:30

Map 42 *

Drop Box	3717 N Ravenswood	7:00
Kinko's	3435 N Western Ave	7:45
Mailbox Plus	2154 W Addison St	6:00
Drop Box	1800 W Larchmont	7:00

Map 43 *

Drop Box	3024 N Ashland	4:00
Mail Boxes Etc	3105 N Ashland	6:00
Drop Box	2940 N Ashland	7:00
Drop Box	2835 N Sheffield	7:30
Kinko's	3524 N Southport	7:30
Drop Box	1300 W Belmont	7:00

Map 44 *

Pak Mail	3176 N Broadway	5:30
Postal Place	3304 N Broadway	6:00
Kinko's	3001 N Clark St	8:00
Drop Box	3660 N LSD	7:30
Drop Box	2800 N Sheridan Rd	7:00
Postal Plus	559 W Diversey	6:00
PostNet	636 W Diversey	6:00

Chicago's lesbian and gay communities are a diverse, politically influential Chicago entity. Just look to the pride pylons lining North Halsted Street, the city's officially recognized gay ghetto, as well as the numerous city politicians who vie for a prime spot in the city's annual gay pride parade, which attracts over 200,000 spectators and participants on the last Sunday in June.

Websites

Pride Time: http://www.pridetime.com
Chicago gay and lesbian information and resource guide for bars and restaurants, music and theater, health and fitness, style, current events, and free weekly prizes.

Horizons Community Services: http://www.horizonsonline.org
Horizons is the Midwest's largest lesbian, gay, bisexual, and transgendered social service agency.

Chicago Area Gay and Lesbian Chamber of Commerce: http://www.glchamber.org/
Chicago's online gay and lesbian business guide offers an index of members, membership info, and supportive businesses.

Chicago's Gay and Lesbian Professional Networking Association: http://www.cpna.org/
Check out the regular events for Chicago's professional gay and lesbian community, join the club, find a job, or read articles about important issues.

Alternative Phone Book: http://www.prairienet.org/apb/
Chicago's Lesbigay Yellow Pages.

About Face Theatre: http://www.aboutfacetheatre.com
About Face Theatre is a group of gay, lesbian, and straight artists committed to the creation of performances that examine queer lives, histories, and experiences. Check their website for performance schedule, tickets, and subscription details. They also have a Youth Theatre group and to be eligible youth must be between the ages of 14 and 20, and must be able to participate in the weekly workshops. Check the site for details.

Alternative Connections: http://www.mygaypartner.com
Your online Chicago gay and lesbian dating service.

Dyke Diva: http://www.dykediva.com
Up-to-date info about what's going on in the lesbian scene in Chicago.

SANGAT: http://hometown.aol.com/youngal/sangat.html
Gay and lesbian organization and support group for the people from India, Pakistan, Bangladesh, Sri Lanka, Nepal, Afghanistan, Iran, Burma, and the rest of the Sub-Continent.

Gay, Lesbian and Straight Education Network (GLSEN): http://members.aol.com/glsenchgo/index.html
This group brings together a wide variety of people who actively care about ending homophobia in schools. Everyone (regardless of occupation or sexual orientation) is welcome to get involved, so check out their site for more info.

Early2Bed: http://www.early2bed.com/pages/home.html
Woman-owned sex shop online; store location at 5232 Sheridan Rd.

Women in the Director's Chair: http://www.widc.org
This organization features lots of lesbian and transgender films and events.

Thousand Waves Spa: http://www.thousandwaves.com/twspa/
This is a women-only spa with a strong lesbian presence (not to be confused with the proverbial "bathhouse.")

Windy City Radio: http://www.windycityradio.com/home.html
Gay radio program on WCKG-Radio, 105.9 on Sunday nights at 10:30 p.m. to midnight

Publications

Pick up a copy of the following publications to find out what's happening around town, from the current political headlines to the most happening clubs. They can be found in gay-friendly bookstores, cafes, bars, and various shops.

Windy City Times: http://www.wctimes.com
Gay and Lesbian news weekly—check this site for happenings around town.

En La Vida: http://www.outlineschicago.com/enlavida.html
Monthly gay, lesbian, bisexual, and transgender publication for Latinos.

Black Lines: http://www.outlineschicago.com/blacklines.html
Expressions from Black gay, lesbian, bisexual, and transgendered life featuring news articles reflections, calendar, arts, and advertising.

Nightspots: http://www.outlineschicago.com/nightlines.html
Articles, astrology, and happenings around town.

Out Guide: http://www.windycitytimes.com/Ooutguide/out1.html
Comprehensive GLBT resource guide with listings for services including carpenters, real estate brokers, accounting services, social services, media, computers, bars, bowling alleys, and restaurants.

Chicago Free Press: http:// www.chicagofreepress.com/
Popular publication with features on political issues, arts, culture, spiritual life, entertainment, and resources lists.

Gay Chicago: http://www.gaychicagomag.com/
One of the city's oldest gay publications with events listings, columns, news, astrology and reviews.

Bookstores

Women & Children First Books: 5233 N. Clark St., 773-769-9299
This 20 year-old lesbian resource in Andersonville is the largest feminist bookstore in the world.

Unabridged Books: 3251 N. Broadway St., 773-883-9119
Located in the heart of the North Side gay community, you will find a well annotated lesbigay section, as well as general books and magazines.

Gerber/Hart Gay and Lesbian Library and Archives: 1127 W. Granville St., 773-381-8030
While not actually a "bookstore," this amazing library houses more than 10,000 books, magazines, newspapers, and videos. For special events including readings and screenings, check the website at www.gerberhart.org.

Barbara's Bookstore: 1110 N. Lake St, Oak Park
Gay-friendly bookstore with a large selection of gay and lesbian fiction and non-fiction titles.

Seminary Cooperative Bookstore: 5757 University Ave., 773-752-4381
Located in Hyde Park, this bookstore has sections on GLBT studies.

57th Street Books: 1301 E. 57th St., 773-684-1300
Another Hyde Park bookstore with a strong GLBT section.

Health Center & Support Organizations

Horizons Community Services: The Midwest's largest lesbian, gay, bisexual, and transgendered social service agency. http://www.horizonsonline.org

Lesbian and Gay Help Line: 773-929-HELP (6 pm until 10 pm)

The Crisis Hotline/Anti-Violence Project: 773-871-CARE

Legal Services: 773-929-HELP, legal@horizonsonline.org

Mature Adult Program: 773-472-6469 ext. 245, perryw@horizonsonline.org

Psychotherapy Services: 773-472-6469 ext. 261, sarag@horizonsonline.org

Youth Services: 773-472-6469, ext. 252, premp@horizonsonline.org

Illinois State HIV/AIDS/STD Hotline: 772-AID-AIDS

AIDS Foundation of Chicago: 411 Wells St., Ste 300, Chicago, IL 60607, 312-922-2322

AIDSCARE: 315 W. Barry, Chicago, IL 60657, 773-935-4663

GLAAD Chicago: P.O. Box 46343, Chicago, IL 60614, 773-871-7633

PFLAG Chicago: P.O. Box 11023, Chicago, IL 60611, 773-472-3079

Howard Brown Health Center: 4025 N. Sheridan Rd., 773-388-8882. Anonymous, free AIDS testing and GLBT Domestic Violence Counseling and Prevention Program

Support Groups: http://www.prairienet.org/apb/Frames.html Many support groups exist for men, women and families in Chicago. Check out the LesBiGay Yellow Pages for more information about the groups.

Lesbian Community Cancer Project 4753 N Broadway, 773-561-4662. Support and resources for lesbians with cancer. Free quit-smoking clinics.

AA – New Town Alano Club 909 W Belmont, 2nd fl. 773-529-0321 Gay and lesbian AA , CA, OA, ACOA, Coda, etc.

Venues

Gay

- **Anvil** • 1137 W Granville St • 773-973-0006
- **Bucks Saloon** • 3439 N Halsted St • 773-525-1125
- **Cell Block** • 3702 N Halsted St • 773-665-8064
- **Charlie's** • 3726 N Broadway St • 773-871-8887
- **Chicago Eagle** • 5015 N Clark St • 773-728-0050
- **Different Strokes** • 4923 N Clark St • 773-989-1958
- **Hideaway** • 7301 W Roosevelt Rd, Forest Park • 708-771-4459
- **Hunter's** • 1932 E Higgins Rd, Elk Grove Village • 847-439-8840
- **Legacy '21** • 3042 W Irving Park Rd • 773-588-9405
- **Little Jims** • 3501 N Halsted St • 773-871-6116
- **Lucky Horseshoe** • 3169 N Halsted St • 773-404-3169
- **Madrigals** • 5316 N Clark • 773-334-3033
- **Manhandler** • 1948 N Halsted St • 773-871-3339
- **Manhole** • 3458 N Halsted St • 773-975-9244
- **North End** • 3733 N Halsted St • 773-477-7999
- **Nutbush** • 7201 W Franklin St, Forest Park • 708-366-5117
- **Second Story Bar** • 157 E Ohio St • 312-923-9536
- **Sidetrack** • 3349 N Halsted St • 773-477-9189
- **Touche** • 6412 N Clark St • 773-465-7400

Lesbian

- **The Closet** • 3325 N Broadway St • 773-477-8533
- **Club Intimus** • 312 W Randolph St • 312-901-1703
- **Lost & Found** • 3058 W Irving Park Rd • 773-463-7599
- **The Patch** • 201 155th St, Calumet City • 708-891-9854
- **Pour House** • 103 155th St, Calumet City • 708-891-3980
- **StarGaze** •5419 N Clark St • 773-561-7363
- **Temptations** • 10235 W Grand Ave, Franklin Park • 847-455-0008

Both

- **Berlin** • 54 W Belmont Ave • 773-348-4975
- **Big Chicks** • 5024 N Sheridan Rd • 773-728-5511
- **Bobby Loves** • 3729 N Halsted St • 773-525-1200
- **Buddies' Bar & Restaurant** • 3301 N Clark St • 773-477-4066
- **Circuit / Rehab** • 3641 N Halsted St • 773-325-2233
- **Clark's on Clark** • 5001 N Clark St • 773-728-2373
- **Club Escape** • 1530 E 75th St • 773-667-6454
- **Cocktail** • 3359 N Halsted St • 773-477-1420
- **Gentry on Halsted** • 3320 N Halsted St • 773-348-1053
- **Gentry on State** • 440 N State St • 312-836-0933
- **Jeffery Pub** • 7041 S Jeffery St • 773-363-8555
- **Roscoe's** • 3356 N Halsted St • 773-281-3355
- **Scot's** • 1829 W Montrose Ave • 773-528-3253
- **Spin Nightclub** • Halsted St & Belmont Ave • 773-327-7711
- **T's Bar & Restaurant** • 5025 N Clark St • 773-784-6000

Map 1 • River North / Fulton Market District

The Blommer Chocolate Co • 600 W Kinzie St • 312-226-7700 Opened in 1939. Eventually became largest commercial chocolate manufacturer in the U.S.

Map 2 • Near North / River North

Courthouse Place • 54 W Hubbard St — This Romanesque-style former courthouse has witnessed many legendary trials.

House of Blues • 329 N Dearborn St • 312-923-2000 — Concert venue, hotel, and bowling alley.

Marina Towers • 300 N State St — Two weird-looking condo buildings nestled on the edge of Chicago River.

Merchandise Mart • 222 Merchandise Mart Plz — Houses furniture showrooms and a small mall.

Sotheby's • 215 W Ohio St • 312-396-9599 — Renowned auction house.

Map 3 • Streeterville / Magnificent Mile

Navy Pier • 600 E Grand Ave — A bastion of Chicago tourism.

Tribune Tower • 435 N Michigan Ave — Check out the stones from famous buildings around the world.

Map 4 • West Loop Gate / Greektown

Dugan's Drinking Emporium • 128 S Halsted St • 312-421-7191 Sports bar in Greektown fantastic beer garden and favorite cop hangout.

Union Station • 200 S Canal St — Built in 1925, the architecture is not to be missed!

Zorba's House Restaurant • 301 S Halsted St • 312-454-1397 — 24-hour Greek food-hangout for cops and hospital workers; everybody ends up here sooner or later.

Map 5 • The Loop

Chicago Board of Trade • 141 W Jackson Blvd — The goddess Ceres tops this deco monolith.

Chicago Board Options Exchange • 400 S La Salle St

Chicago Cultural Center • 78 E Washington • 312-744-FINEART The spot for free lectures, exhibits, concerts and movies.

Chicago Mercantile Exchange • 20-30 S Wacker Dr

Chicago Stock Exchange • 440 S La Salle St

Daley Civic Plaza • 50 W Washington St — Home of Picasso sculpture, Christmas tree ceremony, and alfresco lunches.

Harold Washington Library Center • 400 S State St • 312-747-4300 — The world's largest public library building; nearly 100 works of art on every floor.

Sears Tower • 233 S Wacker Dr • 312-875-9696 — World's tallest building, cool skydeck.

Map 6 • The Loop / Grant Park

Art Institute of Chicago • 111 S Michigan Ave • 312-443-3600 World-class art museum.

Auditorium Building • 430 S Michigan Ave — Designed by Louis Sullivan; on National Register of Historic Places.

Buckingham Fountain • Grant Park, between Balbo & Columbus • 312-747-2474 — Dazzling landmark that boasts a music, light, and water show every hour on the hour until 11 pm.

Fine Arts Building • 410 S Michigan Ave — Frank Lloyd Wright had an office here.

Symphony Center • 22 S Michigan Ave • 312-294-3000 — Classical music headquarters.

Map 7 • South Loop / River City

Old Post Office • 404 W Harrison St — Straddling 90/94 and 290 as they enter downtown, this massive edifice continues to act as a benchmark for traffic reports.

River City • 800 S Wells St — A fluid cement design flop by architect Bartrand Goldberg.

US Postal Distribution Center • 433 W Harrison St — The city's main mail routing center, employing over 6,000 people and operating 24 hours a day

Map 8 • South Loop / Printer's Row / Dearborn Park

Former Elliot Ness Building • 618 S Dearborn St — Former headquarters of Elliot Ness, head of the Untouchables. Ness arranged Al Capone's delivery to prison at the Dearborn Station just down the street, so he could personally view his exit from Chicago. Now it's an insurance agency.

Columbia College Center for Book & Paper Arts • 1104 S Wabash Ave, 2nd Floor • 312-344-6630 — Two galleries feature changing exhibits of handmade books, paper, letterpress, and related objects.

Old Dearborn Train Station • 47 W Polk St — Beautiful turn-of-the-century train station with a lighted clocktower visible for several blocks at the end of Dearborn and Polk. Rich history includes being the station Al Capone was sent from Chicago to prison.

Pacific Garden Mission • 646 S State St — Keepin' it real in the south Loop.

Map 9 • South Loop / S Michigan Ave

Buckingham Fountain • Columbus Dr and East Congress Pkwy — Built of pink marble; inspired by Versailles.

Chicago Hilton and Towers • 720 S Michigan Ave — Check out the frescoes in the lobby; sneak a kiss in the palatial ballroom.

Julian and Doris Wineberg Sculpture Garden • 681 S Michigan Ave — A tranquil spot to ponder traffic on Michigan Ave.

Shedd Aquarium • 1200 S Lake Shore Drive • 312-939-2435 — Marine and freshwater creatures from around the world are on view in this 1929 Classical Greek-inspired Beaux Arts structure.

Map 10 • East Pilsen / Chinatown

Chinatown Square • S Archer Ave — Near S. Wentworth in the Chinatown Square Plaza.

Map 11 • South Loop / McCormick Place

America's Courtyard • South of Adler Planetarium on the lakefront — A spiral of stones that echoes both the milky way and ancient structures. Artists: Denise Milan and Ary R. Perez.

Clarke House • 1827 S Indiana Ave — Built c. 1836 by an unknown architect, this Greek Revival-style home has been relocated twice and is now a designated Chicago landmark. Part of the Prairie Avenue Historic District.

Field Museum • 1400 S Lake Shore Dr • 312-922-9410

Hillary Rodham Clinton Women's Park and Gardens of Chicago • Prairie, between 18th and 19th

Hyatt Regency McCormick Place • 2233 S Dr Martin L King Jr Dr • 312-567-1234

McCormick Place • 2301 S Lake Shore Drive — Hard to miss.

Monument to the Great Northern Migration • S Dr Martin L King Jr Dr, just before Stevenson Expressway — Statue depicts man standing on pile of worn shoes, representing the journey of African-Americans from the south. Artist: Alison Saar.

National Vietnam Veterans Art Museum • 1801 S Indiana Ave • 312-326-0270 — Features art about the war created by Vietnam veterans from all sides of the conflict.

Quinn Chapel, African Methodist Episcopal Church • 2401 S Wabash Ave — Built in 1892, this Victorian Gothic-style church houses Chicago's oldest African-American congregation. The chapel has been host to famous speakers and performers, including George Washington Carter, Martin Luther King, and Patti LaBelle.

Raymond Hilliard Homes • 2030 S State St — Designed by Bertrand Goldberg (also the designer of the nearby River City apartments), this public housing complex has long been admired by architects. Plans are underway to rehab the buildings into upscale rental apartments.

Second Presbyterian Church • 1936 S Michigan Ave — This Gothic Revival-style church, frequented by the wealthy denizens of Prairie Avenue, was built in 1874 by James Renwirk and reconstructed in 1900 by Howard Van Doren Shaw.

Soldier Field • 425 E McFetridge Dr — This concert venue and Chicago Bears stadium is under renovation until 2003.

The Chicago Daily Defender • 2400 S Michigan Ave • 312-225-5656 — Founded in 1905, this became the country's most influential black newspaper through the 1950s. Still in operation, the much-diminished Defender has been at the center of an ownership battle since 1997.

The Wheeler Mansion • 2020 S Calumet Ave • 312-945-2020 — This Second Empire-style mansion now houses a boutique hotel for high-end travelers.

Willie Dixon's Blues Heaven Foundation • 2120 S Michigan Ave • 312-808-1286 — Located in the former Chess Records studio, where several influential 1960s blues and rock albums were recorded, this foundation offers tours, exhibits, and performances, along with workshops and support for emerging musicians. Call for hours.

Women Made Gallery • 1900 S Prairie Ave • 312-328-0038 — This gallery and gift shop, located in the historic Keith House, showcases contemporary women's art Wed, Th, Fri: Noon-7 pm; Sat, Sun: Noon-4 pm

Map 12 • Bridgeport (West)

Library Fountain • W 34th & Halsted

Monastery of the Holy Cross • 3111 S Aberdeen — Have your breakfast served by monks in this bed & breakfast monastery.

Wilson Park • S May & W 34th Pl

Map 13 • Bridgeport (East)

McGuane Park • W 29th St & S Halsted

Richard J Daley House • 3536 S Lowe Ave — Childhood home of Mayor Richard J. Daley.

The Old Neighborhood Italian American Club • 3031 S Shields Ave

Map 14 • Prairie Shores / Lake Meadows

Benches • S Dr Martin L King Jr Dr btn E 33rd-E 35th St
Douglas Tomb State Historical Site • E 35th St & Lake Park (entrance on east side of Lake)
Dunbar Park • S Indiana & E 31st St

Map 15 • Canaryville / Fuller Park

Union Stockyard Gate • Exchange Ave & Peoria St — This limestone gate marks the place that made Chicago the Hog Butcher to the World.

Map 16 • Bronzeville

Fountain • S Drexel Blvd @ E Oakwood Blvd
Historic Walk • S Drexel Blvd & E Hyde Park Blvd
Metcalf Park • S State St @ E 43rd St
Mural • S Cottage Grove Ave & E 41st St
Murals • S Dr Martin L King Jr Dr & E 40th St
Track • S Cottage Grove Ave & E Oakwood Blvd

Map 17 • North Kenwood / Oakland

South Kenwood Mansions • Between S Dorchester (east) and S Ellis, (West), and S Hyde Park Blvd (south) and E 47th (north) — Built in the early 1900s by wealthy businessmen who wanted to flee the cramped North Side. Once in a state of disrepair, the mansions have (mostly) been rehabbed, and are once again the Jewels of the South Side.

Map 18 • Washington Park

DuSable Museum of African-American History • 740 E 56th Pl — Founded in 1961 and dedicated to preserving and honoring African-American culture, the museum is the oldest not-for-profit institution of its kind.
Former Home of Jesse Binga • 5922 S Dr Martin L King Jr Dr — Home of nation's first African-American banker.
Washington Park • E 60th St thru E 51st St from S Cottage Grove Ave to S Dr Martin L King Jr Dr
Washington Park Aquatic Ctr & Refectory • 5531 S Russell Dr

Map 19 • Hyde Park / Woodlawn

Frederick C Robie House • 5757 S Woodlawn Ave — Designed by Frank Lloyd Wright, preservation trust property.
Midway Plaisance Park & Skating Rink • S Ellis Ave & S University Ave, between E 59th St to E 60th St
Rockefeller Memorial Chapel • 1156 E 59th Ave — Authentic English catherdral built in 1928.

Map 20 • Hyde Park East / Jackson Park

Osaka Garden/Wooded Island • Just south of the Museum of Science and Industry, between the West and East Lagoons — A Japanese garden in the middle of Jackson Park—why not?
Promontory Point Park • 5491 S Shore Dr — Picnic with a view.

Map 21 • Wicker Park / Ukrainian Village

Crumbling Bucktown • 1579 N Milwaukee Ave — Structural icon seen from miles away; nucleus of Around the Coyote Arts Festival
Division Street Russian Bath • 1916 W Division St — Treat yourself to an old-school style day at the spa, complete with Swedish massages and granite heating room.
Holy Trinity Orthodox Cathedral and Rectory • 1121 N Leavitt St — Designed by Louis Sullivan to look like Russian provincial catherdrals known to churchgoers when it was built in 1903.
The Coyote Building • 1600 N Milwaukee Ave — This 12-story Art Deco building was built in 1929.
The Flat Iron Building • 1579 N Milwaukee Ave — This distinct triangular-shaped building is a part of the Chicago Coalition of Community Cultural Centers and houses artist studios.
Wicker Park District • Pierce and Hoyne Streets — The homes in this district reflect the style of Old Chicago.

Map 22 • Noble Square / Goose Island

Morton Salt Elston Facility • Elston Ave & Blackhawk St — Has a painting of the famous salt girl.
Nelson Algren Fountain • Division St & Ashland Blvd — Recent, and controversial, addition.
North Avenue Bridge — Wretched traffic jams; river view.
Polish Museum of America • 984 N Milwaukee Ave — Right to life painting on the side.
Pulaski Park/Pulaski Fieldhouse • Blackhawk St & Cleaver St — Has an outdoor swimming pool.
St Stanislaus Kostka Church • 1351 W Evergreen Ave — One of the oldest in Chicago.
Weed St District • Between Chicago River & Halsted St — Several bars and clubs in one area.

Map 23 • West Town / Near West Side

First Baptist Congregational Church • 60 N Ashland Ave — Official Chicago landmark.

Metropolitan Missionary Baptist Church • 2151 W Washington Blvd — Official Chicago landmark.

Ukrainian Cultural Center • 2247 W Chicago Ave — A gathering place to share and celebrate Ukrainian culture.

Ukrainian National Museum • 721 N Oakley Blvd — Museum, library, and archives detail the heritage, culture, and people of Ukraine.

United Center • 1901 W Madison St — Statue of His Airness still draws tourists.

Map 24 • River West / West Town / Near West Side

Eckhart Park/Ida Crown Natatorium • Noble St & Chicago Ave — One of two swimming pools in the area.

Goldblatt Bros Department Store • 1613-35 W Chicago Ave — Official Chicago landmark.

Harpo Studios • 1058 W Washington Blvd • 312-591-9222 — Home of the Oprah Winfrey Show.

Map 27 • Logan Square (South)

Illinois Centennial Monument • 3100 W Logan Blvd — A well-known landmark to orient visitors, some neighbors feel that this eagle-topped obelisk stands for Logan Square.

Map 28 • Bucktown

Margie's Candies • 1960 N Western Ave — This old-fashioned ice cream shop is known all over the world for its nostalgic charm and awesome homemade goodies.

Map 29 • DePaul / Wrightwood / Sheffield

Biograph Theater • 2433 N Lincoln Ave — This was site of the gangster John Dillinger's infamous death in 1934. Today it still functions as one of Chicago's oldest movie theaters.

Courtland Street Drawbridge • 1440 W Cortland St — Built in 1902 by John Ernst Erickson, this innovative leaf-lift bridge changed the way the world built bridges.

McCormick Row House District • 800 blocks of Chalmers, Fullerton, and Belden Streets. — Quaint example of late 19th century urban planning and architecture.

Map 30 • Lincoln Park

Dewes Mansion • 503 N Wrightwood Ave — Ornate historic home done in the German baroque style and built in 1896.

Kauffman Store and Flats • 2312-14 N Lincoln Ave — One of the oldest existing buildings designed by Adler and Sullivan. It's amazing that its characteristic features have survived.

Lincoln Park Boat Club • Cannon Dr/Fullerton Ave

Lincoln Park Conservatory • 2400 N Stockton Dr — Sister to Garfield Park Conservatory. Built in 1891.

Lincoln Park Cultural Center • 2045 N Lincoln Park W

Lincoln Park Zoo • Cannon Dr @ Fullerton Pkwy — Oldest free zoo in the U.S.

Peggy Notebaert Nature Museum • 2430 N Cannon Dr — An oasis for adults and kids to reconnect with nature by playing with wildflowers and butterflies.

Theurer-Wrigley House • 2466 N Lakeview Ave — Early Richard E. Schmidt (and maybe Hugh H.G. Garden) based on late-Italian Renaissance architecture. Also famous because it was later sold to William Wrigley Jr, chewing gum king.

Map 32 • Gold Coast / Magnificent Mile

Water Tower Place and Park • 845 N Michigan Ave — Huge shopping—6 floors—Marshall Field's

Map 33 • Rogers Park West

Bernard Horwich JCC • 3003 W Touhy Ave • 773-761-9100 — Community center, programming for kids/adults, pool/fitness center, senior center, sports leagues.

Croatian Cultural Center • 2845 W Devon Ave • 773-338-3839 — A place where families can relax, socialize and congregate. Intended to benefit the Croatian community in Chicago.

High Ridge YMCA • 2430 W Touhy Ave • 773-262-8300 — Community center, programming for kids/adults, summer activities, child care programs, sport teams, pool.

India Town • Devon street Indian strip — Devon street features Indian and Pakistani shops, grocery stores, restaurants, and more.

Indian Boundary Park • 2500 W Lunt • 773-742-7887 — Petting zoo, tennis courts, chess tables, ice rink, tennis courts, skate park, batting cages, spray pool, community center classes seasonally.

Rogers Park / West Ridge Historical Society • 6424 N Western Ave • 773-764-4078 — Photos / memorabilia / historical documents of the community's history, details it's ethnic diversity, open Wed / Fri 10-5, Th 7pm-9pm, and by appointment.

Thillen's Stadium • Devon and Kedzie — Chicago landmark, 16 softball fields, features little league baseball and various other games and benefits.

Map 33 • Rogers Park West—continued

Warren Park • 6601 N Western Ave • 312-742-7888	Seasonal free entertainment, pony rides, ethnic food festivals, amusement park rides, arts & crafts, Winter sledding hill, baseball diamond, picnic pavilions, dog play areas.

Map 34 • Rogers Park East

Robert A Black Golf Course • 2045 W Pratt • 773-764-4045	The newest of Chicago Park District courses; 2,300-yard, par 33 layout, great choice for all skill levels, perfect for group outings and golf leagues, nine-hole daily fee. This short-distance course plays more difficult that most players predict.

Map 36 • Bryn Mawr

Rosehill Cemetery and Mausoleum • 5800 N Ravenswood Ave	Chicago's historical glitterati entombed among unsurpassed sculpture and architecture.

Map 37 • Edgewater / Andersonville

Ann Sather's Restaurant • 5207 N Clark St	More than a restaurant, a cultural field trip.
Philadelphia Church • 5437 N Clark St	Can't miss neon sign.
Swedish American Museum • 5211 N Clark St	Everything you want to know about Swedish culture, which is more than you thought.
The Belle Shore Hotel Building • 1062 W Bryn Mawr Ave	Once homes to roaring 1920s nightlife, now historic landmarks, restored to their former glory as apartments.

Map 38 • Ravenswood Manor

North Branch Pumping Station • Lawrence and the River	With its 1930s Art Deco façade, it seems like something prettier should be happening here than pumping most of the North Side's sewage.
Paradise • 2910 W Montrose Ave	It's a sushi restaurant. It's a beauty shop. It's a sauna ($12 for as long as you want). It's paradise. Of course, it's a neighborhood landmark.
Ravenswood Manor Park • 4626 N Manor Ave	It's just a tiny triangle wedged between the non-elevated El and several streets, but it is ground zero for garden sales, neighborhood associations, dogs, kids, and any community activity.
River Park • 5100 N Francisco Ave	More than 30 acres of park, including one of the few city canoe launches.

Map 39 • Ravenswood / North Center

St Benedict's Church • 2215 W Irving Park Rd	The namesake of the St. Ben's neighborhood.

Map 40 • Uptown / Sheridan Park / Buena Park

Graceland Cemetery • 4001 N Clark St • 773-525-1105	Chicago famous buried in masterpiece of landscape architecture.
Green Mill Pub • 4802 N Broadway St • 773-878-5552	Live jazz 7 nights a week. Dillinger drank here.
Lakeview Lounge • 5110 N Broadway St • 773-769-0994	Old School Bar—live music weekends. John Dillinger used to drink here—shot and a beer type of joint.
Tattoo Factory • 4408 N Broadway St • 773-989-4077	Tattoos for famous and infamous.
Uptown Theatre • 4707 N Broadway St • 773-561-5700	an acre of seats in a magic city—scheduled to reopen 2004

Map 43 • Wrigleyville/ Lakeview

Southport Lanes • 3325 N Southport Ave	
Vic Theater • 3145 N Sheffield Ave	Drink, watch films, and take in an occasional band at this old theater.
Wrigley Field • 1060 W Addison St	Legendary neighborhood ballpark claims full houses whether the team wins or loses.

Map 44 • Lakeview East

Belmont Rocks • Briar at the lake	Popular lakefront hangout.
Dog Beach • Northern tip of Belmont Harbor	Fun and frolic with your pup.
Totem Pole • Waveland & Belmont Harbor Drive	Where did it come from? Why is it there? Nobody knows.

Make no bones about it, Chicago is a dog's kind of town. Over 750,000 canines live and play in the Windy City. Dogs socialize and exercise their owners daily at designated DFAs (dog friendly areas), shady parks and sprawling beaches.

Dog Friendly Areas

Dog Friendly Areas (DFAs) are parks reserved just for canines. DFA amenities vary by park, but they include doggie drinking fountains; agility equipment; grass, wood chip, pea pebble, and green asphalt surfaces; "time out" fenced-in areas for shy or bad dogs to chill; trash receptacles and doggie bags for, well, not take-out; and bulletin boards and information kiosks to post animal lovers' announcements.

DFAs are managed by the neighborhoods' dog owners' councils and the Chicago Park District. Chicago Police, who have the authority to ticket dog owners who don't leash their pooches or pick up their piles ($500 fine), recognize DFAs as legal areas to let canines run free and poop as they please. However, dog owners must abide by the DFA rules, which include cleaning up after your pooch, ensuring that your dog is fully immunized, de-wormed, licensed and wearing ID tags, and not bringing puppies under four months or dogs in heat into the park. Chicago has seven DFAs.

- **Coliseum Park**, 14th St. & Wabash Ave.
  Long, narrow and fenced-in park where dogs race the passing trains.
- **Dog Lot**, Orleans St. and Ohio St. (southwest corner)
  This park is as creative as its name. Next to the I-90/94 exit ramp, the fenced-in strip of concrete flanked by bushes is better used for rat races than dog exercise.
- **Hamlin Park**, 3035 N. Hoyne Ave. at Wellington Ave. (Map 42). Located in the shady southwest corner, this active L-shaped park appeals to tennis-ball chasers and fetching owners.
- **Margate Park**, 4921 N. Marine Dr. (Map 40)
  Called "pup town" by the canine community, this beloved DFA tends to be grass-worn because of all the doggone fun. Plans are to add trees and a drinking fountain.
- **Walsh Park**, 1722 N. Ashland Ave.; walshparkdogs@aol.com (Map 29). A 4,500-square foot park with grassy area for fetching, with pea gravel and shade.
- **Wicker Park**, 1425 N. Damen Ave. (Map 21)
  Popular pooch as well as dog owner pick-up park. Often packed with dog-walkers wrangling fleets of frisky canines.
- **Wiggley Field**, 2645 N. Sheffield Ave. (Map 29)
  Shaded by El tracks and trees, this model DFA built in 1997 with all the pawpular amenities was Chicago's pilot pooch park. It has a fenced-in doggy obstacle course, a green asphalt surface, drinking fountain, "time out" area, and info kiosk.

Creating a DFA takes a serious grass-roots effort spearheaded by the neighborhood's dog owners. They must organize themselves into an official dog owner council (DOW), get the community to bow to their desires through several surveys and meetings and, most importantly, unleash the support of their alderman, police precinct and park district. For more DFA information call the Park District's Dog Hot Line 312-744-DOGS (3647). Chicago's Dog Advisory Work Group (DAWG) assists neighborhood groups in establishing DFAs, 312-409-2169.

Top Dog Parks and Beaches

Basically, dogs and well-behaved owners are welcome in most of Chicago's parks and on its beaches. Here are some local canines' top picks.

- **Lincoln Park**
  Paws down, the best dog park in town for romping, fetch, and Frisbee. Unofficial "Bark Park" where pet lovers congregate is a grassy area south of Addison St. bound by a fence on the west and the lake's rocky shoreline.
- **Warren Park**
  Rogers Park dogs give a waggly tails up for this DFA's big hill for sprints and lake views.
- **Dog Beach**
  A crescent of sand at the north corner of Belmont Harbor separated from the bike path by a fence, this unofficial dog sand box is always crowded with frolicking Fidos.
- **Horner Park**
  Dog heaven with lots of trees, grass, squirrels to chase, and other pups to meet.
- **Montrose/Wilson Ave. Beach**
  Perfect for pooches to practice dogpaddling as lake water is shallow.
- **Loyola Beach**
  Decent breakwaters for serious paddlers and pooches that dig body surfing.
- **Ohio St. Beach and Olive Park**
  The perfect combo for cross-training canines: Olive Park's fenced-in grassy areas for running and neighboring Ohio St. Beach's calm waters for swim.
- **Promontory Point**
  Radical dog run for daring, buff dogs that dive off the scenic picnic area's rocks into the deep water below.

More Doggone Information

Chicago's canine community keeps up to sniff on doggie doings through *Chicago Tails Magazine* produced by DAWG and *Pet Times* newspaper, 312-337-6976. The definitive dog resource for Chicagoans is Steve Dale's book *Doggone Chicago.*

Map 2 • Near North / River North

			Pricing	Rating
Best Western Inn	125 W Ohio St	312-467-0800	119-145	★★★
Hotel 71	71 E Wacker Dr	312-346-7100	169-229	
Courtyard by Marriott	30 E Hubbard St	312-329-2500	189-250	★★★
Embassy Suites Hotel	600 N State St	312-943-3800	229-289	★★★★
Hampton Inn	33 W Illinois St	312-832-0330	105-159	★★★
Hilton	10 E Grand Ave	312-595-0000	119-269	★★★
Homewood Suites	40 E Grand Ave	312-644-2222	99-209	★★★
House of Blues Hotel Loews	333 N Dearborn St	312-245-0333	119-218	★★★1/2
Lenox House Suites	616 N Rush St	312-337-1000	109-159	★★★
Ohio House Motel	600 N La Salle Dr	312-943-6000	85	
Penisula Chicago Hotel	745 N Rush St	312-337-2888	380-450	★★★★★
Westin River North Chicago	320 N Dearborn St	312-744-1900	169-424	

Map 3 • Streeterville / Magnificent Mile

Allerton Crowne Plaza	701 N Michigan Ave	312-440-1500	169-319	★★★★
Best Western Inn	162 E Ohio St	312-787-3100	99-164	★★★
Embassy Suites Lakefront	511 N Columbus Dr	312-836-5900	119-260	
Fairfield Inn	216 E Ontario St	312-787-3100	119-245	★★★
Fitzpatrick Chicago Hotel	166 E Superior St	312-787-6000	169-269	
Holiday Inn	300 E Ohio St	312-787-6100	119-320	★★★★
Hotel Inter-Continental	505 N Michigan Ave	312-944-4100	239-409	★★★★
Marriott Chicago Downtown	540 N Michigan Ave	312-836-0100	169-229	
Omni Chicago Hotel	676 N Michigan Ave	312-944-6664	269-379	★★★★
Park Hyatt Hotel	800 N Michigan Ave	312-335-1234	270-350	★★★★
Radisson Hotel	160 E Huron St	312-787-2900	109-259	★★★1/2
Red Roof Inn Chicago	162 E Ontario St	312-787-3580	85-106	
Sheraton	301 E North Water St	800-325-3535	129-429	★★★★1/2
W Chicago Lakeshore	644 N Lake Shore Dr	312-943-9200	229	★★★★
Wyndham Chicago	633 N St Clair St	312-573-0300	179-299	★★★★

Map 4 • West Loop Gate / Greektown

Quality Inn	1 S Halsted St	312-829-5000	139-149	★★★

Map 5 • The Loop

Crowne Plaza Silversmith	10 S Wabash Ave	312-372-7696	149-249	★★★★
Hotel Allegro	171 W Randolph St	312-236-0123	139-299	★★★1/2
Hotel Burnham	1 W Washington Ave	312-782-1111	155-230	
Hotel Monaco	225 N Wabash Ave	312-960-8500	145-250	
Palmer House Hilton	17 E Monroe St	312-726-7500	119-379	★★★
Renaissance Chicago Hotel	1 W Wacker Dr	312-372-7200	159-269	
W Hotels Chicago	172 W Adams St	312-332-1200	181-259	

Map 6 • The Loop / Grant Park

Fairmont Hotel	200 N Columbus Dr	312-565-8000	179-349	★★★★1/2
Hyatt Regency Chicago Hotel	151 E Wacker Dr	312-565-1234		★★★★1/2
Marriott Hotels & Resorts	333 N Michigan Ave	312-214-8923	219-369	
Swissotel Chicago	323 E Wacker Dr	312-565-0565	169-399	★★★★1/2

Map 7 • South Loop / River City

Holiday Inn-Downtown West Loop	506 W Harrison St	312-957-9100		★★★

Map 8 • South Loop / Printer's Row / Dearborn Park

Chicago Travelodge Downtown	65 E Harrison St	312-427-8000	95-159	★★★
Ho Jo Inn	720 N La Salle St	312-664-8100	88-103	★★
Hyatt Printer's Row	500 S Dearborn St	312-986-1234	119-275	★★★

Map 9 • South Loop / S Michigan Ave

Hotel	Address	Phone	Pricing	Rating
Best Western Inn	1100 S Michigan Ave	312-922-2900	139-169	★★
Congress Plaza Hotel	520 S Michigan Ave	312-427-3800	129-149	★★★
Essex Inn	800 S Michigan Ave	312-939-2800	69-150	
Hilton & Towers Chicago	720 S Michigan Ave	312-922-4400	159-314	★★★★

Map 11 • South Loop / McCormick Place

Hotel	Address	Phone	*Pricing*	*Rating*
Hyatt Hotels & Resorts	2233 S Dr Martin L King Jr Dr	312-567-1234	289-159	★★★★1/2

Map 14 • Prairie Shores / Lake Meadows

Hotel	Address	Phone	Pricing	Rating
Amber Inn	3901 S Michigan Ave	773-285-1000	72-149	
Bronzeville's First Bed & Breakfast	3911 S Dr MLK Dr	773-373-8081	150-255	(with 3 meals)

Map 16 • Bronzeville

Hotel	Address	Phone	Pricing	Rating
Harlem Hotel	5020 S Michigan Ave	773-536-1640	120-155	

Map 30 • Lincoln Park

Hotel	Address	Phone	Pricing	Rating
Days Inn	1816 N Clark St	312-664-3040	89-129	★★★
Sofitel Water Tower	20 E Chestnut St	312-324-4011	199-249	

Map 32 • Gold Coast / Magnificent Mile

Hotel	Address	Phone	Pricing	Rating
Ambassador West	1300 N State St	312-787-3700	169-249	
Claridge Hotel	1244 N Dearborn St	312-787-4980	139-225	★★★1/2
Doubletree Guest Suites	198 E Delaware Pl	312-664-1100	199-369	★★★★
Drake Hotel	140 E Walton St	312-787-2200	196-395	★★★★
Elms Hotel	18 E Elm St	312-787-4740	51-100	★★★
Four Seasons Hotel Chicago	120 E Delaware Pl	312-280-8800	425-545	★★★★
Millenium Knickerbocker	163 E Walton St	312-751-8100	149-249	★★★★
Omni Ambassador East Hotel	1301 N State Pkwy	312-787-7200	139-199	★★★★
Raphael Hotel	201 E Delaware Pl	312-943-5000	99-209	★★★
Residence Inn	201 E Walton St	312-943-9800	149-189	★★★
Ritz Carlton Hotel	160 E Pearson St	312-266-2343	360-455	★★★★1/2
Seneca Hotel	200 E Chestnut St	312-787-8900	129-209	★★★
Sutton Place Hotel	21 E Bellevue Pl	312-266-2100	189-300	
Talbott Hotel	20 E Delaware Pl	312-944-4970	139-229	★★★★
Tremont	100 E Chestnut St	312-751-1900	99-389	★★★★
Westin Michigan Avenue	909 N Michigan Ave	312-943-7200	169-424	
Whitehall Hotel	105 E Delaware Pl	312-944-6300	149-279	★★★★

Map 34 • Rogers Park East

Hotel	Address	Phone	Pricing	Rating
Sheraton	7300 N Sheridan Rd	773-973-7440		

Map 37 • Edgewater / Andersonville

Hotel	Address	Phone	Pricing	Rating
Lakeside Motel	5440 N Sheridan Rd	773-275-2700	57	

Map 43 • Wrigleyville/ Lakeview

Hotel	Address	Phone	Pricing	Rating
City Suites Hotel Chicago	933 W Belmont Ave	773-404-3400	109-169	

Map 44 • Lakeview East

Hotel	Address	Phone	Pricing	Rating
Best Western Hawthorne Terrace	3434 N Broadway St	773-244-3434	139-185	
Comfort Inn	601 W Diversey Pkwy	773-348-2810	122-135	
Days Inn	644 W Diversey Pkwy	773-525-7010	79-170	
Hotel Majestic	528 W Brompton Ave	773-404-3499	109-169	
Willows	555 W Surf St	773-528-8400	109-169	

Veterinarian

Veterinarian	Address	Phone	Map
Chicago Feline Medical Center	600 N Wells	312-944-2287	2

Delivery & Messengers

Delivery & Messengers	Address	Phone	Map
Deadline Express	449 N Union Ave	312-850-1200	1
On The Fly Courier	131 N Green	312-738-2154	4

Gyms

Gyms	Address	Phone	Map
Chicago Fitness Center	3131 N Lincoln Ave	773-549-8181	43

Locksmiths

Locksmiths	Address	Phone	Map
Gateway Locksmith	multiple locations	800-964-8282	N/A
Amazing Lock Service	739 W Belmont Ave	773-935-8900	44
AASA Locksmith	multiple locations	773-434-4650	N/A
A-AAA Accurate Lock Service	multiple locations	800-734-5156	N/A
A-AAround the Clock	multiple locations	800-281-5445	N/A
Safemasters	614 W Monroe St	312-627-8209	4
Wernick Key & Lock Service	multiple locations	888-937-6425	N/A
Abby Lock Service	multiple locations	888-272-7435	N/A
Always Available	multiple locations	773-478-1960	N/A
Five Star Lock & Key	N/A	773-778-2066	N/A

Plumbers

Plumbers	Address	Phone	Map
Fast Service	multiple locations	773-376-6666	N/A
A Metro Plumbing & Sewer Service	N/A	877-872-3060	N/A
A-AAAA Plumbing & Sewer	N/A	773-282-2878	N/A
A Better Man Plumbing & Sewer	N/A	773-286-9351	N/A
Roto-Rooter	N/A	800-438-7686	N/A
Plumbing & Heating	N/A	773-889-1130	N/A
Sears HomeCentral	N/A	773-737-3580	N/A
Emergency Response	N/A	773-736-3247	N/A
O'Bannon Plumbing & Sewer (Northside)	N/A	773-486-5748	N/A
O'Bannon Plumbing & Sewer (Southside)	N/A	773-862-5112	N/A
Second City Plumbing & Sewer	N/A	773-581-2300	N/A
Southtown Plumbing & Sewer Service	N/A	773-779-0024	N/A
Top Quality Plumbing & Sewer	N/A	773-523-1160	N/A
Elliot Plumbing & Sewer Service	N/A	773-370-9908	N/A
Midwest Plumbing & Sewer	N/A	773.478.1000	N/A
Sunrise Plumbing & Sewer	N/A	773.960.6462	N/A

Copy Shops	*Address*	*Phone*	*Map*
Kinko's	444 N Wells St	312-670-4460	2
Kinko's	540 N Michigan Ave	312-832-0090	3
Kinko's	128 S Canal St	312-258-8833	4
Kinko's	227 W Monroe St	312-609-1128	5
Kinko's	55 E Monroe St	312-701-0730	5
Kinko's	6 W Lake St	312-424-6700	5
Kinko's	1242 S Canal St	312-455-0920	10
Kinko's	1315 E 57th St	773-643-2424	19
Kinko's	1800 W North Ave	773-395-4639	21
Kinko's	2300 N Clybourn Ave	773-665-7500	29
Kinko's	1201 N Dearborn St	312-640-6100	32
Kinko's	3435 N Western Ave	773-755-9000	42
Kinko's	3524 N Southport Ave	773-975-5031	43
Kinko's	3001 N Clark St	773-528-0500	44

Pharmacies	*Address*	*Phone*	*Map*
Walgreens	641 N Clark St	312-587-1416	2
Walgreens	757 N Michigan Ave	312-664-8686	3
Walgreens	111 S Halsted St	312-463-9142	4
Walgreens	501 W Roosevelt St	312-492-8559	7
Walgreens	3405 S Dr ML King Jr Dr	312-326-4058	14
Walgreens	1554 E 55th St	773-667-1177	19
Walgreens	1601 N Wells St	312-642-4008	31
Walgreens	1200 N Dearborn St	312-943-0973	32
Walgreens	7510 N Western St	773-764-1765	33
Osco Drug	5532 N Clark St	773-784-7348	37
Walgreens	3302 W Belmont Ave	773-267-2328	41
Osco Drug	3572 N Elston Ave	773-583-9858	41
Osco Drug	2940 N Ashland Ave	773-348-4155	43
Walgreens	3046 N Halsted St	773-325-0413	44
Walgreens	5625 N Ridge Ave		37
Parkway Drugs	680 N Lake Shore Dr		3
Osco Drug	845 W Wilson St	773-275-7192	40

Chicago's gallery scene keeps growing ever outward from the city's original, and still thriving, gallery district, River North. The abundance of openings on Friday nights make for some cheap dates. Dress in black, grab a glass of wine, and pretend that you belong. When people start looking at you funny, it's time to move on.

Areas codes are 312 unless otherwise noted.

2 • Near North / River North

Akainyah Gallery	357 W Erie St	654-0333
Alan Koppel Gallery	210 W Chicago Ave	640-0730
Aldo Castillo Gallery	233 W Huron St	337-2536
Andrew Bae Gallery	300 W Superior St	335-8601
Ann Nathan Gallery	218 W Superior St	664-6622
Arms Akimbo Gallery	233 W Huron St	654-1968
Australian Exhibition Center	114 W Kinzie St	645-1948
Belloc-Lowndes Fine Art	215 W Huron St	573-1157
Byron Roche Gallery	750 N Franklin St	654-0144
Carl Hammer Gallery	740 N Wells St	266-8512
Carrie Secrist Gallery	300 W Superior St	280-4500
Catherine Edelman Gallery	300 W Superior St	266-2350
Douglas Dawson Gallery	222 W Huron St	751-1961
Eastern Gallery	750 N Franklin St	280-0787
Gescheidle Gallery	300 W Superior St	654-0600
Gwenda Jay/Addington Gallery	704 N Wells St	664-3406
Habatat Galleries	222 W Superior St	440-0288
I Space Gallery	230 W Superior St	587-9976
James Tigerman Gallery	212 W Chicago Ave	337-8300
Jean Albano Gallery	215 W Superior St	440-0770
Judy A Saslow Gallery	300 W Superior St	943-0530
Kass Meridian Gallery	325 W Huron St	266-5999
Kenneth Probst Galleries	46 E Superior	440-1991
Lydon Fine Art	309 W Superior St	943-1133
Lyons Wier Gallery	300 W Superior St	654-8171
Marx-Saunders Gallery	230 W Superior St	573-1400
Mary Bell Gallery	740 N Franklin St	642-0202
Maya Polsky Gallery	215 W Superior St	440-0055
Melanee Cooper Gallery	740 N Franklin St	202-9305
Mongerson Gallery	704 N Wells St	943-2354
Nicole Gallery	230 W Huron St	787-7716
Oskar Friedl Gallery	300 W Superior St	867-1930
Perimeter Gallery	210 W Superior St	266-9473
Peter Bartlow Gallery	44 E Superior	337-1782
Portals	742 N Wells St	642-1066
Primitive Art Works	706 N Wells St	943-3770
Printworks	311 W Superior St	664-9407
RH Love Galleries	40 E Erie St	640-1300
Richard Norton Gallery	612 Merchandise Mart	644-8855
Rita Bucheit Fine Art & Antiques	449 N Wells St	527-4080
Robert Henry Adams Fine Art	715 N Franklin St	642-8700
Roy Boyd Gallery	739 N Wells St	642-1606
Schneider Gallery	230 W Superior St	988-4033
Sonia Zaks Gallery	311 W Superior	943-8440
Stephen Daiter Gallery	311 W Superior St	787-3350
TBA Exhibition Space	230 W Huron St	587-3300
Trowbridge Gallery	703 N Wells St	587-9575
Vale Craft Gallery	230 W Superior St	337-3525
ZG Gallery	300 W Superior St	654-9900
Zolla/Liberman Gallery	325 W Huron St	944-1990
Zygman Voss Gallery	222 W Superior St	787-3300

3 • Streeterville / Magnificent Mile

City Gallery	806 N Michigan Ave	742-0808
Hollis Taggart Galleries	3 E Huron St	475-9300
Kenyon Oppenheimer	410 N Michigan Ave	642-5300
Lipa	160 E Illinois St	329-0812
R S Johnson Fine Art	645 N Michigan Ave	943-1661
RS Johnson Fine Art	645 N Michigan Ave	943-1661
Smith Museum of Stained Glass Windows	600 E Grand Ave	595-7437
The Arts Club of Chicago	201 E Ontario St	787-3997
The Museum of Contemporary Art	220 E Chicago Ave	280-2660

4 • West Loop Gate / Greektown

Fassbender/ Stevens Gallery	835 W Washington Blvd	666-4302
Jan Cicero Gallery	835 W Washington Blvd	733-9551
Saic Gallery 2	847 W Jackson Blvd	563-5162
Thomas McCormick Gallery	835 W Washington Blvd	226-6800

5 • The Loop

Arndt & Partner Gallery	835 W Washington St	432-0708
Donald Young Gallery	933 W Washington St	455-0100
Illinois Art Gallery	100 W Randolph St	814-5322
Vedanta Gallery	835 W Washington St	432-0708

6 • The Loop / Grant Park

Cliff Dwellers Gallery	200 S Michigan Ave	922-8080
Fine Arts Building Gallery	410 S Michigan Ave	913-0537
Hilligoss Gallery	250 N Michigan Ave	755-0300
The Art Institute of Chicago	111 S Michigan Ave	443-3500
The Chicago Architecture Center	224 S Michigan Ave	922-3402 x908

7 • South Loop / River City

Unit B Gallery	1733 S Des Plaines St	491-9384

8 • South Loop / Printer's Row

Art House	43 W Harrison St	708-763-9533
Bella Vista Fine Art Gallery	746 N La Salle St	274-1490

10 • East Pilsen / Chinatown

Gallery Six Four Five	645 W 18th St	455-8976

11 • South Loop / McCormick Place

Woman Made Gallery	1900 S Prarie Ave	328-0038

13 • Bridgeport (East)

MN Gallery	3524 S Halsted St	773-847-0573

19 • Hyde Park / Woodlawn

Art Werk	5300 S Blackstone Ave	773-684-5300
Artisans 21	5225 S Harper Ave	773-288-7450

20 • Hyde Park East / Jackson Park

Hyde Park Art Center	5307 S Hyde Park Blvd	773-324-5520

21 • Wicker Park / Ukrainian Village

Axis Gallery — 1542 N Milwaukee Ave
Carlos E Jimenez Gallery — 2301 W North Ave 773-235-5328
Collage — 1563 N Milwaukee Ave
David Leonardis Gallery — 1352 N Paulina St
Dawning, Art the Gift — 2246 W North Ave
Feitico Gallery — 1821 W North Ave
Fringe Salon — 1437 N Milwaukee Ave 773-862-1000
Gallery 203 — 1579 N Milwaukee Ave
Green Room Gallery — 1375 N Milwaukee Ave 773-227-6512
The Blue Ladder Gallery — 1573 N Milwaukee Ave
Thirteenth Floor Gallery — 2337 W North Ave
TZ Gallery — 1834 W North Ave 773-342-8676
Wood St Gallery & Sculpture Garden — 1239 N Wood St

22 • Noble Square / Goose Island

1112 Gallery — 1112 N Milwaukee Ave
Standard Gallery — 1437 N Bosworth Ave 773-486-1005

23 • West Town / Near West Side

Gallery 406 — 406 N Wood St
Monkey Business Gallery — 1942 W Chicago Ave 773-269-3133
Open-End Art — 2000 W Fulton Market 738-2140
Skylight Gallery — 1956 W Grand Ave 226-2855
Ukrainian Institute of Art — 2318 W Chicago Ave

24 • River West / West Town

ARC Gallery	734 N Milwaukee Ave	733-2787
Arena Gallery	311 N Sangamon St	421-0212
Aron Packer Gallery	118 N Peoria St	226-8984
Artemisia Gallery	700 N Carpenter St	226-7323
Bodybuilder & Sportsman	119 N Peoria St	492-7261
Flatfile Photography Gallery	118 N Peoria St	491-1190
Frederick Baker Gallery	1230 W Jackson Blvd	243-2980
Function + Art	1046 W Fulton Market	243-2780
Gallery 312	312 N May St	942-2500
GR N'Namdi Gallery	110 N Peoria St	587-8362
Intuit Gallery	756 N Milwaukee Ave	243-9088
Julia Friedman Gallery	118 N Peoria St	455-0755
Klein Art Works	400 N Morgan St	243-0400
Monique Meloche Gallery	951 W Fulton Market	455-0299
Peter Miller Gallery	118 N Peoria St	226-5291
Rhona Hoffman Gallery	118 N Peoria St	455-1990
Richard Milliman Fine Art	1364 Grand Ave	432-9900
Rogeramsay Gallery	711 N Milwaukee Ave	491-1400
Schopf Gallery	942 W Lake St	432-1630
Stolen Buick Studio	1303 W Chicago Ave	226-5902
Walsh Gallery	118 N Peoria St	829-3312

25 • Illinois Medical District

Mexican Fine Arts Center — 1852 W 19th St

26 • University Village / Little Italy

Colibri Gallery	2032 W 18th St	733-8431
Jesus Chrysler Gallery	722 W 18th St	935-2885
Polvo Art Studio	1257 W 18th St	217-0350
UIC Gallery 400	1240 W Harrison St	996-6114

28 • Bucktown

Art Gallery Kafe — 1907 N Milwaukee Ave 773-235-2351
Bucktown Fine Arts — 2200 N Oakley Ave
Eclectic Junction — 1630 N Damen Ave
Gallery 1633 — 1633 N Damen Ave
Idao Gallery — 1616 N Damen Ave
Malovat Art Gallery — 1630 N Milwaukee Ave 773-278-8600
Morlen Sinoway-Atelier — 2035 W Wabansia Ave

29 • DePaul / Wrightwood / Sheffield

Chicago Center for the Print — 1509 W Fullerton Ave 773-477-1585
Havana Gallery — 1139 W Webster Ave 773-549-2492
La Llorona Gallery — 1474 W Webster Ave 773-281-8460
Urban Studio — 1450 W Webster Ave 773-832-4350

30 • Lincoln Park

Contemporary Art Workshop	542 W Grant Pl	773-472-4004
Old Town Art Center	1763 N North Park Ave	337-1938

31 • Old Town / Near North

Orca Aart Gallery	812 N Franklin St	280-4975
Thomas Masters Gallery	245 W North Ave	440-2322

32 • Gold Coast / Magnificent Mile

Aaron Gallery	50 E Oak St	943-0660
Billy Hork Galleries	109 E Oak St	337-1199
Colletti Gallery	67 E Oak St	664-6767
FL Braswell Fine Art	73 E Elm St	636-4399
Galleries Maurice Sternberg	140 E Walton	642-1700
Hildt Galleries	943 N State St	255-0005
Richard Gray Gallery	875 N Michigan Ave	642-8877
Richard Reed Armstrong Fine Art	200 E Walton	664-9312
The Hart Gallery	64 E Walton	932-9646
Valerie Carberry Gallery	875 N Michigan Ave	397-9990

37 • Edgewater / Andersonville

Bonfiglio Gallery	5408 N Clark St	773-989-7840
Las Manos Gallery	5220 N Clark St	773-728-8910

39 • Ravenswood / North Center

Peter Jones Gallery — 1806 W Cuyler Ave 773-472-6725

40 • Uptown / Sheridan Park

Beacon Street Gallery — 4131 N Broadway St 773-525-7579

42 • North Center / Roscoe Village

August House Studio — 2113 W Roscoe St 773-327-5644

43 • Wrigleyville/ Lakeview

Bell Studio — 3428 N Southport Ave 773-281-2172
Fourth World Artisans — 3440 N Southport Ave 773-404-5200

Map 1 • River North / River West / Fulton District

Emmit's Irish Pub & Eatery	495 N Milwaukee Ave	312-563-9631	An old school Chicago establishment.
Funky Buddha Lounge	728 W Grand Ave	312-666-1695	See and be seen at this trendy, live music lounge.
Rednofive	440 N Halsted	312-733-6699	Get your groove on.

Map 2 • Near North / River North

Bar Louie	226 W Chicago Ave	312-337-3313	Popular happy hour pick.
Bin 36	339 N Dearborn St	312-755-9463	Wine bar with everything that entails.
Blue Frog Bar & Grill	676 N La Salle St	312-943-8900	Board games and karoake.
Cyrano's Bistrot & Wine Bar	546 N Wells St	312-467-0546	Charming.
Green Door Tavern	678 N Orleans St	312-664-5496	A Chicago landmark; old school classic.
Harry's Velvet Room	56 W Illinois St	312-527-5600	Swank hipster throwback.
Martini Ranch	311 W Chicago Ave	312-335-9500	Tightly packed hipster haven.
Mother Hubbard's	5 W Hubbard St	312-828-0007	Another Rush Street nightmare.
Red Head Piano Bar	16 W Ontario St	312-640-1000	Touristy, but worth it.

Map 3 • Streeterville / Magnificent Mile

Billy Goat Tavern	430 N Michigan Ave	312-222-1525	Home of infamous cheezeboigas.
Dick's Last Resort	435 E Illinois St	312-836-7870	Between Mardi Gras & Hell.
O'Neill's Bar & Grill	152 E Ontario St		A touristy joint with pub food.
Timothy O'Tooles Pub	622 N Fairbanks Ct	312-642-0700	A touristy joint with pub food.

Map 5 • The Loop

Exchequer Pub	226 S Wabash Ave	312-939-5633	Art institute students drink here.
Govnor's Pub	207 N State St	312-236-3696	The place to get sauced after work.
Manhattans	415 S Dearborn St	312-957-0460	Tired of martini bars? Try small but fun Manhattans.
Miller's Pub	134 S Wabash Ave	312-263-4988	A Loop tradition.

Map 6 • The Loop / Grant Park

Houlihan's	111 E Wacker	312-616-FOOD	Rowdy meeting place.

Map 7 • South Loop / River City

Scarlett's Gentleman's	750 S Clinton St	312-986-1300	Strip club.

Map 8 • South Loop / Printer's Row / Dearborn Park

Buddy Guy's Legends	754 S Wabash Ave	312-427-0333	Top notch blues with Cajun food.
Hot House	31 E Balbo Ave	312-362-9707	Eclectic center for international music, from salsa to jazz.
Kasey's Tavern	701 S Dearborn St	312-427-7992	108-year old neighborhood oasis.
South Loop Club	701 S State St	312-427-2787	There's something creepy about this place.
Tantrum	1023 S State St	312-939-9160	Tucked away nicely appointed bar which attracts a lively S. Loop following.

Map 9 • South Loop / S Michigan Ave

Kitty O'Shea's	720 S Michigan Ave	312-294-6860	Guinness Fish and Chips with your Guinness?
Savoy Bar and Grill	800 S Michigan Ave	312-939-1464	Serious drinking in a kooky '50s hotel; early morning breakfast.

Map 11 • South Loop / McCormick Place

Bobby McGee's Sports Bar & Grill	1239 S State St	312-987-1189	
The Cotton Club	1710 S Michigan Ave	312-341-9787	This 1940s Harlem-themed club has a split personality: the Cab Calloway room offers blues/jazz and the Gray Room offers hip hop/urban contemporary. Look for stars on "Talent Tuesday".

Map 13 • Bridgeport (East)

Boston Tavern	451 W 26th St		
Cobblestone's Bar and Grill	514 E Pershing Rd	773-624-3630	A quiet neighborhood bar. Closes early.
Jimbo's Lounge	3258 S Princeton Ave	312-326-3253	Close to Sox park
Puffer's Bar	3356 S Halsted St	773-927-6073	
Redwood Lounge	S Wallace St & W 32nd St		

Map 14 • Prairie Shores / Lake Meadows

Darryl's Den	2600 S State St	312-842-1984	You won't see the light of day.
Mr T's Lounge	3528 S Indiana Ave	312-842-0400	Welcome to the basement.

Map 15 • Canaryville / Fuller Park

Kelley's Tavern	4403 S Wallace St	773-924-0796	
Root End Lounge	230 W Root St	773-285-5280	Laid back bar, '70s party twice monthly.

Map 16 • Bronzeville

New Bonanza Lounge	552 E 47th St	773-538-3200	Laid back blues lounge.
Ritz Lounge	3947 S Dr Martin L King Jr Dr	773-924-8136	Friendly bar with pool, darts, cards and dominoes.

Map 18 • Washington Park

Hank's Lounge	415 E 61st St	773-296-9700	
The Odyssey Cocktail Lounge	211 E Garfield Blvd		

Map 19 • Hyde Park / Woodlawn

Woodlawn Tap	1172 E 55th St	773-643-5516	Popular with students.

Map 20 • Hyde Park East / Jackson Park

The Cove Cocktail Lounge	1750 E 55th St	773-684-1013	

Map 21 • Wicker Park / Ukrainian Village

Bar Thirteen	1944 W Division St	773-394-1313	Upscale lounging at its best.
Borderline	1958 W North Ave	773-278-5138	When you really shouldn't have one more, but you do anyways, you have it here.
Club Foot	1824 W Augusta Blvd	773-489-0379	Amateur DJs spin in comfy neighborhood spot.
Davenport's	1383 N Milwaukee Ave	773-278-1830	Once legendary skanker bar now yuppy fern bar. Whattya gonna do?
Double Door	1572 N Milwaukee Ave	773-489-3160	Wicker Park instution where the Rolling Stones performed.
Empty Bottle	1035 N Western Ave	773-276-3600	Live music dive bar.
Estelle's Cafe & Lounge	2013 W North Ave	773-782-0450	Weird, dark and sticky.
Ezuli	1415 N Milwaukee Ave	773-227-8200	Hip-hop and reggae bar.
Gold Star Bar	1755 W Division St	773-227-8700	Local dive bar.
Holiday Club	1471 N Milwaukee Ave	773-486-0686	Retro bar.
Inner Town Pub	1935 W Thomas	773-235-9795	Wicker dump.
Lava Lounge	859 N Damen Ave	773-772-3355	Good music, good people, good location.
Nick's	1516 N Milwaukee Ave	773-252-1155	
Pontiac Cafe	1531 N Damen Ave	773-252-7767	Hipsters people watch on the huge patio.
Rainbo Club	1150 N Damen Ave	773-489-5999	The original scenester institution.
Red Dog	1958 W North Ave	773-278-5291	Dance club open 'til 4.
Sinibar	1540 N Milwaukee Ave	773-278-7797	Hip-hop lounge.
Subterranean Cafe	2011 W North Ave	773-278-6600	Live music upstairs.
The Note	1565 N Milwaukee Ave	773-489-0011	Live music almost every night.

Map 22 • Noble Square / Goose Island

Big Wig	1551 W Division St	773-235-9100	Salon theme, eclectic entertainment.
Biology Bar	1520 N Fremont St	312-397-0580	Main bar covered in grass.
Circus	901 W Weed St	312-266-1200	Just like it sounds, but slicker.
Crazy Horse Too	1531 N Kingsbury St	312-664-7400	Topless dance club for high-rollers.
Crobar	1543 N Kingsbury St	312-413-7000	Seminal club for house music.
Exit	1315 W North Ave	773-395-2700	Punk rock throwback.
Glow	1615 N Clybourn Ave	312-587-8469	Disco dance club with lounge.
Hot Shots	1440 N Dayton St	312-654-8204	Romanian music.

Map 22 • Noble Square / Goose Island — continued

Joe's	940 W Weed St	312-337-3486	Sports & yuppies.
Mudbug/Trackside	901 W Weed St	312-787-9600	
Slow Down, Life's Too Short	1177 N Elston Ave	773-384-1040	Gimmicky river-front party spot.

Map 23 • West Town / Near West Side

Black Beetle	2532 W Chicago Ave	773-384-0701	Almost as cool as the name.
Cleo's	1935 W Chicago Ave	312-243-5600	Clubby neighborhood lounge.
Sak's Ukrainian Village Restaurant	2301 W Chicago Ave		

Map 24 • River West / West Town / Near West Side

Betty's Blue Star Lounge	1600 W Grand Ave	312-243-1699	Your drunken last chance for love.
Cafe Fresco	1202 W Grand Ave	312-733-6378	Comfy, local environs.
Iggy's	700 N Milwaukee Ave	312-829-4449	Late kitchen—obnoxious wannabe crowd.
Jack's Tap	901 W Jackson Blvd	312-666-1700	From the good folks who brought us the Village Tap.
Matchbox	770 N Milwaukee Ave	312-666-9292	Goes way beyond intimate.
The Tasting Room	1415 W Randolph St	312-942-1313	Swank, low-key wine bar.
Twisted Spoke	501 N Ogden Ave	312-666-1500	Looks more like yuppies than bikers to us.

Map 25 • Illinois Medical District / Heart of Chicago

Cerwood Inn	1759 W Cermak Rd	773-523-9088	
Simpson's	Grenshaw and Western		
White Horse Lounge	2059 W 19th St	312-432-9754	

Map 27 • Logan Square (South)

Fireside Bowl	2646 W Fullerton Ave	773-486-2700	Unbelievably divey punk rock venue keeps threatening to shut down.
Palladium	2047 N Milwaukee Ave	773-342-6604	Disco dreams for the Millennium.
The Winds Cafe	2657 N Kedzie Blvd	773-489-7478	Neighborhood bar smack dab in the middle of the 'hood.

Map 28 • Bucktown

Artful Dodger Pub	1734 W Wabansia Ave	773-227-6859	Young loud crowd, day-glo drinks.
Bar Louie	1704 N Damen Ave	773-645-7500	Beer, wine, mammoth sandwiches.
Charleston Tavern	2076 N Hoyne Ave	773-489-4757	Yuppie dive.
Danny's Tavern	1951 W Dickens Ave	773-489-6457	Whatever it once had, it lost it.
Lemmings	1850 N Damen Ave	773-862-1688	Another yuppie hot spot.
Lincoln Tavern	1858 W Wabansia Ave	773-342-7778	Neighborhood bar.
Marie's Rip Tide Lounge	1745 W Armitage Ave	773-278-7317	Drunk wannabes welcome here.
Northside Cafe	1635 N Damen Ave	773-384-3555	Popular Wicker Park pick-up bar.
Quencher Saloon	2401 N Western Ave	773-276-9730	Low-key bar on the edge of the abyss.
The Map Room	1949 N Hoyne Ave	773-252-7636	International travel theme.

Map 29 • DePaul / Wrightwood / Sheffield

Big John's	1147 W Armitage Ave	773-477-4400	
Charlie's Ale House	1224 W Webster Ave	773-871-1440	Shivers.
Deliliah's	2771 N Lincoln Ave	773-472-2771	Raucous punk rock venue.
Gin Mill	2462 N Lincoln Ave	773-549-3232	College bar.
Green Dolphin Street	2200 N Ashland Ave	773-395-0066	Self-conscious jazz club.
Hog Head McDunna's	1505 W Fullerton Ave	773-929-0944	College-y crowd.
Irish Eyes	2519 N Lincoln Ave	773-348-9548	Small Irish pub.
Jack Sullivan's	2142 N Clybourn Ave	773-549-9009	Sports bar.
Kincade's	950 W Armitage Ave	773-348-0010	Happy hour sports bar.
Kustom	1997 N Clybourn Ave	773-528-3400	Techno dance club.
Local Option	1102 W Webster Ave	773-348-2008	Neighborhood hole-in-the-wall and proud of it.
Lush	948 W Armitage Ave	773-871-8123	Neighborhood lounge.
Red Lion Pub	2446 N Lincoln Ave	773-348-2645	It's haunted!
The Hideout	1354 W Wabansia Ave	773-227-4433	Secret live music gem.
Webster Wine Bar	1480 Webster Ave	773-868-0608	Large selection of wine by the glass.
Wrightwood Tap	1059 W Wrightwood Ave	773-549-4949	Neighborhood tavern.
Zella	1983 N Clybourn Ave	773-549-2910	Great summer seating.

Map 30 • Lincoln Park

Bar Louie	1800 N Lincoln Ave	312-337-9800	
Blu	2247 N Lincoln Ave	773-549-5884	
Corner Pocket	2610 N Halsted St	773-281-0050	Student-y billiards bar.
Game Keepers	1971 N Lincoln Ave	773-549-0400	Where young singles mingle.
Glascott's	2158 N Halsted	773-281-1205	The pub that beckons on sunny afternoons.
GoodBar	2512 N Halsted		Candles, DJ, wine bar.
Hidden Shamrock	2723 N Halsted	773-883-0304	Halsted Street staple.
Kingston Mines	2548 N Halsted St	773-477-4646	Blues club likes you to know which celebrities have visited them recently.
Neo	2350 N Clark St	773-528-2622	
Parkway Tavern	746 W Fullerton Ave	773-327-8164	Sports bar with turtle races!
River Shannon	425 W Armitage Ave	312-944-5087	
Sauce	1750 N Clark St	312-932-1750	Sleek chic place to drink.
Tequila Roadhouse	1653 N Wells St	312-440-0535	Nightmarish.

Map 31 • Old Town / Near North

Burton Place	1447 N Wells St	312-664-4699	Great late night; good bar food.
Dragon Room	809 W Evergreen St	312-751-2900	Sushi/sake bar; Asian dance club.
Hobo's	1446 N Wells St	312-943-5444	Board games and locals.
North Park Tap	313 W North Ave	312-943-5228	Laid-back crowd.
Old Town Ale House	219 W North Ave	312-944-7020	Local flare.
Spoon	1240 N Wells St	312-642-5522	Trendy young crowd.
Weeds	1555 N Dayton St	312-943-7815	Dive with live jazz.

Map 32 • Gold Coast / Magnificent Mile

Bar Chicago	9 W Division St	312-654-1120	Dancing of sorts.
Butch McGuire's	20 W Division St	312-337-9080	Wet T-shirt contests anyone?
Cactus	404 S Wells St	312-922-3830	
Cru Wine Bar	888 N Wabash Ave	312-337-4078	Another little wine bar.
Dublin's	1030 N State St	312-266-6340	Gold Coast pub.
Le Passage	1 E Oak St		
Leg Room	7 W Division St	312-337-2583	Bar food and funky music.
Mothers	26 W Division St	312-642-7251	The mother of frat-boy shenanigans.
She-nanigans	16 W Division St	312-642-2344	Another Rush vicinity hellhole.
Signature Lounge	875 N Michigan Ave	312-787-9596	Unbelievable view from the women's room.
The Hunt Club	1100 N State St	312-988-7887	The ultimate yuppie sports bar.
The Whisky	1015 N Rush St	312-475-0300	Sutton Place Hotel.
Zebra Lounge	1220 N State St	312-642-5140	Garish, cramped piano bar—in other words, it's a hit.

Map 33 • Rogers Park West

Cary's Lounge	2251 W Devon Ave	773-743-5737	Free pool, Karaoke Saturdays, open mic Sundays.
Mark II Chicago	7436 N Western Ave	773-465-9675	Pool tables & dart boards.
McKellin's	2800 W Touhy Ave	773-262-6140	Cozy neighborhood Irish bar.
Mullen's Sports Bar and Grill	7301 N Western Ave	773-465-2113	Food until 1 am (10 pm on Sundays).
Pinewood Inn	2310 W Touhy Ave	773-973-4443	Beer garden open seasonally.

Map 34 • Rogers Park East

Don's Coffee Club	1439 W Jarvis Ave	773-381-5507	
No Exit	6730 N Glenwood Ave		Cafe-bar with live folky music & poetry.

Map 35 • Arcadia Terrace / Peterson Park

Hidden Cove	5336 N Lincoln Ave	773-275-6711	Sports bar w/trivia, darts, and karaoke.
Hollywood Lounge	3301 W Bryn Mawr Ave	773-588-9707	Friendly neighborhood bar with extensive beer selection.

Map 36 • Bryn Mawr

Claddagh Ring	2306 W Foster Ave	773-271-4794	Traditional Irish-American bar with plentiful pub fare.
Leadway Bar & Cafe	5233 N Damen Ave	773-728-2663	Pool hustlers and artistes mingle in Bryn Mawr's latest addition.

Map 37 • Edgewater / Andersonville

Atmosphere	5355 N Clark St	773-784-1100	See and be seen in Andersonville.
Charlie's Ale House	5308 Clark St	773-751-0140	Andersonville's newest yuppie gathering spot.
Edgewater Lounge	5600 N Ashland Ave	773-878-3343	Bluegrass, open mic night, and grub.
George's Cocktail Lounge	646 S Wabash	312-427-3964	Columbia students and faculty quaff in this dive between classes.
Granville Anvil	1137 Granville Ave	773-973-0006	Gay old-timers drink here.
Madrigals	5316 N Clark St	773-334-3033	A gay bar for everyone.
Moody's Pub	5910 N Broadway St	773-275-2696	Beer beer and beer garden.
Ollie's	1064 W Berwyn Ave		A rare quiet neighborhood joint.
Simon's	5210 N Clark St	773-878-0894	Yuppies galore.
StarGaze	5419 N Clark St		Lesbian bar with salsa on Friday nights.

Map 38 • Ravenswood Manor

Lincoln Square Lanes	4874 N Lincoln Ave	773-561-8191	Brews and bowling above a hardware store. Cheap date.
Montrose Saloon	2933 W Montrose Ave		Classic Chicago Old Style. No cell phones, please.
Peek Inn	2825 W Irving Park Rd		Neighborhood joint.

Map 39 • Ravenswood / North Center

Chicago Brauhaus	4732 N Lincoln Ave	773-784-4444	Oktoberfest year round.
Daily Bar & Grill	4560 N Lincoln Ave	773-561-6198	Bar food in retro ambience.
Lyon's Den	1934 W Irving Park Rd	773-871-3757	Live music and comedy.
Resi's Bierstube	2034 W Irving Park Rd	773-472-1749	Wear your leiderhosen.
The Great Beer Palace	4128 N Lincoln Ave	773-525-4906	The name says it all.
The Long Room	1612 W Irving Park Rd	773-665-4500	Friendly and loooooonnnnggg.

Map 40 • Uptown / Sheridan Park / Buena Park

Big Chicks	5024 N Sheridan Rd	773-728-5511	Neighborhood gay bar.
Carol's Pub	4659 N Clark St	773-334-2402	Good ole boys with live music.
Green Mill Pub	4802 N Broadway St	773-878-5552	Jazz, jive, blues—join in! Dillinger drank here.
Holiday Club	4000 N Sheridan Rd	773-348-9600	Hipster spot relocated from Wicker to the uptown frontier.
Hopleaf	5148 N Clark St	773-334-9851	Crowded neighborhood tavern with lots of imported beers.
Lakeview Lounge	5110 N Broadway St	773-769-0994	A shot and a beer, please.

Map 41 • Avondale / Old Irving

Abbey Pub	3420 W Grace St	773-478-4408	Reputable live music venue.
Chief O'Neill's	3471 N Elston Ave	773-473-5263	Pub grub/beer garden/live music.
Christine's Place	3759 N Kedzie Ave	773-463-1768	$2 Guinness/4 am/karaoke/dive.
Mycroft's	2900 W Belmont Ave		Neighborly bar with good jukebox.

Map 42 • North Center / Roscoe Village / West Lakeview

Art of Sports	2444 W Diversey Ave	773-276-7298	More sports than art.
Beat Kitchen	2100 W Belmont Ave	773-281-4444	Live music and decent bar food.
Benedict's	3937 N Lincoln Ave	773-549-5599	Neighborhood spot with food.
Black Rock	3614 N Damen Ave	773-348-4044	Pub with lots of scotch.
Cody's Public House	1658 W Barry Ave	773-528-4050	Friendly neighborhood pub.
Four Moon Tavern	1847 W Roscoe St	773-929-6666	Neighborhood tavern.
Four Treys	3333 N Damen Ave	773-549-8845	One of 5,000 drinking options in this area.
G & L Fire Escape	2157 W Grace St	773-472-1138	Neighborhood tavern.
JT Collins	3358 N Lincoln Ave	773-327-7467	
Martyrs'	3855 N Lincoln Ave	773-404-9494	Big hair live rock throwback.
Mulligan's Public House	2000 W Roscoe St	773-549-4225	Villagers do not go thirsty.
Riverview Tavern & Restaurant	1958 W Roscoe St		Another Roscoe Village watering hole.
Seanchai Public House	2345 W Belmont Ave	773-549-4444	Gritty pub with live DJs on weekends.
Tavern 33	3328 N Lincoln Ave	773-935-6391	
The Hungry Brain	2319 W Belmont Ave		Dumpy trendster dive.
The Village Tap	2055 W Roscoe St	773-883-0817	Fave neighborhood spot.
Tiny Lounge	1814 W Addison St	773-296-9620	It really is tiny.
Xippo	3759 N Damen Ave	773-529-9135	Martini lounge in unlikely 'hood.

Map 43 • Wrigleyville/ Lakeview

Bungalow Bar and Lounge	1622 W Belmont Ave	773-244-0400	Swank little neighborhood spot.
Cubby Bear	1059 W Addison St	773-975-0600	Live music, very hellacious.
Elbo Room	2871 N Lincoln Ave	773-549-5549	Questionable live rock.
Fizz Bar and Grill	3220 N Lincoln Ave	773-348-6000	Yuppie heaven.
Fuel	3724 N Clark St	773-248-3330	Rock star sightings from Metro shows.
Ginger Man Tavern	3740 N Clark St	773-549-2050	Not bad when there's no Cubs game.
Gunther Murphy's	1638 W Belmont Ave	773-472-5139	Eclectic live music.
Higgin's Tavern	3259 N Racine Ave	773-281-7637	Yuppies and drunks.
Jack's Bar & Grill	2856 N Southport Ave	773-404-8400	Classy wine bar.
Justin's	3358 N Southport Ave	773-929-4844	Great bar for Sunday football.
Lakeview Links	3206 N Wilton St	773-975-0505	Now with live music.
Lincoln Tap Room	3010 N Lincoln Ave	773-868-0060	Great mix of people, comfortable couches.
Metro	3730 N Clark St	773-549-0203	Most popular music venue in the city.
Murphy's Bleachers	3655 N Sheffield Ave	773-281-5356	Another Cubbie beer fest.
Raw Bar	3720 N Clark St	773-348-7291	Post-Metro rock star hangout.
Schuba's	3159 N Southport Ave	773-525-2508	Musical acts from far and near.
Sheffield's	3258 N Sheffield Ave	773-281-4989	Outdoor area attracts afternoon revelers.
Slugger's	3540 N Clark St	773-248-0055	Batting cages—some people's heaven, others' hell.
Ten Cat Tavern	3931 N Ashland Ave	773-935-5377	Cute neighborhood spot.
Y*k-zies-Clark	3710 N Clark St	773-525-9200	Loud post-Cubs hangout.

Map 44 • Lakeview East

Charlie's Chicago	3726 N Broadway St	773-871-8887	Gay country and western bar. That's right.
Circuit	3641 N Halsted St	773-325-2233	Nightclub/DJ dancing.
Cocktail	3359 N Halsted St	773-477-1420	Friendly mixed bar with male strippers.
Coyle's Tippling House	2843 N Halsted St	773-528-7569	One of the bigger Lakeview pubs.
Duke of Perth	2913 N Clark St	773-477-1741	Great Irish pub with fish & chips.
Kit Kat Lounge	3700 N Halsted St	773-352-1111	Live drag queen shows.
Little Jim's	3501 N Halsted St	773-871-6116	Gay dive.
Monsignor Murphy's	3019 N Broadway St	773-348-7285	Irish pub.
Roscoe's	3354-56 N Halsted	773-281-3355	Cavernous mingling for the gay sweater set.
Rose & Crown	420 W Belmont Ave	773-248-6654	Irish pub.
Sidetracks	3345-55 N Halsted		Popular showtune sing-a-longs!
Spin	800 W Belmont Ave	773-327-7711	Girl-friendly boy bar, dancing, pool.
The Closet	3325 N Broadway St	773-477-8533	Boy-friendly lesbian bar, 4 am license.
Town Hall Pub	3340 N Halsted	773-472-4405	Unassuming, mixed clientele, live music.

While we love all bookstores, some favorites are: After-Words in River North (check out the basement's gently used books); Rain Dog Books and Savvy Traveller in the Loop; Sandmeyer's in Printer's Row; 57th Street Books in Hyde Park; Barbara's in Old Town; Unabridged Books in East Lakeview; and Women & Children First in Andersonville.

Area codes are those in the map header unless otherwise noted.

1 • River North / Fulton District *(312)*

N Fagin Books	459 N Milwaukee Ave	829-5252

2 • Near North / River North *(312)*

Abraham Lincoln Book Shop	357 W Chicago Ave	944-3085
After-Words	23 E Illinois St	464-1110
B Dalton Bookseller	222 Merchandise Mart Plz	329-1881
Beck's Book Store	50 E Chicago Ave	944-7685
Te-Jays Book Store	53 W Hubbard St	923-9210

3 • Streeterville / Magnificent Mile *(312)*

Barbara's Bookstore	201 E Huron St	926-2665
Barbara's Bookstore	Navy Pier	222-0890
Rand McNally Map & Travel	444 N Michigan Ave	321-1751
Univ of Chicago Bookstore	450 N Cityfront Plaza Dr	464-8650

4 • West Loop Gate / Greektown *(312)*

Barbara's Bestsellers	2 N Riverside Plz	258-8007
Walden Bookstore	500 W Madison St	627-8334

5 • The Loop *(312)*

Afrocentric Book Store	333 S State St	939-1956
Barbara's Bestsellers	233 S Wacker Dr	466-0223
Beck's Book Store	209 N Wabash Ave	630-9113
Beck's Book Store	315 S Plymouth Ct	913-0650
Books a Million	144 S Clark St	857-0613
Borders Books & Music	150 N State St	606-0750
Brent Books & Cards	309 W Washington St	364-0126
Cultural Book Store	100 W Randolph St	214-1314
Graham Crackers Comics	69 E Madison St	629-1810
North Loop Comics	226 S Wabash Ave	236-7331
Prairie Avenue Bookshop	418 S Wabash Ave	922-8311
Psychology Bookstore	20 S Clark St	201-8789
Rand McNally Map & Travel	150 S Wacker Dr Lbby	332-2009
Tower Records/ Video/Books	214 S Wabash Ave	663-0660
Waldenbooks	127 W Madison St	236-8446

6 • The Loop / Grant Park *(312)*

Business Savvy	310 S Michigan Ave	408-0667
Chicago Architecture Fndtn	224 S Michigan Ave	922-3432
Rain Dog Books	404 S Michigan Ave	922-1200
Savvy Traveller	310 S Michigan Ave	913-9800

8 • South Loop / Printer's Row *(312)*

Printers Row Fine & Rare Books	715 S Dearborn St	583-1800
Sandmeyer's Bookstore	714 S Dearborn St	922-2104

9 • South Loop / S Michigan Ave *(312)*

Bariff Shop for Judaica	618 S Michigan Ave	322-1740
Columbia College Bookstore	624 S Michigan Ave	344-7406

10 • East Pilsen / Chinatown *(312)*

Chinese Champion Book & Gift	2167 S China Pl	326-3577
World Journal Bookstore	2116 S Archer Ave	842-8005

11 • South Loop / McCormick Place *(312)*

Paragon Book Gallery	1507 S Michigan Ave	663-5155

14 • Prairie Shores / Lake Meadows *(312)*

Living Word Bookstore	3512 S Dr Martin L King Jr Dr	225-7500

19 • Hyde Park / Woodlawn *(773)*

57th Street Books	1301 E 57th St	684-1300
O'Gara & Wilson	1448 E 57th St	363-0993
Powell's Book Store	1501 E 57th St	955-7780
Scholars Bookstore	1466 E 53rd St	288-6565
Seminary Cooperative	5757 S University Ave	752-4381
University-Chicago Bookstore	970 E 58th St	702-8729

20 • Hyde Park East / Jackson Park *(773)*

Carter & Co	5400 S Hyde Park Blvd	363-5590

21 • Wicker Park / Ukrainian Village *(773)*

Luz A La Familia	2425 W Division St	772-0954
Occult Book Store	1579 N Milwaukee Ave	292-0995
Quimby's Bookstore	1854 W North Ave	342-0910

22 • Noble Square / Goose Island *(312)*

Transitions Book Place	1000 W North Ave	951-7323

23 • West Town / Near West Side *(312)*

Malcolm X College Book Store	1900 W Van Buren St	829-6482
Ukranian Book Store	2315 W Chicago Ave	773-276-6373

25 • Illinois Medical District *(312)*

Logan Medical Ctr Book Store	1910 W Harrison St	733-4544
UIC Medical Bookstore	828 S Wolcott Ave	413-5550

26 • University Village / Little Italy *(312)*

Chicago Textbook	1076 W Taylor St	733-8398

27 • Logan Square (South) *(773)*

New World Resource Ctr	2600 W Fullerton Ave	227-4011

28 • Bucktown *(773)*

Libreria Nsra De Lourves	1907 Milwaukee Ave	342-8890
Minor Arcana	1852 N Damen Ave	252-1389

29 • DePaul / Wrightwood / Sheffield *(773)*

Act I Bookstore	2540 N Lincoln Ave	348-6757
Barnes & Noble	1441 W Webster Ave	871-3610

30 • Lincoln Park (773)

Graham Cracker Comics	2562 N Clark St	665-2010
Tower Records/Video/Books	2301 N Clark St	477-5994

31 • Old Town / Near North (312)

Barbara's Book Store	1350 N Wells St	642-5044

32 • Gold Coast / Magnificent Mile (312)

Abbott Hall Book Ctr	710 N Lake Shore Dr	503-8486
Adonis	6 E Walton St	440-1913
Barnes & Noble	1130 N State St	280-8155
Borders Books & Music	830 N Michigan Ave	573-0564
Chicago Rare Book Ctr	56 W Maple St	988-7246
Children In Paradise	909 N Rush St	951-5437
Europa Books	832 N State St	335-9677
Kabbalah Center	810 N Clark St	664-2256
Newberry Bookstore	60 W Walton St	255-3520
Waldenbooks	900 N Michigan Ave	337-0330

33 • Rogers Park West (773)

India Book House & Journals	2551 W Devon Ave	764-6567
Interbook Russian Book Store	2754 W Devon Ave	973-5536
Iqra Book Ctr	2751 W Devon Ave	274-2665
Russian American Book Store	2746 W Devon Ave	761-3233

34 • Rogers Park East (773)

Beck's Book Store	6550 N Sheridan Rd	743-2281
Mustard Seed Bookstore	1143 W Sheridan Rd	973-7055

35 • Arcadia Terrace / Peterson Park (773)

Covenant Bookstore	3200 W Foster Ave	478-4676

37 • Edgewater / Andersonville (773)

Heritage Books	1135 W Granville Ave	262-1566
Women & Children First	5233 N Clark St	769-9299

40 • Uptown / Sheridan Park (773)

Beck's Book Store	4520 N Broadway St	784-7963
Book Box - Shake, Rattle and Read	4812 N Broadway St	334-5311
Liberia de Hable Hispana	4441 N Broadway St	878-2117

42 • North Center / Roscoe Village (773)

Stern's Psychology Book Store	2004 W Roscoe St	883-5100

43 • Wrigleyville/ Lakeview (773)

Bookworks	3444 N Clark St	871-5318
Chicago Comics	3244 N Clark St	528-1983
Hanley's Bookstore	923 W Belmont Ave	281-9999
Healing Earth Resources	3111 N Ashland Ave	327-8459
Powell's Book Store	2850 N Lincoln Ave	248-1444

44 • Lakeview East (773)

Barnes & Noble	659 W Diversey Pkwy	871-9004
Bookman's Corner	2959 N Clark St	929-8298
Borders Books & Music	2817 N Clark St	935-3909
New & Used Books	2928 N Broadway St	404-5422
Selected Works Bookstore	3510 N Broadway St	975-0002
Unabridged Books	3251 N Broadway St	883-9119

As a rule of thumb, Saturday nights are amateur nights, when every downtown venue is packed with 708s and 847s. City slickers know to go out on weeknights, when covers are cheaper and there's room to breath. While we've done our best to keep current on all the clubs in Chicago, you can appreciate how trends change and establishments frequently open and close. Check *The Reader*, *New City*, *Chicago Magazine*, and *Windy City Times* for the latest on Chicago's club scene.

Area codes are those in the map header unless otherwise noted.

1 • River North / Fulton District (312)

Mickey Finn's	412 N Milwaukee Ave	847-362-8595
Q Nightlife	358 W Ontario St	944-3586
Rednofive & Fifth Floor	440 N Halsted	733-6699

2 • Near North / River North (312)

Andy's	11 E Hubbard St	642-6805
Blue Chicago	736 N Clark St	642-6261
Buzz Club	308 W Erie St	475-9800
Catch 35	35 W Wacker Dr	346-3500
Club 720	720 N Wells St	397-0600
Erik & Me	1 W Illinois St	630-377-9222
Excalibur	632 N Dearborn St	266-1944
Features Bar & Grill	10 W Chicago Ave	630-416-3310
Frankie's Blue Room	16 W Chicago Ave	630-416-4898
Gentry	440 N State St	836-0933
Harry's Velvet Room	56 W Illinois St	527-5600
House Of Blues	329 N Dearborn St	923-2000
House Of Blues Hotel	333 N Dearborn St	245-0333
Howl at the Moon	26 W Hubbard St	863-7427
Magnum's Prime Steakhouse	1701 W Golf	847-952-8755
Minx	111 W Hubbard St	828-9000
Mystique	157 W Ontario St	642-2582
Palaggi's Ristorante Italiano	10 W Hubbard St	527-1010
Redhead Piano Bar	16 W Ontario St	640-1000
Spy Bar	646 N Franklin St	587-8779
Vision	640 N Dearborn St	266-2114
White Star	225 W Ontario St	337-8080

3 • Streeterville / Magnificent Mile (312)

Becco D'Oro Ristorante	160 E Huron St	787-1300
Fitzers Pub	Fitzpatrick Chicago Hotel, 166 E Superior	787-6000
Joe's Be-Bop Cafe & Jazz Emporium	Navy Pier, 600 E Grand Ave	595-5299
Navy Pier Beer Garden	600 E Grand Ave	595-7437
Sayat Nova	157 E Ohio St	773-381-7171

4 • West Loop Gate / Greektown (312)

Blonde	820 W Lake St	226-4500
Chromium	817 W Lake St	666-8106
Metro Deli & Café	Union Station, Canal & Adams	655-0600
Reunion	811 W Lake St	491-9600
Snuggery Saloon & Dining Room	Union Station, Canal & Adams	441-9334

5 • The Loop (312)

Cal's	400 S Wells St	939-9700
Club Mercury	221 W Van Buren St	427-1774
Encore	171 W Randolph St	338-3788

6 • The Loop / Grant Park (312)

Rednofive & Fifth Floor	440 N Halsted	733-6699
Entre Nous	Fairmont Hotel, 200 N Columbus	565-7997
Metropole Room	Fairmont Hotel, 200 N Columbus	565-8000

8 • South Loop / Printer's Row (312)

Blackie's	755 S Clark St	832-1806
Buddy Guy's Legends	754 S Wabash Ave	427-0333
Hothouse	31 E Balbo Ave	362-9707

11 • South Loop / McCormick Place (312)

Chicago Firehouse	1401 S Michigan Ave	786-1401
Club Alphonse	1351 S Michigan Ave	697-0975
Java Oasis	2240 S Michigan Ave	328-1216
The Cotton Club	1710 S Michigan Ave	341-9787
Velvet Lounge	2128 1/2 S Indiana	791-9050

13 • Bridgeport (East) (312)

Puffer's	3356 S Halsted St	773-927-6073

16 • Bronzeville (773)

Checker Board Lounge	423 E 43rd St	624-3240
Some Like It Black Coffee Club	4500 S Michigan Ave	425-7032

21 • Wicker Park / Ukrainian Village (773)

Bar Thirteen	1944 W Division St	394-1313
Big Horse Lounge	1558 N Milwaukee Ave	278-5785
D'Vine	1950 W North Ave	235-5700
Davenport's Piano Bar & Cabaret	1383 N Milwaukee Ave	278-1830
Double Door	1572 N Milwaukee Ave	489-3160
Innjoy	2051 W Division St	394-2066
Lava Lounge	859 N Damen Ave	772-3355
Phyllis' Musical Inn	1800 W Division St	486-9862
Red Dog	1958 W North Ave	278-1009
Reservation Blues	1566 N Milwaukee Ave	645-5200
Sinibar	1540 N Milwaukee Ave	278-7797
Smoke Daddy	1804 W Division St	772-6656
Spareroom	2416 W North Ave	489-3734
Squareone	1561 N Milwaukee Ave	227-7111
Subterranean Cafe & Cabaret	2011 W North Ave	278-6600
Taste	1922 W North Ave	276-8000
Ten56	1056 N Damen Ave	227-4906
The Note	1565 N Milwaukee Ave	489-0011

22 • Noble Square / Goose Island (312)

Big Wig	1551 W Division St	773-235-9100
Biology Bar	1516 N Fremont St	266-1234
Circus	901 W Weed St	266-1200
Crobar the Nightclub	1543 N Kingsbury St	413-7000
Dig	1551 N Sheffield Ave	377-1727
Exit	1315 W North Ave	773-395-2700
Freddy's Rib House	1555 N Sheffield Ave	377-7427
Joe's	940 W Weed St	337-3486
Life's Too Short	1177 N Elston Ave	773-384-1040
Stevie B's	1401 N Ashland Ave	773-486-7427
Zentra	923 W Weed St	787-0400

23 • West Town / Near West Side (312)

Bally Muck	1930 Grand Ave	847-244-5636
Odum	2116 W Chicago Ave	666-0795

24 • River West / West Town (312)

Babalu	1645 W Jackson Blvd	733-3512
Bird's Nest	2500 N Southport Ave	773-472-1502
Carmichael's Chicago Steak House	1052 W Monroe St	433-0025
Crab Street Saloon	1061 W Madison	433-0013
Moretti's	1645 W Jackson Blvd	427-2572
Saussy	1156 W Grand Ave	491-1122

27 • Logan Square (South) (773)

3030	3030 W Cortland St	862-3616
Boulevard Café	3137 W Logan Blvd	384-8600
El Cid	2115 N Milwaukee Ave	252-4747
Fireside Bowl	2646 W Fullerton Ave	486-2700
Lula Café	2537 N Kedzie Ave	489-9554
Planeta Mexico/OK Corral	2047 N Milwaukee Ave	489-0600
Streetside Café	3201 W Armitage Ave	252-9700

28 • Bucktown (773)

Artful Dodger	1734 W Wabansia Ave	227-6859
Clybar	2417 N Clybourn Ave	388-1877
Gallery Cabaret	2020 N Oakley Ave	489-5471
Get Me High Lounge	1758 N Honore St	252-4090
Liar's Club	1665 W Fullerton Ave	665-1110
Quenchers Saloon	2401 N Western Ave	276-9730
The Mutiny	2428 N Western Ave	486-7774

29 • DePaul/Wrightwood/Sheffield (773)

Big House	2354 N Clybourn Ave	435-0130
Bistro Ultra	2239 N Clybourn Ave	529-3300
Copa	1637 N Clybourn	312-642-3449
Deja Vu Bar Room	2624 N Lincoln Ave	871-0205
Gin Mill	2462 N Lincoln Ave	549-3232
Green Dolphin Street	2200 N Ashland Ave	395-0066
Hideout	1354 W Wabansia Ave	227-4433
Irish Eyes	2519 N Lincoln Ave	348-9548
Kustom	1997 N Clybourn Ave	528-3400
McGee's	950 W Webster	549-8200
The (Prop) House	1675 N Elston Ave	486-2390
US Beer Co	1801 N Clybourn	871-7799
Webster Wine Bar	1480 W Webster	868-0608

30 • Lincoln Park *(773)*

B.L.U.E.S.	2519 N Halsted	528-1012
Bar 3	2138 N Halsted	348-3665
Griffin's Public House	2710 N Halsted	525-7313
Hidden Shamrock	2723 N Halsted	883-0304
Katacomb	1909 N Lincoln Ave	312-337-4040
Kingston Mines	2548 N Halsted	477-4646
Lion Head Pub & The Apartment	2251 N Lincoln Ave	348-5100
Neo	2350 N Clark St	528-2622
Park West	322 W Armitage Ave	
Prodigal Son Bar & Grill	2626 N Halsted	248-3093
Second City	1616 N Wells St	
Wise Fools Pub	2270 N Lincoln Ave	929-1300

31 • Old Town / Near North *(312)*

Black Orchid	230 W North Ave, 3rd Fl	944-2200
Cucina Bella	1612 N Sedgwick St	274-1119
Dragon Room	809 W Evergreen Ave	751-2900
Glow	1615 N Clybourn	587-8469
Weeds	1555 N Dayton St	943-7815
Zanies Comedy Club	1548 N Wells St	

32 • Gold Coast / Magnificent Mile *(312)*

Alumni Club	15 W Division St	337-4349
Backroom	1007 N Rush St	751-2433
Carton's Lounge	21 E Chestnut St	664-5512
Dragonfly	1206 N State St	787-7600
Jilly's Retro Club	1009 N Rush St	664-1001
Underground Wonder Bar	10 E Walton	266-7761

33 • Rogers Park West *(773)*

Cary's Lounge	2251 W Devon Ave	743-5737

34 • Rogers Park East *(773)*

Chase Cafe	7301 N Sheridan Rd	743-5650
Cocoabean Expressions	7007 N Glenwood Ave	274-6057
Gateway Bar & Grill	7545 N Clark St	262-5767
Heartland Cafe	7000 N Glenwood Ave	465-8005
No Exit	6970 N Glenwood Ave	743-3355
Red Line Tap	7006 N Glenwood Ave	274-3239

37 • Edgewater / Andersonville *(773)*

Edgewater Lounge	5600 N Ashland Ave	878-3343
Hollywood East	5650 N Broadway St	271-4711
Pumping Company	6157 N Broadway St	743-7994

38 • Ravenswood Manor *(773)*

Candlestick Maker	4432 N Kedzie Ave	463-0158

39 • Ravenswood / North Center *(773)*

Club 950	2122 W Lawrence Ave	878-8241

40 • Uptown / Sheridan Park *(773)*

Aragon	1106 W Lawrence Ave	561-9500
Carol's Pub	4659 N Clark St	334-2402
Green Mill	4802 N Broadway St	878-5552
Joy-Blue	3998 N Southport Ave	477-3330
Riveria	4746 N Racine Ave	275-6800
T's	5025 N Clark St	784-6000

41 • Avondale / Old Irving *(773)*

Chief O'Neill's Pub	3471 N Elston Ave	473-5263

42 • North Center / Roscoe Village *(773)*

Hungry Brain	2319 W Belmont Ave	935-2118
Kitsch'N	2005 W Roscoe St	248-7372
Le Relais	3925 N Lincoln Ave	312-493-6783
Martyrs'	3855 N Lincoln Ave	404-9494
Seanchai	2345 W Belmont Ave	549-4444
Tiny Lounge	1814 W Addison St	296-9620

43 • Wrigleyville/ Lakeview *(773)*

Bar Celona	3474 N Clark St	244-8000
Berlin	954 W Belmont Ave	348-4975
Bottom Lounge	3206 N Wilton St	975-0505
Cherry Red	2833 N Sheffield Ave	477-3661
Cubby Bear	1059 W Addison St	327-1662
Elbo Room	2871 N Lincoln Ave	549-5549
Fizz Bar & Grill	3220 N Lincoln Ave	348-6000
Fly Me To The Moon	3400 N Clark St	528-4033
Fuel	3724 N Clark St	248-3330
Goose Island Brewery	3535 N Clark St	549-9624
Gunther Murphy's	1638 W Belmont Ave	472-5139
Hi-Tops	3551 N Sheffield Ave	348-0009
John Barleycorn	3524 N Clark St	549-6000
Lithium	1124 W Belmont Ave	477-6513
Metro	3730 N Clark St	549-0203
Mullen's	3527 N Clark St	325-2319
Pops For Champagne	2934 N Sheffield Ave	472-1000
Schubas	3159 N Southport Ave	525-2508
Smart Bar	3730 N Clark St	549-4140
Strega Nona	3747 N Southport Ave	244-0990
Trace	3714 N Clark St	477-3400
Uncommon Ground Café	1214 W Grace St	929-3680
Underground Lounge	952 W Newport	327-2739
Vaughan's Pub	2917 N Sheffield Ave	281-8188
Wild Hare	3530 N Clark St	327-4273

44 • Lakeview East *(773)*

Cocktail	3359 N Halsted St	477-1420
Crush	2843 N Halsted	528-7569
Gentry on Halsted	3320 N Halsted	348-1053
Harrigan's	2816 N Halsted	248-5933
Jack's	3201 N Halsted	244-9191
Spin	800 W Belmont Ave	327-7711

The impeccably restored Music Box Theatre, built in 1929, features fantastic Moorish architecture and thumbs up, highbrow cinema. The Three Penny sells cheap tickets to the almost-newest releases. The main theater at McClurg Court Theatre has one of the city's largest screens. Drunken frat-boy audiences at The Vic's Brew & View nights are as annoying as the movies they show.

Movie Theater	*Address*	*Phone*	*Map*
AMC City North	2600 N Western Ave	773-394-1601	28
Biograph Theatre	2433 N Lincoln Ave	773-348-4123	29
Brew & View at the Vic	3145 N Sheffield Ave	312-618-8439	43
Burnham Plaza Theater	826 S Wabash Ave	312-922-1121	8
Chicago Underground Film Festival	3109 N Western Ave	773-327-3456	42
Cineplex Odeon	600 N Michigan Ave	312-255-9340	3
Davis Theatre	4614 N Lincoln Ave	773-784-0893	39
Esquire Theater	58 E Oak St	312-280-0101	32
Facets Multimedia Theatre	1517 Fullerton Ave	773-281-9075	29
Fine Arts Theatre	418 S Michigan Ave	312-939-3700	6
Gene Siskel Film Center	164 N State St	312-846-2800	5
Landmark Century Cinema	2828 N Clark St	773-248-7744	44
Loews Cineplex	1471 W Webster Ave	773-327-3100	29
Logan Theater	2646 N Milwaukee Ave	773-252-0627	27
McClurg Court Theatre	330 E Ohio St	312-642-0723	3
Music Box Theatre	3733 N Southport Ave	773-871-6604	43
Navy Pier IMAX Theatre	700 E Grand Ave	312-595-5629	3
Piper's Alley Loews Cineplex	1608 N Wells St	312-642-7500	31
Sony Theatre	1616 N Wells St	312-642-7500	30
Three Penny Theatre	2424 N Lincoln Ave	773-935-5744	30
Village North Theaters	6746 N Sheridan Rd	773-764-9100	34
Village Theater	1548 N Clark St	312-642-2403	32
Village Theatres Burnham Plaza	826 S Wabash Ave	312-554-9100	8
Water Tower Theater	157 E Chestnut St	312-274-1010	32

The big ones already draw crowds and fleets of school buses. Exercise different parts of your brain at these smaller, interesting museums: David & Alfred Smart Museum, the Oriental Institute, DuSable Museum of African-American History, International Museum of Surgical Science, Mexican Fine Arts Center Museum, ABA Museum of Law, Spertus Museum, and the National Vietnam Veterans Art Museum.

Museum	*Address*	*Phone*	*Map*
A Philip Randolph Pullman Porter Museum	10406 S Maryland Ave	773-928-3935	
ABA Museum of Law	750 N Lake Shore Dr	312-988-5730	32
Adler Planetarium & Astronomy Museum	1300 S Lake Shore Dr	312-922-STAR	11
Arts Club of Chicago	1300 N Dearborn Pkwy	312-944-6250	3
Center for Intuitive & Outsider Art	756 N Milwaukee Ave	312-243-9088	24
Chicago Architecture Foundation	224 S Michigan Ave	312-922-3432	6
Chicago Athenaeum at Schamburg	225 N Michigan Ave	847-895-3950	6
Chicago Children's Museum	700 E Grand Ave	312-527-1000	3
Chicago Historical Society	1601 N Clark St	312-642-4600	32
Clarke House Museum	1827 S Indiana Ave	312-745-0040	11
Das Motorad Museum	1901 S Western Ave	312-738-2269	25
David & Alfred Smart Museum	5550 S Greenwood Ave	773-702-0200	19
DL Moody Museum	820 N La Salle Dr	312-329-4404	31
Du Sable Museum of African-American History	740 E 56th Pl	773-947-0600	18
Field Museum	1400 S Lake Shore Dr	312-922-9410	11
Filipino American Historical Society of Chicago Museum	3952 N Ashland Ave	773-947-8696	43
Frank Lloyd Wright Home & Studio	951 Chicago Ave, Oak Park	708-848-1976	
Glessner House Museum	1800 S Prairie	312-326-1480	11
Hellenic Museum & Cultural Ctr	168 N Michigan Ave	312-726-1234	6
International Monetary Market	1516 N Lake Shore Dr	312-642-6502	32
International Museum of Surgical Science	1524 N Lake Shore Dr	312-642-6502	32
Jane Addams Hull-House Museum	800 S Halsted St	312-413-5353	26
John G Shedd Aquarium	1200 S Lake Shore Dr	312-939-2438	9
Leather Archives & Museum	6418 N Greenview Ave	773-761-9200	34
Mexican Fine Arts Center	1852 W 19th St	312-738-1503	25
Mimi International	56 E Oak St	312-664-6161	32
Museum of Contemporary Art	220 E Chicago Ave	312-280-2660	3
Museum of Holography-Chicago	1134 W Washington Blvd	312-226-1007	24
Museum of Science & Industry	5700 S Lake Shore Dr	773-684-1414	37
Museum Shop of the Art Institute	900 N Michigan Ave	312-482-8275	32
Museum of Contemporary Photography	Columbia College, 600 S Michigan Ave	312-663-5554	9
Museums in the Park	104 S Michigan Ave	312-857-7136	6
National Jazz Museum	1727 S Indiana Ave	312-663-3038	11
National Vietnam Veterans Art Museum	1801 S Indiana Ave	312-326-0270	11
Oriental Institute Museum	University of Chicago, 1155 E 58th St	773-702-9514	19
Pallas Photographica Gallery	319 W Erie St	312-664-1257	2
Peggy Notebaert Nature Museum	2430 N Cannon Dr	773-755-5100	30
Polish Museum of America	984 N Milwaukee Ave	773-384-3352	22
Renaissance Center	5710 N Broadway St	773-722-2900	37
Robie House	5757 S Woodlawn Ave	773-834-1847	19
Rogers Park Historical Society	6424 N Western Ave	773-764-4078	33
Smith Museum of Stained Glass	700 E Grand Ave (Navy Pier)	312-329-6049	3
Spertus Museum	618 S Michigan Ave	312-922-9012	9
Swedish American Museum Center	5211 N Clark St	773-728-8111	37
Terra Museum of American Art	664 N Michigan Ave	312-664-3939	3
The Art Institute of Chicago	111 S Michigan Ave	312-443-3600	6
The Museum of Broadcast Communications	78 E Washington St	312-629-6000	5
The Peace Museum	100 N Central Park Ave	773-638-6450	
Ukrainian Institute of Art	2318 W Chicago Ave	773-227-5522	23
Ukrainian National Museum of Chicago	721 N Oakley Blvd	312-421-8020	23

*Key: $: Under $10 / $$: $10–$20 / $$$: $20–$30 / $$$$: $30+ * : Does not accept credit cards. / † : Accepts only American Express.*

Map 1 • River North / Fulton Market District

Chilpancingo	358 W Ontario St	312-266-9525	$$$	Gourmet Mexican madness.
Iguana Cafe	517 N Halsted St	312-432-0663	$	Internet cafe with bagels and such.
La Scarola	721 W Grand Ave	312-243-1740	$$	Authentic Italian in a super-close atmosphere.
Reza's	432 W Ontario St	312-664-4500	$$	Persian food with not-so-much atmosphere.
Scoozi!	410 W Huron St	312-943-5900	$$	Typical Italian.
Thyme	464 N Halsted	312-226-4300	$$$	Eclectic eating in funky atmosphere.
Zealous	419 W Superior St	312-475-9112	*	Over the top gourmet from Trotter protégé.

Map 2 • Near North / River North

Ace Grill	71 E Wacker	312-346-7100	$$$	Low-key American fare.
Bob Chinn's Crab House	321 N La Salle St		$$$	Worth the wait.
Brasserie Jo	59 W Hubbard St	312-595-0800	*	Swanky French.
Cafe Iberico	739 N La Salle Blvd	312-573-1510	*	Shoulder-to-shoulder tapas joint.
Chicago Chop House	60 W Ontario St	312-787-7100	*	You want chops? They got chops.
Club Lago	331 W Superior St	312-951-2849	$$	Generous servings of basic Italian.
Crofton on Wells	535 Wells St	312-755-1790	*	Pushing the envelope with top regional cuisine.
Cyrano's Bistrot & Wine Bar	546 N Wells St	312-467-0546	*	Steak frites!
Erawan Royal Thai Cuisine	729 N Clark St	312-642-6888	$$$$	Top shelf Thai.
Frontera Grill	445 N Clark St	312-661-1434	*	Rick Bayless's famous cantina—expect to wait.
Gaylord India	678 N Clark St	312-664-1700	*	Indian buffet.
Gene & Georgetti	500 N Franklin St	312-527-3718	*	Big steaks.
Harray Caray's	33 W Kinzie St	312-828-0966	*	Tourist trap for suburban punters.
House of Blues	329 N Dearborn St	312-923-2007	*	Sunday gospel brunch buffet.
Jaipur Palace	22 E Hubbard St	312-595-0911	*	Upscale Indian buffet.
Kevin	9 W Hubbard St	312-595-0055	$$$	Promising new fusion.
Kinzie Chophouse	400 N Wells St	312-822-0191	$$$	Neighborhood steak house.
Klay Oven	414 N Orleans St	312-527-3999	*	Upscale Indian buffet.
Lawry's The Prime Rib	100 E Ontario St	312-787-5000	*	Carnivore's delight.
Linos	222 W Ontario St	312-266-6159	$$$	Old school service at this classic Italian. Closed on Sundays.
Lou Malnati's Pizzeria	439 N Wells St	312-828-9800	*	Famous in a city famous for pizza.
Maggiano's Little Italy	516 N Clark St	312-644-7700	*	Gut-busting family-style Italian.
Magnum's Prime Steakhouse	225 W Ontario St	312-337-8080	*	Classic supper club ambience.
Mr Beef	666 N Orleans St	312-337-8500	$	Get your Italian beef fix at this Chicago classic.
Nacional 27	325 W Huron St	312-664-2727	*	Pan-latin supper club with dance floor. Babaloo!
Narcisse	710 N Clark St	312-787-2675	*	Dripping in luxury in a champagne, foie gras way.
Original Gino's East	633 N Wells St	312-943-1124	*	Great for teenagers.
Pizzeria Due	619 N Wabash Ave	312-280-5110	*	Sister to Pizzeria Uno.
Pizzeria Uno	29 E Ohio St	312-321-1000	*	Legendary Chicago pizza.
Redfish	400 N State St	312-467-1600	$$	Fun Cajun; free beads and good drinks.
Rosebud on Rush	720 N Rush St	312-266-6444	*	A branch of Chicago's legendary old school Italian.
Rumba	351 W Hubbard St	312-222-0770	$$	Burgers, fries, the regular.
Shaw's Crab House & Blue Crab Lounge	21 E Hubbard St	312-527-2722	*	A seafood destination.
Smith & Wollensky	318 N State St	312-670-9900	*	Chicago branch of New York steak emporium.
Sorriso	321 N Clark St	312-644-0283	*	Italian in lovely environs.
Star of Siam	11 E Illinois St	312-670-0100	*	Really good Thai food.
Sullivan's Steakhouse	415 N Dearborn St	312-527-3510	*	Another upscale steakhouse.
Sushi Naniwa	607 N Wells St	312-255-8555	$$	Quality sushi. Great outdoor.
Thai Star Cafe	660 N State St	312-951-1196	*	Scrappy Thai—good food overcomes décor.
Tizi Melloul	531 N Wells St	312-670-4338	*	Exotic setting for Moroccan tangines.
Topolobampo	445 N Clark St	312-661-1434	*	Standard bearer for upscale Mexican.
Vong's Thai Kitchen	6 W Hubbard St	312-644-8664	$$	Thai with a satisfying kick.
Wildfire	159 W Erie St	312-787-9000	*	Fun, trendy American.
Zinfandel	59 W Grand Ave	312-527-1818	$$$	Ethnic American with menu that changes monthly.

Map 3 • Streeterville / Magnificent Mile

Bandera	535 N Michigan Ave	312-644-3524	$$	Lunch above Mag Mile.
Bice Ristorante	158 E Ontario St	312-664-1474	*	Well-regarded Italian.
Billy Goat Tavern	430 N Michigan Ave	312-222-1525	*	Cheezboiga no fries-chips, pepsi, no coke.
Cambridge House Grill	167 E Ohio St	312-828-0600	$	Diner; open late.
Capital Grille	633 N St Clair St	312-337-9400	$$$$	Macho steak & zin.
Cite	Lake Point Tower, 70th fl 505 N Lake Shore Dr	312-644-4050	$$$$	Contemporary with a view.
Dick's Last Resort	435 E Illinois St	312-836-7870	*	Tourist's last memory of the night.
Eli's the Place for Steaks	215 E Chicago Ave	312-642-1393	*	The place for cheesecake.
Emilio's Tapas Sol y Nieve	215 E Ohio St	312-467-7177	*	One of the nicest branches of the local tapas chain.
Hatsuhana	160 E Ontario St	312-280-8808	*	Sushi-up after shopping.
Heaven on Seven	600 N Michigan Ave	312-280-7774	*	Cajun grub and cocktails.
Hot Diggity Dogs	251 E Ohio St	312-943-5598	$*	Walk-up chicawga dawgs.
Indian Garden	247 E Ontario St, 2nd fl	312-280-4910	$$	Good veggie options.
Kamehachi	240 E Ontario St	312-587-0600	*	One of Chicago's top sushi spots.
Les Nomades	222 E Ontario St	312-649-9010	$$$$	Deluxe haute cuisine.
Nomi	Park Hyatt Chicago, 800 N Michigan Ave,	312-335-1234	$$$$	Deluxe French fusion.
Riva	Navy Pier	312-644-7482	*	Touristic fine dining on the Pier.
Ron of Japan	230 E Ontario St	312-644-6500	*	Guilty pleasure teppanyaki.
Sayat Nova	157 E Ohio St	312-644-9159	$$	Armenian.
Tru	676 N St Clair St	312-202-0001	$$$$	Still hot.
Volare	201 E Grand Ave	312-410-9900	$$$	Casual Italian.
Wave	644 N Lake Shore Dr	312-255-4460	*	Trendy W Hotel gruberie is making...you guessed it.

Map 4 • West Loop Gate / Greektown

Artopolis Bakery & Cafe	306 S Halsted St	312-559-9000	$$	Frappes to Mediterranean pizza.
Athena	212 S Halsted St	312-655-0000	$$$	Goddess Athena inspired outdoor and indoor.
Azure	832 W Randolph St	773-455-1400	$$$	Cal-Ital.
Blackbird	619 W Randolph St	312-715-0708	*	Chic les plus ultra.
Bluepoint Oyster Bar	741 W Randolph St	312-207-1222	*	Trendy gulpers.
Byzantium	232 S Halsted St	312-454-1227	$$	Tapas Greek piano bar.
Costa's	340 S Halsted St	312-263-9700	$$$	Greece at its warmest. Have the octopus.
Gold Coast Dogs	2 N Riverside Plz	312-879-0447	*	Gotta have the dogs.
Gold Coast Dogs	Union Station	312-258-8585	*	Gotta have the dogs.
Greek Islands	200 S Halsted St	312-782-9855	$$$	Greek Heaven—not to be missed.
J and C Inn	558 W Van Buren St	312-663-4114	$$$	Dingy outside—best sandwiches in town inside.
Lou Mitchell's	565 W Jackson Blvd	312-939-3111	*	Rub shoulders with local pols at this legendary grill.
Nine Muses	315 S Halsted St	312-902-9922	$$$	Brick bars and backgammon.
Parthenon	314 S Halsted St	312-726-2407	$$$	Creaters of flaming saganaki!
Pegasus Restaurant and Taverna	130 S Halsted St	312-226-3377	$$$	Rooftop garden—Chicago secret!.
Red Light	820 W Randolph St	312-733-8880	*	Trendy pan-Asian.
Robinson's No 1 Ribs	225 S Canal St	312-258-8477	*	Dress-down and dig in.
Roditys	222 S Halsted St	312-454-0800	$$$	Greek lamb since 1972.
Santorini	800 W Adams St	312-829-8820	$$$	Fish, shellfish, and roasted chicken. Yum.
Sushi Wabi	842 W Randolph St	312-563-1224	*	Self-consciously chic sushi.
Vivo	838 W Randolph St	312-733-3379	*	Young, trendy Italian.

Map 5 • The Loop

Atwood Cafe	1 W Washington St	312-368-1900	$$$	High tea with contemporary flair.
Berghoff Restaurant	17 W Adams St	312-427-3170	$$	Chicago icon with hearty German fare.
Billy Goat Tavern	330 S Wells St	312-554-0297	*	Chain of cheezboiga joint made famous by John Belushi.
Everest	440 S La Salle St	312-663-8920	$$$$	High fallutin' food.
French Quarter/Palmer House Hilton	17 E Monroe St	312-621-7363	$$$	Festive Chicago tradition.
Gold Coast Dogs	159 N Wabash Ave	312-917-1677	*	Onion, peppers, pickle spear, tomato, celery salt, mustard.
Gold Coast Dogs	17 S Wabash Ave	312-578-1133	*	Classic dog joint.
Heaven on Seven	111 N Wabash Ave	312-263-6443	$$	Cajun Chicago classic. Closed for dinner.
Italian Village	71 W Monroe St	312-332-4040	$$$	Theater dining tradition.

*Key: $: Under $10 / $$: $10–$20 / $$$: $20–$30 / $$$$: $30+   * : Does not accept credit cards. / † : Accepts only American Express.*

Map 5 • The Loop — continued

La Cantina Enoteca	71 W Monroe St	312-332-7005	*	Pre-show fave.
La Rosetta	70 W Madison St	312-332-9500	*	Family-style Italian.
Miller's Pub	134 S Wabash Ave	312-263-4988	*	Down-to-earth grub in a pub.
Mrs Levy's Delicatessen	233 S Wacker Dr	312-993-0530	*	No surprises here.
Oasis Restaurant	21 N Wabash Ave	312-558-1058	$$*	Middle Eastern hideout inside of a jewelry store.
Quincy Grille on the River	200 S Wacker Dr	312-627-1800	*	Solid new American.
Rhapsody	65 E Adams St	312-786-9911	*	Upscale pre-symphony grub.
Robinson's No 1 Ribs	77 W Jackson Blvd	312-431-1001	*	It ain't about bein' fancy.
Russian Tea Time	77 E Adams St	312-360-0000	$$$	Elegant Russian cuisine.
Taza	39 S Wabash Ave	312-425-9988	*	Fast tasty chicken and mash.
Trattoria No 10	10 N Dearborn St	312-984-1718	$$$	Authentic Italian.
Vivere	71 W Monroe St	312-733-3379	*	Stylish Italian, packed before shows.

Map 6 • The Loop / Grant Park

Art Institute Restaurant on the Park	111 S Michigan Ave	312-443-3600	$$	Lovely, scenic lunch-time dining. Closes at 2:30 pm.
Artist's Cafe	412 S Michigan Ave	312-939-7855	$$*	Students and tourists lunch at this old-time diner.
Bennigan's	150 S Michigan Ave	312-427-0577	$$	The busiest Bennigan's in the world!
Rain Dog Books & Cafe	408 S Michigan Ave	312-922-1200		Killer smoothies keep you from being a starving writer.

Map 7 • South Loop / River City

Bake for Me	608 W Roosevelt Rd	312-957-1994	$	Good coffee and pastries.
Harrison Red Hot	565 W Harrison St	312-341-1979	$	Hot dog stand.
Harrison St Grill	506 W Harrison St	312-957-9100	$$	Holiday Inn burger bar.
Manny's Coffee Shop	1141 S Jefferson St	312-939-2855	$	Famous deli—popular with politicians.
Nick's Grill	518 W Harrison St	312-341-9163	$	Burgers and chicken.
White Palace Grill	1159 S Canal St	312-939-7167	$	Greasy cabbie chow.

Map 8 • South Loop / Printer's Row / Dearborn Park

Bar Louie	47 W Polk	312-347-0000		Upscale bar with one of the best bar kitchens in Chicago. Late kitchen til 1 am.
Blackies	755 S Clark St	312-786-1161	*	A famous burger, lesser-known best breakfast in S. Loop on Fri, Sat, Sun.
Hackneys	733 S Dearborn St	312-939-3870		A specialty burger and onion loaf a northshore legend since 1939; now has a little known outlet in downtown.
Prairie Restaurant	500 S Dearborn St	312-663-1143	$$$$	Stylish heartland dining.
South Loop Club	701 S State St	312-427-2787		Very casual bar resturant with surprisingly good kitchen.
Trattoria Caterina	616 S Dearborn St	312-939-7606		A little touch of Italy, and a great value for Italian.

Map 9 • South Loop / S Michigan Ave

Oysy	888 S Michigan Ave	312-922-1127	$$$	Chic, industrial sushi setting.

Map 10 • East Pilsen / Chinatown

Cugino's, The Original Cheesie Beef	300 W Cermak Rd	312-528-1000	*	
Emperor's Choice	2238 S Wentworth Ave	312-225-8800	$	Start with seafood; finish with tea.
Happy Chef Dim Sum House	2164 S Archer Ave	312-808-3869	$	Entrees priced to try several dishes.
Hong Min	221 W Cermak Rd	312-842-5026	$	Shirimp toast, Mongolian beef, dim sum. Mmm.
Lao Sze Chuan Spice City	2172 S Archer Ave	312-326-5040		Authentic Chinese dishes plus evening karaoke.
Penang	2201 S Wentworth Ave	312-326-6888	$	Malaysian favorites.
Phoenix	2131 S Archer Ave	312-328-0848	$	The best Chinese breakfast in town.
Three Happiness	209 W Cermak Rd	312-842-1964	$	So good it has a junior restaurant nearby. Long waits for dim sum.
Won Kow	2237 S Wentworth Ave	312-842-7500	$	Cheap, tasty dim sum.

Map 11 • South Loop / McCormick Place

Chef Luciano	49 E Cermak Rd	312-326-0062	$	Walk-in restaurant with eclectic entrees; Italian/African/Cajun influences.
Chicago Firehouse Resturant	1401 S Michigan Ave	312-786-1401		Transformed Chicago firehouse complete with pole and fine dining.
Gioco	1312 S Wabash Ave	312-939-3870		Great Italian dining.
NetWorks (at Hyatt Regency McCormick Place)	2233 S Dr Martin L King Jr Dr	312-567-1234	$$	Contemporary American with a focus on Chicago specialties.

Map 12 • Bridgeport (West)

Johnny O's	3465 S Morgan St	773-927-1011	*	
Mexico Steak House	2983 S Archer Ave	773-254-5151		
Polo's Nut & Candy Cafe	3322 S Morgan St	773-927-7656		

Map 13 • Bridgeport (East)

Bridgeport Restaurant	3500 S Halsted St	773-247-8977		
Dox's Place	600 W Pershing Rd	773-927-0350	*	24-hour grill.
Ferro's Homemade Italian Lemonade	200 W 31 St	312-842-0702	*	
Franco's Ristorante	300 W 31st St	312-225-9566		Family-style Italian near Sox park.
Furama	2828 S Wentworth Ave	312-225-6888	*	Outskirts of Chinatown, great dim sum and karaoke to boot!
Graziano's Ristorante	605 W 31st St	312-326-1399		
Healthy Food Restaurant	3236 S Halsted St	312-326-2724	*	Sauerkraut soup is a must.
Kevin's Hamburger Heaven	554 W Pershing Rd	773-924-5771	*	Hamburgers and milkshakes.
Offshore Steak House	480 W 26th St	312-842-1362	$$	Great deals, simple setting.
Phil's Pizza	3551 S Halsted St	773-523-0947	*	Pizza-rific.
Sugar Shack	630 W 26th St	312-949-1153	*	
Wing Yip Chop Suey	537 W 26th	312-326-2822	*	Nader bumper sticker on window.

Map 14 • Prairie Shores / Lake Meadows

Blue Sea Drive Inn	427 E Pershing Rd	773-285-3325	$*	Fast food and carry out.
Bronzeville Market & Deli	339 E 35th St	312-225-2988	$	Simple, convenient, easy, and old-fashioned.
Chicago Rib House, The	3851 S Michigan Ave	773-268-8750	$*	It is named like that for a reason. All day lunch.
Fisher Fish & Chicken	3901 S Dr ML King Jr Dr	773-924-4444	$*	The catfish is worth the price.
Hong Kong Delight	327 E 35th St	312-842-2929	$$*	Not quite like being there, but close enough.
Mississippi Rick's	3351 S Dr ML King Jr Dr	312-791-0090	$*	Fish and tips, all kinds of meat with a little on the side.

Map 16 • Bronzeville

Gladys Luncheonette	4527 S Indiana Ave	773-548-4566	*	Soul food legend.
Harold's Chicken Shack	307 E 51st St	773-373-9016	$*	Fries, bread, and chicken.
Harold's Chicken Shack	364 E 47th St	773-285-8362	$*	It may say #7 but it is #1 around here.

Map 17 • North Kenwood / Oakland

Kenny's Ribs & Chicken	1461 E Hyde Park Blvd	773-241-5550		Cheap and good to go.
Lake Shore Cafe	4950 S Lake Shore Drive	773-288-5800		Good continental.

Map 18 • Washington Park

Ms Lee's Good Food	205 E Garfield Blvd	773-752-5253	$*	It is good.
Rose's BBQ Chicken	5426 S State St	773-268-3401	$*	Don't mind the floor, it's the sauce.

Map 19 • Hyde Park / Woodlawn

Calypso Cafe	5211-C S Harper Ave	773-955-0229	$$	Good Caribbean. Great drinks.
Daley's Restaurant	805 E 63rd St	773-643-6670	$$*	The mayor ought to try this place.
Dixie Kitchen and Bait Shop	5225-A S Harper Ave	773-363-4943	$$	A little taste of the South.
Kikuya Japanese Restaurant	1601 E 55th St	773-667-3727	*	Best sushi in the neighborhood.
La Petite Folie	1504 E 55th St	773-493-1394	$$	The only haute cuisine in the neighborhood. The most expensive in the area, but worth it.
Leona's	1228 E 53rd St	773-363-2600	$$	Huge portions of good Italian.
Maravilla's Mexican Restaurant	5211 S Harper Ave	773-643-3155	$	Cheap, good Mexican. Stinging salsa. Open late.
Medici on 57th	1327 E 57th St	773-667-7394	$	The essence of life at U of C.

*Key: $: Under $10 / $$: $10–$20 / $$$: $20–$30 / $$$$: $30+   * : Does not accept credit cards. / † : Accepts only American Express.*

Map 19 • Hyde Park / Woodlawn — continued

Mellow Yellow	1508-10 E 53rd St	773-667-2000	$	Comfort food for morning and night.
Noodles Etc	1460 E 53rd St	773-947-8787	$	Great, cheap Asian.
Rajun Cajun	1459 E 53rd St	773-955-1145	$	Cheap, good Indian and vegetarian.
Ribs N Bibs	5300 S Dorchester Ave	773-493-0400	$	Finger lickin'. Wear the bib.
Salonica Restaurant	1438 E 57th St	773-752-3899	$	Where to go the morning after.

Map 20 • Hyde Park East / Jackson Park

Cedars of Lebanon	1618 E 53rd St	773-324-6227	*	Good cheap Middle Eastern.
Jackson Harbor Grill	6401 S Coast Guard Dr	773-288-4442	$$	Go just for the location.
Morry's Deli	5500 S Cornell Ave	773-363-3800	*	Good on the go.
Nile Restaurant, The	1611 E 55th St	773-324-9499	*	Varied Middle Eastern.
Orly's Cafe	1660 E 55th St	773-643-5500	*	Stick to the Mexican. Have a margarita.
Piccolo Mondo	1642 E 56th St	773-643-1106	*	Best Italian in the area.

Map 21 • Wicker Park / Ukrainian Village

Bluefin	1952 W North Ave	773-394-7373	$$$	Upscale, trendy sushi bar.
Bongo Room	1470 N Milwaukee Ave	773-489-0690	$	Great breakfast spot, expect to wait on weekends.
Cafe Absinthe	1958 W North Ave	773-278-4488	$$$$	Outrageously expensive and chi-chi.
Cold Comfort Cafe & Deli	2211 W North Ave	773-342-1998	$$	Freshly made deli sandwiches; groceries.
D'Vine Restaurant & Wine Bar	1950 W North Ave	773-235-5700	$$$$	Another place to be seen and blow your paycheck.
Feast	1616 N Damen Ave	773-235-6362	$$$	Popular for Sunday brunch.
Half & Half	1560 N Damen Ave	773-489-6220	$$	Breakfast "cuisine."
Hi Ricky	1852 W North Ave	773-276-8300	$	Pan-Asian.
Las Palmas	1835 W North Ave	773-289-4991	$	Great al fresco dining and atrium seating.
Leo's Lunchroom	1809 W Division St	773-276-6509	*	Tiny BYOB—great for breakfast, lunch or dinner.
Leona's	1936 W Augusta Blvd	773-292-4300	*	Popular branch of local pizza chain.
Lulu's Hot Dogs	1000 S Leavitt St	312-243-3444	*	
Mas	1670 W Division St	773-276-8700	$$	Stylish Latin cooking, dinner only.
Mirai Sushi	2020 W Division St	773-862-8500	$$	Chic dining and good sushi.
MOD	1520 N Damen Ave	773-252-1500	$$	Contemporary American. Hipster destination.
Ohba	2049 W Division St	773-772-2727	$$$	Global tidbits in stylish setting.
Pacific Cafe	1619 N Damen Ave	773-862-1988	$$	Inexpensive sushi/Japanese.
Piece	1927 W North Ave	773-772-4422	$$	"Designer" pizza joint.
Pontiac Cafe	1531 N Damen Ave	773-252-7767	$	Old pumping station, great people watching.
Settimana Cafe	2056 W Division St	773-394-1629	*	Thai the summer patio.
Smoke Daddy	1804 W Division St	773-772-6656	$	Barbecue and blues.
Soju	1745 W North Ave	773-793-5444	$$$	Fancy Korean barbecue.
Souk	1552 N Milwaukee Ave	773-227-9110	$$	Middle Eastern with belly dancers and hookahs.
Soul Kitchen	1576 N Milwaukee Ave	773-342-9742	$	Contemporary soul food.
Spring	2039 W North Ave	773-395-7100	$$$$	Vogue, overpriced Asian.
Sultan's Market	2057 W North Ave	773-235-3072	$	Cheap Middle Eastern, groceries.
Thai Lagoon	2223 W North Ave	773-489-5747	$$	Great Thai, funky atmosphere.

Map 22 • Noble Square / Goose Island

Corosh	1072 N Milwaukee Ave	773-235-0600	$$	Italian and pub fare, great patio.
El Barco Mariscos Seafood	1035 N Ashland Blvd	773-486-6850	$$	Outdoor seating, terrific ceviche.
Hilary's Urban Eatery	1500 W Division St	773-235-4327	$$	Salmon cakes to die for.
Hollywood Grill	1609 W North Ave	773-395-1818	$	Where the hipsters and drunks dry out.
Luc Thang	1524 N Ashland Blvd	773-395-3907	$	Thai with Chinese and Vietnamese touches.
Watusi	1540 W North Ave	773-862-1540	$$$	Pan-Latin in chic environs.

Map 23 • West Town / Near West Side

China Dragon Restaurant	2008 W Madison St	312-666-3766	*	Dependably fantastic Chinese.
Darkroom	2210 W Chicago Ave	773-276-1411		New York strip, glazed salmon, mac and cheese, and BYOB.
Dionises Restaurant & Cafe	510 N Western Ave	312-243-7330		Mexican supper club with dancing.
Il Jack's Italian Restaurant	1758 W Grand Ave	312-421-7565		Neighborhood Italian.
Munch	1800 W Grand Ave	312-226-4914		Laid-back, funky brunch place.
Old Lviv	2228 W Chicago Ave	773-772-7250	*	Eastern European buffet.
Privata Cafe	1936 Chicago Ave	773-394-0662		Eclectic Mexican-Italian cuisine, brunch buffet.
Tecalitlan Restaurant	1814 W Chicago Ave	773-384-4285		Popular family-style, Mexican restaurant.

Map 24 • River West / West Town / Near West Side

160 Blue	160 N Loomis St	312-850-0303	$$$	Ameri-French and owned by Michael Jordan.
Bone Daddy	551 Ogden Ave	312-226-6666	*	Ribs and, um, ribs.
Breakfast Club, The	1381 W Hubbard St	312-666-2372	$$	Brunch and then some.
Crab Street Saloon	1061 W Madison	312-433-0013	$$$	East-coast style seafood experience.
Flo	1434 W Chicago Ave	312-243-0477	$$	Mexican-influenced breakfast in relaxed atmosphere.
Hacienda Tecalitlan	820 N Ashland Blvd	312-243-1166	$$	Beautiful, authentic interior; amazing margaritas.
Ina's	1235 W Randolph St	312-226-8227	*	Special occasion breakfasts. Try the scrapple.
Jerry's Sandwiches	1045 W Madison	312-563-1008	$	Fresh and slightly gourmet concoctions.
La Borsa	375 N Morgan St	312-563-1414	$$$	Not-too-traditional Italian.
La Sardine	111 N Carpenter St	312-421-2800	*	Snug French bistro.
Marche	833 W Randolph St	312-226-8399	$$$	Theatrical French brasserie dining.
Moretti's	1645 W Jackson Blvd	312-850-0208		Pizzeria with garden patio.
Wishbone	1001 W Washington	312-850-2663	$$	Comfort food, comfort folks.

Map 25 • Illinois Medical District / Heart of Chicago

Carnitas Uruapan Restaurant	1725 W 18th St	312-226-2654	*	Carnitas muy necesitas.
El Charco Verde	2253 W Taylor St	312-738-1686	$	A Mexican favorite.

Map 26 • University Village / Little Italy / Pilsen

Al's Number 1 Italian Beef	1079 W Taylor St	312-226-4017	$*	Where's the beef? Right here.
Cafe Viaggio	1435 W Taylor St	312-226-9009	$$	A variety of pasta, chicken and veal.
Carm's Beef and Snack Shop	1057 W Polk St	312-738-1046	$*	Italian subs and sausages.
Chez Joel	1119 W Taylor St	312-226-6479	$$$	Delicious French cuisine in Little Italy.
Francesca's on Taylor	1400 W Taylor St	312-829-2828	$$	Loud, bustling dining room.
Genarro's	1352 W Taylor St	312-243-1035	$	Standard fare served in generous portions.
New Rosebud Cafe	1500 W Taylor St	312-942-1117	$	Popular with the United Center crowd.
Nuevo Leon	1515 W 18th St	312-421-1517	$	Real-deal Mexican grub in Pilsen.
Siam Pot	1509 Taylor St	312-733-0760	$	Reasonable Thai in large amounts.
Taj Mahal	1512 W Taylor St	312-226-6546	$$	Affordable Indian.

Map 27 • Logan Square (South)

Abril Mexican Restaurant	2607 N Milwaukee Ave	773-227-7252	$$	Tacos and tequila.
Boulevard Cafe	3137 W Logan Blvd	773-384-8600	$$	Eat, drink and be merry!
Cafe Bolero	2252 N Western Ave	773-227-9000	$$	Tasty Cuban fare.
Choi's Chinese Restaurant	2638 N Milwaukee Ave	773-486-8496	$$	Good, fresh Chinese food.
El Cid	2116 N Milwaukee Ave	773-252-4747	$	Authentic Mexican for the masses.
El Nandu	2731 N Fullerton Ave	773-278-0900	$$	Argentinian delicacies mixed with music.
Johnny's Grill	2545 N Kedzie Blvd	773-278-2215	$*	Diner food for the grunge crowd.
Lula Cafe	2537 N Kedzie Blvd	773-489-9554	$$*	Pan-ethnic nouveau for hipsters.

Map 28 • Bucktown

Cafe Bolero	2252 W N Western	773-227-9000	$$$	Spicy Cuban food and music.
Cafe De Luca	1721 N Damen Ave	773-342-6000	$$	Café and Italian sandwiches.
Cafe Matou	1848 N Milwaukee Ave	773-384-8911	$$$	Fantastic French food, dodgy locale.
Club Lucky	1824 W Wabansia Ave	773-227-2300	$$	Age-old Italian joint.
Glory	1952 N Damen Ave	773-235-7400	$$	New England cuisine, whatever that is.
Jambalaya's	1653 N Damen Ave	773-289-3678	$	Tiny Creole café and sandwich shop.
Jane's	1655 W Cortland St	773-862-5263	*	Good-for-you gourmet.
Le Bouchon	1958 N Damen Ave	773-862-6600	*	Affordable, crowded French.
Northside Cafe	1635 N Damen Ave	773-384-6337	$$	Bucktown institution; outdoor seating.
Phlair	1935 N Damen Ave	773-772-3719	$$	Creative New American with good wine list.
Roong Thai Restaurant	1633 N Milwaukee Ave	773-252-3488	$$	Tasty Thai.
Silver Cloud Club & Grill	1700 N Damen Ave	773-489-6212	$$	Comfort food and drinks.
Zoom Kitchen	1646 N Damen Ave	773-227-7000	$$	Cafeteria style dining.

Map 29 • DePaul / Wrightwood / Sheffield

Buffalo Wild Wings	2464 N Lincoln Ave	773-868-9453	$	Sports bar with wings.
Charlie's Ale House	1224 W Webster Ave	773-871-1440	*	Yuppies eat and drink here.
Clarke's Pancake House & Restaurant	2441 N Lincoln Ave	773-472-3505	$	Great pancake and omelet spot.
Demon Dogs	944 W Fullerton Ave	773-281-2001	$*	Classic Chicago Dogs.
Goose Island Wrigleyville	1800 N Clybourn Ave	312-915-0071	$	Pub grub at its best.

*Key: $: Under $10 / $$: $10–$20 / $$$: $20–$30 / $$$$: $30+   * : Does not accept credit cards. / † : Accepts only American Express.*

Map 29 • DePaul / Wrightwood / Sheffield — continued

Green Dolphin Street	2200 N Ashland Ave	773-395-0066	$$$$	Live jazz club and contemporary American.
John's Place	1202 W Webster Ave	773-525-6670	$	Healthy comfort food.
Lindo Mexico	2642 N Lincoln Ave	773-871-4832	*	Sunny Mexican.
Red Lion Pub	2446 N Lincoln Ave	773-348-2695	*	It's haunted!
Salt & Pepper Diner	2575 N Lincoln Ave	773-525-8788	$*	Retro burger joint.
Shine & Morida	901 W Armitage Ave	773-296-0101	$$	Chinese and Japanese all-in-one.
Twisted Lizard, The	1964 N Sheffield Ave	773-929-1414	*	Yuppie Mexican.

Map 30 • Lincoln Park

Aladdin Cafe	2269 N Lincoln Ave	773-871-7327	*	Dine-in or take-out hummos hut.
Ambria	2300 N Lincoln Park W	773-472-5959	*	Luxe French with impeccable service.
Asiana	2546 N Clark St	773-296-9189	$$$$	Veggie vietnamese noodles.
Athenian Room	807 W Webster Ave	773-348-5155	$	Casual Greek dining.
Cafe Ba-Ba-Reeba!	2024 N Halsted St	773-935-5000	*	Noisy, bustling tapas joint.
Cafe Bernard	2100 N Halsted St	773-871-2100	*	Charming French.
Charlie Trotter's	816 W Armitage Ave	773-248-6228	$$$$	World renowned, dinner only.
Dunlays on Clark	2600 N Clark St	773-883-6000	$$$	Upscale American.
Emilio's Tapas	444 Fullerton Pkwy	773-327-5100	*	Cavernous branch of local tapas chain.
Escargot	1962 N Halsted St	773-281-4211	$$	Casual French spot by Eric Aubriot.
Frances	2552 N Clark St	773-248-4580		Inventive deli.
Geja's Cafe	340 W Armitage Ave	773-281-9101	*	Romantic fondue with live flamenco.
King Crab	1816 N Halsted St	312-280-8990	$$$	Reliable fish and sea food.
L'Olive	1629 N Halsted St	312-573-1515	$$$	Great pre-theatre Marrakesh dining.
Mon Ami Gabi	2300 N Lincoln Park W	773-348-8886	*	Ambria's more casual neighbor.
Nookies, Too	2114 N Halsted St	773-327-1400	*	24-hour grill.
O' Fame	750 W Webster Ave	773-929-5111	*	Nice neighborhood casual Italian.
Original Pancake House	2020 N Lincoln Park W	773-929-8130	*	Breakfast-y grill.
Piattini	934 W Webster	773-281-3898	$$	Italian tapas.
Ranalli's	1925 N Lincoln Ave	312-642-4700	*	Huge patio for summertime quaffing.
RJ Grunts	2056 Lincoln Park W	773-929-5363	$$	Great grub.
Salvatore's Ristorante	525 W Arlington Pl	773-528-1200	*	Cute neighborhood Italian.
Sushi O Sushi	346 W Armitage Ave	773-871-4777		
Taco Burrito Palace #2	2441 N Halsted St	773-248-0740	$*	Speedy Mexican.
Tilli's	1952 N Halsted St	773-325-0044	$$	Cute staff and good food.
Toast	746 W Webster Ave	773-935-5600	$$	Made for brunching.
Twin Anchors	1655 N Sedgwick St	312-266-1616	$$	Regulars will vouch for the ribs.
Via Emilia Ristorante	2119 N Clark St	773-248-6283	*	Elegant Italian, nice wine list .
Vinci	1732 N Halsted St	312-266-1199	*	Homemade pasta raises the bar.
Wiener's Circle, The	2622 N Clark St	773-477-7444	*	Classic Chicago hot dog stand.
Zucco	543 W Diversey Pkwy	773-248-7263	$$	Cosy Italian.

Map 31 • Old Town / Near North

Bistrot Margot	1437 N Wells St	312-587-3660	$$$$	Great date place.
CHIC Cafe	361 W Chestnut St	312-873-2032	*	Gourmet prix fixe by culinary students.
Cucina Bella Osteria & Wine Bar	1612 N Sedgwick St	312-274-1119	$$*	Solid Italian; wine bar.
Fireplace Inn, The	1448 N Wells St	312-664-5264	$$$	Popular spot to watch sports.
Fresh Choice	1534 N Wells St	312-664-7065	$*	Sandwich and smoothie king.
Kamehachi	1400 N Wells St	312-664-3663	$$$	Sushi favorite with upstairs lounge.
Kiki's Bistro	900 N Franklin St	312-335-5454	*	Stylish French.
Las Pinatas	1552 N Wells St	312-664-8277	$$	Festive atmosphere, fantastic food.
MK	868 N Franklin St	312-482-9179	*	Very stylish.
O'Brien's	1528 N Wells St	312-787-3131	$$$	Best outdoor in Old Town.
Old Jerusalem	1411 N Wells St	312-944-0459	$$	Cheap, good food.
Topo Gigio Ristorante	1516 N Wells St	312-266-9335	$$$	Crowded reliable Italian. Big outdoor.

Map 32 • Gold Coast / Magnificent Mile

Ashkenaz	12 E Cedar St	312-944-5006		Chicago's true Jewish deli.
Bistro 110	110 E Pearson St	312-266-3110	$$$	Popular Sunday jazz brunch.
Cheesecake Factory, The	875 N Michigan Ave	312-337-1101	$$	40+ kinds of cheesecake.
Cru Wine Bar & Cafe	888 N Wabash Ave	312-337-4001	*	Cool, funky wine and cheese.
Dave & Buster's	1030 N Clark St	312-943-5151	*	Chuck E. Cheese for grown-ups.
Gibson's Steakhouse	1028 N Rush St	312-266-8999	$$$$	If you love steak, get a reservation.
Johnny Rockets	901 N Rush St	312-337-3900	$	Jukebox and malts—outdoor seating, late night eating.
Le Colonial	937 N Rush St	312-255-0088	$$$	Vietnamese/French fare.

McCormick 's & Schmick's	41 E Chestnut St	312-397-9500	$$$$	Seafood chain that outdoes itself on portions and taste.
Mike Ditka's	100 E Chestnut St	312-587-8989	$$$	The place for Ditka, Chicago sports, and meat.
Original Pancake House	22 E Bellevue Pl	312-642-7917	$$*	The apple waffle/pancake is right!
Pane Caldo	72 E Walton St	312-649-0055	$$$$	Tucked away genius Italian trattoria.
Pump Room, The	Omni Ambassador East Hotel, 1301 N State Pkwy	312-266-0360	$$$$	Chicago old school tradition. Dress code.
Signature Room at the 95th	875 N Michigan Ave	312-787-9596	*	It's the view. Proposal hot spot.
Spiaggia	940 N Michigan Ave	312-280-2755	$$$$	One of Chicago's best—gorgeous lake view and Italian cuisine.
Tavern on Rush	1031 N Rush St	312-664-9600	$$$$	Summer mainstay, American menu.
Tempo	6 E Chestnut St	312-943-4373	*	24/7 patio seating and huge menu.
Tsunami	1160 N Dearborn St	312-642-9911	$$$	Sushi and sake in a club-like atmosphere.
Whiskey Bar and Grill	1015 N Rush St	312-475-0300		Great summer place. Hip and trendy folks galore.

Map 33 • Rogers Park West

Angus	7555 N Western Ave	773-262-8844	$$	Steak and seafood. Surprisingly fancy.
Cafe Montenegro	6954 N Western Ave	773-761-2233	*	Greek-accented coffeeshop.
Delhi Darbar Kabab House	6403 N California Ave	773-338-1818	$	Open 24-hours everyday, Indian/Pakistani.
Desi Island	2401 W Devon Ave	773-465-2489		Think corner diner, but spicy.
Fluky's	6821 N Western Ave	773-274-3652	$*	"Famous" hot dog joint, breakfast, lunch, and dinner, outdoor seating.
Ghandi India Restaurant	2601 W Devon Ave	773-761-8714	*	Family style north and south Indian fare.
Gitel's Kosher Bakery	2745 W Devon Ave	773-262-3701	*	Baked goods and pastries, always fresh, carry-out.
Good Morgan Kosher Fish Market	2948 W Devon Ave	773-764-8115	*	Fish market/restaurant in the Devon kosher strip (kosher restaurant).
Hashalom	2905 W Devon Ave	773-465-5675	$*	Israeli/Moroccan, Kosher, BYOB, closed Sat/Sun.
Tiffin, The Indian Kitchen	2536 W Devon Ave	773-338-2143	$$	A more upscale Indian restaurant.
Udupi Palace	2543 W Devon Ave	773-338-2152	$	Pure vegetarian Indian food, low-fat, not too spicy.
Viceroy of India	2520 W Devon Ave	773-743-4100	$$	Elegantly stylish Indian restaurant, separate half for fast-food/carryout, features both meat and vegetarian dishes.

Map 34 • Rogers Park East

Deluxe Diner	6349 N Clark St	773-743-8244	$*	Retro-styled greasy spoon.
El Famous Burrito	7047 N Clark St	773-465-0377	$*	Mexican treats for the college crowd.
Ennui Cafe	6981 N Sheridan Rd	773-973-2233	$*	Tasty tidbits.
Heartland Cafe	7000 N Glenwood Ave	773-465-8005	$$	Eclectic health food.
Panini Panini	6764 N Sheridan Rd	773-761-7775	$$*	Italian flavor for the North Side.
Tien Tsin	7018 N Clark St	773-761-2820	$$	Great Chinese food for the family.

Map 35 • Arcadia Terrace / Peterson Park

Charcoal Delights	3139 W Foster Ave	773-583-0056	$*	The name says it all.
Fondue Stube	2717 W Peterson Ave	773-784-2200	*	Fun fondue!
Garden Buffet	5347 N Lincoln Ave	773-728-1249	*	Korean/Japanese with huge buffet and sushi bar.

Map 36 • Bryn Mawr

El Tipico	1836 W Foster Ave	773-878-0839		Neighborhood hangout with semi-authentic Mexican food.
Fireside Restaurant & Lounge	5739 N Ravenswood Ave	773-878-5942		Diverse crowd and eclectic menu from ribs to pizza.
Max's Italian Beef	5754 N Western Avenue	773-989-8200		Chicago institution; home of the pepper-and-egg sandwich.
San Soo Gap San Korean Restaurant and Sushi House	5247 N Western Ave	773-334-2115		Do-it-yourself Korean barbeque at 4 am.

Map 37 • Edgewater / Andersonville

Andies	5253 N Clark St	773-784-8616	*	Fresh middle eastern in airy atmosphere.
Ann Sather	5207 N Clark St	773-271-6677	*	Andersonville landmark—Swedish inspired food.
Carson's Ribs	5970 N Ridge Ave	773-271-4000	*	They say ribs, but it's really the pork chops.
Francesca's Bryn Mawr	1039 W Bryn Mawr Ave	773-506-9261	$$	Dined in an SRO before?

*Key: $: Under $10 / $$: $10–$20 / $$$: $20–$30 / $$$$: $30+ * : Does not accept credit cards. / † : Accepts only American Express.*

Map 37 • Edgewater / Andersonville — continued

Jin Ju	5203 N Clark St	773-334-6377	$$$	Upscale Korean.
La Tache	1475 W Balmoral Ave	773-334-7168	$$	Neighborhood French bistro.
Moody's Pub	5910 N Broadway St	773-275-2696	$*	Burgers only, but the best.
Pasteur	5525 N Broadway St	773-878-1061	$$$$	Easy to imagine you're in Vietnam 50 years ago.
Pauline's	1754 W Balmoral Ave	773-561-8573	$*	Weekend breakfast hotspot; try the famous five-egg omelet.
Reza's	5255 N Clark St	773-561-1898	$$	Many Persian options, leftovers for lunch tomorrow.
Room, The	5900 N Broadway St	773-989-7666	$$$	Wear black, BYOB, eat fresh seafood.
Svea	5236 N Clark St	773-275-7738	$*	Adorable, tiny Swedish diner.
Tomboy	5402 N Clark St	773-907-0636	$$$	Loud, hip and fun, BYOB.

Map 38 • Ravenswood Manor

Arun's	4156 N Kedzie Ave	773-539-1909	$$$$	Worldwide rep for four-star prix fixe Thai.
Lutz Continental Cafe	2458 W Montrose Ave	773-478-7785	$$	If Grandma was German, she served these pastries.
Noon-O-Kabab	4661 N Kedzie Ave	773-279-8899	$	Bring doggie bag for day-after lunch.
Penguin, The	2723 W Lawrence Ave	773-271-4924	$*	High-fat, authentic Argentine ice cream (empanadas and pizza, too, but go straight for dessert).
Thai Little Home Cafe	4747 N Kedzie Ave	773-478-3944	$	Two rooms + one lunch buffet = less than $10.

Map 39 • Ravenswood / North Center

Cafe 28	1800 W Irving Park Rd	773-528-2883	$$	Trendy Cuban.
Cafe Selmarie	4729 N Lincoln Ave	773-989-5595	$$	Bakery/café.
Chicago Brauhaus	4732 N Lincoln Ave	773-784-4444	$$	Live German band!
Daily Bar & Grill	4560 N Lincoln Ave	773-561-6198	$	Bar food in retro ambiance.
Garcia's	4749 N Western Ave	773-769-5600	$	Mexican/Tex-Mex with great shakes.
Grecian Taverna	4761 N Lincoln Ave	773-878-6400	$$	Greek.
Jury's Food & Drink	4337 N Lincoln Ave	773-935-2255	$	Neighborhood pub.
La Boca della Verita	4618 N Lincoln Ave	773-784-6222	$$	Cozy Italian café.
O'Donovan's	2100 W Irving Park Rd	773-478-2100	$	Three words: Dollar Burger Night.
Opart Thai House	4658 N Western Ave	773-989-8517	$	Cheap, tasty Thai BYOB
Pangea	1935 W Irving Park Rd	773-665-1340	$$$	Contemporary American.
She She	4539 N Lincoln Ave	773-293-3690	$$$$	Upscale/eclectic American.
Tartufo Restaurante	4601 Lincoln Ave	773-334-7820	$$	Traditional Italian.
Woody's	4160 N Lincoln Ave	773-880-1100	$$	Ribs 'n' wings 'n' other sticky eats.

Map 40 • Uptown / Sheridan Park / Buena Park

Andies	1467 W Montrose Ave	773-348-0654	$$	Middle Eastern food in Babylonian surroundings.
Atlantique	5101 N Clark St	773-275-9191	*	Fancy neighborhood seafood.
Bale French Bakery	5018 N Broadway St	773-561-4424	$	French/Asian bakery and sandwiches.
Don Quijote	4761 N Clark St	773-769-5930	$*	Burritos as big as your head.
Frankie J's An American Theatre and Grill	4437 N Broadway St	773-769-2959	$$$	Laugh and eat.
Furama	4936 N Broadway St	773-271-1161	*	Dim sum with karaoke.
Golden House Restaurant	4744 N Broadway St	773-334-0406	$	Pancakes and ambience next to the river.
Holiday Club	4000 N Sheridan Rd	773-348-9600	$$*	The Rat Pack is back! With food.
La Donna	5146 N Clark St	773-561-9400	*	Friendly, tasty Italian.
Magnolia Cafe	1224 W Wilson	773-728-8785	$$	Magnolias in an American bistro.
Smoke Country House	1465 W Irving Park Rd	773-327-0600	$$	Great barbecue on the north side (imagine that!).
Tokyo Marina	5058 N Clark St	773-878-2900	*	Sushi in a pinch.

Map 41 • Avondale / Old Irving

Chief O'Neill's Pub	3471 N Elston Ave	773-583-3066	*	Excellent traditional pub fare.
Clara's	3159 N California Ave	773-539-3020	$*	Ultimate cheap greasy spoon.
IHOP	2818 W Diversey Ave	773-342-8901	$	Open 24-hours.
La Finca	3361 N Elston Ave	773-478-4006	$	Servicable Mexican, margaritas.
N	2977 N Elston Ave	773-866-9898	$$	Argentinian tapas.
Rancho Luna del Caribe	2554 W Diversey Ave	773-772-9333	$$	Carribean supper club.
Taqueria Trespazada	3144 N California Ave	773-539-4533	$*	Tasty, cheap tacos & salsas—no atmosphere.

Map 42 • North Center / Roscoe Village / West Lakeview

Brett's Cafe Americain	2011 W Roscoe St	773-248-0999	$$$	Go for brunch or dessert. Great bread basket.
Costello Sandwich & Sides	2015 W Roscoe St	773-929-2323	$	Yummy baked sandwiches.
El Tinajon	2054 W Roscoe St	773-525-8455	$$	Good, cheap Guatemalan. Great mango margaritas.
Four Moon Tavern	1847 W Roscoe St	773-929-6666	$	Neighborhood tavern. Cozy back room. Thespian crowd.
Hot Doug's	2314 W Roscoe St	773-348-0326	$*	Gourmet "encased meat" emporium.
Kitsch'n on Roscoe	2005 W Roscoe St	773-248-7372	$$	Clever retro food and tiki bar. Friendly staff.
La Mora	2132 W Roscoe St	773-404-4555	$$	Neighborhood Mediterranean-influenced Italian.
Lee's Chop Suey	2415 W Diversey Ave	773-342-7050	$*	Chop suey and booze.
Piazza Bella Trattoria	2116 W Roscoe St	773-477-7330	$$$	Neighborhood Italian.
Riverview Tavern & Grill	1958 W Roscoe St	773-248-9523	$$	Frat food and beer.
Thai Linda Cafe	2022 W Roscoe St	773-868-0075	$$	Standard-issue neighborhood Thai.
Victory's Banner	2100 W Roscoe St	773-665-0227	$	Best vegetarian in the city, with toga-clad waitstaff.
Village Tap	2055 W Roscoe St	773-883-0817	$	Beer garden and good bar food.
Wishbone	3300 N Lincoln Ave	773-549-2663	$$	Southern and soul food paradise. Go early for brunch.

Map 43 • Wrigleyville/ Lakeview

Addis Abeba	3521 N Clark St	773-929-9383	*	Ethiopian finger food.
Ann Sather	929 W Belmont Ave	773-348-2378	*	Warm, family friendly ambience, Swedish comfort food.
BD's Mongolian BBQ	3330 N Clark St	773-325-2300	$$*	Stir-fry your own creations.
Bistrot Zinc	1131 N State St	312-337-1131	$$*	Quiet elegance.
Blue Bayou	3734 N Southport Ave	773-871-3330	$$	New Orleans-themed, in case you couldn't guess.
Cafe Le Loup	3348 N Sheffield Ave	773-248-1830	*	BYOB casual French.
Coobah	3423 N Southport Ave	773-528-2220	$$	Trendy Latin spot near Music Box.
Cy's Crab House	3819 N Ashland Ave	773-883-8900	*	Persian-tinged seafood emporium.
Heaven on Seven	3478 N Clark St	773-477-7818	$$*	An epicurean jaunt to N'Orleans. Yum.
Leona's	3215 N Sheffield Ave	773-327-8861	*	Flagship of the belt-buckle loosening chain.
Little Bucharest	3001 N Ashland Ave	773-929-8640	*	Free limo rides!
Mama Desta's Red Sea	3218 N Clark St	773-935-7561	$$*	No forks at this authentic Ethiopian restaurant.
Menagerie	1232 W Belmont Ave	773-404-8333	$$$	Styish fusion.
Matsuya	3469 N Clark St	773-248-2677	*	One of the best on Sushi Row.
Mia Francesca	3311 N Clark St	773-281-3310	$$*	Contemporary Italian date place.
Moti Mahal	1031-35 W Belmont Ave	773-348-4392	*	So-so Indian buffet in shabby environment. Popular all the same.
Orange	3231 N Clark St	773-549-4400	*	Super stylish brunches.
Outpost, The	3438 N Clark St	773-244-1166	*	Hey mate, dining from Down Under.
Pepper Lounge	3441 N Sheffield Ave	773-665-7377	*	Loungy late-night dining. Smoker friendly.
PS Bangkok	3345 N Clark St	773-871-7777	*	Popular neighborhood Thai that delivers.
Shiroi Hana	3242 N Clark St	773-477-1652	$$*	Tastiest sushi ever.
Standard India	917 W Belmont Ave	773-929-1123	*	Yet another Indian buffet.
Technicolor Kitchen	3210 N Lincoln Ave	773-665-2111	$$$	Eclectic fusion. Try the alligator wontons.
Tombo Kitchen	3244 N Lincoln Ave	773-244-9885	$$	Modern, very good sushi. Try the eel.
Wrigleyville Dog	3737 N Clark St	773-296-1500	$*	Hot dog heaven.

Map 44 • Lakeview East

Angelina	3561 N Broadway St	773-935-5933	$$$	Casual, romantic Italian.
Ann Sather	3411 N Broadway St	773-305-0024	*	Airy branch of local comfort food chain.
Anna Maria Pasteria	3953 N Broadway St	773-929-6363	*	Cute, neighborhood Italian, casual date spot.
Arco de Cuchilleros	3445 N Halsted St	773-296-6046	$$$	Intimate tapas; great Sangria.
Chicago Diner	3411 N Halsted St	773-935-6696	$$	A vegetarian institution.
Clark Street Dog	3040 N Clark St	773-281-6690	$*	24-hour hot dogs and cheese fries.
Cornelia's Restaurant	750 W Cornelia Ave	773-248-8333	*	Neighborhood casual dining institution.
Duke of Perth	2913 N Clark St	773-477-1741	*	Fish and chips.
Erwin, an American Cafe & Bar	2925 N Halsted St	773-528-7200	$$$$	Elegant.
Half Shell	676 W Diversey Pkwy	773-549-1773	*	Casual raw bar.
Jack's on Halsted	3201 N Halsted St	773-244-9191	$$$$	Great wine list.
Kit Kit Lounge & Supper Club	3700 N Halsted St	773-525-1111	*	Drag shows while you dine.
La Creperie	2845 N Clark St	773-528-9050	$$	Live French music.
Las Mananitas	3523 N Halsted St	773-528-2109	$$	Lethal margaritas.
Mark's Chop Suey	3343 N Halsted St	773-281-9090	$	The BEST eggrolls.
Melrose, The	3233 N Broadway St	773-327-2060	$$	24-hour diner.
Nancy's Original Stuffed Pizza	2930 N Broadway St	773-883-1977	*	Seedy pizza parlor.
Nookie's Tree	3334 N Halsted St	773-248-9888	$*	24-hour diner.
Yoshi's Cafe	3257 N Halsted St	773-248-6160	$$$	Franco-Japanese fusion.

Map 2 • Near North / River North

Jazz Record Mart	444 N Wabash Ave	312-222-1468	Jazz lover's emporium.
Mary Wolf Gallery	705 Dearborn St	312-588-1478	Unusual oils, including lots of Chicago scenes.
Mig and Tig Furniture	549 N Wells St		Classic well made furniture.
Montauk	223 W Erie St		The most comfortable sofas.
Paper Source	232 W Chicago Ave		Great paper and invitations.

Map 3 • Streeterville / Magnificent Mile

Chicago Place	700 N Michigan Ave		Upscale mall.
Decoro	224 E Ontario St	312-943-4847	Fine Asian antiques and fine furnishings.
Garrett Popcorn Shop	670 N Michigan Ave		Everything you could possibly think of related to popcorn!
Niketown	669 N Michigan Ave		Nike label sports clothing.
Rand McNally Store	444 N Michigan Ave		Map store.
Virgin Megastore	540 N Michigan Ave		Music, books, videos, DVDs.

Map 4 • West Loop Gate / Greektown

Athenian Candle Co	300 S Halsted St	312-332-6988	Candles, curse-breakers, Greek trinkets and more.
Athens Jewelry	310 S Halsted St	312-258-8018	Island gold.
Greek Town Gifts	330 S Halsted St	312-263-6342	Music, T-shirts, hats—everything Greek!

Map 5 • The Loop

Afrocentric Bookstore	333 S State St	312-939-1956	The authority on Afrocentic literature.
American Music World	333 S State St		The place to go if you're looking to buy an instrument.
Carson Pirie Scott	1 S State St		Department store.
Crows Nest Records	333 S State St	312-341-9196	Excellent selection of world music, classical, and jazz.
Gallery 37 Store	66 E Randolph St		Speciality gifts.
Jeweler's Mall	7 S Wabash Ave		Jewelry.
Marshall Field's	111 N State St		Department store.
Ragstock	226 S Wabash Ave	312-694-1778	Funky vintage clothes and trendy irregulars.
Rock Records	175 W Washington St	312-346-3489	Good CD store.
Sears	2 N State St		Department store.

Map 6 • The Loop / Grant Park

Art & Artisians	108 S Michigan Ave		Art gallery.
Museum Shop of the Art Institute	111 S Michigan Ave		Art Institute gift shop.
Poster Plus	200 S Michigan Ave		Vintage posters and custom framing.
Precious Possessions	28 N Michigan Ave		Mineral shop.
Rain Dog Books and Café	408 S Michigan Ave		Awesome used books and geek-chic clientele.
The Savvy Traveller	310 S Michigan Ave		Travel.

Map 7 • South Loop / River City

Chicago Vintage Motor Carriage	700 S Des Plaines St	312-589-2708	Antique cars shown by appointment.
Fishman's Fabrics	1101 S Des Plaines St	312-922-7250	Huge fabric wholesaler.
Joseph Adam's Hats	544 W Roosevelt Rd	312-829-8899	Haberdashery and menswear.
Lee's Foreign Car Service	727 S Jefferson St	312-663-0823	Import parts and service.

Map 8 • South Loop / Printer's Row / Dearborn Park

Kozy's Bike Shop	600 S LaSalle St	312-360-0020	Bikes and accessories in a fun loft setting.
Printer's Row Fine and Rare Books	715 S Dearborn St	312-583-1800	Fine and rare books.
Sandmeyer's Book Store	714 S Dearborn St	312-922-2104	Dream come true if you love books and atmosphere.

Map 9 • South Loop / S Michigan Ave

Bariff Shop	618 S Michigan Ave		Unique Hanukkah gifts.
Clancy's Market	1130 S Michigan Ave		Grab snacks for a picnic in the park; new icon needed.

Map 10 • East Pilsen / Chinatown

Chinatown Bazaar	2221 S Wentworth Ave	312-225-1088	Part clothing store, part knick-knack shop.
Chinatown Furniture	2326 S Canal St	312-236-1712	Beautiful, ornate furniture.
Pacific Imports	2200 S Wentworth Ave	312-808-0456	Mostly home furnishings.
Sun Sun Tong	2260 S Wentworth Ave	312-842-6398	Stock up on Chinese herbs and teas.
Ten Ren Tea & Ginseng Co	2247 S Wentworth Ave	312-842-1171	The only place to buy ginseng.
Woks 'n' Things	2234 S Wentworth Ave	312-842-0701	Stir-fry utensils and cookware.

Map 11 • South Loop / McCormick Place

Blossoms of Hawaii	1631 S Michigan Ave	312-922-0281	Florist.
Blue Star Auto Stores	2001 S State St	312-225-0717	All your auto needs.
Re-Cycle Bicycle shop	1465 S Michigan Ave	312-987-1080	Bike shop, obviously.
Waterware	1829 S State St	312-225-4549	Designer plumbing fixtures.
Y'lonn Salon	1802 S Wabash Ave	312-225-9247	Beauty salon.

Map 12 • Bridgeport (West)

Bridgeport Antiques	2963 S Archer Ave		Antiques.

Map 13 • Bridgeport (East)

Accutek Printing & Graphics	260 W 26th St		Printing and copying needs.
Ace Bakery	3200 S Halsted St		Excellent breads and pastries.
Augustine's Spiritual Goods	3114 S Halsted St		Mystical and religious knick-knacks.
Bridgeport News Travel & Tours	3252 S Halsted St		Travel store.
Chicago Technical Center	3500 S Emerald Ave		Computers.
Health King Enterprises Chinese Medicinals	238 W 31st St		Natural remedies.
Let's Boogie Records & Tapes	3321 S Halsted St		Music.
Modern Bookstore	3118 S Halsted St		Books.
Petals From Heaven Flowers	244 W 31st St		Flower shop.

Map 14 • Prairie Shores / Lake Meadows

Ashley Stewart	3455 S Dr Martin L King Jr Dr		Women's clothing.
Avenue	3427 S Dr Martin L King Jr Dr		Modern plus-size clothes.
Living Word Book Store	3512 S Dr Martin L King Jr Dr		Books.
SMW Flea Market	3852 S Indiana Ave		Unique gifts and housewares.

Map 16 • Bronzeville

Alvin's Watch Repair	4317 S Cottage Grove Ave		Watch repair including batteries and bands.
Chicago Furniture Co	4238 S Cottage Grove Ave		Furniture store.
Dollar Junction	4701 S Cottage Grove Ave		Lots of items for a dollar or less.
Issues Barber & Beauty Salon	3958 S Cottage Grove Ave		Beauty salon.
Parker House Sausage Co	4601 S State St		All types of sausages.
The African Hair & Weaving Center	428 E 47th St		When you want your 'do to be fierce.

Map 17 • North Kenwood / Oakland

Coop's Records	1350 E 47th St		Music.
South Shore Decor	1328 E 47th St		Wall coverings, paint and blinds and window treatments.

Map 19 • Hyde Park / Woodlawn

57th Street Books	1301 E 57th St	773-684-1300	Brainy independent bookstore.
Artisans 21	5240 S Harper Ave	773-643-8533	Art gallery.
Brush Strokes	1369 E 53rd St		Paint-it-yourself pottery.
Calla Lily Gift Shop	5225 S Harper Ave		Speciality gifts.
Cohn & Stern For Men	1500 E 55th St		Men's accessories.
Dr Wax Records and Tapes	5225-D S Harper Ave		Old-style vinyl.
Freehling Pot & Pan Co	1365 E 53rd St		Pots and pans.
Futons N More	1370 E 53rd St		Futons 'n more.
O'Gara and Wilson	1448 E 57th St		Rare and out-of-print books.
Powell's Bookstore	1501 E 57th St		Famous bookstore.
Tony's Sports	1308 E 53rd St		Sporting goods.
Wesley's Shoe Corral	1506 E 55th St		Shoes.
Wheels and Things	5210-E S Harper Ave		Bike sales and repairs.

Map 20 • Hyde Park East / Jackson Park

Art's Cycle Sales & Service	1636 E 55th St	773-363-7524	Bike sales and repairs.
Mothaland Books, Art and Culture	1635 E 55th St	773-955-6969	Books, gifts celebrating African-American life.

Map 21 • Wicker Park / Ukrainian Village

Asian Essence	2025 1/2 W North Ave		Homewares with an Asian flavor.
Asrai Garden	1935 W North Ave		Flowers and garden.
Chop Sooee Hair	2109 W Division St	773-262-3212	Rock star 'dos served here.
City Soles/Niche	2001 W North Ave		Excellent shoe store.
DeciBel Audio	1407 N Milwaukee Ave	773-862-6700	New and used stereo.
Lille	1923 W North Ave		Great little things for the home.
Noir	1746 W Division St		Upscale clothing and accessories.
Paper Doll	1747 W Division St		Paper and cards.
Quimby's Bookstore	1854 W North Ave		Books and music.
Reckless Records	1532 N Milwaukee Ave		Mostly indie music—new and used.
The Silver Room	1410 N Milwaukee Ave		Clothing and accessories.

Map 22 • Noble Square / Goose Island

Balloonz Special Event Décor	1121 N Ashland Blvd		Specializing in helium balloons.
Casa Loca Furniture	1130 N Milwaukee Ave		Household furniture hecho en Mexico.
Dusty Groove Records	1120 N Ashland Blvd		Vinyl and CDs. Specializes in funk, soul, rare groove, now sound, and world music.
Eastern Mountain Sports (EMS)	1000 W North Ave		Everything for sports and outdoor fun.
Expo Design Center	1500 N Dayton St		
Olga's Flower Shop	1041 N Ashland Blvd		Flowers for all occasions.
Restoration Hardware	938 W North Ave		Fancy housewares.
Right-On Futon	1184 N Milwaukee Ave		Need a new bed? Check this place out!

Map 23 • West Town / Near West Side

Alcala's	1733 W Chicago Ave		Western-wear emporium sells boots, jeans and cowboy hats.
Decoro Studio	2000 W Carroll St	312-850-9260	Lot filled with Asian antiques and furniture.
Donofrio's Double Corona Cigars	2058 W Chicago Ave		Brian Donofrio sells very fine imported cigars.
Edie's	1937 W Chicago Ave		Hip, vintage threads for the underground.
H&R Sports	1741 W Chicago Ave		Soccer gear.
Salvage One Architectural Artifacts	1840 W Hubbard St		Warehouse of antique, vintage and salvaged architectural pieces for home/loft restoration.
Through Maria's Eyes	1953 W Chicago Ave		Eclectic vintage store.
Tomato Tattoo	1855 W Chicago Ave		Every hip strip needs a tattoo parlor.

Map 24 • River West / West Town / Near West Side

Arrow Vintage	1452 W Chicago Ave		Antiques.
Hollis Funk	949 W Fulton Market		Cool housey stuff.
Upgrade Cycle Works	1128 W Chicago Ave		Bikes, accessories and servicing.
Xyloform	1423 Chicago Ave		

Map 26 • University Village / Little Italy / Pilsen

Scafuri Bakery	1337 W Taylor St	312-733-8881	The secret's in the bread.

Map 27 • Logan Square (South)

MegaMall	2502 N Milwaukee Ave		Tube socks, sunglasses, gold necklaces… One-stop shopping!
Threads, Inc	2327 N Milwaukee Ave	773-276-6411	Resale clothes and furniture.

Map 28 • Bucktown

Bleeker Street Antiques	1946 N Leavitt St		Fine selection of antiques.
Eclectic Junction	1630 N Damen Ave		House and home.
Gypsy	2131 N Damen Ave		House and home.
Jean Alan	2134 Damen Ave		House and home.
Pagoda Red	1714 N Damen Ave		House and home.
Pavilion Antiques	2055 N Damen Ave		Antique furniture.
Red Balloon Company	2060 N Damen Ave		A unique store for children—toys, clothes and furniture.
Vagabond Books & Gear	2010 N Damen Ave	773-227-6140	Travel books and accessories.
Viva La Femme	2115 N Damen Ave	773-772-7429	Style beyond size.
Yardifacts	1864 N Damen Ave		Flowers and garden.

Map 29 • DePaul / Wrightwood / Sheffield

Active Endeavors	935 W Armitage Ave		Playing sports or heading into the great outdoors, this is your place for gear.
Isabella Fine Lingerie	2150 N Seminary Ave		Fine after-hours wear.
Jayson Home & Garden	1885 & 1911 N Clybourn Ave		Flowers and garden.
Jolie Joli	2131 N Southport Ave		Clothing and accessories.
Tabula Tua	1015 W Armitage Ave		Housewares.
Uncle Dan's	2440 N Lincoln Ave	773-477-1918	One-stop shopping for survivalists.
Wine Discount Center	1826 1/2 N Elston	773-489-3454	Wine warehouse—free tastings every Saturday.

Map 30 • Lincoln Park

Art & Science	1971 N Halsted St		Beauty salon.
Coconuts Music & Movies	2747 N Clark St		Music, DVDs, videos.
Cynthia Rowley	808 W Armitage Ave		Apparel and accessories.
Ethan Allen	1700 N Halsted St		Furniture store.
Gallery 1756	1756 N Sedgwick St		Fine art.
GNC	2740 N Clark St		General Nutrition Center.
Kwik Mart	2427 N Clark St		Grocery store.
Lori's Designer Shoes	824 W Armitage Ave		Designer shoes.
Sally Beauty Supply	2723 N Clark St		Wholesale for stylists. License ID needed.
Triangle Gallery of Old Town	1763 N North Park Ave		Don't miss their openings.

Map 31 • Old Town / Near North

Atom Antiques	1219 N Wells St		Unusual antique items, free parking!
Barbara's Bookstore	1350 N Wells St		Knowledgeable, friendly staff at this great bookstore.
Crate & Barrel Outlet Store	800 W North Ave		Housewares.
Etre	1361 N Wells St		Upscale boutique.
Fleet Feet Sports	210 W North Ave		The staff watches you run to make sure the shoes fit.
Fudge Pot	1532 N Wells St		A chocolate institution.
Jumbalia	1427 N Wells St		Great gift store.
Old Town Gardens	1555 N Wells St		Beautiful plants and flowers.
See Hear Music	217 W North Ave		Discount music store.
Sofie	1343 N Wells St		Chic boutique.
The Spice House	1512 N Wells St		Spice up your cooking.
Vagabonds Boutique	1357 N Wells St		Reasonably priced trendy jewelry and clothes.
Village Cycle	1337 N Wells St	312-751-7488	Good urban cycling store.

Map 32 • Gold Coast / Magnificent Mile

Anthropologie	1120 N State St		Hip clothing and knick-knacks.
Barney's New York	25 E Oak St		Upscale boutique, clothing and accessories.
BCBG	103 E Oak St		Apparel and accessories.
Bloomingdales	900 N Michigan Ave		Upscale department store.
Bravco Beauty Center	43 E Oak St		For those who like to be pampered.
Chanel at the Drake Hotel	935 N Michigan Ave	312-787-5000	Classic, expensive clothing, accessories and fragrances.
Elements	102 E Oak St		Cool housey stuff.
Europa Books	832 N State St		International magazines.
Frette	41 E Oak St		European furniture and accessories.
G'bani	949 N State St		Shoes.
Gucci	900 N Michigan Ave		Tom Ford's alluring and provocative clothes and accessories.
Hear Music	932 N Rush St		Music and books.
MAC	40 E Oak St		Fabulous make-up.
Nicole Miller	63 E Oak St		Female fashion.
Portico	834 N Rush St		Homewares.
Prada	30 E Oak St		Expensive but delightful clothing and accessories.
Pratesi	67 E Oak St		Linens.
Tod's	121 E Oak St		Clothing.
Ultimate Bride	106 E Oak St, 2nd Fl		Bridal gear.
Ultimo	114 E Oak St		Apparel and accessories.
Urban Outfitters	935 N Rush St		Retro clothing, nifty gifts and cool accessories.
Water Tower	845 N Michigan Ave		Marshall Fields.

Map 33 • Rogers Park West

Cheesecakes by JR	2841 W Howard St	773-465-6733	Over 20 flavors of cheesecakes, full bakery, retail and wholesale, same location for over 20 years, special West Rogers Park treat!
Chicago Harley Davidson	6868 N Western Ave	773-338-6868	American classic motorcycles and all the gear that you need to match—leather jackets, hats, T-shirts, gifts, pet gear, etc.
Office Mart	2801 W Touhy Ave	773-262-3924	Combination office supply store and an internet coffee shop.
Snoop Shop Too	2742 W Touhy Ave	773-262-0444	Pick out a ceramic piece and paint it! The shop will glaze and fire your work of art. Perfect for parties or just a relaxing afternoon.
Taj Sari Palace	2553 W Devon Ave	773-338-0177	Beautiful Indian clothing and accessories.
Z'Afrique	7156 N California Ave	773-274-5236	Unique African art and jewelry, small neighborhood shop.

Map 34 • Rogers Park East

Mar-Jen Discount Furniture	1536 W Devon Ave	773-338-6636	Cheap futons, dorm furniture.

Map 37 • Edgewater / Andersonville

Broadway Antique Mart	6130 N Broadway St		Great modern pieces as well as art deco and arts and crafts.
Early to Bed	5232 N Sheridan Rd	773-271-1219	Woman-oriented grown-up toys. Boy friendly.
Gethsemane Garden Center	5739 N Clark St		Flowers and garden.
Paper Trail	5309 N Clark St		Paper and cards.
Surrender	5225 N Clark St		Health and beauty.
The Acorn Antiques & Uniques	5241 N Clark St		Antiques.
Women & Children First	5233 N Clark St		World's biggest feminist book and music store.

Map 39 • Ravenswood / North Center

Architectural Artifacts	4325 N Ravenswood Ave	773-348-0622	Renovator's dream.
Different Strummer	4544 N Lincoln Ave	773-751-3398	Guitars and such.
Glass Art & Decorative Studio	4507 N Lincoln Ave	773-561-9008	Stained glass and gifts.
Laurie's Planet of Sound	4639 N Lincoln Ave	773-271-3569	Funky CD shop.
Play It Again Sports	2102 W Irving Park Rd		Sporting goods.
Timeless Toys	4749 N Lincoln Ave	773-334-4445	Old fashioned toys.

Map 40 • Uptown / Sheridan Park / Buena Park

Eagle Leathers	5005 N Clark St	773-728-7228	Come to daddy.
Tai Nam Market Center	4925 N Broadway St	773-275-5666	Vietnamese. Very good.
Wilson Broadway Mall	1114 W Wilson Dr	773-561-0300	Socks, shoes, ethnic shopping, music, luggage—it's all here.

Map 42 • North Center / Roscoe Village / West Lakeview

Antique Resources	1741 W Belmont Ave		Large inventory of antique furniture.
Father Time Antiques	2108 W Belmont Ave		Antiques store.
Glam to Go	2002 W Roscoe St	773-525-7004	Girly-girls get pampered.
Good Old Days Antiques	2138 W Belmont Ave		Antiques and treasures.
Lynn's Hallmark	3353 N Lincoln Ave		Cards, stationary, and gift wrap.
Serendipity	2010 W Roscoe St		Gifts.
Toy Town	1903 W Belmont Ave		Toys.

Map 43 • Wrigleyville/ Lakeview

Bookworks	3444 N Clark St	773-871-5318	Friendly, well-organized used books.
Disc Revival	3182 N Clark St	773-404-4955	Super-cheap used CDs.
Midwest Pro Stereo	1613 W Belmont Ave	773-975-4250	DJ equipment, fog machines, strobe lights.
Namascar	3946 N Southport Ave	773-472-0930	Yoga accessories.
Ragstock	Belmont & Dayton	773-868-9263	Vintage resale and trendy off-price clothes.
Uncle Fun	1338 W Belmont Ave	773-477-8223	Cramped and crazy retro toys and novelties.

Map 44 • Lakeview East

Century Mall	2828 N Clark St		Most notable occupants include the cinema and Bally's Fitness.
Equinox	3401 N Broadway St	773-281-9151	Gifts and glassware—great X-mas ornament selection.
Evil Clown Compact Discs	3418 N Halsted St		The best hand-picked rare disc selection.
Gallimaufry Gallery	3345 N Halsted St		Artisan crafts including instruments, incense, stone fountains.
GayMart	3457 N Halsted St		Gay barbie and other homo kitsch and gifts.
The Brown Elephant Resale	3651 N Halsted St		Resale boutique benefits Howard Brown Health Clinic.
Toyscape	2911 N Broadway St		Hours of fun at this quirky toy store.
Unabridged Bookstore	3251 N Broadway St		Helpful bookstore with great travel, kids and gay sections.

Chicago has a rich theatrical tradition ranging from the birth of improv at venerable Second City to the creation of the fiery, intense acting style known as Chicago Style by John Malkovich and Gary Sinise, co-founders of Steppenwolf Theatre Company. Chicago's revitalized Loop Theater District boasts several new and renovated theaters, including the Chicago Theater, Cadillac Palace Theater, the Ford Center-Oriental Theater, and the new Goodman Theater. The League of Chicago Theatres operates Hot Tix booths that sell tickets to participating productions at half-price. An updated list of available shows is posted daily at www.hottix.org. Booths (which also offer full-price tickets through Ticketmaster) are located in Chicago at 78 W. Randolph; the Chicago Water Works Visitor Center, 163 E. Pearson; and the Tower Records stores at 2301 N. Clark and 214 S. Wabash.

Theater	*Address*	*Phone*	*Map*
About Face Theatre	1222 W Wilson Ave	773-784-8565	44
Apollo Theater Center	2540 N Lincoln Ave	773-935-6100	29
Arie Crown Theatre	2301 S Lake Shore Dr	312-791-6190	11
Athenaeum Theatre	2936 N Southport Ave	773-935-6860	43
Auditorium Theatre	50 E Congress Pkwy	312-902-1500	5
Bailwick Repertory	1229 W Belmont Ave	773-883-1090	43
Boxer Rebellion Theater	1257 W Loyola Ave	773-465-7325	34
Breadline Theatre Group	1802 W Berenice Ave	773-327-6096	42
Briar Street Theatre	3133 N Halsted St		44
Broadway in Chicago	22 W Monroe St	312-902-1400	5
Cadillac Place Theatre	151 W Randolph St	312-902-1400	5
Chicago Dramatists	1105 W Chicago Ave	847-217-0691	24
Chicago Music & Dance Theatre	205 E Randolph St	312-629-8696	5
Chicago Theatre Restoration	175 N State St	312-372-5422	5
Chopin Theater	1543 W Division St	866-468-3401	22
City Lit Theater Co	1020 W Bryn Mawr Ave	773-293-3682	37
Civic Opera House	20 N Wacker Dr	312-419-0033	5
Comedy Sportz	2851 N Halsted St	773-549-8080	44
Congress Theatre	2135 N Milwaukee Ave	773-252-4000	27
Cornservatory	4210 N Lincoln Ave	312-409-6435	39
Court Theatre	5535 S Ellis Ave	773-753-4472	19
Dance Center of Columbia College	1306 S Michigan Ave	312-344-8300	11
Emma & Oscar Getz Theatre	62 E 11th St		11
Famous Door Theatre	3212 N Broadway St	773-871-3000	44
Free Street Program	1419 W Blackhawk St	773-772-7248	22
Goodman Theatre	170 N Dearborn St	312-443-3800	5
Griffin Theatre Co	5404 N Clark St	773-769-2228	37
Healthworks Theatre	3171 N Halsted St	773-929-4260	44
ImprovOlympic	3541 N Clark St	773-880-0199	43
Ivanhoe Theater	180 E Pearson St	773-975-7171	32
Jose Rizal Center	1332 W Irving Park Rd	773-293-2787	40
Lakeshore Theatre	3175 N Broadway St	773-472-3492	44
Lifeline Theatre	6912 N Glenwood Ave	773-761-4477	34
Live Bait Theater	3914 N Clark St	773-871-1212	43

Theater	*Address*	*Phone*	*Map*
Lookinglass Theater	821 N Michigan Ave	773-477-9257	43
Mary-Arrchie Theatre Co	731 W Sheridan Rd	773-871-0442	44
Mercury Theater	3745 N Southport Ave	773-325-1700	43
Merle Reskin Theatre	60 E Balbo Ave	312-922-1999	8
Methadome Theatre	4437 N Broadway St	773-758-4249	40
National Pastime Theater	4139 N Broadway St	773-327-7077	40
Neo-Futurarium	5152 N Ashland Ave	312-409-1954	37
Noble Fool Theater	16 W Randolph St	312-726-1156	5
O'Rourke Center for the Performing Arts	1145 W Wilson	773-878-9761	40
Orchestra Hall at Symphony Center	220 S Michigan Ave	312-294-3000	6
Oriental Theatre	24 W Randolph St		5
Performance Loft	656 W Barry Ave	773-320-7985	44
Performing Arts Chicago	410 S Michigan Ave	312-663-1628	6
Playground Improv Theatre	3341 N Lincoln Ave	773-871-3793	42
Profiles Theatre	4147 N Broadway St	773-549-1815	40
Prop Theatre	4225 N Lincoln Ave	773-719-4914	39
Puppet Parlor	1922 W Montrose Ave	773-774-2919	39
Raven Theatre Co	6157 N Clark St	773-338-2177	33
Red Orchid Theatre	1531 N Wells St	312-943-8722	31
Ren Hen Productions	5123 N Clark St	773-728-0599	40
Royal George Theatre	1641 N Halsted	312-988-9000	30
Scrap Mettle Soul	4600 N Magnolia Ave	773-275-3999	40
Shakespeare Reperatory	800 E Grand Ave	312-595-5656	3
Shubert Theatre	22 W Monroe St	312-977-1710	5
St Sebastian Players	1621 W Diversey Pkwy	773-404-7922	43
Stage Left Theatre	3408 N Sheffield Ave	773-883-8830	43
Steep Theatre Company	3902 N Sheridan Rd	312-458-0722	43
Steppenwolf Theatre Co	1650 N Halsted	312-335-1650	30
Stolen Buick Studio	1303 W Chicago Ave		24
Storefront Theatre	66 E Randolph St	312-742-8497	5
Strawdog Theatre Co	3829 N Broadway St		44
The Second City	1616 N Wells St	312-337-3992	30
The Space	4829 N Damen Ave	773-297-2745	39
Theatre 355	355 E Chicago Ave	847-741-0532	3
Theatre Building	1225 W Belmont Ave	773-327-5252	43
Time Line Theatre Co	615 W Wellington Ave	773-281-8463	44
Tommy Gun's Garage Dinner Theatre	1239 S State St	312-461-0102	11
Trap Door Productions	1655 W Cortland St	773-384-0494	28
Viaduct Theater	3111 N Western Ave	773-913-6471	42
Vic Theatre	3145 N Sheffield Ave	773-472-0366	43
Victory Gardens Theatre	2257 N Lincoln Ave	773-549-5788	30
Vittum Theater	1012 N Noble St	773-342-4141	22
Wing & Groove Theatre	1935 W North Ave	773-342-3575	21
WNEP Theatre	3209 N Halsted	773-755-1693	44

Essential Phone Numbers

General

All emergencies **911**
AIDS Hotline 800-342-AIDS
Animal-Cruelty Society 312-644-8338
Chicago Dental Referral Service 312-836-7305
Chicago Department of Housing 773-285-5800
City of Chicago Board of Elections 312-269-7900
Dog License (City Clerk) 312-744-6875
Driver's Licenses 312-793-1010
Emergency Services 312-747-7247
Employment Discrimination 312-744-7584
Gas Leaks 312-240-7000
Income Tax (Illinois) 800-732-8866
Income Tax (Federal) 800-829-3676
Legal Assistance 312-332-1624
Mayor's Office 312-744-4000
Parking (City Stickers) 312-744-6861
Parking Ticket Inquiries 312-744-7275
Report Crime in Your Neighborhood 312-372-0101
Passports 312-341-6020
Police Assistance (non-emergency) 311
Social Security 800-772-1213
Streets and Sanitation 312-744-5000
Telephone Repair Service 888-611-4466
Voter Information 312-269-7900
Water Main Leaks 312-744-7038

Helplines

Alcoholics Anonymous 312-346-1475
Alcohol, Drug and Abuse Helpline 800-234-0420
Alcoholism and Substance Abuse 312-988-7900
Domestic Violence Hotline 800-799-7233
Drug Care, St. Elizabeth's 773-278-5015
Gamblers Anonymous 312-346-1588
Illinois Child Abuse Hotline 800-252-2873
Narcotics Anonymous 708-848-4884
Parental Stress Services 312-372-7368
Runaway Switchboard 800-621-4000
Sexual Assault Hotline 888-293-2080
United Way Community Information and Referral 312-876-0010
Violence – Anti-Violence Project 773-871-CARE

Complaints

Better Business Bureau of Chicago 312-832-0500
Consumer Fraud Division (Attorney General's Office) 312-814-3000
Chicago Department of Consumer Services 312-744-9400
Citizen's Utility Board 800-669-5556
Department of Housing Inspection Complaints 312-747-1500
Mayor's Office 312-744-4000
Postal Service Complaints 312-983-8400

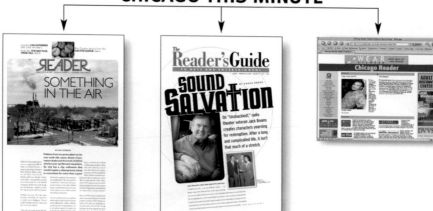

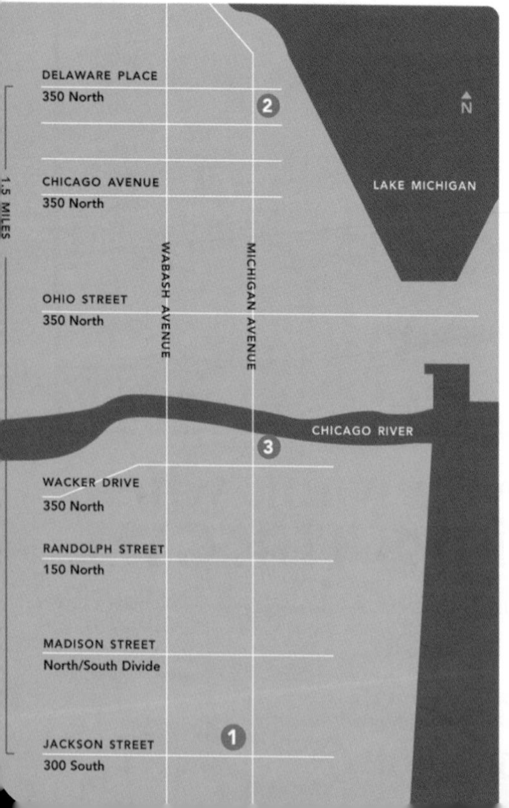

Pick a neighborhood, take a tour.

Our 70 different boat, bus, bike, and walking tours cover neighborhoods from Beverly to Winnetka. And our trained volunteer docents make our tours the real deal—narrated, not scripted; led by Chicago enthusiasts, not just-another-day-at-the-office tour guides.

For details, visit www.architecture.org/tours or our ArchiCenter Shops at:

1. **The Santa Fe Building**
   224 South Michigan Avenue
2. **The John Hancock Center**
   875 North Michigan Avenue
3. For our famous **Architecture River Cruise**, you can also stop by the CAF/Mercury dock at the southeast corner of the Michigan Avenue Bridge, May through October.

CHICAGO ARCHITECTURE FOUNDATION

The city is our museum

Street Index

Street Index

E

F

G

H

I

Street Index